THE GIANT
1001
PUZZLE BOOK

General Editor: Robert Allen

Random House
Puzzles & Games

INTRODUCTION

Did you know that, apart from romantic fiction, puzzling forms the largest sector of the publishing business? Are you surprised? Of course you aren't! Unless you were a puzzler yourself you would never have strayed beyond the front cover. Let's face it – you're hooked. I know exactly how you feel because I've been fascinated by puzzles for many years. To be honest I prefer making them up to solving them myself but as a puzzle writer I've learnt to appreciate what goes into constructing a really satisfying conundrum. I didn't write any of the puzzles in this book, so I can tell you that they really are an impressive and varied collection. They include logic problems (both the long, classic puzzles and a large number of quick ones that are just the right size for solving over a cup of coffee), picture puzzles, visual reasoning enigmas, number problems, mazes, physical problems, and mathematical crosswords. You can browse through the book for five minutes and solve a quick puzzle or spend a whole day on one of the real biggies. We have awarded three levels of difficulty (indicated by dots in the headings – the more dots, the more difficult the puzzle) to give you a rough guide to how long the puzzles will take you. Don't be put off by a difficult puzzle! The difficulty is purely subjective and you may find that the ones we struggled with are just a breeze for you. I hope and believe that you will get many, many hours, weeks, and months of fun from this book. Happy puzzling!

1 HEADS AND TAILS

The diagram shows four coins issued in different reigns by rulers of Monetaria. Can you name the monarch whose head appears on the obverse of each of the coins lettered A to D, describe its reverse design and say in which year it was minted?

1 No female monarch reigned in Monetaria during the 18th century.
2 The coin from the reign of Karl II bears the crossed swords on its reverse.
3 The heraldic dragon appears on coin A, which wasn't issued by William V.
4 The head on the obverse of coin D is that of Josef III.
5 The 1785 coin's reverse shows the value in a wreath of laurel leaves.
6 The coin dated 1865 is somewhere to the right of the one whose reverse design is the shield of Monetaria.

Monarchs: Josef III, Karl II, Maria, William V
Reverse designs: crossed swords, heraldic dragon, shield, wreath of laurels
Dates: 1745, 1785, 1825, 1865

A   B   C   D

Ruler: _____
Reverse: _____
Date: _____

2 DOMINO DEAL

A standard set (0–0) to (6–6) is laid out below. Each domino is placed so that the larger number will be on the bottom:
i.e.   3   not   6
       6   3

Those top numbers show the four numbers which form the top half of each domino in that column. The bottom numbers, below the grid, give the four bottom numbers for that column. The seven numbers on the left show the numbers which belong in that row. Can you cross-reference the facts and deduce where each domino has been placed? 3*6 is given as a start.

'TOP' NUMBERS

| 13 | 01 | 01 | 01 | 00 | 12 | 00 |
| 55 | 24 | 24 | 23 | 14 | 36 | 26 |

| 0 0 1 2 2 3 5 | | | | | | 3 | |
| 2 2 4 4 5 5 6 | | | | | | 6 | |

| 0 2 2 2 3 5 6 |
| 3 4 4 5 6 6 6 |

| 0 0 0 1 1 3 3 |
| 0 1 2 3 3 3 5 |

| A 0 1 1 1 4 4 4 |
| 1 4 5 5 5 6 6 |

| 55 | 23 | 14 | 04 | 24 | 13 | 23 |
| 56 | 35 | 56 | 66 | 46 | 46 | 56 |

'BOTTOM' NUMBERS

3 PEN PALS

Five school friends went their separate ways to seek their fortunes. They had agreed to write to each other from time to time, but not to be bound by any 'take turns' approach. In their first year after graduation it turned out that:

From AL ■
To: BOB
CHRIS
DON
ED

From BOB ■
To: AL
CHRIS
DON
ED

From DON ■
To: AL
BOB
CHRIS
ED

From CHRIS ■
To: AL
BOB
DON
ED

From ED ■
To: AL
BOB
CHRIS
DON

1 Chris wrote twice as many letters to Gainor as he did to Insley, who wrote twice as many to Al as to Ed.
2 Gainor received twice as many letters from Don as he did from Bob, who wrote four to Insley.
3 Al wrote more to Gainor than he did to Jarrett, who received three letters from Chris.
4 Harkness wrote more to Chris than Chris wrote to Harkness.
5 Don received twice as many letters form Farley as he did from Harkness.
6 No one wrote the same number to any two of the others. Each wrote and received ten letters.

Can you give each writer's surname and say how many letters (at least one) he sent to each of the others?

4 SIX SQUARES

The six squares seen highlighted at the top right-hand corner of the grid are repeated in only one other place. Can you see where?

5 THE WHEEL THING

Which two of the pictures below form a matching pair?

6 TSUNAMI

The numbers alongside each row or column tell you how many blocks of black squares are in a line. For example: 2, 3, 5 tells you that from left to right (or top to bottom) there is a group of two black squares, then at least one white space, then a group of three black squares, then at least one white shape, then a group of five black squares. Each block of black squares on the same line must have at least one white square between it and the next block of black squares.

Sometimes it is possible to tell which squares are going to be black without reference to other lines or columns. In the example below, we can deduce that any block of six black squares must incorporate the two central squares.

6 ⬜⬜⬜⬜⬛⬜⬜⬜⬜⬜

Can you complete this Tsunami puzzle, to reveal the hidden pattern or picture?

Row clues (top to bottom):
- 3 1
- 2 3
- 1 1 6
- 2 3 1 1
- 1 2 7
- 1 1 1 5
- 1 1 2 2 4
- 1 2 1 1 4
- 2 3 1 1 1 2
- 2 4 2 3
- 2 11
- 1 3 6
- 1 7
- 1 1 7
- 1 3 4 3
- 1 1 1 2 3
- 1 1 2 3
- 1 1 4 3
- 2 3 1 1
- 3 3 3
- 10 3
- 1 6 3
- 1 6
- 1 7
- 2 1 6

(c) Conceptis Puzzles   UK10516

7 NUMBER SEARCH

The number 123456 appears just once in this grid, running in either a forward or backward direction, either vertically, horizontally or diagonally. Can you locate it?

8 SMALL HOLDINGS

When Ivan The Not-too-bad-really decided to divide a spare kingdom between four faithful followers, he stipulated that each should hold an identically shaped chunk of territory, the same size as every other. Each, of course, was to have just one castle and one farm. Can you show Ivan's Estate Agent, Manfromm The Prudential, how to achieve his master's wishes?

9 LETTER MAZE

The object is to pass through the maze and reach the exit at the top. No diamond may be passed through more than once in any one move nor may you leave a diamond by the gap you came in by. You must not enter diamonds that contain the letters you are told to avoid.

1. Move 4 diamonds. Avoid A, C and F.
2. Move 3 diamonds. Avoid C, E and G.
3. Move 5 diamonds. Avoid A and E.
4. Move 3 diamonds. Avoid C.
5. Move 4 diamonds. Avoid C, D and E.
6. Move 5 diamonds. Avoid B and F.
7. Move 5 diamonds. Avoid C and G.
8. Move 2 diamonds. Avoid B.
9. Move 2 diamonds. Avoid A, C and G.
10. Move 3 diamonds. Avoid A, B and E.

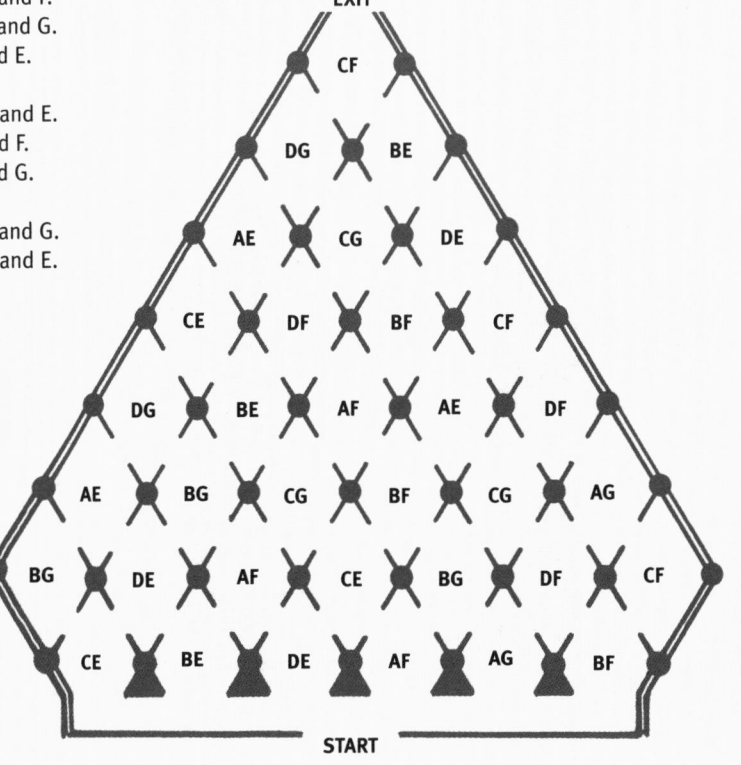

10 DROP-OUT

The hippie is trying to choose a waistcoat. In the picture on the right, he's made his choice. Which one did he buy?

11 BIG BREAK

A snooker break is made up by potting red balls (maximum 15) which are each followed by one of six different colours, the point values of the balls are:

- RED 1
- YELLOW 2
- GREEN 3
- BROWN 4
- BLUE 5
- PINK 6
- BLACK 7

Snooker player Bob Basher made a break of 70, which ended when he failed to pot a red. In the break he potted the same number of blue and brown and one more pink than yellow, potting all four colours in the break and no other colours.

How was the break compiled?

12 SEQUENCE

Which butterfly (a, b, c, d) comes next in this sequence?

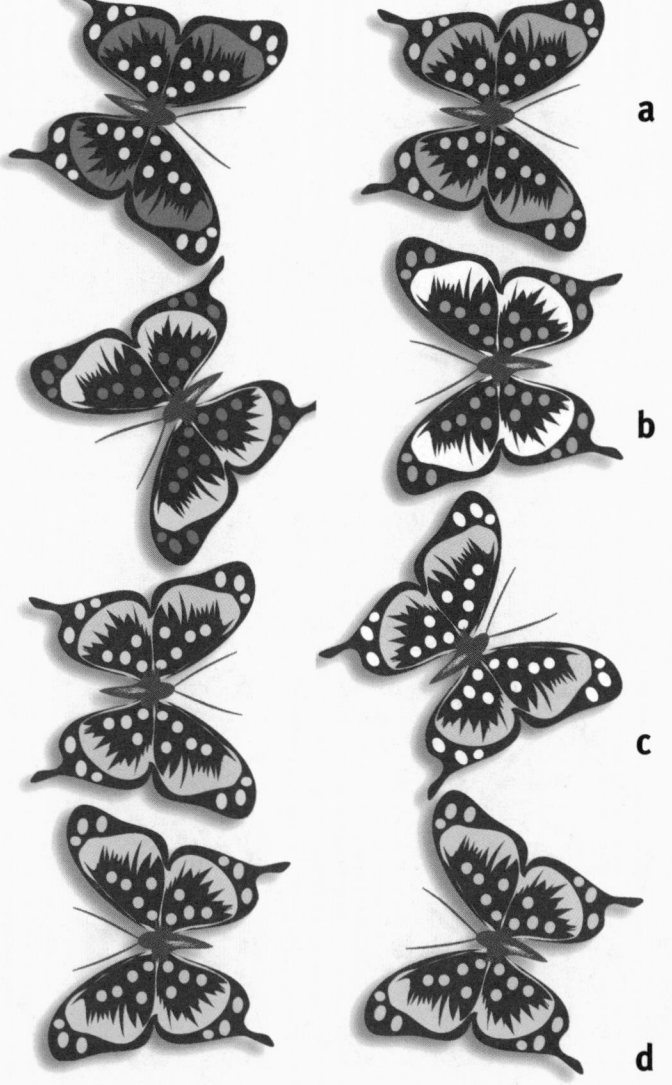

a

b

c

d

13 DOMINO DEAL

A standard set (0–0) to (6–6) is laid out below. Each domino is placed so that the larger number will be on the bottom:

i.e.   3   not   6
           6   3

Those top numbers show the four numbers which form the top half of each domino in that column. The bottom numbers, below the grid, give the four bottom numbers for that column. The seven numbers on the left show the numbers which belong in that row. Can you cross-reference the facts and deduce where each domino has been placed? 3*6 is given as a start.

'TOP' NUMBERS

| | 13 | 00 | 01 | 02 | 01 | 01 | 02 |
	55	13	12	24	2̶3̶	44	36
0 0 1 1 3 4 6							
1 3 4 4 5 6 6							
1 2 2 2 3̶ 3 5				3			
2 2 3 5 5 5 6̶				6			
0 0 1 2 2 3 5							
2 3 4 5 6 6 6							
0 0 0 1 1 4 4							
0 1 3 4 4 5 6							

| 44 | 11 | 23 | 36 | 03 | 22 | 34 |
| 56 | 55 | 56 | 66 | 4̶6̶ | 45 | 56 |

'BOTTOM' NUMBERS

14 SIX SQUARES

The six squares seen highlighted at the top right-hand corner of the grid are repeated in only one other place. Can you see where?

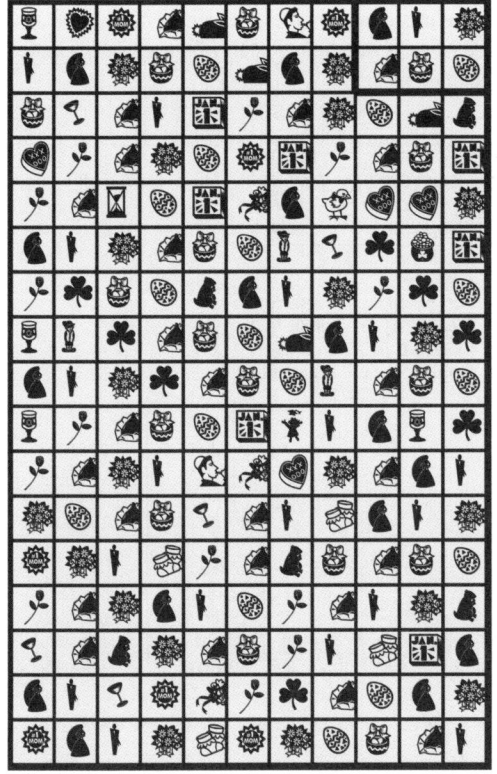

15 TSUNAMI

The numbers alongside each row or column tell you how many blocks of black squares are in a line. For example: 2, 3, 5 tells you that from left to right (or top to bottom) there is a group of two black squares, then at least one white space, then a group of three black squares, then at least one white shape, then a group of five black squares. Each block of black squares on the same line must have at least one white square between it and the next block of black squares.

Sometimes it is possible to tell which squares are going to be black without reference to other lines or columns. In the example below, we can deduce that any block of six black squares must incorporate the two central squares.

6 ☐☐☐☐☐■☐☐☐☐☐

Can you complete this Tsunami puzzle, to reveal the hidden pattern or picture?

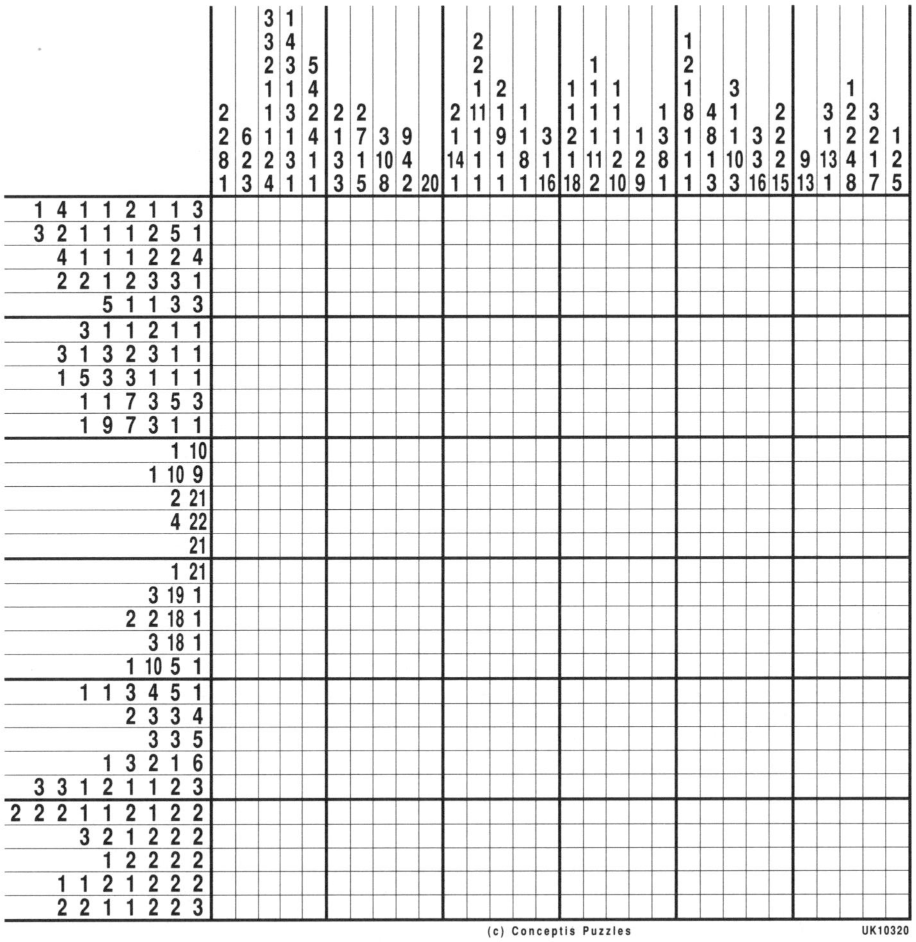

Row clues (top to bottom):
- 1 4 1 1 2 1 1 3
- 3 2 1 1 1 2 5 1
- 4 1 1 2 2 4
- 2 2 1 2 3 3 1
- 5 1 1 3 3
- 3 1 1 2 1 1
- 3 1 3 2 1 1
- 1 5 3 3 1 1 1
- 1 1 7 3 5 3
- 1 9 7 3 1 1
- 1 10
- 1 10 9
- 2 21
- 4 22
- 21
- 1 21
- 3 19 1
- 2 2 18 1
- 3 18 1
- 1 10 5 1
- 1 1 3 4 5 1
- 2 3 3 4
- 3 3 5
- 1 3 2 1 6
- 3 3 1 2 1 1 2 3
- 2 2 2 1 1 2 1 2 2
- 3 2 1 2 2 2
- 1 2 2 2 2
- 1 1 2 1 2 2 2
- 2 2 1 1 2 2 3

(c) Conceptis Puzzles   UK10320

16 ABC

Each line, across and down, is to have each of the letters A, B and C, and two empty squares. The letter outside the grid shows the first or second letter in the direction of the arrow. Can you fill in the grid?

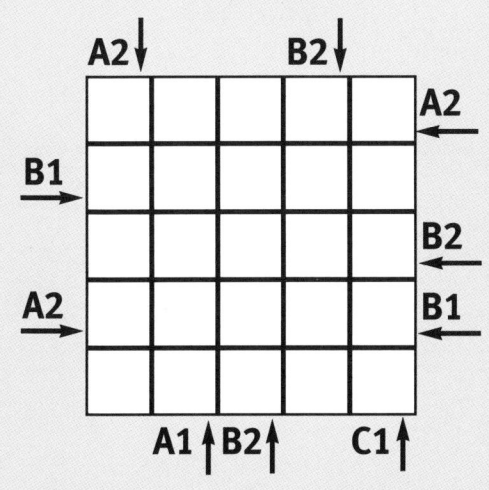

17 COUNTING HOUSE

In Colourland, where the currency rate is 100 cents to the Colourland dollar, the national bank issues coins of a large range of different (and decidedly strange!) denominations, which are distinguishable only by their colour. From the information shown in the four boxes below, can you calculate the individual values of just four of these coins: red, blue, yellow and green?

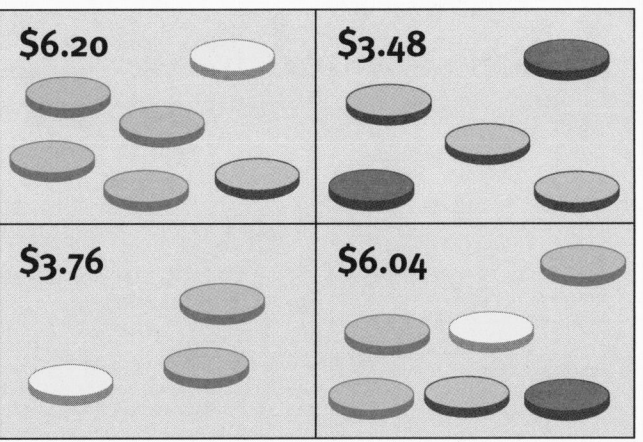

At the Little Appenin local fair a plant stall had a display of 25 potted plants. Four customers each bought five plants – taking one from each row and each column. So with just five plants left, each was given a free gift of a plant type she had not already bought. Madge was given the plant next to one of the ferns she purchased. The picture shows one plant bought by each customer. The chart indicates how many of some plants each purchased. At the end of it all, which plant was left on the table and which pots did each buy or was given?

18 ODD POT

	Azalea	Begonia	Cactus	Fern
Jackie			3	
Kim				3
Laura		3		
Madge			2	2

19 BOWLING TEAM

The members of the Basham bowling team make a splendid sight. Can you identify these four colourful characters?
1 Tom the dustman is not the chap sporting the long beard.
2 The postman is not Alf who wears a monocle.
3 George is not the milkman who even bowls in his panama hat.

ALF	
BLACKSMITH	DOCTOR
LAWYER	MAIL MAN
BEARD	CRAVAT
MONOCLE	PANAMA

GEORGE	
BLACKSMITH	DOCTOR
LAWYER	MAIL MAN
BEARD	CRAVAT
MONOCLE	PANAMA

FRED	
BLACKSMITH	DOCTOR
LAWYER	MAIL MAN
BEARD	CRAVAT
MONOCLE	PANAMA

TOM	
BLACKSMITH	DOCTOR
LAWYER	MAIL MAN
BEARD	CRAVAT
MONOCLE	PANAMA

20 NUMBER SEARCH

The number 12478 appears just once in this grid, running in either a forward or backward direction, either vertically, horizontally or diagonally. Can you locate it?

21 PAY, STAY AND GO AWAY

Lucy Tayble climbed out of her Rolls Royce and stared at the parking meter. A helpful attendant came up.

'Can I assist you, Ma'am?'

'Certainly not. I was merely wondering how many different ways there were to put in this ridiculous charge of 50 cents.'

'There must be hundreds.'

'No, it's less than that, even though putting in 5 cents then 10 cents is not the same as 10 cents then 5 cents.' The attendant's brain was beginning to spin. 'Isn't it?', he asked. 'Of course not. If one were to drop one's first coin down that drain there, one would rather lose 5 cents than 10 cents, wouldn't one? "I suppose one, err I, would. Did you get the answer?'

'No, you interrupted me. Work it out and tell me when I get back.'

And off Lucy went, knowing that once again she had avoided paying to park and that the attendant would be too busy to notice!

So, how many ways are there to put 50 cents into the machine?

CHARGES		
50C PER HOUR ONLY 5C AND 10C COINS ACCEPTED		
	5C	10C

22 DOMINO DEAL

A standard set (0–0) to (6–6) is laid out below. Each domino is placed so that the larger number will be on the bottom:

i.e.   3   not   6
         6   3

Those top numbers show the four numbers which form the top half of each domino in that column. The bottom numbers, below the grid, give the four bottom numbers for that column. The seven numbers on the left show the numbers which belong in that row. Can you cross-reference the facts and deduce where each domino has been placed? 3*6 is given as a start.

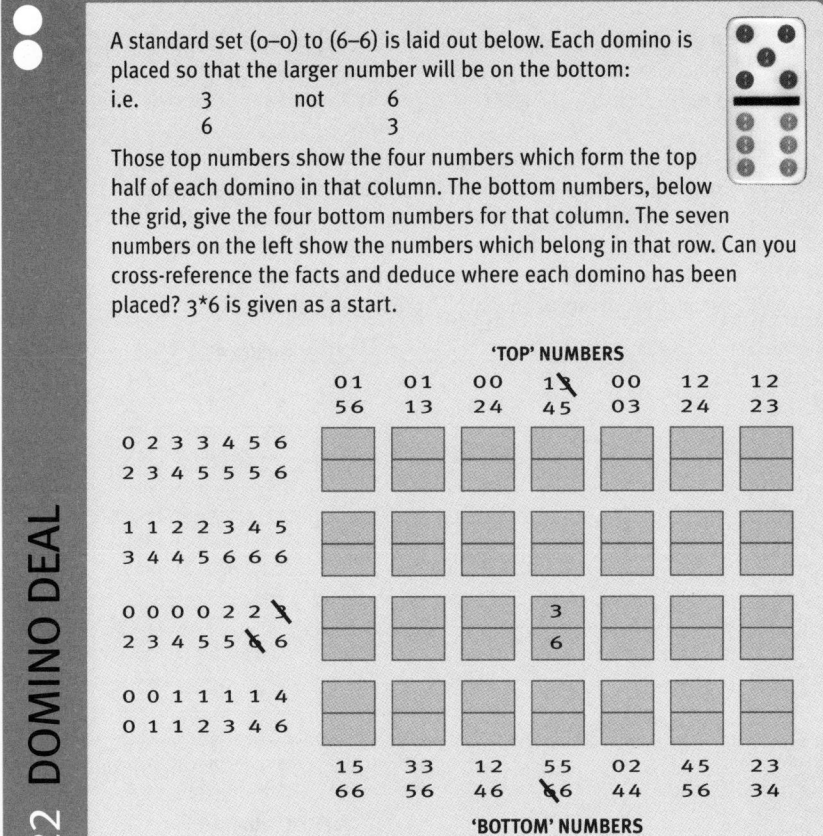

'TOP' NUMBERS

	01 56	01 13	00 24	1̶ 45	00 03	12 24	12 23
0 2 3 4 5 6 / 2 3 4 5 5 5 6							
1 1 2 2 3 4 5 / 3 4 4 5 6 6 6							
0 0 0 0 2 2 ✗ / 2 3 4 5 5 ✗ 6			3 6				
0 0 1 1 1 1 4 / 0 1 1 2 3 4 6							

	15 66	33 56	12 46	55 ✗6	02 44	45 56	23 34

'BOTTOM' NUMBERS

23 TSUNAMI

The numbers alongside each row or column tell you how many blocks of black squares are in a line. For example: 2, 3, 5 tells you that from left to right (or top to bottom) there is a group of two black squares, then at least one white space, then a group of three black squares, then at least one white shape, then a group of five black squares. Each block of black squares on the same line must have at least one white square between it and the next block of black squares. Sometimes it is possible to tell which squares are going to be black without reference to other lines or columns. In the example below, we can deduce that any block of six black squares must incorporate the two central squares.

6 ▢▢▢▢▢■■▢▢▢▢▢

Can you complete this Tsunami puzzle, to reveal the hidden pattern or picture?

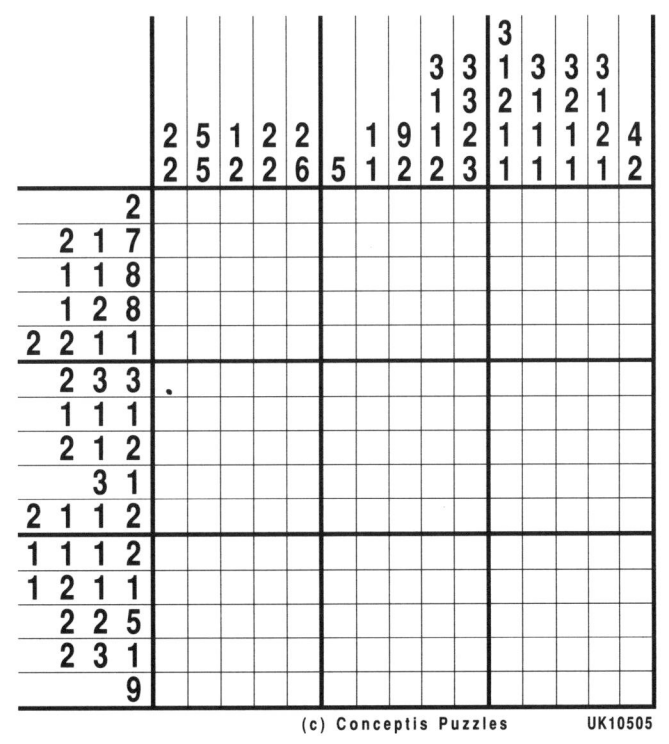

(c) Conceptis Puzzles   UK10505

24 CELL STRUCTURE

The object is to create white areas surrounded by black walls, so that:

• Each white area contains only one number
• The number of cells in a white area is equal to the number in it
• The white areas are separated from each other with a black wall
• Cells containing numbers must not be filled in
• The black cells must be linked into a continuous wall
• Black cells cannot form a square of 2x2 or larger

1		2	3		
				2	
3			3		
				2	
2		1			
					2
	1			2	2
		6			
		1		1	
4				2	1

25 DOMINO DEAL

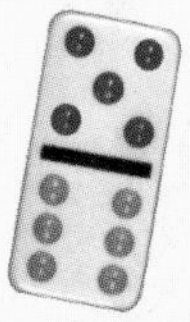

A standard set (0–0) to (6–6) is laid out below. Each domino is placed so that the larger number will be on the bottom:

i.e. 3 not 6
      6   3

Those top numbers show the four numbers which form the top half of each domino in that column. The bottom numbers, below the grid, give the four bottom numbers for that column. The seven numbers on the left show the numbers which belong in that row. Can you cross-reference the facts and deduce where each domino has been placed? 3*6 is given as a start.

'TOP' NUMBERS

| 00 | 01 | 01 | 01 | 04 | 01 | 12 |
| 14 | 23 | 23 | 22 | 56 | 35 | ~~34~~ |

Rows (left numbers):

1 1 1 1 2 3 4
2 3 4 4 4 5 6

0 0 1 3 3 5 5
1 3 4 5 5 5 6

0 0 0 1 2 2 ~~5~~
0 1 3 3 4 5 ~~6~~   (cell: 3 / 6)

0 0 2 2 4 4 6
2 2 5 6 6 6 6

'BOTTOM' NUMBERS

| 13 | 23 | 02 | 34 | 34 | 44 | 14 |
| 56 | 56 | 25 | 56 | 56 | 66 | ~~56~~ |

26 COLOUR BLIND

Police Officer Friendly's informer, Slippery Sid, is none too helpful when it comes to pointing out which of various colourful characters keeps their car behind which coloured garage door. The only thing that we do know is that no garage has either a door, car or an owner's name with the same colour in it. From Sid's statement see if you can fill in the form correctly.

LEFT

Owner
Car Make
Car Colour

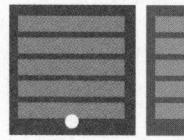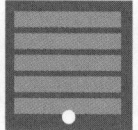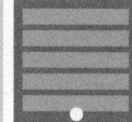

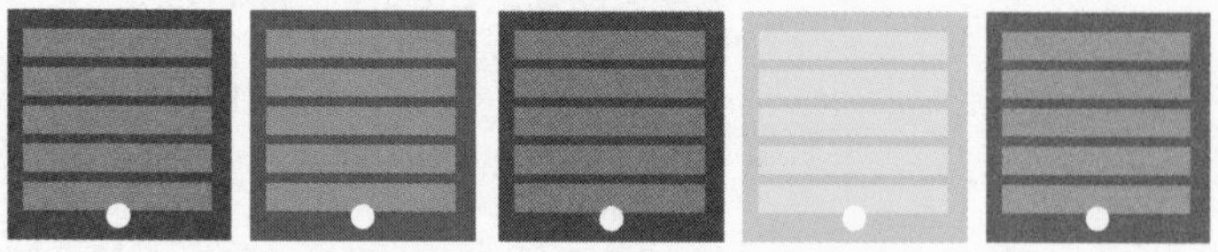

The red car is two places to the left of the Jaguar and the grey car is one place to the right of Mr Grey's car, which isn't a VW. Mr Green's car, the Lancia and the blue car are in adjoining garages but none has a red door and the green car, the Skoda and Mr Pink's car are also in adjoining garages with the named make being the middle car in each case. There is also an Opel, Mr Blue and Mr White are the other two owners and the other car colour is white.

27 FRAME UP

Henry is a faithful supporter of Coppleton Basketball Club and he attends matches whenever possible. He has decided that the supporters should have some recognition and he has persuaded Madge, one of the ladies providing refreshments, to take a photo. Henry is in position F and your job is to provide the other names. Left and right are as you look at the photo, and in front and behind are not necessarily directly so unless stated, ie, it is true to say that A is behind K.

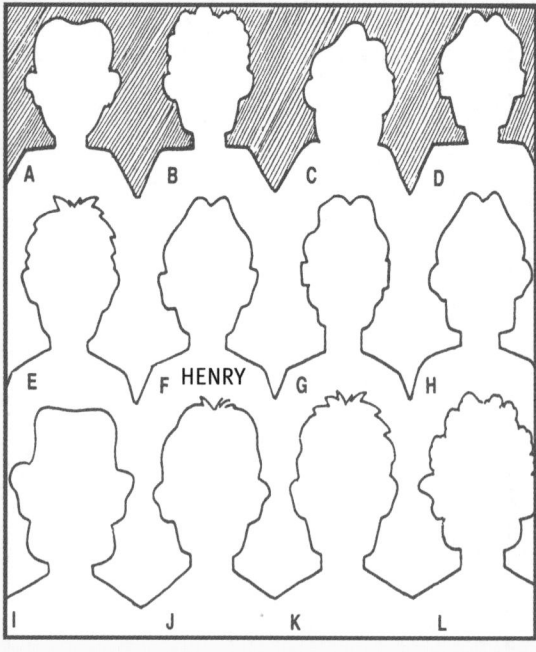

1 Agnes is behind Emily and to the right of Isaac.
2 David is behind Joyce and to the right of Keith.
3 Isaac is behind David and to the right of Lydia.
4 Clive is to the right of Beryl and behind Lydia.
5 Grace is to the left of Isaac and in front of Agnes.
6 Beryl is in front of Felix and to the right of Joyce.
7 Keith is to the right of Henry and behind Agnes.

28 NUMBER JIG

Insert the figures into the grid. One has been done for you.

3 figures
130
191
219
233
354
419
463
507
588
671
690
~~807~~
876
935

4 figures
2190
3253
8491
9725

5 figures
12663
13002
19309
20393
26205
29994
31069
31155

32194
33062
40134
48181
50242
50551
52104
53606
60885
62271
65018
77123
83118
89031
90460

91203
92186
93661
93906

6 figures
110375
452706
546371
680935
790020

At the Little Appenin local fair a plant stall had a display of 25 potted plants. Four customers each bought five plants – taking one from each row and each column. So with just 5 plants left, each was given a free gift of a plant type they hadn't already bought. One plant bought by each customer is shown. The chart indicates how many of some plants each purchased. The columns are counted from the left as you look. (For non-gardeners the begonia is yellow; the azalea is pink and the other two are, hopefully, obvious.) At the end of it all, which plant was left on the table and which pots did each buy or was given free?

	Azalea	Begonia	Cactus	Fern
Kevin	2			2
Len		2		2
Mary	3			
Norma			3	

29 ODD POT

30 SQUARE NUMBERS

The numbers 1–25 are entered randomly in a 5 x 5 square so that no two consecutive numbers are adjacent in any direction, or in the same row or column. Column 1 contains four multiples of 5, but not 20, which is in the same row as 5. C3 is one lower than A2 which is four lower than B1 which is one higher than E2 which is one higher than A3 which is a prime number. B4 plus D3 equals D5; E3 plus A5, which are consecutive numbers, equals A4; C2 is an even number. B3, which is one higher than E4, is twice C4; B5 is a multiple of C5, which is not 1. 7 is in the same line diagonally as 8, and 6 is immediately below an even number, whilst 8 is below an odd number. 22 is below and diagonally adjacent to 2 which is in the same row as 14. If the long diagonal from top left to bottom right contains only one odd number, can you complete the grid?

	1	2	3	4	5
A					
B					
C					
D					
E					

31 LOGI-5

Each line, across and down, is to have each of the letters A, B, C, D and E, appearing once each. Also, every shape – shown by the thick lines – must also have each of the letters in it. Can you fill in the grid?

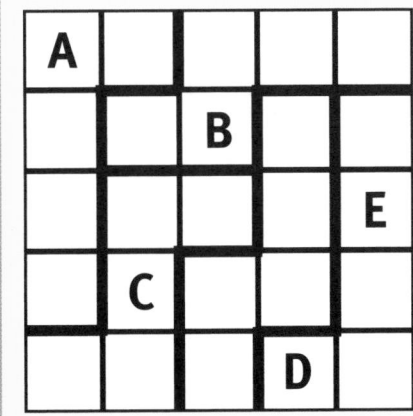

32 ON THE SCENE

Each of the six objects in the lower boxes can be found in one of the lettered squares in the big picture. Find these squares and transfer the letters to the little boxes below. You should spell out the name of a world – famous university.

34 NINE NUMBERS

Place a number from 1 to 9 in each empty cell so that each row, each column and each 3 x 3 block contains all the numbers from 1 to 9.

	2	6				8	1	
3			7		8			6
4				5				7
	5		1		7		9	
		3	9		5	1		
	4		3		2		5	
1				3				2
5			2		4			9
	3	8				4	6	

33 DATE WITH A PLATE

Four couples in Celebration Road have each invited another couple round for a small dinner party. Each party is on a different day. By crossing out the names which do not fit on each invitation and circling those that do, can you name each couple hosting each event and the names of their two guests?

1 Tim is going out the day after Don. Alf is entertaining Dot the day after Joy's dinner party. One hostess is May.
2 Liz's dinner party is on Sunday. Les is going out the day before Jim's dinner party.
3 Fay is not married to Bob who is going out on Friday and neither is the guest of Joy who is not married to Jim.
4 Pam and Tom are married but are not the couple entertaining Kay on Saturday.

Thur.

JOY LIZ   MAY PAM
ALF JIM   SAM TOM
DOT FAY   KAY SUE
BOB DON   LES TIM

Fri.

JOY LIZ   MAY PAM
ALF JIM   SAM TOM
DOT FAY   KAY SUE
BOB DON   LES TIM

Sat.

JOY LIZ   MAY PAM
ALF JIM   SAM TOM
DOT FAY   KAY SUE
BOB DON   LES TIM

Sun.

JOY LIZ   MAY PAM
ALF JIM   SAM TOM
DOT FAY   KAY SUE
BOB DON   LES TIM

DAY	FROM SHE	& HE	TO SHE	& HE

35 TOFFEE TRAUMA

Guide Greedy Gordon through the maze to collect as many toffees as possible before the end, without going back over his own tracks.

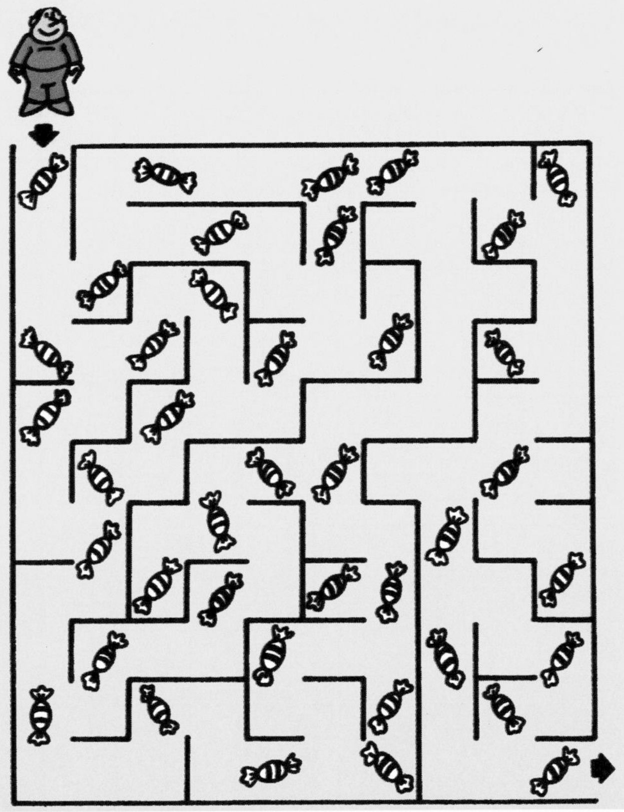

36 COLOUR BLIND

Police Officer Friendly's informer, Slippery Sid, is none too helpful when it comes to pointing out which of various colourful characters keeps their car behind which coloured garage door. The only thing that we do know is that no garage has either a door, car or an owner's name with the same colour in it. From Sid's statement see if you can fill in the form correctly.

LEFT

Owner
Car Make
Car Colour

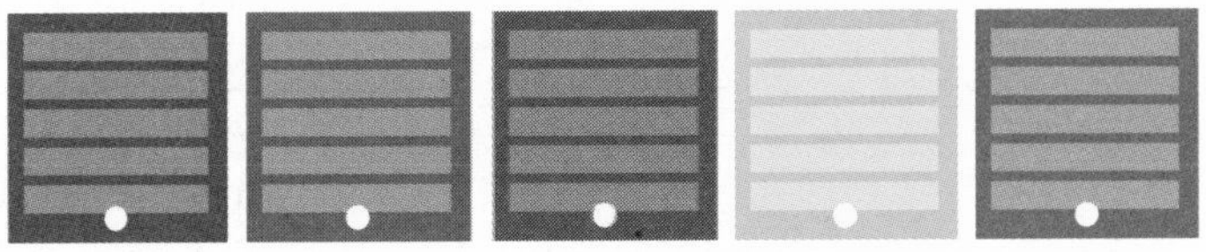

Mr Grey's car is between the red car and the Toyota. The blue car and the Lada are in adjoining garages, neither is Mr Green's car, and none of these is behind the yellow door. The white car is between the Ford and Mr Red's car, and none of these is behind the blue door. Mr White owns the Renault, which is not a red car and is to the left of both Mr Green's car and the black car. There is also a grey car and a Nissan and Mr Black is the other owner.

37 TSUNAMI

The numbers alongside each row or column tell you how many blocks of black squares are in a line. For example: 2, 3, 5 tells you that from left to right (or top to bottom) there is a group of two black squares, then at least one white space, then a group of three black squares, then at least one white shape, then a group of five black squares. Each block of black squares on the same line must have at least one white square between it and the next block of black squares.

Sometimes it is possible to tell which squares are going to be black without reference to other lines or columns. In the example below, we can deduce that any block of six black squares must incorporate the two central squares.

6 □□□□■■□□□□

Can you complete this Tsunami puzzle, to reveal the hidden pattern or picture?

	3	1 2 1	1 5 1	2 1 3 2	5 6	7 4	2 1 4 1 1	1 4 1 1 2	1 4 2 1	1 1 1 1 1	1 4 3 2	1 4 3 2	1 1 1 5	1 4 1	1 4 1	2 1 1	1 1 3	1 2 2	1 2 1	3 1
9																				
3 1																				
3 1																				
15																				
2 2 2 2																				
2 2 2 2																				
4 15																				
1 1 1 1 1																				
8 3 2																				
6 3 2																				
4 3 2																				
6 5																				
2 1 2 2																				
2 1 2 2																				
1 5 1																				

38 MAZE MYSTERY

Travel from the entrance to the exit of the maze, filling the path completely to create a picture.

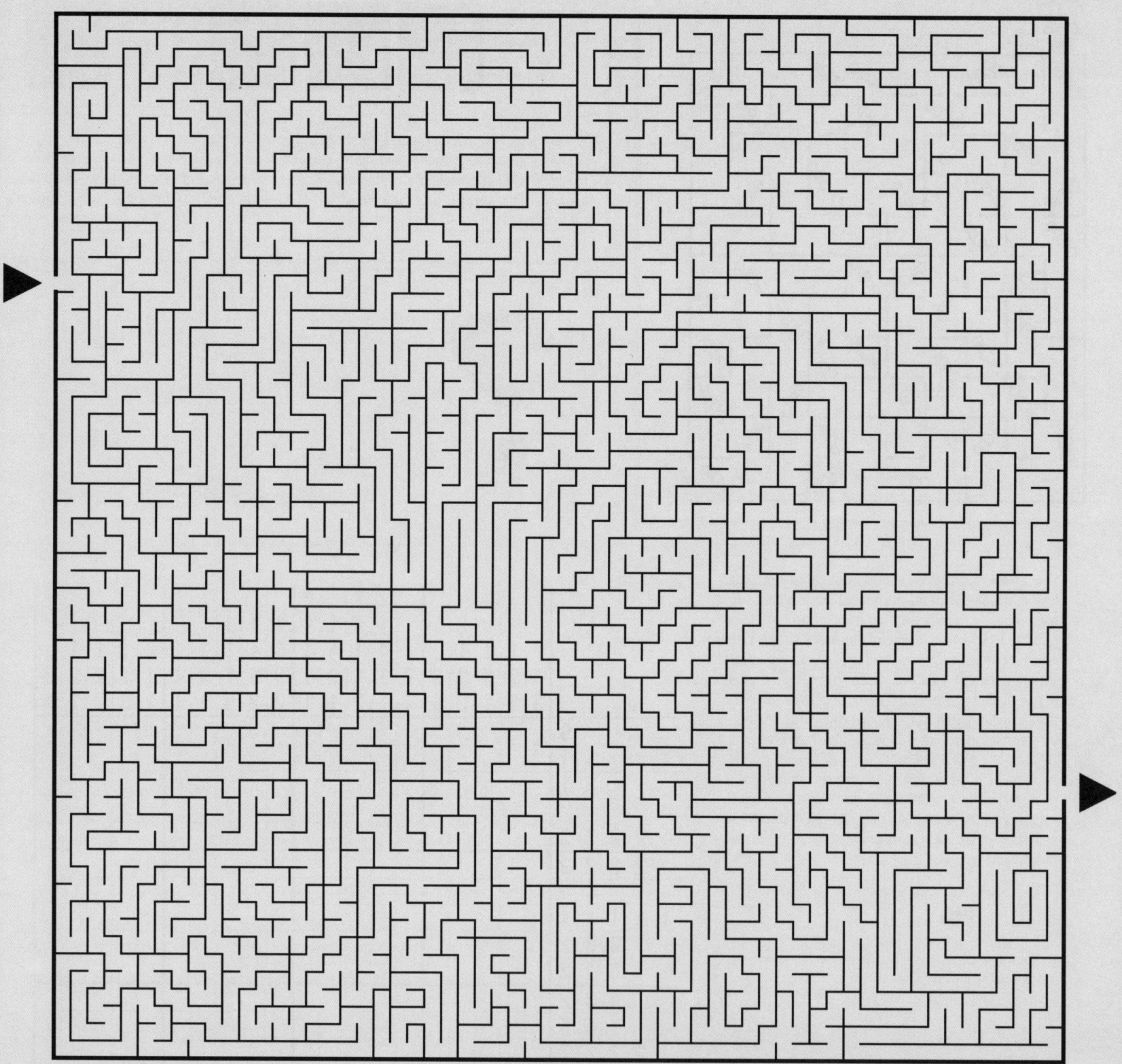

39 DOMINO SEARCH

A set of dominoes has been laid out, using numbers instead of dots for clarity, but the lines which separate the dominoes have been left out. Can you show where each domino in the set has been placed? You may find the check grid useful as each domino is identified by its number pair and the appropriate box can be ticked when the domino has been located. To give you a start 5*2 has been marked in.

6	1	0	3	4	3	4	1
1	6	6	3	6	5	2	2
2	0	3	1	2	3	5	1
1	3	4	2	6	1	1	0
5	4	2	6	0	5	2	5
3	0	4	0	4	6	4	4
0	3	6	0	2	5	5	5

Check grid rows: 0, 1, 2, 3, 4, 5, 6 — with X marked at row 5.
Columns: 0 1 2 3 4 5 6

40 DOTTY DILEMMA

Connect adjacent dots with vertical or horizontal lines so that a single loop is formed with no crossings or branches. Each number indicates how many lines surround it, while empty cells may be surrounded by any number of lines.

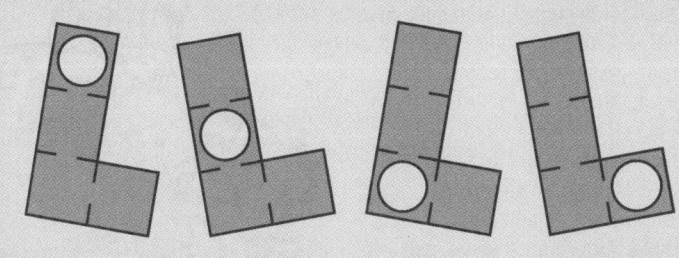

41 COLOUR BLIND

Police Officer Friendly's informer, Slippery Sid, is none too helpful when it comes to pointing out which of various colourful characters keeps their car behind which coloured garage door. The only thing that we do know is that no garage has either a door, car or an owner's name with the same colour in it. From Sid's statement see if you can fill in the form correctly.

LEFT
Owner
Car Make
Car Colour

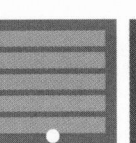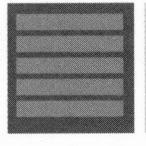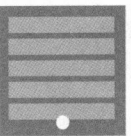

Mr Brown's car, which is next to both the BMW and the black one, is not the Fiat, which is next to both the brown car and Mr White's. The Volvo is two places to the right of the grey car and the Audi which is not Mr White's is two places to the left of Mr Grey's car. There are also both a red and green car, Mr Black and Mr Green are the other two owners and the final make of car is a Ford.

42 WHERE THE L?

Twelve L shapes like the ones below have been fitted into a rectangular shape. Each L has one hole, and there are three of each type in the rectangle. No two pieces of the same type are adjacent, even at a corner. They fit together so well that the spaces between pieces do not show. From the locations of the holes, can you tell where each L is?

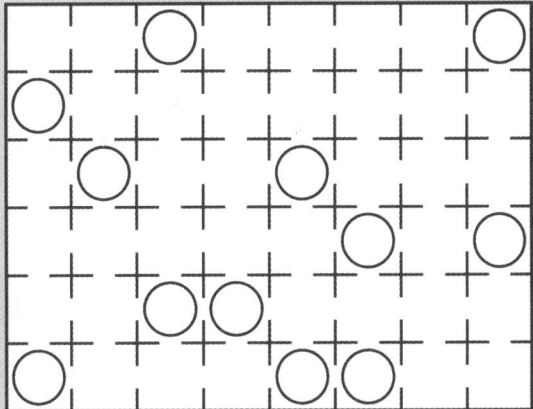

43 PATTERN MAKER

Can you place the numbered blocks into the grid to form the pattern shown? The blocks may be placed horizontally or vertically, and may be turned round.

4	6	4	3
3	3	2	2
5	5	5	4
6	4	2	6
5	6	3	2

5	6

4	2

3	2

6	4

3	6

5	4

3	4

5	3

2	5

2	6

44 IT FIGURES

Place a number from 1 to 9 in each empty cell so that the sum of each vertical or horizontal block equals the number at the top or on the left of that block. Numbers may only be used once in each block.

45 BLACK AND WHITE

In a negative, everything which is really black appears white and everything which is really white appears black.

Can you see which one of the three boots A, B and C is shown as a negative?

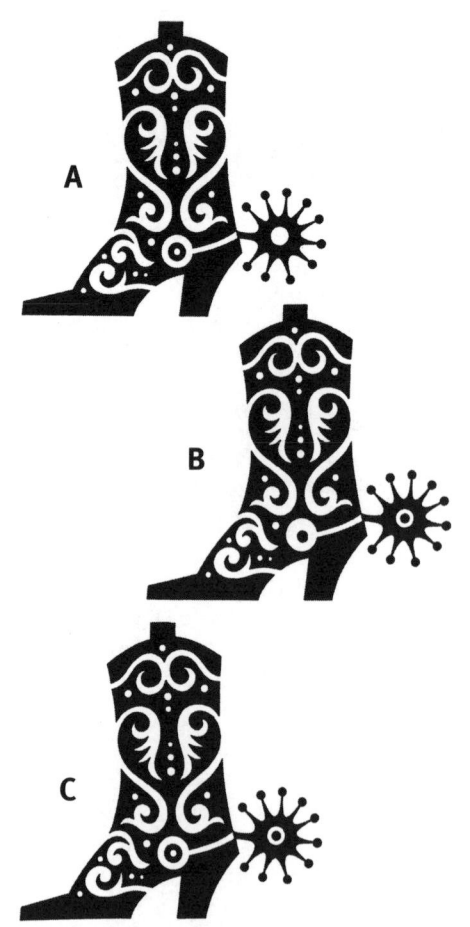

A

B

C

46 POKER PLACES

These seven regulars of a weekly poker school have developed a ritual for deciding where each man will sit. They form a line, host at the front. He selects a seat and sits down. The others move clockwise around the table in line, passing three empty chairs and sitting at the next empty chair. This continues until all are sat down. For tonight's game, we can tell you that: Malcolm was directly in front of the doctor and directly behind Lionel in the line. Jerry who was next in line after the mail man is sat with Keith on his right hand and the financier on his left hand. The jockey was the third man in the line. He sat next door to neither the salesman or Gus who were next to each other in the line and are next to each other at the table. The bookmaker sat down next after Syd. The baker who was two places earlier in the line than Wilf is seated two places clockwise from him. Can you work out the occupation of each man and place him at the table?

HINT: Number the men in the line 1 to 7 and work out first where each 'number' is sat. Then work out who can't be in each seat.

47 HAT CHECK

Which silhouette exactly matches the cowboy with the air-conditioned stetson?

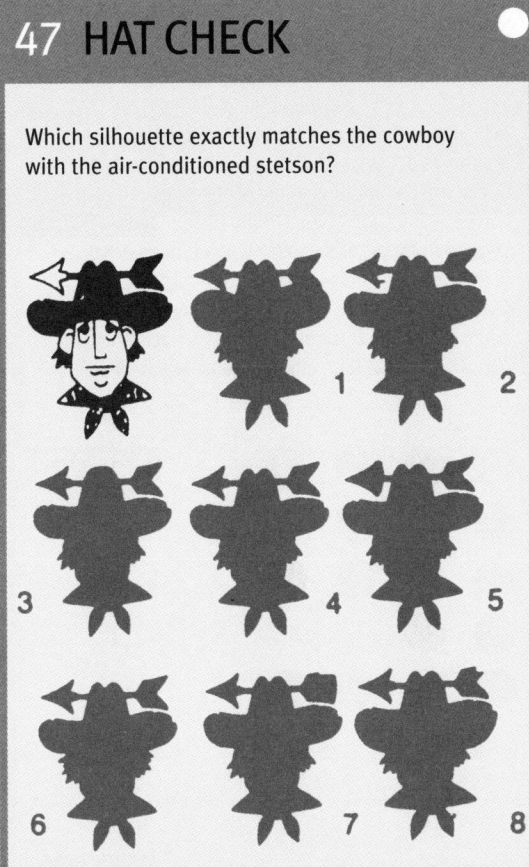

49 TOGA PARTY

Each figure differs from the other three by one extra detail. Can you spot all four extra details?

48 CRAZY MAZE

Can you find your way through this mad scientist's smoky maze?

50 TAKING STEPS

During their vacation at Pantings (with reduced rates for the anniversarily challenged), three couples became close friends. In the two dances recorded here, nobody danced with his/her spouse and each had a different partner for each dance.
The couples were:

FOXTROT
Andrew and the lady from New York.
Floe's husband and Mrs Gould.
Mr Hedges and Colin's wife.

WALTZ
Brian and the lady from Kansas City.
Dolly's husband and the lady from New Orleans.
Mr Jacobs and Edna.

Can you name each married couple and say where they came from?

51 DOMINO SEARCH

A set of dominoes has been laid out, using numbers instead of dots for clarity, but the lines which separate the dominoes have been left out. Can you show where each domino in the set has been placed? You may find the check grid useful as each domino is identified by its number pair and the appropriate box can be ticked when the domino has been located. To give you a start 6*4 has been marked in.

0	0	1	5	4	5	2	6
1	0	5	3	6	1	4	2
3	5	0	4	5	3	4	1
2	5	6	5	6	1	3	6
2	3	2	3	2	4	3	6
0	0	5	0	2	1	0	6
4	3	6	1	1	4	2	4

52 CODE MASTER

Just follow the rules of that classic puzzle, Master Mind, to crack the colour code. The first number tells you how many of the pegs are exactly correct – the right colour in the right place(✓✓). The second number tells you how many pegs are the correct colour but are not in the right place(✓). Colours may be repeated in the answer. By comparing the information given by each line, can you work out which colour goes in which place?

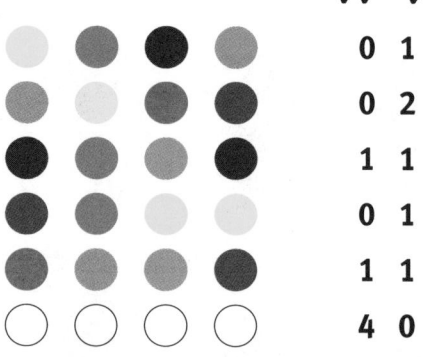

	✓✓	✓
	0	1
	0	2
	1	1
	0	1
	1	1
	4	0

53 CELL STRUCTURE

The object is to create white areas surrounded by black walls, so that:
• Each white area contains only one number
• The number of cells in a white area is equal to the number in it
• The white areas are separated from each other with a black wall
• Cells containing numbers must not be filled in
• The black cells must be linked into a continuous wall
• Black cells cannot form a square of 2 x 2 or larger

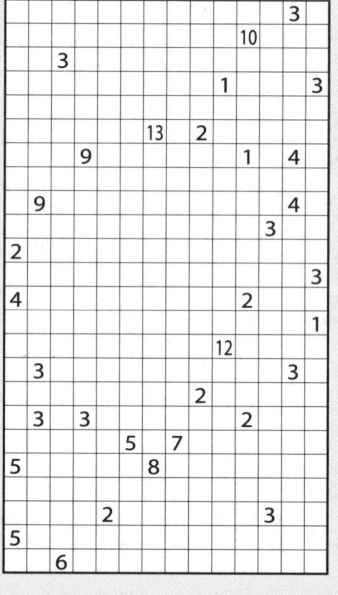

54 WHERE THE L?

Twelve L shapes like the ones below have been fitted into an oblong shape. Each L has one hole, and there are three of each type in the square. No two pieces of the same type are adjacent, even at a corner. They fit together so well that the spaces between pieces do not show. From the locations of the holes, can you tell where each L is?

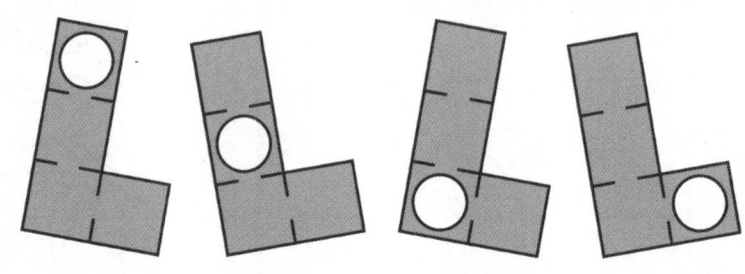

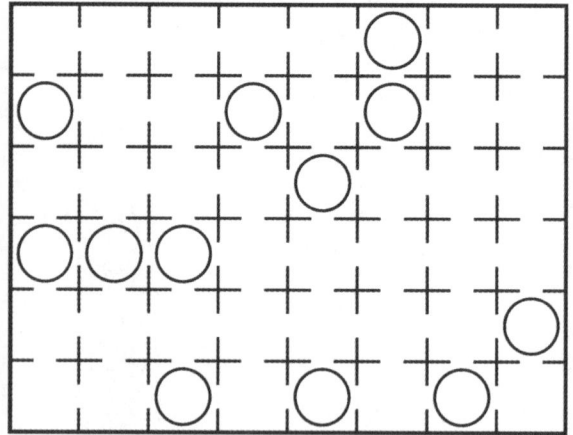

55 STICKY TIME

There are 30 squares here of various sizes. Remove nine matchsticks, so that *no squares exist at all.*

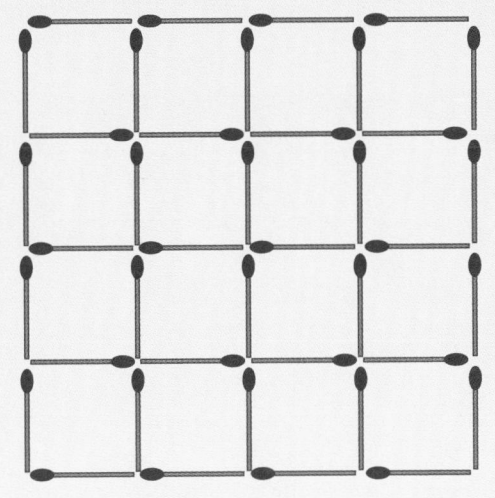

56 I ON U!

Nanotec, launchers of such great software as Peephole2001, have hired IonU Surveillance Ltd to report on members of staff making illegal use of company facilities. Within hours, four hapless souls were on the carpet. Sean de Lear sent the fax but not to Burnley. The phone call was to Canada. Mother was contacted in Accrington and Wilf Hickset contacted Denmark. Neither the connection to the bookmaker in Burnley nor the one via the Internet was made by Rhoda Luck. Tania Hyde's e-mail was not the message to the car salesman as a man sent that.

CONTACT	EMPLOYEE	METHOD	PLACE
Bookmaker			
Car Sales			
Mother			
Partner			

57 SIX-PACK

By packing numbers in the empty spaces, can you make the numbers in each of the 16 hexagons add up to 25? No two numbers in each hexagon may be the same and you can't use zero. We've started you off.

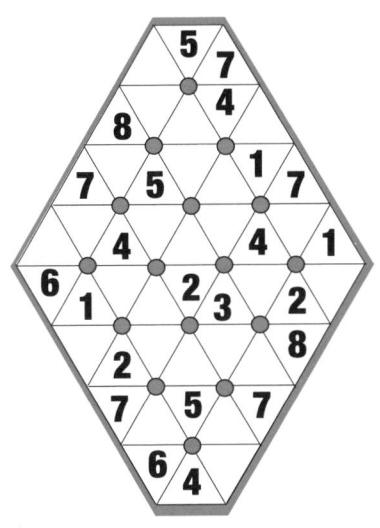

58 LIFE ON THE OCEAN WAVE

Which one of the numbered prints did the stamp create?

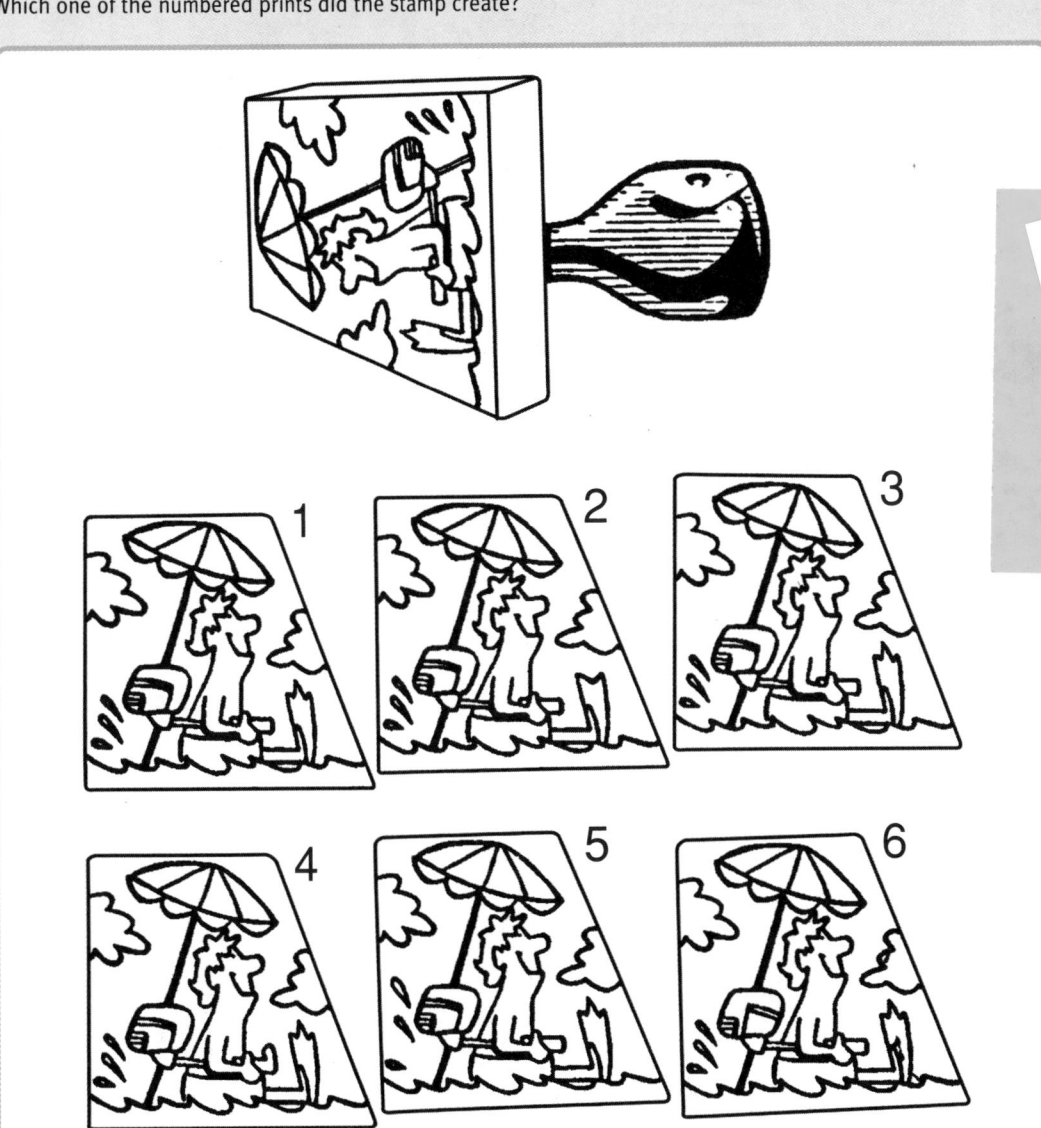

59 CUT BACK

The first three pictures A, B, C form a sequence. Which of the pictures D, E and F is the correct one to continue the pattern?

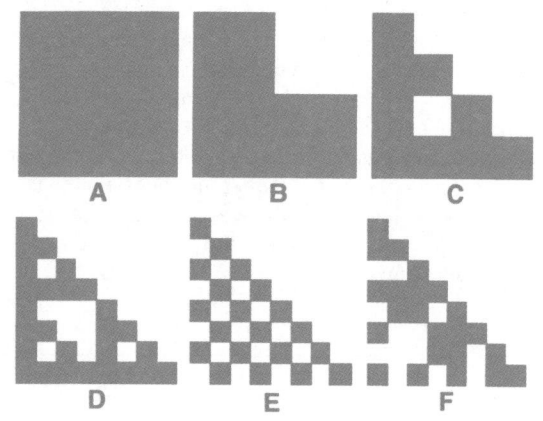

61 BOOK BORROWING

The top shelf shows books at the start of the day, when Puzzleton Library opened. The bottom shelf shows books at the end of the day, when Puzzleton Library closed. During the day the books were all studied by various people who replaced them in different positions and one was borrowed and taken home. Can you discover which is missing?

62 NINE NUMBERS

Place a number from 1 to 9 in each empty cell so that each row, each column and each 3 x 3 block contains all the numbers from 1 to 9.

	6	3			2	4	1	
4			5		8			7
8			1		3			6
9	8	7				1	4	
				3				
	2	4				6	9	5
7			2		1			4
6			3		9			1
	1	8	4			7	3	

60 NUMBER JIG

Fit the numbers into the grid. One has been done for you.

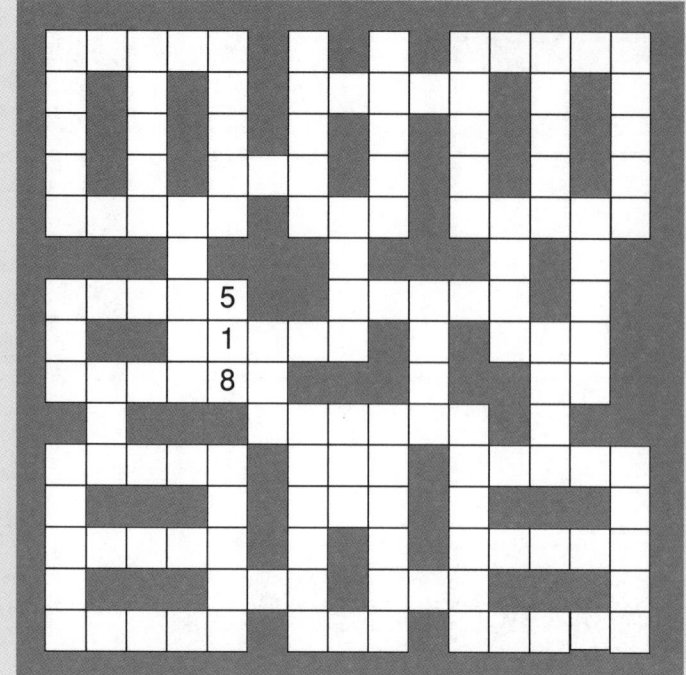

3 figures

102
190
240
299
347
372
518
593
609
656
825
911
964

4 figures

3581
6617

8570
9360

5 figures

12756
14099
18200
18808
24971
28146
31927
32481
32810
33264
34079
36638
41703
42036
43026

43312
50721
53904
60049
63491
70950
73624
81955
83013
92538
94270
94407

6 figures

142807
431296
552881
784399
872366

63 MAZE MYSTERY

Travel from the entrance to the exit of the maze, filling the path completely to create a picture.

64 BOXES

Pattern A when cut out and folded along the straight lines will make a cube-shaped box. This folded box is shown in figures 1 and 2 but in each case one face is left blank. Can you fill in the missing symbols which should appear on the blank faces? When you have done this, repeat the same procedure with pattern B and figures 3 and 4.

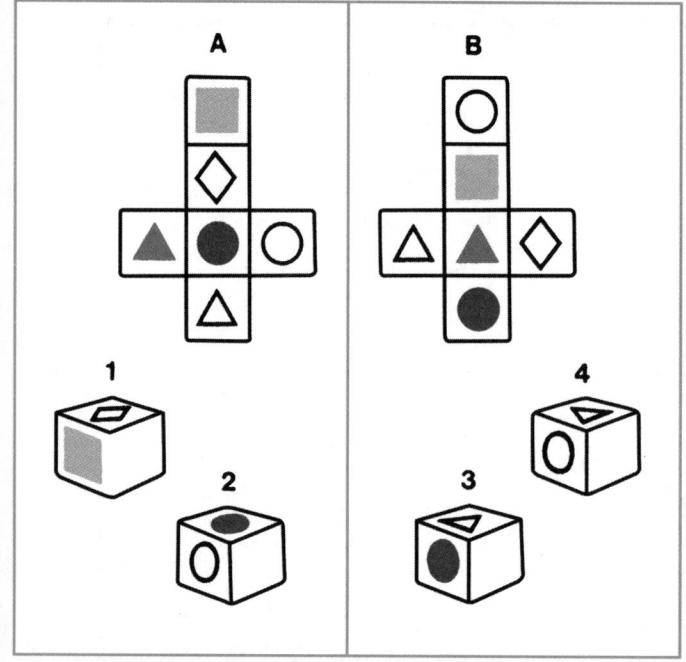

65 ONE TO TEN

In this tangle of numbers, can you find a path which passes through all the numbers from 1 to 10? The numbers must run consecutively.

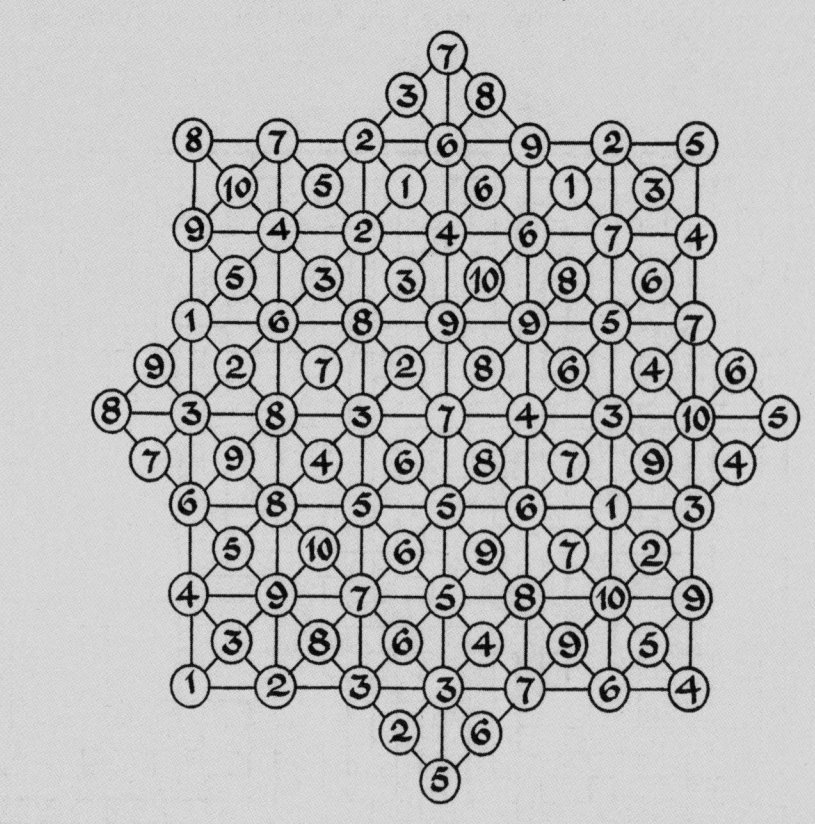

66 DOMINO SEARCH

A set of dominoes has been laid out, using numbers instead of dots for clarity, but the lines which separate the dominoes have been left out. Can you show where each domino in the set has been placed? You may find the check grid useful as each domino is identified by its number pair and the appropriate box can be ticked when the domino has been located. To give you a start 0*9 has been marked in.

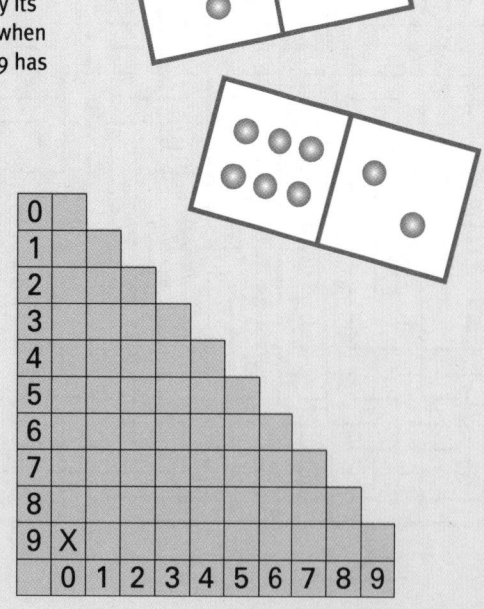

8	0	3	2	7	9	8	0	9	7	9
7	4	7	1	1	2	2	4	9	3	6
8	3	5	8	2	3	0	9	0	5	0
4	4	4	9	6	2	4	3	7	8	3
8	0	0	3	8	1	6	0	8	6	3
4	1	8	9	2	5	8	5	8	9	2
1	2	3	5	9	5	7	2	3	1	4
5	7	5	7	6	7	1	6	1	6	6
1	7	9	6	5	4	5	2	0	3	1
0	5	0	7	6	6	9	4	2	1	4

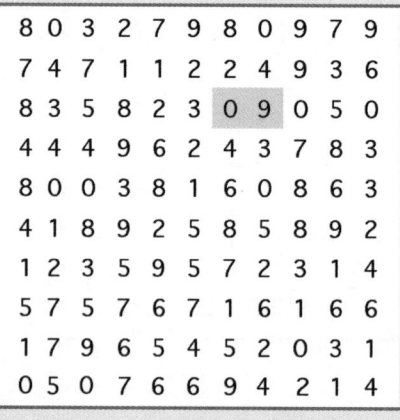

67 CELL STRUCTURE

The object is to create white areas surrounded by black walls, so that:
• Each white area contains only one number
• The number of cells in a white area is equal to the number in it
• The white areas are separated from each other with a black wall
• Cells containing numbers must not be filled in
• The black cells must be linked into a continuous wall
• Black cells cannot form a square of 2 x 2 or larger

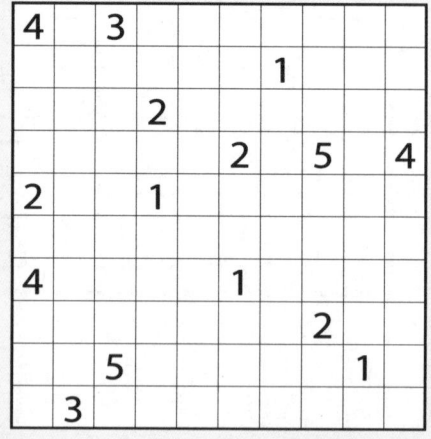

68 SHORT ORDER

These six souls are happy couples – can you put a name to each and match up the pairs?

1 Art is heavier than Alice's date.
2 Bill's date is taller than Chuck's date.
3 Chuck is heavier than Beth's date.
4 Chuck's date is taller than Cathy.

69 BOX CLEVER

Using just two straight lines, can you divide this box into three segments, each containing six differently coloured crayons?

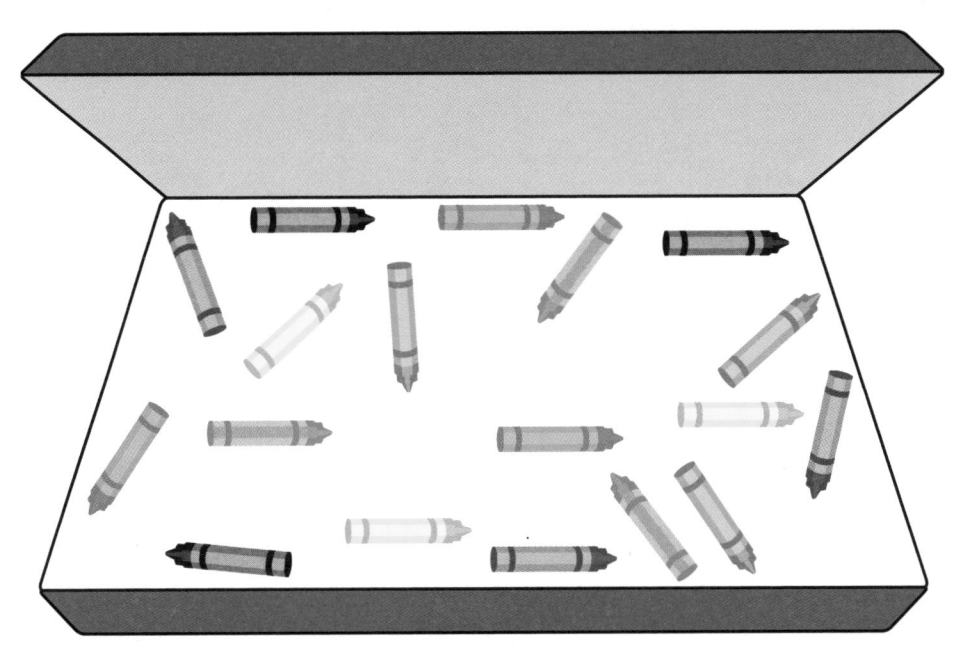

70 IT FIGURES

Place a number from 1 to 9 in each empty cell so that the sum of each vertical or horizontal block equals the number at the top or on the left of that block. Numbers may only be used once in each block.

71 BIG BREAK

A snooker break is made up by potting red balls (maximum 15) which are each followed by one of six different colours. The point values of the balls are:-

 RED 1

 YELLOW 2

 GREEN 3

 BROWN 4

 BLUE 5

 PINK 6

 BLACK 7

Snooker player Bob Basher made a break of 74, which ended when he failed to pot a red. In the break he potted more blacks than browns and more blues than pinks, potting all four colours in the break, each a different number of times.

How many of each colour ball were potted?

72 21s

Obeying the normal rules of arithmetic, with the numbers given, using only where necessary +, −, x, or ÷, make the resulting calculations equal 21.

$$6 \quad 3 \quad 9 \quad 6 = 21$$

$$4 \quad 4 \quad 2 \quad 3 = 21$$

$$3 \quad 5 \quad 10 \quad 4 = 21$$

73 TRILINES

Can you divide this square into six sections, each containing three pairs of different symbols, by drawing three straight lines? The lines must run from one reference number to another on the other side of the square.

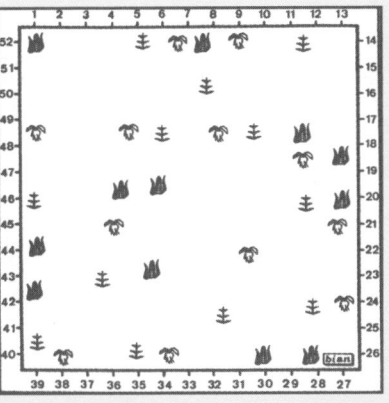

74 TEA FOR TWO

Which two teapots are exactly identical?

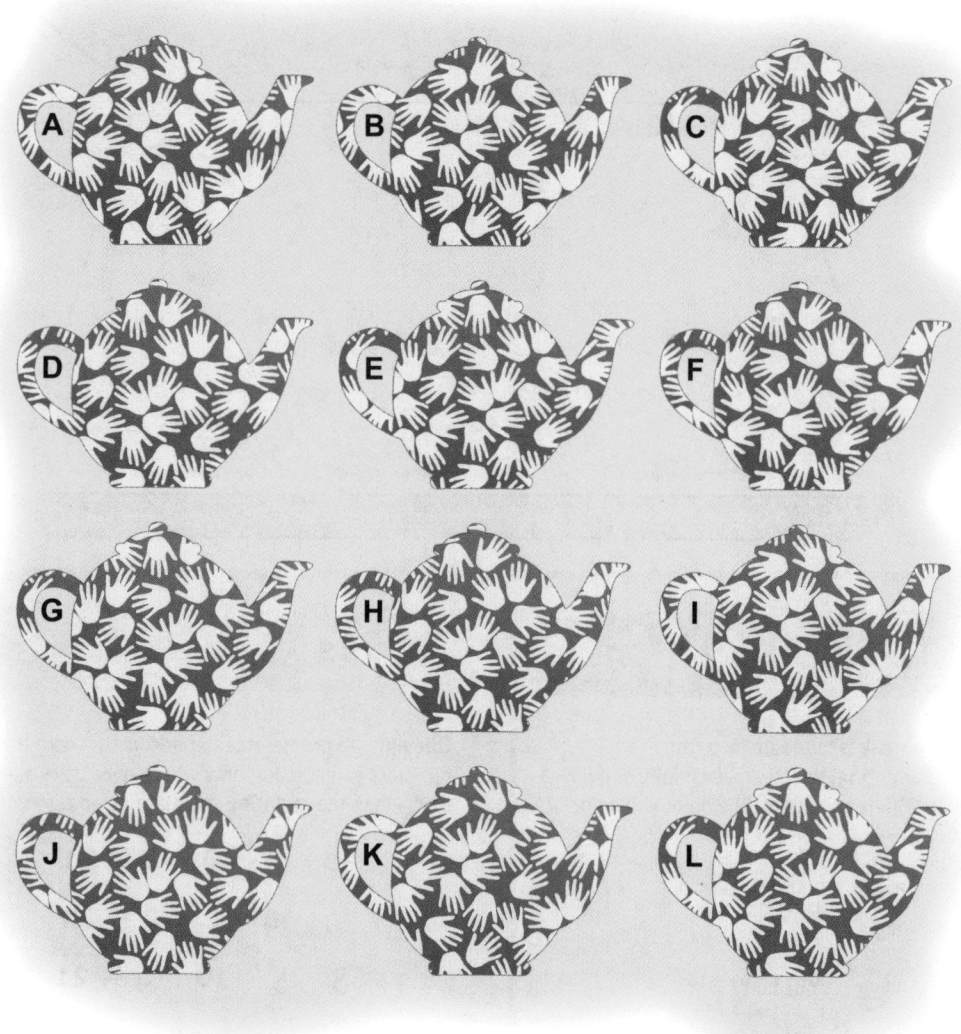

75 LOGI-5

Each line, across and down, is to have each of the letters A, B, C, D and E, appearing once each. Also, every shape – shown by the thick lines, must also have each of the letters in it. Can you fill in the grid?

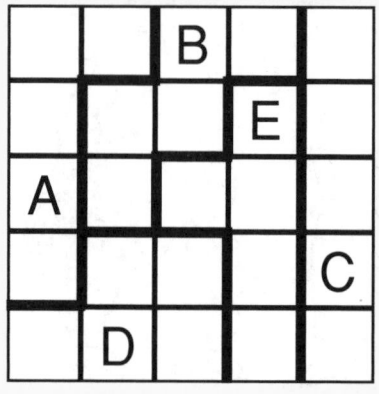

76 ABC

Each line, across and down, is to have each of the letters A, B and C, and two empty squares. The letter outside the grid shows the first or second letter in the direction of the arrow. Can you fill in the grid?

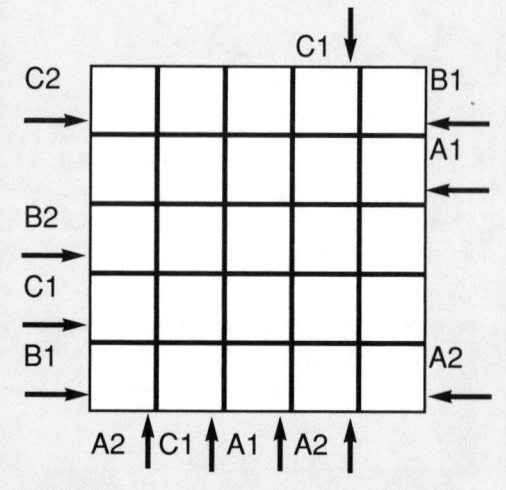

77 LOGI-TILES

Following the first diagram, there is a logical rule that determines how the next block is to be filled in. Given these three blocks, can you colour in the fourth?

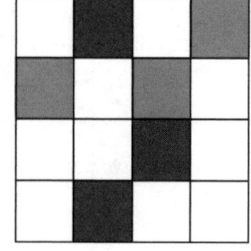 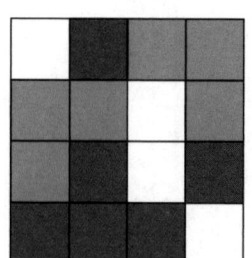  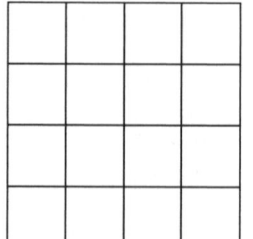

78 NUMBER JIG ●●

Fit the numbers into the grid. One has been done for you.

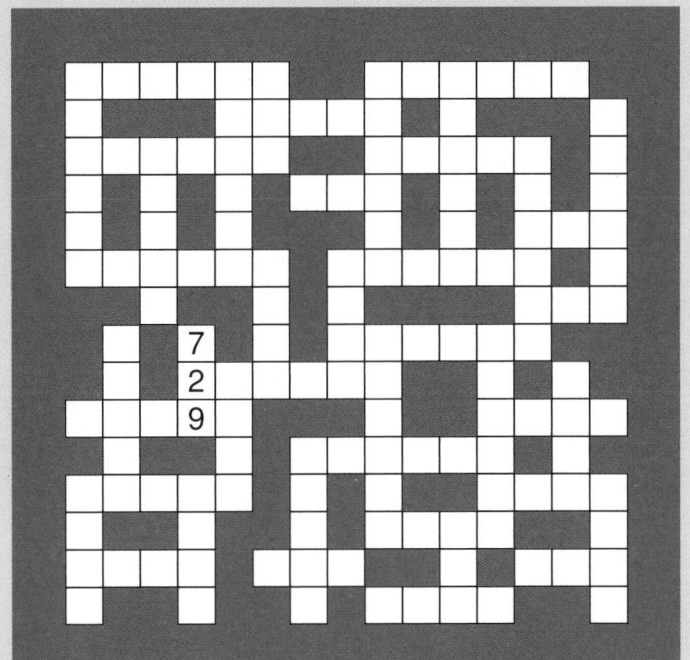

3 figures	5325	6 figures
178	6193	125507
281	7274	234006
302	8180	324318
348	9162	352810
583	9383	363909
633		416332
~~729~~	**5 figures**	439114
904	11091	455232
	20585	506342
4 figures	28614	514368
1992	40106	625331
2231	53046	679073
3146	61859	724300
4535	83123	802202
5190		832192
5218		926452

79 WHERE THE L?

Twelve L shapes like the ones below have been fitted into a square shape. Each L has one hole, and there are three of each type in the square. No two pieces of the same type are adjacent, even at a corner. They fit together so well that the spaces between pieces do not show. From the locations of the holes, can you tell where each L is?

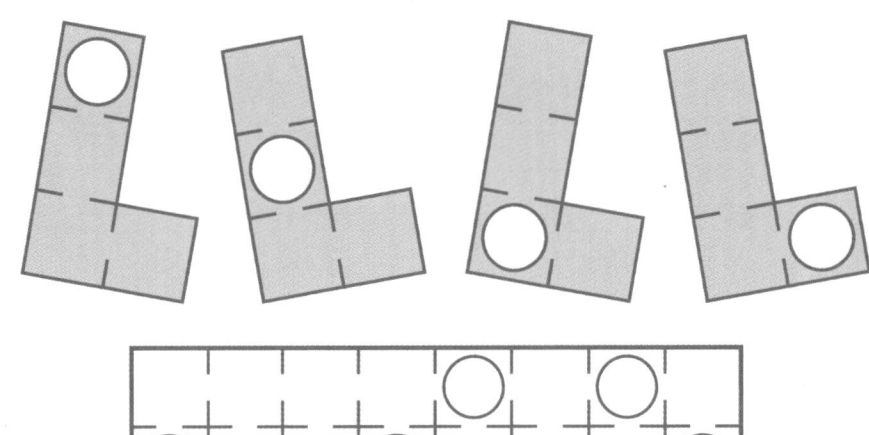

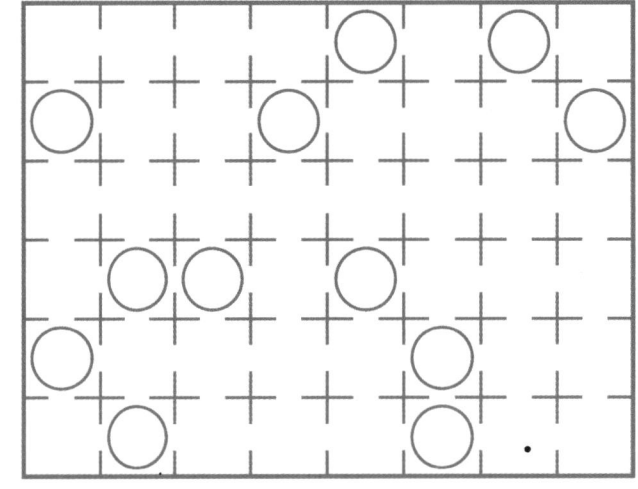

80 NINE NUMBERS

Place a number from 1 to 9 in each empty cell so that each row, each column and each 3 x 3 block contains all the numbers from 1 to 9.

2	5			4			7	1
7			9		1			2
		6		7		5		
	6		2		4		1	
4		1				2		3
	9		6		8		5	
		5		2		8		
9			7		5			4
6	3			8			2	5

81 SET SQUARE ●●

All the digits from 1 to 9 are used in this grid, but only once. Can you work out their positions in the grid and make the sums work? We've given two numbers to start you off.

	+		÷	5	=	1
+	■	x	■	x		
	+		÷		=	6
−	■	−	■	−		
7	+		−		=	5
=		=		=		
3		6		2		

25

At Come Prancing's Annual Dance Gala, four couples reprised the Latin-American section from the previous week's Amateur Finals. As the gala was a fancy dress affair, at least the ladies could now wear more each than they had between them in the competition and the men could remove the rose stems from between their punctured gums. This time round, nobody danced with his/her spouse and each had a different partner in each dance. From these pairings, hastily made as the couples twirled faster than a cheerleader's baton, can you identify each married couple and the costume each is sporting?

CHA-CHA	RUMBA	TANGO
Pirate & Ann	Jester & Mark's wife	Fairy's husband & Rose
Mr Turner & Mrs Young	Steve & Ballerina	Eskimo & King's wife
Rose's husband & Leila	Mr Turner & Nurse	Jester & Norman's wife
John & Mrs Downs	Norman & Cowgirl	Mr West & Zoe

82 TAKING STEPS

83 EASY AS ABC

Each row and column originally contained one A, one B, one C, one D and two blank squares. Each letter and number refers to the first or second of the four letters encountered when travelling in the direction of the arrow. Can you complete the original grid?

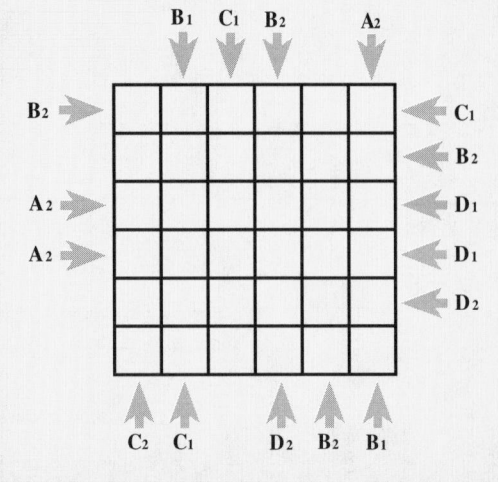

84 NINE NUMBERS

Place a number from 1 to 9 in each empty cell so that each row, each column and each 3 x 3 block contains all the numbers from 1 to 9.

			9	5	6	4		
		6					8	2
		8		4	9			5
	4	6	1		3	5		7
2				5				8
3		5	7		9	2	6	
4		8	9		7			
1	2				8			
	6	7	3	4				

85 HIGH CARDS

Five cards have been laid out, all are between Ace and Ten. All four suits are represented. No three of the cards form a consecutive sequence of numbers.

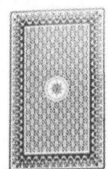 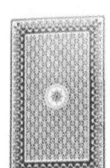   

The total value of Red cards is the same as the total value of Black cards.
The total value of Hearts is 12.
The even-value cards have a total four higher than the sum of the odd-value cards.
The Club has a lower value than the Spade. The lowest card is a Diamond.
Which five cards have been dealt?

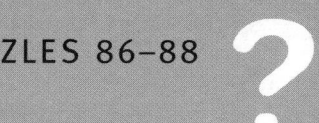

86 COG-ITATION

In which direction will each of the lettered weights move when the figure pulls the rope?

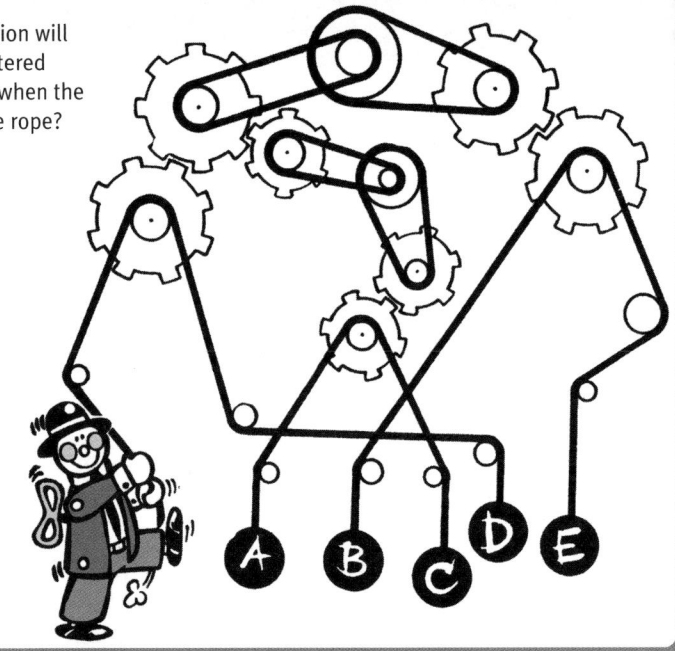

87 NUMBER JIG

Fit the numbers into the grid. One has been done for you.

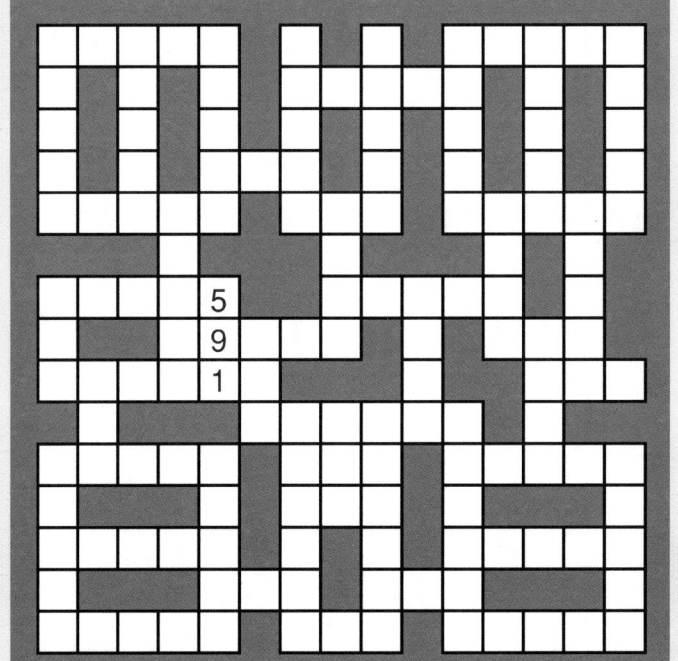

3 figures		
165	6912	68688
168	9553	71206
248		71209
364	**5 figures**	71301
381	10211	78800
400	10860	80035
550	15131	83247
591	15771	89905
610	20185	91206
702	27761	91324
883	32198	98801
892	32909	
956	34848	**6 figures**
983	35016	280376
	39246	330514
4 figures	40118	483321
1336	50106	615229
5193	50662	861234
	60345	
	62320	

88 ALL FALL DOWN

Which of the falling girls are identical?

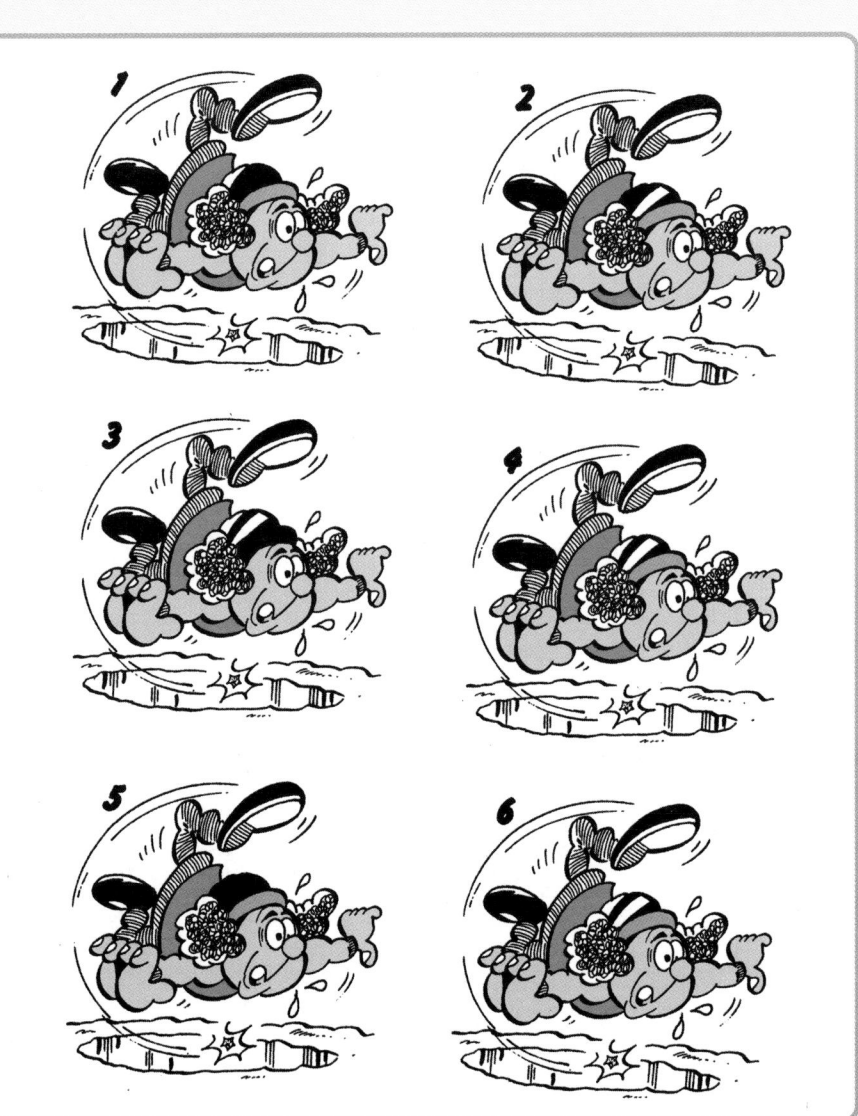

89 MAZE MYSTERY

Travel from the entrance to the exit of the maze, filling the path completely to create a picture.

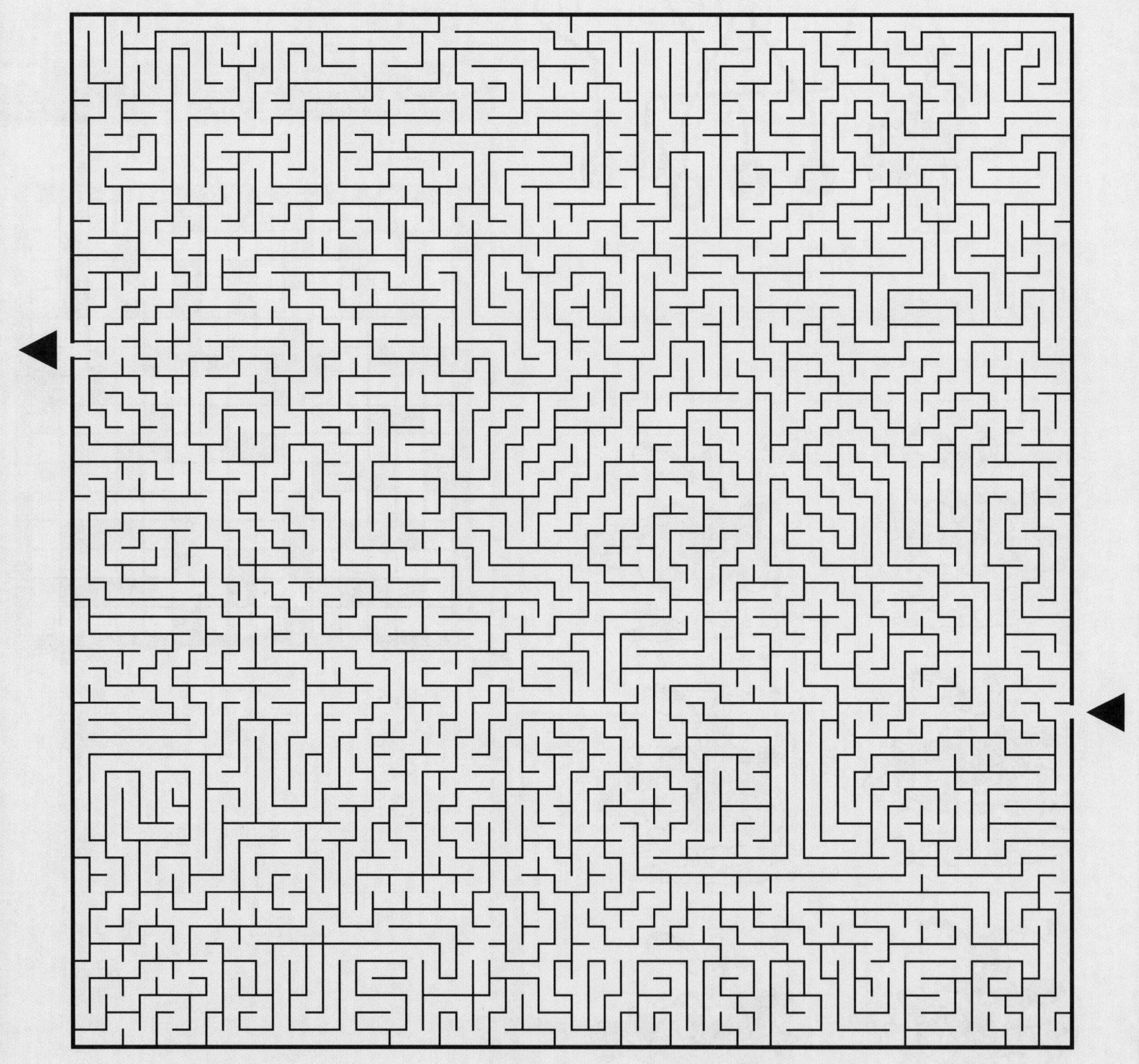

90 DOMINO SEARCH

A set of dominoes has been laid out, using numbers instead of dots for clarity, but the lines which separate the dominoes have been left out. Can you show where each domino in the set has been placed? You may find the check grid useful as each domino is identified by its number pair and the appropriate box can be ticked when the domino has been located. To give you a start, 0*9 has been marked in.

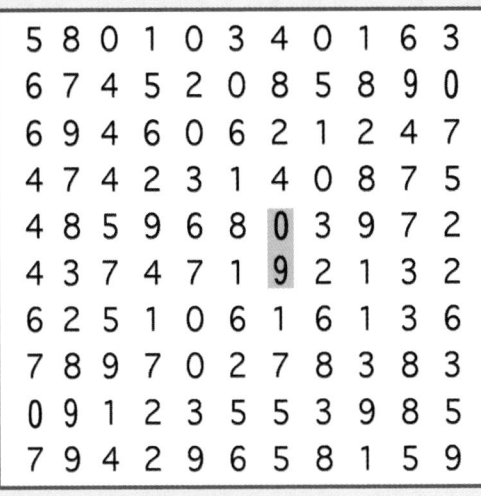
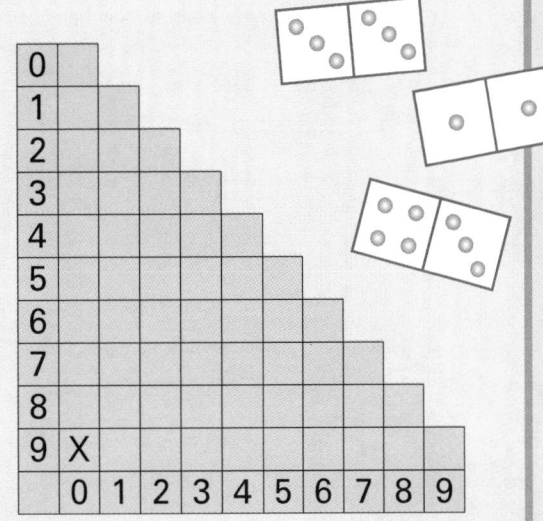

91 LOGI-5

Each line, across and down, is to have each of the five colours appearing once each. Each colour must also appear just once in each shape, shown by thick lines. Can you colour in this crazy quilt, or mark each square with its correct letter B, G, R, V or Y?

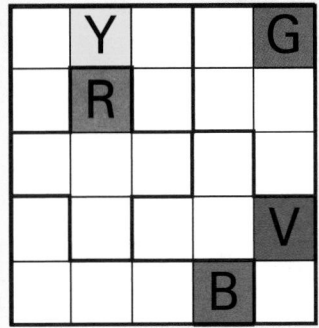

92 TAKE NOTE

Something's gone wrong with Tony's saxophone. He wants to play a tune but can't produce a note. Can you find ten musical notes hidden somewhere in this picture so that Tony can start to play?

93 ON THE SPOT

Can you place the dominoes into the grid so that the four vertical, four horizontal and both diagonal rows each have a spot total of eleven?

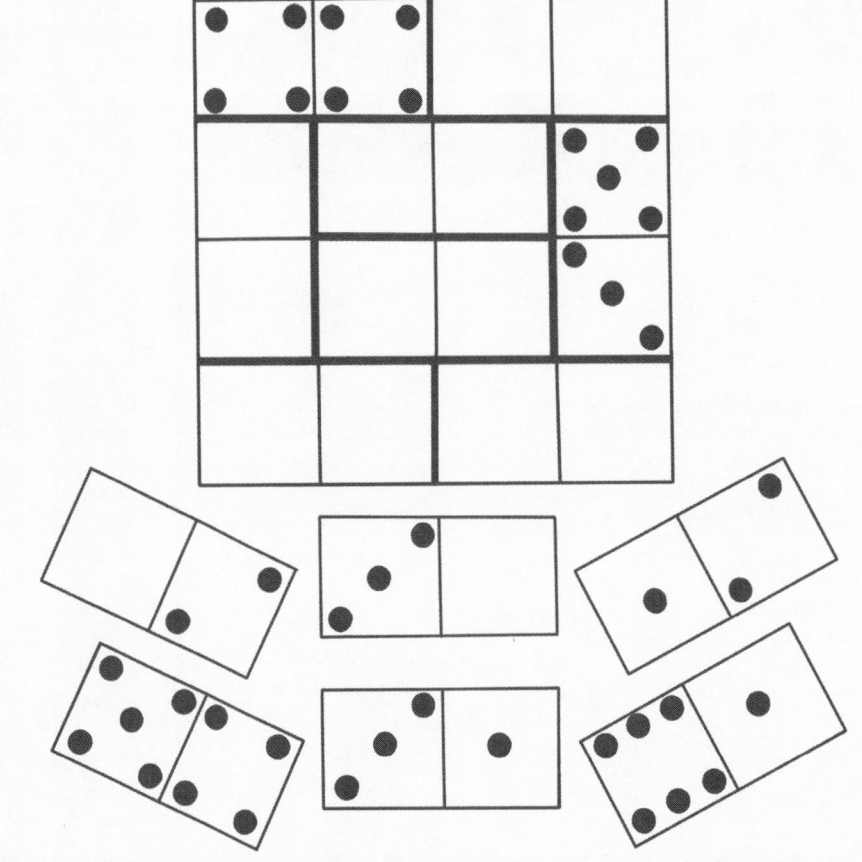

94 DOTTY DILEMMA

Connect adjacent dots with vertical or horizontal lines so that a single loop is formed with no crossings or branches. Each number indicates how many lines surround it, while empty cells may be surrounded by any number of lines.

```
. . 3 . 3 . . . . . 0 . .
. . . . . . 1 . 3 . . 3 . . 1
. 0 . 2 . . . . . . . . . . 2
. . . . . . 1 . 0 . 2 . . .
. . . 3 . . . . . . 3 . . 3 . 3
. . . 2 . 3 . . . . . . . . . 0
. . . . . . 0 . . 3 . 2 . . .
. 2 . . . . . . . . . . 2 . 3
. 3 . . 2 . . 3 . 0 . . . . .
. . . . 0 . . . . . . 0 . 2 .
```

96 NUMBER JIG

Fit the numbers into the grid. One has been done for you.

3 9 6

3 figures
128
285
~~396~~
586
793
861
950

4 figures
1218
1809
2237
3354
4026
5302
6195

6233
8139
9303

5 figures
25510
32165
51995
78163
92851

6 figures
108392
122589
210101
329406
403625

411074
525008
606340
726493
783914
803103
895105
938118

7 figures
1438116
2117055
3248813
5246319
5360241
8302269
9372688

95 DOMINO DEAL

A standard set (0–0 to 6–6) is laid out below. Each domino is placed so that the larger number will be on the bottom:
i.e.
```
    3        not     6
    6                3
```

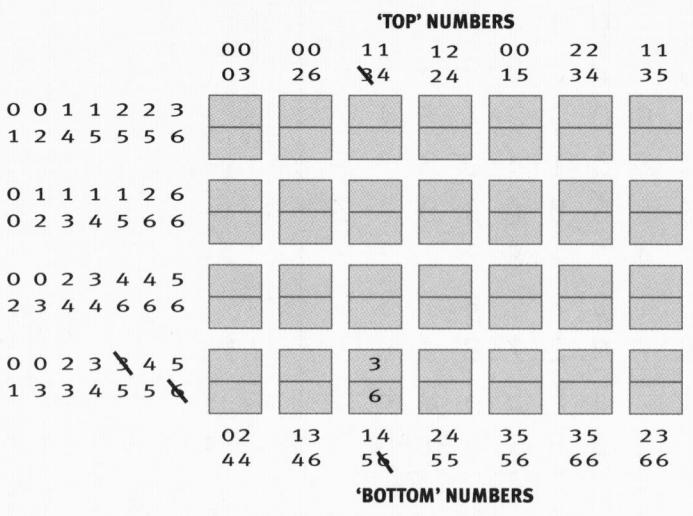

Those TOP NUMBERS show the four numbers which form the top half of each domino in that column. The BOTTOM NUMBERS, below the grid, give the four bottom numbers for that column. The seven numbers on the left show the numbers which belong in that row. Can you cross-reference the facts and deduce where each domino has been placed? 3*6 is given as a start.

'TOP' NUMBERS

| | 00 | 00 | 11 | 12 | 00 | 22 | 11 |
	03	26	~~14~~	24	15	34	35
0 0 1 1 2 2 3 / 1 2 4 5 5 5 6							
0 1 1 1 1 2 6 / 0 2 3 4 5 6 6							
0 0 2 3 4 4 5 / 2 3 4 4 6 6 6							
0 0 2 3 ~~4~~ 4 5 / 1 3 3 4 5 5 ~~6~~			3 / 6				
	02	13	14	24	35	35	23
	44	46	~~5~~	55	56	66	66

'BOTTOM' NUMBERS

97 SIX GEESE-A-LAYING

When the six geese were finally trapped and boxed they settled down and began laying eggs, in nests numbered 1 to 6. Next morning, Miss T Hyde discovered that:

1 Only two of the birds laid the same number of eggs as the number of the box each was in.
2 Twenty-one eggs were laid altogether, no two birds laying the same number. No bird failed to lay any.
3 Clarissa, who was on one end, laid half as many eggs as were laid by both Brenda and the goose in box 5 added together.
4 Deirdre laid twice as many eggs as her box number. Her neighbour on one side, Felicity, laid two less eggs than Edwina who was Deirdre's neighbour on the other side.
5 The goose to the right of Abigail laid 3 eggs which was less than were laid in box 1.

Naturally, that golden egg was the only one laid by that remarkably gifted bird. Can you name her, and say in which box Miss Hyde will find her fortune? (Right is as you face the nests.)

98 POLYGON POSER

Which are the only two pieces that will fit together perfectly, to form a blue copy of this white shape?

A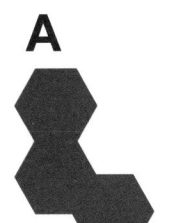

B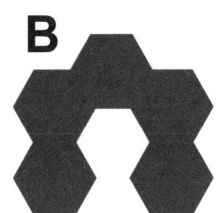

C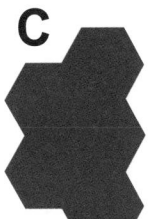

D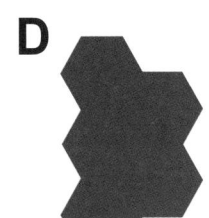

E

F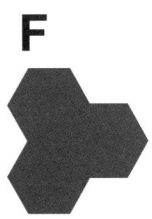

G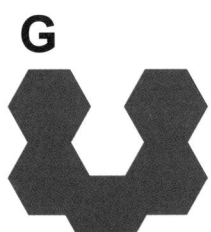

H

99 NUMBER JIG

Fit the numbers into the grid. One has been done for you.

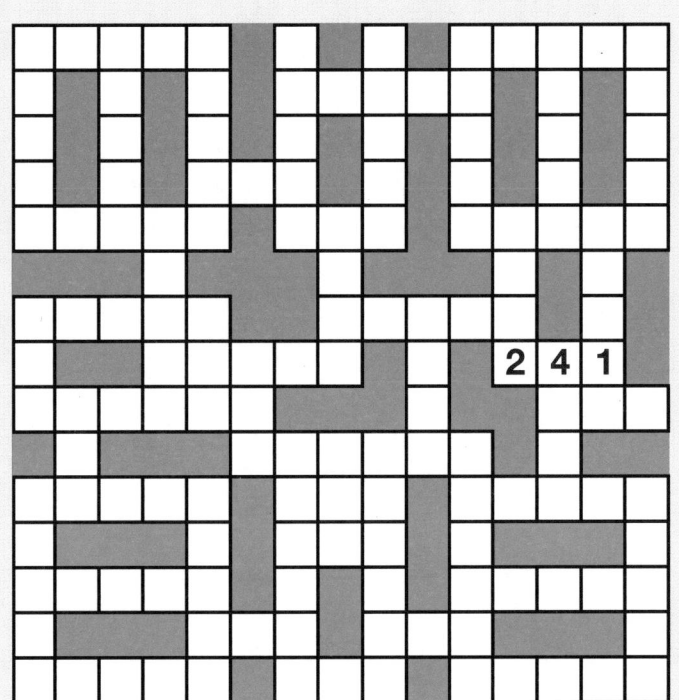

3 figures	4245	60826
116	7443	63091
170		67768
241	**5 figures**	71910
249	13598	74783
306	15348	79805
353	19281	82001
423	24467	82697
551	25732	83728
582	28906	90723
614	30714	92200
779	35543	93014
821	36772	
954	44596	**6 figures**
970	48190	116238
	49647	250867
4 figures	52673	268982
1298	52739	646903
3302	53509	934516

100 NINE NUMBERS

Place a number from 1 to 9 in each empty cell so that each row, each column and each 3 x 3 block contains all the numbers from 1 to 9.

2	6				3			1
				8		4		7
	8	3	7			9		
1					5			
	9			4			8	
		2						3
		8			2	6	9	
6		4		1				
5			6				2	8

101 PATTERN MAKER

Can you place the numbered blocks into the grid to form the pattern shown? The blocks may be placed horizontally or vertically, and can be turned round.

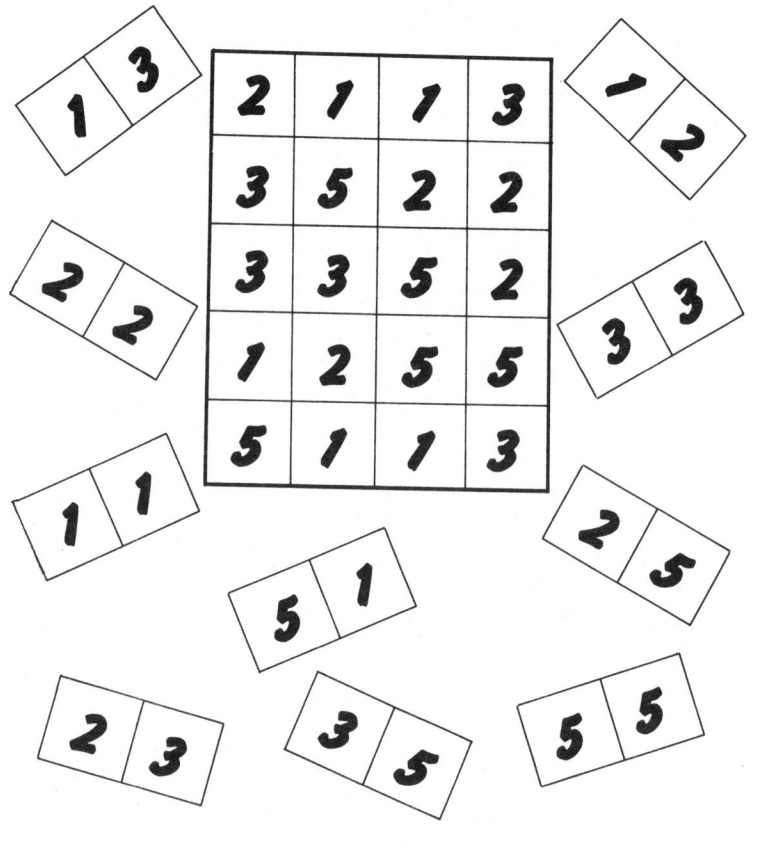

103 ROPED INTO IT!

When the man pulls the rope which weights will go down and which will go up?

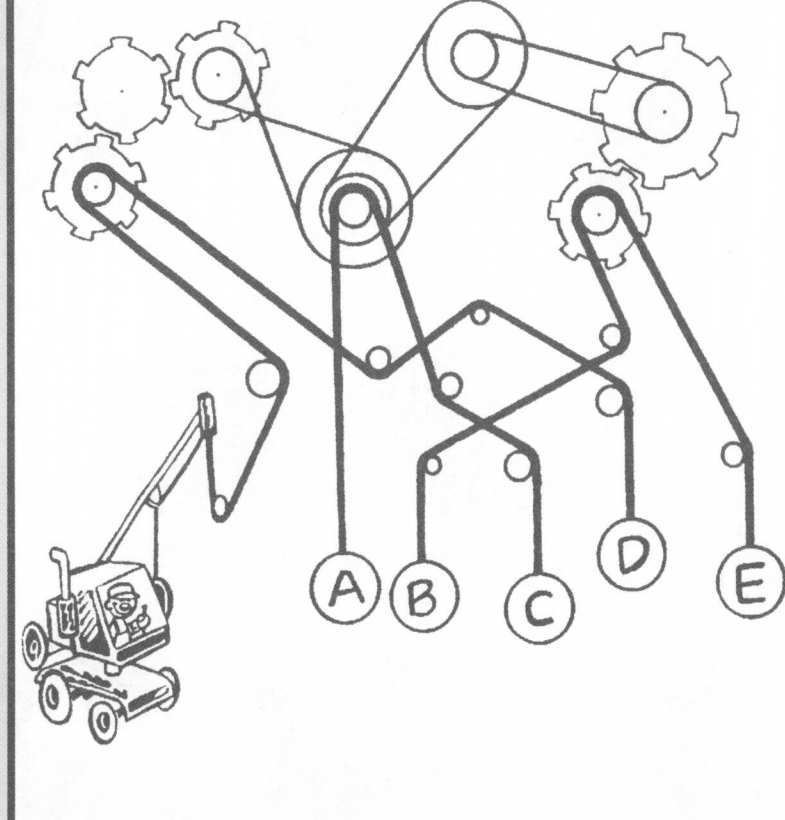

102 METEOR MUDDLE

In the picture on the left there are seven flying saucers flying through a meteorite storm. When they returned one was missing. Can you work out which one?

104 LONELY VIGILS ●●●

In the later years of the Roman occupation of Britain, the garrisons in the legionary fortresses were much depleted. In Deva, for example, they could spare only one man at a time to guard each of the four walls. From the clues given, can you indicate in the diagram the name of the soldier on each wall, his home country and the number of years he had served in his legion?

Clues

1 The wall patrolled by Blunderbuss was opposite the one whose guard had twelve years' service; he was not Rictus.
2 The man on the south wall was neither Voluminus nor the one from Syria.
3 The man from Gallia had been assigned to the west wall; the one from Africa had eleven years' service behind him; and the man on the north wall had served for nine years.
4 The duty centurion making a clockwise tour of the walls would have come across Hiatus next after the man from Germania; neither of these was the longest serving legionary.

Names: Blunderbuss; Hiatus; Rictus; Voluminus
Countries: Africa; Gallia; Germania; Syria
Years' service: 9, 10, 11, 12

Starting tip: Work out who has served for twelve years.

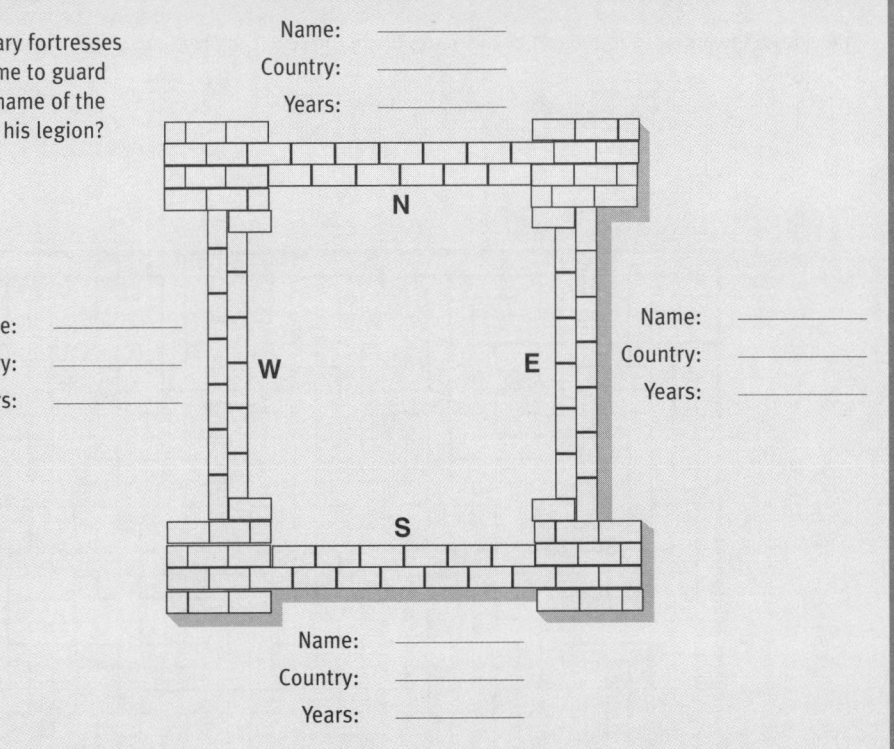

Name: ———
Country: ———
Years: ———

Name: ———
Country: ———
Years: ———

Name: ———
Country: ———
Years: ———

Name: ———
Country: ———
Years: ———

105 LOGI-5 ●

Each line, across and down, is to have each of the letters A, B, C, D and E, appearing once each. Also, every shape – shown by the thick lines – must also have each of the letters in it. Can you fill in the grid?

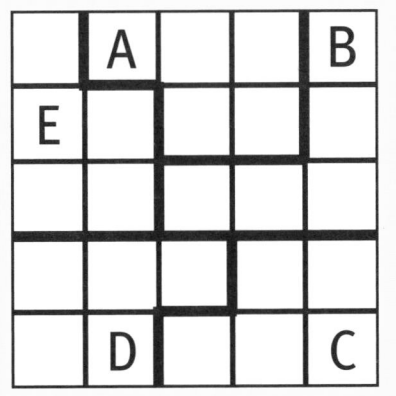

106 NUMBER SQUARES ●●

Find the following numbers in the grid in a square formation. The first set has been found for you. Take care, some digits may be mixed up within the square.

4	2	0	4	3	9	3	1	3	8
8	3	5	8	5	1	2	4	0	4
9	1	4	6	1	8	2	0	5	7
2	7	3	0	3	8	9	3	9	
5	0	9	6	8	2	4	2	1	4
9	7	2	1	7	5	3	6	5	8
3	1	4	9	2	8	0	2	3	2

3159   2890   6523   9713
4531   7681   0483

107 SET SQUARE ●●

All the digits from 1 to 9 are used in this grid, but only once each. Can you work out their positions in the grid and make the sums work? We've given two numbers to start you off.

108 NINE NUMBERS ●

Place a number from 1 to 9 in each empty cell so that each row, each column and each 3 x 3 block contains all the numbers from 1 to 9.

8			7					2
	6	4		2	8			
	5			3			1	
	1		5		4		2	
2		5				6		7
	3		2		7		5	
	2			1			3	
		9	7		3	4		
3				4				8

109 MAZE MYSTERY

Travel from the entrance to the exit of the maze, filling the path completely to create a picture.

110 LOGI-5

Each line, across and down, is to have each of the five colours appearing once each. Each colour must also appear just once in each shape, shown by thick lines. Can you colour in this crazy quilt, or mark each square with its correct letter B, G, R, V or Y?

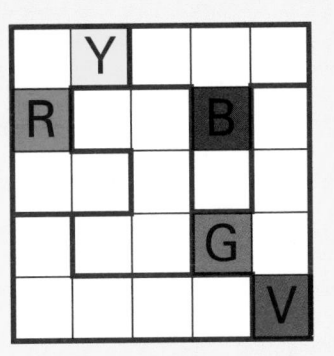

WHERE THE L?

Twelve L-shapes like the ones shown have been inserted in the grid. Each L has one hole in it. There are three pieces of each of the four kinds shown below and any piece might be turned or flipped over before being put into the grid. No two pieces of the same kind touch, even at a corner. The pieces fit together so well that you cannot see the spaces between them; only the holes show. Can you tell where the Ls are?

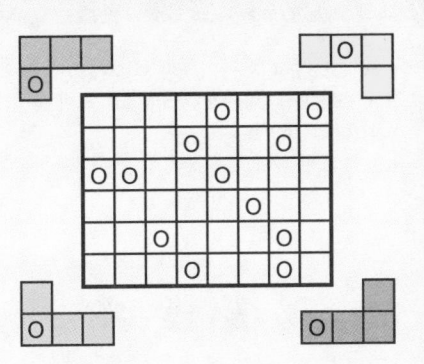

111 MISTLING OUT

Letting down the company's structural barriers at Amalgamated Scrufflinks office party last week produced predictable results. Five males, armed with alcohol and mistletoe, set out for closer contact with a lady than ever is possible at departmental meetings. Experience, though, has also armed each lady...

1 The director pursued the personnel officer who is not I Noah who invited her mistletoe waver to meet her husband who was just looming large in the doorway. H Bee-Pensill is not the general manager.

2 The secretary suggested to her pursuer that he listen to a tape recording she had made at last year's party but this was to neither D Veeus nor the driver.

3 E Stender was offered a look at the file reporting his inflated expenses but by neither J Beecy nor the typist.

4 F Ishent is a director but was not the lady pursued by the salesman or the one who stopped A Hound in his tracks by getting him drunk.

5 C Nutting is the clerk who was after neither the general manager nor G Purrs who was harrassed by the accountant who is not A Hound or E Stender.

6 It was the salesman who had his picture taken just as he leered into action but he is not B Pushie who is not the driver.

	ACCOUNTANT	CLERK	DIRECTOR	DRIVER	SALESMAN	F ISHENT	G PURRS	H BEE-PENSILL	I NOAH	J BEECY	DIRECTOR	GEN. MANAGER	PERSONNEL OFF.	SECRETARY	TYPIST	GET DRUNK	MEET HUSBAND	PLAY TAPE	SHOW FILE	TAKE PICTURE
A HOUND																				
B PUSHIE																				
C NUTTING																				
D VEEUS																				
E STENDER																				
GET DRUNK																				
MEET HUSBAND																				
PLAY TAPE																				
SHOW FILE																				
TAKE PICTURE																				
DIRECTOR																				
GEN. MANAGER																				
PERSONNEL																				
SECRETARY																				
TYPIST																				
F ISHENT																				
G PURRS																				
H BEE-PENSILL																				
I NOAH																				
J BEECY																				

HE	JOB	SHE	JOB	PLOY

113 TAKE FIVE

Can you complete the 5 x 5 block so that each of the following symbols appears in all vertical and horizontal lines?

Symbols:

◆ ■ ✚ ● ▲

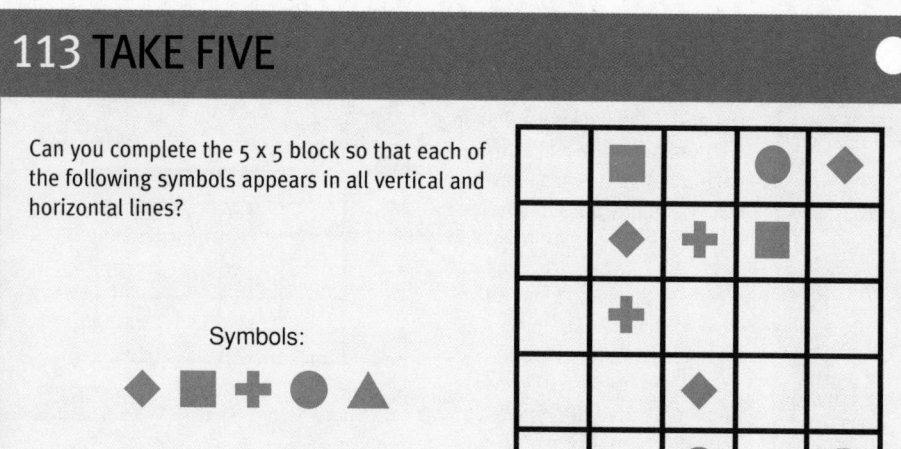

114 ISLAND HOPPING

Each circle containing a number represents an island. The object is to connect each island with vertical or horizontal bridges so that:
* The number of bridges is the same as the number inside the island.
* There can be up to two bridges between two islands.
* Bridges cannot cross islands or other bridges.
* There is a continuous path connecting all the islands.

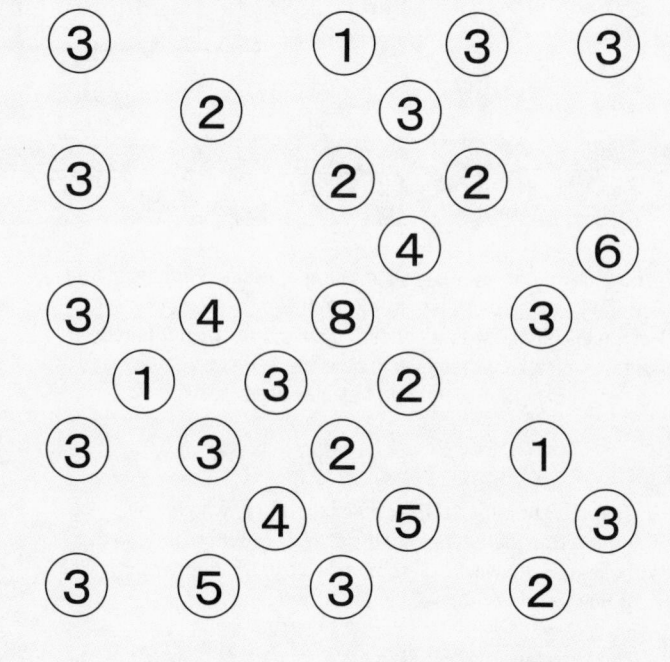

115 NUMBER JIG

Fit the numbers into the grid. One has been done for you.

3 figures	4 figures		
172	2933	37304	86261
296	3461	39610	92065
317	6514	39792	93371
366	9943	40013	93770
413		42618	
541	5 figures	48887	6 figures
552	11903	49980	493918
622	14712	50468	763081
673	15704	52789	876421
707	21014	67158	933016
745	26817	72422	946152
818	29306	72431	
820	29317	73538	
914	30115	75368	
		77213	

116 FIT TOGETHER

Which are the only two pieces which will fit together perfectly, to form a complete circle?

117 ON THE SPOT

Can you place the dominoes into the grid so that the four vertical, four horizontal and both diagonal rows each have a spot total of ten?

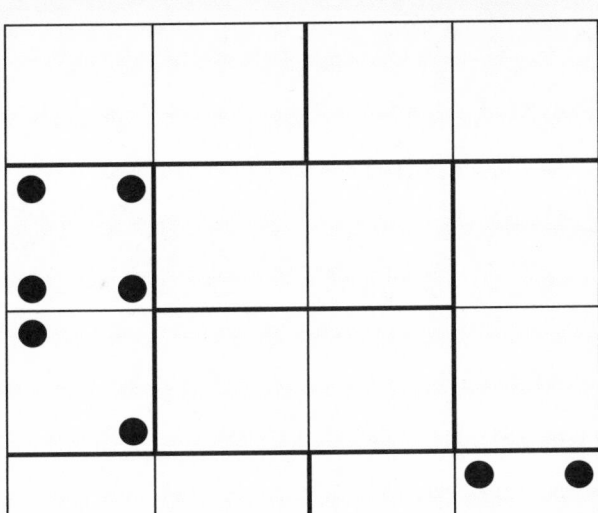

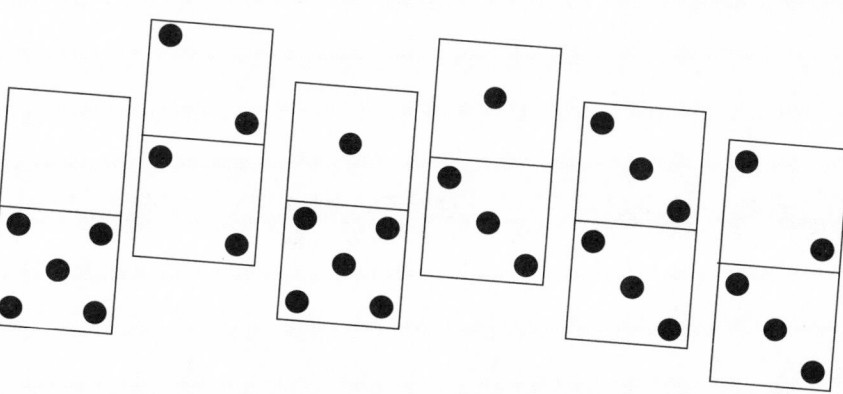

118 LOGI-5

Can you place the letters A, B, C, D, E, one to each square so that every line across and down contains each letter once and every shape made from five squares also has each letter once?

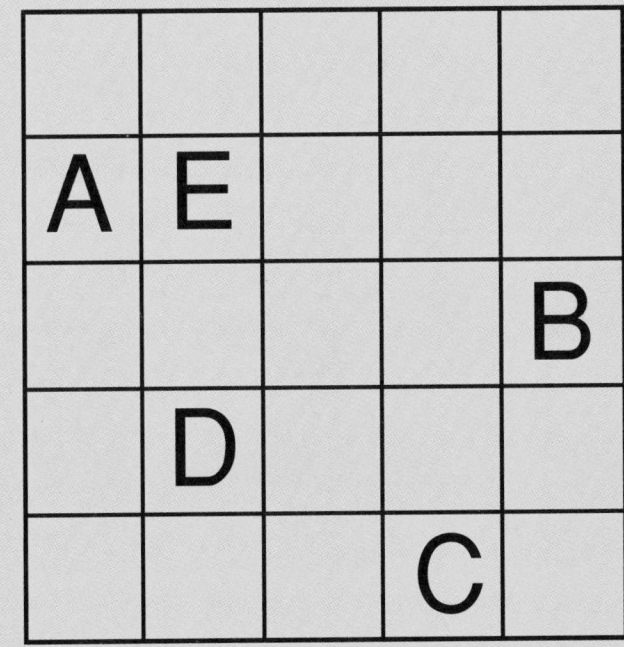

119 STOCKING FILLER

Three friends have been shopping in Weale and each bought three little presents to put in their children's Christmas stockings. Between them they bought three oranges, costing a penny each, three boxes of dates, costing twopence each, and three wooden tops costing threepence each. They did not make identical purchases; Mrs Featherbed spent exactly twice as much as Mrs Greengage and Mrs Flowerpot did not buy all three wooden tops. Who bought what?

LADY	ORANGES	DATES	TOPS

120 ABC

Each line, across and down, is to have each of the letters A, B and C, and two empty squares. The letter outside the grid shows the first or second letter in the direction of the arrow. Can you fill in the grid?

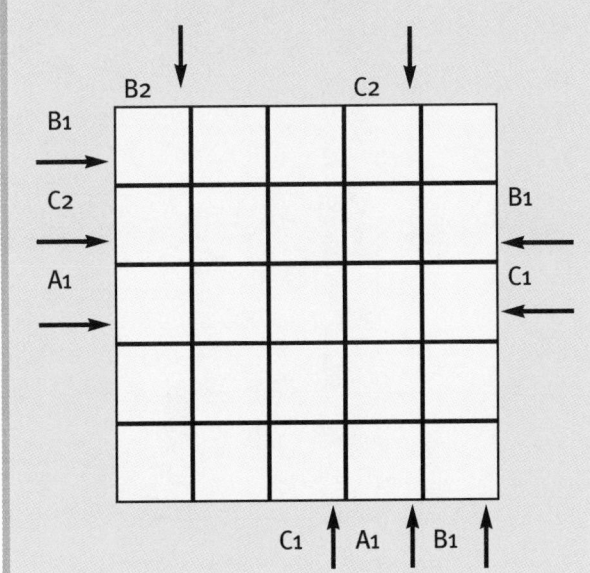

37

121 FIT TOGETHER

Which are the only three pieces which will fit together perfectly, to form a complete polygon?

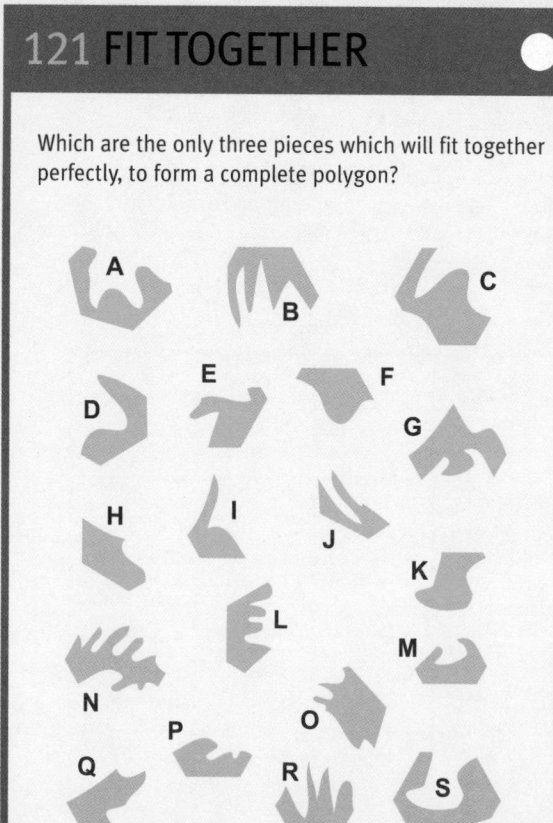

122 CAROUSEL

The merry-go-round at the fair, turning clockwise, has 16 single seats, all occupied – they too are numbered clockwise.

1 is opposite 9, 2 is opposite 10 etc. Christine is directly opposite Alice, whose one-digit seat is not no. 1 or 9; Mary's number is three lower than Joan's, and Enid's is two lower than George's.

As they turn, Peter is immediately behind Jerry, whose number is two lower than Daisy's. Bernard is one place ahead of Tom and directly opposite Kate, whose number is higher.

Freddy is one place behind Jack, whose one-digit number (not no. 1) is three lower than Charley's.

Lottie's number is divisible by three, and is one higher than Kate's.

The initial of the name of the child in seat 1 comes earlier in the alphabet than that of the child in seat 16, while the names of the children in seats 3, 10 and 14 do not begin with J.

George's seat number is prime, and is higher than Charley's, which is not prime. 1 is considered prime.

Can you locate each child?

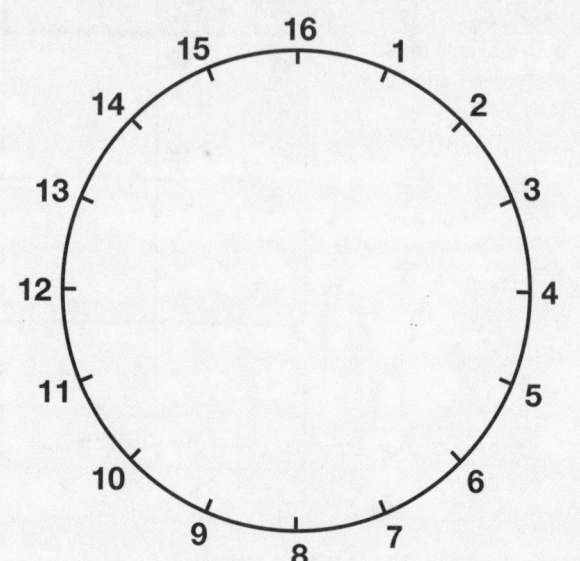

123 IT FIGURES

Place a number from 1 to 9 in each empty cell so that the sum of each vertical or horizontal block equals the number at the top or on the left of that block. Numbers may only be used once in each block.

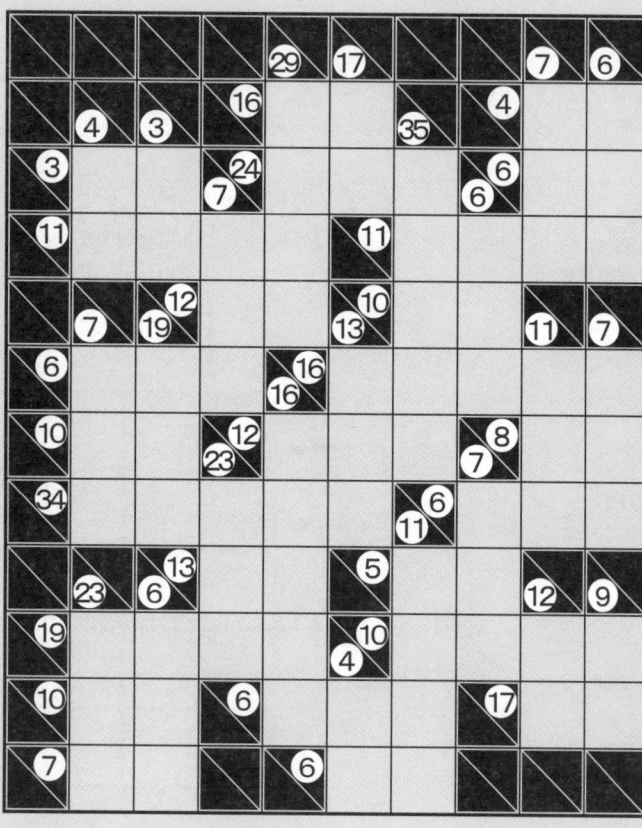

124 DOUBLE DUTCH

Theo Versteylan, a tulip grower from Zuidelijk, was found murdered. He had been hit on the head with one of his own clogs. Commissaris Van Drijver of the Amsterdam police was despatched to investigate. Five suspects are discovered but they all claim alibis from each other. The facts listed may sound like so much double Dutch, but from them Van Drijver was able to deduce that one suspect did not have an alibi. Can you?

1   Hein was not with Roel or Rudig unless Jan was with Wouter.

2   Jan was not with Roel or Wouter unless Hein was with Rudig.

3   Roel was not with Jan or Rudig unless Hein was with Wouter.

4   Rudig was not with Jan or Wouter unless Hein was with Roel.

5   Wouter was not with Hein or Roel unless Jan was with Rudig.

125 LOGI-PATH

Use your deductive reasoning to form a pathway from the box marked START to the box marked FINISH moving in either direction horizontally or vertically (but not diagonally). The number at the beginning of every row or column indicates exactly how many boxes in that row or column your pathway must pass through. The small diagram is given as an example of how it works.

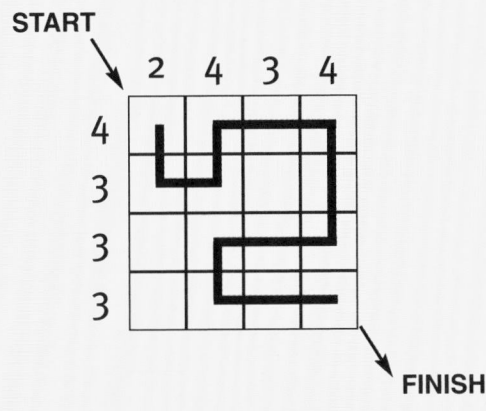

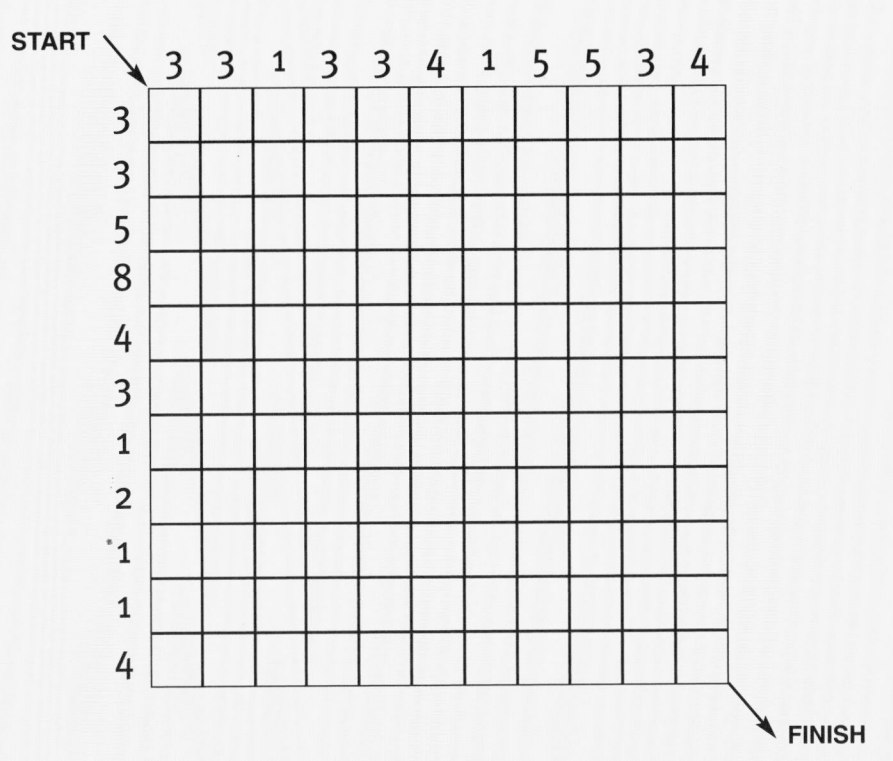

126 AROUND THE CLOCK

Tick, tock! Starting from picture 9, can you put these pictures in time order?

127 MARATHON MAN

Can you help this long-distance runner find his way to the flag?

128 DOTTY DILEMMA

Connect adjacent dots with vertical or horizontal lines so that a single loop is formed with no crossings or branches. Each number indicates how many lines surround it, while empty cells may be surrounded by any number of lines.

```
 0 1   3   0 2     2
 2       3     0 3
     3  2
    0 2     2 2  3
         3  3   3 1
  2 0   2   1
    2   2 0     0 1
           3   1
  0 1     2     3
 1    1 3   3   0 1
```

129 ISLAND HOPPING

Each circle containing a number represents an island. The object is to connect each island with vertical or horizontal bridges so that:
* The number of bridges is the same as the number inside the island.
* There can be up to two bridges between two islands.
* Bridges cannot cross islands or other bridges.
* There is a continuous path connecting all the islands.

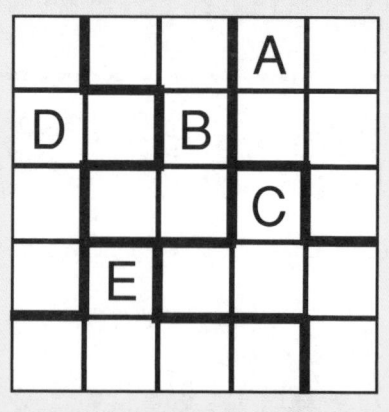

130 BIG BREAK

A pool break is made up by potting red balls (maximum 15) which are each followed by one of six different colours. The point values of the balls are:

- RED 1
- YELLOW 2
- GREEN 3
- BROWN 4
- PINK 6
- BLUE 5
- BLACK 7

Pool player Bob Basher, otherwise known as the Bristol Breeze, made a break of 69, which ended when he failed to pot a red. In the break he potted one less black than blue and one more brown than yellow, potting only these four colours in the break. Can you work out how the break was compiled?

131 LOGI-5

Each line, across and down, is to have each of the letters A, B, C, D and E, appearing once each. Also, every shape – shown by the thick lines – must also have each of the letters in it. Can you fill in the grid?

```
              A
 D     B
           C
    E
```

132 NUMBER JIG

Fit the numbers into the grid. One has been done for you.

3 figures
150
344
391
629
782
(888)
943

4 figures
1622
2191
3160
3731
4570

5768
5921
7726
8273
9801

5 figures
13804
14630
27403
28135
78836

6 figures
187332
228433
314517
341712
410355
435127
467169
637901
643115
729362
862561
910266
955925

7 figures
1230172
2482077
5273559
5613984
6157248
9102626
9921349

888

133 MAZE MYSTERY

Travel from the entrance to the exit of the maze, filling the path completely to create a picture.

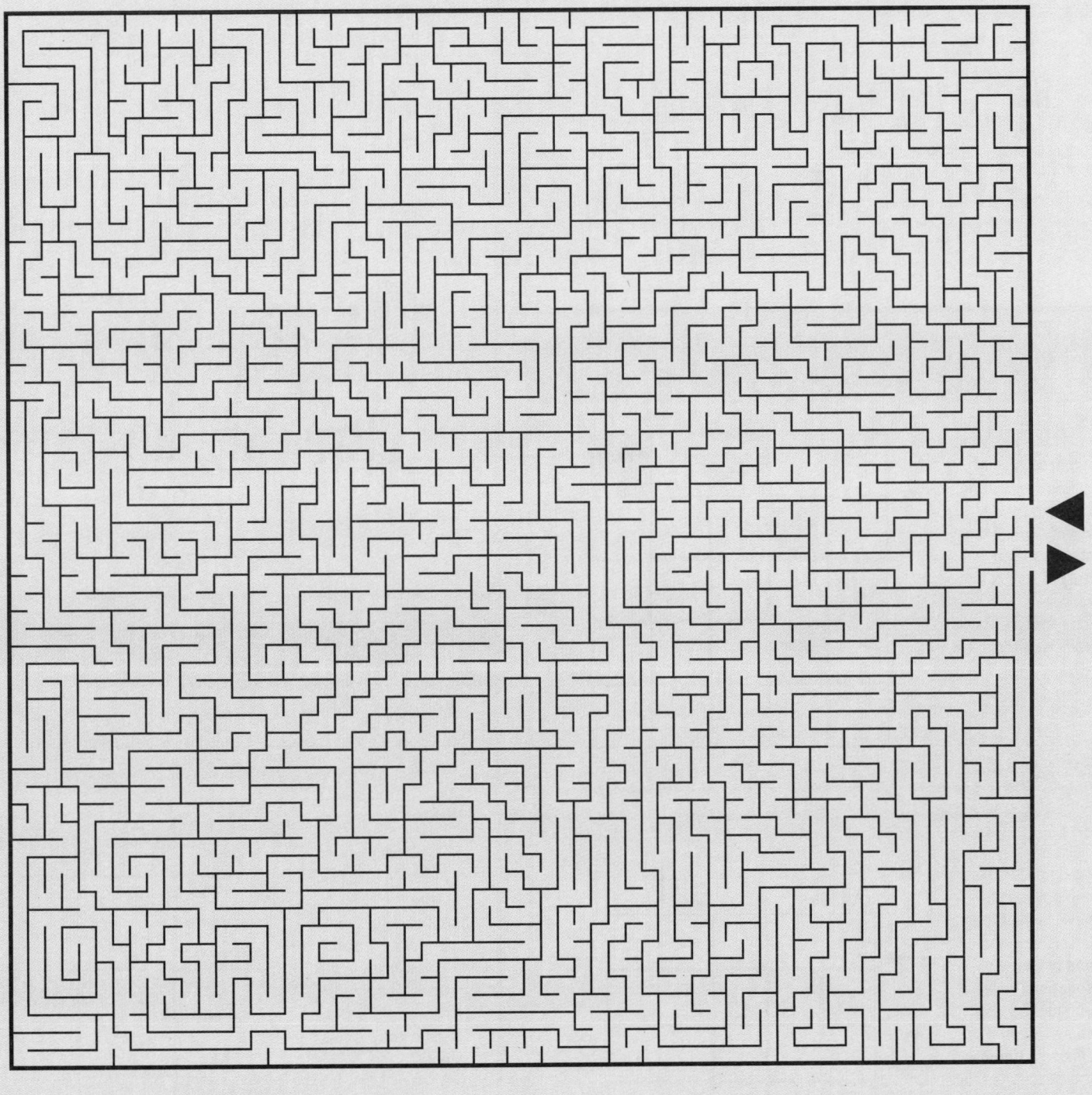

134 ON THE SPOT

Can you place the dominoes into the grid so that the four vertical, four horizontal and both diagonal rows each have a spot total of nine?

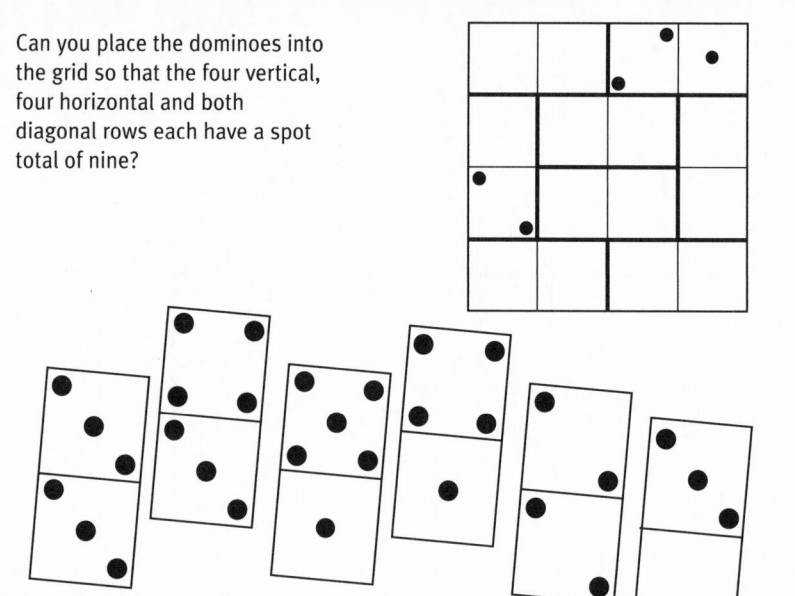

135 LOGI-5

Each line, across and down, is to have each of the five colours appearing once each. Each colour must also appear just once in each shape, shown by thick lines. Can you colour in this crazy quilt, or mark each square with a letter by which the colour can be identified?

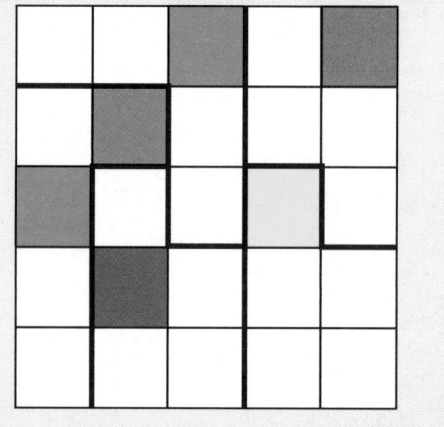

136 ABC

Each line, across and down, is to have each of the letters A, B and C, and two empty squares. The letter outside the grid shows the first or second letter in the direction of the arrow. Can you fill in the grid?

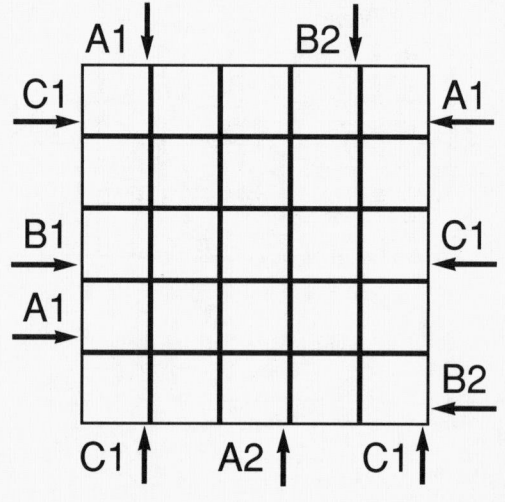

137 BEARED RIDDEN

Goldie Locks was not alone in wreaking havoc at the Bears' semi-detached pad in Dingley Dell. Four companions helped her cause devastation by sampling a different cereal each, breaking an item of furniture and crashing out in each of the family's beds. Goldie Locks was not the one who broke the table and slept in Papa Bear's bed; nor did Cilla Field who ate Bran Bits. The one who broke the chair ate Chafflakes but neither she nor Cilla slept in Fred Bear's bed which was claimed by the one who smashed the sideboard. Cher Noble slept in Mama Bear's bed but is not the one who flattened the desk. Wyn Frith did not eat the Ricypops but Dawn Ray did try the Weetybricks. Neither slept in Teddy Bear's bed. The one who ate Muesli Munch broke the bookcase but did not sleep in Carmen Bear's cot or Teddy Bear's bed.

Who slept in each bed, what did he/she eat for breakfast and what did he/she break?

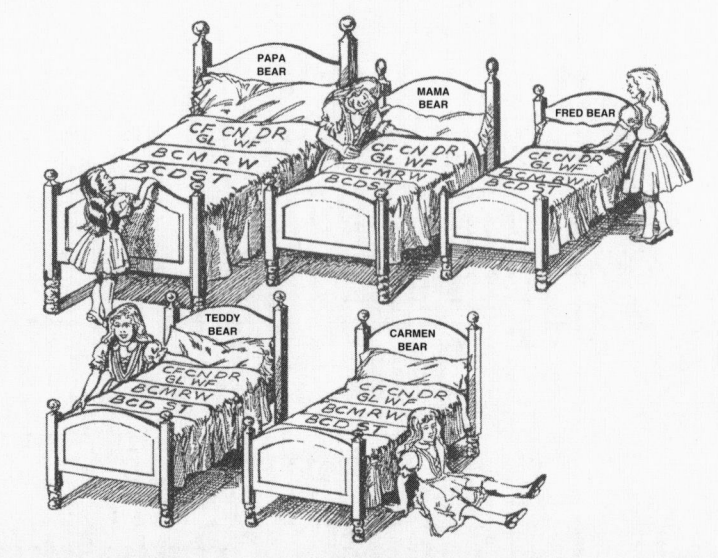

138 POCKET LOGIC

Three girls in class 2ZZ at Grabham High have received Valentine cards from three boys. Can you post the details into the summary grid?

Clues

1 Marian did not receive a card from Gary.
2 Alan and Ian sent cards to the same girl who was not Ava.
3 David and Henry sent cards to the same girl who was not Marian.
4 Brian and Eric sent cards to the same girl who was not Gladys.

	ALAN	BRIAN	COLIN	DAVID	ERIC	FRANK	GARY	HENRY	IAN
AVA CRUSH									
GLADYS MIGN									
MARIAN KYND									
GARY									
HENRY									
IAN									
DAVID									
ERIC									
FRANK									

GIRL	BOY	BOY	BOY

140 SAFE BET

This is a strange safe. Answer all the questions and the combination will appear in the shaded boxes.

ACROSS

1 Multiply *24 down* by 3
5 Add 1,000 to *1 across*
7 Square *4 down*
8 Multiply *23 down* by 3
12 Add 3 to *4 down*
14 Square *1 across*
18 Square *5 across*
19 Anagram of digits of *8 across*
21 Add *3 down* to *4 down*
26 Subtract 24,142 from *8 down*
27 Next in series 4,267, 4,317, 4,367,…
28 Subtract *4 down* from *27 across*, then subtract 5

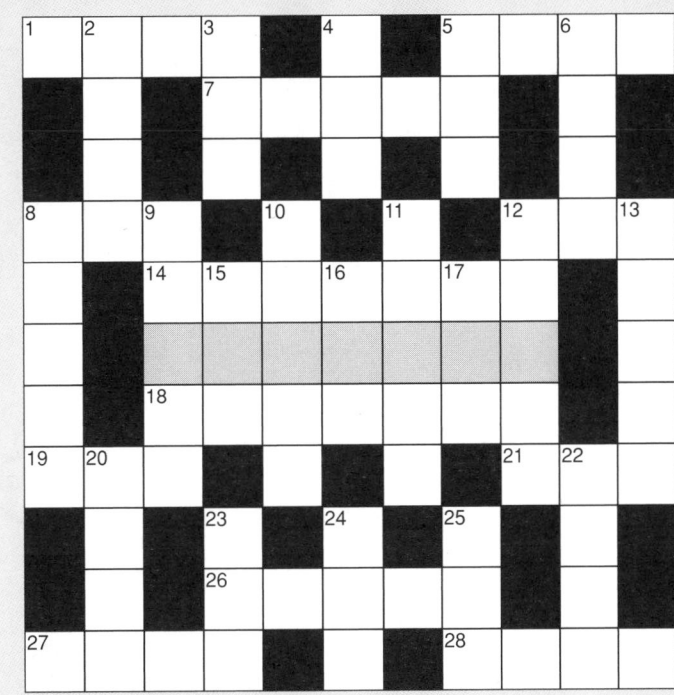

DOWN

2 Square the last two digits of *8 down*
3 Square root of 44,100
4 Second, third and fourth digits of *26 across*
5 Subtract 1 from *3 down*
6 Multiply *23 down* by 10
8 Add 45 to *13 down*
9 Subtract 2,802 from *12 down*
10 3 per cent of 1,229,700
11 Add 23,000 to *10 down*
12 Add 4,043 to *7 across*
13 Multiply *8 across* by *23 down* and subtract 5,967
15 Subtract 314 from *16 down*
16 Add 318 to *17 down*
17 Square root of 244,036
20 Add *1 across* to *5 across*
22 Next in series 1,611, 1,701, 1,791,…
23 Divide *20 down* by 32, then add 10
24 Square root of 163,216
25 Twice *23 down*

139 NINE NUMBERS

Place a number from 1 to 9 in each empty cell so that each row, each column and each 3 x 3 block contains all the numbers from 1 to 9.

1		4		6		2		
	4	3		8	9			
	7		1			3		
	1		7		5		4	
6			2					3
	3		1		9		5	
	2		8			9		
		8	9		7	2		
	4		2		1		6	

141 DOMINO SEARCH

A set of dominoes has been laid out, using numbers instead of dots for clarity, but the lines which separate the dominoes have been left out. Can you, armed with a sharp pencil and keen brain, show where each domino in the set has been placed? You may find the check grid useful as each domino is identified by its number pair and the appropriate box can be ticked when the domino has been located.

3	1	3	4	1	3	1	4
1	4	1	4	5	6	0	6
1	3	5	0	5	2	6	5
6	5	2	4	2	3	2	4
0	0	0	2	0	5	6	5
6	4	0	6	2	5	6	0
1	4	2	1	2	3	3	3

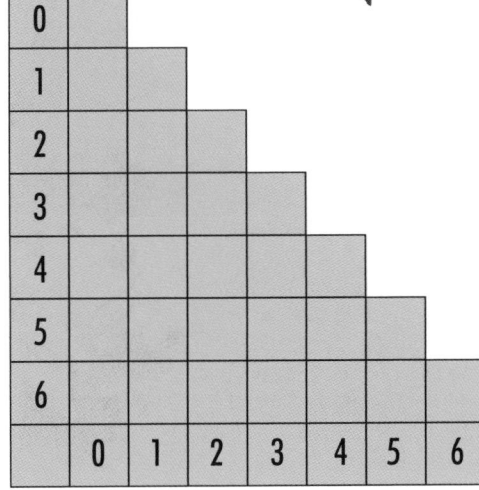

142 ON THE SPOT

Can you place the dominoes into the grid so that the four vertical, four horizontal and both diagonal rows each have a spot total of eight?

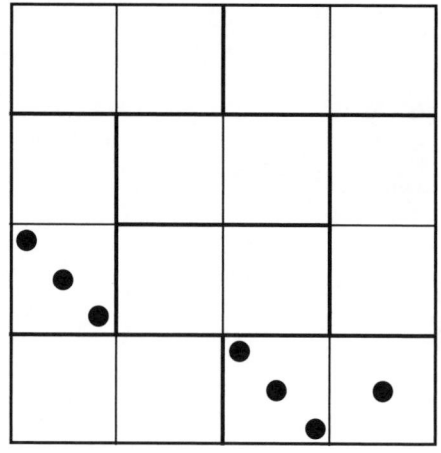

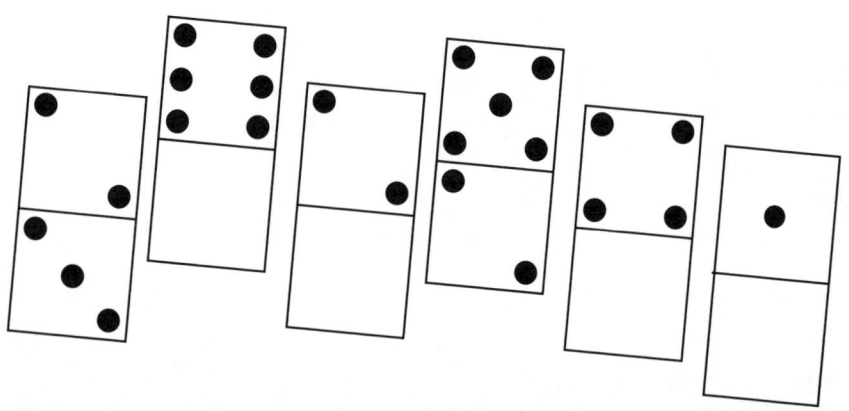

143 PUPPY POWER

When the dog pulls the rope which weights will go down and which will go up?

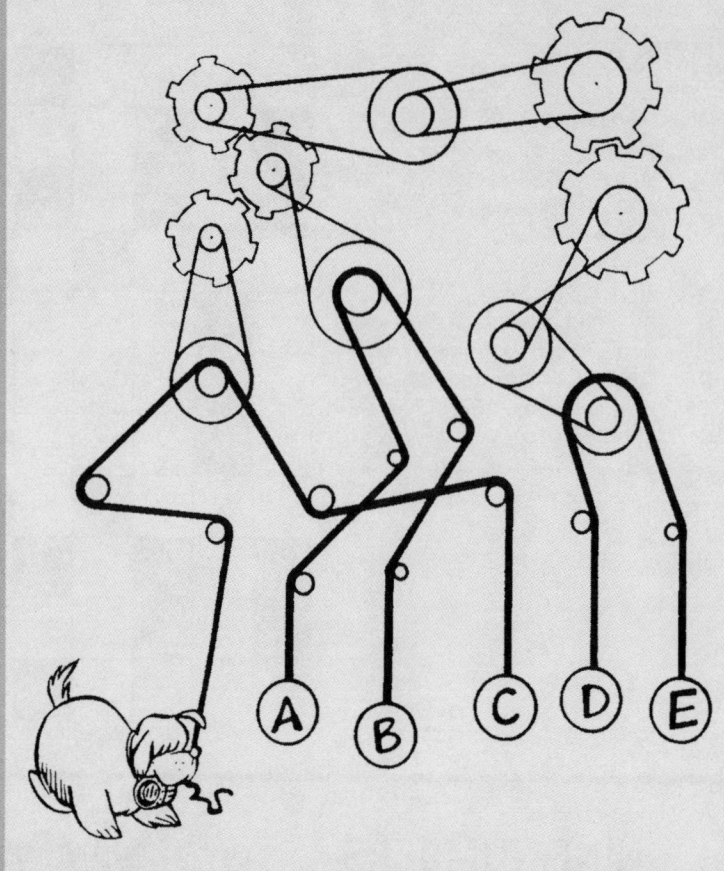

144 FLOWER POWER

Patriotic Pete sells bunches of red, white and blue flowers in the market. Some bunches have just a single colour, some have two and some a mixture of all three. If he brings along a total of 80 bunches, can you work out how many bunches have flowers of all three colours?

Half the bunches contain red flowers and a quarter of the bunches have both blue and white. There is one more bunch with red flowers only than there are with both blue and white but no red. The total number of those with both red and white but no blue and red and blue but no white is five greater than the number containing red only. How many bunches have all three colours?

145 BIG BREAK

A pool break is made up by potting red balls (maximum 15) which are each followed by one of six different colours. The point values of the balls are:

- RED 1
- YELLOW 2
- GREEN 3
- BROWN 4
- PINK 6
- BLUE 5
- BLACK 7

Pool player Bob Basher, otherwise known as the Bristol Breeze, made a break of 71, which ended when he failed to pot a red. In the break he potted two more pinks than greens and two more yellows than blues, potting only these four colours in the break. Can you work out how the break was compiled?

146 PATTERN MAKER

Can you place the numbered blocks into the grid to form the pattern shown? The blocks may be placed horizontally or vertically, and may be turned around.

0	1	3	2
1	2	3	2
2	2	0	0
1	1	1	0
3	3	0	3

0 1		0 3
2 2	1 3	3 3
0 2	1 2	0 0
1 1		3 2

147 SPOT THE DIFFERENCE

Can you tell which one of these pictures is different from the others?

148 ACROSS THE BOARD

Can you place the numbered blocks into the grid to form the pattern shown? The blocks may be placed horizontally or vertically, and can be turned round.

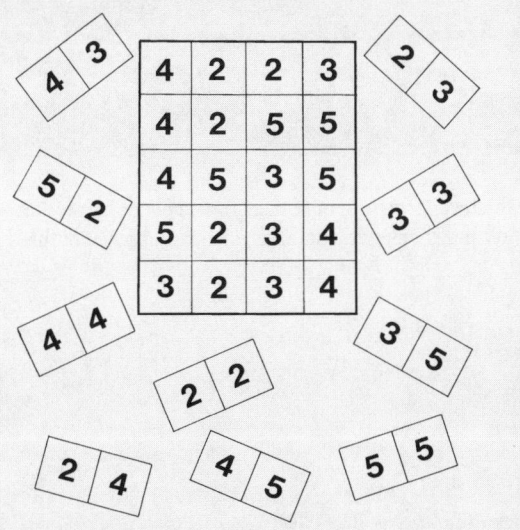

149 TEE TIME

Three old-timers play a weekly game of golf on the Golden Lawns 18-hole, par 72, course. Each score at every hole falls into one of five categories. Each golfer gets a different result, greater than zero in each category. Also, no category has the same result for another player, i.e., if a player has two eagles, he has a different number in the other four and no other player has two eagles. With the score details below and the information given can you fill in their card? Nick's bogeys were the same as Barry's pars and Parnell's double bogeys and together they totalled the same as Parnell's pars which were one more than Nick's birdies which were one more than Barry's double bogeys which were the same as Parnell's eagles and these last two together totalled Barry's birdies. The total number of eagles was more than the double bogeys but less than the bogeys.

	Eagle −2	Birdie −1	Par 0	Bogey +1	Double Bogey +2	FINAL SCORE
Parnell Darma						
Nick Jackliss						
Barry Clayer						

150 ABC

Each line, across and down, is to have each of the letters A, B and C, and two empty squares. The letter outside the grid shows the first or second letter in the direction of the arrow. Can you fill in the grid?

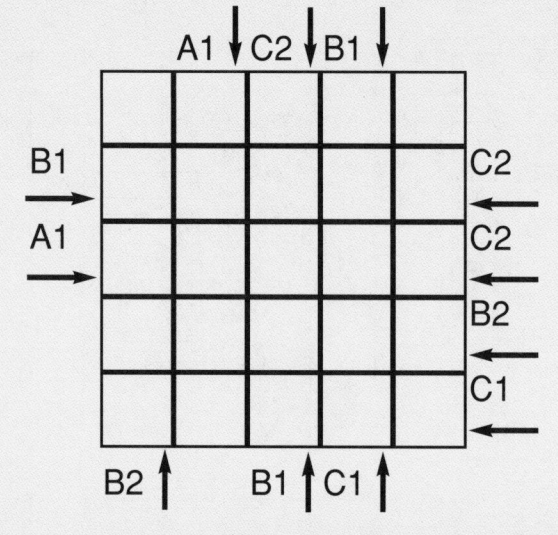

151 21S

Obeying the normal rules of arithmetic, with the numbers given, using only where necessary +, –, x, or ÷, make the resulting calculations equal 21.

9 (3 2) 6 = 21   7 4 9 9 = 21

(3 5 8) 3 = 21

152 FILLING IN

Each of the nine empty boxes contains a different digit from 1 to 9. Each calculation is to be treated sequentially rather than according to the 'multiplication first' system. Can you fill in the empty boxes?

	+		÷		= 2
÷		+		x	
	+		−		= 5
+		−		−	
	x		÷		= 6

= 6   = 6   = 9

153 DOMINO SEARCH

A set of dominoes has been laid out, using numbers instead of dots for clarity, but the lines which separate the dominoes have been left out. Can you, armed with a sharp pencil and keen brain, show where each domino in the set has been placed? You may find the check grid useful as each domino is identified by its number pair and the appropriate box can be ticked when the domino has been located.

2	4	3	3	0	3	3	1
4	1	1	6	1	6	4	3
5	2	4	5	4	4	1	5
4	2	0	1	5	3	5	2
3	6	2	0	4	6	0	1
3	2	1	0	0	5	5	2
6	6	2	6	5	0	6	0

154 MAZE MYSTERY

Travel from the entrance to the exit of the maze, filling the path completely to create a picture.

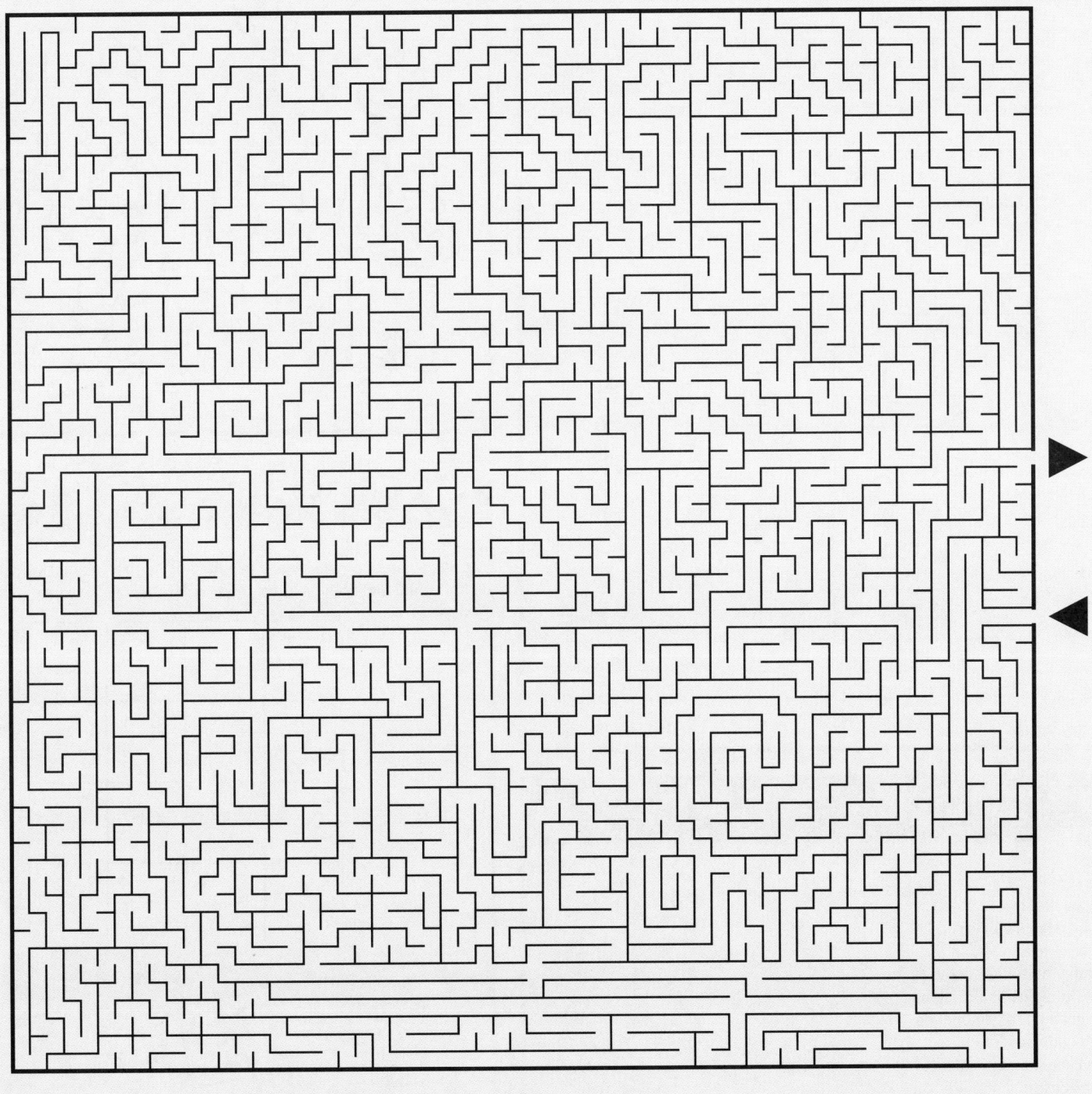

155 MAIL MAN'S PROBLEM

The old houses in the community have always caused a problem for mail men – the house numbers seem to bear no relationship to their positions around a central square. So to help all new mail men on that round learn where each number is, the following puzzle is given to them.

The houses are numbered from 1 to 24, and the position of each letter in the diagram indicates the front of its respective house. P, Q and R – along with S, T and U – are all odd numbers; both of these sets of three add up to the same total, which is two more than the total of F's and G's numbers – F's being twice G's. The total of numbers J, K, L, M and N is ten more than that of A, B, C, D and E. W, X and Y add up to twenty more than the total of S, T and U.

House B is No. 20. Nos. 5 and 7 have west-facing frontages, but they're not adjacent. C's number is half that of D's, which is half that of E's. C and D add up to A's number. X's number is four times W's, V's is nineteen less than Z's, which is twice H's. N's number is one more than Z's and two more than K's, which is one-and-a-half times that of J.

E's number is four more than A's, and T's is greater than U's, which is greater than S's. No. 2 is somewhere due west of No. 10, and No. 7 is somewhere due north of No. 5. Where is each number?

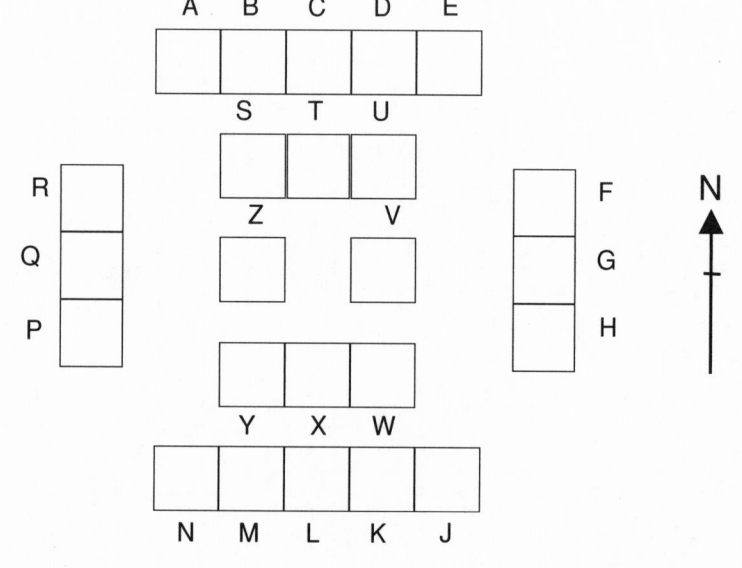

158 ISLAND HOPPING

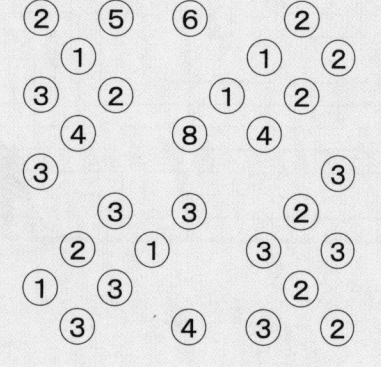

Each circle containing a number represents an island. The object is to connect each island with vertical or horizontal bridges so that:
* The number of bridges is the same as the number inside the island.
* There can be up to two bridges between two islands.
* Bridges cannot cross islands or other bridges.
* There is a continuous path connecting all the islands.

156 AGE GROUP

Can you calculate the age of each of these men from the following information? B is twice as old as D. The difference in age of A and B is the same as the difference in age between C and D, while the difference in age between A and C is half the difference in age between B and D. None of the men is older than forty or younger than twenty, and A is older than C.

157 ON THE SPOT

Can you place the dominoes into the grid so that the four vertical, four horizontal and both diagonal rows each have a spot value of nine?

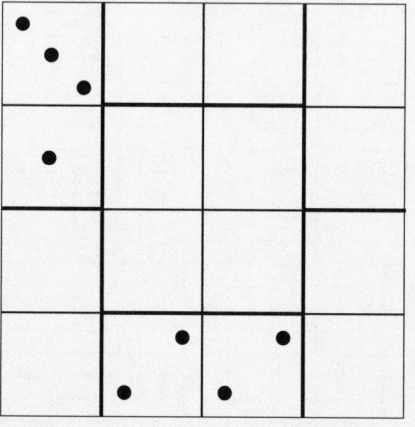

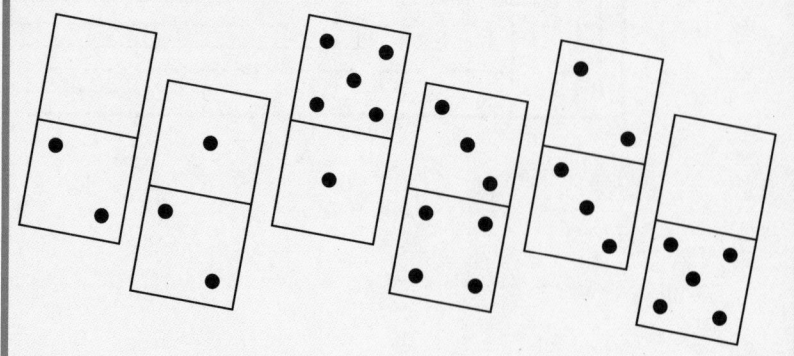

159 BLOOMERS

Charlie Dimwit's garden centre, Bloomers, has a fine display of pot plants for sale. Four gardeners each took ten pots from the stand. Each gardener took a different number of pots of the colours they selected. After they had taken their pots there were an equal number of each colour left over. From the information given can you work out what each gardener selected?

Mary bought two more green than yellow and together this was twice Dawn's red, which were the same as John's yellow. Neither man bought any green but Dawn bought twice as many green as John bought red. John who bought no violet bought two more blue than yellow. Alan bought no red and Mary bought no blue. Dawn bought one more yellow than blue.

160 SIX-PACK

By packing numbers in the empty spaces, can you make the numbers in each of the sixteen hexagons add up to 25? No two numbers in each hexagon may be the same and you can't use zero. We've started you off.

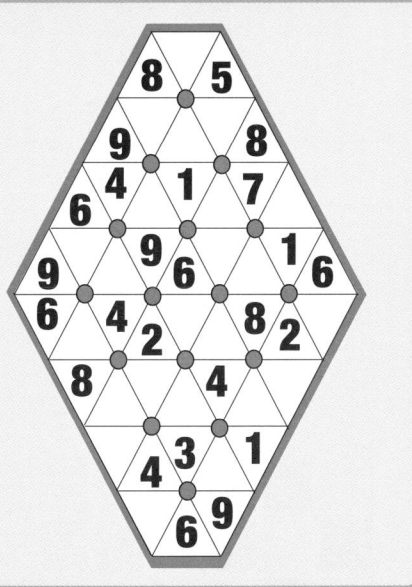

161 IT'S MAGIC

This magic square can be completed using the numbers from 61 to 85 inclusive. To give you a start, in each square with a black corner dot, all the even digits have been entered. In a plain square all the odd digits have been entered. Can you complete the square so that the five numbers in each row, column and diagonal add up to the magic total? The total—and close your eyes now if you don't want to be told—is 365.

●	6	●		●
	●		8 2	●
8 ●	6	7 1	8 ●	
7	6 ●	3 6	●	7
6 ●	7 ●	2	7 9 8 ●	

163 ENGINE DRIVER

There are eight differences between these two pictures – can you discover them all?

162 SET SQUARE

All the digits from 1 to 9 are used in this grid, but only once. Can you work out their positions in the grid and make the sums work? We've given two numbers to start you off.

	+	4	−		= 5
+		+		−	
	−		+		= 2
÷		−		x	
	+		÷	2	= 5
=		=		=	
5		5		8	

164 DOUBLE PUZZLE

Roll up folks, for our special sale offer—two puzzles for the price of one!

Puzzle One: Each colour has been given a value from 1 to 7. Given the totals at the end of each line, can you work out the value of each colour?

Puzzle Two: The picture is a layout of a set of colour dominoes—just like ordinary dominoes but with colours instead of spots. Can you draw in the lines to show each separate domino?

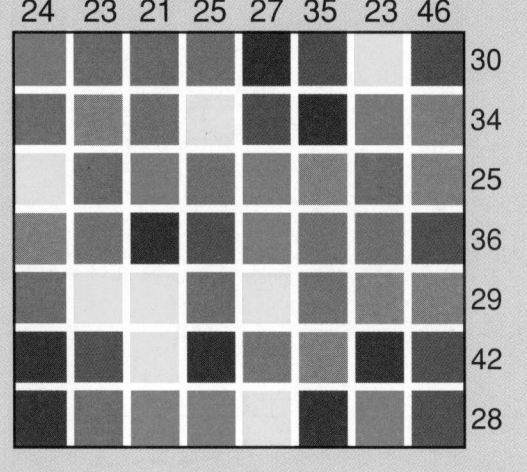

165 WELL SPOTTED

The number in each circle tells you how many of it and its touching neighbours are to be filled in.

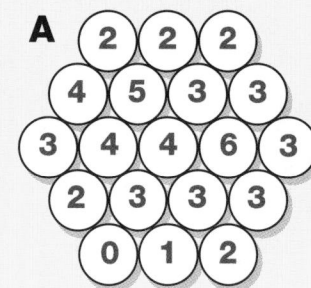
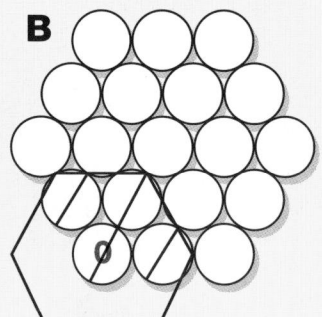
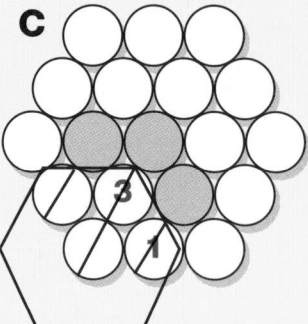

In our example, A, the zero gives a start – put lines through it and its neighbours (B). Three circles can now be filled (C) – lightly, though so the numbers can still be read...

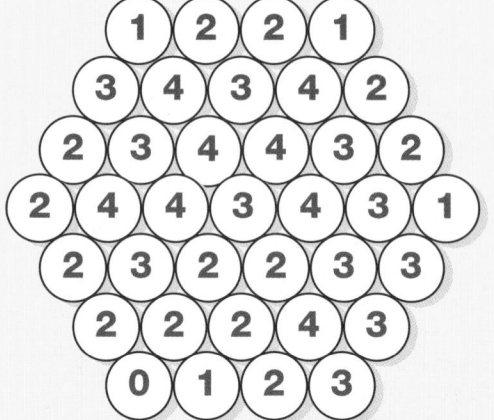

166 NUMBER JIG

Fit the numbers into the grid. One has been done for you.

3 figures
109
388
(460)
472
699
702
980

4 figures
1372
1626
3019
3491
4590
6395
7424
7677
8118
9103

5 figures
32094
36125
39942
60841
82160

6 figures
100341
122074
335642
382772
412979

420799
430216
543748
710327
786243

793612
813730
918622

7 figures
1505213
2188663
4623963
4956134
7026471
8146072
9783288

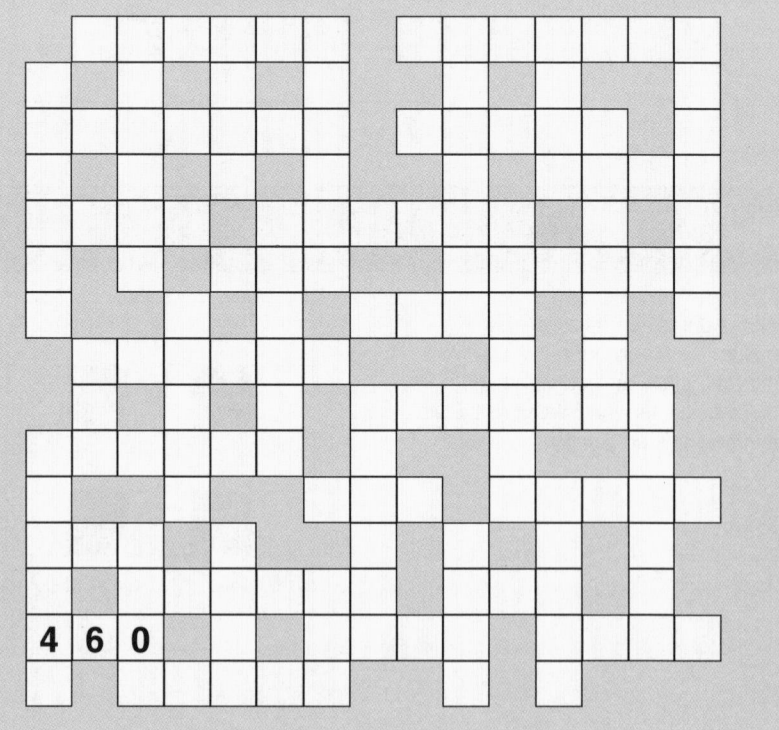

167 DOMINO SEARCH

A set of dominoes has been laid out, using numbers instead of dots for clarity, but the lines which separate the dominoes have been left out. Can you, armed with a sharp pencil and keen brain, show where each domino in the set has been placed? You may find the check grid useful as each domino is identified by its number pair and the appropriate box can be ticked when the domino has been located. To give you a start 7*9 is given.

Hint: Look near the bottom left corner – which is the only domino that goes there?

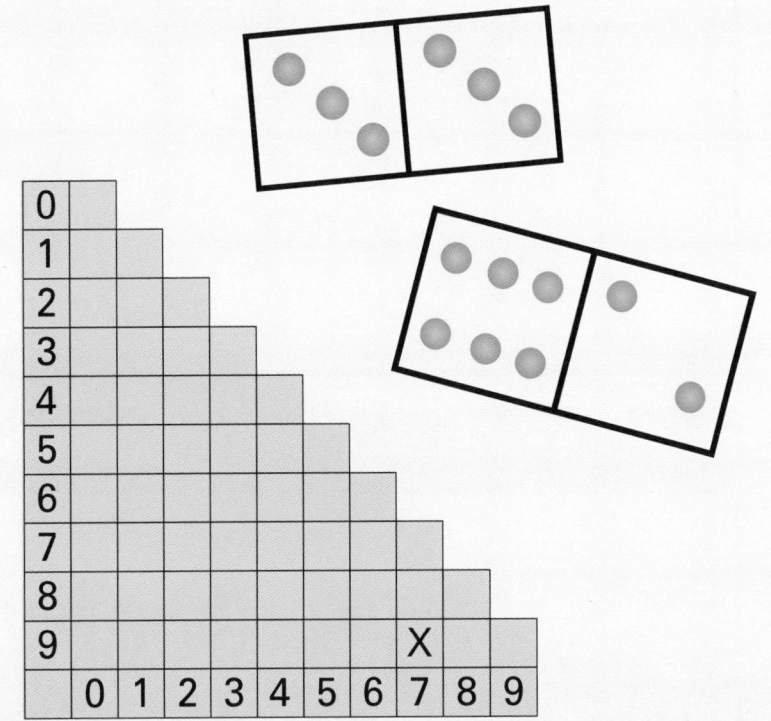

0										
1										
2										
3										
4										
5										
6										
7										
8										
9							X			
	0	1	2	3	4	5	6	7	8	9

8	2	8	1	0	5	2	8	5	0	1
8	7	3	7	4	4	6	3	3	9	3
0	4	4	2	7	3	8	9	2	7	0
3	5	1	6	8	4	0	9	2	3	4
1	8	3	8	0	6	0	5	8	1	4
1	6	0	9	1	3	6	5	6	6	7
9	7	5	6	6	2	0	2	5	0	7
0	4	5	9	9	6	7	1	5	1	4
1	7	3	2	7	9	6	5	7	2	9
4	1	5	9	9	4	8	3	2	8	2

168 KARL KRACK'S CIRCUS

Karl Krack, who owns a small travelling circus, believes that variety is the spice of life and for each show he alters the order of his eight acts. Can you work out what the order will be for tonight's performance?

No act is next to another with the same initials. The Clever Clowns come two acts after Fred the Fire-eater and two acts before Senor Pedro's Poodles. Jim the Juggler comes three acts before the Agilles Acrobats but he does not open the show. The Flying Fortresses come four acts after Madame Poll's Parrots, but not immediately before the Poodles. The Crazy Carvellos are not the final act.

1	2	3	4
5	6	7	8

169 DOUBLE PUZZLE

Roll up folks, for our special sale offer – two puzzles for the price of one!

Puzzle One: Each colour has been given a value from 1 to 7. Given the totals at the end of each line, can you work out the value of each colour?

Puzzle Two: The picture is a layout of a set of colour dominoes – just like ordinary dominoes but with colours instead of spots. Can you draw in the lines to show each separate domino?

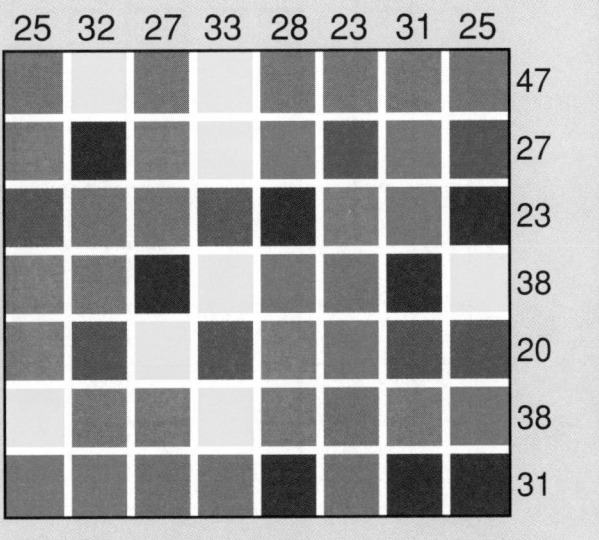

Column totals: 25 32 27 33 28 23 31 25

Row totals: 47 27 23 38 20 38 31

170 FLOWER POWER

Patriotic Pete sells bunches of red, white and blue flowers in the market. Some bunches have just a single colour, some two and some a mixture of all three. If he brings along a total of 80 bunches, can you work out how many bunches have flowers of all three colours? The number of bunches with both red and blue but no white is the same as that with blue only and together they total the number with both red and white but no blue. The number with white only is double that with all three, which is one less than red only, which is the same as that with both blue and white but no red. Fifty-five bunches had white flowers in them.

171 BATTLESHIPS

Do you remember the old game of battleships? These puzzles are based on that idea. Your task is to find the vessels in the diagram. Some parts of boats or sea squares have already been filled in, and a number next to a row or column refers to the number of occupied squares in that row or column. The boats may be positioned horizontally or vertically, but no two boats or parts of boats are in adjacent squares – horizontally, vertically or diagonally.

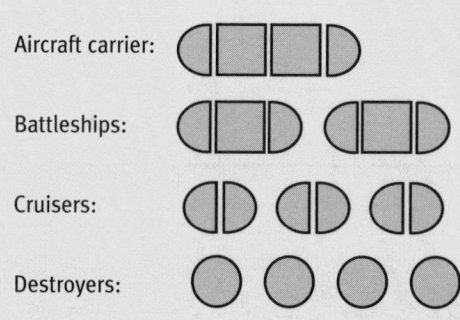

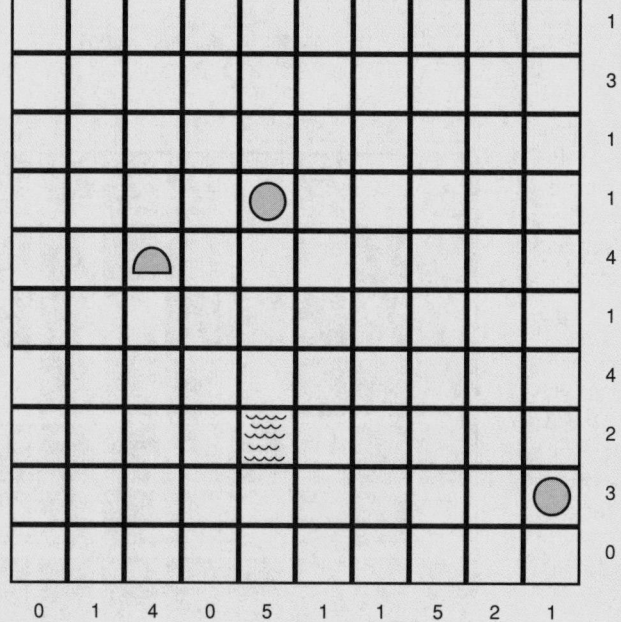

172 ON THE SPOT

Can you place the dominoes into the grid so that the four vertical, four horizontal and both diagonal rows have a spot total of eight?

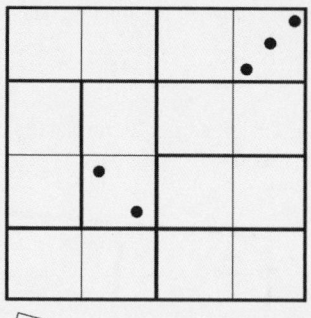

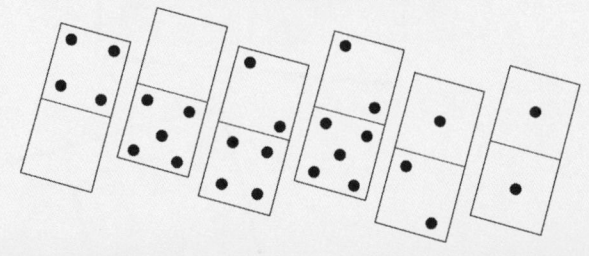

173 PAINT BOXES

In each of the pictures on the right, there is a different amount of paint dripping from the brush. Starting with picture F, can you put these pictures in order, so that in each new picture the paint drip is larger than before?

174 NINE NUMBERS

Place a number from 1 to 9 in each empty cell so that each row, each column and each 3 x 3 block contains all the numbers from 1 to 9.

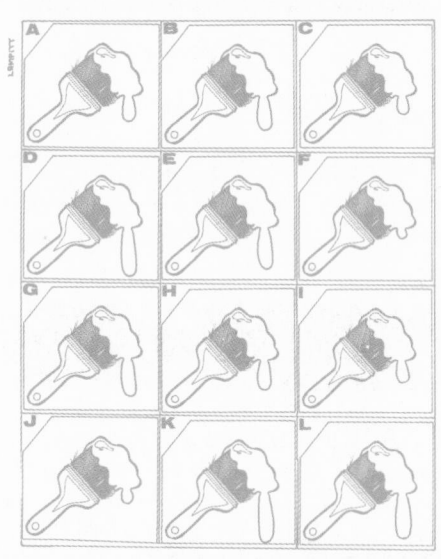

175 NUMBER JIG

Fit the numbers into the grid. One has been done for you.

3 figures
106
204
301
567
605
723
818
(919)

4 figures
1010
1853
2380
3123
4017
4190

5111
6037
7283
8093
8866
9171

5 figures
41528
43150
55073
60523
71375
81797
90173

6 figures
105921
166927
224466
299102
337473
344353
403044
413013
513397
523149
620732
668896
723378
789121
836343
977027

176 DOMINO SEARCH

A set of dominoes has been laid out, using numbers instead of dots for clarity, but the lines which separate the dominoes have been left out. Can you, armed with a sharp pencil and keen brain, show where each domino in the set has been placed? You may find the check grid useful as each domino is identified by its number pair and the appropriate box can be ticked when the domino has been located. To give you a start 2*9 is given.

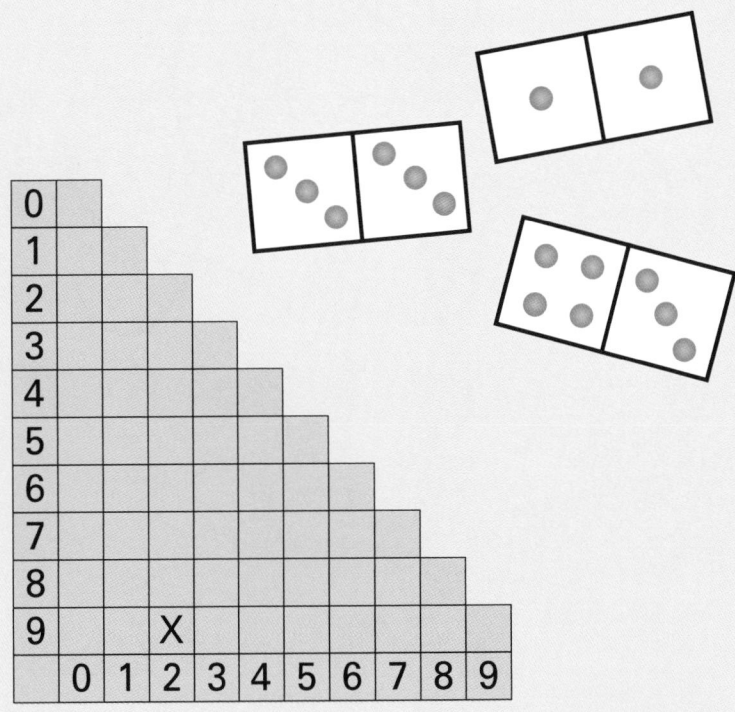

4	7	2	9	9	2	5	6	3	7	2
4	3	7	0	4	1	2	2	0	4	7
0	9	8	5	9	9	3	8	3	1	9
0	5	3	6	4	6	1	4	6	8	8
6	6	3	0	7	7	5	5	2	6	0
7	5	1	9	3	4	1	1	4	1	9
9	0	6	6	1	0	0	1	5	8	3
8	1	2	5	8	7	2	7	3	1	2
4	0	8	5	9	4	5	2	7	8	6
3	4	3	9	5	8	0	7	6	8	2

177 IT FIGURES

Place a number from 1 to 9 in each empty cell so that the sum of each vertical or horizontal block equals the number at the top or on the left of that block. Numbers may only be used once in each block.

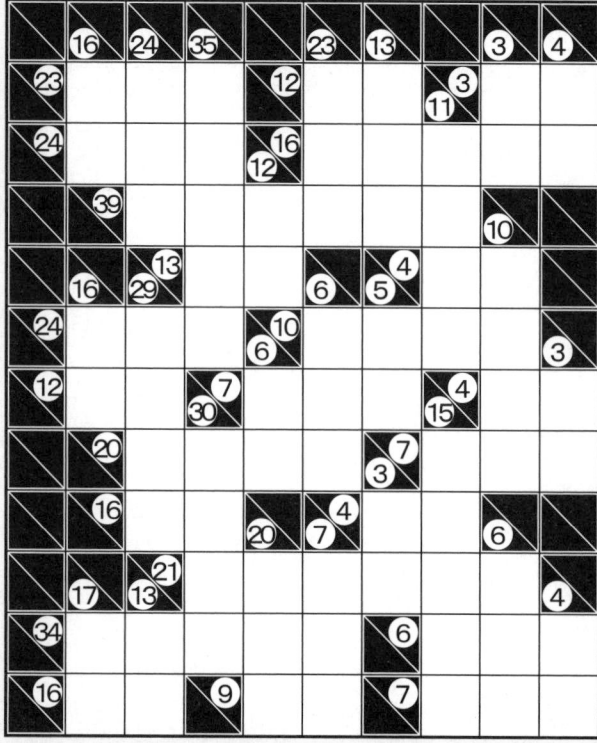

178 FLOWER POWER

Patriotic Pete sells bunches of red, white and blue flowers in the market. Some bunches have just a single colour, some two and some a mixture of all three. If he brings along a total of 80 bunches, can you work out how many bunches have flowers of all three colours?

There are 16 bunches with both blue and red and of these the number with no white is the same as that with white only, which is one less than the number with blue only and the total of the blue only and white only is the same as that of the ones with both red and white but no blue. Of the 47 bunches containing red flowers only 12 had just the one colour.

180 CAKE RACE

These joggers are so pleased with themselves for doing some exercise over Christmas that they've decided to treat themselves to extra helpings of cake when they get back. Follow the trails to discover which runner is after each cake.

179 LOGI-TILES

Following the first diagram, there is a logical rule that determines how the next block is to be filled in. Given these three blocks, can you colour in the fourth?

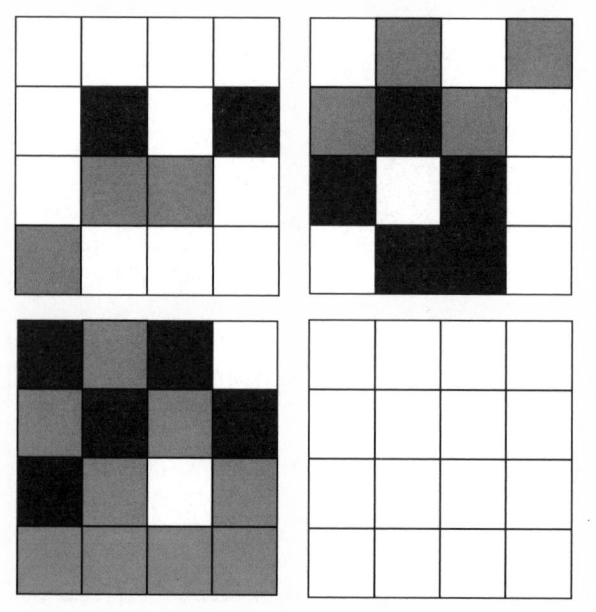

181 OUT WEST

Towards the end of the last century in Wichita USA, the main street was becoming quite well established, as our drawing of the first five buildings in that street shows. From the following clues, can you discover the name of each establishment and the name of the proprietor? By eliminating with an X any initial letter in the Answer Block, which does not apply, you will eventually arrive at the full answer.

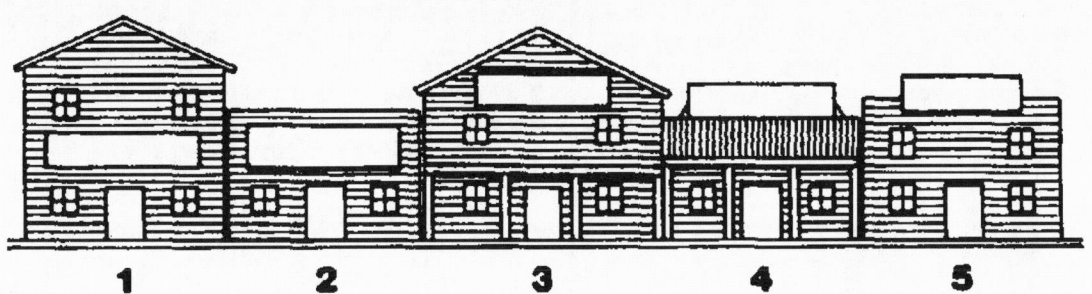

1   2   3   4   5

1. Frank Foster is at No. 2 but he does not run the Trading Post.
2. Jesse Jones is not the proprietor of No. 3.
3. The number of Jesse Jones's building is smaller than the number allocated to Chuck Carson's Saloon which is not No. 5.
4. The Bank is at No. 4 but the Trading Post is not No. 1.
5. Rocky Rawlings is not the manager of the Bank. The Wells Fargo office is not No. 2.
6. The Jail is one of the buildings but is Dave Dalton the Sheriff?

NUMBER	PROPRIETOR	BUILDING
1	C D F J R	B J S T W
2	C D F J R	B J S T W
3	C D F J R	B J S T W
4	C D F J R	B J S T W
5	C D F J R	B J S T W

182 NINE NUMBERS

Place a number from 1 to 9 in each empty cell so that each row, each column and each 3 x 3 block contains all the numbers from 1 to 9.

5	7						2	4
9	8						1	3
			3	7				
2	3			8	9			
7	6						8	5
			4	6			3	7
			9	2				
8	1						4	6
5	2					1	7	

183 EASY AS ABC

Each row and column originally contained one A, one B, one C, one D and two blank squares. Each letter and number refers to the first or second of the four letters encountered when travelling in the direction of the arrow. Can you complete the original grid?

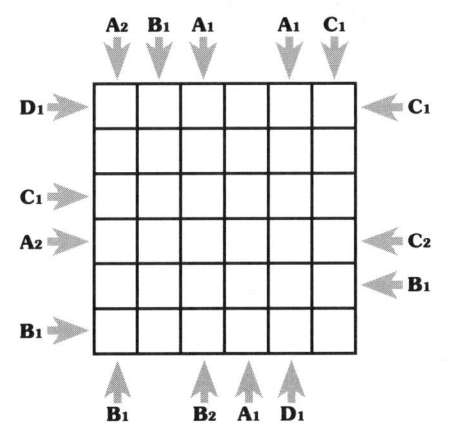

184 SIX-PACK

By packing numbers in the empty spaces, can you make the numbers in each of the 16 hexagons add up to 25? No two numbers in each hexagon may be the same and you can't use zero. We've started you off.

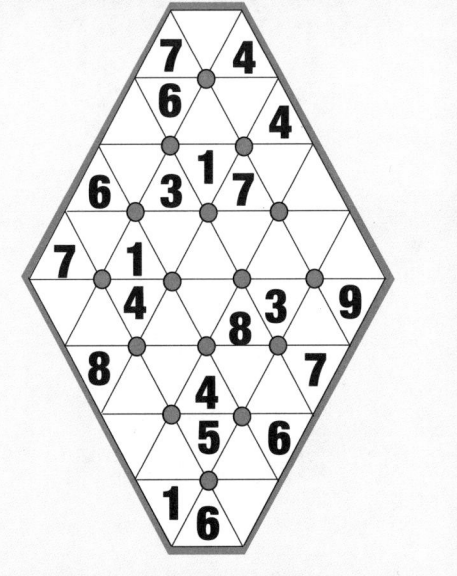

185 SET SQUARE

All the digits from 1 to 9 are used in this grid, but only once. Can you work out their positions in the grid and make the sums work? We've given two numbers to start you off.

	+	7	−		=	2
+		+		−		
	+		−		=	1
−		÷		+		
1	x		−		=	3
=		=		=		
9		2		3		

186 EASY AS ABC

Each row and column originally contained one A, one B, one C, one D and two blank squares. Each letter and number refers to the first or second of the four letters encountered when travelling in the direction of the arrow. Can you complete the original grid?

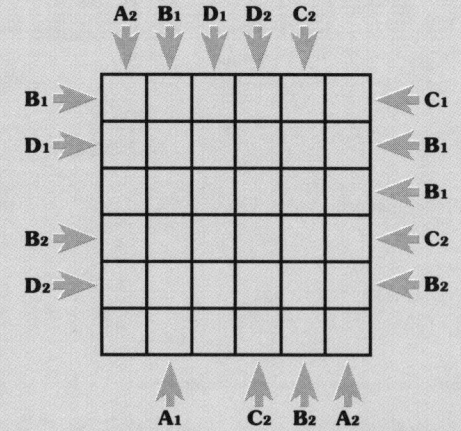

187 KNOT SO

Can you work out which tangles will form a knot, and which will not?

188 DOLLY THE CLONE

Which two of the pictures form a matching pair?

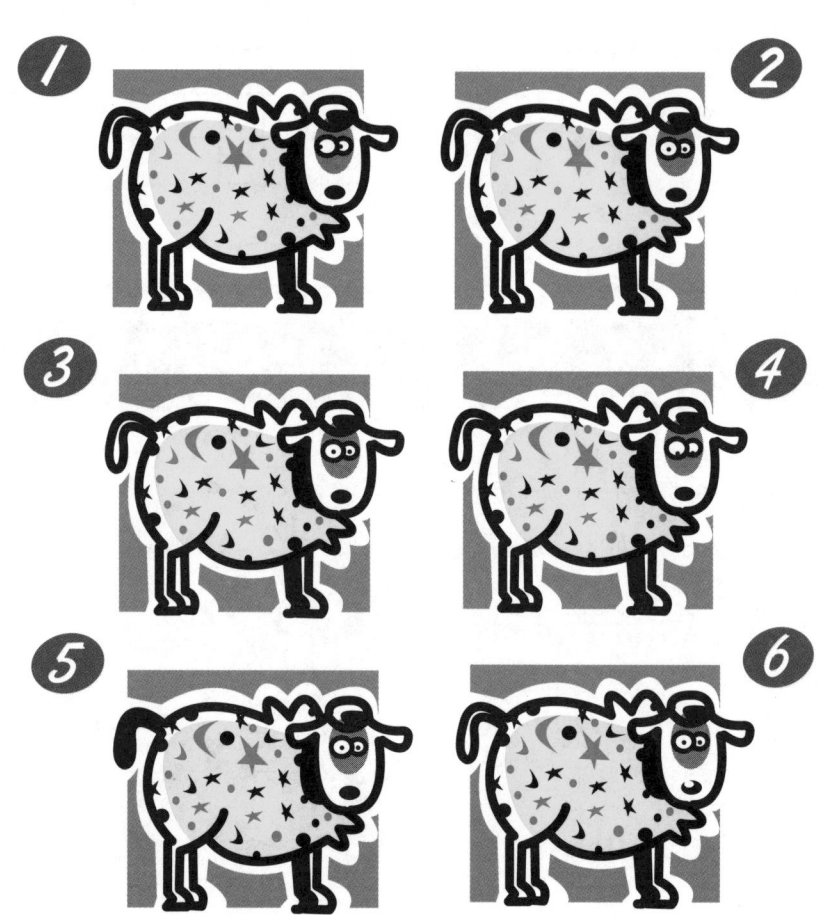

189 TRICOUNT

How many triangles can you find in this figure?

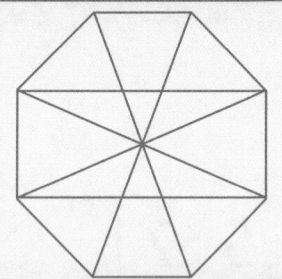

190 TEACUP TWINS

Can you match up the teacups into identical pairs?

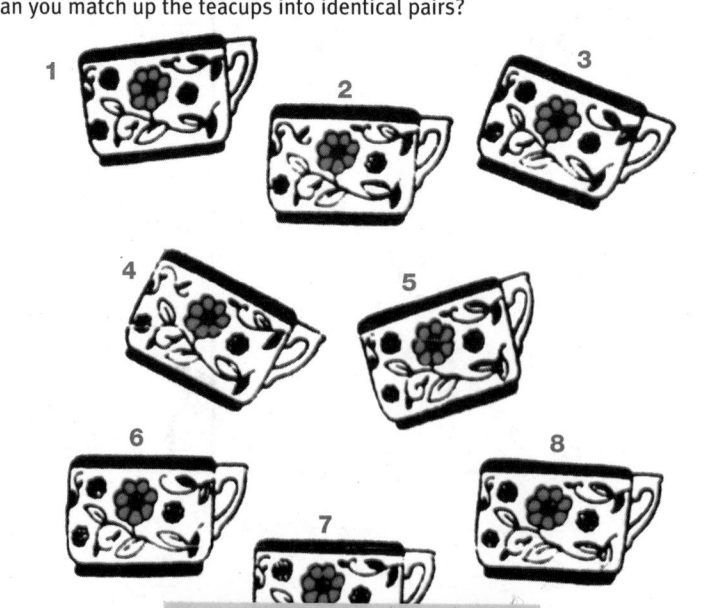

191 BIG BREAK ●●

A snooker break is made up by potting red balls (maximum 15) which are each followed by one of six different colours. The point values of the balls are:

● RED 1   ● BROWN 4   ● BLUE 5

○ YELLOW 2   ○ PINK 6

● GREEN 3   ● BLACK 7

In this next frame, Bob made a break of 85, which ended when he failed to pot a red. In the break he potted one more black than green and two more pink than blue, potting all four colours in the break and no other colours. How many of each colour ball were potted?

192 PATTERN MAKER ○

Can you place the numbered blocks below into the grid on the right to form the pattern shown? The blocks may be placed horizontally or vertically, and may be turned around.

3665
4434
0005
6533
0645

65		45
63	53	46
34	30	50
60		40

193 GIVING IT THE BOOT ●●

Four boys were fishing in a shallow stream, each wearing a different coloured pair of boots. From the clues given below, can you identify the boys in positions 1 to 4, and work out the colour of the boots each was wearing?

Clues

1 The boy in the red boots is somewhere to the left of Shaun, whose surname is not Brook.
2 Darren Poole is somewhere to the right of the youth in the brown boots.
3 Wader number 3 is Johnny, but the surname of the boy in position 2 is not Burne.
4 The green boots are worn by a boy wading alongside Garry, while Waters is standing next to his friend whose boots are black.

First name: _____

Surname: _____

Boots: _____

First names: Darren; Garry; Johnny; Shaun
Surnames: Brook; Burne; Poole; Waters
Boots: black; brown; green; red

Starting tip: Start by working out the first name of the boy in position 1.

194 NUMBER JIG ●●

Fit the numbers into the grid. One has been done for you.

3 figures
161
358
444
(483)
560
809
942

4 figures
1108
2921
3250

4230
6307
6323
6519
8243
8313
9054

5 figures
27328
39902
48326
71166

73014

6 figures
103600
175050
235798
326419
384104
403647
409214
524939
538018
640882

713648
810123
932100

7 figures
1638425
2152260
4236909
5990304
6539112
6603299
9013302

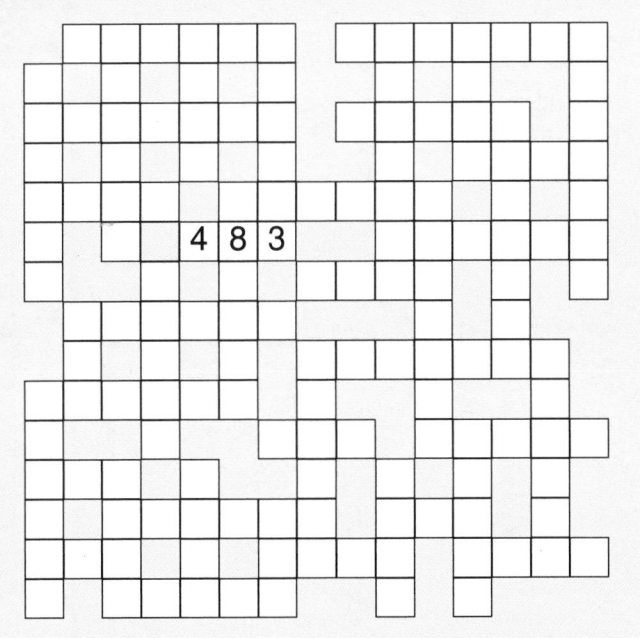

195 HORSE SHOW

Which one of the happy horses cast this shadow?

196 ON THE SPOT

Can you place the dominoes in the grid so that the four vertical, four horizontal and both diagonal rows each have a spot total of eight?

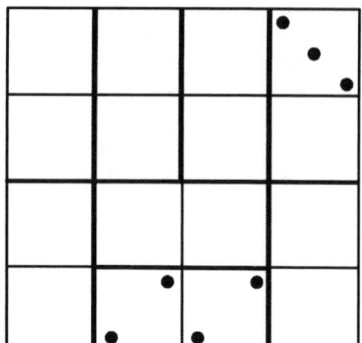

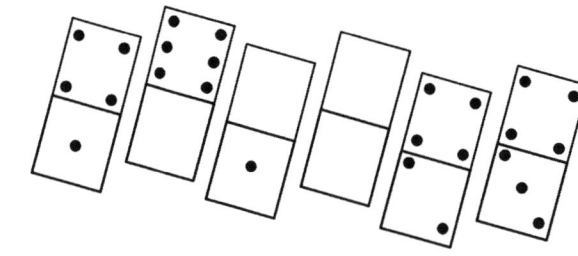

197 BLOOMERS

Charlie Dimwit's garden centre, Bloomers, has a fine display of pot plants for sale. Four gardeners each took ten pots from the stand. Each gardener took a different number of pots of the colours they selected. After they had taken their pots there were an equal number of each colour left over. From the information given can you work out what each gardener selected?

The two 'A' gardeners bought seven blues between them. George bought twice as many yellows as reds. The two ladies each bought the same number of yellows. Barbara bought no blues or violets. The two men bought half the sold number of blues but neither bought any greens. Anne bought one more green than violets and the total of the two was one more than Barbara's reds. Albert also bought some fertilizer.

198 ISLAND HOPPING

Each circle containing a number represents an island. The object is to connect each island with vertical or horizontal bridges so that:
* The number of bridges is the same as the number inside the island.
* There can be up to two bridges between two islands.
* Bridges cannot cross islands or other bridges.
* There is a continuous path connecting all the islands.

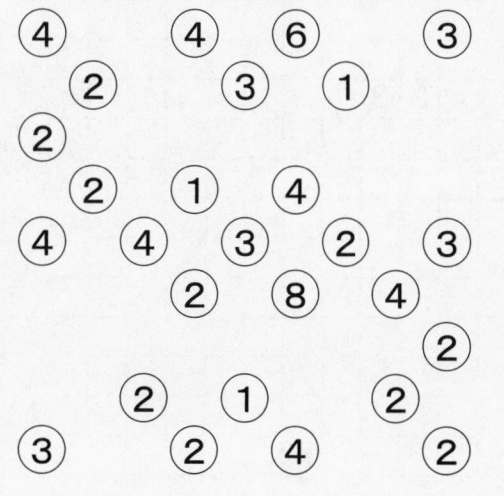

199 DOMINO SEARCH

A standard set of dominoes has been laid out, using numbers instead of dots for clarity. Using a sharp pencil and a keen brain, can you draw in the lines to show where each domino has been placed? You may find the check grid useful – crossing off each domino as you find it.

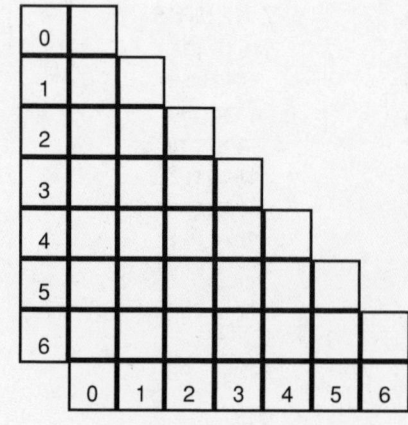

1	2	4	5	2	3	2	3
1	5	6	4	4	2	3	1
1	4	2	2	1	0	3	4
2	5	1	6	5	6	3	3
3	5	4	6	6	2	5	1
0	5	3	6	4	6	1	0
0	4	5	0	6	0	0	0

200 MAZE MYSTERY

Travel from the entrance to the exit of the maze, filling the path completely to create a picture.

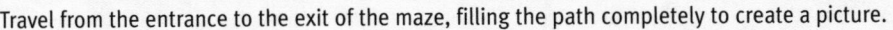

201 IT FIGURES

Place a number from 1 to 9 in each empty cell so that the sum of each vertical or horizontal block equals the number at the top or on the left of that block. Numbers may only be used once in each block.

202 KNOT SO

Can you work out which of these ropes will form a knot when their ends are pulled, and which will not?

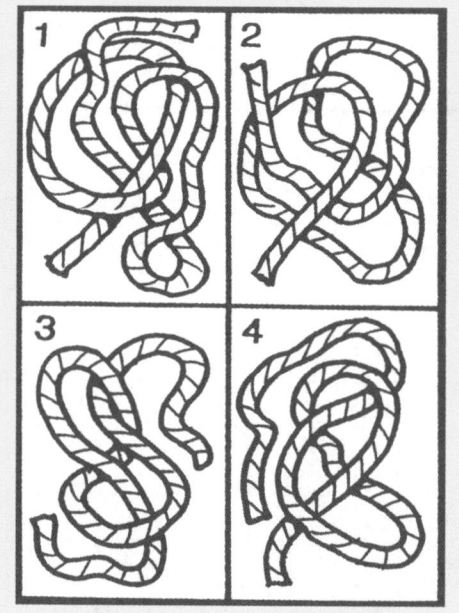

203 MATCH THAT

Rearrange these matches to make 14 squares.

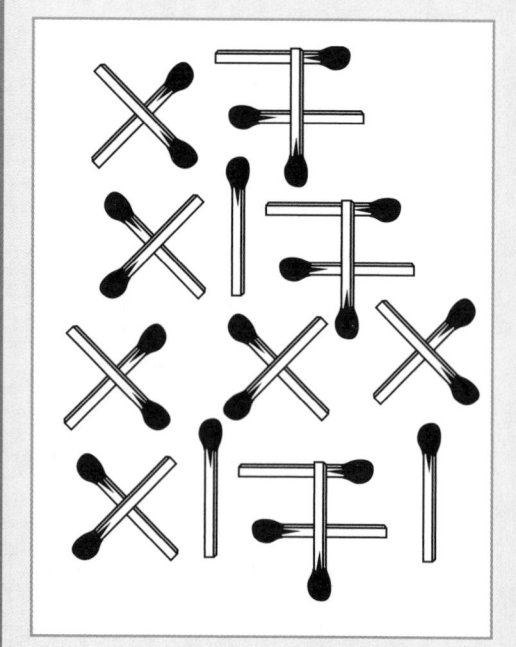

204 ALPHABET ECHO

In the grid, each letter of the alphabet appears twice and there are four blanks. Neither the same or any two consecutive letters of the alphabet appear in the same row, column or diagonal. A and Z are not treated as consecutive in this puzzle. Beside each row and column appear two numbers; the black number shows how many vowels appear in that row or column and the blue number shows how many of the letters are in the first half of the alphabet i.e. A–M. Using the additional clues below, can you fill in the grid?

Letters which are repeated:
In the first four rows   D, F, M, P, S, U, Y
In the last four rows   A, C, L, O, Q, T
In the first four columns   B, D, G, K, N, Q, R, V
In the last four columns   C, E, H, I, M, O, P, S, U, X, Z
In successive rows   D, F, M, O, P, Q, S, U, Y
In successive columns   B, H, I, K, X, Z

JRY and FIR read diagonally downwards. One column contains three blanks but there are none in the left-hand column. One G is in the top row but there are no Bs in row 6.

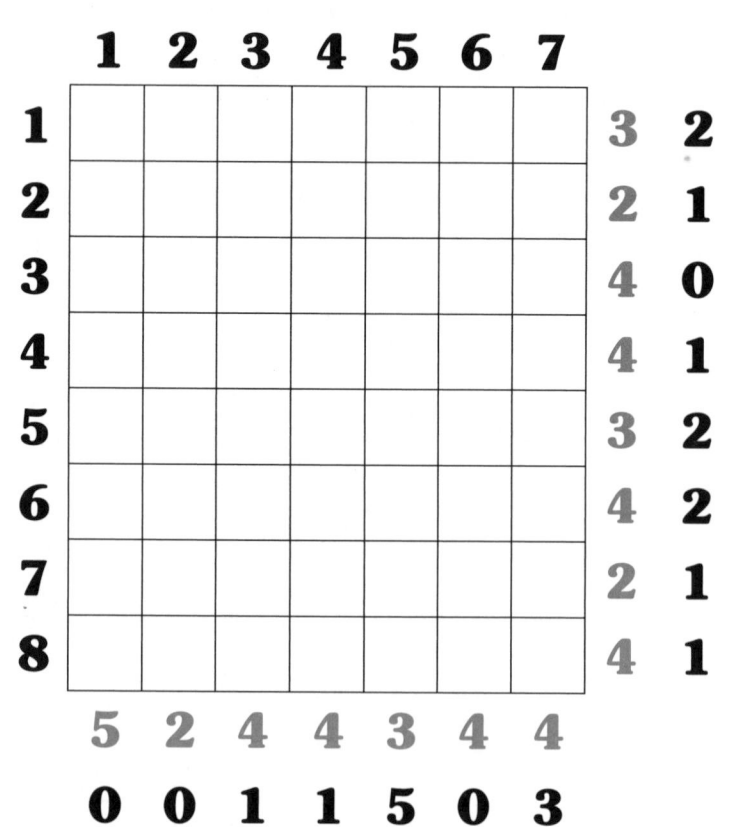

205 CELL STRUCTURE

The object is to create white areas surrounded by black walls, so that:
• Each white area contains only one number
• The number of cells in a white area is equal to the number in it
• The white areas are separated from each other with a black wall
• Cells containing numbers must not be filled in
• The black cells must be linked into a continuous wall
• Black cells cannot form a square of 2 x 2 or larger

```
        4
    2       3
    4           5
  3               4
1   4
      1 7
    4       3
  4               1
    4
1                 4
    4
11      7           16
  2 4       6 4

      2       3

    7       6

    4       7

  4     3
  3     1
```

206 STAR STUDENTS

In a magazine article, three popular Albion-TV personalities talk about their time at university, studying for careers which they never pursued after getting into television. From the clues given below, can you work out each woman's full name, what she does on Albion-TV and what she trained to be originally?

Clues

1 It wasn't Donna who was trained as a teacher.
2 Miss Knight is host of Albion-TV's popular Saturday evening quiz show Go For It!
3 Laura is a newsreader, presenting Albion-TV's flagship 9.00pm summary every weekday.
4 Susan Niven never had any ambition to be a nurse.
5 It isn't the one-time student teacher who now presents current affairs programmes for Albion-TV.

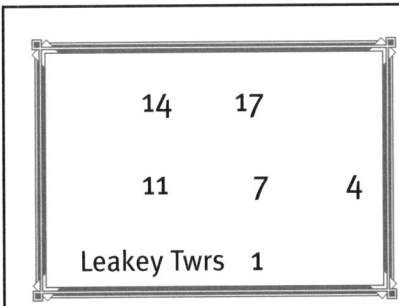

	Knight	Niven	Robins	Newsreader	Presenter	Quiz host	Nurse	Lawyer	Teacher
Donna									
Laura									
Susan									
Nurse									
Lawyer									
Teacher									
Newsreader									
Presenter									
Quiz host									

FIRST NAME	SURNAME	TV CAREER	STUDIED AS

207 TOP APARTMENT

The brass number plate for the apartments in Leakey Towers was bought from the Nutting-Fitz Hardware Store. This place never has exactly what anyone wants, so the locals have to make do with what they get. Young vandals have already ensured that one apartment number needs replacing. What should it be?

```
    14      17

    11      7       4

Leakey Twrs    1
```

208 BLACK AND WHITE

A question frequently asked is – "How many squares are there on a chessboard?" It's a pretty old question as well, so if you're young enough not to have heard it before, it is worth finding out now! (No, it isn't 64, is it?)

What isn't asked quite so often is – "How many squares are there on a chessboard which are more black than white?" Can you work that out?

209 DOTTY DILEMMA

Connect adjacent dots with vertical or horizontal lines so that a single loop is formed with no crossings or branches. Each number indicates how many lines surround it, while empty cells may be surrounded by any number of lines.

```
. . . . . . . . . .
  0     2 1     1
  3     3     2     0
      3         2
    0       1 3     2
  1     0       3     2
  1     3     1     0
    1     2 1     3
      1         1
  3     2     1     2
      3     3 3     3
```

210 HEDGE YOUR BETS

Can you draw the boundary lines on this estate so that each plot is the same size as each of the others and each contains a house, a cat, a dog and a tree?

211 STRAWBERRY SHARES

Can you carve up this ornate cake, cutting along the intersecting lines only, to produce eight equal sized portions? Each portion is to be decorated with 1 piece of chocolate, 1 iced star, a blob of cream and 1 strawberry.

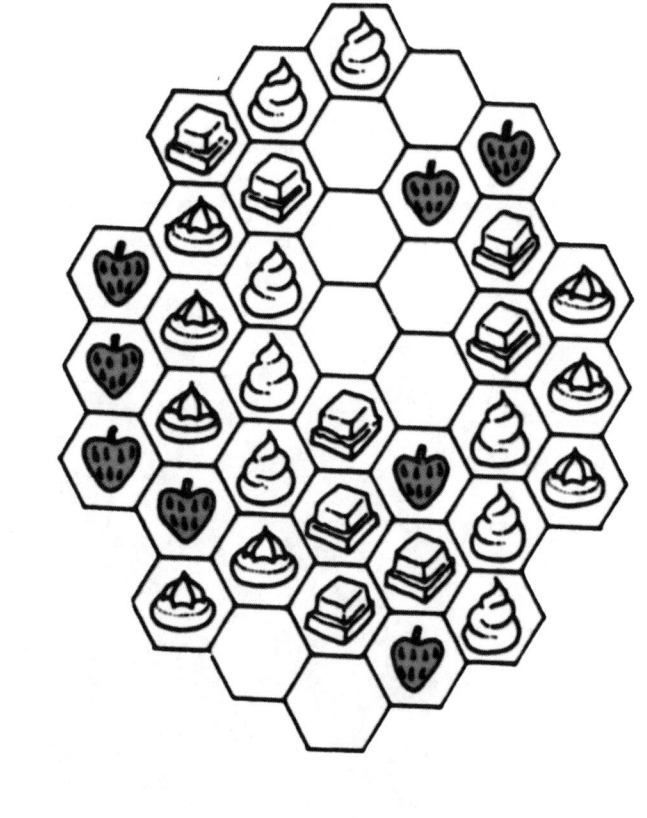

212 PYROTECHNIC PAIRS

Find the matching pair of fireworks?

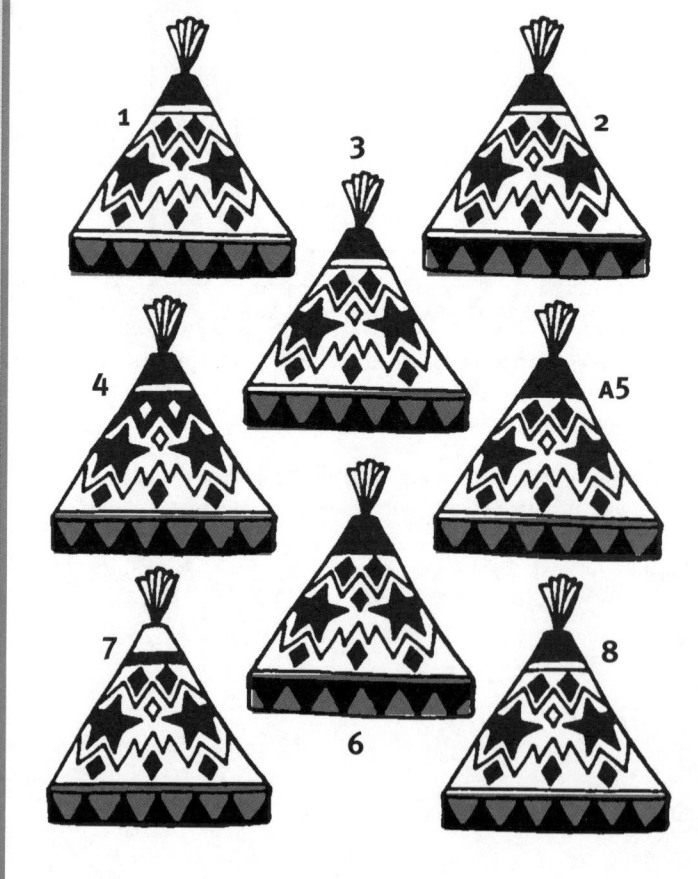

213 SQUARE THE CIRCLE

Divide the 6 x 6 square into four identical pieces so that one circle appears on each piece.

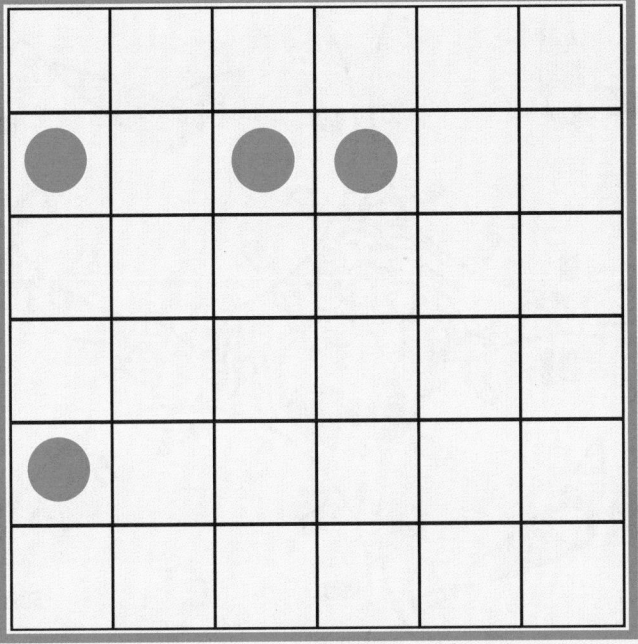

214 TENTACKLE

Eight children are camping out, two to each tent, and some have given us a couple of clues as to how to find them. The trouble is their directions are as bad as their cooking and in each case only one direction is true whilst the other is an exact opposite, so that East should read West, etc. Directions are not necessarily exact so North could be North, Northeast or Northwest. To help you one child is already tucked into a sleeping bag.

Owen says: I'm West of Rob and South of Pete
Sam says: I'm East of Vince and North of Nick
Vince says: I'm West of Nick and South of Tom
Will says: I'm East of Vince and North of Rob

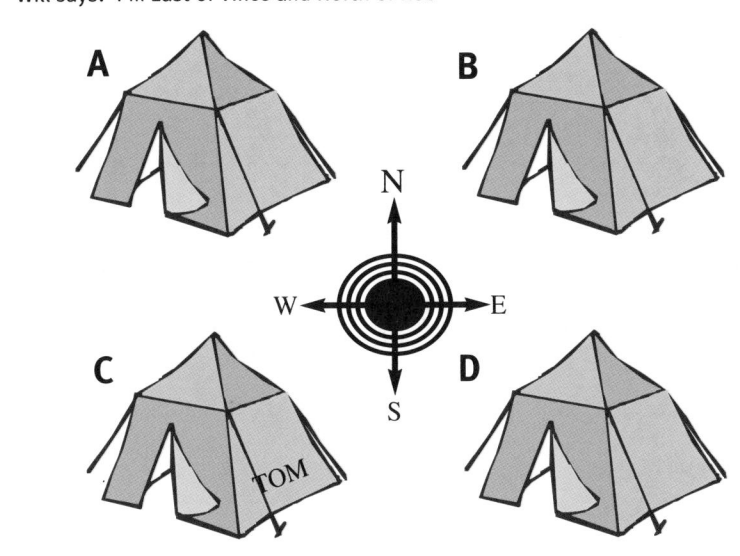

215 FACE VALUES

There are three faces hidden somewhere in this picture – can you find them?

216 SIX PACK

By packing numbers in the empty spaces, can you make the numbers in each of the 16 hexagons add up to 25? No two numbers in each hexagon may be the same and you can't use zero. We've started you off.

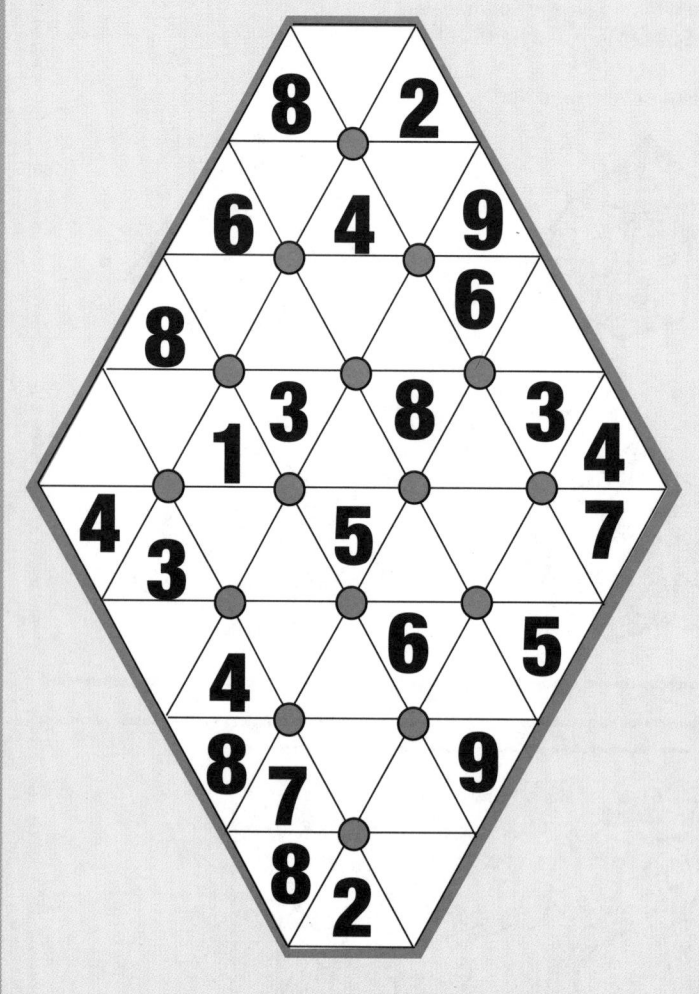

217 TIME PLEASE

Look at the three clocks, then work out what the last clock should say to continue the sequence. Can you draw in the hands correctly?

218 DOMINO SEARCH

A standard set of dominoes has been laid out, using numbers instead of dots for clarity. Using a sharp pencil and a keen brain, can you draw in the lines to show where each domino has been placed? You may find the check grid useful – crossing off each domino as you find it.

1	2	4	5	1	1	1	3
6	2	2	5	6	2	5	3
2	1	2	5	6	3	6	3
2	6	4	5	0	4	0	4
0	3	0	5	6	0	0	0
5	3	6	5	4	4	6	3
3	1	4	1	4	0	1	2

219 SET SQUARE

All the digits from 1 to 9 are used in this grid, but only once. Can you work out their positions in the grid and make the sums work? We've given two numbers to start you off.

	+	4	−		=	6
−	■	+	■	+		
	+		−	3	=	8
+	■	−	■	−		
	+		−		=	9
=		=		=		
6		2		9		

220 COMMUNITY VIEWS

Three friends who were artists each produced a work showing a different feature of the community they all lived in. From the clues given below, can you identify the three, say which view each chose to depict, and work out the medium in which each worked?

Clues

1 Ms Frame chose the local church as her subject.
2 Rosalind, whose surname is not Canvass, produced the oil painting.
3 The windmill was the subject of the watercolour painting, which was not the work of Nadine.
4 The pond was not the view selected by the artist who favoured pen and ink for her picture.

	Canvass	Frame	Pallett	Pond	Local church	Windmill	Oils	Pen and ink	Watercolour
Josephine									
Nadine									
Rosalind									
Oils									
Pen and ink									
Watercolour									
Pond									
Local church									
Windmill									

FIRST NAME	SURNAME	VIEW	MEDIUM

221 FLOWER POWER

Patriotic Pete sells bunches of red, white and blue flowers in the market. Some bunches have just a single colour, some two and some a mixture of all three. If he brings along a total of 80 bunches, can you work out how many bunches have flowers of all three colours?

The number of bunches with both red and white flowers is the same as that with both blue and white but no red. The number of bunches with only white flowers is the same as that with only red and the number of bunches with only blue flowers is the same as that with both red and blue but no white. Forty bunches contain red flowers, 49 bunches contain white and 44 contain blue. There are 38 bunches with just one colour in them.

222 NINE NUMBERS

Place a number from 1 to 9 in each empty cell so that each row, each column and each 3 x 3 block contains all the numbers from 1 to 9.

		9	7	4				
		2					5	
			3	6				1
	7				1	9		3
3		6				5		7
4		2	3				8	
9			4	5				
	5				3			
		4	1	2				

223 WHERE THE L?

Sixteen L shapes like the ones below have been fitted into a square shape. Each L has one hole, and there are four of each type in the square. No two pieces of the same type are adjacent, even at a corner. They fit together so well that the spaces between pieces do not show. From the locations of the holes, can you tell where each L is?

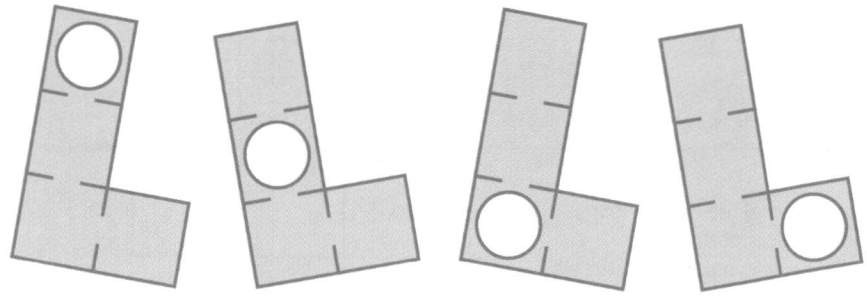

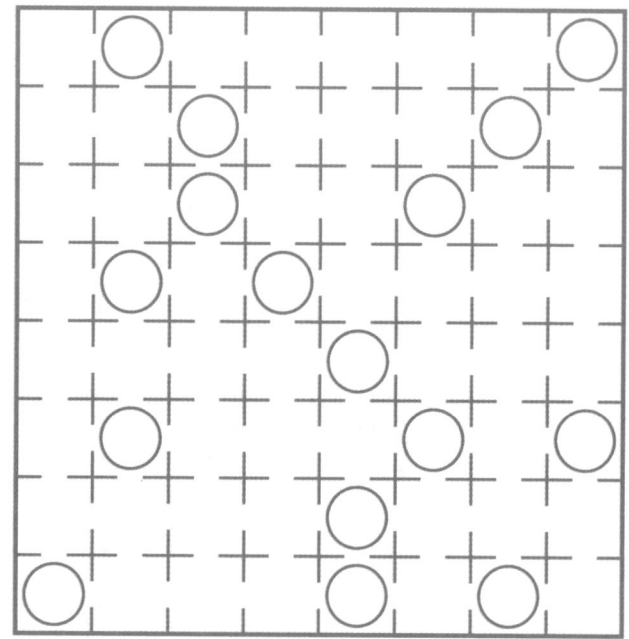

224 IN THE PICTURE

Only two of the lettered dogs match the portrait. Which are they?

225 ROUND TRIP

We have made a round trip through the dots in the grid, visiting each dot once and returning to the start. Part of our path is shown; can you deduce the rest?

HINT: Once a dot has two lines leaving it, it can't have any more. Show this by hash lines xxxx.

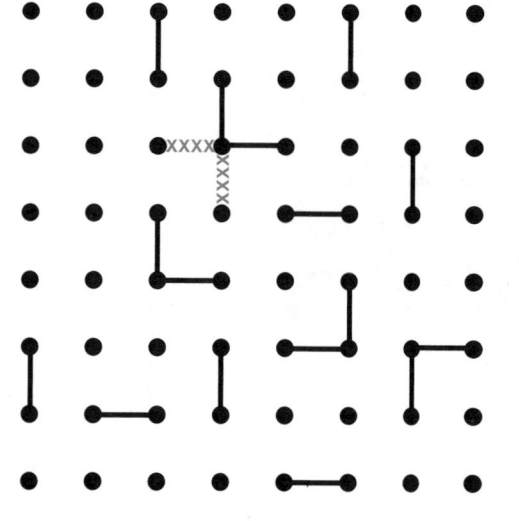

226 ISLAND HOPPING

Each circle containing a number represents an island. The object is to connect each island with vertical or horizontal bridges so that:
• The number of bridges is the same as the number inside the island.
• There can be up to two bridges between two islands.
• Bridges cannot cross islands or other bridges.
• There is a continuous path connecting all the islands.

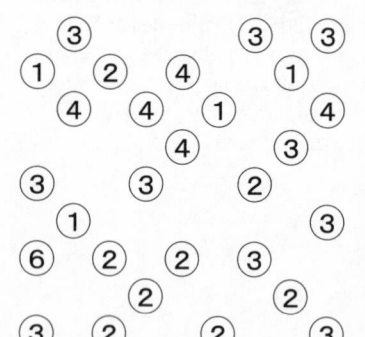

227 ARTIST'S PALETTE

Which one of the numbered boxes has been removed from this culinary scene?

228 NUMBER JIG

Fit the numbers into the grid. We have done one for you.

3 figures
214
311
362
~~401~~
421
637
729

4 figures
1714
1762
2773
3018
3707
3979
4233
6913
7326
9032

5 figures
37022
48206
48221
48872
79491

6 figures
102331
193767
212669
312943
404331
466278
476236
618243
721426
739998
760636
920307
943201

7 figures
1382916
2361712
2719383
4216072
5173484
6377028
8920973

229 FILLING IN

Each of the nine empty boxes contains a different digit from 1 to 9. Each calculation is to be treated sequentially rather than according to the 'multiplication first' system. Can you fill in the empty boxes?

	x		÷		= 2
+	■	x	■	x	
	÷		+		= 10
÷	■	÷	■	−	
	+		−		= 3
= 2		= 2		= 6	

230 BLOOMERS

Charlie Dimwit's garden centre, Bloomers, has a fine display of pot plants for sale, an equal number of each colour. Four gardeners each took ten pots from the stand. Each gardener took a different number of pots of the colours they selected. After they had taken their pots there were an equal number of each colour left over. From the information given can you work out what each gardener selected?

Brian who bought no yellows, bought the same number of reds as Pete did violets and this was double Gloria's yellows. Green was the only colour bought by all four; all the other colours were bought by three gardeners. The two 'B' gardeners bought the same number of green pots and together these were one more than Gloria's red pots which was the same as Beth's violet pots. Brian bought the same number of violets as Gloria did greens and this was two less than Brian's blues. Pete bought no reds.

231 STICKY TIME

These 16 sticks make five squares. Can you work out how to move *just two sticks* to leave four squares? The squares you leave must all be the same size and we said move not throw away. Don't leave any loose ends either.

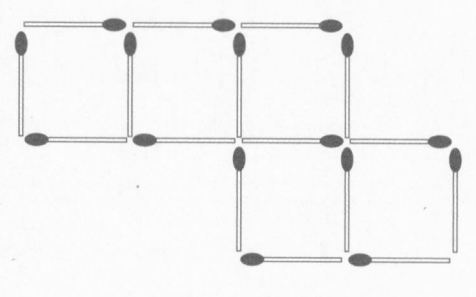

232 PATTERN MAKER

Can you place the numbered blocks into the grid to form the pattern shown? The blocks may be placed horizontally or vertically, and can be turned round.

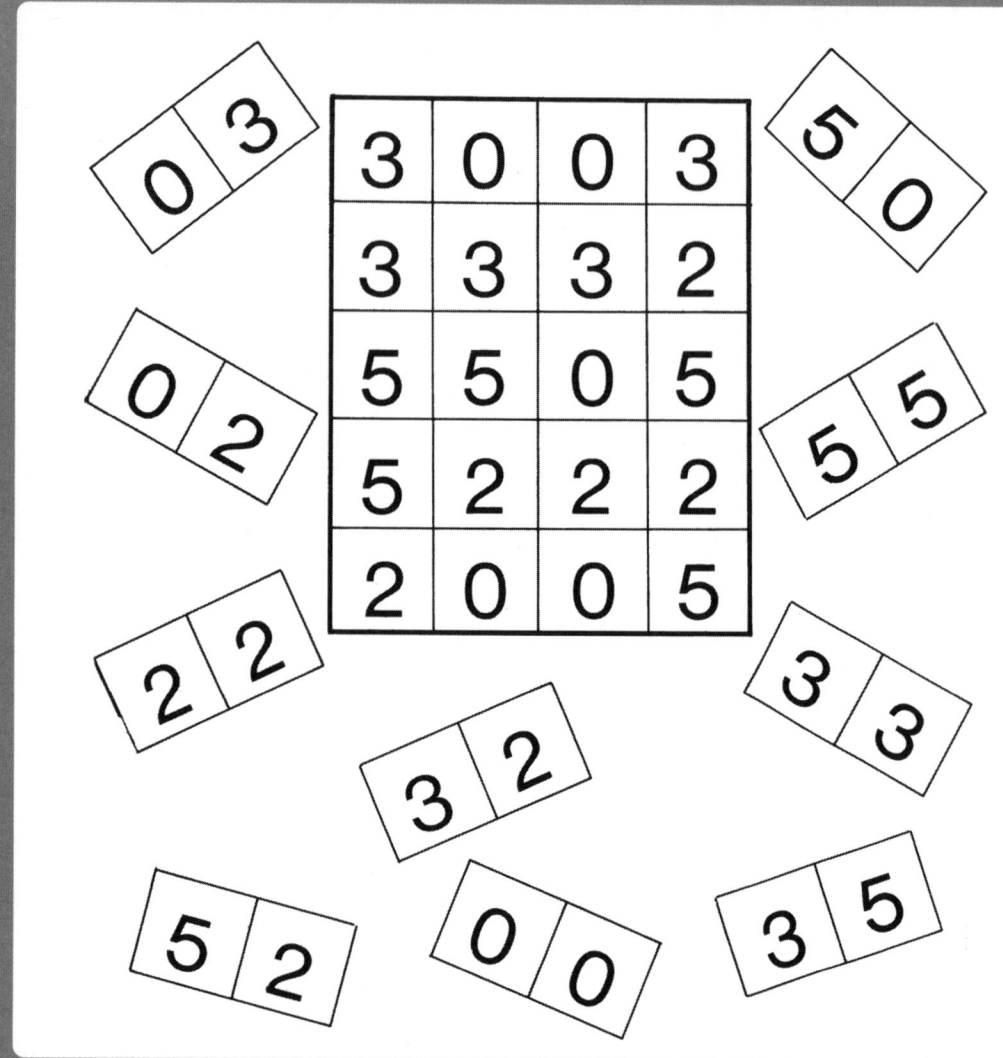

233 END OF THE LINE

There are eight differences between these two pictures – can you find them all?

234 SKI MAZE

Soppy Sally has let her skis slide down the ski slope (try saying that fast!). Can you find the way through the maze from Sally to the skis?

START

FINISH

235 COG-ITATE

Which one of the two contacts will be touched when the mechanic turns the handle as shown?

236 EASY AS ABC

Each row and column originally contained one A, one B, one C, one D and two blank squares. Each letter and number refers to the first or second of the four letters encountered when travelling in the direction of the arrow. Can you complete the original grid?

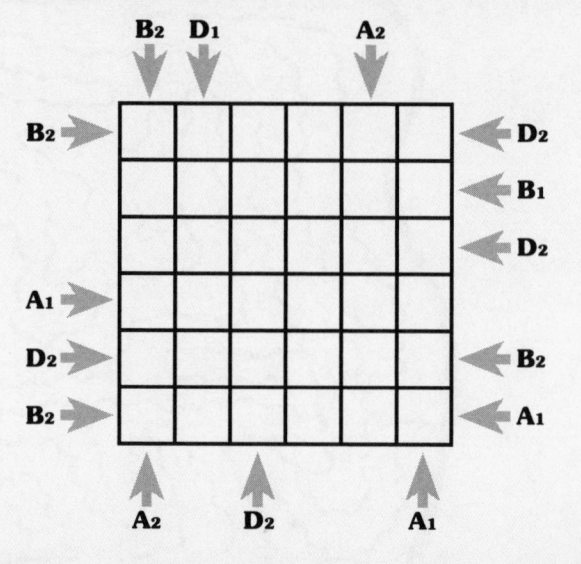

237 FILLING IN

Each of the nine empty boxes contains a different digit from 1 to 9. Each calculation is to be treated sequentially rather than according to the 'multiplication first' system. Can you fill in the empty boxes?

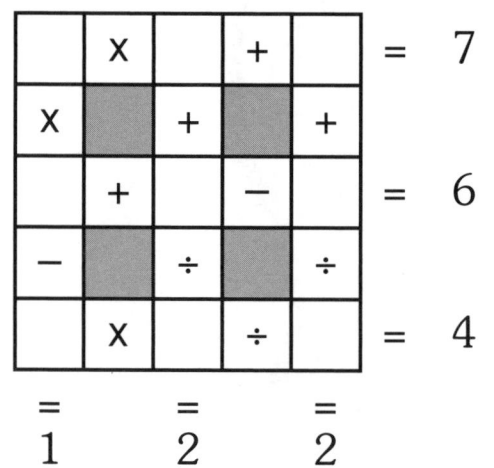

238 DOMINO SEARCH

A standard set of dominoes has been laid out, using numbers instead of dots for clarity. Using a sharp pencil and a keen brain, can you draw in the lines to show where each domino has been placed? You may find the check grid useful – crossing off each domino as you find it.

```
6 4 5 3 3 3 4 5
0 0 6 6 0 3 2 1
3 0 2 5 2 6 4 2
6 1 3 2 2 5 5 1
0 6 0 5 0 4 3 1
5 4 1 5 0 2 4 4
4 1 2 1 3 6 1 6
```

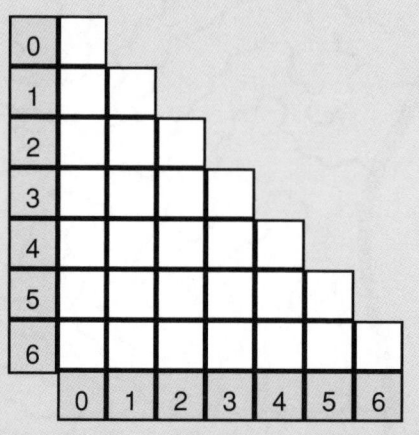

239 SQUARE FILL

How many squares, of all sizes, are more black than white in this picture?

240 RIGHT NUMBER

How many rectangles are there in this picture? (Remember, squares count as rectangles.)

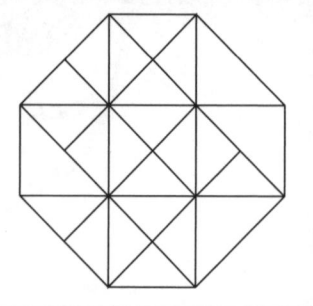

241 BLOOMERS

Charlie Dimwit's garden centre, Bloomers, has a fine display of pot plants for sale. Four gardeners each took ten pots from the stand. Each gardener took a different number of pots of the plants they selected. After they had taken their pots there was an equal number of each plant left over. From the information give below can you work out what each gardener selected? In case you are tempted to rush along to Bloomers, the gardenias are now sold out!

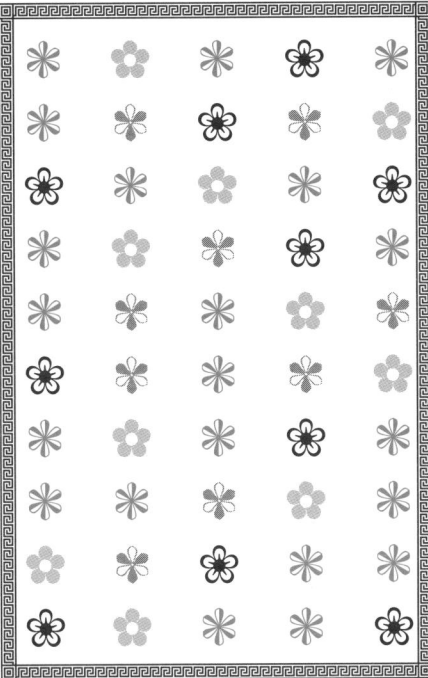

Connie bought twice as many African violets as begonias and the same number of begonias as Debbie who bought two less African violets than begonias. Arthur bought half the number of begonias as Barry bought cyclamens and Barry bought no begonias. Debbie was the only one not to buy cyclamens and Arthur bought no African violets but twice as many jasmines as Barry.

242 FLOWER POWER

Mucky Mouse has got a new camera and he's been busy snapping some flowers. Can you sort his photos into five matching pairs?

243 FRAME UP

It's that time of year again and the Mail Office has taken on extra staff for the forthcoming rush, John has persuaded his fellow recruits at Kimbledown to appear in a photo before exhaustion sets in and he himself is in position G. Left and right are as you look at the photo, and in front and behind are not necessarily directly so unless stated, i.e., it is true to say that A is behind K.

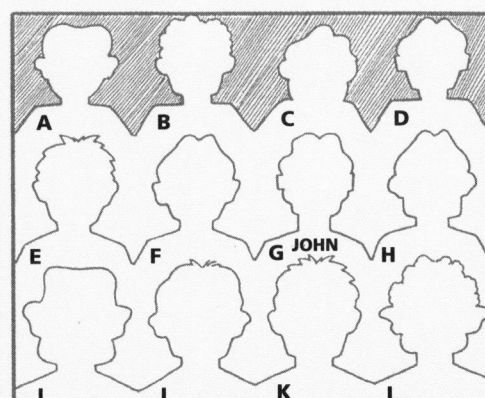

1 Fred is not next to Cleo and is not in an end position.
2 Gwen is in an end position and is behind Karl.
3 Edna is to the left of Lucy and to the right of Babs.
4 Alan is behind Dave and next to Fred.
5 Hugh is to the right of Irma and immediately in front of Edna.
6 Dave is to the right of Karl and in front of Irma.
7 Cleo is next to Lucy and they are behind John.

244 MOSTLY GHOSTS

Can you see which one of the four shadows belongs to the rabbit in the top left-hand corner?

A

B

C

D

246 DOTTY DILEMMA

Connect adjacent dots with vertical or horizontal lines so that a single loop is formed with no crossings or branches. Each number indicates how many lines surround it, while empty cells may be surrounded by any number of lines.

```
       2 0 1         1
  2 3 2               1
       2   2 3   2
  2     1   2 0   1
  2   0           3
     3           3     1
    2   2 3   2       0
    2   3 1   1
  2               3 1 3
  0       2 3 3
```

245 NUMBER JIG

Fit the numbers into the grid. One has been done for you.

2
2
8

3 figures
105
228
270
412
539
643
811
927

4 figures
2659
3107
3918
3990
4183
4277
5019
5134
5912
6108
6724
7193
7228

7830
8334
8655
9092

5 figures
11349
13296
15010
24511
32550
35012
38921
39369
44347
47075
58133
62735
70322
76074
83054
85154
93824

6 figures
120944
385581
527463
553925
729310
932408

247 CELL STRUCTURE

The object is to create white areas surrounded by black walls, so that:
* Each white area contains only one number
* The number of cells in a white area is equal to the number in it
* The white areas are separated from each other with a black wall
* Cells containing numbers must not be filled in
* The black cells must be linked into a continuous wall
* Black cells cannot form a square of 2x2 or larger

	2		3						3
						3			
			3			3	4	1	
5		2							
	4			5					
					5				
						4			3
					2				
3	4		3						
					2		1		
2			3			3			
	1			2					4
3		5							
					3	2		3	
		3							
3	4								
		4							
		5				4			
						1		3	
3	3	3		5					
	1								
3					5	4			

248 WHAT A CRACKER

Four celebratory souls are about to pull arms from sockets, wait in vain for the non-existent crack and see what expensive luxury lies hidden in each 50 cent cracker. Can you pull apart the clues, cross off the impossible and leave each cracker displaying the name of the owner, gift, motif and colour?

1 Paul has the cracker numbered two higher than Yapp's whose silver cracker is decorated with reindeer.

2 Jock has cracker No. 2 which does not have the knife in it. The gold cracker is neither No. 1 nor the one with the tinsel decoration which was given to a lady.

3 Cracker No. 3 has stars on it but is not ruby in colour. Cole was not given this one but the one with the picture in it.

4 The cracker decorated with cakes has the scarf in it which is for neither Tricia nor Williams.

5 Audrey is not Lewis and neither has the cracker with the biro nor No. 4 which is bronze in colour.

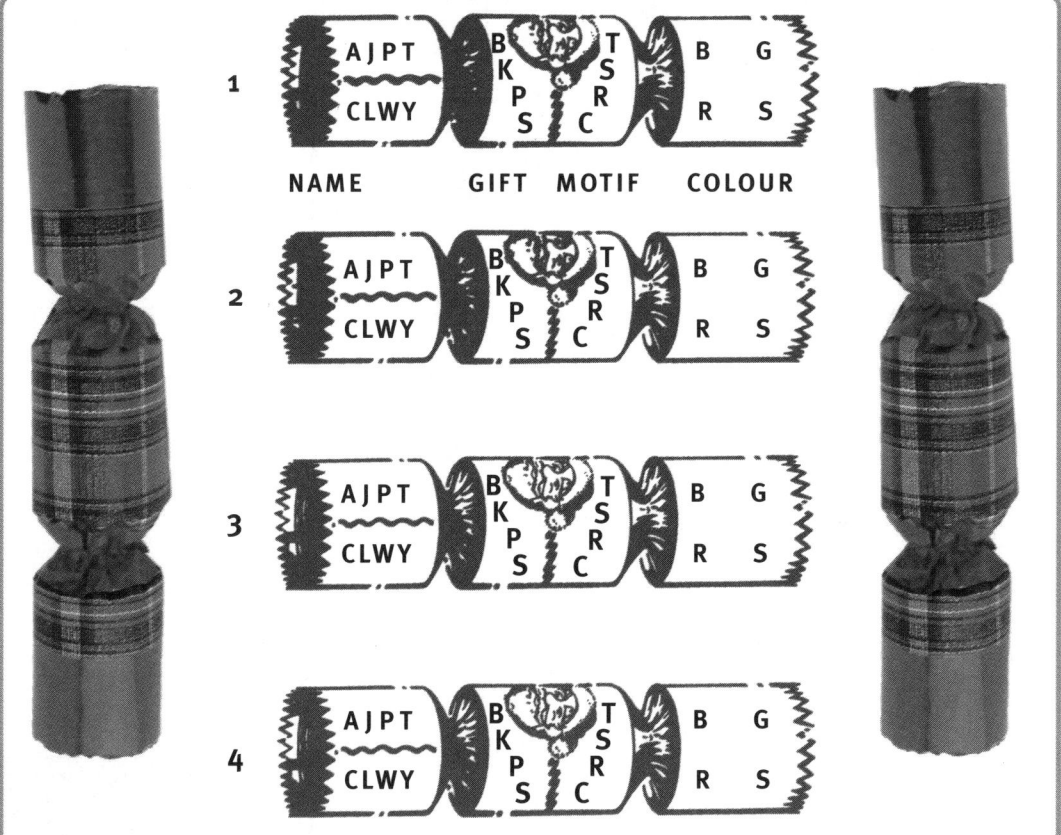

249 COG-ITATE

Which of the four weights will rise and which will fall when the handle is turned as shown?

250 FLOWER POWER

Patriotic Pete sells bunches of red, white and blue flowers in the market. Some bunches have just a single colour, some two and some a mixture of all three. If he brings along a total of 80 bunches, can you work out how many bunches have flowers of all three colours?

The number of bunches with both red and blue flowers but no white is the same as the number with red only and the number of bunches with both blue and white but no red is the same as the number with blue only and this is equal to the total number of bunches with red only and with both red and white but no blue. Three times as many bunches have white flowers only as have all three colours. Twenty-nine bunches contained red flowers and 41 bunches contained blue.

251 IN DEEP WATER

Which one of these numbered prints has been developed from the negative?

252 WHERE THE L?

Sixteen L shapes like the ones below have been fitted into a square shape. Each L has one hole, and there are four of each type in the square. No two pieces of the same type are adjacent, even at a corner. They fit together so well that the spaces between pieces do not show. From the locations of the holes, can you tell where each L is?

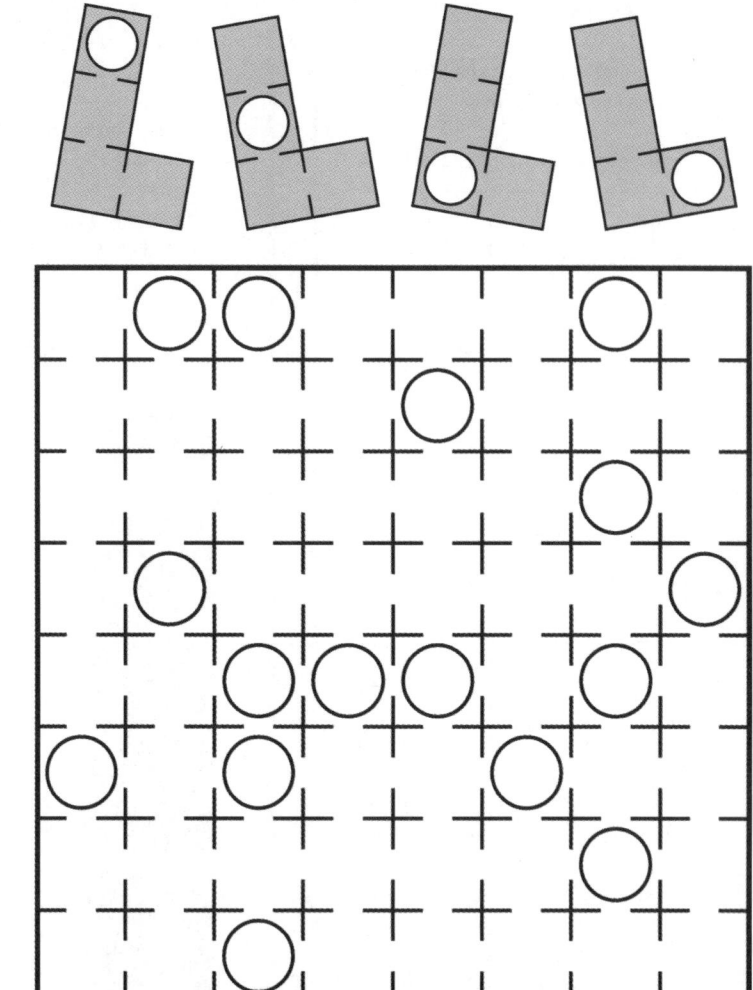

253 FILLING IN

Each of the nine empty boxes contains a different digit from 1 to 9. Each calculation is to be treated sequentially rather than according to the 'multiplication first' system. Can you fill in the empty boxes?

	÷		+		=	7
X		+		+		
	X		÷		=	12
−		÷		÷		
	+		−		=	1
=		=		=		
5		3		1		

254 BIRD BOXES

Can you see which one of the four boxes contains the pieces of the bird shown below?

255 WELL SPOTTED

The number in each circle tells you how many of it and its touching neighbours are to be filled in.

In our example, A, the zero gives a start – put lines through it and its neighbours (B). Three circles can now be filled (C) – lightly, though so the numbers can still be read…

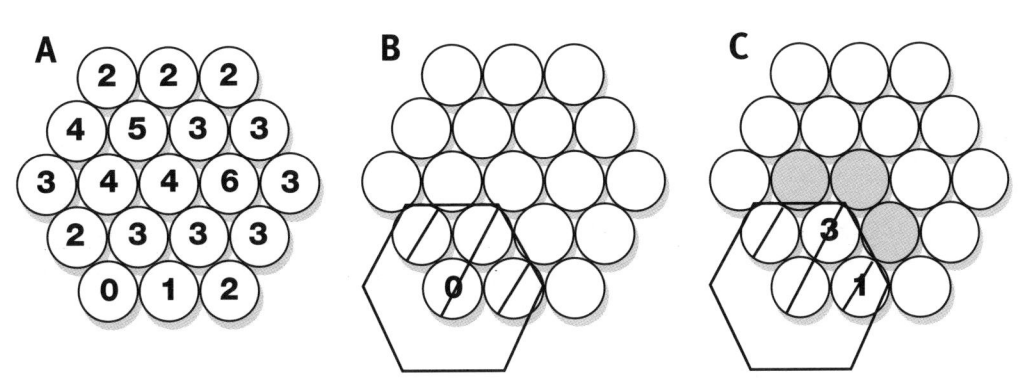

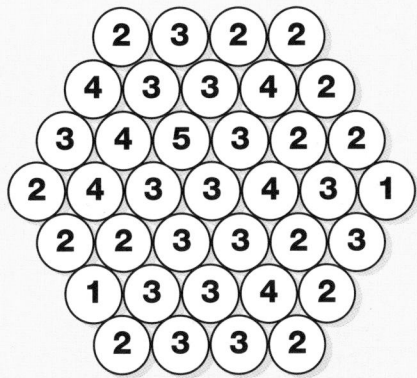

256 PIXELATED PICS

1	2	3
8	X	4
7	6	5

The numbers in the squares tell you how many of it and its neighbours are to be filled in. A square can have up to eight neighbours. Using logic alone, can you fill in the pixels and create an admirable portrait?

0		0		2		5		5		2		0		0
	1		4		6		6		6		3		0
0		4		7		5		7		8		2		0
	4		8		4		5		8		7		2
2		7		4		6		7		7		7		3
	7		6		6		6		3		6		8
3		6		7		6		3		3		6		4
	3		5		6		2		2		2		3
0		1		5		3		2		3		1		0
	0		0		3		2		1		2		0
0		0		1		3		3		4		1		0
	0		0		1		3		5		3		0
0		2		3		3		5		6		3		2
	4		6		6		4		4		5		5
4		8		9		8		5		6		7		6
	8		8		9		6		5		4		6
4		7		7		8		8		8		6		6
	4		4		8		7		7		4		6
1		2		4		8		8		8		6		6
	0		0		4		5		5		3		4

257 STAR LINES

With one continuous line, join up all the circles (starting from Pisces) and, with another continuous line, join up all the triangles (starting from Gemini). The lines must not cross!

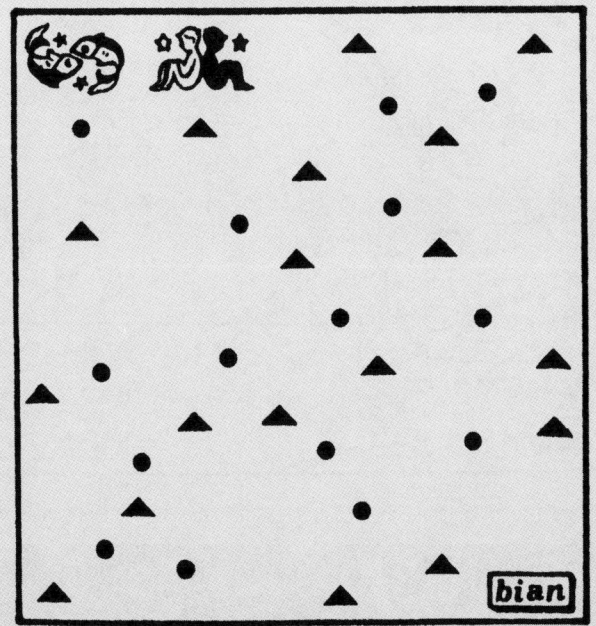

258 21s

Obeying the normal rules of arithmetic, with the numbers given, using only where necessary +, −, x, or ÷, make the resulting calculations equal 21.

2   (12   3)   9 = 21   2   11   11   10 = 21

5   3   8   2 = 21   12   10   5   3 = 21

259 SPOT THE DIFFERENCE

Can you spot the ten differences between these two pictures?

260 NUMBER SQUARES

Can you complete the grids with the aid of the numbers given, so that all sums, whether horizontal or vertical, are correct? (Please note that each sum should be treated separately.)

64	÷		=		+		=	56
−		+		−		÷		−
	÷		=		+	4		=
=		=		=		=		=
	÷		=	4	×			=
+		×		+		+		−
	−	4	=		+			=
=		=		=		=		=
41	−		=		+		=	27

261 NINE NUMBERS

Place a number from 1 to 9 in each empty cell so that each row, each column and each 3 x 3 block contains all the numbers from 1 to 9.

							5	4
	5	4				6		
3			2			7		
			1	7			4	8
7	3			4	9			
		1			7			9
	5				3	2		
2	9							

262 RINGING IN THE CHANGES

Karl Krack, who owns a small travelling circus, believes that variety is the spice of life and for each show he alters the order of his eight acts. Can you work out what the order will be for tonight's performance? The Flying Fortresses will perform immediately after Jim the Juggler and Fred the Fire-eater is immediately before the Crazy Carvellos. The Clever Clowns are in action three acts after Senor Pedro's Poodles and three acts before the Agilles Acrobats. Madame Poll's Parrots are two acts after the Flying Fortresses.

1	2	3	4
5	6	7	8

263 HARE PLAY

Which two of the pictures below form a matching pair?

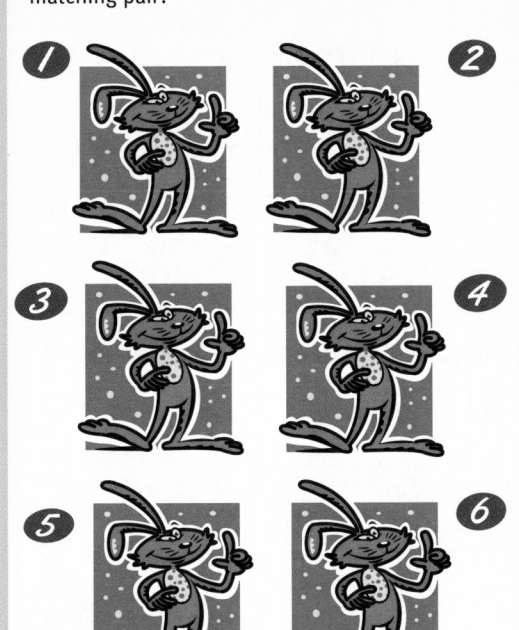

1 2 3 4 5 6

264 ACE IN PLACE

The cards Eight to King of each suit, together with the Ace of Hearts, have been placed in a five by five square. Figures and letters to the values – 8, 9, T, Q, K and suits – C, D, H, S have been placed at the end of each line across and down. With the Ace in place and the fact that the two cards shown at the top left belong in the shaded squares, can you work out the unique place for each card?

| 8 H | T C |

			T Q / Q K / C C / C C	J 8 / Q 9 / K 9 / C C / C D	8 T / 9 K / Q K / D D / H S	8 T / J J / K J / D D / H S	8 / J T / A / 9 / H C / H S	8 9 / J K / J A / C D / H S
8 J / J Q / D D / D D S							
8 J / K A / T H / C D / C H				(shaded)			A H
9 J / T K / C S / H H / S							
8 9 / Q Q / C S / H S / D S							(shaded)
9 T / T K / C H / H S / C S							

265 STICKY TIME

Using just these six matchsticks, can you make 12 right-angled triangles?

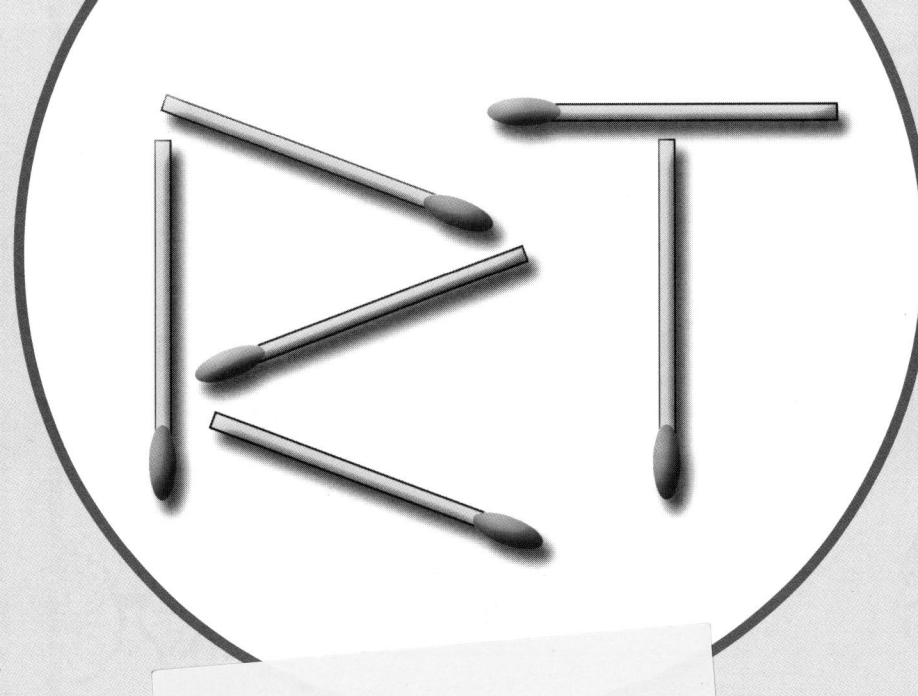

266 DOTTY DILEMMA

Connect adjacent dots with vertical or horizontal lines so that a single loop is formed with no crossings or branches. Each number indicates how many lines surround it, while empty cells may be surrounded by any number of lines.

```
·  3 1 0  ·  1 0 2  ·
· 3      · 3          ·
·          ·  3       3 ·
·  0 2 0  ·  2 3 1  ·
· 1      · 3          ·
·          ·  3       0 ·
·  3 0 2  ·  1 3 3  ·
· 1      · 3          ·
·          ·  2       3 ·
·  3 3 1  ·  0 1 0  ·
```

267 ROOM TO MANOEUVRE

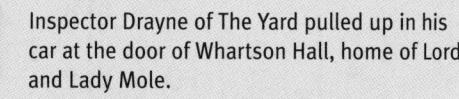

Inspector Drayne of The Yard pulled up in his car at the door of Whartson Hall, home of Lord and Lady Mole.

He entered the Hall. Swiftly his eyes travelled round the interior. Not waiting for them to come back, he stepped blindly forward and tripped over a scullery maid.

A large butler helped him to his feet.

"This way, sir. The body is waiting for you in the library."

Passing through another door, Drayne stopped in horror. He had seen death before many times – but never like this. The body of Lord Mole lay on a Persian rug – his head was caked in a thick, glutinous yellow liquid. It was obvious he had been battered to death.

Drayne turned to the local detective who was leaning against a Constable.

"Where was each person at the time of the murder?"

The detective cleared his throat, cleaned his glass eye and varnished his nails.

"Lady Mole says she was in the card room; the Hon. Reginald Ackney in the billiard room; Reverend Rash, the lounge; Lance O'Boyle, the morning room. Miss Felicity Bytes was in the study. Spott, the butler, and Wicklow, the maid, were in the cloak room."

"Thank you. Now it's obvious that...."

A sobbing interrupted his train of thought which went off into a siding.

The maid he had tripped over was having her arm set in plaster but Drayne was sure her tears were not for that. He looked at her, stern but kindly.

"Please, sir. I was told to say we were together by Mr Spott. But we wasn't."

"Were you alone?"

"If you please, sir, yes, sir."

An inner light in Drayne's mind signalled green and his train of thought shunted back into consciousness.

"Not only was Wicklow here, lying" he said, "but I know for a fact that not one of you was in the room you claimed to be in. And each of you was alone – except one – the murderer!"

Seven heads fell.

"I shall now take a statement from each of you and it had better be the truth this time."

It was.

Lady Mole recalled that Reverend Rash was in a room next to hers but Wicklow was not.

The Honourable Reginald, who thought himself frightfully good with numbers, was in a room with fewer doors than the one Her Ladyship was in but more than the one occupied by Lance O'Boyle.

Reverend Rash seem flustered. "Well, yes. I'm sure there was a lady in one room next to mine and a man in another. But I don't know who was in the third – you see, the door to that room was shut at the time."

Felicity Bytes stated candidly that Reverend Rash had not been in the lounge as she had been in a room next to it.

Spott declared that he had not been in a room adjacent to either Wicklow or the Honourable Reginald. He also confirmed that there was no door between the billiard room and the study.

Wicklow sobbed out between her tears that Mr O'Boyle had been in a room next to hers.

Drayne was stumped. The security camera replay showed him well out of his crease. He wrung his hands and then his wife. She agreed to warm his dinner in the oven – it was a ham salad.

To the assembled suspects he had but one thing to say. "I haven't a clue who was in the library – will somebody please confess?"

No one did, so-whodunnit?

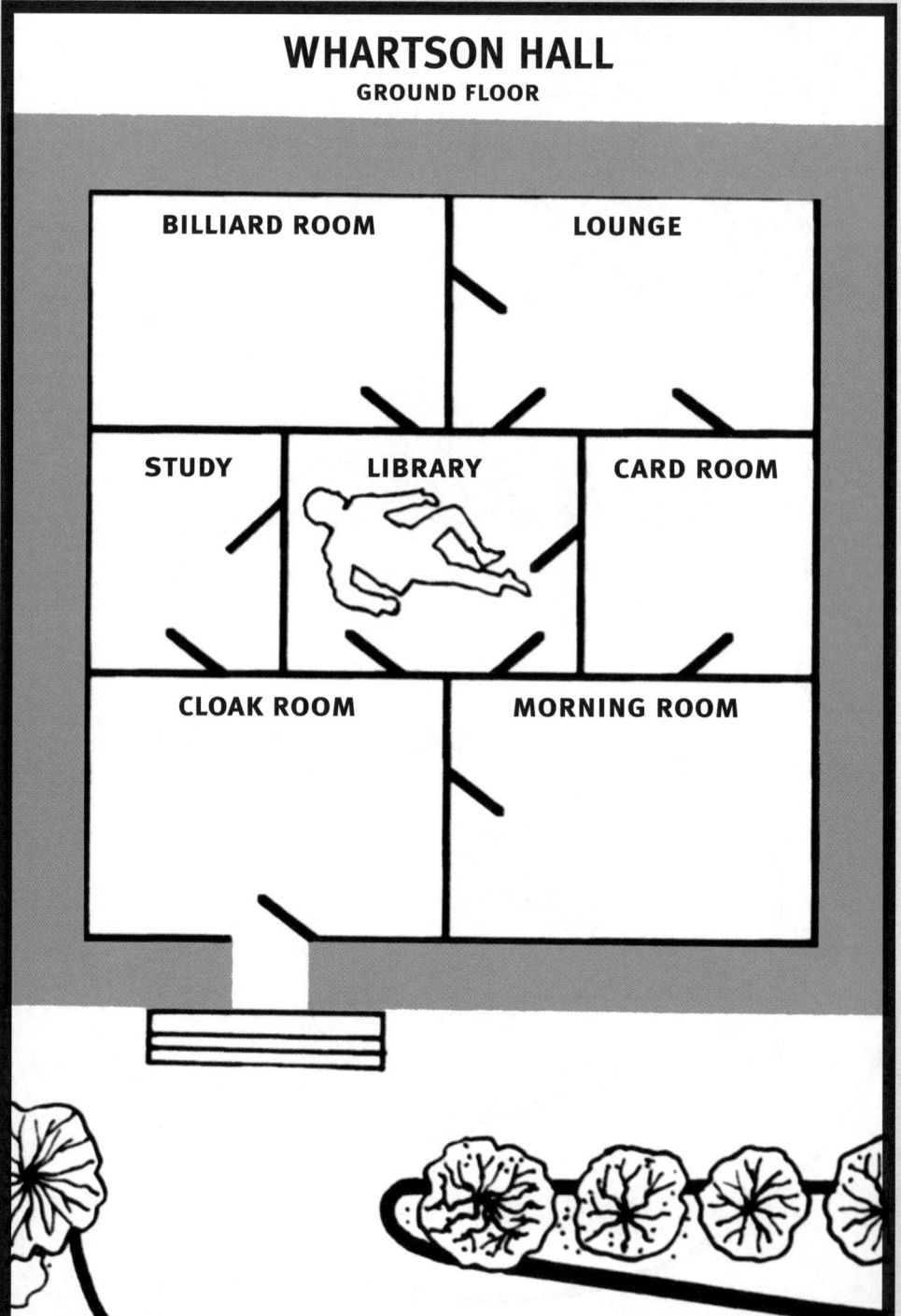

268 ISLAND HOPPING

Each circle containing a number represents an island. The object is to connect each island with vertical or horizontal bridges so that:
* The number of bridges is the same as the number inside the island
* There can be up to two bridges between two islands
* Bridges cannot cross islands or other bridges
* There is a continuous path connecting all the islands.

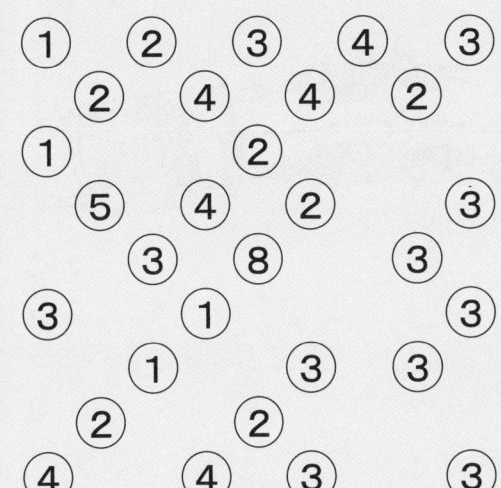

269 ILLOGI-5

Clever Trevor is trying to compile a little logical puzzle – the idea is that each line across and down has each letter A, B, C, D, E once only. Also, each shape of five squares also has the letters A to E once only. After hours of effort and wasted paper, he still hasn't managed to find a suitable arrangement. Can you end the misery by proving, quite simply, that the task is impossible?

270 LOGIQUATIONS

In the following problems the digits 0 to 9 are represented by letters. Within each separate puzzle the same letter always represents the same digit. Can you find the correct values each time so that all sums, both horizontal and vertical, are correct? There is a clue to help start you off.

$$
\begin{array}{ccccccc}
ABC & \times & DE & = & EFCE \\
+ & & + & & - \\
GHJG & - & EDH & = & GKGF \\
\hline
FDEB & - & EFJ & = & GGDA \\
\end{array}
$$

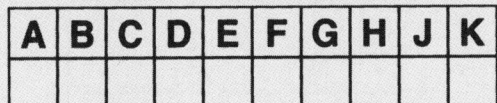

A	B	C	D	E	F	G	H	J	K

Clue: AC is a square

271 GAME SET AND MATCH

Which two of the pictures below form a matching pair?

272 SET PIECES

Which one of these broken televisions used to look exactly like the complete one?

273 BRICK UP

The numbers on the bottom row of bricks are random. Above that, every number on each brick is made up – following some simple rule – from the TWO numbers on the bricks directly below it. Can you work out what the rule is and put the right number on the top brick?

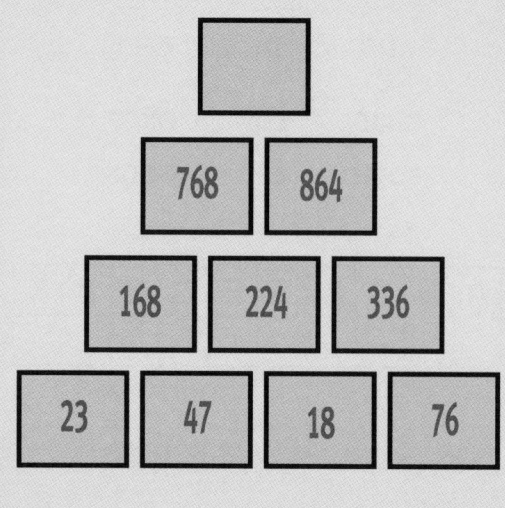

274 DEAR DEER

As usual Rudolph is in the lead as Santa's sleigh speeds down the M1. From the patrolling policeman's notes, can you name the reindeer in each of the other eight positions?

1 Cupid is Cornet's right-hand partner but Donner is further forward than, and on the opposite side to, Dasher.

2 Blitzen is further back than Dancer who, in turn, is further back than Prancer and directly in front of Vixen.

3 Cornet is directly in front of Dasher who is on the opposite side to the one both Vixen and Donner are on.

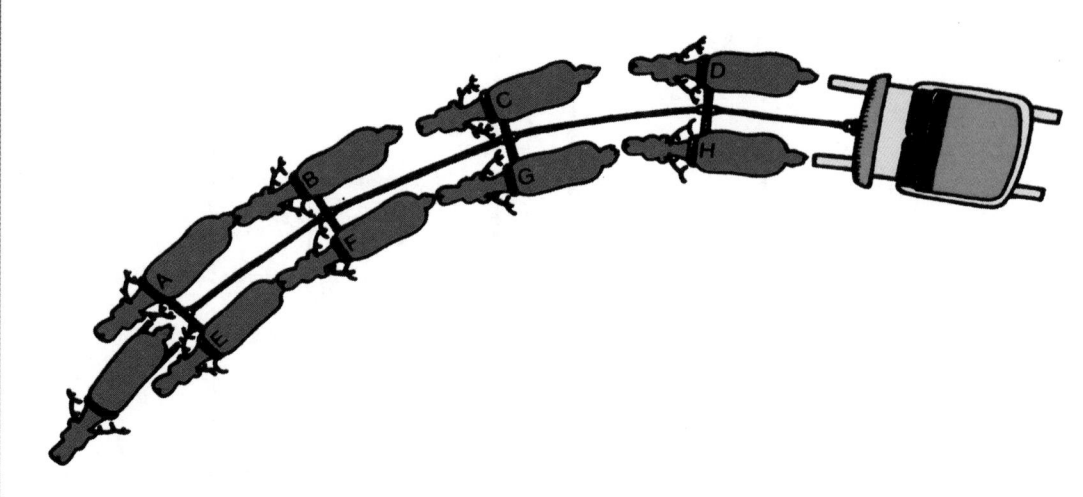

275 COG-ITATE

When the handle is turned in the direction shown, which two of the four weights will rise and which two will fall?

276 EASY AS ABC

Each row and column originally contained one A, one B, one C, one D and two blank squares. Each letter and number refers to the first or second of the four letters encountered when travelling in the direction of the arrow. Can you complete the original grid?

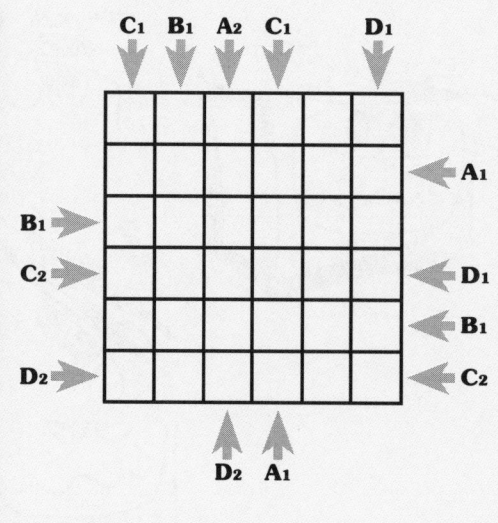

277 DOUBLE DUCKS

Can you spot three pairs of identical ducks and say which two are totally different from the others?

278 NUMBER JIG

Fit the numbers into the grid. One has been done for you.

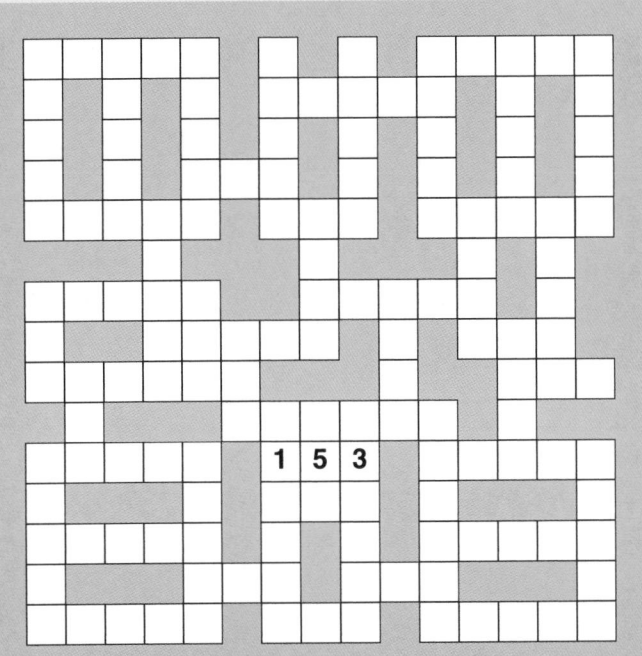

3 figures	5 figures	95422
~~153~~	10123	97324
247	12101	99283
285	13452	
318	24539	**6 figures**
396	26908	293492
407	28930	615454
562	31243	734537
564	34074	868789
628	38620	918466
630	41773	
741	46789	
779	47504	
856	51234	
962	51848	
	58907	
4 figures	61953	
1578	65678	
1646	67768	
2108	71234	
3704	72062	
	77678	
	82129	
	83103	
	86115	

279 TENTACKLE

Eight children are camping, two to each tent, and some have given us a couple of clues as to how to find them. The trouble is their directions are as bad as their cooking and in each case only one direction is true whilst the other is an exact opposite, so that East should read West etc. Directions are not necessarily exact so North could be North, Northeast or Northwest. To help you, one child is already tucked into a sleeping bag.

Kate says: I'm West of Jenny and South of Sally.
Megan says: I'm East of Lisa and South of Naomi.
Rita says: I'm West of Megan and South of Kate.
Sally says: I'm West of Paula and North of Lisa.

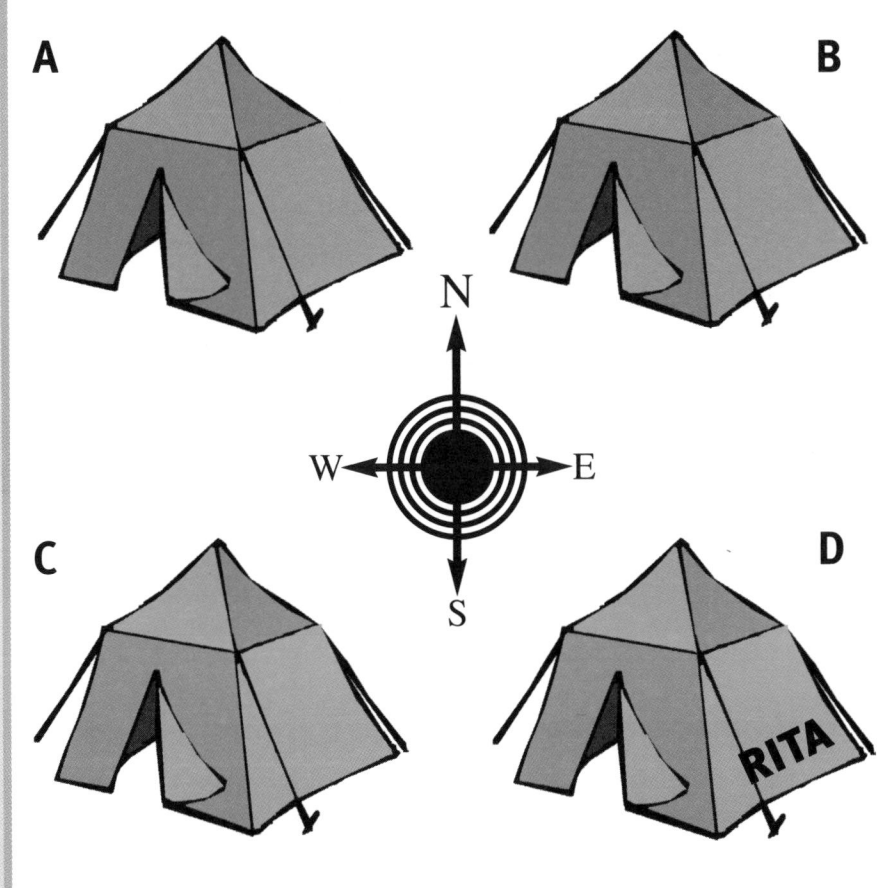

280 STICKY TIME

These 13 sticks have been placed to form four squares. Can you remove three sticks then move two of those left to form just *two* squares?

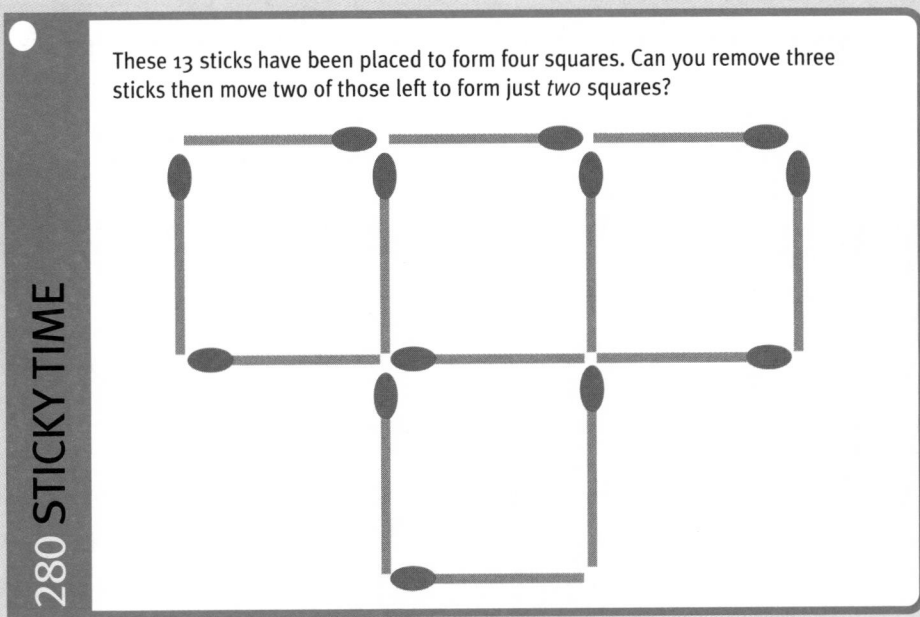

281 FIDDLEHAM APARTMENTS

The super of these notorious apartments continues to confuse visitors with his addiction to Invicta's game Master Mind. Instead of 'Smith's in Apartment X, buddy.' he hands the visitor a list of current residents and asks him to make guesses as to who is in each apartment. He then marks the line of guesses with two numbers:

First: how many are exactly right – the correct name on the right door.
Second: how many of the names are correct for that floor but are on the wrong door.
The only other information he gives is that each surname can only occur on one floor – if Smith is on the ground floor, that name can't be on either of the other two floors. However, the same name can occur more than once on the same floor.
From the 12 guesses below and the list of names on the right, can you work out the correct name for each flat?

NAMES OF RESIDENTS
Carrol, Davies, Edgely, Farmer, Grimes, Harris, Innish, Jenkin, Levers

#					Right apartment and floor	Right floor only
1	Grimes	Jenkin	Farmer	Farmer	0	2
2	Carrol	Levers	Farmer	Edgely	1	1
3	Innish	Harris	Carrol	Davies	0	2
4	Grimes	Edgely	Farmer	Jenkin	0	2
	I	J	K	L		
5	Levers	Levers	Grimes	Grimes	0	2
6	Grimes	Harris	Grimes	Davies	1	3
7	Innish	Grimes	Grimes	Levers	1	1
8	Grimes	Carrol	Jenkin	Innish	1	0
	E	F	G	H		
9	Edgely	Levers	Edgely	Levers	2	2
10	Innish	Davies	Innish	Levers	1	0
11	Jenkin	Edgely	Levers	Davies	1	1
12	Grimes	Davies	Levers	Grimes	0	1
	A	B	C	D		

Answer grid columns: I J K L / E F G H / A B C D

282 ROUND TRIP

We have made a round trip through the dots in the grid, visiting each dot once and returning to the start. Part of our path is shown. Can you deduce the rest?

HINT: Once a dot has two lines leaving it, it can't have any more. Show this by hash lines xxxx.

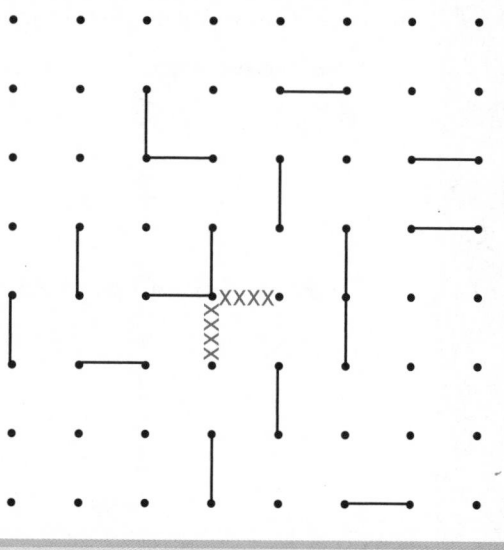

283 DOTTY DILEMMA

Connect adjacent dots with vertical or horizontal lines so that a single loop is formed with no crossings or branches. Each number indicates how many lines surround it, while empty cells may be surrounded by any number of lines.

```
                    2 0
  2 3 0 2   1     3
                2       2
    2 1 3     3
  0         2     1 3
    3 0       2         2
      3       2 1 2
    3     1
    1     2   3 2 3 3
      3 1
```

284 HEART ON HIS SLEEVE

Can you spot the eight differences between these two pictures?

285 ISLAND HOPPING

Each circle containing a number represents an island. The object is to connect each island with vertical or horizontal bridges so that:
• The number of bridges is the same as the number inside the island
• There can be up to two bridges between two islands
• Bridges cannot cross islands or other bridges
• There is a continuous path connecting all the islands.

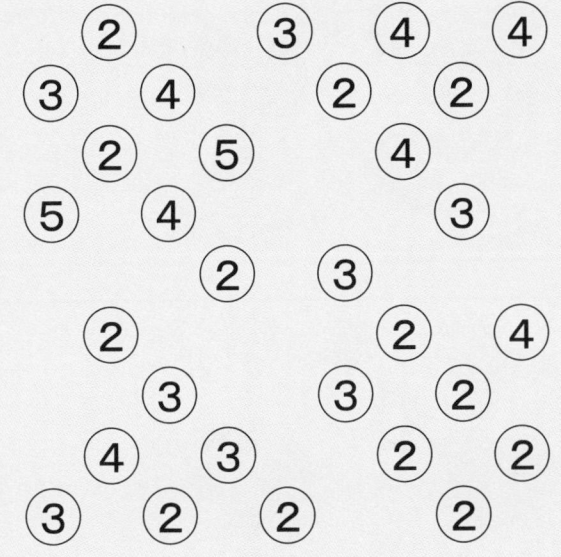

286 FOUR-WHEEL FROLIC

There are six differences in the pictures below. Can you spot them?

287 BLOOMIN' MARVELLOUS

There are six differences between these two pictures.
Can you find them all?

288 NINE NUMBERS

Place a number from 1 to 9 in each empty cell so that each row, each column and each 3 x 3 block contains all the numbers from 1 to 9.

					9	1		
	4	2	1					7
3			5				6	
2							4	
		1				9		
	6							5
	5			6				1
	7				3	5	2	
		8	9					

289 CUBE IT

Inside the circle are three views of the same cube.
Which of the lettered shapes can be folded up to make this cube?

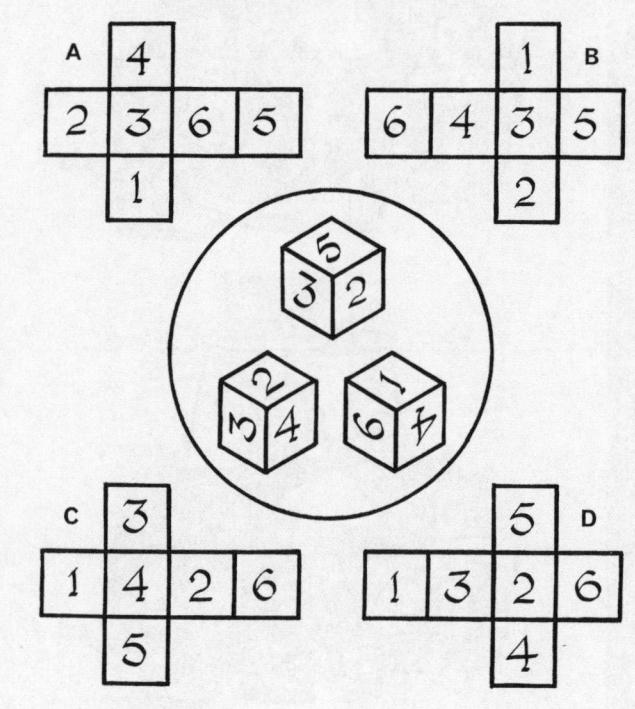

290 ROUND TRIP

We have made a round trip through the dots in the grid, visiting each dot once and returning to the start. Part of our path is shown; can you deduce the rest?

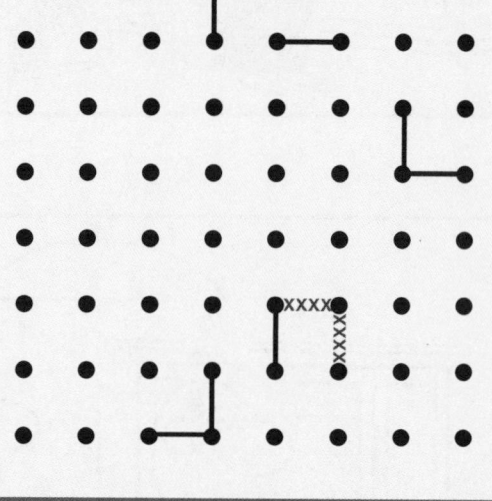

291 DOTTY DILEMMA

Connect adjacent dots with vertical or horizontal lines so that a single loop is formed with no crossings or branches. Each number indicates how many lines surround it, while empty cells may be surrounded by any number of lines.

```
. . . . 2 0 . 3 . 1 . .
3 0 . . . . . . . 3 . .
. . . 3 . 2 . 3 3 . . .
. 3 . 3 . . 1 . . . . 3
. . . . . 2 1 2 . 3 . 2
3 . 3 . . 1 2 2 . . . .
3 . . . . 2 . . 0 . 3 .
. . . . 3 2 . 1 . 1 . .
. . 3 . . . . . . 3 3 .
. . 3 . 1 . 2 1 . . . .
```

292 MAZE MYSTERY

Travel from the entrance to the exit of the maze, filling the path completely to create a picture.

293 SPOT THE DIFFERENCE

How quickly can you discover the ten differences between these two pictures?

294 FIGUREWORK

Just fit these numbers into the grid.

3 figures		9 figures
129	785	182763544
172	905	273611773
173	936	296724217
216	987	419728652
219		612186177
272	**4 figures**	
273	1107	
292	3722	
334	4171	
361	7853	
362		
371	**7 figures**	
611	1012392	
619	2618282	
620	6661761	
651		
671		
716		

295 ROUND TRIP

We have made a round trip through the dots in the grid below, visiting each dot once and returning to the start. Part of our path is shown; Can you deduce the rest?

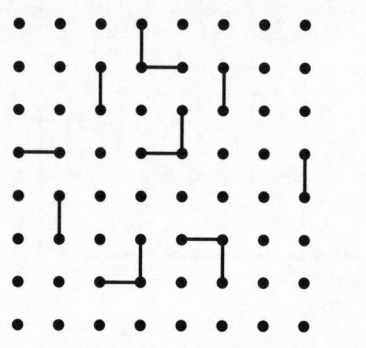

296 ACE IN PLACE

The cards Eight to King of each suit, together with the Ace of Hearts, have been placed in a 5 x 5 square. Figures and letters showing the values – 8, 9, T, J, Q, K and suits – C, D, H, S have been placed at the end of each line across and down. With the Ace in place and the fact that the two cards shown at the top left belong in the shaded squares, can you work out the unique place for each card?

297 SPOT THE DIFFERENCE

One of these footballers looks different from all the others. Can you spot the odd one out?

298 CUBE IT

Which two of the numbered pieces will fit together to make cube A?

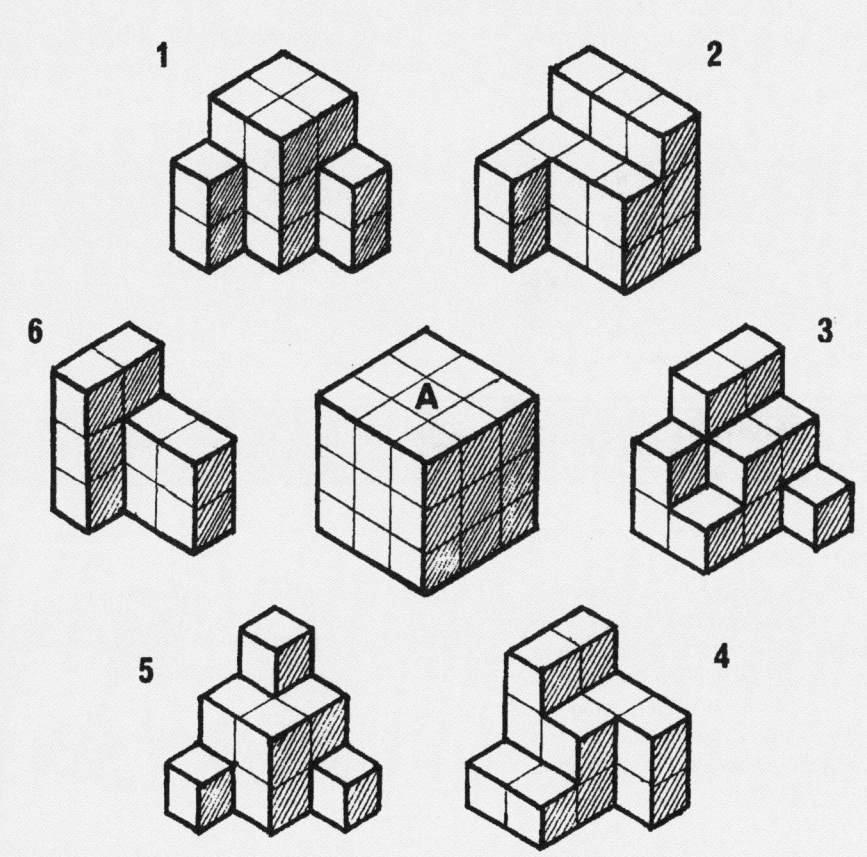

299 IT FIGURES

Place a number from 1 to 9 in each empty cell so that the sum of each vertical or horizontal block equals the number at the top or on the left of that block. Numbers may only be used once in each block.

300 DOMINO DEAL

A standard set (o – o) to (6 – 6) is laid out below. Each domino is placed so that the larger number will be on the bottom:

i.e.   3   not   6
         6   3

Those top numbers show the four numbers which form the top half of each domino in that column. The bottom numbers, below the grid, give the four bottom numbers for that column. The seven numbers on the left show the numbers which belong in that row. Can you cross-reference the facts and deduce where each domino had been placed?

3*6 is given as a start.

'TOP' NUMBERS

	01 23	00 25	01 23	13 35	01 24	01 14	02 46
0 1 2 4 4 5 6 / 1 5 5 5 6 6 6							
0 0 1 1 1 3 3 / 0 2 2 3 5 5 6	3 / 6						
0 0 0 2 2 2 3 / 1 2 3 3 4 4 4							
0 1 1 2 3 4 5 / 3 4 4 5 6 6 6							
	15 66	24 55	12 56	23 46	35 56	34 46	03 46

'BOTTOM' NUMBERS

301 PROFESSIONAL PARTNERS

Each of the six persons mentioned has at least one sibling in the group and has exactly one spouse in the group. Each person is a member of one of the professions mentioned. No one shares a profession with a sibling or a spouse.

Here are the names with some other facts:

1 Neither Alice nor Dave is a surgeon.
2 Betty's sister's husband is an accountant.
3 Carol's husband's brother is an accountant.
4 Ed's wife is a surgeon, and so is Ed's sibling's spouse.
5 Frank's wife's brother is a lawyer.

You are now invited to identify the pre-marriage family groups, the marriages, and the profession of each person.

302 TRILINES

Can you draw three straight lines, each one drawn from one edge to another, so that it divides the box into five plots each containing two different fruits?

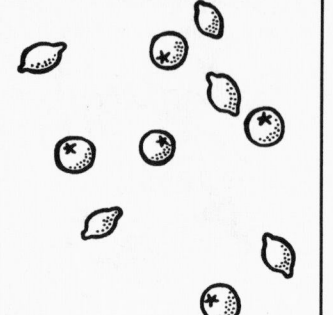

303 WHERE THE L?

Sixteen L-shapes like the ones on the right have been inserted into a square shape. Each L has one hole, and there are four of each type in the square. No two pieces of the same type are adjacent, even at a corner. They fit together so well that the spaces between pieces do not show. From the locations of the holes, can you tell where each L is?

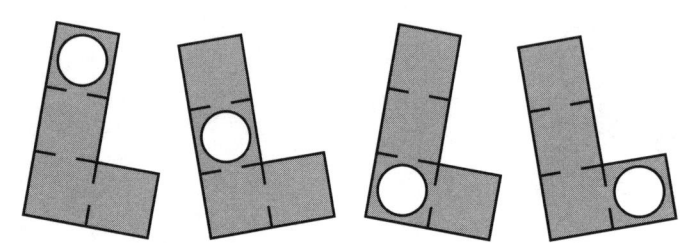

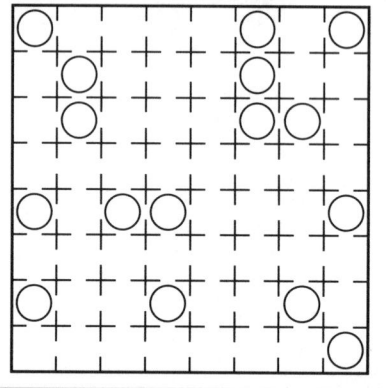

304 FUNNY BUNNY

These nine pieces can be put together to make up the rabbit shown in the middle. However, three of them are slightly wrong. Can you see which three they are?

305 ACE IN PLACE

The cards Eight to King of each suit, together with the Ace of Hearts, have been placed in a 5 x 5 square. Figures and letters showing the values – 8, 9, 10, J, Q, K and suits C, H, D, S, have been placed at the end of each line across and down. With the Ace in place and the fact that the two cards shown at the top left belong in the shaded squares, can you work out the unique place for each card?

306 MAZE MYSTERY

Travel from the entrance to the exit of the maze, filling the path completely to create a picture.

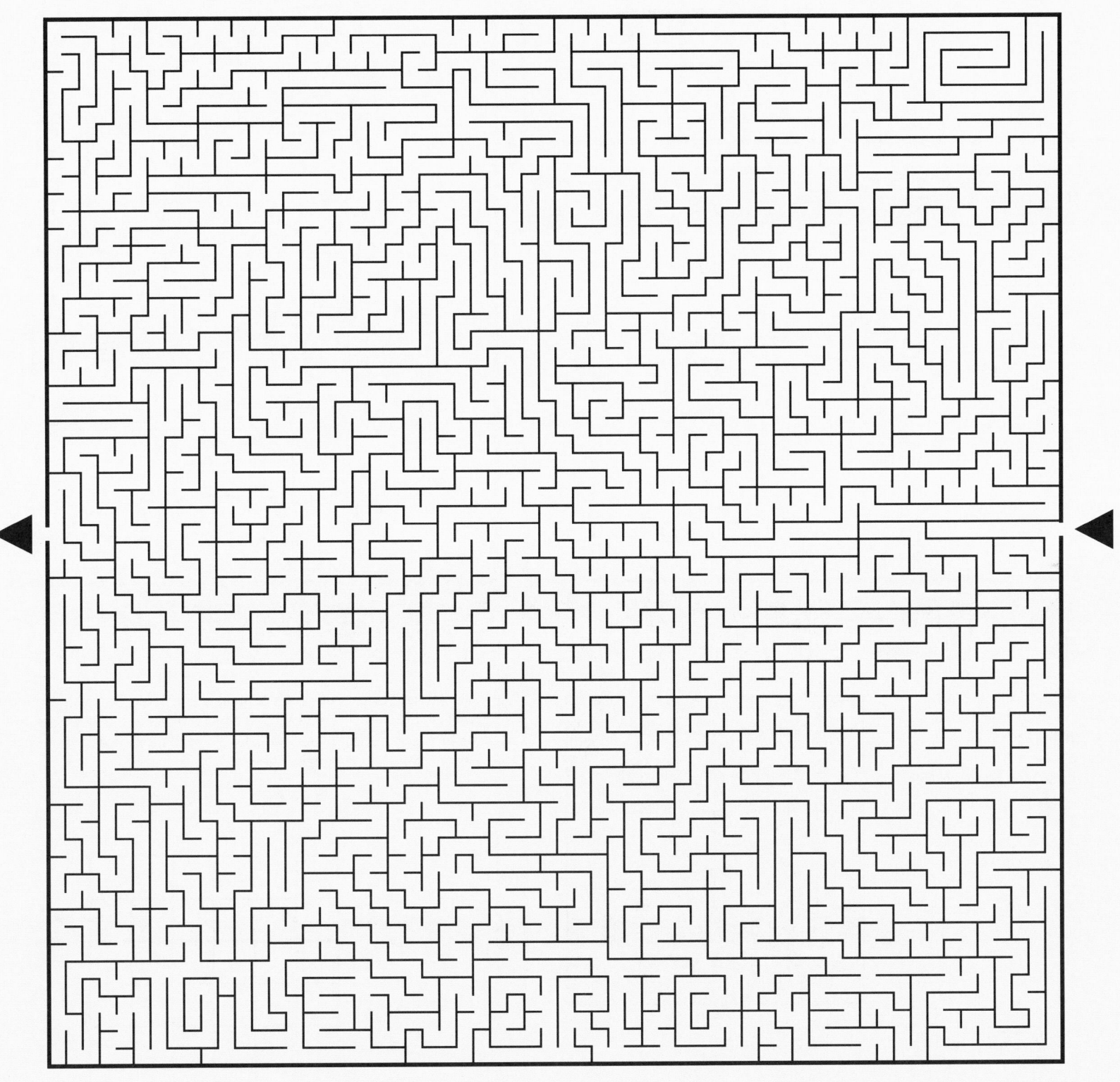

307 LOGI-5

Each line, across and down, is to have each of the letters A, B, C, D and E, appearing once each. Also, every shape – shown by the thick lines – must also have each of the letters in it. Can you fill in the grid?

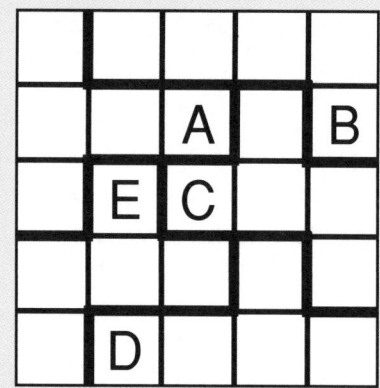

309 ALPHACIPHER

The numbers 1 to 26 have been allocated randomly to the letters of the alphabet. The letter values of the words have been added together to give the word values. For example, in GOLF, G might equal 15, O 12, L 20 and F 7, or any other combination of four numbers totalling 54. The theme this time is the phonetic alphabet. What is the value of ZULU?

ALPHA	68	NOVEMBER	64
BRAVO	59	OSCAR	56
CHARLIE	63	PAPA	48
DELTA	57	QUEBEC	68
ECHO	45	ROMEO	36
FOXTROT	68	SIERRA	54
GOLF	54	TANGO	53
HOTEL	52	UNCLE	50
INDIA	56	VICTOR	47
JULIET	75	WHISKEY	99
KILO	47	X-RAY	46
LIMA	30	YANKEE	65
MIKE	34		

308 ARTIST'S MAZE

Can you work your way through this maze, starting from the flower at the top and finishing at the bottom of the chair?

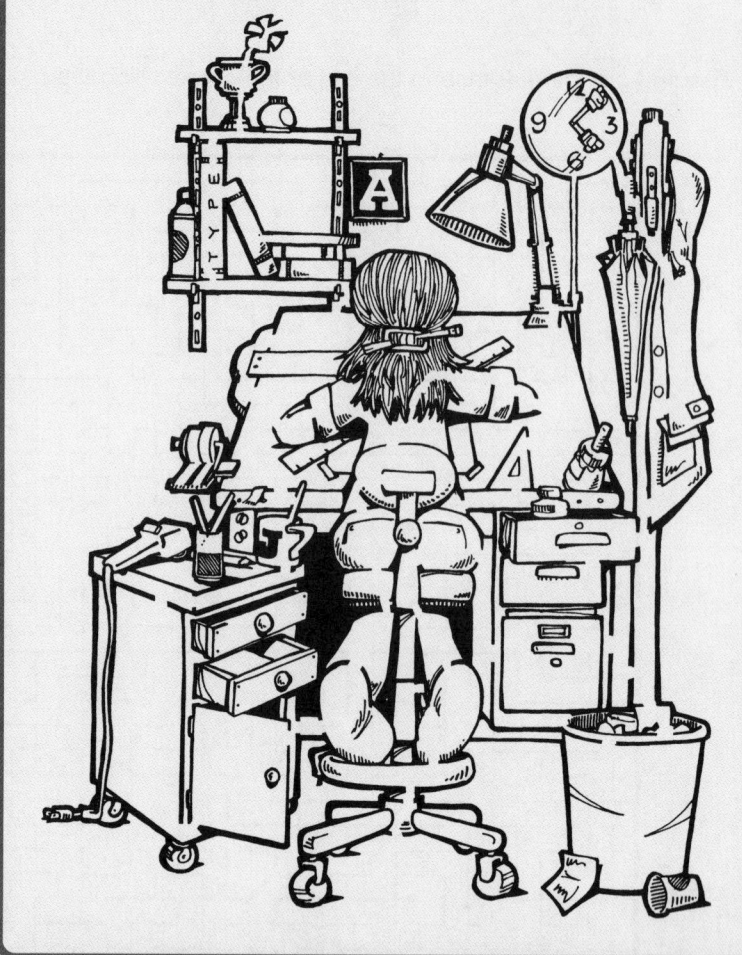

310 WHERE THE L?

Sixteen L-shapes like the ones below have been inserted into a square shape. Each L has one hole, and there are four of each type in the square. No two pieces of the same type are adjacent, even at a corner. They fit together so well that the spaces between pieces do not show. From the locations of the holes, can you tell where each L is?

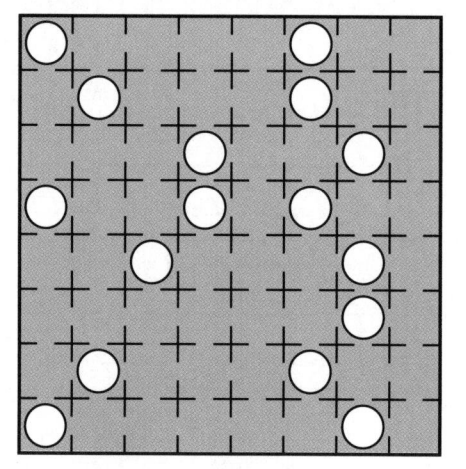

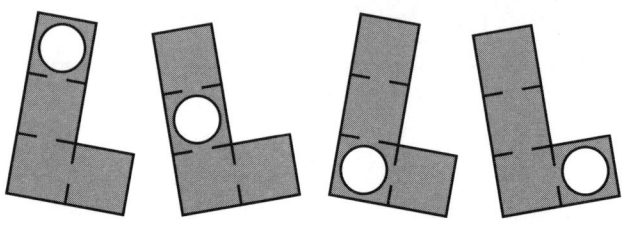

311 EASY AS ABC

Each row and column originally contained one A, one B, one C, one D and two blank squares. Each letter and number refers to the first or second of the four letters encountered when travelling in the direction of the arrow. Can you complete the original grid?

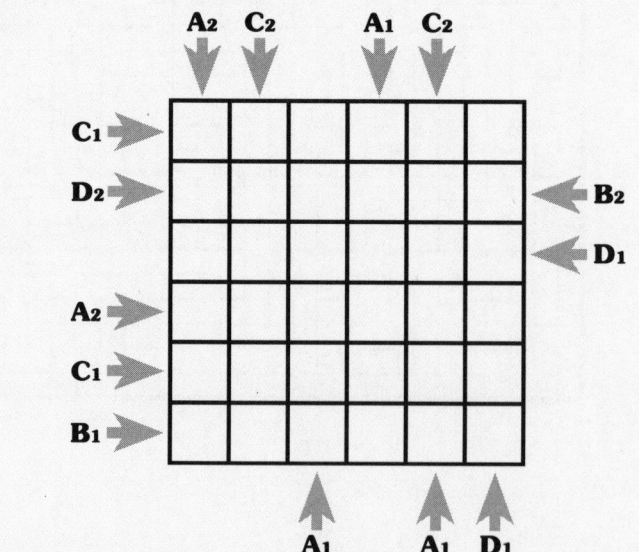

312 DOUBLE PUZZLE

Roll up folks, for our special sale offer of two puzzles for the price of one!

Puzzle One: Each colour has been given a value from 1 to 7. Given the totals at the end of each line, can you work out the value of each colour?

Puzzle Two: The picture is a layout of a set of colour dominoes – just like ordinary dominoes but with colours instead of spots. Can you draw in the lines to show each separate domino?

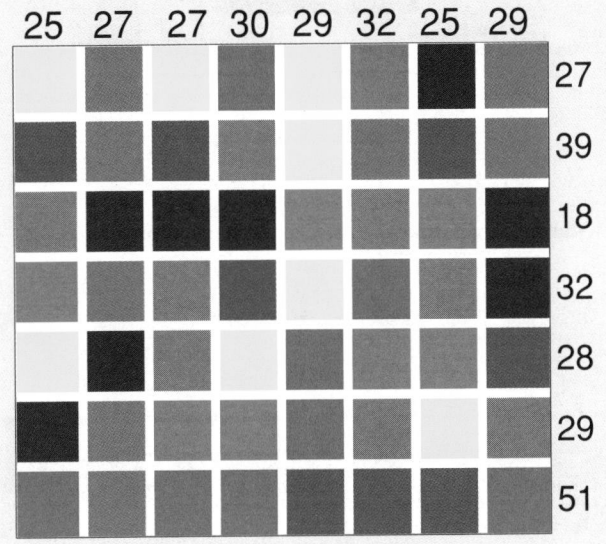

314 HAPPY HOUNDS

Can you see which one of the five pieces at the bottom will fit into the arrowed gap in the jigsaw? It's trickier than it looks!

313 CUBISM

Which two cubes can be constructed from the template?

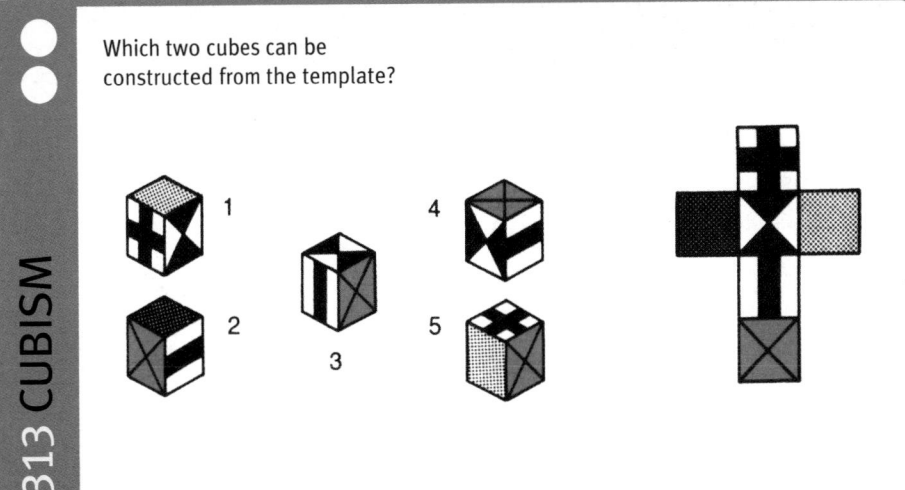

315 STRAPPED

The six straps leading from the central hexagon each contain three different instances of the numbers 1 to 18. From the clues given below, can you place each number in the correct position on the correct strap?

Clues

1 The six innermost numbers total 64.

2 The single-digit middle number on strap A minus the number outside it produces the outermost number on strap F.

3 There are just two even numbers, one of which is the outermost one, on strap E, but only one on strap F.

4 5 is the innermost number on strap D; the 7 is not on the strap directly opposite.

5 17 and 12 are separated by the 1 on one of the straps.

6 The 10 on one strap, which is immediately next to the 16, is in the same relative position as the 3 on another, but the 6 is further away from the centre than the 15 on an adjacent strap.

7 Strap C, which has only one two-digit number on it, does not contain the 1 or 2, which corresponds in its position with the 13 on another strap.

8 The largest of the three numbers on strap B is not its innermost one; the outermost one is a lower number than the innermost number of the strap opposite, which is ten higher than the corresponding number on strap F.

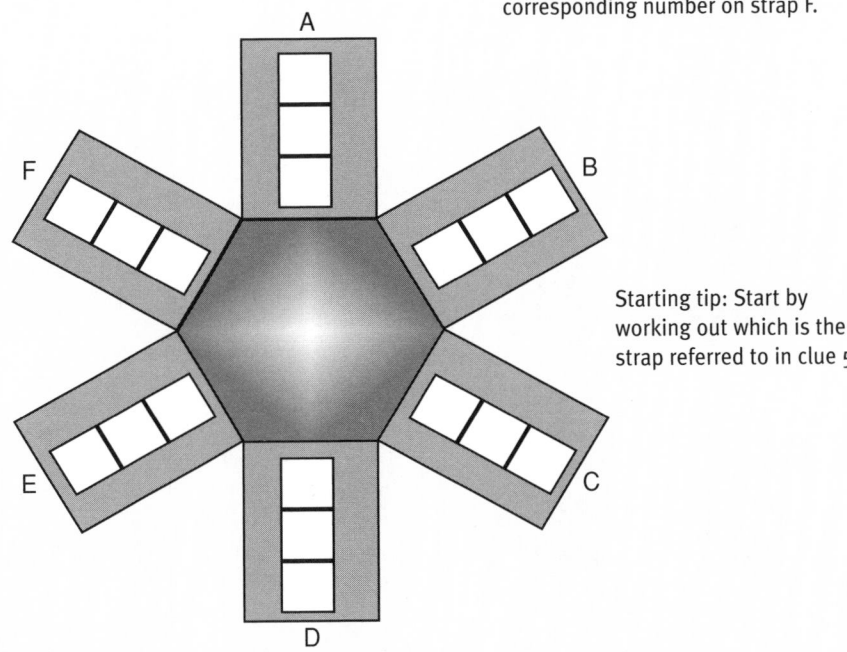

Starting tip: Start by working out which is the strap referred to in clue 5.

91

316 NUMBER BOX

Just fit the numbers into the grid.

3 figures	5 figures
244	41322
432	42071
433	
456	**7 figures**
459	4224545
521	4312344
522	4321345
565	5443099
623	7450975
625	7654456
662	
674	**11 figures**
742	43136777786
774	43973953013
853	55443135666
894	56562523451
	68575856944
	75714244524

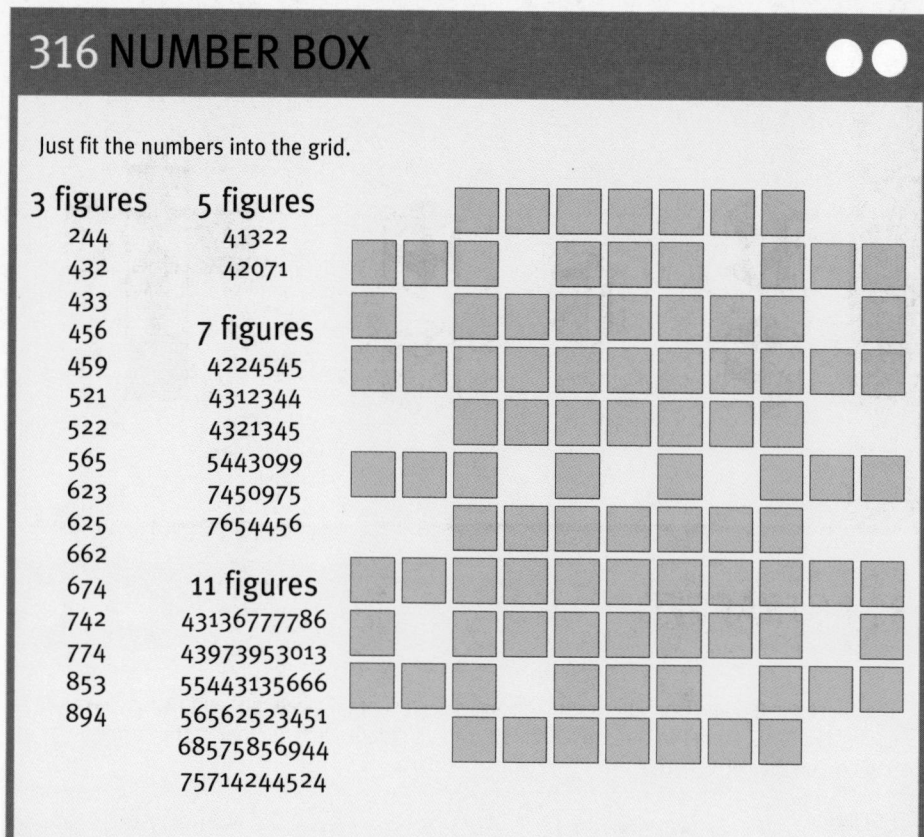

318 WEIGHED UP

How many cans are needed to make the third pair of scales balance?

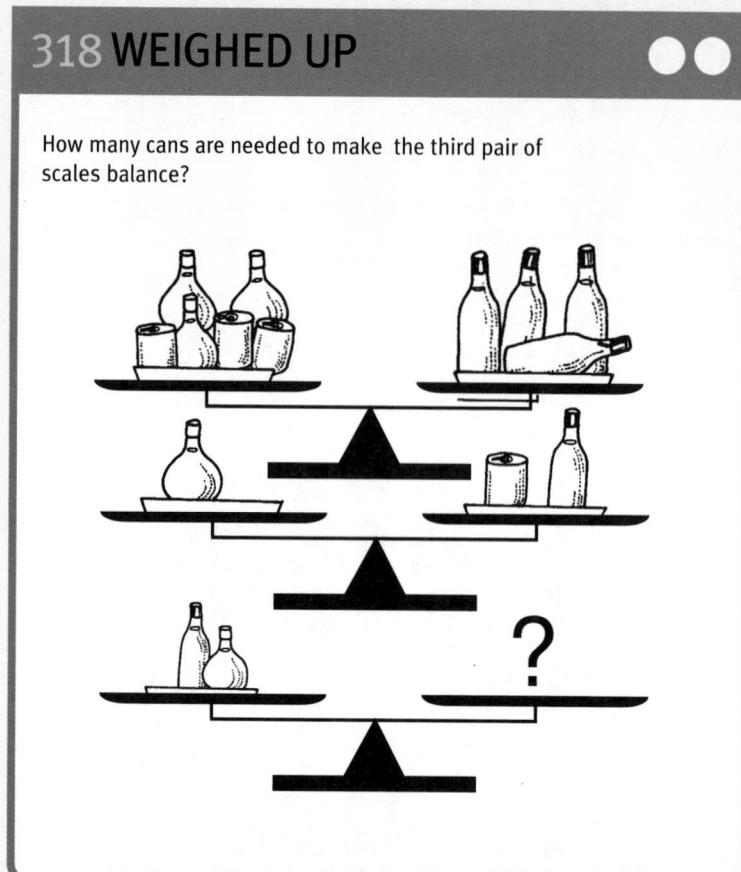

317 WANTED!

The sheriff is sure that one of the ten men shown is the wanted outlaw in the poster in the top right-hand corner. Can you help identify the suspects?

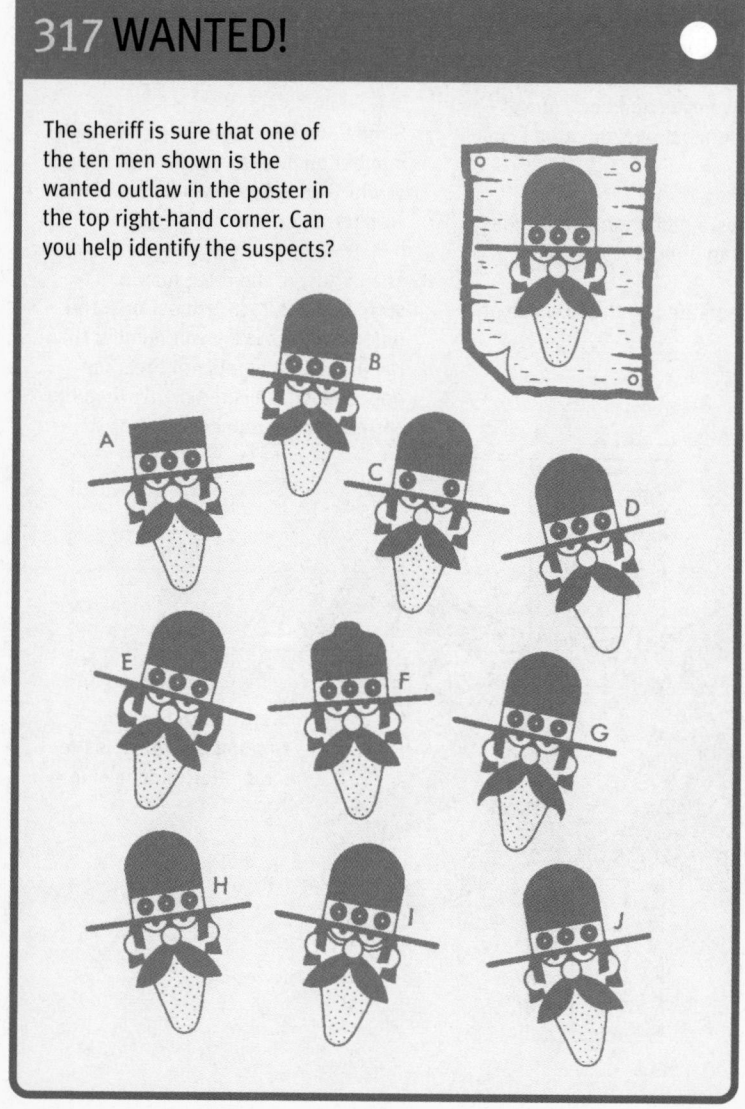

319 DOTTY DILEMMA

Connect adjacent dots with vertical or horizontal lines so that a single loop is formed with no crossings or branches. Each number indicates how many lines surround it, while empty cells may be surrounded by any number of lines.

```
0     2 0     3   1
  2       2     1
2   3       3 0
    1   3           1
    3     0   1 0   2
2   2 3   1       1
1           1   2
    3 3       0     1
  2       3       1
2   1     2 1     3
```

320 LINE UP

Snuffy's Gang found themselves in a police identification parade last week after one of their number committed a spot of smash-and-grab. He was witnessed making a slow getaway, mainly because he was hampered by the weight of the brick, which he had grabbed instead of the jewellery. The guilty party was picked out as standing fourth from the left. From the notes made by a raw recruit to the force, can you name the hapless villain? Snuffy was further left than Clogger and further right than Basher. Alf was not next to Wilf who was not next to Snuffy who was not next to Clogger. If Basher was not on one end then Wilf was not next to Clogger.

322 MATCH THAT

This star has five points and is made of ten matches. Remove one match and rearrange the others to make a nine-pointed star.

321 WHERE THE L?

Sixteen L shapes like the ones below have been fitted into a square shape. Each L has one hole, and there are four of each type in the square. No two pieces of the same type are adjacent, even at a corner. They fit together so well that the spaces between pieces do not show. From the locations of the holes, can you tell where each L is?

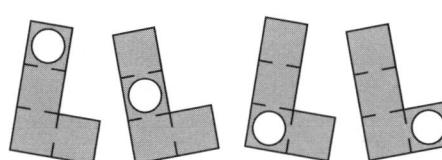

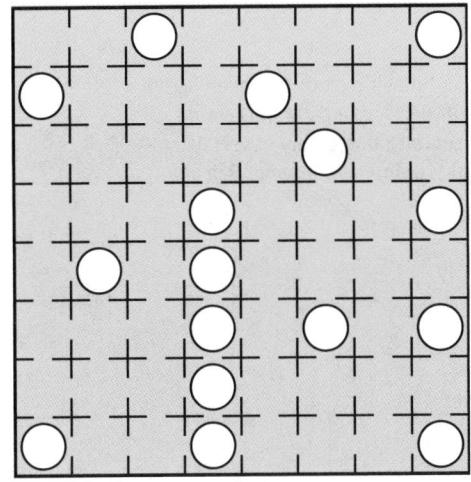

323 TEAM PLAY

As the winter bowls season continues at Tinsbury, we report on two matches in the Mixed Fours competition. The final scores were 24–21 and 17–12. From the odds and ends, can you roll your mental jack along the green and draw an accurate line as to the members of each team of four and who won against whom?

1 Each team consisted of two ladies and two gents.
2 Pete was not in John's losing team, which scored more shots than Pauline's but less than Doris'.
3 Dennis, who was not playing with or against Philip, was in the side which scored least shots of any team.

4 Reg's team won their game but not against the team which included both Janet and Pamela.
5 Joan's team won their game against Deirdre's. Neither was skipped by Rita, who won her game.

REG

PAMELA	PAULINE
PETE	PHILIP
JANET	JIM
JOAN	JOHN
DAVE	DEIRDRE
DENNIS	DORIS

RITA

PAMELA	PAULINE
PETE	PHILIP
JANET	JIM
JOAN	JOHN
DAVE	DEIRDRE
DENNIS	DORIS

RON

PAMELA	PAULINE
PETE	PHILIP
JANET	JIM
JOAN	JOHN
DAVE	DEIRDRE
DENNIS	DORIS

ROSE

PAMELA	PAULINE
PETE	PHILIP
JANET	JIM
JOAN	JOHN
DAVE	DEIRDRE
DENNIS	DORIS

324 EASY AS ABC

Each row and column originally contained one A, one B, one C, one D and two blank squares. Each letter and number refers to the first or second of the four letters encountered when travelling in the direction of the arrow. Can you complete the original grid?

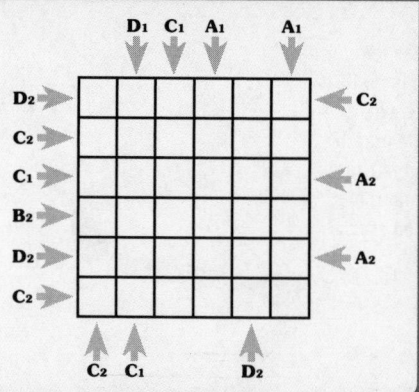

325 NINE NUMBERS

Place a number from 1 to 9 in each empty cell so that each row, each column and each 3 x 3 block contains all the numbers from 1 to 9.

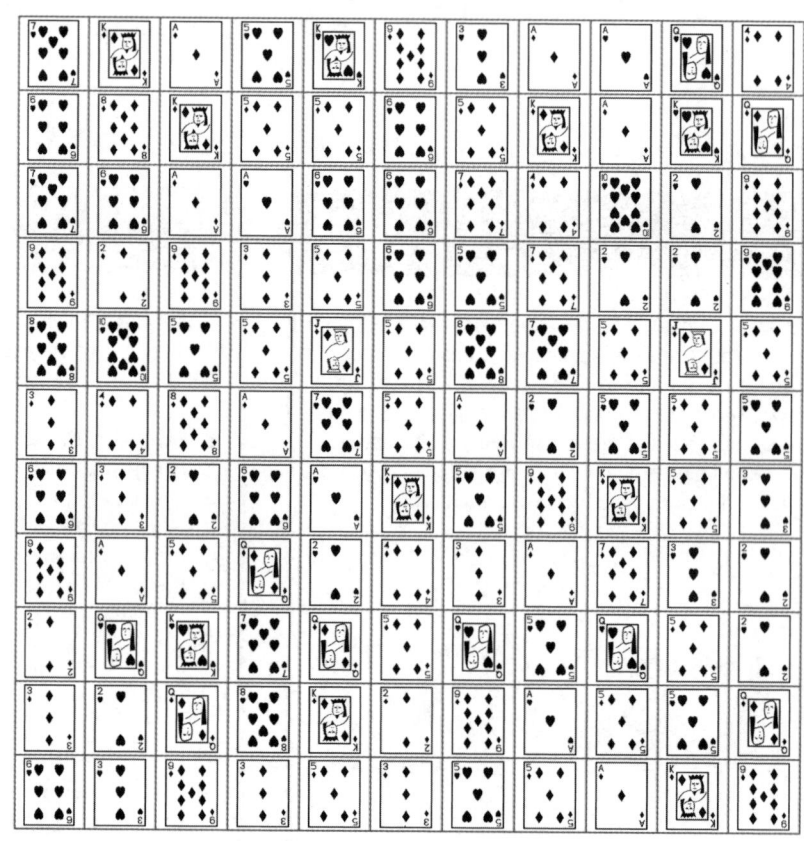

326 LOGI-PICK

Following the first diagram, there is a logical rule that determines how the next block is to be filled in. Given these three blocks, can you colour in the fourth?

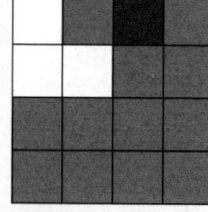

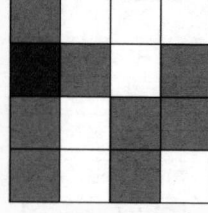

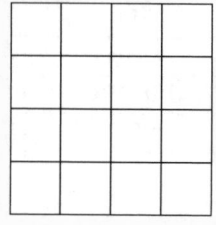

327 CARDSHARP

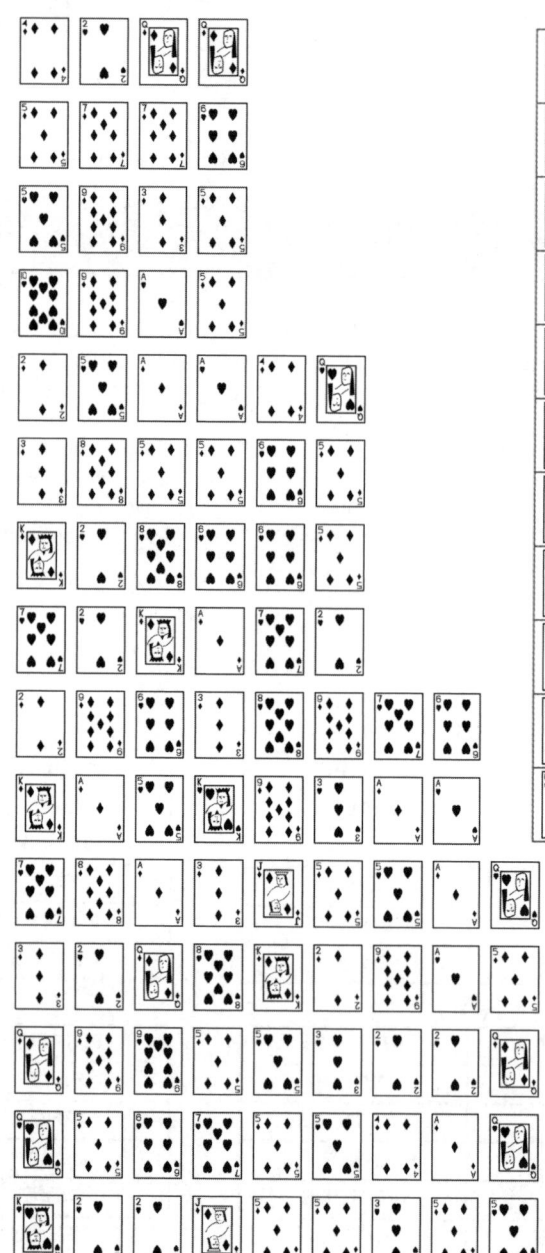

Each of these 16 lines of playing cards has been laid in the grid, running in either a forwards or backwards direction, either horizontally, diagonally or vertically – but always in a straight, uninterrupted line. Can you locate them all?

328 OLD HAUNTS

Each of these five ghosts, one of whom is supposedly Mr Windham and another is Blanche Legh, is reputed to haunt a notable property. Can you put a name to each apparition, say where it just may be seen and what special feature distinguishes it from all the other unnerving manifestations to be found at houses open to the public?

1 It is a man who strolls around Claydon House looking for his hand – sent back there without the rest of him after being cut off at the battle of Edgehill.
2 Anne Boleyn is neither ghost A nor the lady who infests Lyme Park. The papers were hidden in the wall at Ham House which is not haunted by ghost E.
3 Take care when driving to Blickling Hall as the ghost sits in a coach with her head in her lap – the horses are headless too. What state the coach driver is in, we shudder to think.
4 Ghost B is the one still searching for his favourite library books – perhaps because the fines due must now outweigh the nation's National Debt.
5 Ghost E is not that of Elizabeth Dysart or the ghost of Felbrigg.
6 Neither Sir Edmund Verney nor the lady in white

who follows her husband's funeral procession is ghost B or C.

GHOST	OF	AT	FEATURE
A			
B			
C			
D			
E			

330 SET SQUARE

All the digits from 1 to 9 are used in this grid, but only once. Can you work out their positions in the grid and make the sums work? We've given two numbers to start you off.

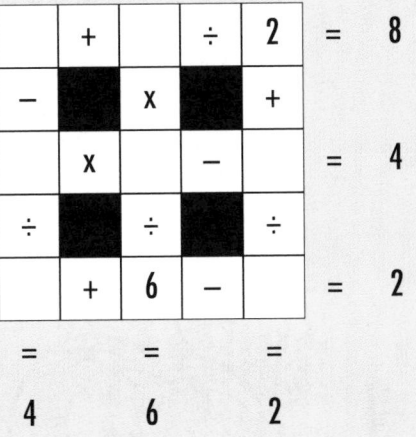

329 ISLAND HOPPING

Each circle containing a number represents an island. The object is to connect each island with vertical or horizontal bridges so that:
* The number of bridges is the same as the number inside the island
* There can be up to two bridges between two islands
* Bridges cannot cross islands or other bridges
* There is a continuous path connecting all the islands

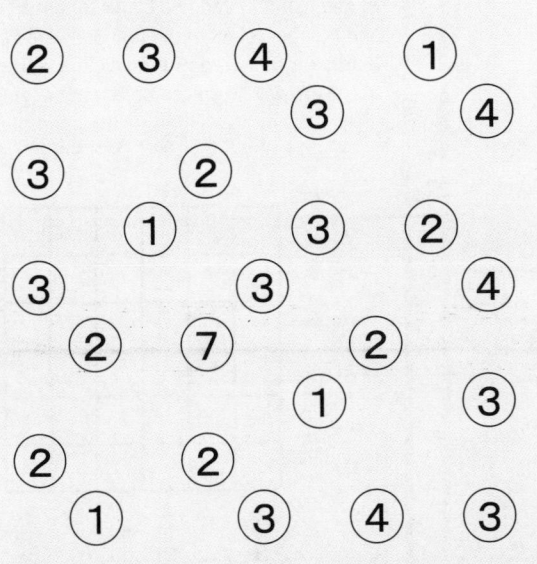

331 COG-ITATE

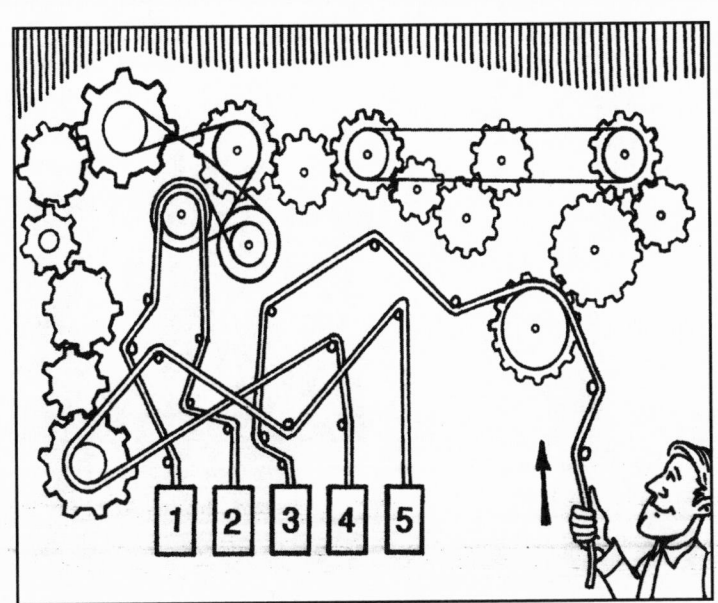

Can you see which two weights will rise and which three will fall when the man releases the tension as shown?

332 SPOT THE DIFFERENCE

Can you spot the ten differences between these two pictures?

333 DOTTY DILEMMA

Connect adjacent dots with vertical or horizontal lines so that a single loop is formed with no crossings or branches. Each number indicates how many lines surround it, while empty cells may be surrounded by any number of lines.

```
· · · 0 · · 1 · 3 ·
· · · 3 · · · 2 · 3 ·
· 2 0 · · 1 1 · · · ·
· · · · 0 · · 3 · 2 1
· · · 2 · 1 · 1 · · ·
· · 2 1 · · · · 1 · 3
· · · · 3 · 1 2 · 1 ·
· 2 · 1 · 1 · · · 2 ·
· 0 · · · 2 · 3 2 · ·
· · 3 2 · 1 · · · · 2
· 2 · · · · 2 · 1 · 2
· · 2 · 0 3 · 2 · · 3
· 3 · 3 · · · · 2 3 ·
· · · 1 · 3 · 2 · · ·
· 1 3 · 1 · · 1 · · ·
· · · · 2 0 · · 2 0 ·
· · 3 · 0 · · · 0 · ·
· 3 · · 2 · · 3 · · ·
```

334 DOUBLE PUZZLE

Roll up folks, for our special sale offer – two puzzles for the price of one!

Puzzle One: Each colour has been given a value from 1 to 7. Given the totals at the end of each line, can you work out the value of each colour?

Puzzle Two: The picture is a layout of a set of colour dominoes – just like ordinary dominoes but with colours instead of spots. Can you draw in the lines to show each separate domino?

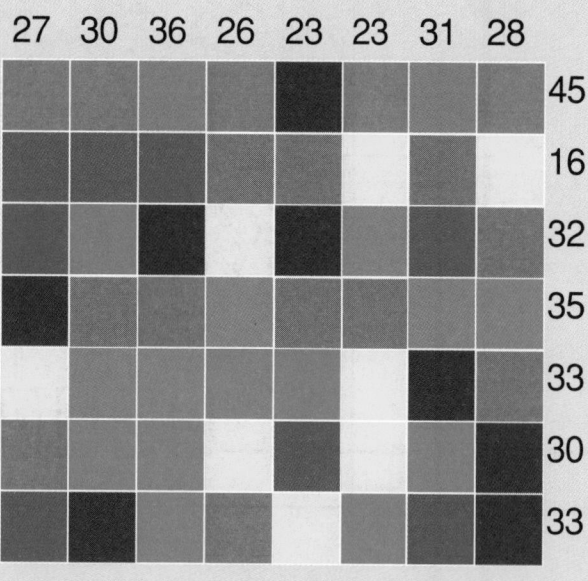

27	30	36	26	23	23	31	28	

Row totals: 45, 16, 32, 35, 33, 30, 33

335 EASY AS ABC

Each row and column originally contained one A, one B, one C, one D and two blank squares. Each letter and number refers to the first or second of the four letters encountered when travelling in the direction of the arrow. Can you complete the original grid?

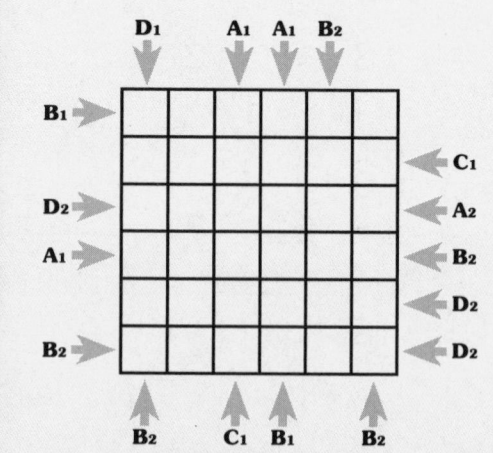

Top: D₁ A₁ A₁ B₂

Left: B₁, D₂, A₁, B₂

Right: C₁, A₂, B₂, D₂, D₂

Bottom: B₂, C₁, B₁, B₂

336 SHELL NEVER MAKE IT!

Can you help Tamara the Tortoise find her way to the finish?

FINISH LINE

337 IT FIGURES

Place a number from 1 to 9 in each empty cell so that the sum of each vertical or horizontal block equals the number at the top or on the left of that block. Numbers may only be used once in each block.

338 CUBISM

Which cube is the finished product of the main illustration?

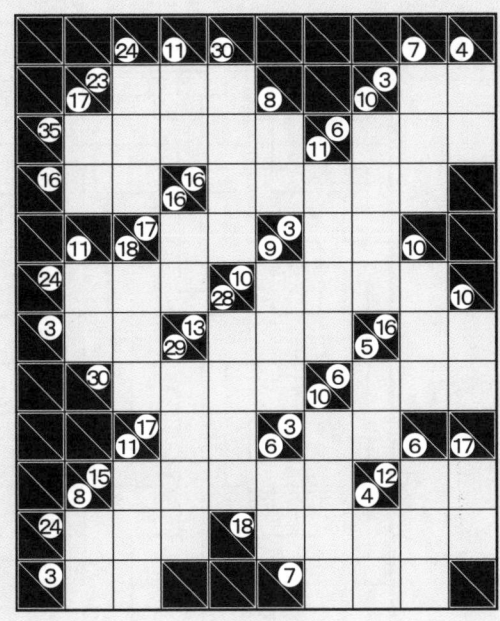

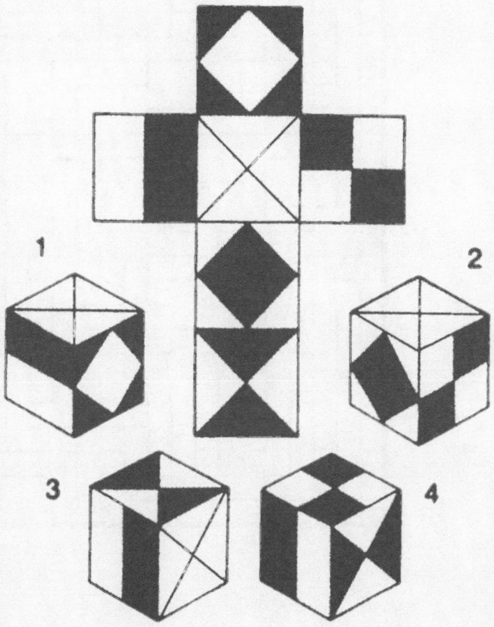

1

2

3

4

339 MAZE MYSTERY

Travel from the entrance to the exit of the maze, filling the path completely to create a picture.

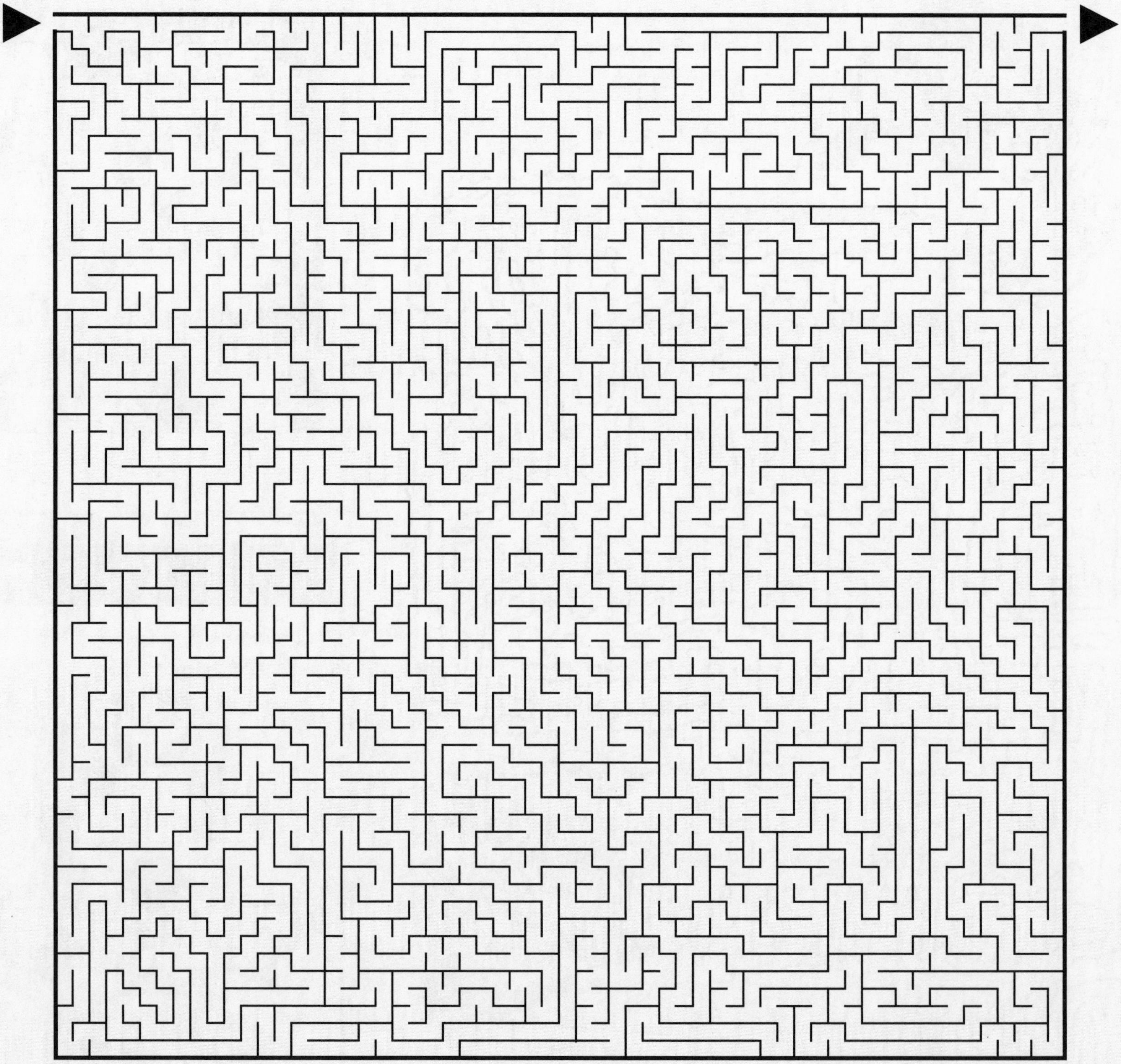

340 MISSING PIECE

Can you tell which one of the four pieces completes the picture of Butch the bulldog?

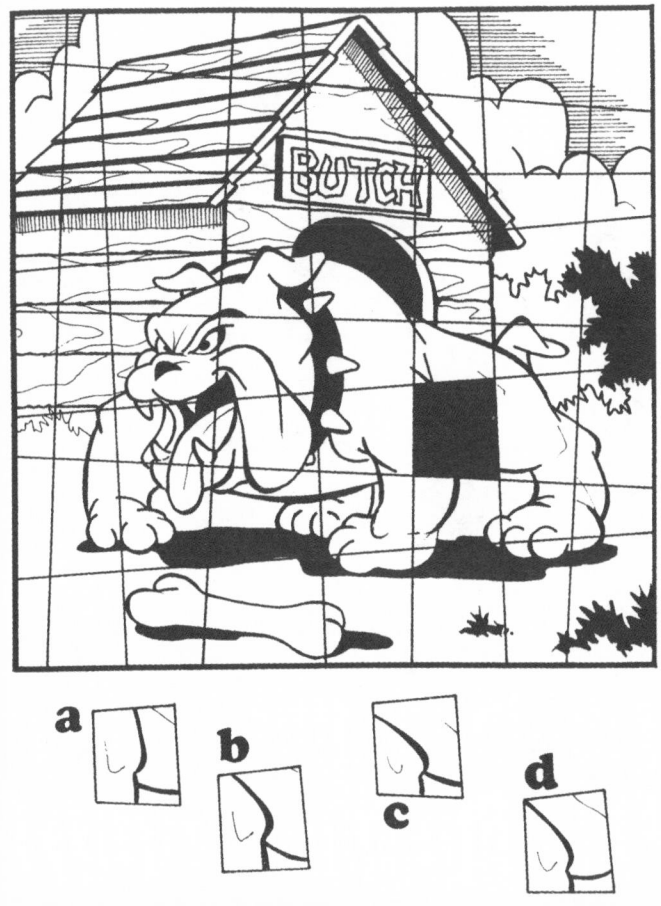

341 SPANISH HIGHS

As Columbus and his not-so-merry crew head for the edge of the unknown, attention at the Spanish Court has turned to lighter matters. Each of these four noble suitors is enamoured of an upper-crust lady and has the marriage contract in hand. Can you put the right names on each portion of parchment? Manuel is courting Maria who is not Sutaz or Meeya. Neither Pancho or Sancho is Fign-Diaz who is marrying neither Juanita nor Nidjota. Isabella da Bolla is being pursued by neither Manuel nor Pancho nor Mucho. Herole is after Meeya who is not Rosa who is not marrying Ghiaz. None of these three weddings is the one involving Juan.

342 EASY AS ABC

Each row and column originally contained one A, one B, one C, one D and two blank squares. Each letter and number refers to the first or second of the four letters encountered when travelling in the direction of the arrow. Can you complete the original grid?

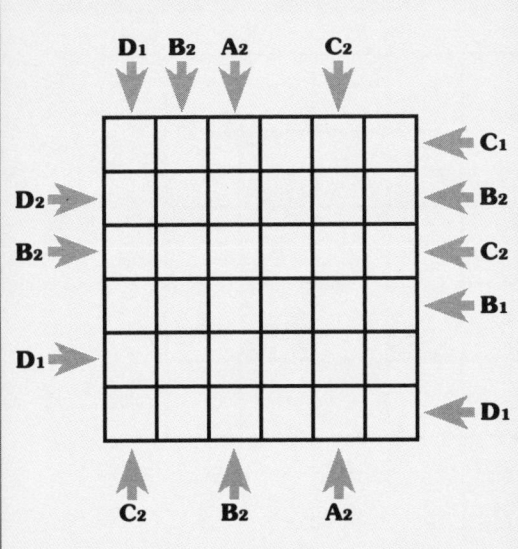

343 LOGI-PATH

Use your deductive reasoning to form a pathway from the box marked START to the box marked FINISH moving in either direction horizontally or vertically (but not diagonally). The number at the beginning of every row or column indicates exactly how many boxes in that row or column your pathway must pass through. The small diagram is given as an example of how it works.

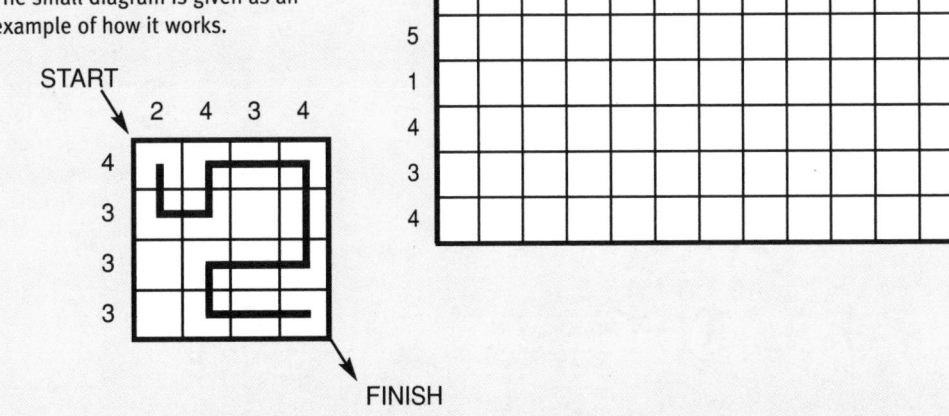

344 BATTLESHIPS

Do you remember the old game of battleships? These puzzles are based on that idea. Your task is to find the vessels in the diagram. Some parts of boats or sea squares have already been filled in, and a number next to a row or column refers to the number of occupied squares in that row or column. The boats may be positioned horizontally or vertically, but no two boats or parts of boats are in adjacent squares – horizontally, vertically or diagonally.

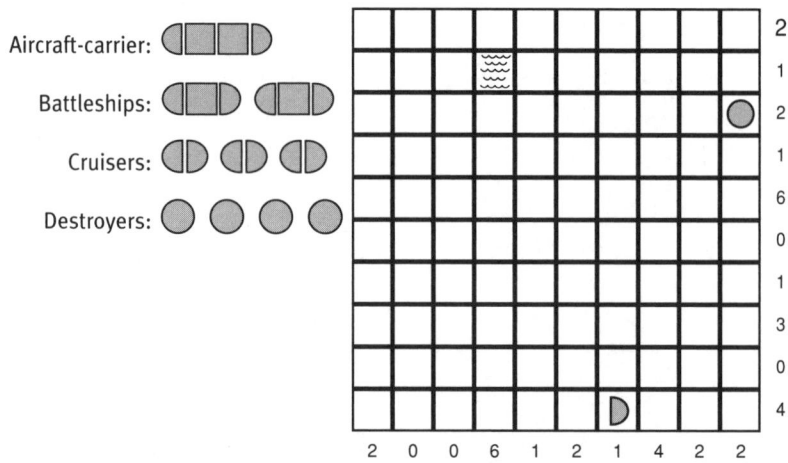

Aircraft-carrier:
Battleships:
Cruisers:
Destroyers:

2
1
2
1
6
0
1
3
0
4

2 0 0 6 1 2 1 4 2 2

345 WELL SPOTTED

The number in each circle tells you how many of it and its touching neighbours are to be filled in.

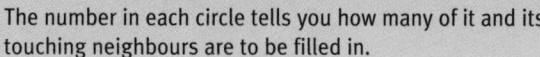

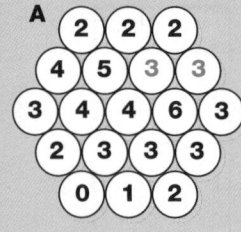
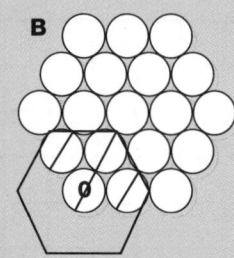
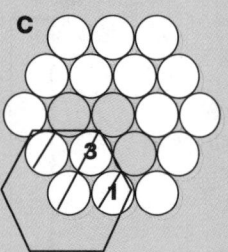

In our example, A, the zero gives a start – put lines through it and its neighbours (B). Three circles can now be filled (C) – lightly, though so the numbers can still be read...

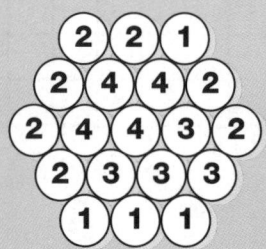

346 ODD ONE OUT

Can you see which rabbit is the odd one out?

347 FILLING IN

Each of the nine empty boxes contains a different digit from 1 to 9. Each calculation is to be treated sequentially rather than according to the 'multiplication first' system. Can you fill in the empty boxes?

	+		÷		= 2
+		−		÷	
	−		×		= 8
−		×		+	
	÷		−		= 2

= 4   = 9   = 4

348 WHAT'S THEIR LINE?

Four celebrity panellists, aided and abetted by that helpful host, Robin Robertson, have guessed the jobs done by four guests. Can you sign in, please, with each guest's full job title and the name of the celebrity who revealed all?

1   Ken's occupation was guessed by Gerta and he is neither the Hocker nor the Crimper's. No one was a Crimper's Hocker.
2   Miles did not realise Ann was a Slant. Wanda guessed the Posset, which was not Connie's occupation.
3   One occupation was Fledger's Cringe.
4   A lady panellist guessed Taddler's.

Clue 1 has been entered for you.

GERTA

~~ANN~~	~~CONNIE~~
~~ENA~~	KEN
~~CRIMPER'S~~	FLEDGER'S
GRUTTLER'S	TADDLER'S
CRINGE	~~HOCKER~~
POSSET	SLANT

MILES

ANN	CONNIE
ENA	~~KEN~~
CRIMPER'S	FLEDGER'S
GRUTTLER'S	TADDLER'S
CRINGE	HOCKER
POSSET	SLANT

NOAH

ANN	CONNIE
ENA	~~KEN~~
CRIMPER'S	FLEDGER'S
GRUTTLER'S	TADDLER'S
CRINGE	HOCKER
POSSET	SLANT

WANDA

ANN	CONNIE
ENA	~~KEN~~
CRIMPER'S	FLEDGER'S
GRUTTLER'S	TADDLER'S
CRINGE	HOCKER
POSSET	SLANT

349 ISLAND HOPPING

Each circle containing a number represents an island. The object is to connect each island with vertical or horizontal bridges so that:
*   The number of bridges is the same as the number inside the island
*   There can be up to two bridges between two islands
*   Bridges cannot cross islands or other bridges
*   There is a continuous path connecting all the islands

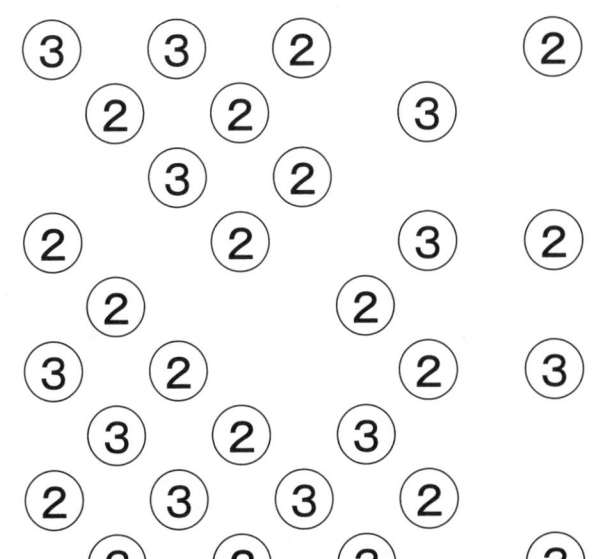

350 RADIO DAYS

Untangle the lines to discover which of the old radios is connected to which plug.

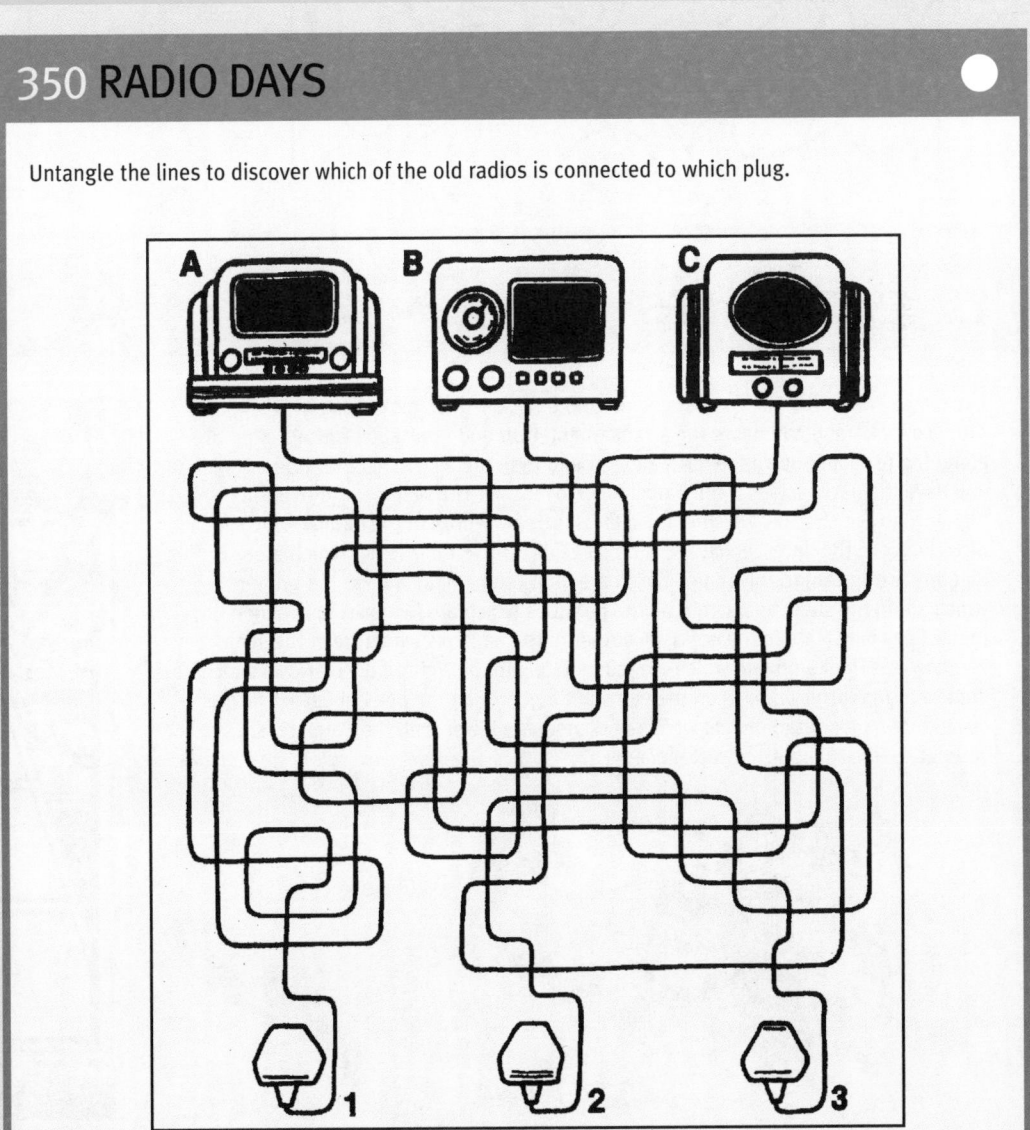

351 SILHOUETTE

Shade all the shapes which contain a dot to reveal a hidden picture.

353 TWO OF A KIND

Can you decide which three objects do not make a pair?

352 FRUIT AND VEG

The display on Gert's stall is changed around daily, partly to make yesterday's produce look fresh. Whatever the arrangement, fruit and vegetables always alternate along the rows and down the lines and left and right are as you gaze on wondering if you have the nerve to ask if the bananas are over-ripe. The radishes are two rows higher than the cherries which are two lines further right than the turnips which are directly above the dates which are two places directly left of the figs which are diagonally adjacent to the apples which are in the same line down as the grapes which are in the same line across as the potatoes which are two lines to the right of the lychees which are in the opposite corner to the bananas which are in the same line down as the kumquats which are immediately to the right of the marrows which are lower and further right than the yams but higher than the peas which are further left than the illustrated onions which, of course, are lower than the watercress. Can you put everything in its correct place?

354 ISLAND HOPPING

Each circle containing a number represents an island. The object is to connect each island with vertical or horizontal bridges so that:

* The number of bridges is the same as the number inside the island.
* There can be up to two bridges between two islands.
* Bridges cannot cross islands or other bridges.
* There is a continuous path connecting all the islands.

355 WELL SPOTTED

The number in each circle tells you how many of it and its touching neighbours are to be filled in.

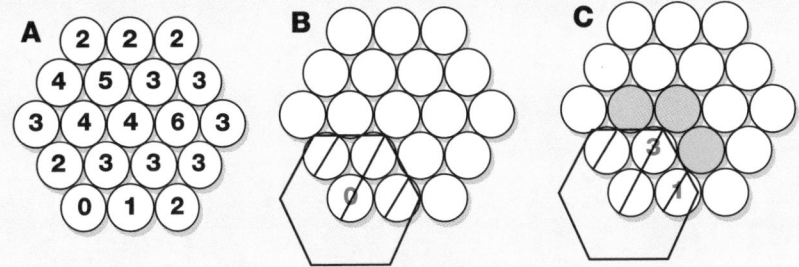

In our example, A, the zero gives a start – put lines through it and its neighbours (B). Three circles can now be filled (C) – lightly, though so the numbers can still be read...

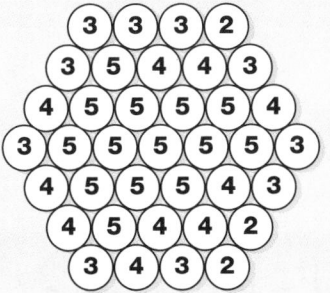

356 TAKE FIVE

Complete the following block of 25 circles so that each of the five road signs appears in all horizontal and vertical lines. To get you started we have filled in nine circles.

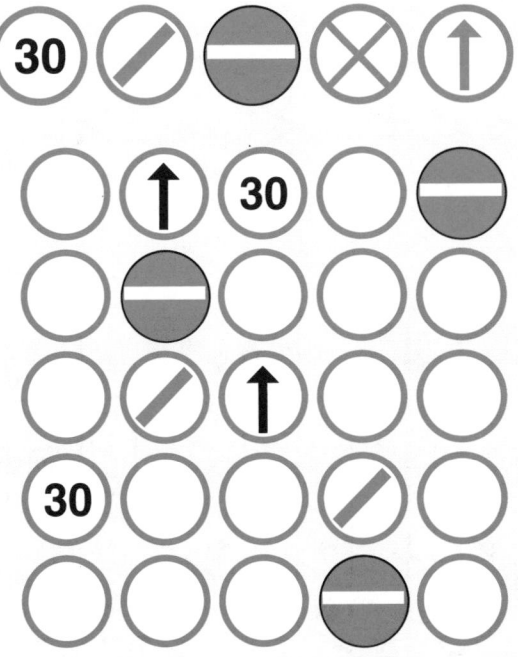

357 SQUARE PAIRS

This picture of Old Father Time contains five pairs of identical squares. Can you find them?

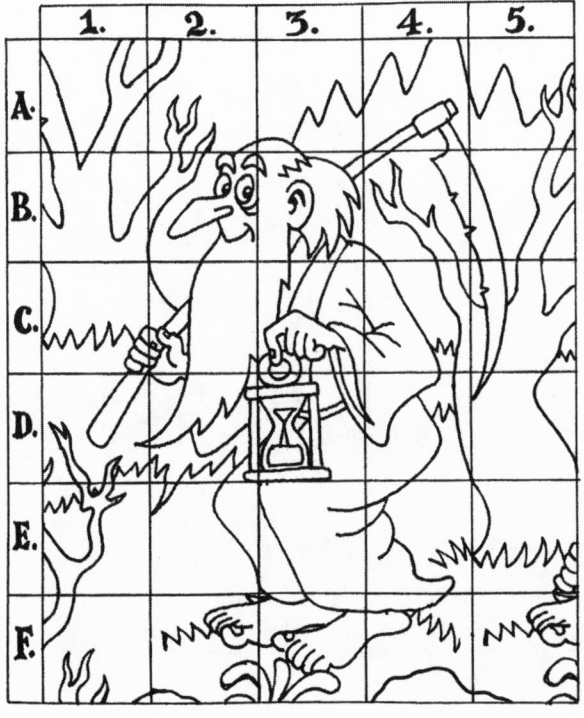

358 NUMBER KROSS

See how quickly you can fit all these numbers into the grid. We've filled one figure in to start you off.

3 figures	5 figures	6 figures
227	11658	140448
301	12932	140747
312	20818	200174
402	21015	321904
513	30030	366336
607	31526	391074
823	31703	419838
905	40307	426198
	50334	463515
4 figures	53614	626206
1601	61392	710521
2247	63579	741029
3431	73713	824513
4152	81605	885198
5423	87352	903529
6000	99703	928174
8998		
~~9634~~		

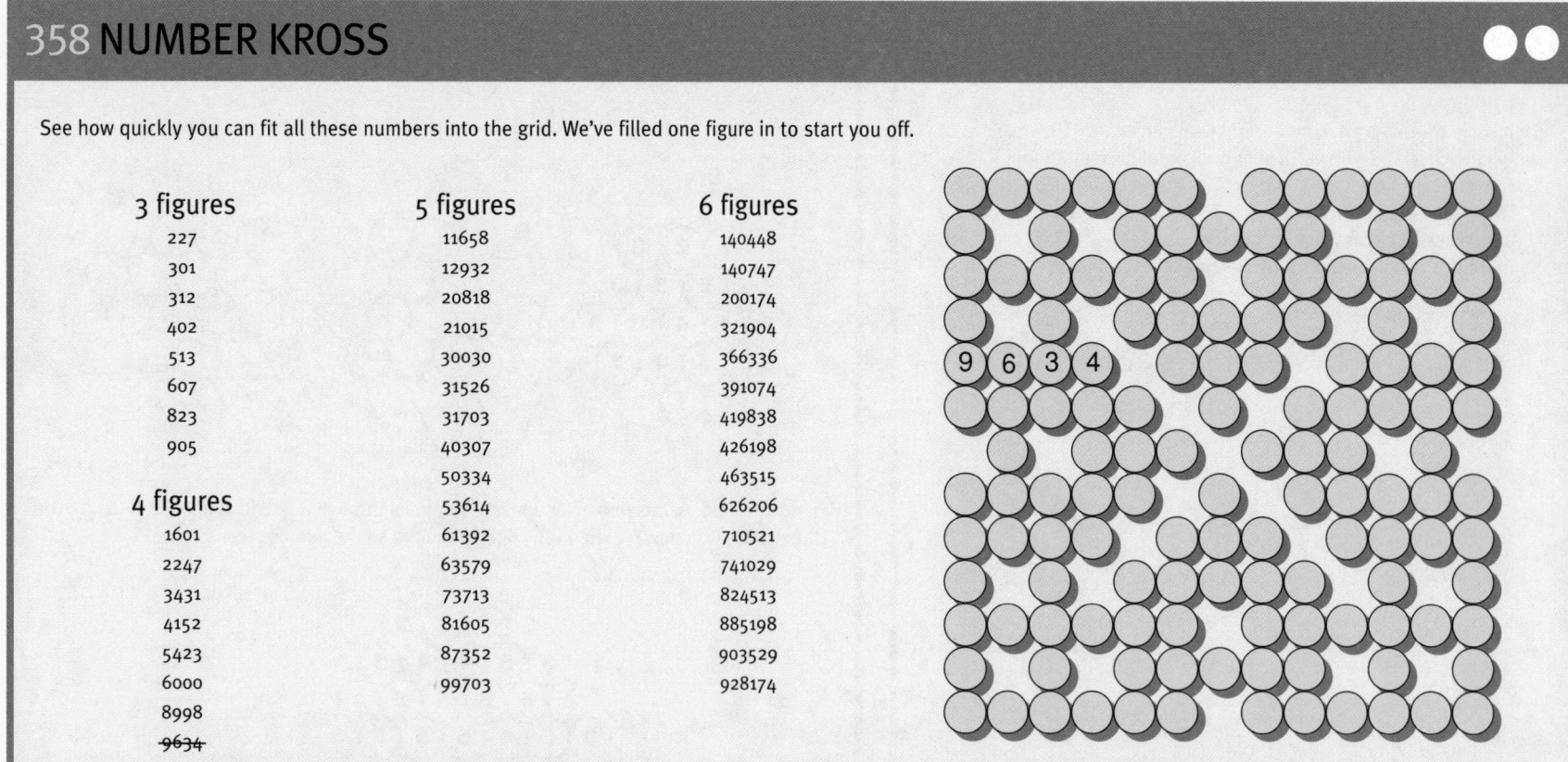

359 A LITTLE DEVIL

See how quickly you can spot which letter appears here three times.

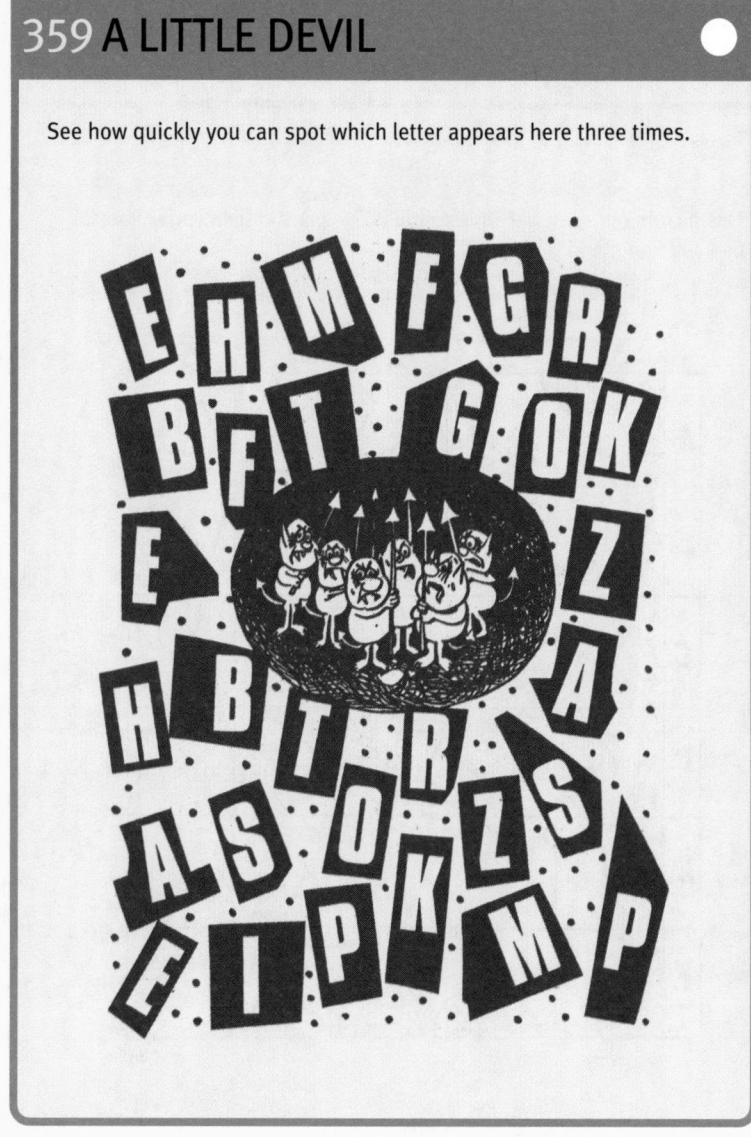

360 CUBE ROUTE

The symbols on each face have a meaning – Up, Down, Right or Left. But each sign has a different meaning on each of the three faces. Thus, whatever is, say, up on the top face cannot be up on the left face or the right face. There is a meaning for each symbol which will lead to a unique path joining Start (S) to End (E) and which passes through all three faces. Can you let your brain do the logical walking and make the journey?

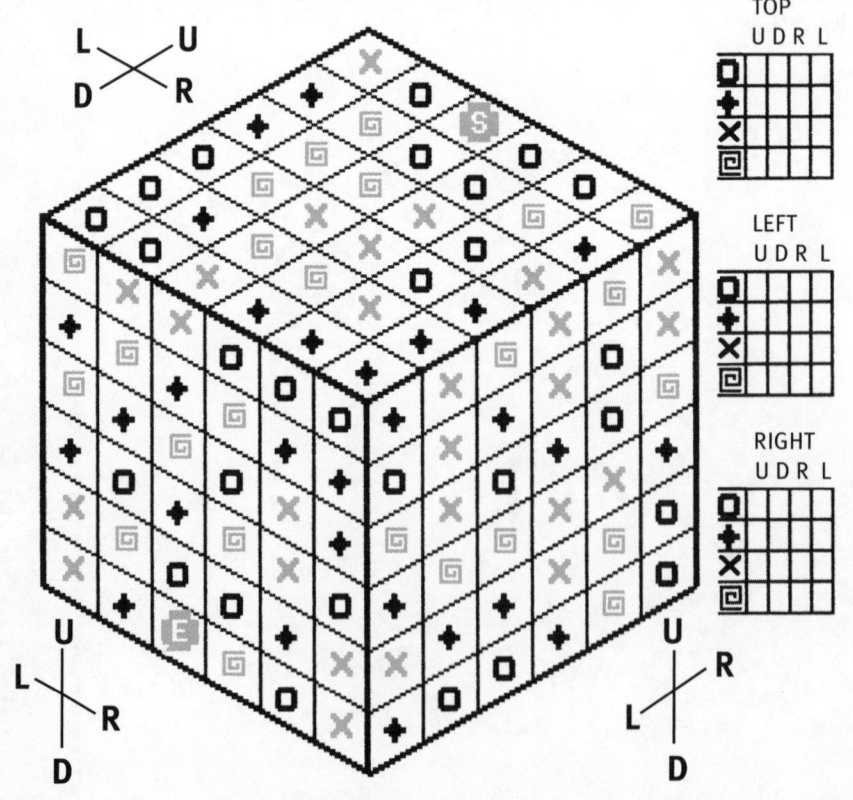

361 MENTAL BLOCKS ●●

Which two of the numbered pieces will fit together to make cube 'A'?

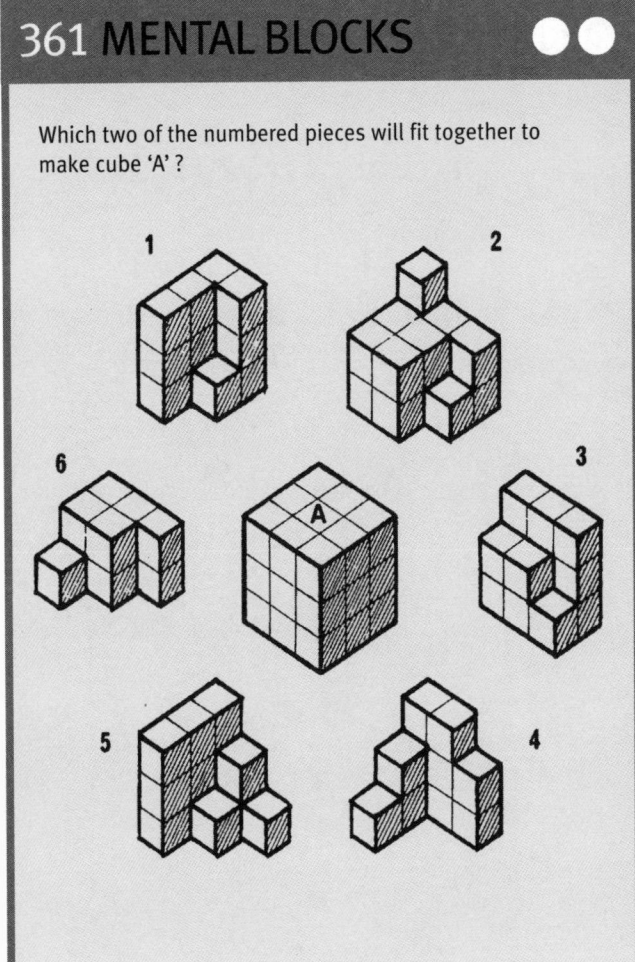

363 CIRCLE OF DIGITS ●●●

The figure below consists of three concentric circles divided into eight sectors; the three single-figure numbers in each sector add up to 15. The circles will be referred to as outer, middle and inner and one number in the inner has been inserted to give you a start. From the clues given, can you insert all the other numbers?

Clues

1 The only 0 appears in the outer circle, where there is no 1 or 3; there is no 9 in the middle and no number is repeated in any sector or circle.

2 All the numbers in sectors A and B are odd; B outer is one more than C inner and one less than H middle, which is one more than H inner; B inner is one less than G outer.

3 The 6 in the outer circle is diagonally opposite the 6 in the inner.

4 C inner is double D inner, while D outer is double D middle; F outer is double F middle, which is double G middle and the same as C outer; E outer is the same as A middle.

Starting tip: Work out the number in C inner.

362 VIDEO RENTAL ●●

Will nothing stop the video boom? These four shops have just opened, to add to the dozen already cluttering Lampwick's side streets. Can you record a summary as to the customer at each shop and the film being rented?

1 D Cryer is at Rent 'N' Rave but is not hiring Gosh! Or Whew!
2 Just Flicks are not hiring out to A Blinkon whose choice is Wow!
3 B Dee-High is not the one choosing Gosh!
4 C Nitt is not at More Movies who are not renting out Wow!

JUST FLICKS

A BLINKON	B DEE-HIGH
C NITT	D CRYER
GOSH!	HEY!
WHEW!	WOW!

MORE MOVIES

A BLINKON	B DEE-HIGH
C NITT	D CRYER
GOSH!	HEY!
WHEW!	WOW!

NITE RATES

A BLINKON	B DEE-HIGH
C NITT	D CRYER
GOSH!	HEY!
WHEW!	WOW!

RENT 'N' RAVE

A BLINKON	B DEE-HIGH
C NITT	D CRYER
GOSH!	HEY!
WHEW!	WOW!

364 EASY AS ABC ●

Each row and column originally contained one A, one B, one C, one D and two blank squares. Each letter and number refer to the first or second of the four letters encountered when travelling in the direction of the arrow. Can you complete the original grid?

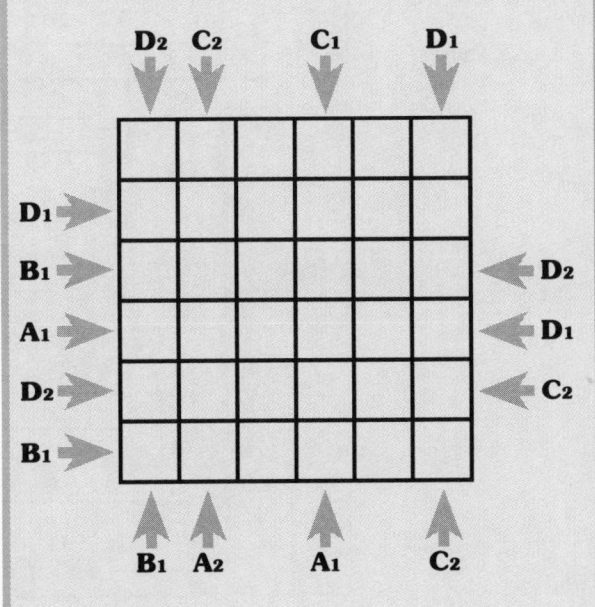

365 STAMP DUTY

Which one of the numbered prints has been made by the stamp?

 1
 2
 3
 4
 5
 6

366 MAZE-WAYS

Each obstacle along the path carries a penalty as shown in the key in the middle. Can you travel from A to B while incurring a total of 40 penalty points?

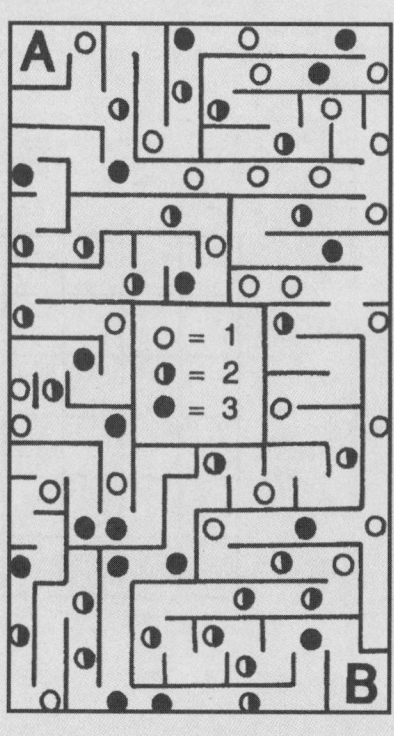

367 DOTTY DILEMMA

Connect adjacent dots with vertical or horizontal lines so that a single loop is formed with no crossings or branches. Each number indicates how many lines surround it, while empty cells may be surrounded by any number of lines.

```
·  ·  ·  ·  ·  ·  ·  ·  ·  ·  ·  ·  ·
 1  3        1  2  1  2  2
· 1· ·  · 3· ·  ·  ·  ·  ·  ·  ·  ·
 2     ·  1·    1  3  1
· · 1  3· ·  3·    · 2· ·
 2·   3·  1·    3· ·
 2    · 1  2·    · 2· 3·
 0·       ·  3·    · 2·
 2     · 0  3  1     · 0
 2·    · 3·       ·  1·
 3           · 2·    · 0·
 1        · 2  1  2     · 1·
 2·   · 2·       ·  1·
 2  · 3·    · 2  3·    1·
   · 0·  · 3  2·    1
 2     2·     1  1
  0  2  3        1     · 1·
               1     · 1·
 2  1  2  2  2        1  2
```

368 MOUNT CUBIC

There are six possible directions which will take you from the centre of one face across an edge to the next face on the mountain. Each direction has been given a number from 1 to 6. Can you work out which direction has which number and so find your way from base to peak?

369 A BRIDGE TOO FAR

Eight men and eight women are playing bridge at four tables, as shown. At the game in hand, dummy is in a different position at each table, and the contract at each is in a different suit and for a different number of tricks – this number also differs in each case from the table number. With the following clues, can you position each person, and also say who is dummy and name the contract being played at each table?

Roger (South) is dummy on his table, which is numbered one lower than Connie's and one higher than Harry's, both of whom are in a different position from Roger and from each other, neither being dummy. Fred and Gordon are partners on the remaining table. Alan (West) is on a table where the contract is 4 Spades. Tessa (dummy) is one table anti-clockwise from Eddie, at whose table the contract is for one trick more than on table 1.

Dummy on table 4 is the person whose name comes first alphabetically on that table. Jane and Dot are in the same position at different tables whose numbers are two apart; this is also true of Kate and Lola, the first-named in each case being at the lower-numbered table. From his seat Peter, who is not on table 2, can see table 2, but not table 4; his contract is in Diamonds, while Michael's table is going for Hearts, but one fewer.

Susie (dummy) has Jane on her left and Harry on her right; her partner is Peter, and the contract is for one more trick than the table number. Connie has Dot on her left, who is not in the same position as Fred. Tessa, whose table is playing a red-suit contract, is in the same relative position as Babs.

	Table 1	Table 2	Table 3	Table 4
N				
E				
S				
W				
Contract				

370 TEE TIME

Three old timers play a weekly game of golf on the Golden Lawns 18-hole, par 72, course. Each score at every hole falls into one of five categories. Each golfer gets a different result (excluding zero) in each category. Also, no category has the same result for another player, i.e., if a player has two eagles, he has a different number in the other four and no other player has two eagles. With the score details below and the information given can you fill in their card?

	Eagle −2	Birdie −1	Par 0	Bogey +1	Double Bogey +2	FINAL SCORE
Parnell Darma						
Nick Jackliss						
Barry Clayer						

Nick got twice as many eagles as birdies and together they added up to Barry's pars which were one more than his double bogeys. The number of Parnell's eagles and Barry's bogeys was the same and the total of the two was the same as that of Nick's bogeys added to his lesser number of double bogeys. The total of Parnell's pars and bogeys was one less than Nick's pars and Barry got one less eagles than bogeys whilst Parnell got one more birdie than double bogeys which was the same as Nick's eagles and also Barry's birdies.

371 LOGI-5

Can you place the letters A, B, C, D, E, one to each square so that every line across and down contains each letter once and every shape made from five squares also has each letter once?

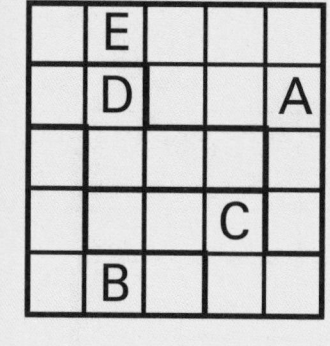

372 CELL STRUCTURE

The object is to create white areas surrounded by black walls, so that:
* Each white area contains only one number.
* The number of cells in a white area is equal to the number in it.
* The white areas are separated from each other with a black wall.
* Cells containing numbers must not be filled in.
* The black cells must be linked into a continuous wall.
* Black cells cannot form a square of 2 x 2 or larger.

373 FILLING IN

Each of the nine empty boxes contains a different digit from 1 to 9. Each calculation is to be treated sequentially rather than according to the 'multiplication first' system. Can you fill in the empty boxes?

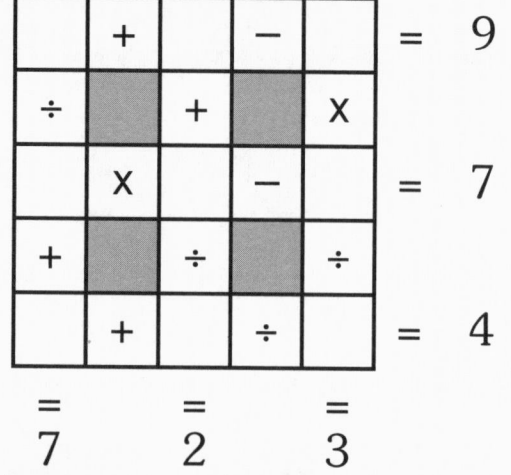

374 DOMINO DEAL

A standard set (0 – 0) to (6 – 6) is laid out below. Each domino is placed so the that the larger number will be on the bottom:

i.e.   3   not   6
        6   3

Those top numbers show the four numbers which form the top half of each domino in that column. The bottom numbers, below the grid, give the four bottom numbers for that column. The seven numbers on the left show the numbers which belong in that row. Can you cross-reference the facts and deduce where each domino had been placed? 1*5 is given as a start.

'TOP' NUMBERS

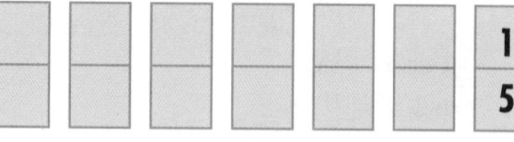
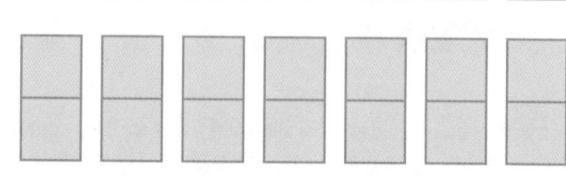

'BOTTOM' NUMBERS

375 LOGI-5 ●

Can you place the letters A, B, C, D, E, one to each square so that every line across and down contains each letter once and every shape made from five squares also has each letter once?

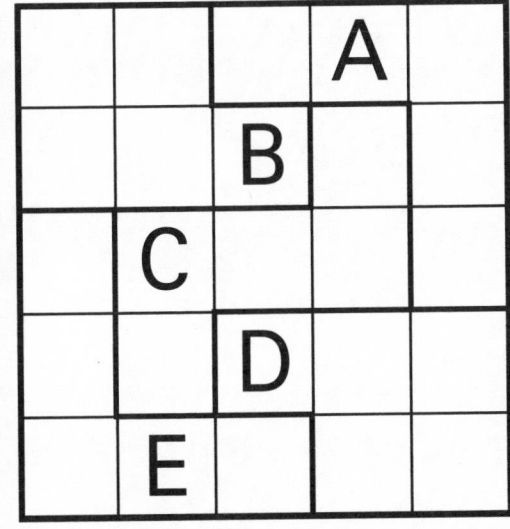

377 THE SPECIAL FIVE ●●●

Although PA Lette, the Netherlipp artist, has sold or given away most of his paintings, he still keeps five, for various sentimental reasons, on one of his walls. From the clues below, can you indicate in the diagram the title and date of the picture at each position?

1. The picture painted in 1976 hangs directly next to and right of one of a building.

2. There is a larger gap in dates between the paintings at positions A and B than between those at positions D and E. The painting at position A is earlier than the one at B; and the painting at E is earlier than the one at D.

3. The picture entitled Lower Woods is directly next to and left of the one painted in 1988.

4. The date of the picture of St Aidan's Church is immediately between that of the picture at position C and that of Fiddler's Brook, which is more than one place to the right of the picture of St Aidan's Church.

5. The Old Mill was painted during the decade preceding that when PA Lette painted Crane Bay.

Titles: Crane Bay, Fiddler's Brook, Lower Woods, St Aidan's Church, The Old Mill

Dates: 1964, 1976, 1981, 1988, 1992

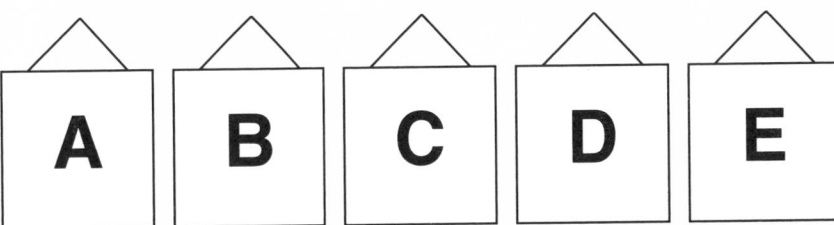

376 PACKED LUNCHES ●●

Four office colleagues, bored with trying to think up new variations for their packed lunches, devised a sharing scheme. In the afternoon, each was randomly allocated a sandwich filling, crisp flavour and piece of fruit that he/she would bring in next day. From the clues given, can you work out what each had last Monday?

1. Freddie ate salt and vinegar crisps, and the person, not Felix, who ate a chicken salad sandwich together with cheese and onion crisps did not also have a peach.

2. The cheese and tomato sandwich was eaten by the person who also ate an apple.

3. Felicity who ate the egg mayonnaise sandwich is not the person who had both the ready-salted crisps and the orange.

4. For your vital information, the remaining items on the menu were: ham and mustard sandwiches, prawn cocktail crisps and a banana – any of which may, or may not have been consumed by Fiona.

NAME	SANDWICH	CRISPS	FRUIT

378 DOGGY DUOS ●

Can you put these dogs into four identical pairs?

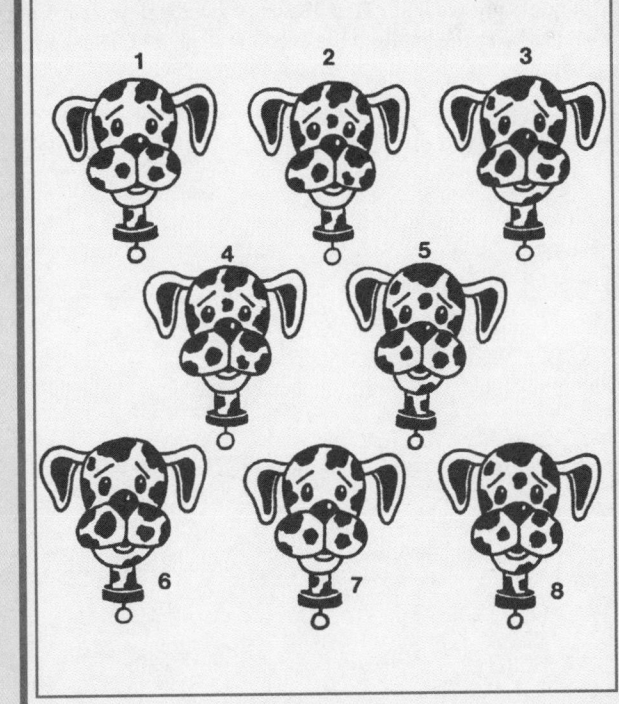

379 JOIN THE POTS

Can you put together the broken pots to make up five complete ones?

381 ISLAND HOPPING

Each circle containing a number represents an island. The object is to connect each island with vertical or horizontal bridges so that:

* The number of bridges is the same as the number inside the island
* There can be up to two bridges between two islands
* Bridges cannot cross islands or other bridges
* There is a continuous path connecting all the islands

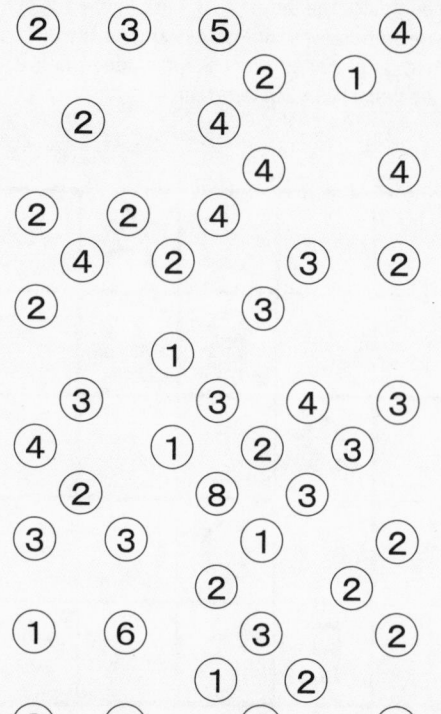

380 THE CHAMPIONS CUP

These soccer teams all got through to the quarter-final stage of this major cup competition, much to the delight of their numerous fans who had followed the progress of each team. From the clues given, can you work out the draw for all the stages up to the final and the eventual winners? Chelsea who played and beat Norwich, won one more game than Watford. Southampton lost to the team that played Everton in the semi-finals. Arsenal won one more game than Liverpool, Everton, who won one more game than Arsenal, never met either Chelsea or Spurs.

Quarter-finals   Semi-finals   Final   Winner

382 ACE IN PLACE

		T T	8 8	8 J	8 T	9 9
J	K	J K	9	J	T ~~A~~	9
C	D	Q C	Q C 9 K	J Q	Q Q ~~H~~	K K D
		C H	C H H S	D D H S	D H S	D C D C
		H H	S	S		S
9 T	C H	████				
J J	S S					
J Q	S S					
8 T	C C					
T	D D					
J Q	D D					
9 9	C D					
Q K	H H					
Q	H H					
8 T	C C				A	
K	C D				H	
K ~~A~~ ~~H~~	S					
8 8	D H					████
T	H					
J K	S S					

The cards Eight to King of each suit, together with the Ace of Hearts, have been placed in a 5 x 5 square.

Figures and letters showing the values – 8, 9, T, J, Q, K and suits – C, D, H, S have been placed at the end of each line across and down. With the Ace in place and the fact that the two cards shown at the top left belong in the shaded squares, can you work out the unique place for each card?

383 DOMINO DEAL

A standard set (0 – 0) to (6 – 6) is laid out below. Each domino is placed so the that the larger number will be on the bottom:

i.e.
3   not   6
6   3

Those top numbers show the four numbers which form the top half of each domino in that column. The bottom numbers, below the grid, give the four bottom numbers for that column. The seven numbers on the left show the numbers which belong in that row. Can you cross-reference the facts and deduce where each domino has been placed?

3*6 is given as a start.

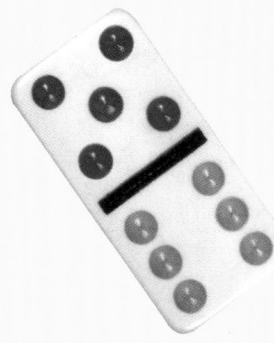

0 1 1 1 4 5 6
1 2 3 4 5 6 6

1 1 2 ~~2~~ 3 3 4
2 3 4 5 5 5 ~~6~~

0 0 1 2 2 4 5
1 2 4 4 5 6 6

0 0 0 0 2 2 3
0 3 3 4 5 6 6

'TOP' NUMBERS

01	00	23	01	01	00	11
26	22	45	15	2~~3~~	34	34
				3		
				6		
23	23	45	12	13	04	34
56	46	55	46	~~6~~6	56	56

'BOTTOM' NUMBERS

111

384 DOTTY DILEMMA ●●

Connect adjacent dots with vertical or horizontal lines so that a single loop is formed with no crossings or branches. Each number indicates how many lines surround it, while empty cells may be surrounded by any number of lines.

```
1   3   12  3   0
      3       1
3     2     1     2
    2   0 3   1
0     3     1     2
  1               1
3     1     3     1
    1   1 2   2
1     2     3     3
3     1     0     1
      3   2 1   3
1     3     0     0
  1               1
3     2     3     1
      3   2 2   2
3     3     2     1
      2       2
3   1   0 2   3   3
```

385 COG-ITATE ●●

Can you work out which weights will rise, and which will fall when the man pulls the rope?

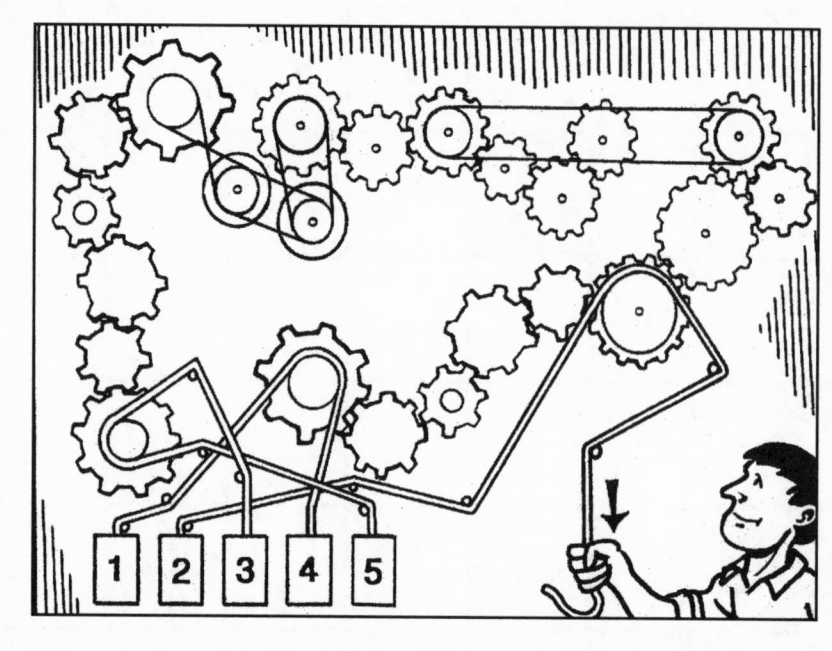

386 OFF YOUR ROCKER ●

In a negative, everything which is really white appears black and everything which is really black appears white. Can you see which one of the four lettered rocking-horses is shown as a negative in the top left-hand corner?

387 CUBE IT ●●

Inside the circle are three views of the same cube. Which of the lettered shapes can be folded up to make the cube?

A
```
    4
2   1   5   3
    6
```

B
```
        2
6   4   3   1
        5
```

C
```
    2
4   3   6   5
    1
```

D
```
    4
3   2   6   5
    1
```

388 HOT AIR

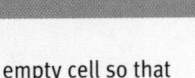

If you looked up into the sky last month, you may have seen five hot air balloons, each advertising a different product. Just in case you didn't, the clues here will enable you to say who was flying each patterned balloon, discover the product being advertised by each, and state the material from which the basket underneath each was made.

1 D. Hytes flew the balloon advertising chocolate, but it was not tartan nor was its basket made from burlap.
2 G. Nears flew the brickwork patterned balloon, but not to advertise tea.
3 The balloon with the straw basket was flown by C. Vyewes but its pattern was neither spots nor tartan.
4 The striped balloon was used to advertise coffee but its basket was not made from either straw, wood or burlap.
5 Neither the balloon with the brickwork design, nor the one flown by E. Bargum had a plastic basket, which was on the balloon advertising cars.
6 F. Tathort, gas and fibreglass complete the line-up.

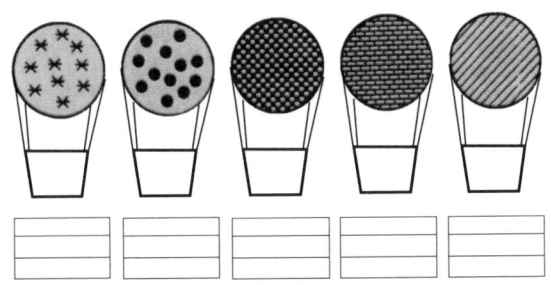

389 NINE NUMBERS

Place a number from 1 to 9 in each empty cell so that each row, each column and each 3 x 3 block contains all the numbers from 1 to 9.

	8		5				2	
1				7		9		6
	3				4			
		5						3
	7						8	
2					1			
			1				4	
6		2		9				5
	4				3		9	

390 BREAKTHROUGH

See how quickly you can break this grid down into the 28 dominoes from which it was formed.

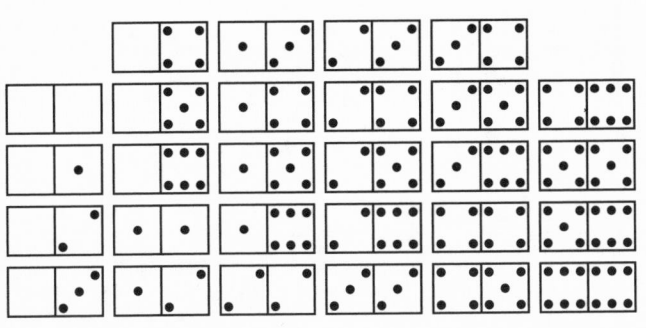

0	0	3	6	4	2	3
3	4	4	4	4	5	2
0	5	5	0	5	5	6
4	3	3	6	6	6	2
4	5	3	0	5	1	3
6	2	2	0	1	1	1
1	5	2	0	2	4	1
1	3	6	6	2	1	0

391 FILLING IN

Each of the nine empty boxes contains a different digit from 1 to 9. Each calculation is to be treated sequentially rather than according to the 'multiplication first' system. Can you fill in the empty boxes?

	+		−		= 8
−		+		×	
	−		×		= 4
+		÷		÷	
	−		×		= 8
= 8		= 3		= 2	

392 LOGIQUATIONS

In the following problems the digits 0 to 9 are represented by letters. Within each separate puzzle the same letter always represents the same digit. Can you find the correct values each time so that all sums, both horizontal and vertical, are correct? There is a clue to help start you off.

CLUE: AB + EC = DF

ABCD	+	EFGH	=	CBJE
−		−		−
JKE	+	AJCK	=	EHJH
BBE	+	AEE	=	HJD

A	B	C	D	E	F	G	H	J	K

393 DOUBLE DANDY

Which two fancily dressed fellows are exactly alike?

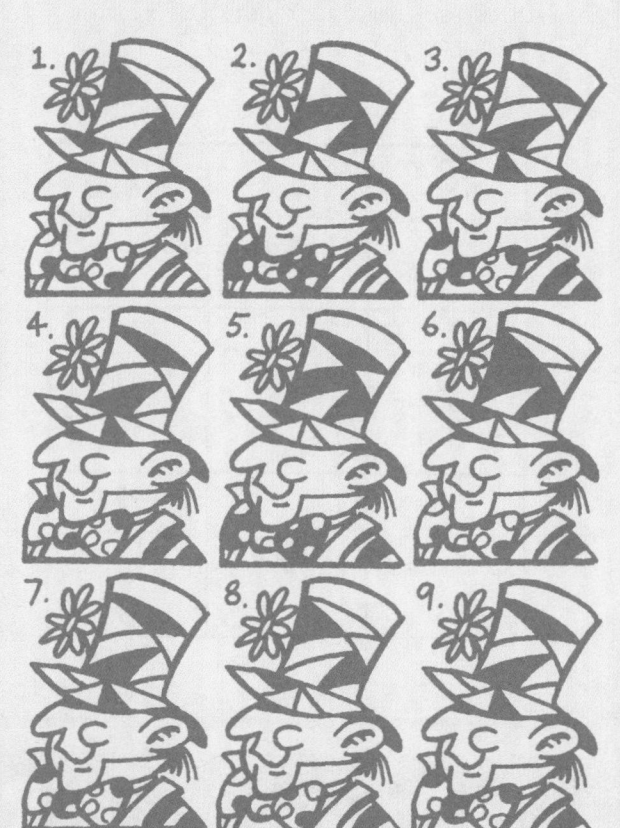

395 COURT ORDER

Of the eight Kings and Queens in a pack of cards, four are lined up here. In these clues *TO THE RIGHT/LEFT* means *NEXT DOOR* and not anywhere beyond.

There's a King to the right of a King.
There's a King to the left of a Queen.
There's a Queen to the left of a King.
There's a Queen to the right of a Spade.
There's a Spade next to a Spade.
There's a Club to the left of a Heart.
There's a Club to the right of a Spade.
Can you identify each card?

394 SPLIT LIZARDS

Can you put together the split lizards to make up four whole ones?

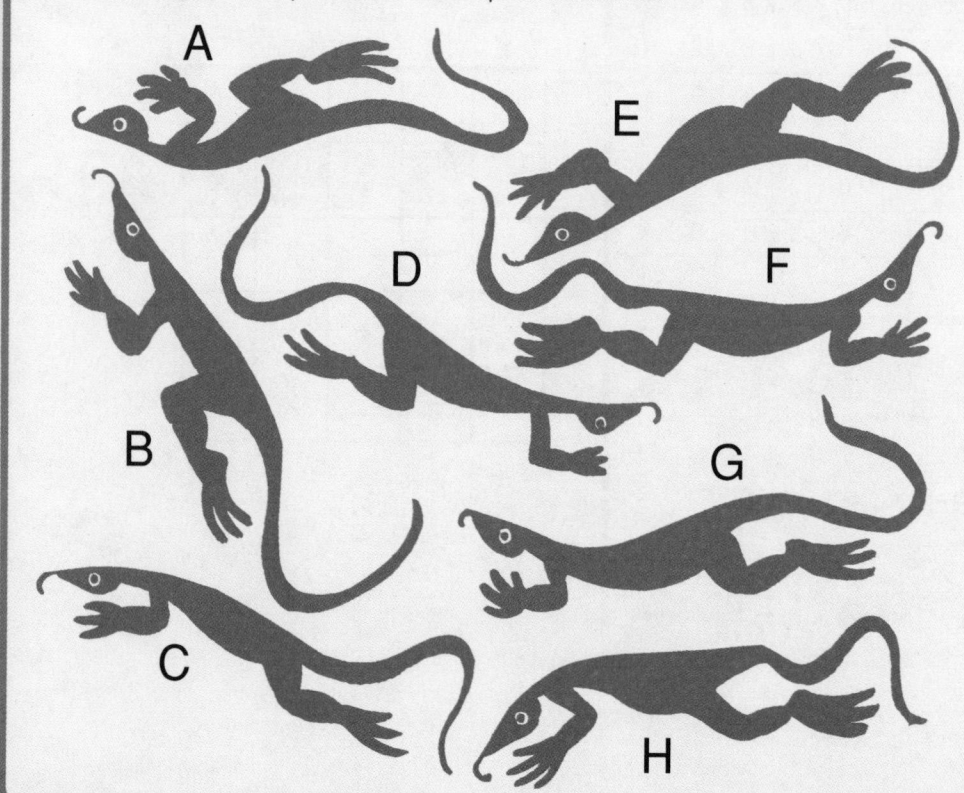

396 DOTTY DILEMMA

Connect adjacent dots with vertical or horizontal lines so that a single loop is formed with no crossings or branches. Each number indicates how many lines surround it, while empty cells may be surrounded by any number of lines.

397 ISLAND HOPPING

Each circle containing a number represents an island. The object is to connect each island with vertical or horizontal bridges so that:

* The number of bridges is the same as the number inside the island.
* There can be up to two bridges between two islands.
* Bridges cannot cross islands or other bridges.
* There is a continuous path connecting all the islands.

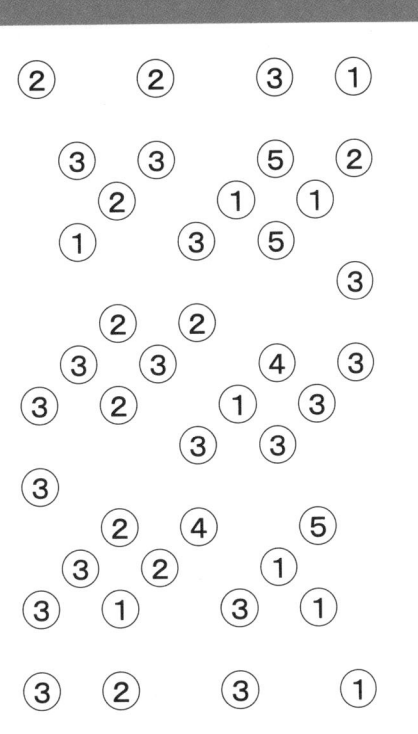

398 PIECE OF CAKE

Four of the letter domino segments can be put together to make a complete 'cake', in which adjacent faces match. Which four segments would make the 'cake' shown?

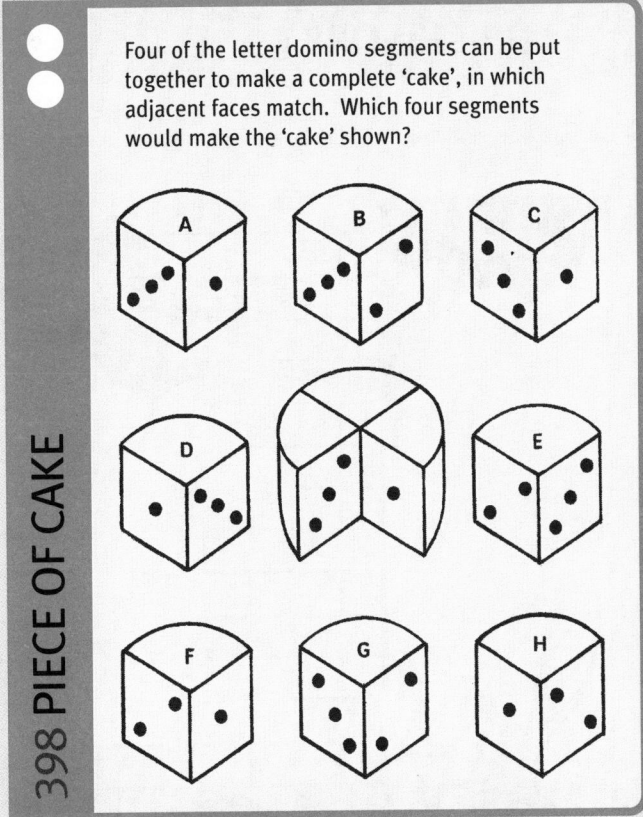

399 IN FLIGHT

Six international jet-setters are enjoying a transatlantic flight. From these details can you name the person in each seat and give his/her business?

The three in the window seats are Ms Baddand, the male model and Ella. None of these is the author.

The three in an aisle seat are her Ladyship, Waylite and the magician. None of these is the tourist who is directly in front of a lady.

In consecutively numbered seats, going upwards, are Ron, the croupier and Ghote. None of these is Stewart who is sitting further back than both Mrs Vatripp and Mahatma who are not side by side.

Smayde is next to Hess who is directly behind Adelia who is in an adjacent-numbered seat to the director in seat No.2 and his snores are beginning to bother her.

400 BIG BREAK

A snooker break is made up by potting red balls (maximum 15) which are each followed by one of six different colours. The point values of the balls are:

 1  2 3 4  5 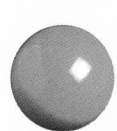 6  7

In his next frame, Bob made a break of 71, which ended when he failed to pot a red. In the break he potted one more pink than greens and one more blue than yellows, potting all four colours in the break (none of which was black or brown). How many of each colour ball were potted?

115

401 BRICKWORK

Can you work out how many bricks are missing from this wall?

403 SPOT THE DIFFERENCE

Can you spot the ten differences between these two pictures?

402 NINE NUMBERS ●●

Place a number from 1 to 9 in each empty cell so that each row, each column and each 3 x 3 block contains all the numbers from 1 to 9.

				6	9			4
	8				4			
2						8		
						3	2	
	4			8			5	
	9	6						
		3						9
			5				6	
5			2	7				

404 LOGI-5

Can you place the letters A, B, C, D, E, one to each square so that every line across and down contains each letter once and every shape made from five squares also has each letter once?

A	E			
			C	
				D
B				

405 KNOTTY PROBLEM

No wonder this chap's looking puzzled – this piece of string seems to be in a real mess! Can you work out how many knots will appear if the two ends are pulled tightly?

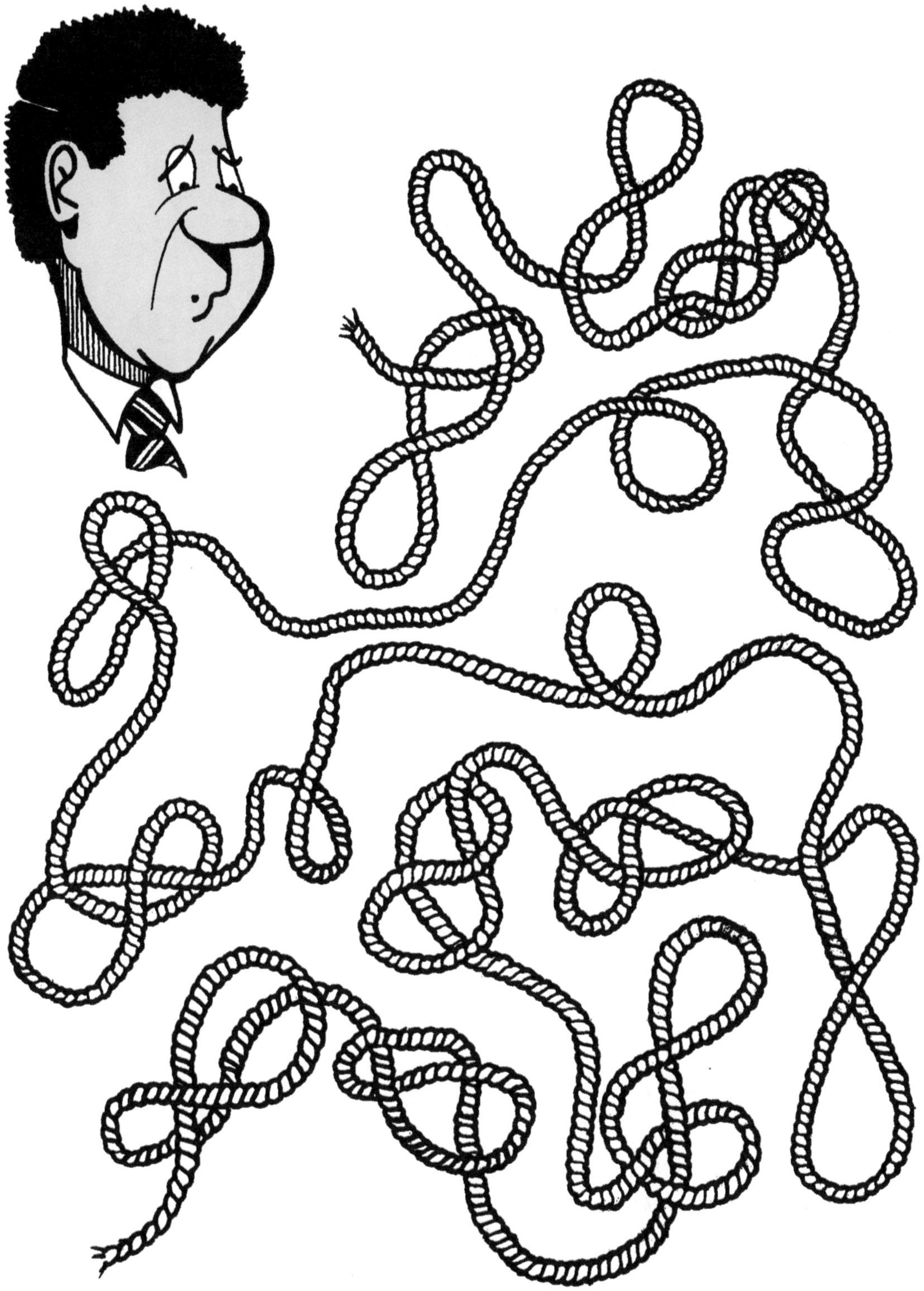

406 DOTTY DILEMMA

Connect adjacent dots with vertical or horizontal lines so that a single loop is formed with no crossings or branches. Each number indicates how many lines surround it, while empty cells may be surrounded by any number of lines.

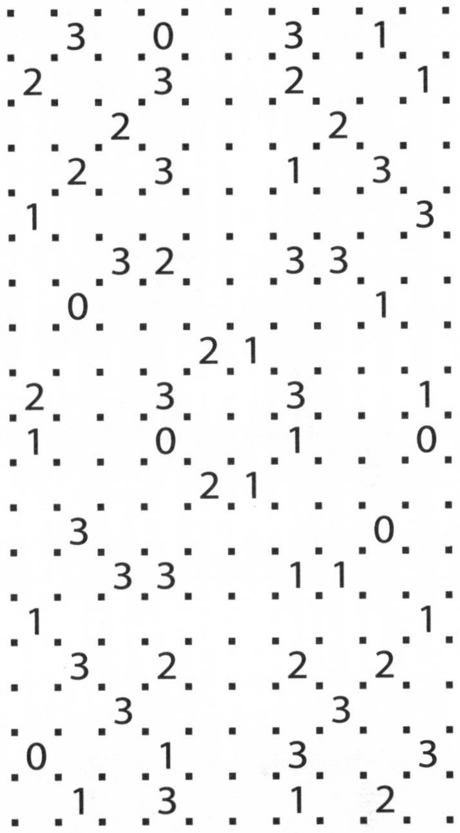

```
  3   0     3   1
2     3   2       1
    2       2
    2   3   1   3
1                 3
    3 2     3 3
  0             1
        2 1
2     3     3     1
1     0     1     0
        2 1
  3             0
    3 3     1 1
1                 1
  3   2     2   2
    3       3
  0     1   3     3
  1   3     1   2
```

407 COG-ITATE

Can you work out which weights will rise, and which will fall when the man releases the rope?

117

408 TOTTERING TOWERS ● ●

These piles of bricks aren't the random results of child's play – but clues to the final, at present, blank tower on the right. Like the rest, that tower has one brick in each of the six colours.

The numbers below each heap tell you two things:
(a) How many adjacent pairs of bricks are actually correct in the final tower.
(b) How many adjacent pairs of bricks make a correct pair but the wrong way up.
So:

 would score one on the first number if the final tower had green directly above yellow. It would score one on the second number if the final tower had yellow on top of green. From all of this, can you create the tower before it finally topples?

PAIRS					
Correct	0	1	0	2	5
Reversed	1	1	1	0	0

409 MOONLIGHTING ●

From anywhere on the Earth, lovers can gaze up at the night sky and see the Moon. Each day it rises and sets. But if you were having a party on the Moon – what would the Earth be doing? Would it rise and set each day; never rise or never set?

EARTH,.........
DEARTH,.........
WORTH,......
SCURF,...........

410 HAIR STYLES ● ●

A saleslady and two others have reached that tedious stage of hairdressing – the hour under the drier. Teresa (who is sitting in the middle) is older than the redhead but younger than the programmer. Mavis is younger than the blonde. Rachel is older than the brunette. The programmer is sitting on the right hand of the secretary's older sister. Can you identify each lady and give her occupation and hair colour?

411 PATH-O-LOGICAL

Use your deductive reasoning to form a pathway from the box marked START to the box marked FINISH moving in either direction horizontally or vertically (but not diagonally). The number at the beginning of every row or column indicates exactly how many of the boxes in that row or column your pathway must pass through. A small diagram is provided to serve you as an example.

Start

	5	1	1	10	3	3	7	2	1	2
5										
3										
3										
3										
5										
4										
1										
1										
4										
6										

Finish

Start

	2	4	3	4
4				
3				
3				
3				

Finish

412 MIND JOGGER

Can you discover which of the numbered cards will fit on card A to complete the sum?

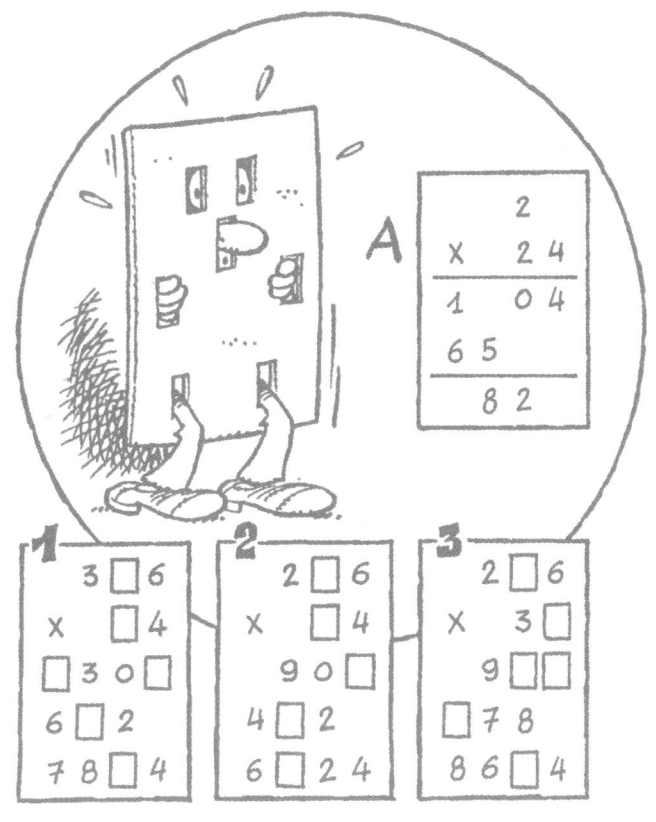

```
      2
  x  24
  1  04
  6 5
  ─────
    8 2
```

A

1.
```
  3 □ 6
  x   □ 4
  □ 3 0 □
  6 □ 2
  7 8 □ 4
```

2.
```
  2 □ 6
  x   □ 4
      9 0 □
  4 □ 2
  6 □ 2 4
```

3.
```
  2 □ 6
  x   3 □
      9 □ □
  □ 7 8
  8 6 □ 4
```

413 OFFSIDE

Which two of the numbered pictures have been taken from picture A?

A

 1

 3

2

 8

5

4

6

7

414 TEE TIME

Three old-timers play a weekly game of golf on the Golden Lawns 18-hole, par 72, course. Each score at every hole falls into one of five categories. Each golfer gets a different result in each category. Also, no category has the same result for another player, ie, if a player has two eagles, he has a different number in the other four and no other player has two eagles. With the score details below and the information given, can you fill in their card?

Parnell, who did not get the fewest pars, got one more eagle than bogey and the two added up to his number of birdies. This number was the same as Barry's pars which were two fewer than his birdies and two more than his double bogeys. Nick got twice as many pars as birdies and twice as many birdies as double-bogeys of which he had the same number as Barry's eagles. This number was one more than Barry's number of bogeys which was two less than his double bogeys.

	Eagle −2	Birdie −1	Par 0	Bogey +1	Double Bogey +2	FINAL SCORE
Parnell Darma						
Nick Jackliss						
Barry Clayer						

415 IT FIGURES

Place a number from 1 to 9 in each empty cell so that the sum of each vertical or horizontal block equals the number at the top or on the left of that block. Numbers may only be used once in each block.

416 BIRD BRAIN

Which one of these ostriches is holding the diagram with the most triangles on it?

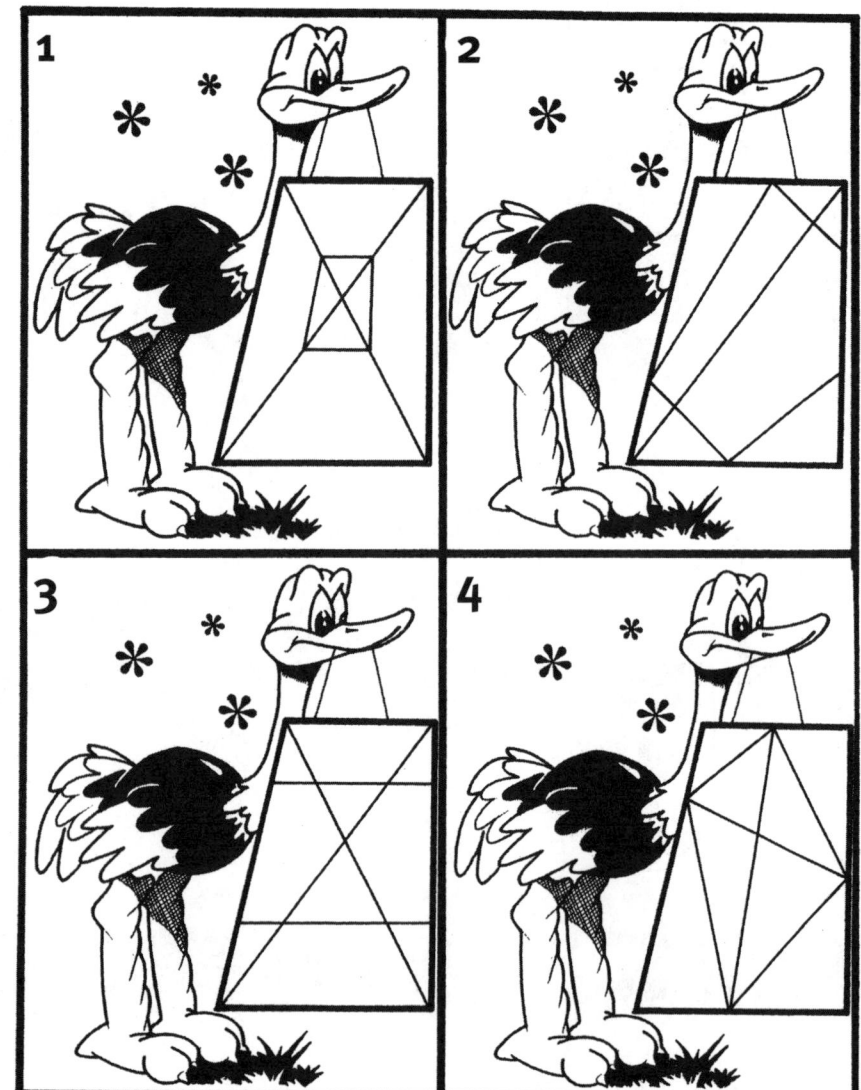

417 ISLAND HOPPING

Each circle containing a number represents an island. The object is to connect each island with vertical or horizontal bridges so that:
* The number of bridges is the same as the number inside the island.
* There can be up to two bridges between two islands.
* Bridges cannot cross islands or other bridges.
* There is a continuous path connecting all the islands.

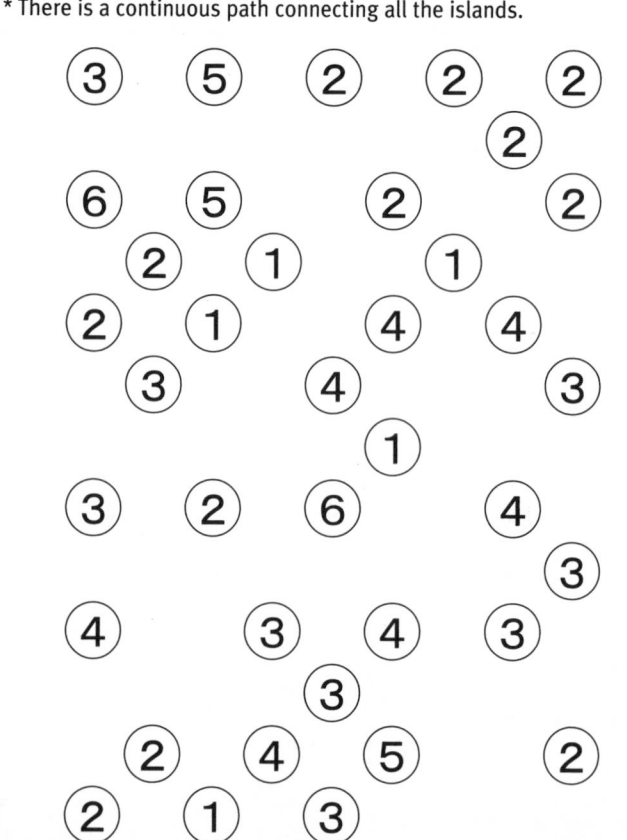

418 KARL KRACK'S CIRCUS

Karl Krack, who owns a small travelling circus, believes that variety is the spice of life and for each show he alters the order of his eight acts. Can you work out what the order will be for tonight's performance? The Clever Clowns will come immediately after the Flying Fortresses and two acts before the Crazy Carvellos and Jim the Juggler is three acts before Fred the Fire-eater and two acts after Madame Poll's Parrots. Senor Pedro's Poodles are more than two later in the programme than the Agilles Acrobats.

1	2	3	4
5	6	7	8

419 STICKY TIME

Move *two* matches only so that you end up with the cherry *outside* the glass.

420 RACER FACES

Talk about being two-faced! Can you match up these speedsters' halves correctly?

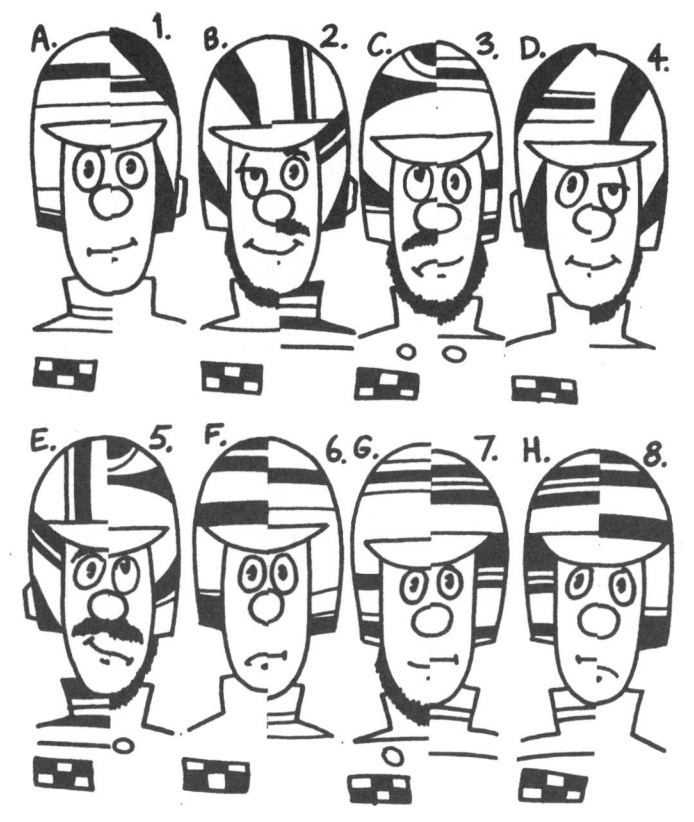

421 PIE-EYED

Before this clown receives the cream pie in the face, can you show him how to divide it into *eight* parts with only *three cuts*?

No, pieces can't be piled up on top of each other – any movement and the cream will escape!

422 DOMINO SEARCH

A standard set of dominoes has been laid out, using numbers instead of dots for clarity. Using a sharp pencil and a keen brain, can you draw in the lines to show where each domino has been placed? You may find the check grid useful – crossing off each domino as you find it.

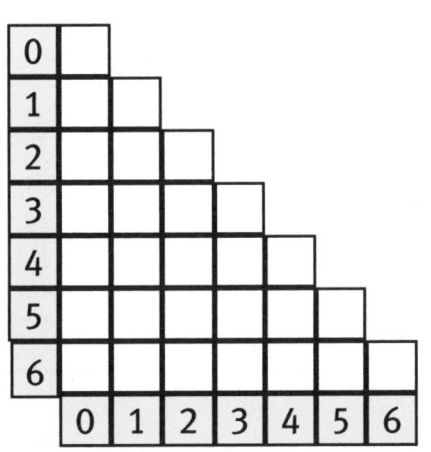

423 MENTAL BLOCKS

Which two of the numbered pieces will fit together to make cube A?

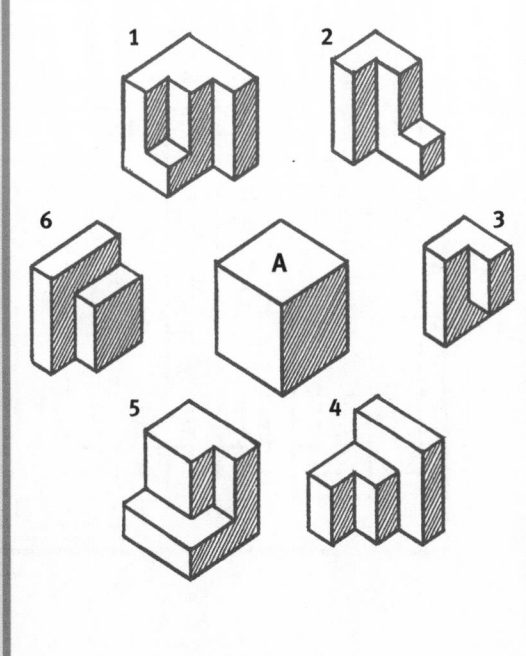

424 MAZE MYSTERY

Travel from the entrance to the exit of the maze, filling the path completely to create a picture.

425 INTERESTING

How can you legally arrange matters so that your body is buried on the day before you die?

1715–1830

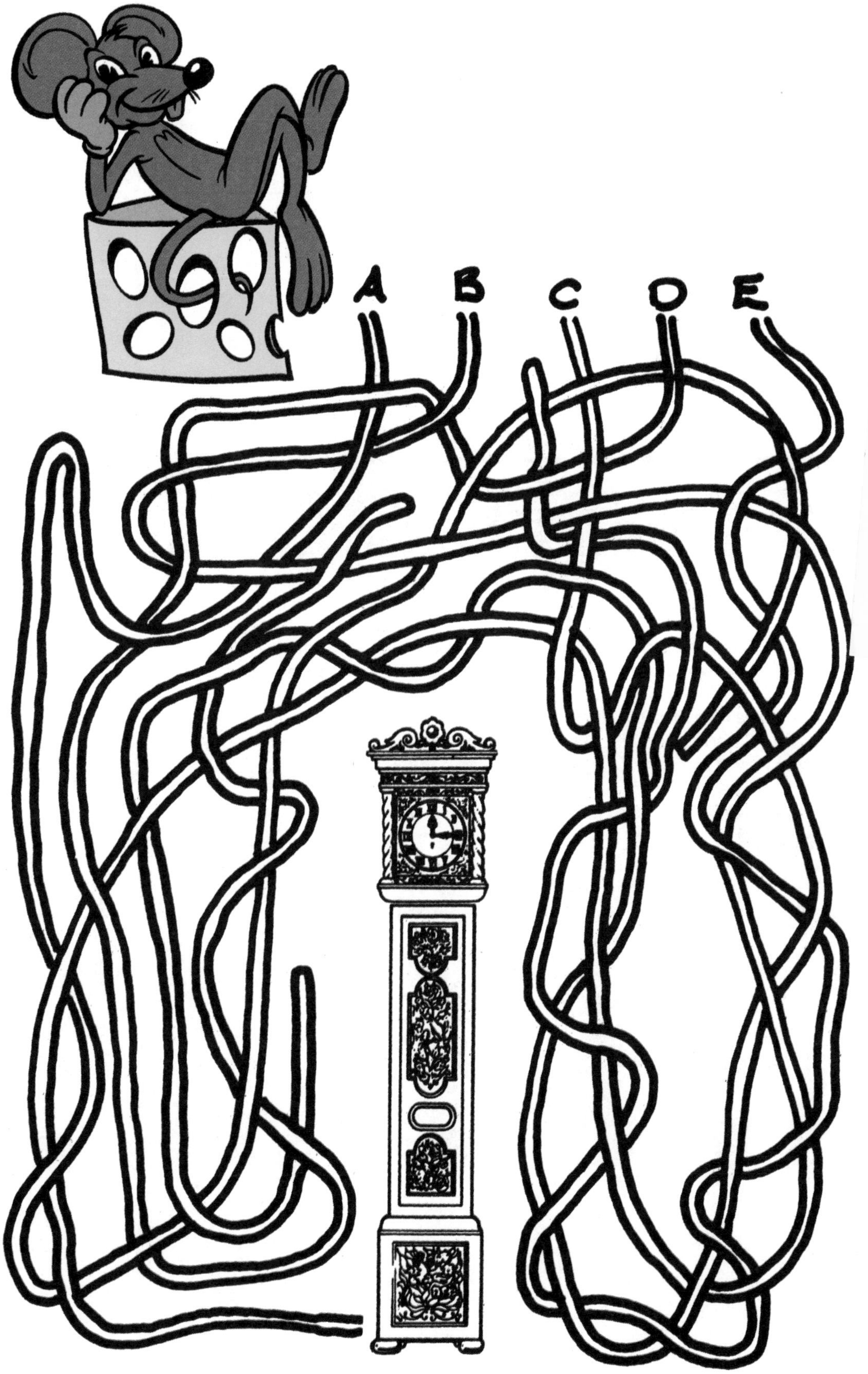

427 NINE NUMBERS ●●

Place a number from 1 to 9 in each empty cell so that each row, each column and each 3 x 3 block contains all the numbers from 1 to 9.

	5				1	9		
	4			2			7	
1			8					3
	9	2						6
	1			5			8	
4				9	5			
5				6				7
	9		3				1	
		1	7			6		

428 ANTIPATHETIC ●

A reluctant ant, not wanting to be sent out on yet another food gathering journey, decided to take the longest route back to the nest. Such is its tiny brain, though, that it will only go along the edges of the patio tiles and will not go over any part of its path more than once. What was the longest way home?

426 CHEESE STRAWS

Which one of these lettered paths will lead the mouse to the clock?

A   B   C   D   E

429 PARTY TIME

Party time and the table is all set up with eight coloured cakes in position waiting for the children to sit down and tuck in. From the information below can you work out where each child will be sitting?

At Sharon and Paul's party, boys and girls are seated alternately and no child is sitting next to another with the same number of letters in his/her name. The child on one side of the yellow cake has one more letter in his/her name than the child on the other side. Fiona is on one side of the brown cake (chocolate flavour!), which is not where Bob is sitting. Amy is sitting next to Martin but neither has a pink cake. Chloe does not have an orange cake and Jack is not next to the child with the green cake.

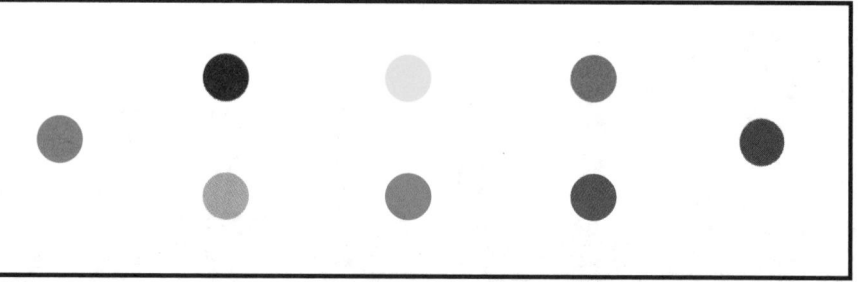

431 TOTTERING TOWERS

These piles of bricks aren't the random results of child's play – but clues to the final, at present, blank tower on the right. Like the rest, that tower has one brick in each of the six colours.

The numbers below each heap tell you two things:
(a) How many adjacent pairs of bricks are actually correct in the final tower.
(b) How many adjacent pairs of bricks make a correct pair but the wrong way up.
So:

 would score one on the first number if the final tower had green directly above yellow. It would score one on the second number if the final tower had yellow on top of green. From all of this, can you create the tower before it finally topples?

PAIRS					
Correct	2	1	0	0	5
Reversed	0	0	2	0	0

430 NUMBER KROSS

See how quickly you can fit all these numbers into the grid. We've filled one figure in to start you off.

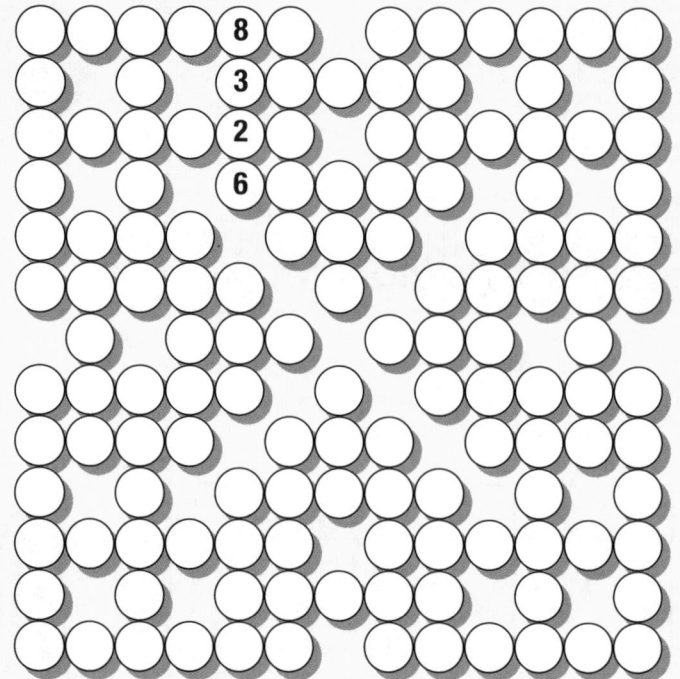

3 figures	5 figures	6 figures
217	10439	107989
226	14756	134871
304	24514	172351
421	27190	212806
572	30947	213071
815	46023	316293
874	55326	341268
907	57147	453527
	60175	551108
4 figures	61513	572215
1740	67329	581941
1783	73346	661630
6137	84168	676869
7576	89224	713954
7657	90718	819201
8326	97179	971329
9083		
9447		

432 ISLAND HOPPING

Each circle containing a number represents an island. The object is to connect each island with vertical or horizontal bridges so that:
* The number of bridges is the same as the number inside the island.
* There can be up to two bridges between two islands.
* Bridges cannot cross islands or other bridges.
* There is a continuous path connecting all the islands.

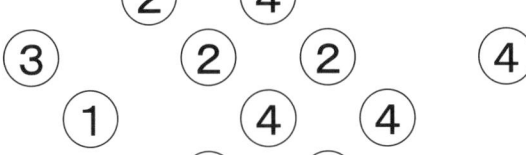

433 DRUM ROLL

In a negative, everything which is really black appears white and everything which is really white appears black. Can you tell which one of the seven kettledrums is shown as a negative in the top left-hand corner?

434 BREAKTHROUGH

See how quickly you can break this grid down into the 28 dominoes from which it is formed.

2	0	2	1	1	0	1
6	6	3	3	2	2	0
4	3	5	4	2	6	6
0	0	0	4	4	6	3
1	6	5	4	5	5	1
6	0	3	5	2	5	4
0	4	3	5	5	1	2
3	4	1	3	2	1	6

125

435 DOTTY DILEMMA

Connect adjacent dots with vertical or horizontal lines so that a single loop is formed with no crossings or branches. Each number indicates how many lines surround it, while empty cells may be surrounded by any number of lines.

```
· · · · · · · · · · · · · · · ·
· · 3 · · · · 3 · · · · · ·
· 2 3 0 1 · · · 0 · · · · ·
· · · · · · · 3 2 0 · ·
· · 0 2 1 1 · · · · · · ·
· · 1 · 2 · · · · · · ·
· · 3 · 1 · · 3 0 · · ·
· 2 2 1 2 · · · 2 · ·
· · · · · · · · · 2 ·
· 1 2 · · 2 1 · · 3 ·
· 0 · · 3 2 · · 3 1 ·
· 3 · · · · · · · · ·
· 2 · · 3 2 0 1 · · ·
· 2 1 · · 0 · · 1 · ·
· · · · · 2 · · 1 · ·
· · · · 0 1 2 2 · · ·
· 1 3 3 · · · · · · ·
· · 2 · · · 1 3 3 3 ·
· 1 · · 1 · · · · ·
```

436 NINE NUMBERS

Place a number from 1 to 9 in each empty cell so that each row, each column and each 3 x 3 block contains all the numbers from 1 to 9.

7			3	4				5
		2			5			
		1				6		
2				1			7	
3								8
		4			2			9
		5					1	
			6			9		
4				7	8			2

437 EASY AS ABC

Each row and column originally contained one A, one B, one C, one D and two blank squares. Each letter and number refers to the first or second of the four letters encountered when travelling in the direction of the arrow. Can you complete the original grid?

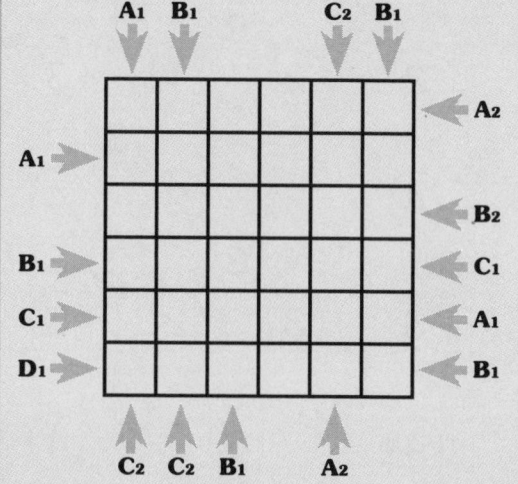

438 LOGI-PATH

Use your deductive reasoning to form a pathway from the box marked START to the box marked FINISH moving in either direction horizontally or vertically (but not diagonally). The number at the beginning of every row or column indicates exactly how many boxes in that row or column your pathway must pass through. The small diagram is given as an example of how it works.

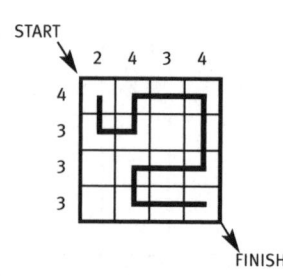

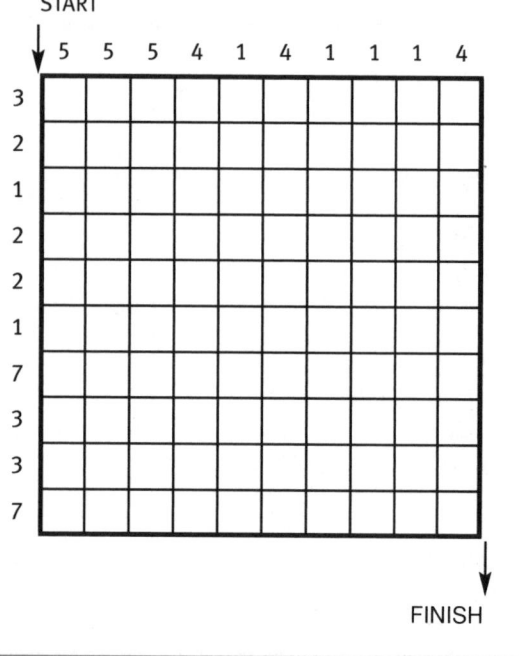

START

	5	5	5	4	1	4	1	1	1	4
3										
2										
1										
2										
2										
1										
7										
3										
3										
7										

FINISH

439 ODD ONE OUT

All of these aliens are odd, but which one is the odd one out?

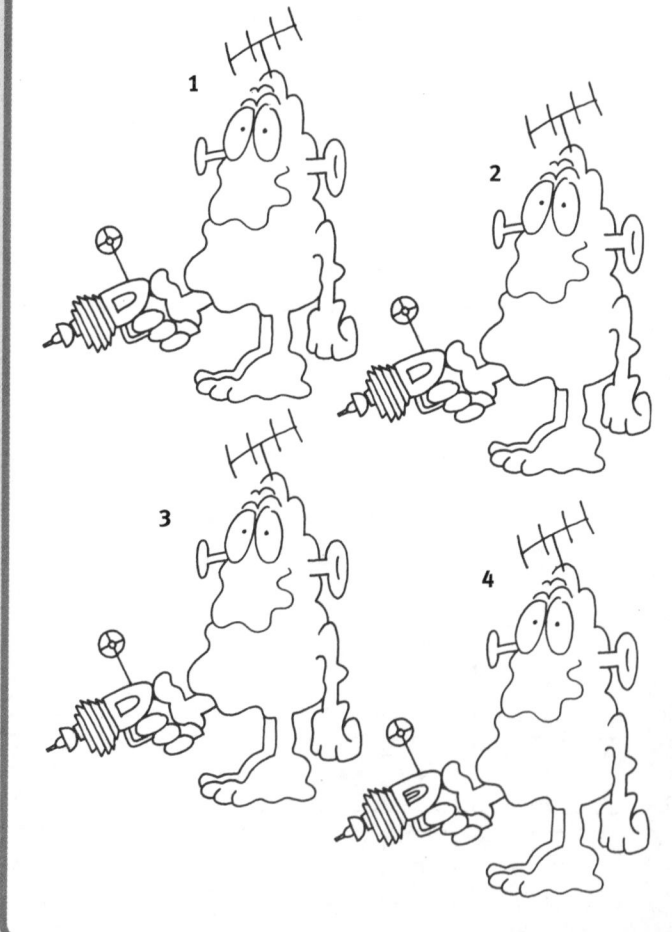

440 MOUSE HUNT

This greedy mouse has been raiding the jar of candy. Can you put the fourteen numbered pictures of the jar in the correct order, to show the candy gradually disappearing? Picture 9 is the first, because the jar in that picture contains the most candy.

441 LOGIMAZE

The grid is a symbol maze through which you must find a route by moving from one symbol to another according to the progression of the code sequence indicated in figure A. You can start anywhere on the edge of the grid but you must start on a Santa, proceed to the opposite side of the grid (repeating the sequence as often as necessary) and end on a stocking. You can move up, down, left or right, but not diagonally.

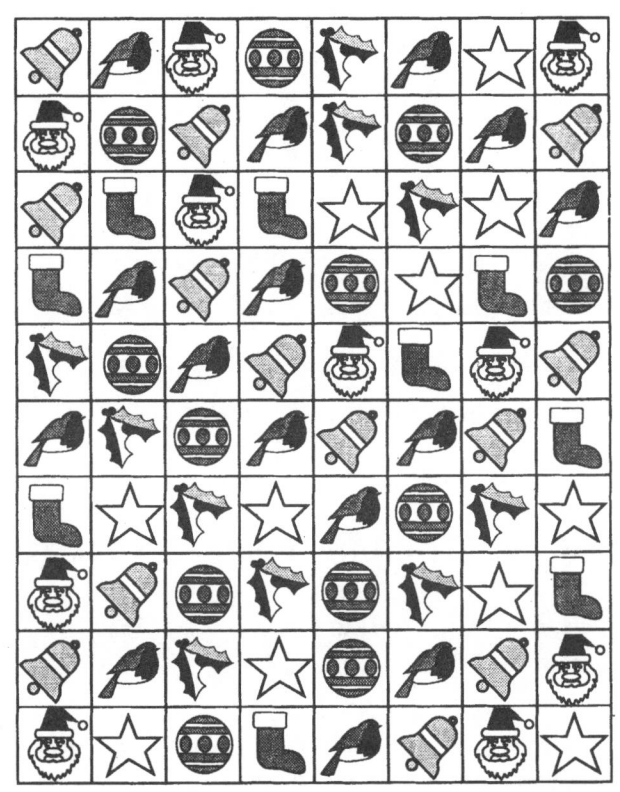

442 BREAKTHROUGH

See how quickly you can break this grid down into the 28 dominoes from which it was formed.

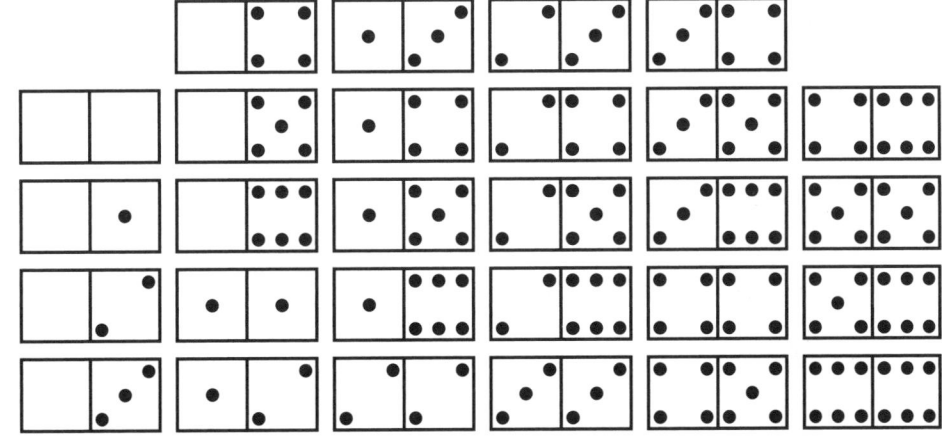

2	6	0	6	0	5	3
3	3	3	5	5	6	5
6	2	0	4	1	6	6
3	2	1	4	4	3	4
5	2	4	1	1	1	6
2	3	0	2	3	2	4
5	4	1	0	0	1	6
5	0	1	0	4	5	2

443 NUMBER KROSS

See how quickly you can fit all these numbers into the grid. We've filled one figure in to start you off.

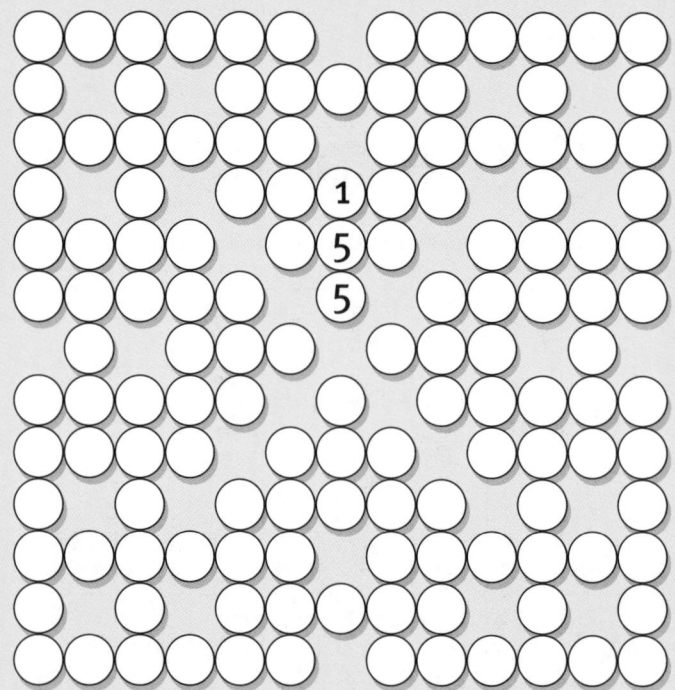

3 figures	5 figures	6 figures
155	12321	123456
179	12807	183547
281	24932	210987
377	30405	215032
488	31255	317506
560	42716	345678
662	45616	403582
757	51726	456489
	61140	504119
4 figures	63422	511433
1746	71050	665544
2000	74828	667686
3584	82710	766665
4738	85947	824332
5666	91606	856472
6656	91717	901570
7863		
8122		

444 SPOT THE DIFFERENCE

Can you spot the ten differences between these two pictures?

445 EASY AS ABC

Each row and column originally contained one A, one B, one C, one D and two blank squares. Each letter and number refers to the first or second of the four letters encountered when travelling in the direction of the arrow. Can you complete the original grid?

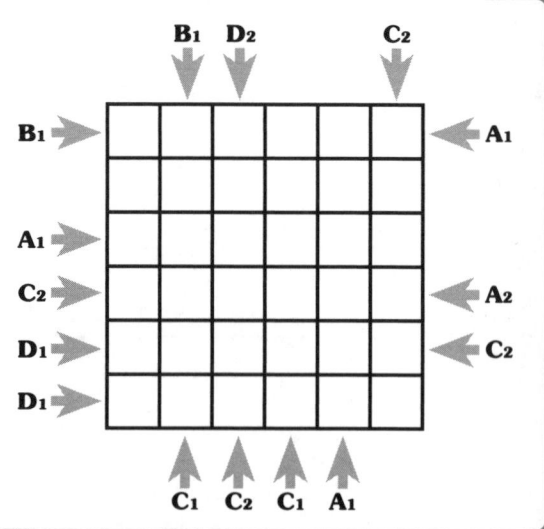

446 NINE NUMBERS

Place a number from 1 to 9 in each empty cell so that each row, each column and each 3 x 3 block contains all the numbers from 1 to 9.

	8			1			6	
	1			5				8
7					1			
	3							4
2			6			7		
5					3			
	4							1
1			2			5		
	6			7			2	

447 IT FIGURES

Place a number from 1 to 9 in each empty cell so that the sum of each vertical or horizontal block equals the number at the top or on the left of that block. Numbers may only be used once in each block.

448 DOTTY DILEMMA

Connect adjacent dots with vertical or horizontal lines so that a single loop is formed with no crossings or branches. Each number indicates how many lines surround it, while empty cells may be surrounded by any number of lines.

```
2 2 1 1 3 1 1 3
                   3
3 2 0 2 0 2 1 2
 1
3 3 2 1 2 2 2 3
                   1
3 1 1 0 2 3 2 2
 2
3 1 2 3
          2 1 3 3
                 0
3 2 0 2 2 3 1 1
 2
2 3 1 0 3 1 1 3
                   1
2 2 2 2 2 2 2 2
 1
3 1 3 1 2 2 1 2
```

449 TOTTERING TOWERS

These piles of bricks aren't the random results of child's play – but clues to the final, at present, blank tower on the right. Like the rest, that tower has one brick with each of the six letters.
The numbers below each heap tell you two things:
(a) How many adjacent pairs of bricks are actually correct in the final tower.
(b) How many adjacent pairs of bricks make a correct pair but the wrong way up.

So:

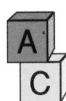 would score one on the first number if the final tower had an A directly above a C. It would score one on the second number if the final tower had C on top of A. From all of this, can you create the tower before it finally topples?

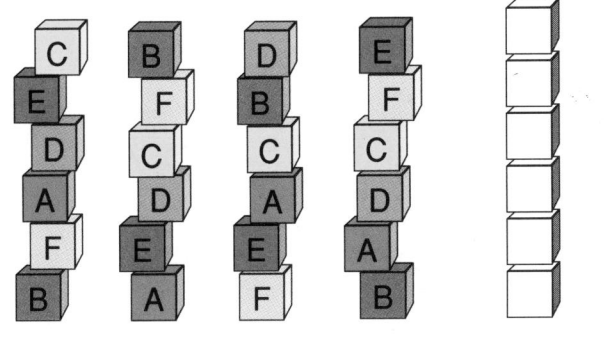

PAIRS

Correct	1	0	0	0	5
Reversed	0	0	2	0	0

450 CELL STRUCTURE

The object is to create white areas surrounded by black walls, so that:
* Each white area contains only one number.
* The number of cells in a white area is equal to the number in it.
* The white areas are separated from each other with a black wall.
* Cells containing numbers must not be filled in.
* The black cells must be linked into a continuous wall.
* Black cells cannot form a square of 2 x 2 or larger.

							4
	3		2				
2					2		3
				4			
	4		2				3
					3		
					2		3
3		3					

451 ISLAND HOPPING

Each circle containing a number represents an island. The object is to connect each island with vertical or horizontal bridges so that:
* The number of bridges is the same as the number inside the island.
* There can be up to two bridges between two islands.
* Bridges cannot cross islands or other bridges.
* There is a continuous path connecting all the islands.

① (2) (3) (2) (4) (1)

(2) (2) (7) (3)

(2) (1) (1)

(3) (2) (3) (2)

(3) (2) (1)

(3) (2) (8) (3)

(4) (5)

(4) (4)

(1) (2) (6) (2)

(4) (2) (3)

(1) (1) (4) (1)

(2) (2) (1)

(2) (2) (2) (3)

(1) (2) (4) (4) (3)

452 PLUMB BLUFF!

Which of the numbered boilers belongs in the plumbing system shown?

453 NINE NUMBERS

Place a number from 1 to 9 in each empty cell so that each row, each column and each 3 x 3 block contains all the numbers from 1 to 9.

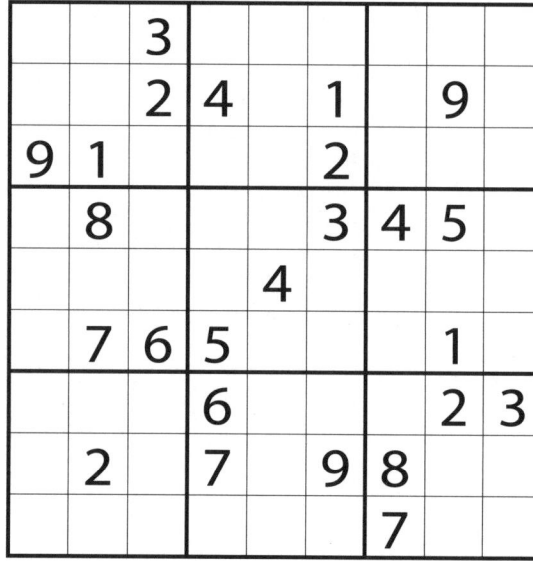

	3							
	2	4		1		9		
9	1			2				
	8				3	4	5	
			4					
	7	6	5				1	
		6				2	3	
	2		7		9	8		
						7		

454 WATER SPORTS

The architect and four of his friends swim in the same pool. Mark and the dentist both swim laps in the morning. Karl and Mr Harkness sometimes dive together in the afternoons. Mr Jones recently considered the idea of making up a swimming team, using the five of them. He observed that:

* In the 100 metre freestyle – both Mr Harkness and Mr Gainor are slower than Mark.
* Both Mr Harkness and Otto are faster than the economist.
* In the backstroke only Neil is willing to swim more than 50 metres, and Karl will not compete at all.
* In the 50 metres backstroke Mr Ives is faster than Mark. Mark, Otto, and Luke are all slower than the barber. Mark is faster than the critic.
* In the breaststroke the critic, the dentist, and the economist are all slower than Mr Franklin. Luke is faster than Mr Ives.
* As to springboard diving: Mr Franklin, Mark and Karl are the three best divers.

Can you identify all five men, giving names and occupations?

455 BEAR MAZE

Can you find your way through this maze, starting from the top and finishing at the bottom?

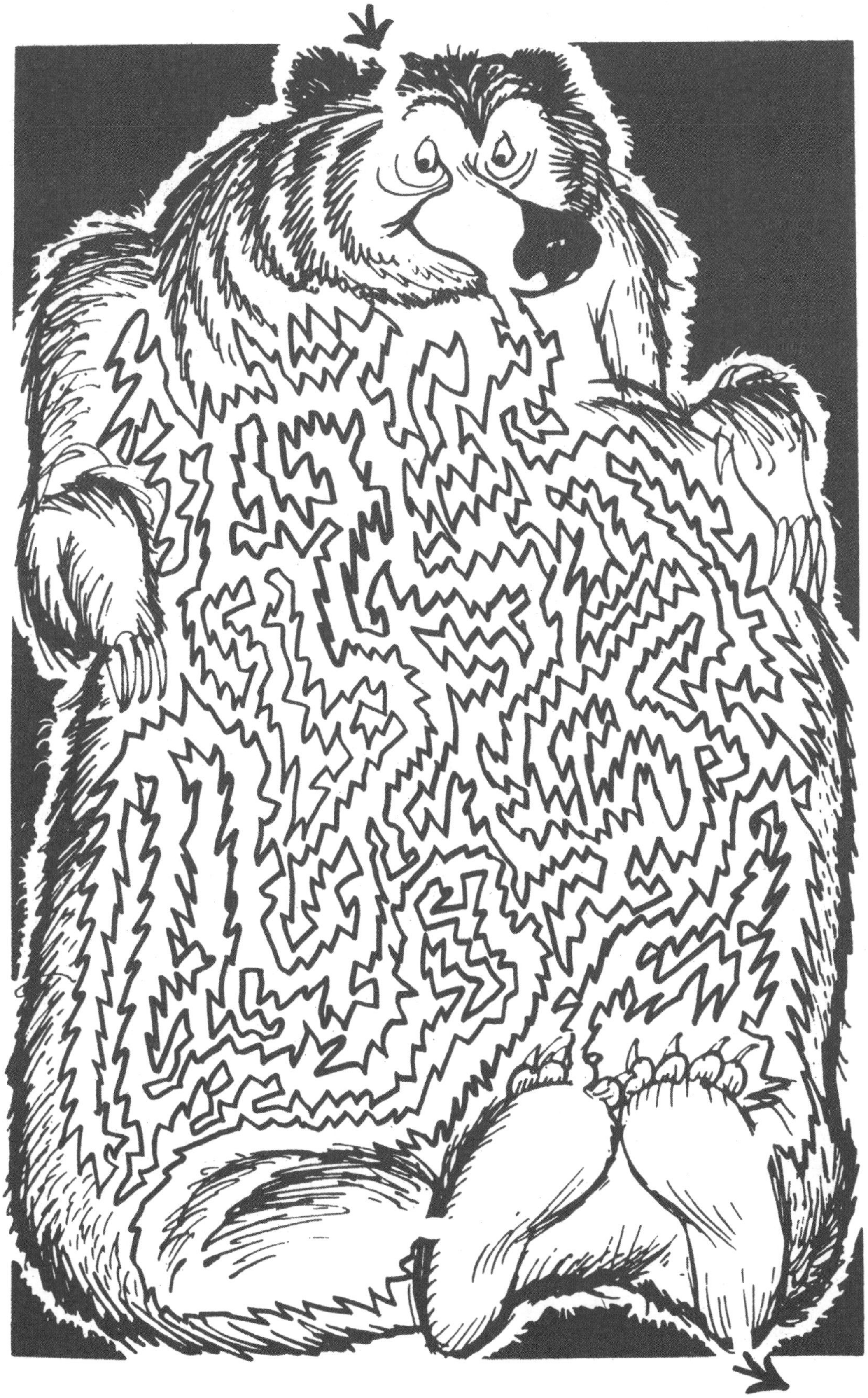

456 DOTTY DILEMMA

Connect adjacent dots with vertical or horizontal lines so that a single loop is formed with no crossings or branches. Each number indicates how many lines surround it, while empty cells may be surrounded by any number of lines.

		2		2		3		0	
2		3		3		1			3
0		1		2			3		
		3			2			2	1
2			0			3			
			1		3		3	2	2
1	0	3	2		2				
					2		3	1	1
	3	1	2	3					
					3	3	1	3	
2	1	0		2					
				3		2	0	1	2
1	0	3		2		2			
			1			2			2
2	1			1			2		
		1			0		3		2
3			3		1		3		3
	3		3		2		1		

457 SQUARE LETTERS

The letters of the alphabet, excluding Z, are entered randomly into a 5 x 5 square so that no two consecutive letters are in the same row or column, or in a diagonal in any direction.

The letters NQG can be read downwards as can TMO. Square E5 is a vowel. D is immediately left of V and immediately above I, which is not in column 2. Row D begins and ends with a vowel, the first alphabetically preceding the latter. Q and T are at opposite ends of a row, and K and S are at the top and bottom respectively of a column. U is diagonally immediately below W. E and R can both be seen on the same long diagonal. C is diagonally adjacent to H; Y is to the immediate right of F, and X is in a corner square.
Can you locate each letter?

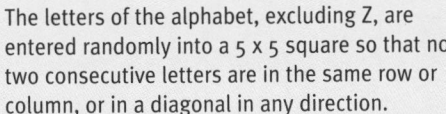

	1	**2**	**3**	**4**	**5**
A					
B					
C					
D					
E					

458 LOGI-PATH

Use your deductive reasoning to form a pathway from the box marked START to the box marked FINISH moving in either direction horizontally or vertically (but not diagonally). The number at the beginning of every row or column indicates exactly how many boxes in that row or column your pathway must pass through. The small diagram is given as an example of how it works.

START →

	2	4	3	4
4				
3				
3				
3				

→ FINISH

START

	4	3	7	4	3	6	1	4	1	1	4	1
4												
3												
1												
1												
1												
4												
1												
1												
5												
5												
3												
10												

→ FINISH

459 STRUCTURE MAZE

Can you find your way through this maze?

START →

FINISH →

460 UPSTAIRS, DOWNSTAIRS

A group of eight people are playing Murder in the Dark and each has hidden in a separate room. Your job is to find them. You are looking at the house from the side and the front and back are as shown. Adjacent rooms share a wall on the same floor. To help you on your way one person has already been found.

1. Fred is not adjacent to Enid.
2. Hebe is directly above Bess.
3. Alan is not directly above Gina.
4. Dave is not adjacent to Enid.
5. Fred is in a back room.
6. Enid is directly below Cary.
7. Dave is on the same side as Gina.

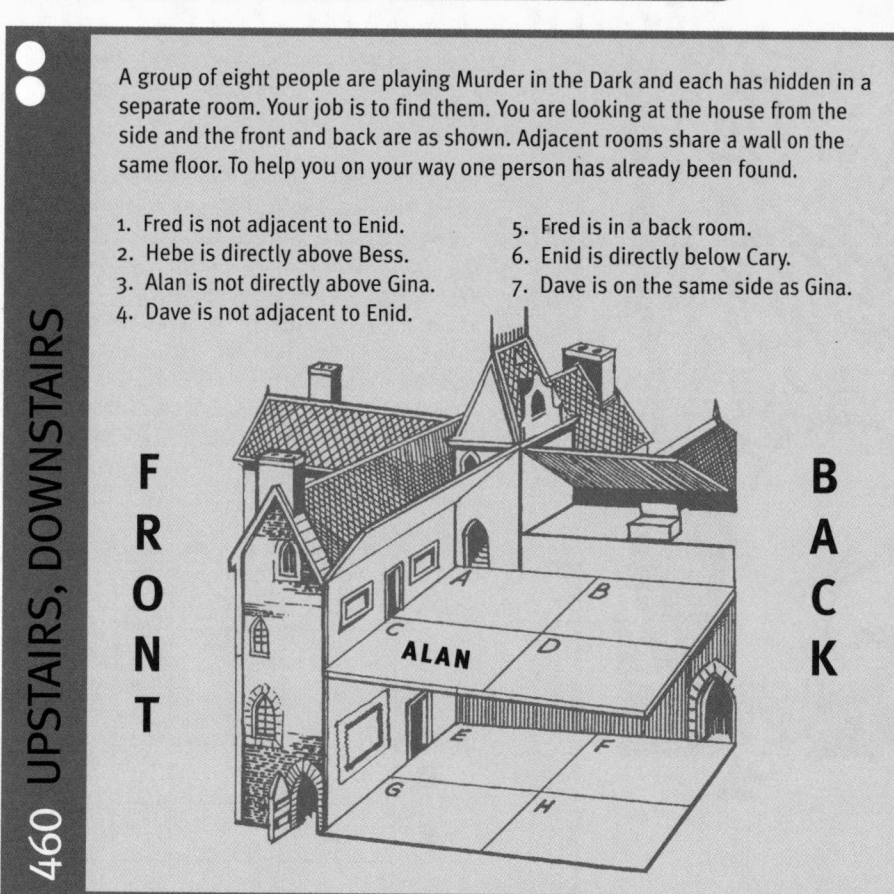

FRONT

BACK

461 CODEMASTER

Can you crack the code and say which of these six pictures has been hidden in each empty box?
The two numbers to the right of each row of pictures tells you first, how many pictures are in the right place and second, how many of the pictures are right but in the wrong place. The answer may have the same picture more than once. Just follow the rules of that classic game Master Mind and you'll soon get the picture.

Pictures				Right place	Wrong place
				2	0
				0	2
				2	1
				0	1
				2	1

462 NUMBER KROSS

See how quickly you can fit all these numbers into the grid. We've filled one figure in to start you off.

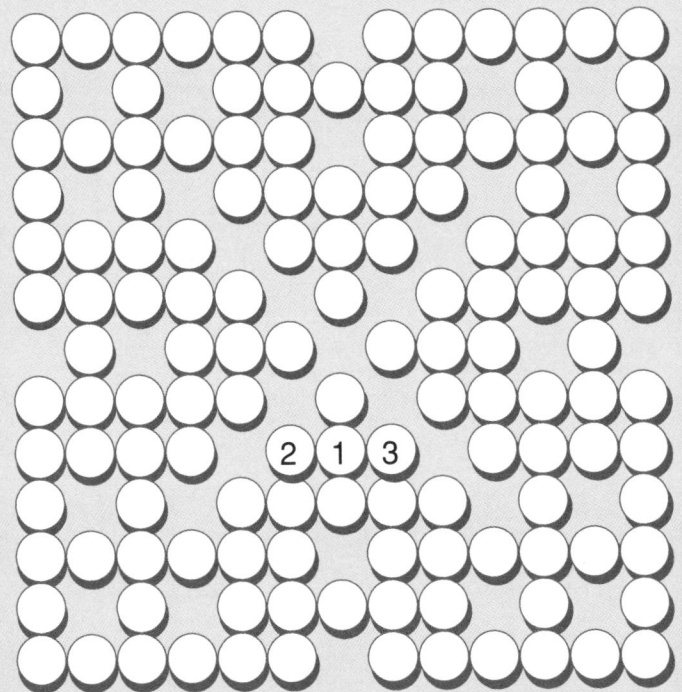

3 figures	5 figures	6 figures
~~213~~	10679	100200
412	19658	121314
547	20184	212223
623	29017	243444
721	33401	312111
736	35709	344071
837	40233	453324
941	43581	463322
	49832	515253
4 figures	57689	543210
3552	69177	624896
4174	71705	635343
5342	78905	703891
6219	81507	776976
7280	87174	884271
7475	91370	921404
8749		
9293		

463 COMPLETE THE SQUARE

Complete the square, using the set of tiles given, so that the same numbers can be read left to right and downwards starting at any point on the diagonal top left to bottom right.

7 5   3 6   4 3   0 3 3

4 8 4   4 0 4   0 3 5

4 2 4

1 3 1 3

7 8 0 2

8 5 6 2

6 8 4 4

2 5 9 0

1 3

1 3 2

4 9 2

464 A MATTER OF BERTH

Farmer Nure's small campsite has four plots which at the moment are occupied by 18 tourists from four families. Each immobile home is labelled West, North, East and South which is the caravan nearest to you as you peer through the nettles.

1 Between them, two caravans have two less campers than the total housed in the two motorvans. No van has more than six berths.

2 There are more Larkitts than Spencers and neither family is the one occupying the East plot.

3 There are more Groves than there are in the family from Frumley.

4 The Huggins family is in the South caravan and their family size is one smaller than the size of the family from Welmside.

5 There are more from Tyneham than from Cheaphill and neither family has booked into a motorhome.

465 MAZE MYSTERY

Travel from the entrance to the exit of the maze, filling the path completely to create a picture.

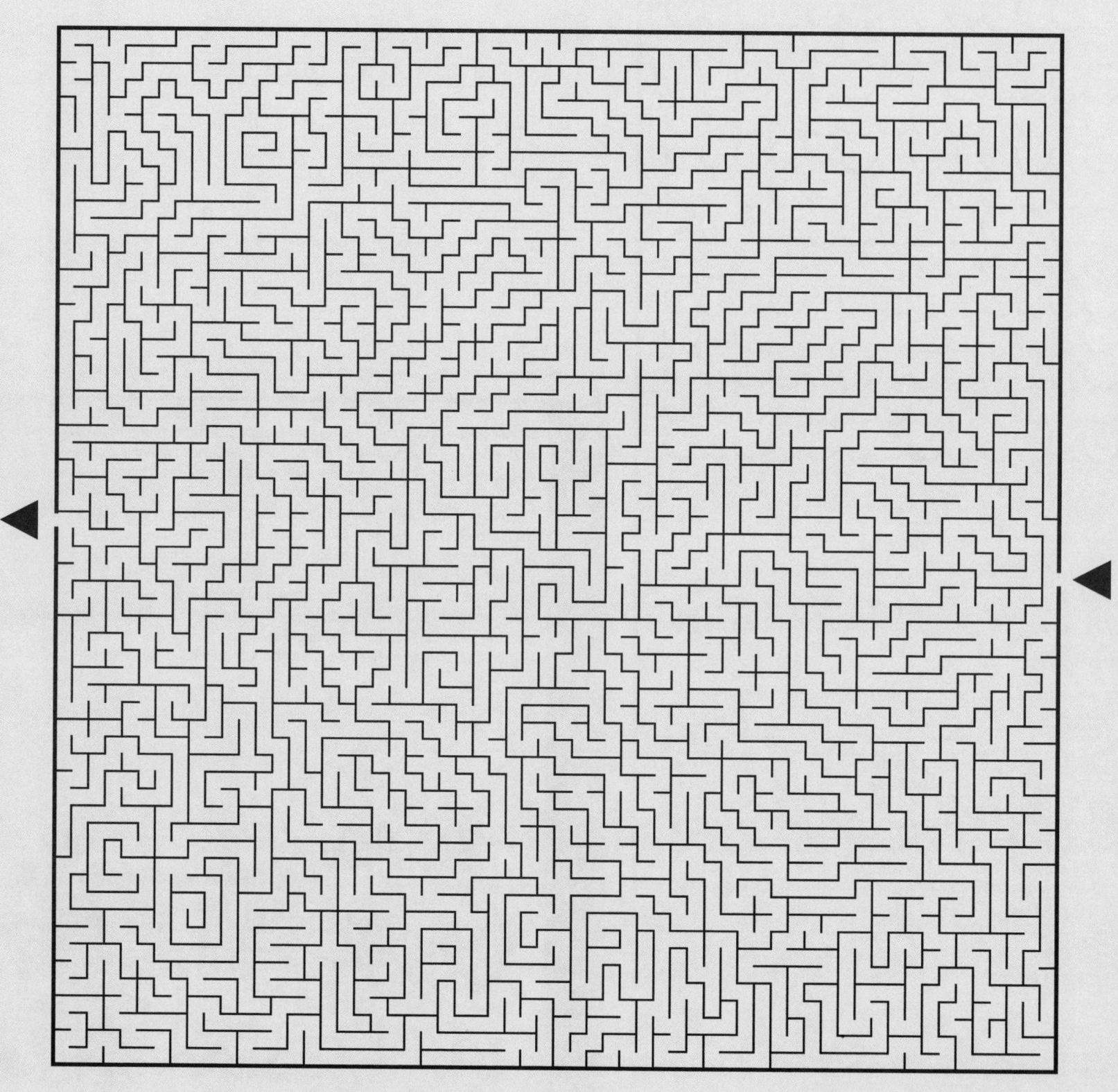

466 ACE IN PLACE

The cards Eight to King of each suit, together with the Ace of Hearts, have been placed in a 5 x 5 square. Figures and letters of the values – 8, 9, T, J, Q, K and suits – C, D, H, S have been placed at the end of each line across and down. With the Ace in place and the fact that the two cards shown at the top left belong in the shaded squares, can you work out the unique place for each card?

467 DOTTY DILEMMA

Connect adjacent dots with vertical or horizontal lines so that a single loop is formed with no crossings or branches. Each number indicates how many lines surround it, while empty cells may be surrounded by any number of lines.

468 OFF TO UNI

Four school friends are off to different universities to take different courses. Can you complete the enrolment form with each girl's full name, subject and destination?

1 Barbara who is not Moore is studying Physics but not at Princeton.
2 Diana is not Jones who is neither the student going to Harvard nor the one studying Chemistry.
3 The student reading Maths at Yale is not Moore.
4 Clare Taylor is at MIT but is not the student reading Biology who is not Brown nor is either of these Anna.

FORENAME	SURNAME	SUBJECT	UNIVERSITY

469 NINE NUMBERS

Place a number from 1 to 9 in each empty cell so that each row, each column and each 3 x 3 block contains all the numbers from 1 to 9.

			5					3
	1				9			
		2		6				
8				7		5		
	6						1	
	9		3					4
			1		8			
	7					2		
4				9				

135

470 KARL KRACK'S CIRCUS

Karl Krack, who owns a small travelling circus, believes that variety is the spice of life and for each show he alters the order of his eight acts. Can you work out what the order will be for tonight's performance?

The Flying Fortresses are three acts after Fred the Fire-eater who is not the opening act. The Clever Clowns are two acts before Jim the Juggler who is not the closing act. The Agilles Acrobats are on immediately after the Crazy Carvellos but are before Senor Pedro's Poodles which are two acts before Madame Poll's Parrots.

1	2	3	4
5	6	7	8

472 MISMATCHES

The numbers 1–10 are to be entered in the top row of boxes, so that none is in its correct numerical position, counting from left to right, and no two consecutive numbers are adjacent to each other. The letters A–J are to be entered in the bottom row, so that none is in its correct alphabetical position, left to right, none is below its correct number (A=1 B=2 etc.), and no two consecutive letters, and no vowels, are adjacent. The number 1 is not with letter I; the letter below 9 is one place earlier in the alphabet than that below 8. The second number from the left is three higher than the number of the letter below it; the eighth number from the left is two lower than the number of its letter. The left-hand number is two lower than the right-hand number; the left-hand letter is three later in the alphabet than the right-hand letter. The fourth and seventh from the left are vowels – the numbers above them total 10. 10 is somewhere left of A; 8 is somewhere left of D; 2 is somewhere right of E, and 4 is somewhere right of C. The third letter from the left is three earlier in the alphabet than the sixth. There is one box between 4 (left) and D, and one between A (left) and 7. Can you match numbers and letters?

474 LOGIPICK

Following the first diagram, there is a logical rule that determines how the next block is to be filled in. Given these three blocks, can you colour in the fourth?

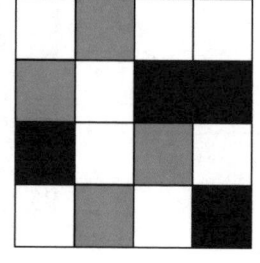   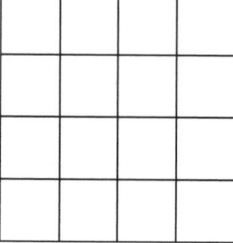

471 NINE NUMBERS

Place a number from 1 to 9 in each empty cell so that each row, each column and each 3 x 3 block contains all the numbers from 1 to 9.

						5	8	4
	2	3						
6	7			1			3	
4				2				
1								9
				3				7
	3			4			2	6
			3	7				
	5	8	9					

473 DOTTY DILEMMA

Connect adjacent dots with vertical or horizontal lines so that a single loop is formed with no crossings or branches. Each number indicates how many lines surround it, while empty cells may be surrounded by any number of lines.

```
  0        3      3
1 2   3 3  3    2 0
      3    0  3
      3  1    1
3 1 3      3     1 0 3
  1
0     2   1 2        1
2   3 2 3    0 2    0
  2    0    3    1
  1   1 1 3 3 2    3
    2            2
0    3 1   2 1    3
1    2 1     2 1  2
  3              2
    3   1 3 3  2    3
  2   3    3    1
3     1 2  1  0 3    0
1    3  3 3  2    1
      3
  2 3 2    1      2 1 3
      3   3 2 2
         0 3    1
2 0   3   1  3    3 3
  3       1    0
```

475 FOOTBALL CRAZY

Can you tell which two different balls appear three times in this picture?

476 LOGI-5

Each line, across and down, is to have each of the five colours appearing once each. Each colour must also appear just once in each shape, shown by thick lines. Can you colour in this crazy quilt, or mark each square with its correct letter B, G, R, V or Y?

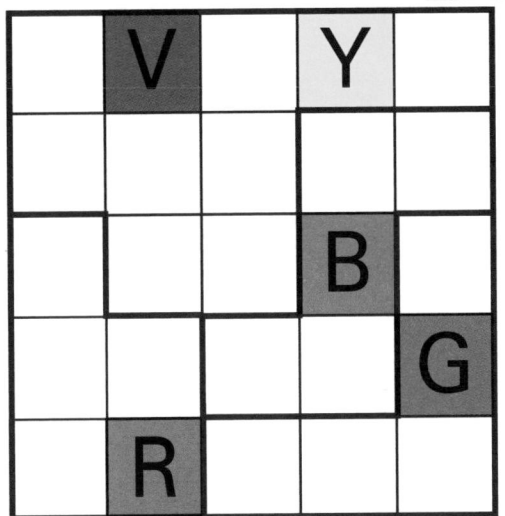

	V		Y	
			B	
				G
	R			

477 CODE MASTER

Just follow the rules of that classic puzzle, Master Mind, to crack the number code. The first number tells you how many of the digits are exactly correct – the right digit in the right place (✓✓). The second number tells you how many digits are the correct number but are not in the right place (✓). By comparing the information given by each line, can you work out which number goes in which place?

✓✓ ✓

2	5	9	4	0	1
4	3	6	9	0	1
0	5	9	8	1	2
7	2	1	0	1	1
5	9	7	1	0	2

478 TOTTERING TOWERS ●●

These piles of bricks aren't the random results of child's play – but clues to the final, at present, blank tower on the right. Like the rest, that tower has one brick with each of the six letters.

The numbers below each heap tell you two things:
(a) How many adjacent pairs of bricks are actually correct in the final tower.
(b) How many adjacent pairs of bricks make a correct pair but the wrong way up.

So: would score one on the first number if the final tower had an A directly above a C. It would score one on the second number if the final tower had C on top of A. From all of this, can you create the tower before it finally topples?

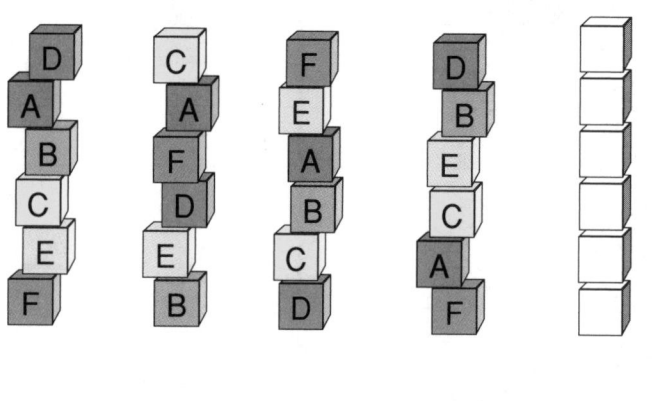

PAIRS					
Correct	0	0	0	1	5
Reversed	0	3	1	1	0

479 BITS AND PIECES ●

Which one of the numbered pieces can be used to repair the cat's tankard?

480 BATTLESHIPS ●●

Do you remember the old game of battleships? These puzzles are based on that idea. Your task is to find the vessels in the diagram. Some parts of boats or sea squares have already been filled in, and a number next to a row or column refers to the number of occupied squares in that row or column. The boats may be positioned horizontally or vertically, but no two boats or parts of boats are in adjacent squares – horizontally, vertically or diagonally.

Aircraft carrier:
Battleships:
Cruisers:
Destroyers:

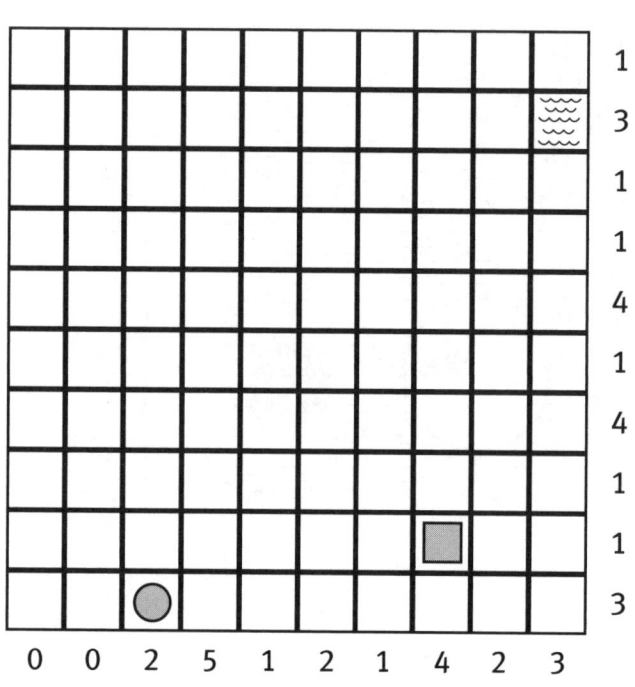

481 NINE NUMBERS ●●●

Place a number from 1 to 9 in each empty cell so that each row, each column and each 3 x 3 block contains all the numbers from 1 to 9.

		9				8		
6	1			7			9	
	2				5			
		1		2				7
	5					4		
8		3		4				
	9				3			
7			6			2	8	
4				5				

482 NUMBER KROSS

See how quickly you can fit all these numbers into the grid. We've filled one figure in to start you off.

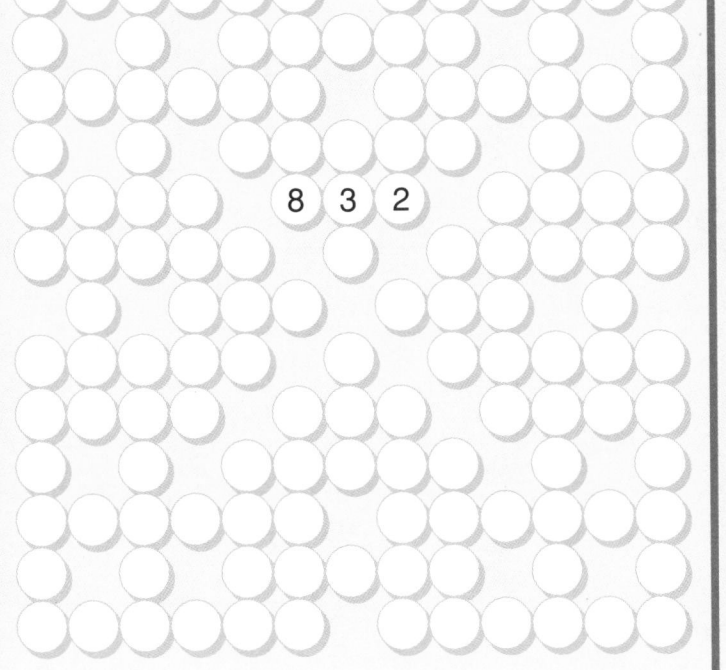

8 3 2

3 figures	5 figures	6 figures
161	10703	116285
256	11802	162564
378	23326	216432
430	29110	263646
562	30879	357874
656	37207	384858
777	41296	412241
832	42407	478439
	59275	538458
	60417	583218
	69292	645444
4 figures	70596	715227
1133	79828	759657
1762	80903	843358
2656	89134	958555
3675	97126	967864
4864		
5254		
6047		
8398		

483 BUBBLE TROUBLE

How many bubbles has this breathless girl blown?

484 TRACERY MAZE

Can you find your way through this maze?

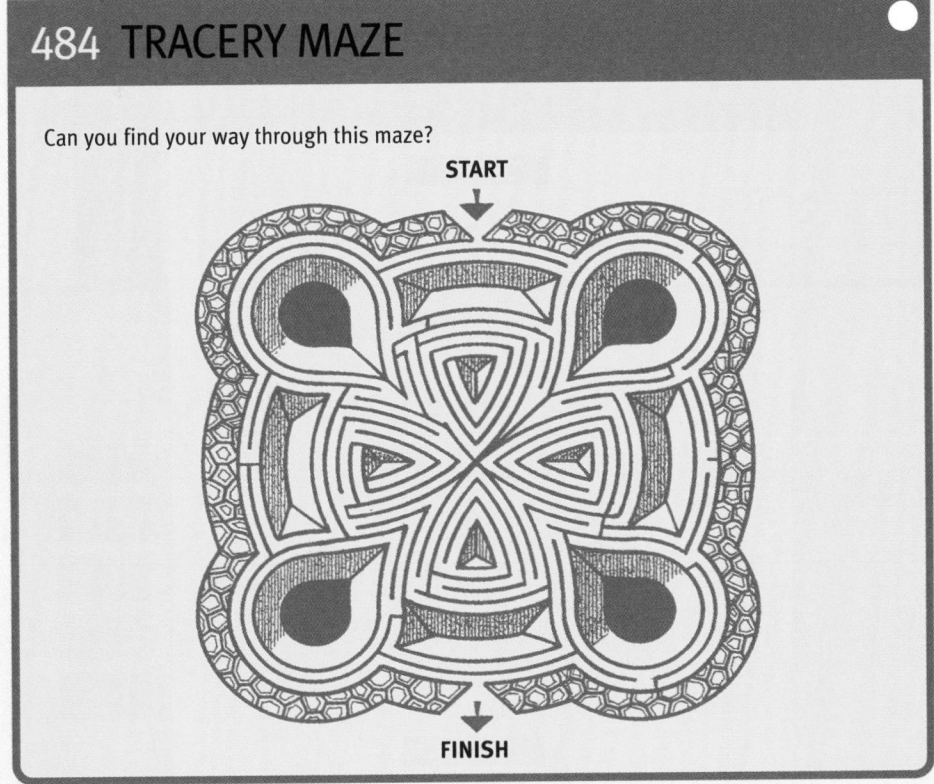

START

FINISH

485 NUMBER KROSS

See how quickly you can fit all these numbers into the grid. We've filled one figure in to start you off.

3 figures	5 figures	6 figures
180	13131	151617
215	15209	170154
~~309~~	20415	278145
405	21775	279156
581	31001	313108
618	33403	351057
747	40756	417934
941	43519	428496
	50221	543716
4 figures	57391	601537
1152	67890	629313
2145	69104	656667
3576	70395	770198
4336	71878	854352
5174	82701	931867
6713	90417	990173
7564		
8105		

486 PIXELATED PICS

The numbers in the squares tell you how many of it and its neighbours are to be filled in. A square can have up to eight neighbours.

1	2	3
8	X	4
7	6	5

Using logic alone and the filled cell, can you fill in the pixels and create a celebratory still-life?

0		2		1		2		1		0		1		2
	2		4		1		3		1		1		3	
0		6		3		1		3		2		3		1
	3		5		1		1		3		3		1	
2		4		3		0		1		4		1		0
	3		3		3		0		3		3		0	
3		3		3		0		0		3		0		0
	3		3		3		0		3		3		0	
3		2		3		1		1		5		1		0
	3		1		3		1		6		6		1	
3		0		3		5		6		9		6		2
	4		2		4		4		6		6		4	
3		4		5		6		4		3		3		2
	6		6		3		2		1		0		1	
3		4		5		4		3		1		2		2
	4		2		3		1		3		2		4	
3		0		3		3		1		3		5		2
	3		0		3		0		2		6		3	
3		3		4		2		2		5		3		0
	3		3		2		1		4		3		0	

487 EASY AS ABC

Each row and column originally contained one A, one B, one C, one D and two blank squares. Each letter and number refers to the first or second of the four letters encountered when travelling in the direction of the arrow. Can you complete the original grid?

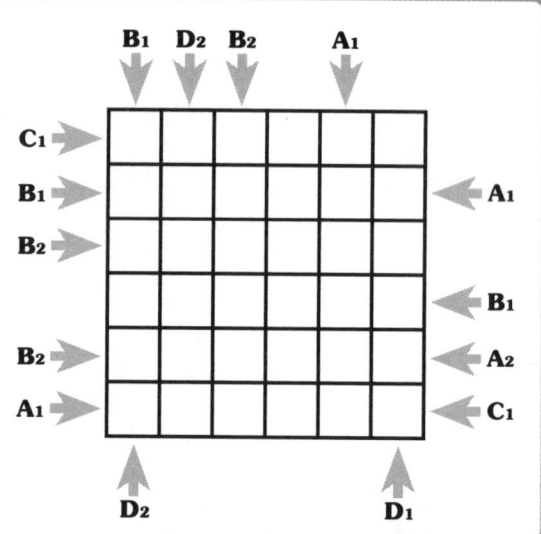

488 CODE MASTER

Just follow the rules of that classic puzzle, Master Mind, to crack the number code. The first number tells you how many of the digits are exactly correct – the right digit in the right place (✓✓). The second number tells you how many digits are the correct number but are not in the right place (✓). By comparing the information given by each line, can you work out which number goes in which place?

✓✓ ✓

2	4	3	1	5	0	2
8	2	1	3	4	2	0
1	9	6	2	7	1	3
6	4	1	7	9	0	4
7	5	9	6	8	1	2

489 NINE NUMBERS

Place a number from 1 to 9 in each empty cell so that each row, each column and each 3 x 3 block contains all the numbers from 1 to 9.

				2	3	4	9	
1				6	8			
2								
5	8							
9	4			7			6	3
							2	5
								1
			9	4				7
	6	3	2	5				

490 DOTTY DILEMMA

Connect adjacent dots with vertical or horizontal lines so that a single loop is formed with no crossings or branches. Each number indicates how many lines surround it, while empty cells may be surrounded by any number of lines.

```
. 3 . 3 .   . 2 . 3 .   . 1 . 3 .
  3 . 3 .   . 3 . 2 .   . 3 . 3
. 1 . 1 .   . 2 . 2 .   . 1 . 1 .
  3 . 3 .   . 3 . 3 .   . 3 . 1

. 3 . 1 .   . 0 . 1 .   . 1 . 3 .
  3 . 3 .   . 1 . 1 .   . 1 . 3
. 3 . 1 .   . 1 . 1 .   . 3 . 1 .
  1 . 3 .   . 0 . 1 .   . 1 . 1

. 0 . 1 .   . 0 . 3 .   . 3 . 3 .
  1 . 1 .   . 3 . 0 .   . 3 . 1
. 0 . 1 .   . 0 . 3 .   . 1 . 1 .
  1 . 1 .   . 3 . 0 .   . 3 . 3

. 3 . 3 .   . 1 . 1 .   . 2 . 3 .
  0 . 3 .   . 1 . 1 .   . 2 . 2
. 3 . 3 .   . 1 . 1 .   . 2 . 3 .
  0 . 3 .   . 1 . 0 .   . 3 . 3

. 1 . 1 .   . 3 . 3 .   . 1 . 1 .
  1 . 1 .   . 0 . 3 .   . 0 . 1
. 1 . 1 .   . 3 . 3 .   . 0 . 1 .
  0 . 1 .   . 0 . 3 .   . 1 . 1
```

492 IT FIGURES

Place a number from 1 to 9 in each empty cell so that the sum of each vertical or horizontal block equals the number at the top or on the left of that block. Numbers may only be used once in each block.

491 TOTTERING TOWERS

These piles of bricks aren't the random results of child's play – but clues to the final, at present, blank tower on the right. Like the rest, that tower has one brick in each of the six colours.
The numbers below each heap tell you two things:
(a) How many adjacent pairs of bricks are actually correct in the final tower.
(b) How many adjacent pairs of bricks make a correct pair but the wrong way up.

So: 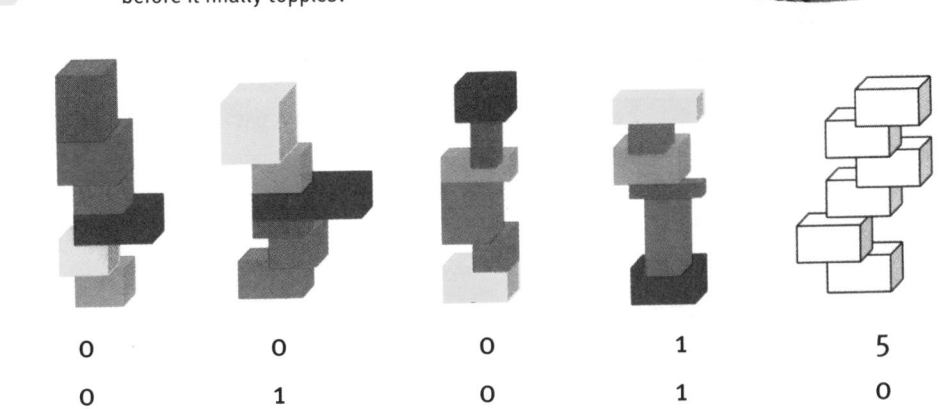 would score one on the first number if the final tower had green directly above yellow. It would score one on the second number if the final tower had yellow on top of green. From all of this, can you create the tower before it finally topples?

PAIRS					
Correct	0	0	0	1	5
Reversed	0	1	0	1	0

493 SHIP MATES

Can you pair up each of these pictures with its identical twin?

494 PAPER CHASE

Which one of the four paths must this rabbit run along in order to pick up the greatest number of pieces of paper?

495 CELL STRUCTURE

The object is to create white areas surrounded by black walls, so that:
* Each white area contains only one number.
* The number of cells in a white area is equal to the number in it.
* The white areas are separated from each other with a black wall.
* Cells containing numbers must not be filled in.
* The black cells must be linked into a continuous wall.
* Black cells cannot form a square of 2 x 2 or larger.

	1	2			1	
3	4			2		3
					3	
			2			
2		3				
				2		2
1						3
	2			2		

496 DIS-ENGAGED

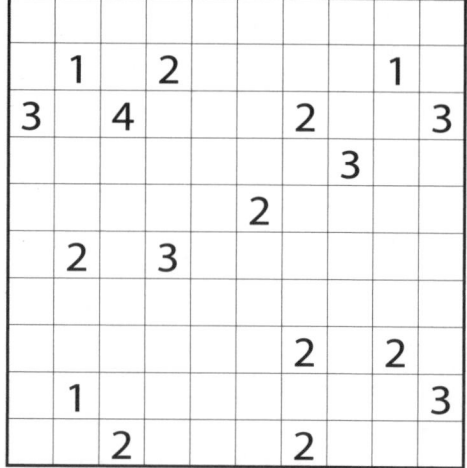

Not for the first time, the Engagements column of the South Fork Gazette has upset the parents of several brides-to-be. After the computer threw a fit, attempts by Herbert, the school-leaver screen-minder, just added to the confusion. The result was that, when the printed version hit the news-stands, no name in each announcement actually belonged with any of the other three. Can you name the now not-so-happy couples?

ENGAGEMENTS

The engagement is announced between:

Ann Chovies & Ed Lynes.
Ann Noble & Frank Copes.
Bella Daball & Frank Stamps.
Cher Chovies & Horace Stamps.
Cher Noble & Gary Baldy.
Bella Brakes & Ed Baldy.
Dawn Brakes & Horace Copes.
Cher Brakes & Frank Lynes.

497 CAROUSEL

The Carousel is a popular ride with the toddlers at Orles Fair. There are eight different animals on it and, so that the children don't get bored with it, Sid Slick, the owner, changes the positions of the animals each day. With the position of the horse given and the knowledge that the animals face and move in a clockwise direction, see if you can use the clues to work out the positions of each animal and child on today's ride.

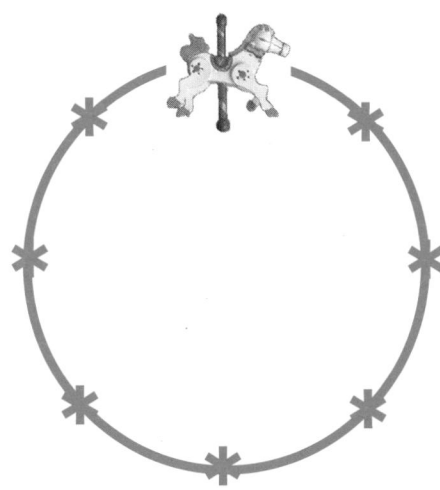

1 No child is either next to or opposite another with the same initial.
2 Biddie is opposite the camel and two places in front of Robin.
3 Brian is opposite the zebra and two places behind the unicorn.
4 The emu is opposite Simon and immediately behind Tess's animal, which is opposite the peacock.
5 Tom is opposite the horse, but is not next to either the peacock or Simon.
6 There is also a dragon on the Carousel, Sheila is one of the riders and both birds have girls sitting on them.
7 The elephant is two places in front of Rose.

498 CUBE ROUTE

The symbols on each face have a meaning – Up, Down, Right or Left. Each sign has only one meaning which is the same for every face. There is a direction for each symbol which will lead to a unique path joining Start (S) to End (E) and which passes through all three faces. Can you let your brain do the logical walking and make the journey?

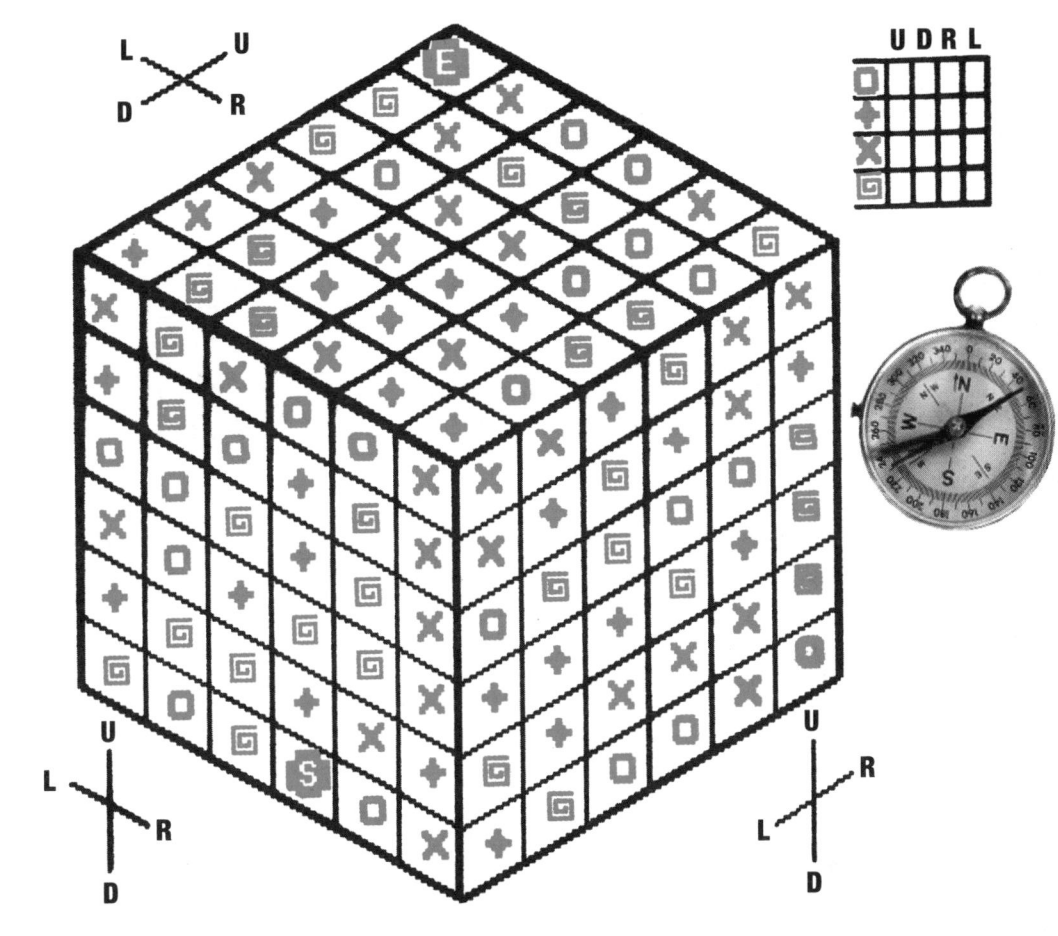

499 NINE-CARD TRICK

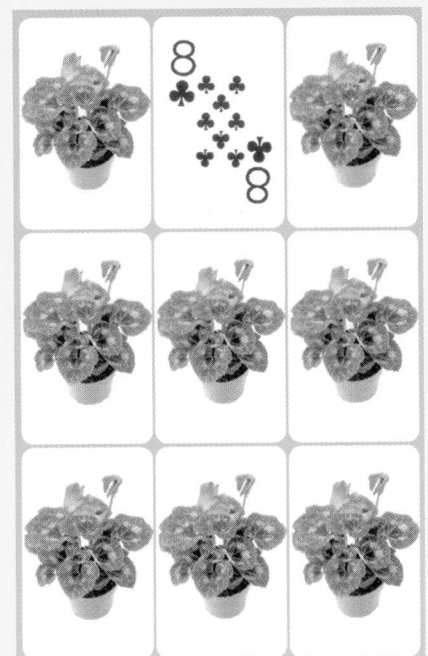

Cards numbered from 2 to 10, which is not in the right-hand column, are set out as shown in the diagram with one card face up.

The numbers on any three cards in a line, vertically, horizontally or diagonally, add up to the same total. No card shares an edge with one of its own colour or a corner with one of its own suit and also there are more Diamonds than Hearts. Can you correctly identify the other eight cards?

500 SUM COLUMNS

Move as few numbers as possible so that both columns have the same total!

0	5
8	7
4	9
2	1
3	6
17	**28**

501 TENTACKLE

Eight children are camping, two to each tent, and some have given us a couple of clues as to how to find them. The trouble is their directions are as bad as their cooking and in each case only one direction is true whilst the other is an exact opposite, so that East should read West etc. Directions are not necessarily exact so North could be North, Northeast or Northwest. To help you one child is already tucked into a sleeping bag.

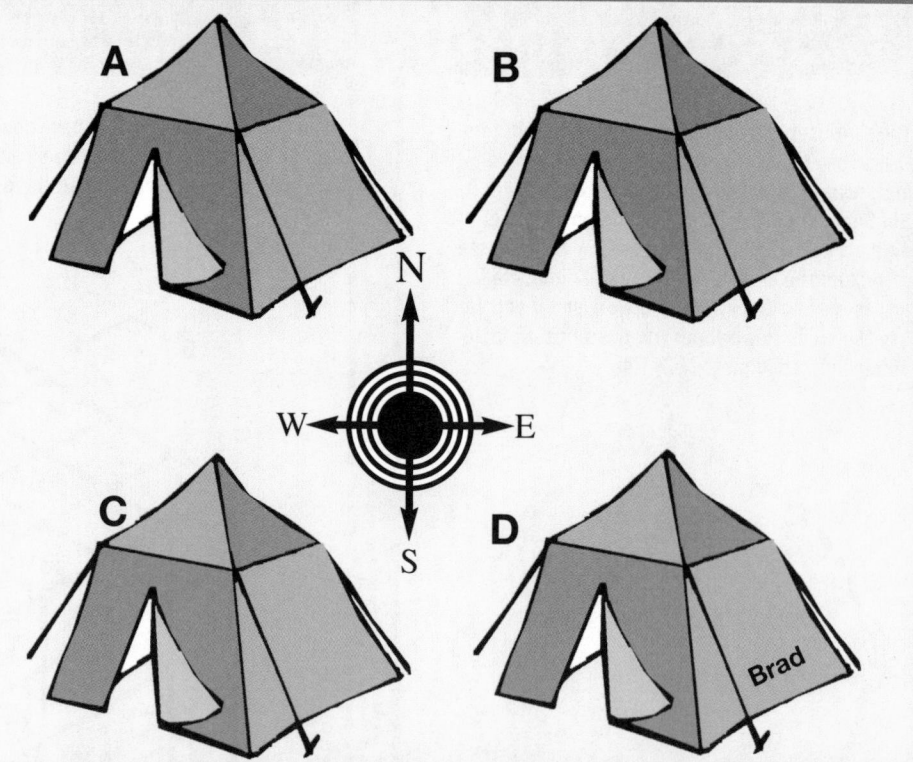

Alvin says: "I'm East of Harvey and South of Dexter."
Dexter says: "I'm West of Frank and North of Elmer."
Frank says: "I'm West of Conrad and North of Brad."
Gary says: "I'm West of Elmer and South of Harvey."

502 CODE MASTER

Just follow the rules of that classic puzzle, Master Mind, to crack the number code. The first number tells you how many of the digits are exactly correct – the right digit in the right place (✓✓). The second number tells you how many digits are the correct number but are not in the right place (✓). By comparing the information given by each line, can you work out which number goes in which place?

					✓✓	✓
3	1	0	4	5	1	1
0	8	1	9	2	0	2
1	4	5	9	7	1	3
3	6	4	5	7	1	2
4	5	2	8	6	1	1

503 EASY AS ABC

Each row and column originally contained one A, one B, one C, one D and two blank squares. Each letter and number refers to the first or second of the four letters encountered when travelling in the direction of the arrow. Can you complete the original grid?

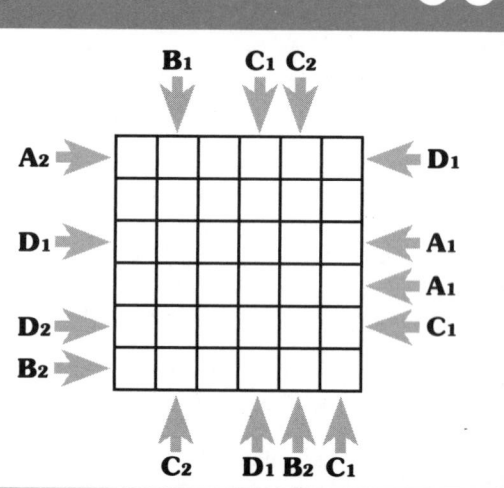

504 CARDS ON THE TABLE

The 13 cards of a suit plus 2 Jokers are shuffled and dealt in a line. No two consecutive cards are adjacent, no Joker or court card is at either end, and no two court cards are adjacent.

Ace is two places left of Queen, 2 is two places left of 8, one Joker two left of 3, the other Joker somewhere left of both, and between 6 (left) and 10. 7 is two left of 4, Jack two right of King, 5 somewhere right of 9, which is somewhere right of 7, which is somewhere right of 10.

Ace is left of 7.

The 7th and 10th cards from the left are even (Ace = 1, King = 13, Q = 12, Jack = 11 and a Joker is neither odd nor even). The Queen is left of the King. The 3rd and 10th cards from the left total 12, as do the 8th and 15th.

Can you locate each card?

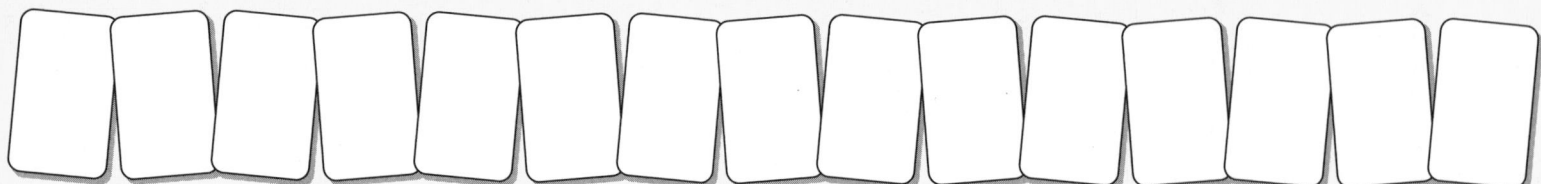

505 NETWORK

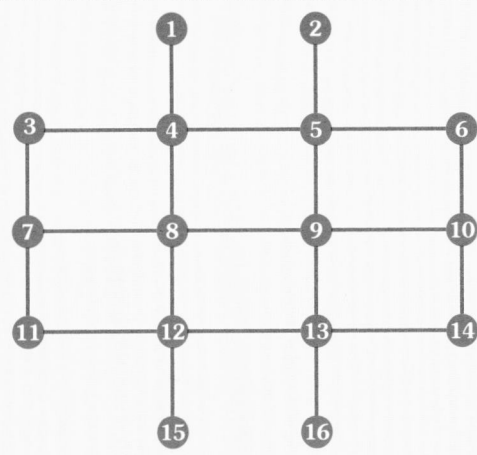

The letters A–P are to be arranged in the diagram, with one letter allocated to each point, so that no two consecutive letters are connected by any direct line i.e., 1–15 or 7–10. F is to the left of, and in the same horizontal line as I, which is above C. H and D are both somewhere left of B though not necessarily in the same line. P is somewhere higher than J, O somewhere higher than F, H somewhere higher than M and L somewhere higher than E but not necessarily in the same line.

B is diagonally adjacent to G and A is diagonally adjacent to C. N is the greatest distance possible from O.

L is immediately left of I, G immediately left of K, J immediately left of C and D immediately left of O.

If the positions of the letters E and F add up to 17 can you place each letter in its correct position?

506 DOTTY DILEMMA

Connect adjacent dots with vertical or horizontal lines so that a single loop is formed with no crossings or branches. Each number indicates how many lines surround it, while empty cells may be surrounded by any number of lines.

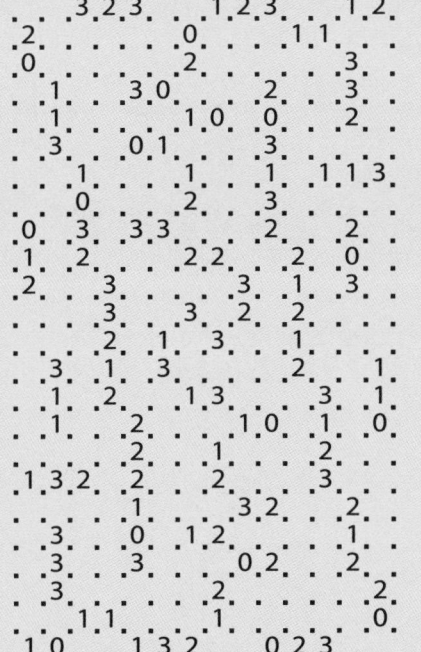

508 POLICE SQUAD

Siren screaming, Frank Drabin pulled his squad car into the side of the road, demolishing three trash cans and a pizza stand. He raced into the building, gun drawn, took the stairs three at a time and gave them back two at a time. Finally he turned into a square hallway and crouched down behind an aspidistra.

"What have we got, Ed?"

A nearby rubber plant shook its leaves.

"We got a gunman or gunmen, Frank. We also have one informer who tipped us off."

"Where are they?"

"We're not sure – but somewhere in the five rooms leading off this landing."

"Well, just open 'em up one at a time and go in blasting."

"No can do, Frank. We've almost used our quota of bullets for the month and we don't want to hit the informer."

"I see someone's been playing games – put notices on the doors."

"Yeah – before we got here. They're trying to confuse us."

"Each stuck a note on his door and maybe on an empty door as well. The notice on the informer's door is entirely true. The notice on any gunman's door is completely false."

"And the empty rooms?"

"The notice may be either entirely true or entirely false."

"So where's the gunman/men?"

Rm 2 has a gunman. Rm 4 is empty. **1**

Room 1 is empty. The note on door 4 is false. **2**

There is a gunman in Rm 5. Rm 2 is empty. **3**

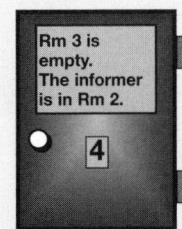

Rm 3 is empty. The informer is in Rm 2. **4**

The sign on door 3 is false. The informer is in Rm 2. **5**

507 TALENT SPOTTING

Once the electronic scoreboard had fused at Mutlins Camp Talent Night, chaos was the result. Later that evening, six Purple Coats stopped smiling at holidaymakers and tried to work out the score. Here's what each thought:

The dancer was 6th. The escapologist won.
The impressionist was 4th. The magician was 6th.
The escapologist was 3rd. The baritone was 6th.

The baritone was 4th. The comedian was 3rd.
The dancer was 4th. The magician was 2nd.
The dancer was 5th. The comedian was 4th.

Each actually had one position correct and one wrong in his/her pair of statements. At that point, they gave up. But with your puzzling skill, can you work out the place in which each contestant finished?

509 PARTY TIME ●●

Party time and the table is all set up with eight coloured cakes in position waiting for the children to sit down and tuck in. From the information below can you work out where each child will be sitting?

At Lisa's birthday party boys and girls are alternately seated. Tom has the yellow cake on one side and is opposite a 'D' child. John and Jenny are next to each other but neither is next to the blue cake. Moira has the orange cake on one side and Dan on the other. Moira is not opposite Gwen who is not next to Dick.

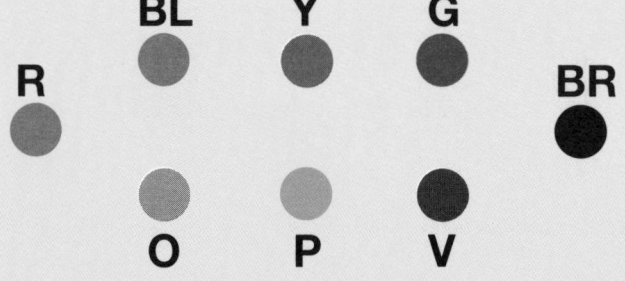

511 LOGI-5 ●●

Each line, across and down, is to have each of the five colours appearing once each. Each colour must also appear just once in each shape, shown by thick lines. Can you colour in this crazy quilt, or mark each square with its correct letter B, G, R, V or Y?

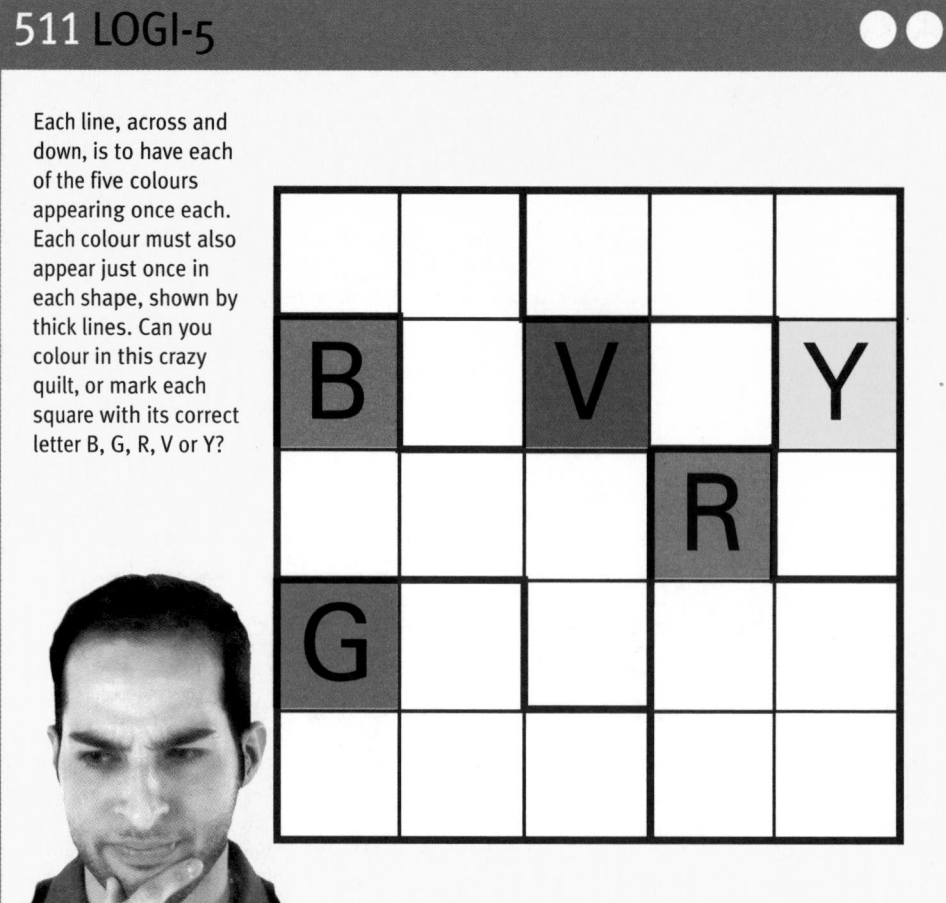

510 NUMBER KROSS ●●

See how quickly you can fit all these numbers into the grid. We've filled one number in to start you off.

3 figures
115
242
301
429
706
743
816
929

4 figures
1557
2154
3918
4177
5172
6855
7050
9230

5 figures
10201

17926
21223
22107
32379
37135
41327
41670
51078
53071
60606
71230
72325
80128
91837
91917

6 figures
107000
167245
214412
314253

393794
403958
455514
503040
514171
644721
671517
701419
715926
804717
958473
981739

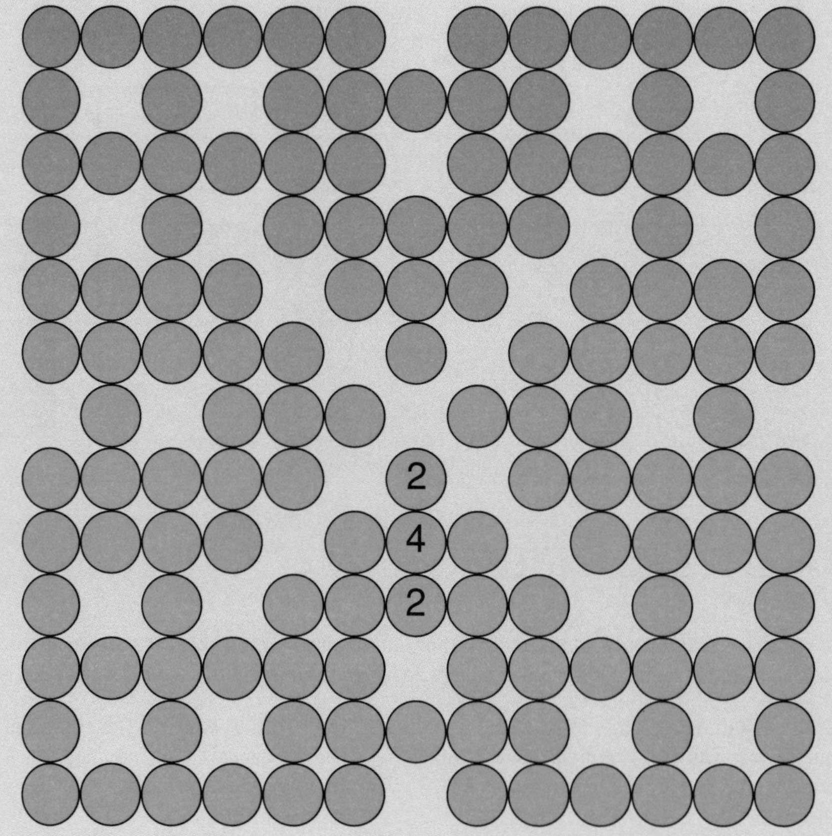

146

Travel from the entrance to the exit of the maze, filling the path completely to create a picture.

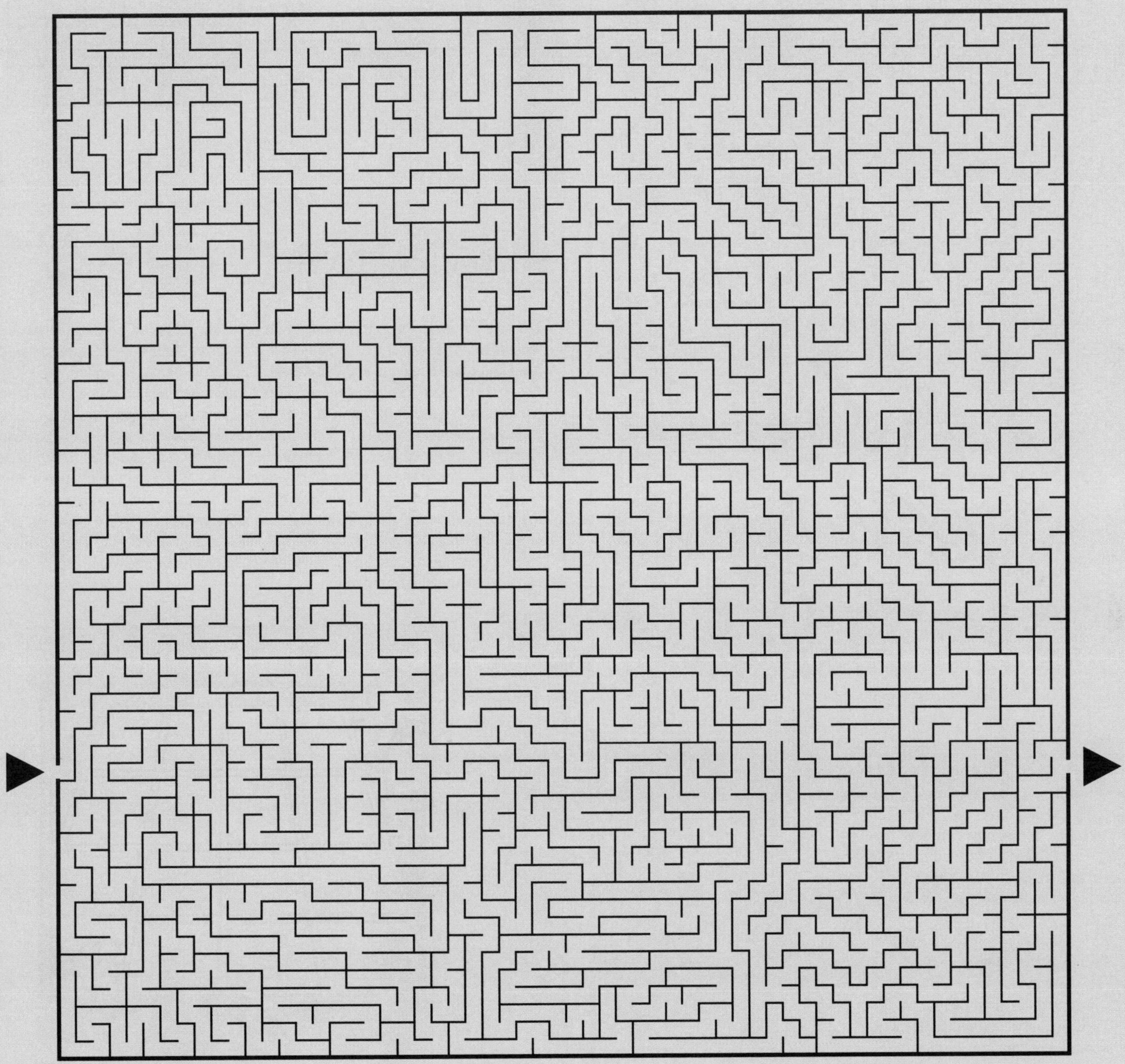

513 ALL OF A FLUTTER

Bean's fancy-dress costume has attracted lots of butterflies! Can you see which type of butterfly is the only one to appear three times in this picture?

515 EASY AS ABC

Each row and column originally contained one A, one B, one C, one D and two blank squares. Each letter and number refers to the first or second of the four letters encountered when travelling in the direction of the arrow. Can you complete the original grid?

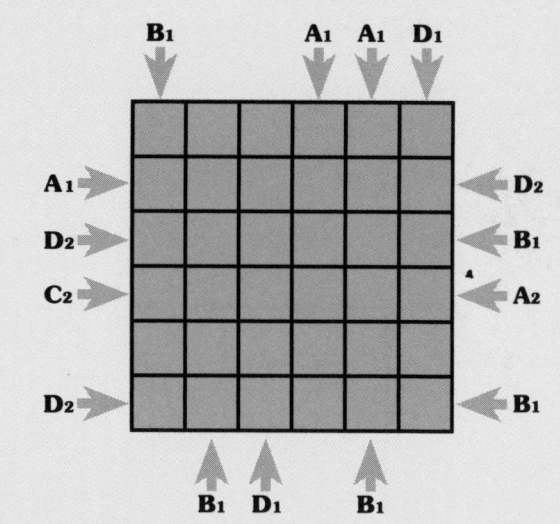

516 FRUIT AND VEG

The display on Gert's stall is changed around daily, partly to make yesterday's produce look fresh. Whatever the arrangement, fruit and vegetables always alternate along the rows and down the lines and left and right are as you gaze on wondering if you have the nerve to ask if the dates are ripe. The turnips are one line to the right of the bananas which are in the same line down as the marrows which are in the same line across as the lychees which are not in the same line across as the potatoes which are directly above the apples which are further to the left and lower than the peas which are directly below the cherries which are two lines to the right of the yams which are higher than and one place to the left of the watercress which is directly to the left of the kumquats which are one line down from the grapes which are two lines to the right of the figs which are higher than but not in the same line down as the radishes which are one place below and one place to the right of the turnips which are three rows higher than the illustrated onions.

514 CELL STRUCTURE

Each circle containing a number represents an island. The object is to connect each island with vertical or horizontal bridges so that:
* The number of bridges is the same as the number inside the island.
* There can be up to two bridges between two islands
* Bridges cannot cross islands or other bridges.
* There is a continuous path connecting all the islands.

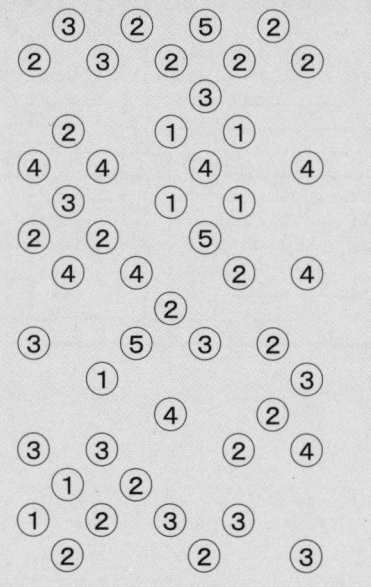

517 NUMBER KROSS

3 figures	5 figures	6 figures
152	10576	101316
234	20231	210211
387	23327	252426
489	30213	305306
516	37733	395446
(650)	40006	414342
713	41425	420395
834	50139	515253
	50289	537219
4 figures	61577	625773
1918	63414	636669
2227	70318	747176
3514	71902	773355
4530	78470	817512
5995	80817	918317
6130	91532	995033
7476		
8104		

See how quickly you can fit all these numbers into the grid. We've filled one number in to start you off.

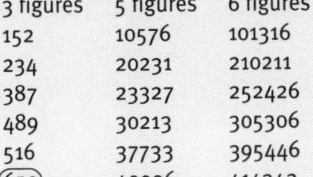

518 LINE UP

Can you follow a continuous black line in this picture from the arrow by the camera to the arrow by the bird's tail? No jumping over gaps!

519 DOTTING DILEMMA

Connect adjacent dots with vertical or horizontal lines so that a single loop is formed with no crossings or branches. Each number indicates how many lines surround it, while empty cells may be surrounded by any number of lines.

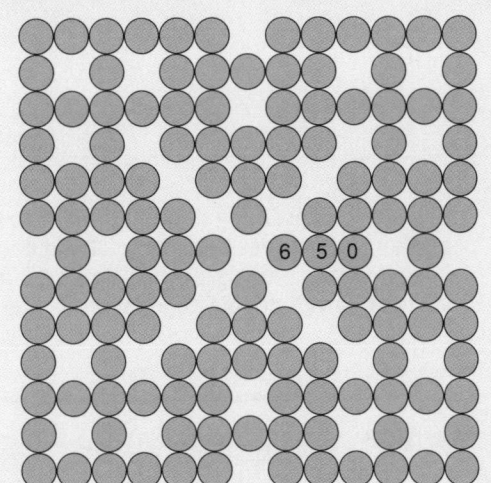

520 ARMS AND THE MAN

The Grand-Duke Hans Niess-und-Bumpzer-Dazi had a very long pedigree, giving rise to the four quarterings on his coat-of-arms. From the clues given below, can you name the creature depicted in each of the quarters numbered 1 to 4, say in which colour it is displayed, and name the Middle-European family whose arms were introduced into the Grand-Duke's family's as a result of various dynastic marriages over the centuries?

Clues

1 The pink elephant, badge of a family of noted drinkers, appears in the quarter directly above the one inherited from the Klotzky family arms.

2 The creature which is depicted in black has appeared on the Grand-Ducal arms since Hans' grandfather married the eldest daughter of Count von Plonka.

3 The lion of the Muddelkopfs, which is not orange, is to be seen in an odd-numbered quarter of the arms.

4 The dragon is immediately to the right of the blue creature.

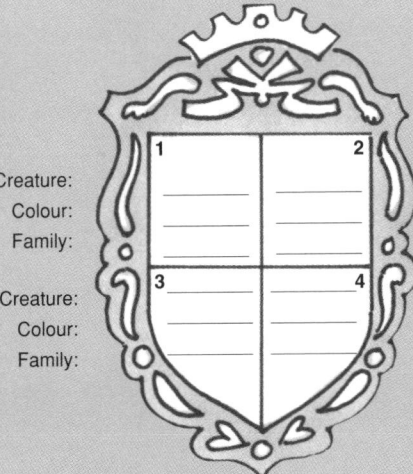

Creature:
Colour:
Family:

Creature:
Colour:
Family:

Creatures: dragon; eagle; elephant; lion
Colours: black; blue; orange; pink
Families: Klotzky; Muddelkopf; Nitwitz; von Plonka

Starting tip: Begin by identifying the creature depicted in quarter number 4.

521 TEE TIME

Three old timers play a weekly game of golf on the Golden Lawns 18-hole, par 72, course. Each score at every hole falls into one of five categories. Each golfer gets a different result, greater than zero in each category. Also, no category has the same result for another player, i.e., if a players has two eagles, he has a different number in the other four and no other player has two eagles. With the score details below and the information given, can you fill in their card?

	Eagle −2	Birdie −1	Par 0	Bogey +1	Double Bogey +2	FINAL SCORE
Parnell Darma						
Nick Jackliss						
Barry Clayer						

Barry scored one more par than bogeys and together they came to one more than Nick's pars. Nick got both the most eagles and double bogeys and together they equalled Parnell's pars. Barry got twice as many birdies as Nick did eagles and these were two less than Parnell's birdies. Altogether there were 20 pars. The total number of birdies was two less than the total number of bogeys and double bogeys. Nick's birdie score was not the same as either Parnell's bogey score or Barry's double bogey score.

522 SHORT AND SNAPPY

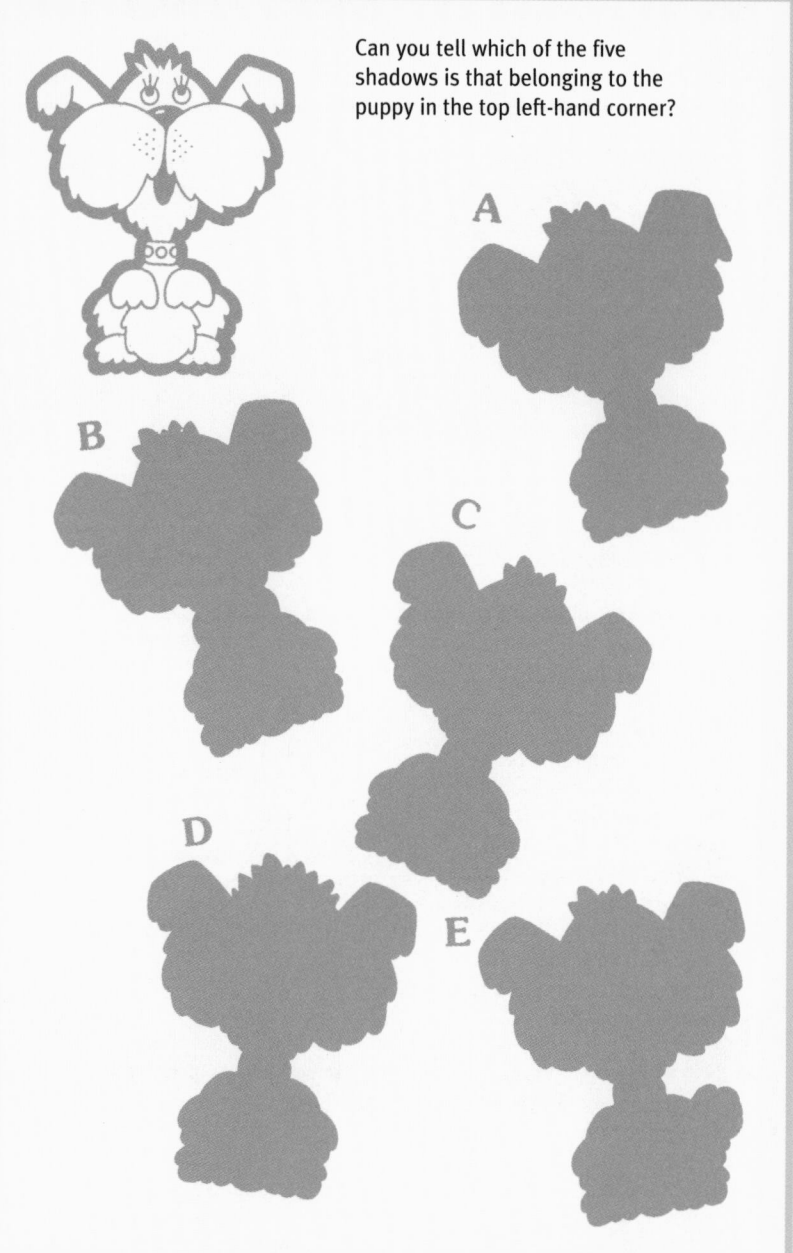

Can you tell which of the five shadows is that belonging to the puppy in the top left-hand corner?

A

B

C

D

E

523 CELL STRUCTURE

Place a number from 1 to 9 in each empty cell so that the sum of each vertical or horizontal block equals the number at the top or on the left of that block. Numbers may only be used once in each block.

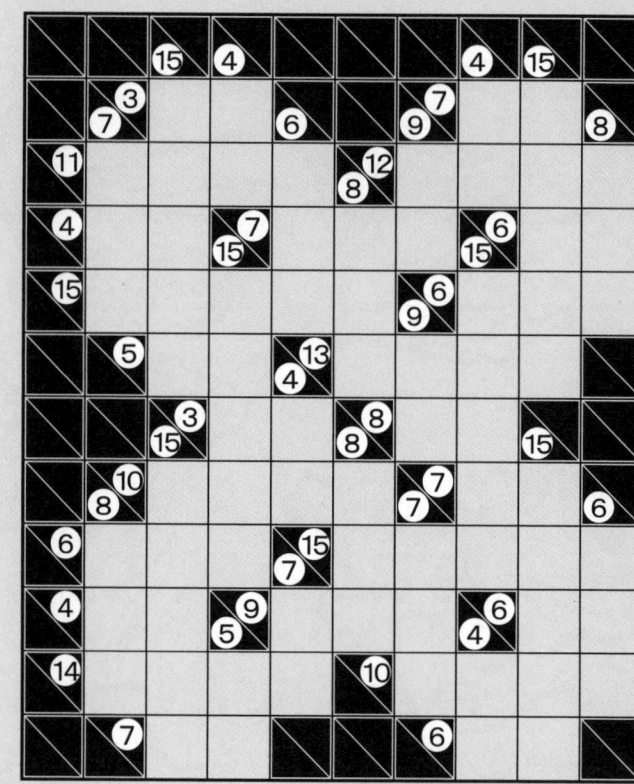

524 BATTLESHIPS

Do you remember the old game of battleships? These puzzles are based on that idea. Your task is to find the vessels in the diagram. Some parts of boats or sea squares have already been filled in, and a number next to a row or column refers to the number of occupied squares in that row or column. The boats may be positioned horizontally or vertically, but no two boats or parts of boats are in adjacent squares – horizontally, vertically or diagonally.

Aircraft carrier:

Battleships:

Cruisers:

Destroyers:

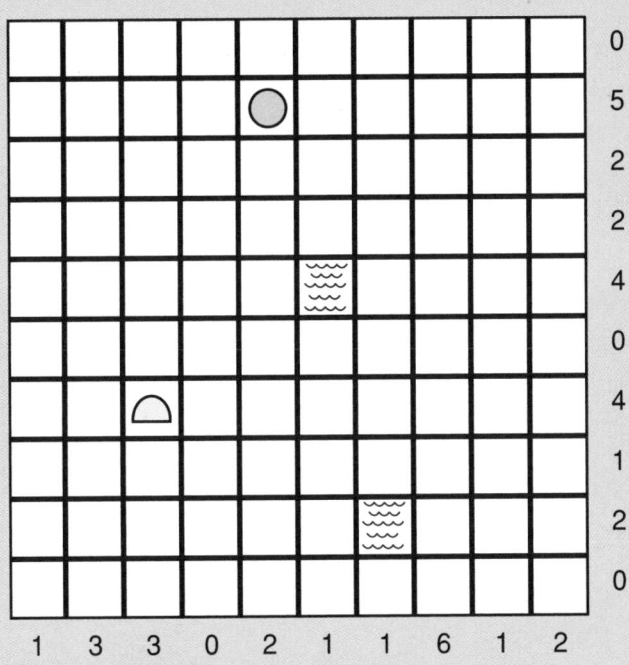

525 FLOWER POWER

There are eight differences between these two pictures – can you spot them?

526 ON COURSE

Four employees at Hall-Thumms Digital Co, have recently taken work-related courses run by Gerta Leggup's Updating Agency. From the clues, can you give, with a high degree of confidence, a summary showing each employee's name, course and cost?

Clues
1 Zebedee's course cost $200 less than Dougal's which cost $50 less than Holmes' which cost $200 more than was paid for Speedy Searching.
2 Brian's course cost more than Wexford's which, at $400 per day, was not the cheapest.
3 Advanced Surfing cost $200 more than Brown's course which cost $50 less than Florence's.
4 Dalgliesh's course cost $50 less than Novice Newsgroup which cost $250 more than Browsing For Beginners.

FORENAME	SURNAME	COURSE	COST
Brian			
Dougal			
Florence			
Zebedee			

527 CARDS ON THE TABLE

The 13 cards of a suit, plus two jokers, are shuffled and dealt in a line. No suit card is in its correct position, counting left to right, whether you begin with the Ace or both the Jokers. No court cards are adjacent to each other or to any Joker.

There is one card separating the Jokers, which are both right of all the court cards and Ace, one of which is on the extreme left. 8 is two places left of 9, Ace two left of 3, 6 two left of 2, Queen two left of Jack, 10 two left of 8, 4 three left of the first Joker from the left, King three left of Ace, 6 four left of 5, first Joker four right of the Queen.

The 4th, 7th and 10th cards from the left are odd, the 5th, 9th and 13th are even (Jokers are neither odd nor even).

Can you locate each card?

528 BREAKTHROUGH

See how quickly you can break this grid down into the 28 dominoes from which it is formed.

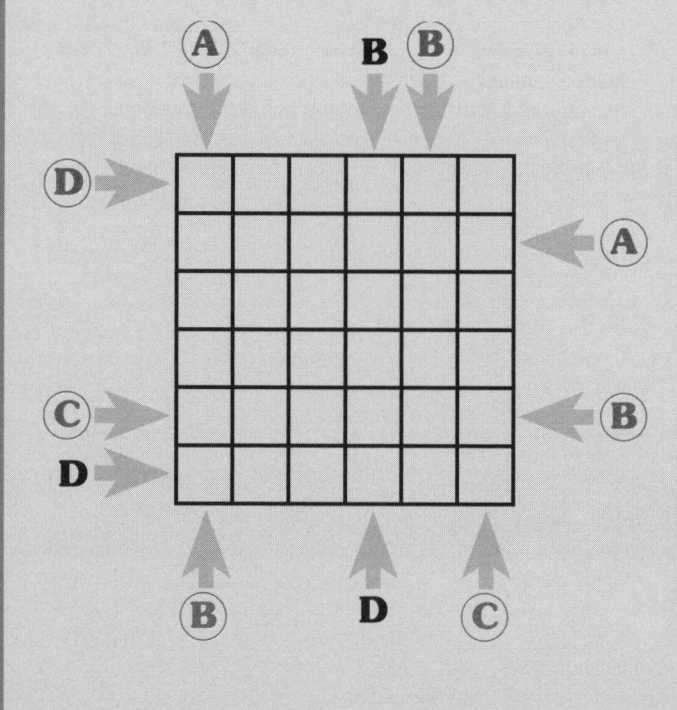

0	5	6	3	2	5	4
0	5	6	2	2	1	5
2	0	0	6	5	2	1
1	5	5	3	3	2	3
5	1	4	2	3	2	6
4	0	4	3	4	4	4
0	6	1	3	0	1	6
6	6	1	1	3	4	0

529 EASY AS ABC

Each row and column in this grid originally contained one A, one B, one C, one D and two blank squares. Each black letter refers to the first of the four letters encountered when travelling in the direction of the arrow, while each blue circled letter refers to the second of the four letters encountered when travelling in the direction of the arrow. Can you complete the original grid?

530 SHADY CHARACTER

Shade in every part of this picture that contains a vowel. What do you see?

531 AGEING FAST

Sam's mother is 63. How old is Sam if her mother is now three times as old as Sam was when her mother was as old as Sam is now? Quick—before they get any older!

532 IN THE ABSTRACT

The Museum of Modern Sculpture in Storbury has a small gallery devoted to the work of abstract sculptor Ivor Screwloose. From the clues given below, can you name the works lettered A to D in the diagram, and say in which season of which year each was produced?

Clues

1 Sculpture B represents *Dichotomy*, perhaps reflecting Ivor's state of mind in the non-leap year in which it was sculpted.

2 *Enchantment* was completed in Fall.

3 *Sorrow* was not sculpted in 1994.

4 As you look at the diagram, the sculpture named *Revenge* was completed two years after the one to its left, but earlier than the Spring sculpture, which is somewhere to its right.

5 None of the works was completed in the Summer of 1992.

Sculptures: *Dichotomy; Enchantment; Revenge; Sorrow*
Seasons: Spring; Summer; Fall; Winter
Years: 1990; 1992; 1994; 1996

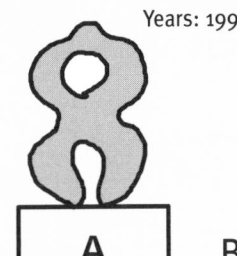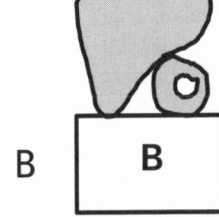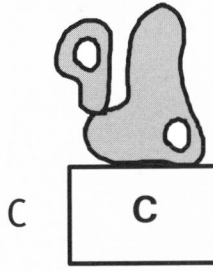

A [A]   B [B]   C [C]   D [D]

Name: _____ _____ _____ _____

Season: _____ _____ _____ _____

Year: _____ _____ _____ _____

Starting tip: Begin by placing *Revenge*.

---

533 FLYING HIGH

Can you see which of these five balloons contains two of each of the different symbols?

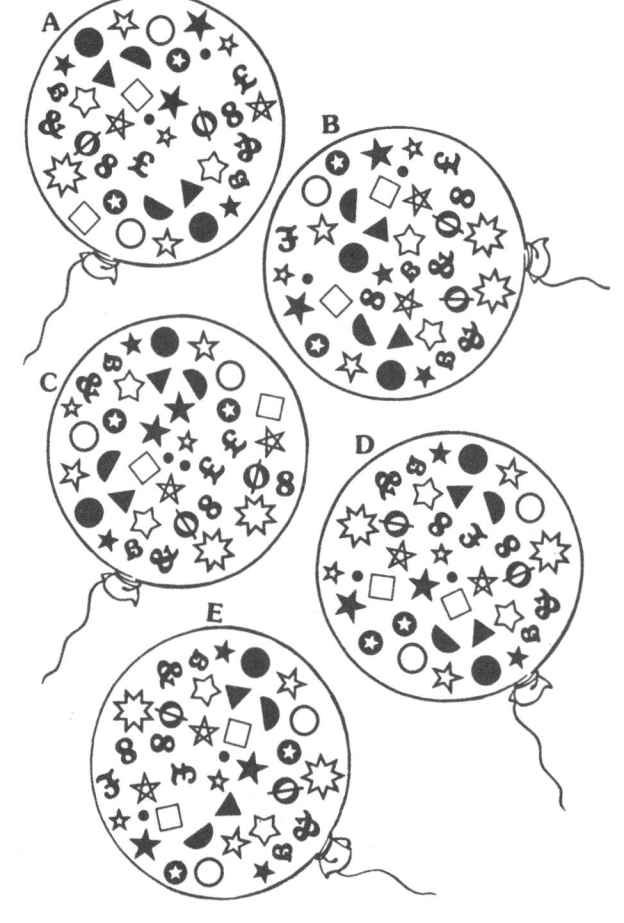

---

534 CODE MASTER

Just follow the rules of that classic puzzle Master Mind, to crack the number code. The first number tells you how many of the digits are exactly correct – the right digit in the right place (✓✓). The second number tells you how many digits are the correct number but are not in the right place (✓). By comparing the information given by each line, can you work out which number goes in which place?

					✓✓	✓
6	5	2	7	1	1	2
4	3	0	8	9	1	0
9	1	2	5	9	1	3
3	0	1	7	4	2	0
6	3	7	6	2	0	2

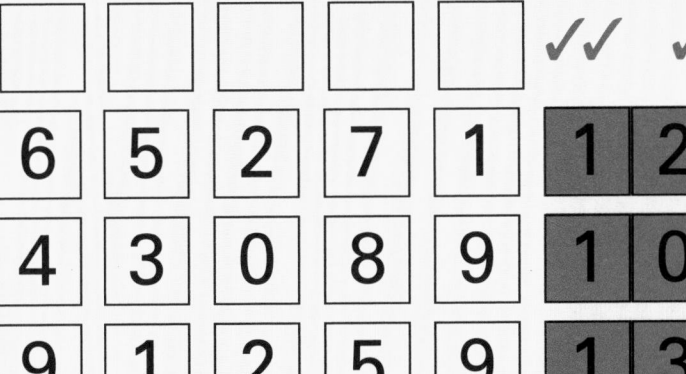

535 FILLING IN

Each of the nine empty boxes contains a *different* digit from 1 to 9. Each calculation is to be treated sequentially rather than according to the 'multiplication first' system. Can you fill in the empty boxes?

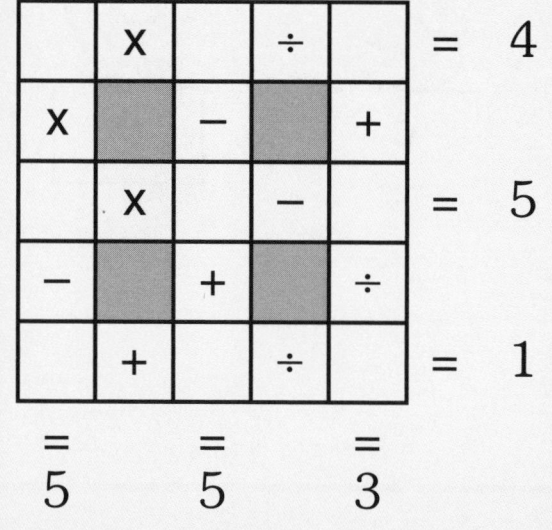

	X		÷		=	4
X		−		+		
	X		−		=	5
−		+		÷		
	+		÷		=	1

= 5   = 5   = 3

536 CROSSNUMBER QUICKIE

1A = 122 x 5A
5A is a prime number
6A = 101 x 4A
1D = 101 x 5D
2D is a square number
3D = 4A x 2D
7, 8 and 9 do not appear in the solution.

Historical clue: Death of Shakespeare.
The year can be read in the lightly shaded squares.

1	2		3
4			
		5	
6			

537 ROSES, ROSES

The delivery boy at Just Blooms flower shop was told to take half a dozen dozen roses to the wedding of Ms Green and six dozen dozen to the silver wedding of Mrs Grey. Knowing that six is half a dozen he delivered the same number to each place. Did he do right?

538 IN THE CLOUDS

Which one of the numbered lines leads to this cloud?

539 MAZE MYSTERY

Travel from the entrance to the exit of the maze, filling the path completely to create a picture.

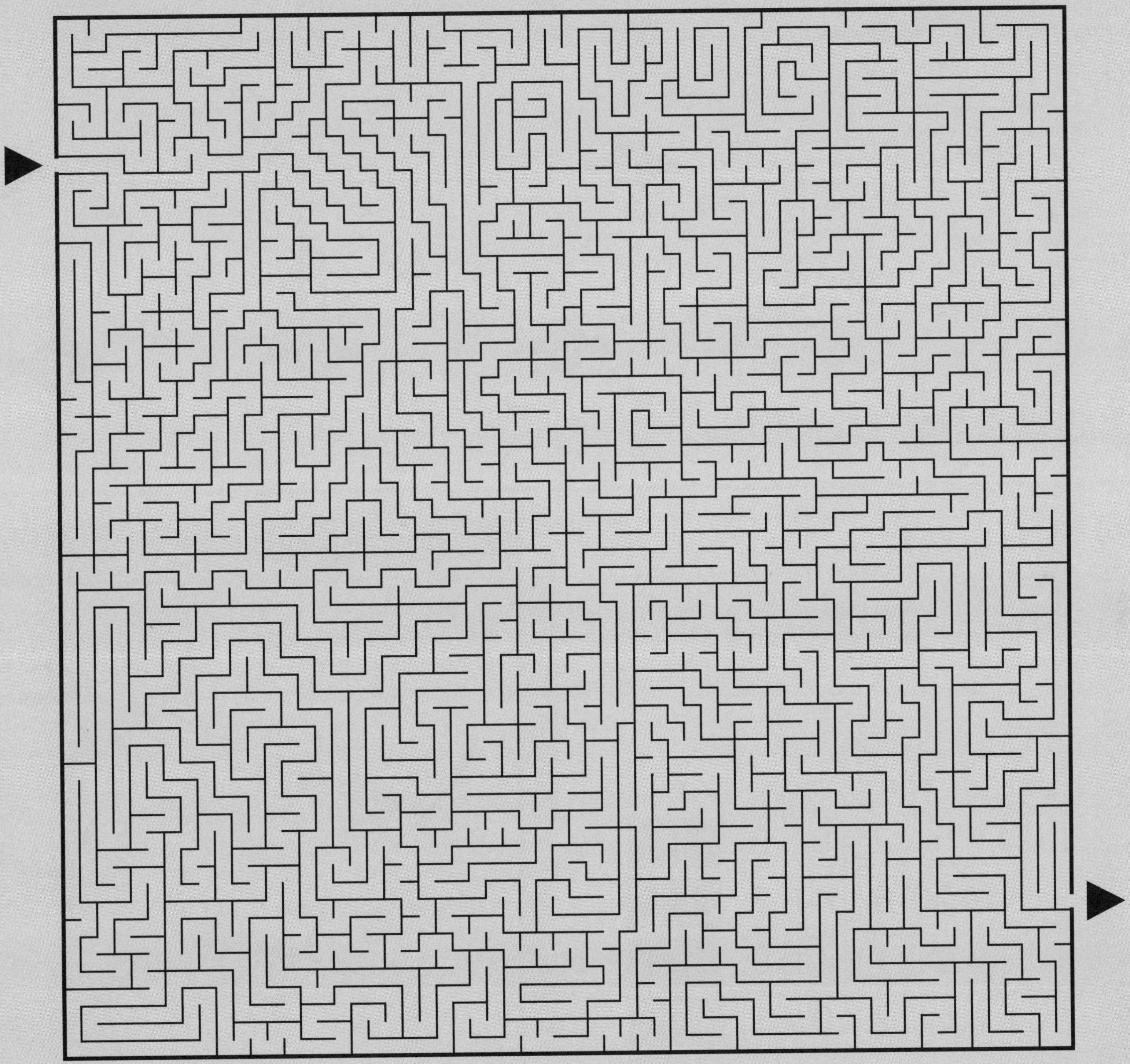

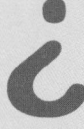

540 ACTION STATIONS

A city's Metro system consists of four lines, one running north to south, one east to west, and two crossing these diagonally, all passing through the central interchange station at Nelson Square. From the clues given below, can you work out the colour in which lines 1 to 4 are depicted on the plan posted up at every station, and name the terminus stations on each line, entering your answers in the spaces provided? NB The terms western and eastern apply to any of the three termini in each of those directions.

Clues

1 One of the diagonal lines runs from The Unicorn to Gradwell, which is the next terminus clockwise from Wallgate.

2 The blue line forms a right angle at Nelson Square with the one whose western terminus is Molton Park.

3 The red line bears a number two higher than the one whose eastern terminus is Riverhead.

4 Potterfield is indicated on the plan by a letter two further down the alphabet than Lampwick.

5 Castlebridge is not on the green line.

6 The two terminus stations on the blue line do not have names containing the same number of letters.

Colours: blue; green; red; yellow
Stations: Castlebridge; Gradwell; Lampwick; Molton Park; Potterfield; Riverhead; The Unicorn; Wallgate

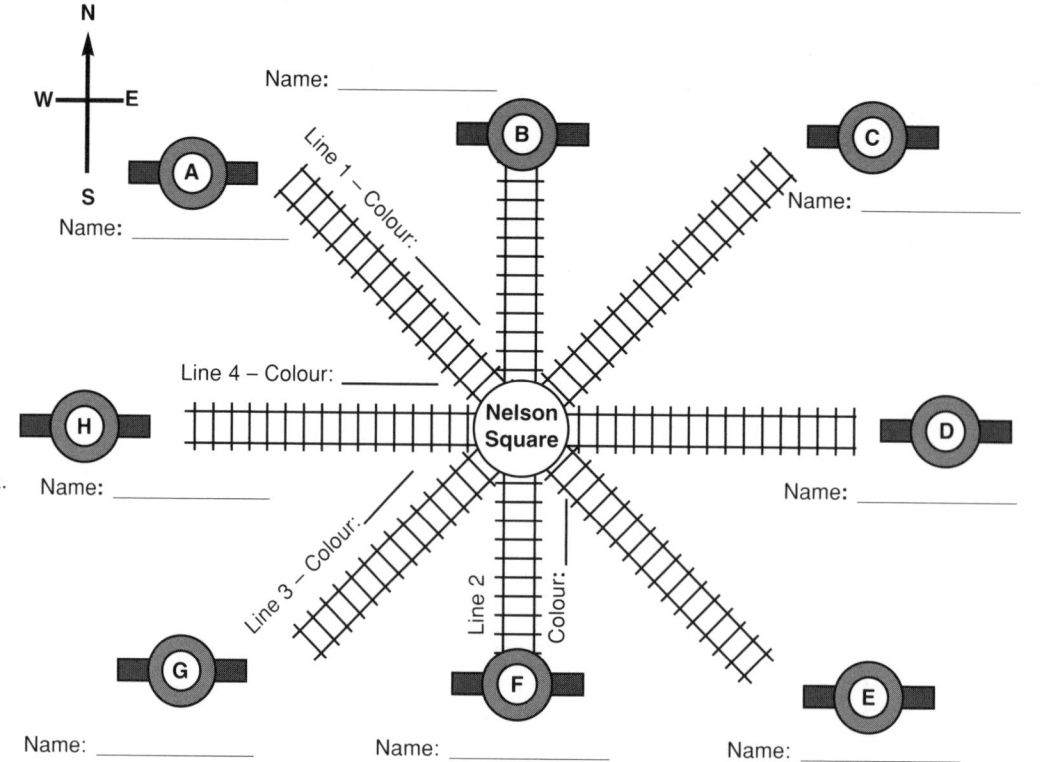

Name: _____
Name: _____
Name: _____
Name: _____
Name: _____
Name: _____
Name: _____
Name: _____

Line 1 – Colour: _____
Line 4 – Colour: _____
Line 3 – Colour: _____
Line 2 – Colour: _____

Nelson Square

Starting tip: Begin by working out which station is Riverhead.

541 CODE MASTER

Just follow the rules of that classic puzzle, Master Mind, to crack the number code. The first number tells you how many of the digits are exactly correct – the right digit in the right place (✓✓). The second number tells you how many digits are the correct number but are not in the right place (✓). By comparing the information given by each line, can you work out which number goes in which place?

					✓✓	✓
4	5	2	8	9	1	1
1	2	6	4	3	2	2
7	0	1	4	9	1	1
8	5	2	0	1	1	1
2	0	4	5	8	0	3
5	8	2	3	6	1	2

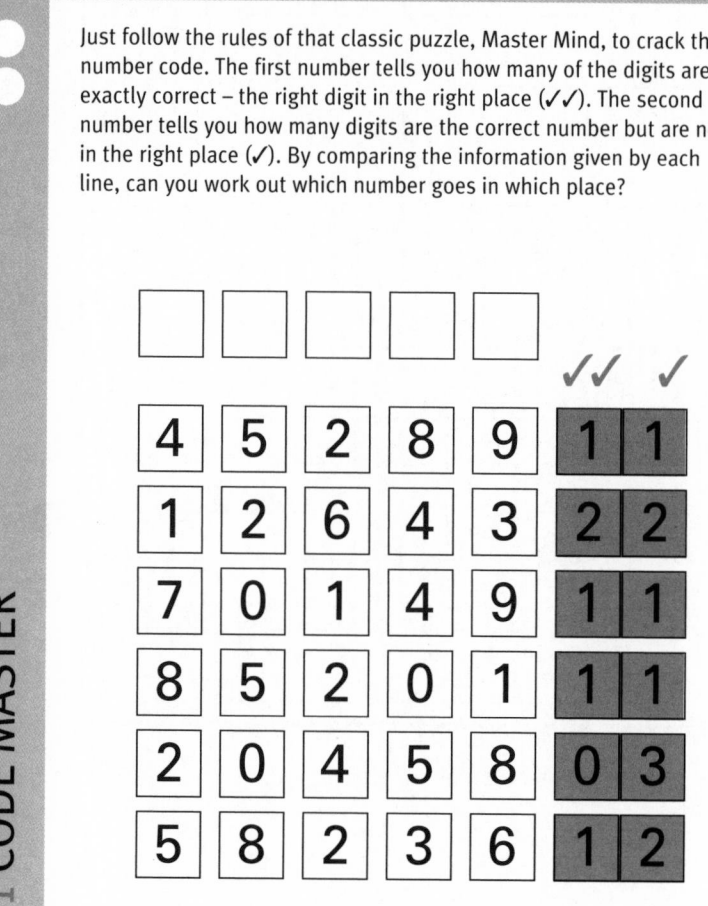

542 ODD ONE OUT

Which one of these panicky cats is different from all the others?

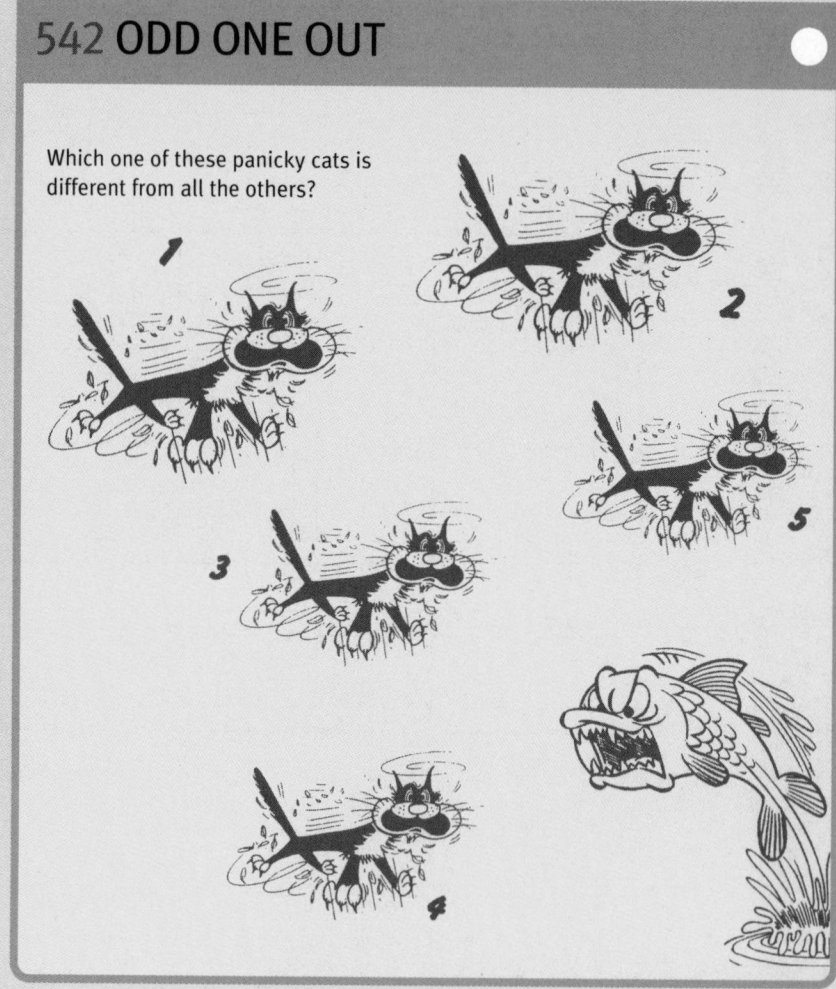

1
2
3
4
5

543 FAIR PRICE

Simple Simon met a pieman, going to the fair. Said Simple Simon to the pieman, "How much is your ware?" Said the pieman to Simple Simon, "It's seven pennies for each of these, and eight pennies for each of those." Simple Simon paid ninety seven pennies, for some of these and some of those. How many of each had he chosen ?

544 SEVEN ALL

7 x 7 is 49

So, without using a calculator, just how quickly can you find the answer to:

$$7\,7\,7 \times 7\,7\,7$$

545 FILLING IN

Each of the nine empty boxes contains a digit from 1 to 9. As is our usual practice, each calculation is to be treated sequentially rather than according to the 'multiplication and division first' system. Can you fill in the empty boxes?

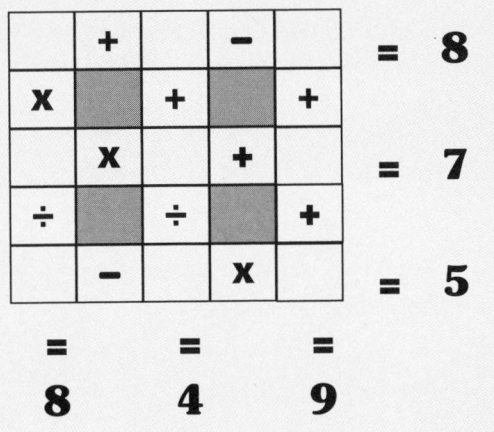

546 WHAT A KNIGHTMARE

Join the dots from 1 to 135 to find out why this nervous knight wishes he'd stayed at home this morning.

547 BATTLESHIPS

● ● ●

Do you remember the old game of battleships? This puzzle is based on that idea. Your task is to find the six vessels in the diagram. Some parts of boats or sea squares have already been filled in, and a number next to a row or column refers to the number of occupied squares in that row or column. A row or column with nothing next to it does not necessarily mean that there are no ship parts there. The boats may be positioned horizontally or vertically, but no two boats or parts of boats are in adjacent squares – horizontally, vertically or diagonally.

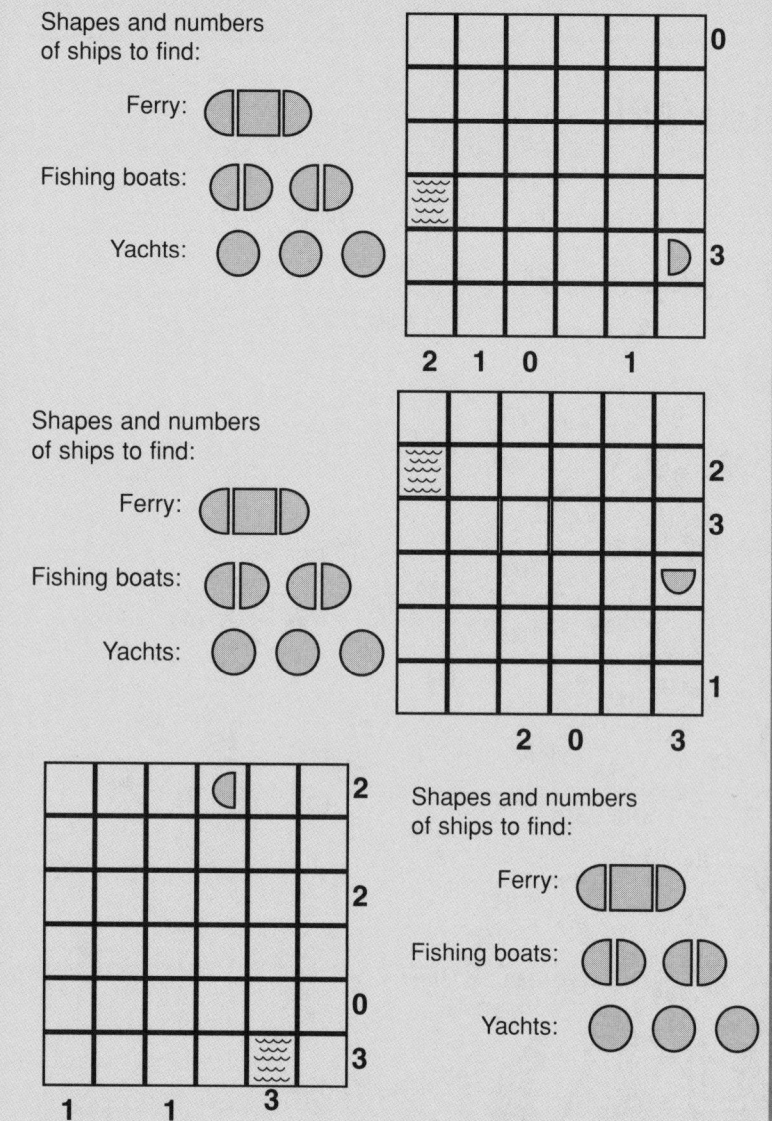

Shapes and numbers of ships to find:

Ferry:

Fishing boats:

Yachts:

Shapes and numbers of ships to find:

Ferry:

Fishing boats:

Yachts:

Shapes and numbers of ships to find:

Ferry:

Fishing boats:

Yachts:

549 NINE NUMBER

○
○
○

Place a number from 1 to 9 in each empty cell so that each row, each column and each 3 x 3 block contains all the numbers from 1 to 9.

3					5			
		9	6	8				
	1			4				7
	6		2					
	7	5				1	3	
					9		4	
2			3			8		
				1	7	9		
	4						6	

548 CASTING LOTS

● ● ●

Peregrine Cupick, who had had some experience as a professional provincial theatre director, came on retirement to live in Netherlipp and offered his services to the Netherlipp Players, who, duly impressed, acceded to his casting decisions for his first production of A Midsummer Night's Dream with unprecedented docility. However, the roles he assigned to the five leading male members were not the ones they had hoped for and he had tried them out at a reading round a table; from the clues given below, can you work out which actor sat where, what part he was given and which role he would have preferred?

Clues

1 Lime sat next clockwise after the man who had aspired to be Quince and opposite the one who was given the part of Demetrius.

2 Pitt's place was next clockwise after that of the man chosen to be Lysander and opposite that of the one who wanted to be Lysander.

3 The man cast as Oberon was next left to the one who got the part of Demetrius; the latter was opposite the actor who had set his heart on being Oberon.

4 Lynes sat next right to the man who wanted to play Bottom and opposite the one who was given the role of Quince.

5 Green was next clockwise after the selected Bottom and next anti-clockwise from the selected Oberon and was opposite the actor who was next left to the would-be Quince.

Actors: Flood; Green; Lime; Lynes; Pitt
Roles: Bottom; Demetrius; Lysander; Oberon; Quince

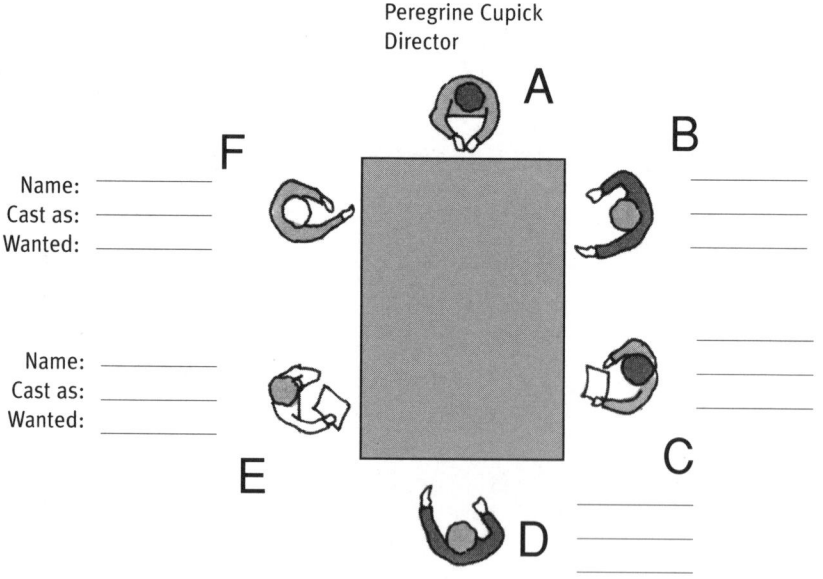

Peregrine Cupick
Director

Name: _____
Cast as: _____
Wanted: _____

Name: _____
Cast as: _____
Wanted: _____

Starting tip: Work out the name of the actor at D.

550 STAMP COLLECTION

Which one of the numbered marks has been made with this stamp?

552 BATTLESHIPS

Do you remember the old game of battleships? These puzzles are based on that idea. Your task is to find the vessels in the diagram. Some parts of boats or sea squares have already been filled in, and a number next to a row or column refers to the number of occupied squares in that row or column. A row or column with nothing next to it does not necessarily mean that there are no ship parts there. The boats may be positioned horizontally or vertically, but no two boats or parts of boats are in adjacent squares – horizontally, vertically or diagonally.

Shapes and numbers of ships to find:

Oil tanker:

Ferries:

Fishing boats:

Yachts:

Now try these two smaller, but no less tricky, versions of Battleships.

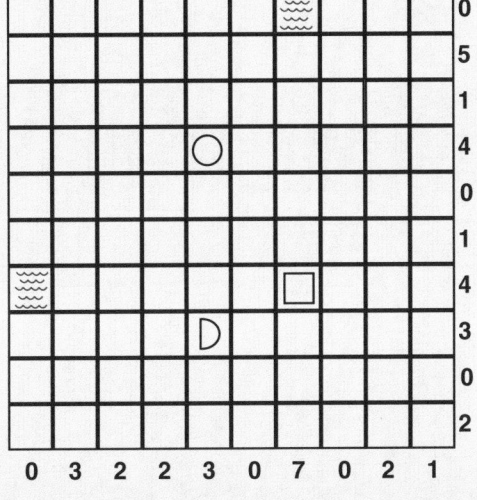

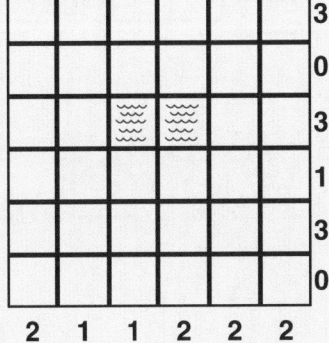 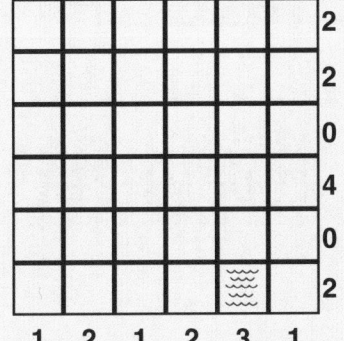

Shapes and numbers of ships to find:

Ferry:

Fishing boats: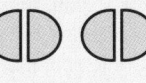

Yachts:

551 DOTTY DILEMMA

Connect adjacent dots with vertical or horizontal lines so that a single loop is formed with no crossings or branches. Each number indicates how many lines surround it, while empty cells may be surrounded by any number of lines.

553 ALL ABOARD

Which one of the numbered prints was made from the stamp?

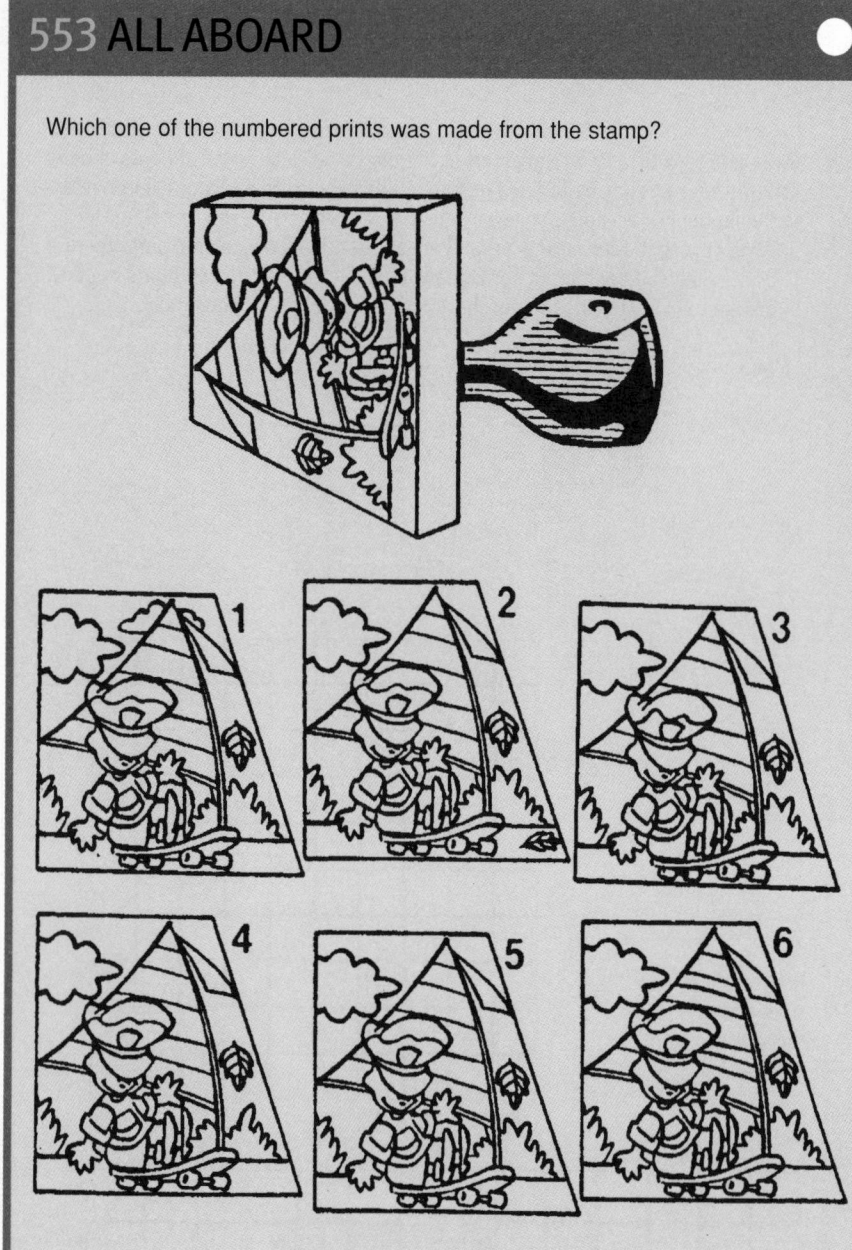

554 THE NUMBERS GAME

Each of the squares in the diagram numbered 1 to 6 contains one of those six numbers, one of the first six letters of the alphabet, and one of the Roman numbers I to VI. From the clues given below, can you place the correct three items in each square?

Clues

1 Taking the six letters A to F as representing their numerical position in the alphabet, none of the squares contains its own letter or number of either type, and no two equivalent numbers or letters appear in any of the squares.

2 The C is in the square immediately to the left of the Roman II.

3 The D appears in the square above that containing the 4. The B is in the square above that containing the III.

4 The 3 is in the square above the VI. The 5 is not in square 2.

5 The 6 appears in the same square as the V. The F appears in the same square as the IV. The I appears in the same square as the E.

6 The Arabic number in square 5 is larger than its Roman companion.

Numbers: 1; 2; 3; 4; 5; 6
Letters: A; B; C; D; E; F
Roman numbers: I; II; III IV; V; VI

	1	2	3
Arabic:	_____	_____	_____
Letter:	_____	_____	_____
Roman:	_____	_____	_____
	4	5	6
Arabic:	_____	_____	_____
Letter:	_____	_____	_____
Roman:	_____	_____	_____

Starting tip: Start by placing the Roman VI.

555 CODE MASTER

Just follow the rules of that classic puzzle, Master Mind, to crack the number code. The first number tells you how many of the digits are exactly correct – the right digit in the right place (✓✓). The second number tells you how many digits are the correct number but are not in the right place (✓). By comparing the information given by each line, can you work out which number goes in which place?

					✓✓	✓
9	5	8	3	4	0	1
7	8	6	0	2	2	2
2	7	8	5	3	1	2
4	6	3	8	2	1	2
6	3	2	7	5	0	3
1	9	4	0	6	0	2

556 IT'S MAGIC

This magic square can be completed using the numbers from 32 to 56 inclusive. To give you a start the first row has all its even digits entered, the second row all its odd digits, the third row even again, the fourth odd and the fifth even. Can you complete the square so that the five numbers in each row, column, and diagonal add up to the magic total? The total—close your eyes if you don't want to be told—is 220.

2		4 6	4 8	
5 1	5 3	3 5	3 7	
4 0	4 2	4		6
5	3	3		5	7
4		0	2		4 4

557 SNAKES AND LADDERS

Which one of the lettered cubes can be made from the unfolded pattern?

559 NUMBER KROSS

See how quickly you can fit all these numbers into the grid. We've filled one number in to start you off.

3 figures	4656	43049	206317
142	5483	57182	241327
216	6122	66278	367687
(425)	7901	66978	423458
511	8234	73842	454288
635		74256	519619
732	**5 figures**	83445	637452
848	16539	88640	678902
920	17822	96780	767893
	27383		775406
4 figures	29743		822538
1968	34551	**6 figures**	862728
2075	37894	120816	904111
3545	42345	134565	941157

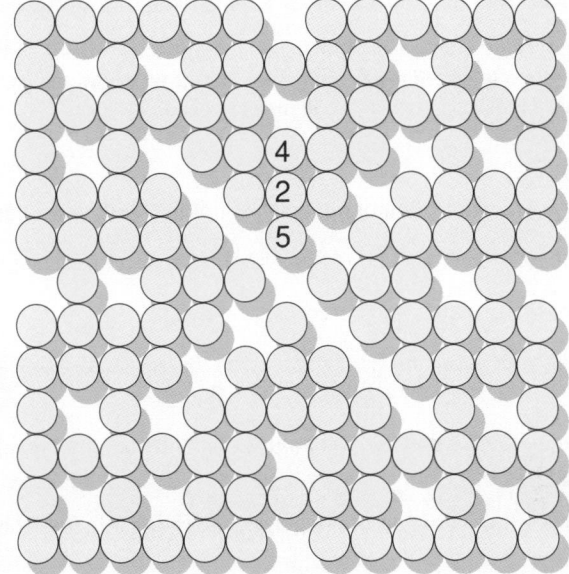

558 CHANGING PLACES

Do you recall Alice's cleaning lady who never puts things back in their proper places? This week it was the six cushions on Alice's capacious sofa which she relocated. From the clues given below, can you establish their original and revised positions?

Clues

1 The gold cushion was moved as many places to the right as the red was to the left; the green was moved in the same direction as the gold, but by a shorter distance, while the pink was moved one fewer place to the left than the red.

2 The green took the place of the turquoise and the turquoise the place of the blue, moving one fewer place left than the blue did right, but more than one more than the green.

3 Neither the green nor the turquoise was at either end both before and after the cleaning operation; the green should have been next left to the turquoise but finished up more than two places to the right of it; the blue should have been next left to the pink but finished up more than two places to the right of it.

4 Alice would never have placed the pink and red next to each other.

Colours: blue, gold, green, pink, red, turquoise

Original: _____

New: _____

Starting tip: Work out the original colour of the cushion at F.

560 SQUARED AWAY

In how many different ways can these three pieces form a 3 x 3 square? The pieces are numbered on the front and the back, so they can be turned over. Rotations and reflections of the final numbered square are not counted as different.

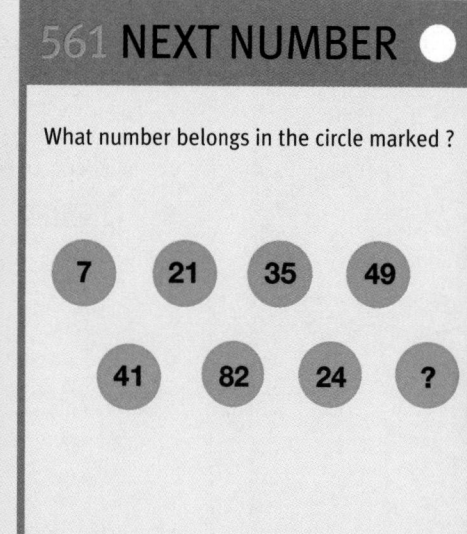

561 NEXT NUMBER

What number belongs in the circle marked ?

7   21   35   49

41   82   24   ?

562 SEARCH PARTY

Four of the six shapes at the top can be found in the main picture. Can you spot their whereabouts?

564 IT CAME TO PASS ●●●

The diagram illustrates a delightful passing movement involving seven members of a soccer team during a recent televised match. From the clues given below, can you work out the names of the seven players who took part in the move in their correct order?

Clues

1 Garry, who was in the opponents' half of the field, received a pass from O'Casey.

2 Clyde Johnson received the ball from Darren, and passed it to Marchant.

3 Steve is the player numbered 2 in the diagram.

4 David, who is not the goalkeeper, was the provider of the telling pass to Mike, who is not in the same half of the pitch as Bennett.

5 Peter, who received the ball from Glenn, was not the provider of the pass received by Donovan.

6 Swann is the surname of the player numbered 3 in the diagram.

First names: Clyde; Darren; David; Garry; Mike; Peter; Steve
Surnames: Bennett; Donovan; Glenn; Johnson; Marchant; O'Casey; Swann

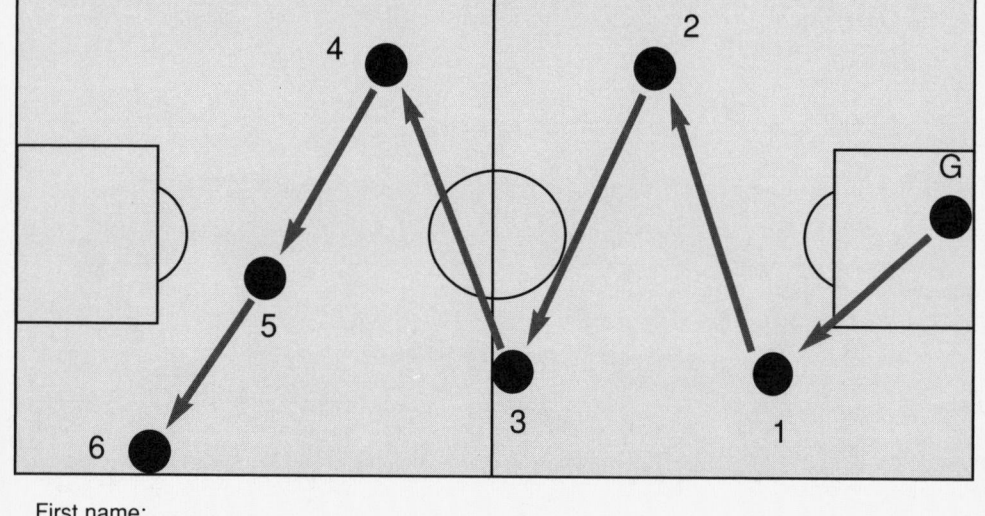

First name: _____ _____ _____

Surname: _____ _____ _____

Starting tip: Begin by working out the first name of the goalkeeper who started the move.

563 WIRED UP

Which of the four plugs should be inserted in the socket to operate the razor?

565 DOT-TO-DOT

Join the dots from 1 to 33 to reveal the hidden picture.

566 BLACK OUT

Can you decide which three of the fifteen vases are shown in silhouette at the top?

568 CODE MASTER

Just follow the rules of that classic puzzle. Master Mind, to crack the number code. The first number tells you how many of the digits are exactly correct – the right digit in the right place (✓✓). The second number tells you how many digits are the correct number but are not in the right place (✓). By comparing the information given by each line, can you work out which number goes in which place?

					✓✓	✓
5	4	2	7	0	2	0
8	4	2	3	1	0	2
1	9	5	2	8	0	2
4	0	7	3	6	0	3
8	6	9	4	7	1	1
5	6	3	8	0	1	1

569 BOX NUMBER

What number belongs in the box marked ?

```
5 — 8 — 6
        |
0 — 4 — 4

8 — ?
```

570 DOTTY DILEMMA

Connect adjacent dots with vertical or horizontal lines so that a single loop is formed with no crossings or branches. Each number indicates how many lines surround it, while empty cells may be surrounded by any number of lines.

567 BATTLESHIPS

Do you remember the old game of battleships? This puzzle is based on that idea. Your task is to find the 10 vessels in the diagram. Some parts of boats or a sea square have already been filled in, and a number next to a row or column refers to the number of occupied squares in that row or column. A row or column with nothing next to it does not necessarily mean that there are no ship parts there. The boats may be positioned horizontally or vertically, but no two boats or parts of boats are in adjacent squares – horizontally, vertically or diagonally.

Shapes and numbers of ships to find:
Oil tanker:
Ferries:
Fishing boats:
Yachts:

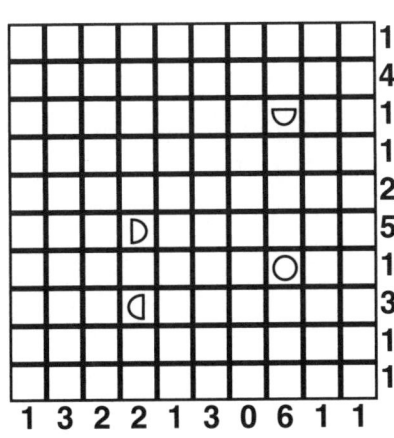

Shapes and numbers of ships to find:
Oil tanker:
Ferries:
Fishing boats:
Yachts:

571 WIRED UP

Which of the four plugs is connected to the chainsaw?

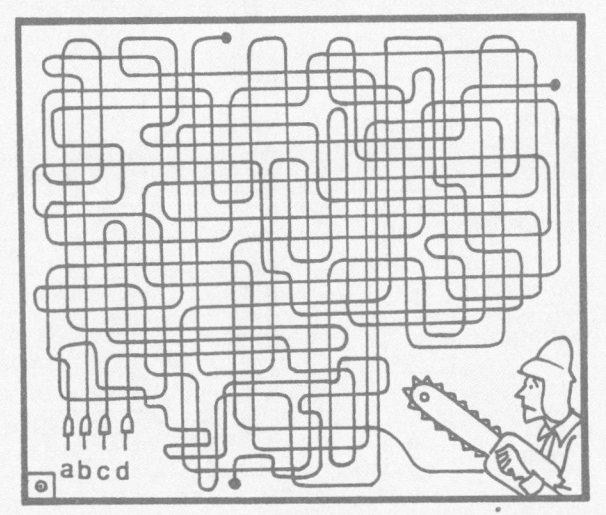

a b c d

163

572 COMMONWEALTH GAMES

● ● ●

Four house-sharing students from the University of Goatsferry's School of Medicine, finding themselves short of money on a cold, wet evening, decided to stay home and play a game – but they spent all their time arguing about which game they should play! From the clues given below, can you fill in on the drawing the name and country of origin of each student, and the game they wanted to play?

Clues

1 The student who wanted to play Monopoly was seated immediately clockwise of Rajendra Patel, who comes from India.

2 The Canadian student who wanted to play mah-jong wasn't Matt Scott.

3 The student from Barbados wasn't the one who wanted to play Trivial Pursuit, who wasn't in seat B.

4 The student in seat C wanted to play Scrabble.

5 Beverly McBain, who is not Australian, was in seat A.

Students: Beverly McBain; Jayne Bailey; Matt Scott; Rajendra Patel
Countries: Australia; Barbados; Canada; India
Games: mah-jong; Monopoly; Scrabble; Trivial Pursuit

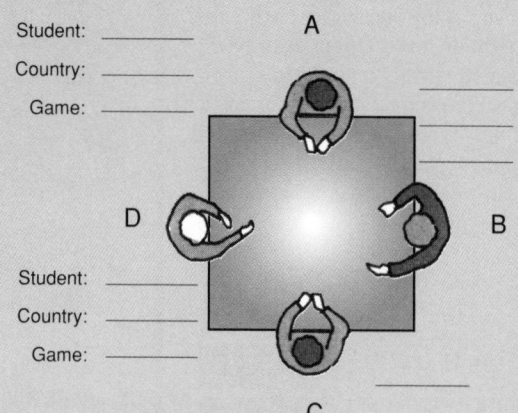

Student: _____
Country: _____
Game: _____

A

D   B

Student: _____
Country: _____
Game: _____

C

Starting tip: Work out which game student B wanted to play.

575 NUMBER KROSS

● ●
●

See how quickly you can fit all these numbers into the grid. We've filled one number in to start you off.

3 figures	1948	16422	82759	471017
110	2587	22212	85177	520293
228	3118	25719	92056	588289
342	4419	32023	96145	630580
(534)	6720	35081		640658
618	7732	49887	6 figures	731290
720	8313	50450	156414	772042
840	9821	54578	246647	834015
935		63958	272674	897613
	5 figures	70598	309220	900510
4 figures	16334	76756	402631	913097

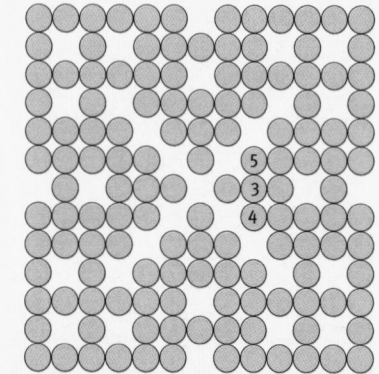

573 MASTERMIND BANDITS

● ● ●

The one-armed bandits in the puzzle-mad land of Enigmatica are different from those we might be familiar with in amusement arcades and on seaside piers. To play this version of the game, punters pull the handle and the four rollers spin and stop to reveal four fruits. The window next to the rollers then lights up to reveal how well that spin matches up with the jackpot line hidden by a shield at the bottom of the fruit machine. An X in the results window indicates that one roller is exactly correct, that is, a right fruit on the right roller. An O indicates that one fruit is correct in that it appears in the winning combination, but is on the wrong roller. Enigmaticans are given four pulls of the handle and then have to deduce the winning jackpot combination. Below is a machine at that final stage of the game after the four pulls of the handle. Can you emulate the good people of Enigmatica and work out the details of the winning line hidden beneath the jackpot shield?

Symbols:

Cherry

Orange

Lemon

Grapefruit

Banana

Pear

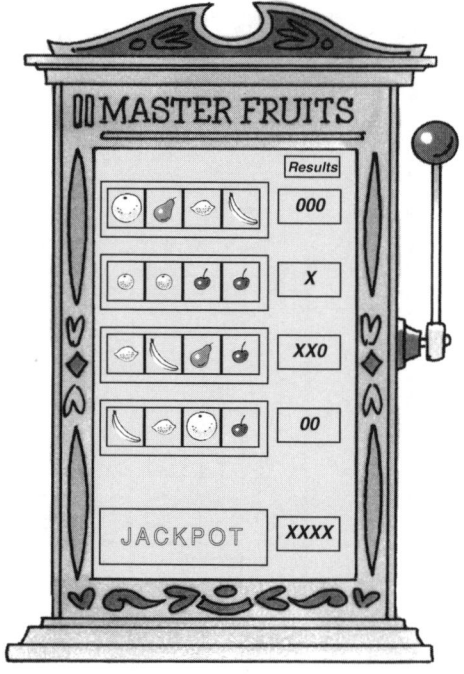

574 SUIT YOURSELF

● ● ●

Based on an idea by J. E. T. Thorne of Sanderstead

Four women recently enjoyed a bridge evening in the course of which they all had to defend their bids, some more boldly than others. From the clues given, can you indicate in the diagram each woman's position at the table and the number and suit of her bid?

Clues

1 Mrs Evans' bid was higher than that of the player on her left but one less than that of her partner; neither of them bid Diamonds, the one who did bidding one higher than the player at South.

2 Mrs Jennings was next left to the player whose suit was Hearts, but whose bid was not 6.

3 Mrs Scott's partner bid an odd number of No Trumps, while she herself made an even-numbered bid though not in Spades.

4 Mrs Ryan neither played North nor made a bid of 5.

Players: Mrs Evans; Mrs Jennings; Mrs Ryan; Mrs Scott
Suits: Diamonds; Hearts; No Trumps; Spades
Bids: 3; 4; 5; 6

North   East

Player: _____
Suit: _____
Bid: _____

West   South

Player: _____
Suit: _____
Bid: _____

Starting tip: Narrow down the possibilities for the bids of Mrs Evans and her partner and then their seats.

Travel from the entrance to the exit of the maze, filling the path completely to create a picture.

577 IT FIGURES

Place a number from 1 to 9 in each empty cell so that the sum of each vertical or horizontal block equals the number at the top or on the left of that block. Numbers may only be used once in each block.

580 TWINNED-UP

This boy would like to buy a spinning top identical to the one he's holding. Which one will he choose?

578 COLOUR CHAOS

The day after Dreadnought Bathroom Supplies Ltd had held their annual dinner-dance, six enraged customers phoned to complain that the six supposedly matching elements of their new bathroom suites had in fact been delivered in six different colours: avocado, dove, lemon, mango, peach and rose.

At 9.35am, Fenella, the DBS receptionist, contemplated the full complaints sheet and hoped that she would remain undisturbed until home time. The calls had started at 9.05am and had come at five-minute intervals. She noticed that in some consecutive boxes on her sheet the initial letters of the colours spelt out words.

The Soap family had PAR in their row of colours and the same word also appeared in a column. The Faucett family had LAD in their row and the Lathers had PAD. There was LAMP reading somewhere down the shower-tray column and LAP was to be seen in another column. The Waters family phoned some time after the Soaps, but fifteen minutes before the Lather household. The Tubbs family had been sent a lemon bath and they phoned some time before the Faucetts and some time after the Flannell family. The peach bidet was noted ten minutes after the rose cistern, but ten minutes before the mango basin. The dove lavatory was noted ten minutes after the peach basin, but ten minutes before the avocado bath. Can you complete Fenella's complaints sheet?

Time	Customer	Basin	Bath	Bidet	Cistern	Lavatory	Shower
9.05							
9.10							
9.15							
9.20							
9.25							
9.30							

579 CYCLE OF MISHAPS

The diagram shows the cross section of a difficult stage of an international cycle race, during which various riders had to drop out at the points marked 1 to 7. From the clues given below, can you name the rider who dropped out at each position, and pinpoint the reason for his withdrawal from the race?

Clues

1 One rider's pedal snapped due to metal fatigue; this was two points beyond the one where Dirk had to drop out.

2 The name of the rider who withdrew at point 6 appears in the alphabetical list immediately before that of the one whose chain broke.

3 Roland dropped out next but one before the rider whose wheel became buckled.

4 It was at point 3 that one injury-prone rider twisted his ankle.

5 Yves' flat tyre caused him to withdraw at an even-numbered location.

6 Michel was obliged to abandon the race at point 4 on the plan.

7 The rider at point 5 has a longer name than the man whose suspect knee gave way, who not Bjorn.

8 Victor was not the rider who suffered a disabling attack of migraine during the race.

Riders: Bjorn; Dirk; Gino; Michel; Roland; Victor; Yves
Reasons for withdrawal: buckled wheel; chain broke; flat tyre; knee gave way; migraine attack; pedal snapped; twisted ankle

Rider: _____ ____ ____ ____ ____ ____ ____

Reason: _____ ____ ____ ____ ____ ____ ____

Starting tip: Begin by working out at which point Yves had to drop out.

581 ACE IN PLACE

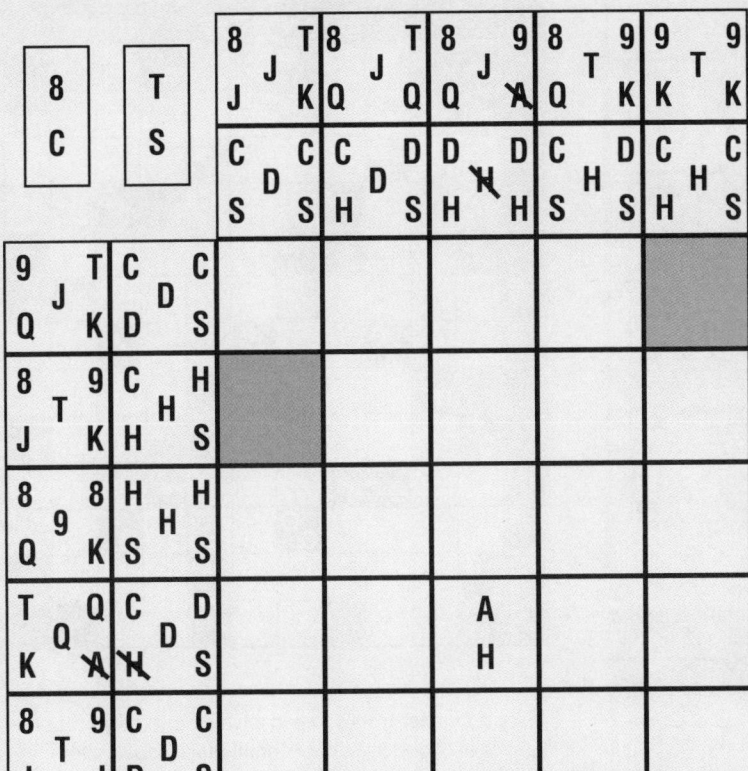

The cards Eight to King of each suit, together with the Ace of Hearts have been placed in a 5 x 5 square. Figures and letters showing the values 8, 9, 10, J, Q, K and suits C, H, D, S have been placed at the end of each line across and down. With the Ace in place and the fact that the two cards shown at the top left belong in the shaded squares, can you work out the unique place for each card?

582 POSER

The artist has made five mistakes while trying to paint an exact portrait of the model. Can you spot the five errors?

583 SEARCH PARTY

Four of the six shapes at the top are hidden in the main picture. Can you work out which ones and whereabouts they appear?

584 CODE MASTER

Just follow the rules of that classic puzzle, Master Mind, to crack the colour code. The first number tells you how many of the pegs are exactly correct – the right colour in the right place (✓✓). The second number tells you how many pegs are the correct colour but are not in the right place (✓). Colours may be repeated in the answer. By comparing the information given by each line, can you work out which colour goes in which place?

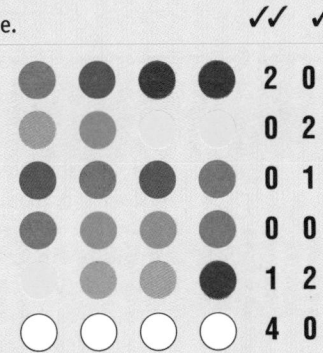

585 ARMS AND THE MAN

Four hereditary peers own the coats of arms featured in the diagram. From the clues given below, can you name the owner of each of the shields lettered A to D, say which heraldic device appears on each, and work out the background colour of each coat of arms?

Clues

1 Lord Rackham's shield features a turkey, in cryptic reference to one of his remote ancestors' heroic deeds in that land against the infidel during the Crusades; it is somewhere to the left of the blue coat of arms.

2 The yellow shield is somewhere to the right of the one depicting an eagle, which can be seen alongside Lord Bertram's arms in the diagram.

3 The lion does not feature on Lord Mallender's coat of arms.

4 The background colour of shield C is green.

5 Shield A is the coat of arms of Lord Liversedge.

Peers: Lord Bertram; Lord Liversedge; Lord Mallender; Lord Rackham
Devices: eagle; lion; stag; turkey
Colours: blue; green; red; yellow

A   **B**   **C**   **D**

Peer: _____
Device: _____
Colour: _____

Starting tip: Begin by working out the colour of shield A.

167

586 TWIN SET

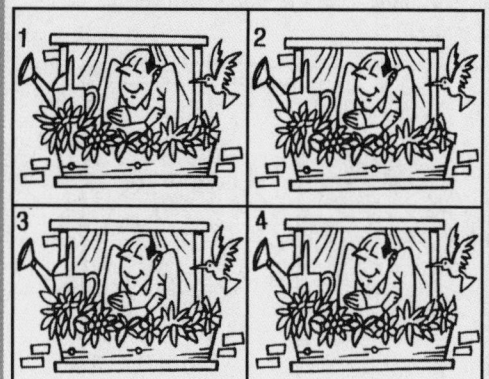

Two of the pictures above are identical. Can you spot the 'twins' and the different detail in each of the remaining pictures?

587 FOURSOME

This woman would like to buy four identical vases. Which design will she choose?

588 IT FIGURES

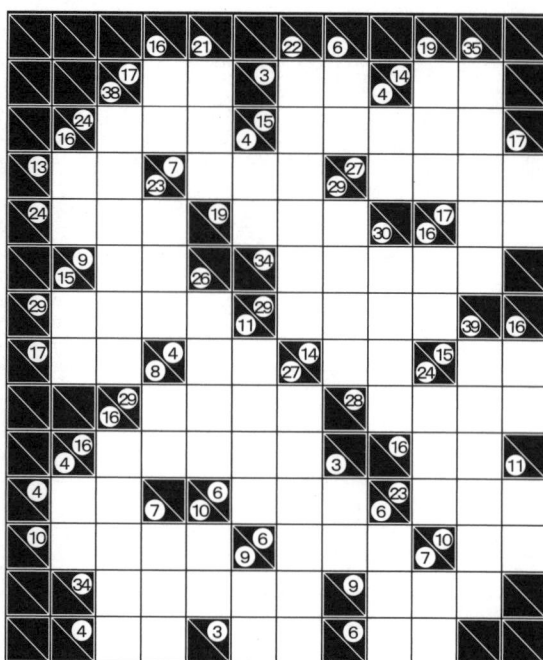

Place a number from 1 to 9 in each empty cell so that the sum of each vertical or horizontal block equals the number at the top or on the left of that block. Numbers may only be used once in each block.

589 DOT-TO-DOT

Join the dots from 1 to 40 to reveal the hidden picture.

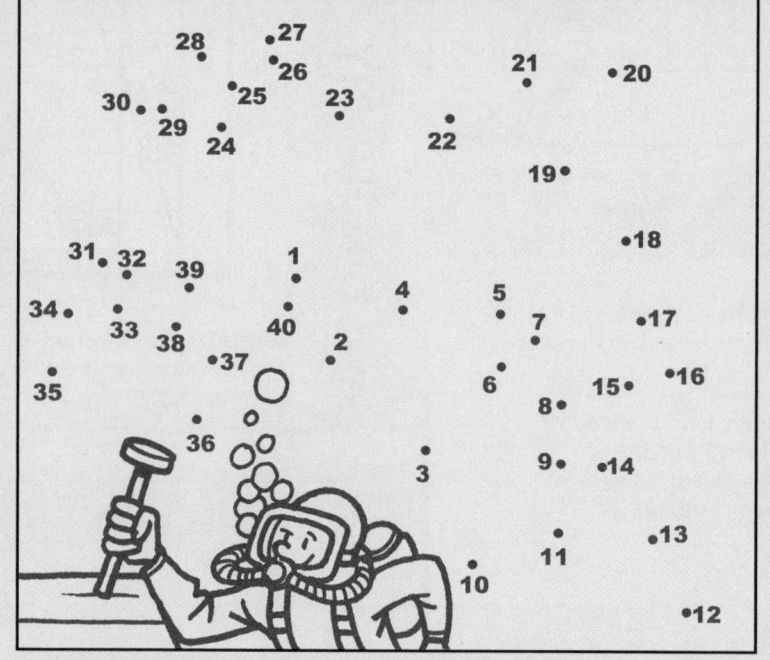

590 SILHOUETTE

Shade in every fragment containing a dot – and what have you got?

591 CODE MASTER

Just follow the rules of that classic puzzle, Master Mind, to crack the colour code. The first number tells you how many of the pegs are exactly correct – the right colour in the right place (✓✓) The second number tells you how many pegs are the correct colour but are not in the right place (✓). Colours may be repeated in the answer. By comparing the information given by each line, can you work out which colour goes in which place?

				✓✓	✓
				1	0
				0	2
				1	1
				1	1
				0	1
				4	0

592 DOTTY DILEMMA

Connect adjacent dots with vertical or horizontal lines so that a single loop is formed with no crossings or branches. Each number indicates how many lines surround it, while empty cells may be surrounded by any number of lines.

```
  3 2       1 3       2 1
3   1   3     3   2     0
1     3   1     3   2     1
  2 0       2 2       1 2
      3         3
  3 2             2 1
1     2   2     3   2     2
3     3   3     3   1     3
  1 3       1 0       2 2
      0           0
  2 2       1 1       3 1
2     3   1     2   1     2
1     1   2     1   2     3
  1 3       0 3       3 3
      0           0
  1 3       1 2       3 2
2     2   1     0   1     3
0     3   3     1   2     3
  1 1       2 2       2 3
      1           3
  3 1       3 0       0 1
1     3   2     3   2     3
2     3   1     1   2     1
  2 3       3 3       3 3
```

593 BATTLESHIPS

Do you remember the old game of battleships? These puzzles are based on that idea. Your task is to find the vessels in the diagram. Some parts of boats or sea squares have already been filled in, and a number next to a row or column refers to the number of occupied squares in that row or column. The boats may be positioned horizontally or vertically, but no two boats or parts of boats are in adjacent squares – horizontally, vertically or diagonally.

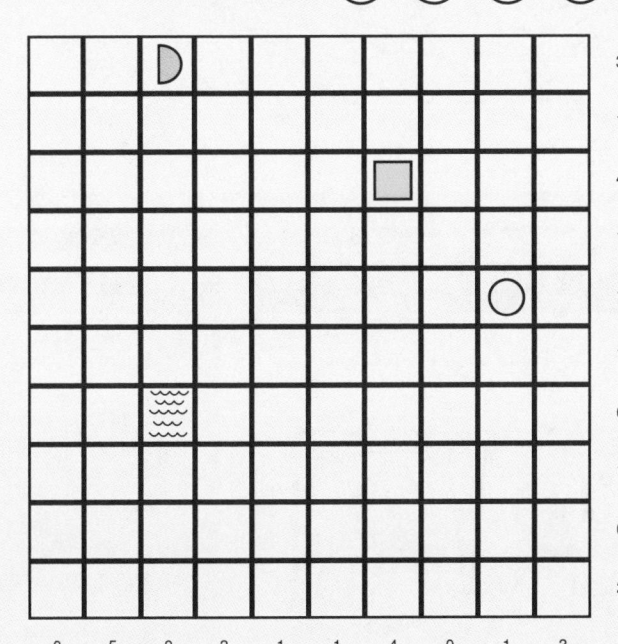

594 KEEPING IN TOUCH

Diana was an inveterate letter-writer, keeping in touch with all her former school friends by post on a regular basis. The other day she wrote four letters to friends in different parts of the country. From the clues given below, can you fill in the full names and the town which appeared on each envelope lying on the table in the positions numbered 1 to 4?

Clues

1. Betty's letter is immediately to the right of the one addressed to Mrs Hardy.
2. Letter 2 is about to wing its way to Nantwich; it is not the one addressed to Mrs Riley.
3. Jenny's name appears on the envelope containing letter 3; she does not live in Hull.
4. The letter to Cardiff is somewhere to the left on the table of the one addressed to Sally.
5. Mrs Dukes is destined to receive letter 1.

First names: Betty; Jenny; Jill; Sally
Surnames: Dukes; Hardy; Markham; Riley
Towns: Cardiff; Hull; Ipswich; Nantwich

	1	2	3	4
First name:	_____	_____	_____	_____
Surname:	_____	_____	_____	_____
Town:	_____	_____	_____	_____

Starting tip: Start by working out which letter is addressed to Mrs Hardy.

595 SILHOUETTE

Shade in every fragment containing a dot – and what have you got?

596 TRILINES

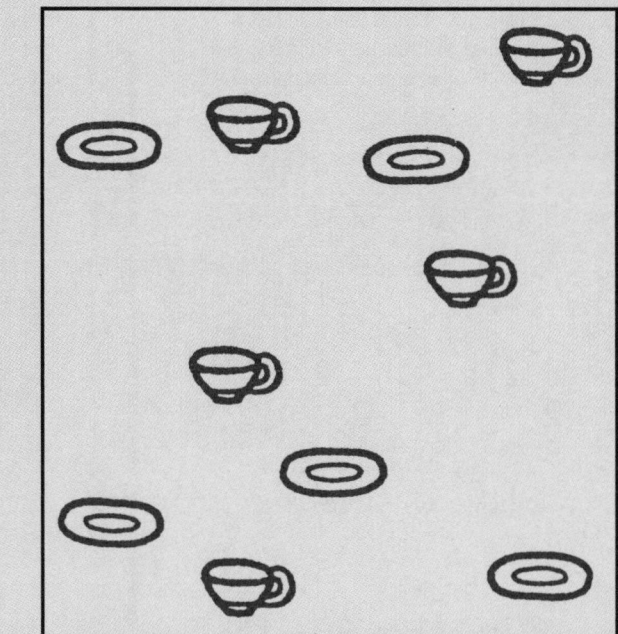

Can you draw three straight lines, each one drawn from one edge to another, so that they divide the box into five sections each containing a cup and a saucer?

597 SNAPSHOT

Can you work out which of nine photographs is an exact replica of the model?

598 MARKING THE CHANGES

Mr Prendergast, who teaches maths at Netherlipp High, always has four coloured pens in his top pocket. A pupil, whose mind kept drifting away from considering the implications of Pythagoras, noticed that each day this week up to Thursday no pen stayed in the same position. His observations are embodied in the clues which should enable you to work out the position of each pen on each day.

Clues

1 On Monday the blue was next left to the red but on Thursday the red was next left to the blue.

2 The green was in the same place on Monday as the red on Wednesday and in the same place on Tuesday as the black on Wednesday.

3 The green was one place further left on Wednesday than on Tuesday and one place further left on Thursday than on Monday.

4 On Tuesday the red was third from the left.

Colours: black; blue; green; red

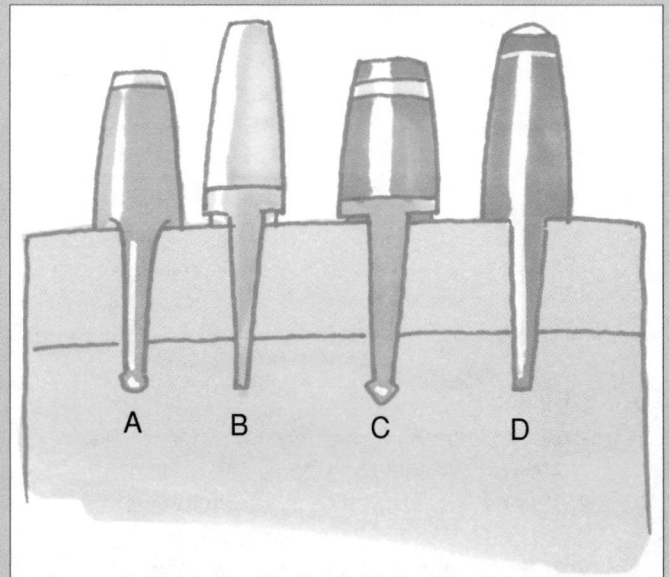

Monday: ———— ———— ———— ————
Tuesday: ———— ———— ———— ————
Wednesday: ———— ———— ———— ————
Thursday: ———— ———— ———— ————

Starting tip: Work out the colour of pen D on Thursday.

599 BAKE ME A CAKE

The cake stall is always popular at the monthly church fund-raising event. This month the four cakes at the front of the stall, numbered 1 to 4 in the diagram, were sold within seconds of the opening. From the clues given below, can you describe each cake, and name the woman who made it and the one who bought it?

Clues

1 Thelma bought the cake made by Mary, which was immediately to the right of the chocolate cake on the table.

2 Betty did not make the fruit cake, which was not bought by Linda, and Jean's cake was not number 4.

3 Cake 2 was made by Eileen.

4 The ginger sponge cake was in position 3 on the stall.

5 The jelly sponge was next but one on the table to the cake bought by Hilary.

Cakes: chocolate; ginger sponge; fruit cake; jelly sponge
Cake bakers: Betty; Eileen; Jean; Mary
Buyers: Hilary; Linda; Sarah; Thelma

Cake: ____ ____ ____ ____
Made by: ____ ____ ____ ____
Bought by: ____ ____ ____ ____

Starting tip: Start by numbering the chocolate cake.

600 STRICTLY FOR THE BIRDS

The women in four neighbouring semi-detached houses each cooked a different bird for their family's Christmas dinner, though all followed it up with the traditional Christmas pudding. From the clues given below, can you identify the cook at each of the houses numbered 6 to 12, and say which bird her family dined on?

Women: Beryl; Denise; Elaine; Molly
Surnames: Bird; Carver; Fowler; Legge
Birds: chicken; duck; goose; turkey

Clues

1 Denise Carver's house is the other half of the one where the duck was cooked.

2 The Fowler family dined on turkey, but not at number 8.

3 The Birds live at number 6; the woman who cooked their dinner is not Elaine.

4 Beryl lives at a house numbered two higher than the one where the family enjoyed a goose for their Christmas dinner.

5 The traditionalists at number 10 ate their usual chicken at dinner-time on Christmas Day.

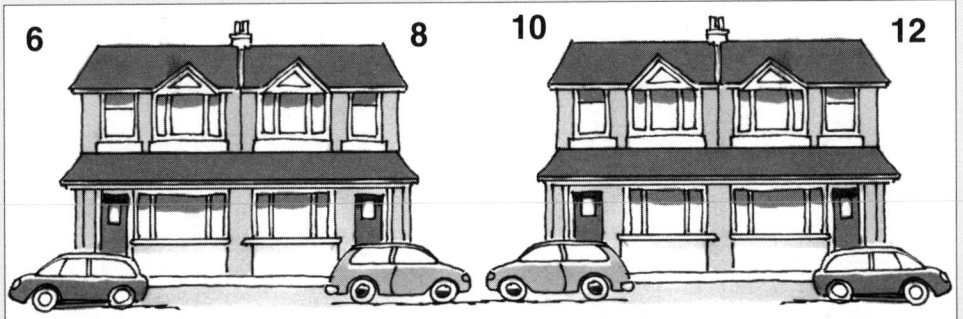

Woman: ____ ____ ____ ____
Surname: ____ ____ ____ ____
Bird: ____ ____ ____ ____

Starting tip: Start by working out the first name of Mrs Bird.

601 MAZE MYSTERY

Travel from the entrance to the exit of the maze, filling the path completely to create a picture.

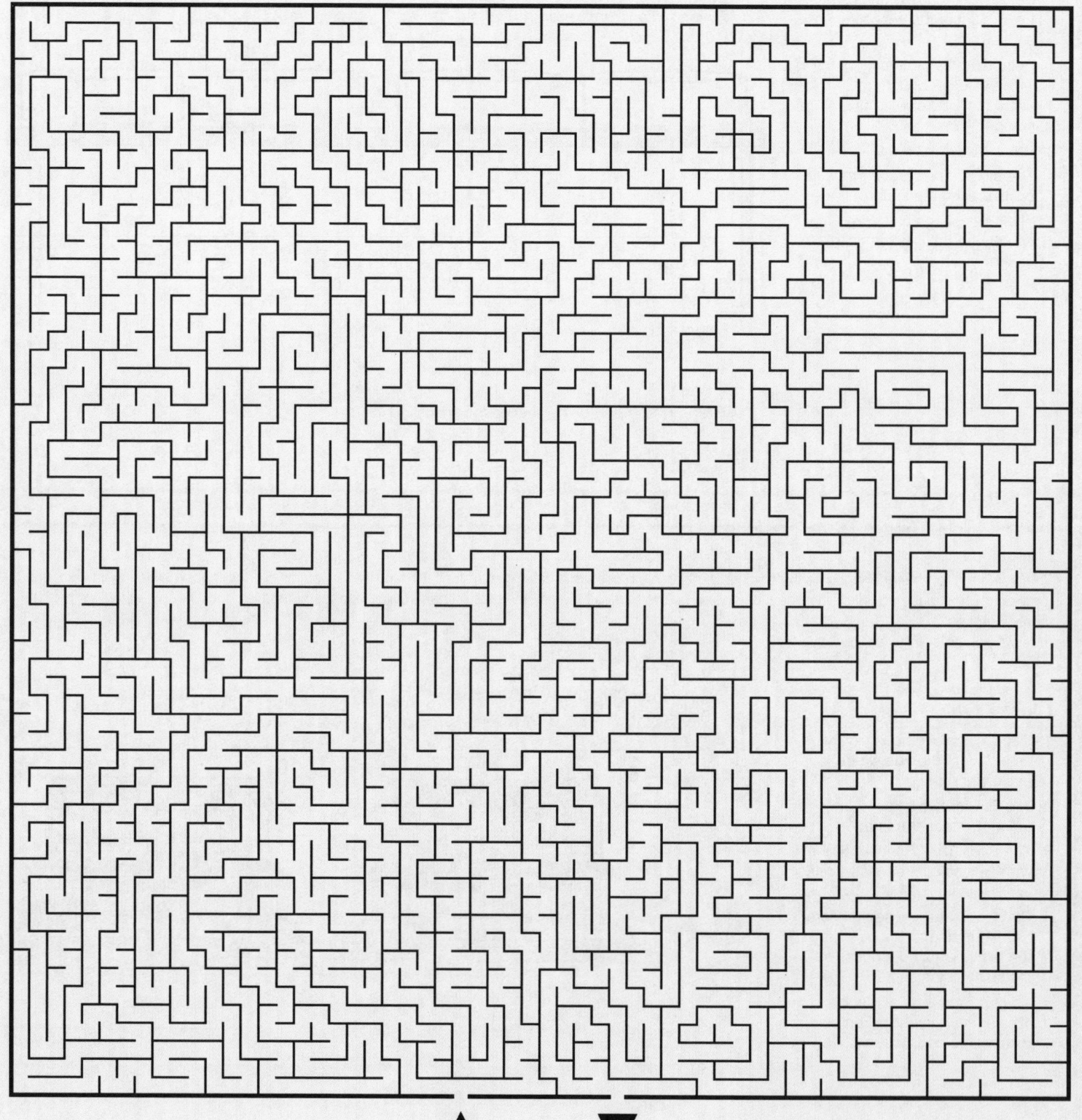

602 LITTLE AND LARGE

In this puzzle, the little numbers are large and the large numbers are little! Each little number from 1 to 9 is to be placed into the boxes, one per box.

Each larger number in the boxes is the sum of the little number that goes in it plus the little number in each box with which it shares an edge.

So the corner squares have two neighbours, the rest along the sides, three and the square in the middle has four. From the little larger numbers given, and the large little numbers already placed, can you fill in the rest?

14	16	15
3		
24	29	21
16	21	15
		4

603 CODE MASTER

Just follow the rules of that classic puzzle, Master Mind, to crack the colour code. The first number tells you how many of the pegs are exactly correct – the right colour in the right place (✓✓).

The second number tells you how many pegs are the correct colour but are not in the right place (✓). Colours may be repeated in the answer.

By comparing the information given by each line, can you work out which colour goes in which place?

		✓✓	✓
● ● ○ ○		1	1
● ● ● ●		2	0
○ ○ ● ○		1	1
● ● ● ●		2	1
● ○ ● ●		0	2
○ ○ ○ ○		4	0

604 WHAT'S YOUR GAME?

Andy Player is giving board games to all his friends this Christmas and at the moment the parcels are stacked up in the corner of his living room as shown in the drawing. From the clues given below, can you work out who each parcel is addressed to, and which game is in it?

Clues

1 The Longs' present is immediately below the one intended for the Dixons.
2 Parcel E contains the game Andy's giving John and Laura Smith.
3 The *Advantage* game is in contact with just one other present, the one meant for the Woods.
4 The present addressed to Mike and Fran Brown is immediately above the *Terminator* game and immediately below the backgammon set; the latter is not next but one in the stack to the Fields' present.
5 The *X-Words* game which Andy has bought for Frank and Carol Allen is not at the bottom of the pile.
6 The elaborate Roman-style chess set, which is not parcel G, is between the presents Andy is giving to the Fields and to the Kings, neither of which is next to the parcel addressed to the Smiths.
7 Parcel C contains the game *Stonewall*; the *Hippodrome* horse-racing game isn't in parcel F.

Presents for: Allens; Browns; Dixons; Fields; Kings; Longs; Smiths; Woods
Games: *Advantage*; backgammon; chess; *Grand Tour*; *Hippodrome*; *Stonewall*; *Terminator*; *X-Words*

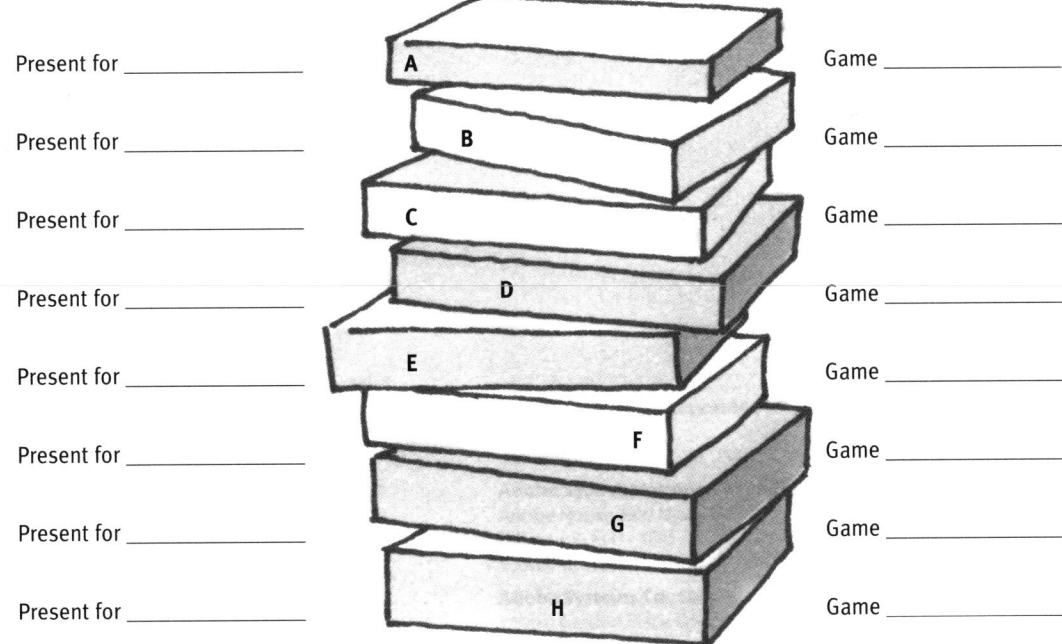

Present for _____   A   Game _____

Present for _____   B   Game _____

Present for _____   C   Game _____

Present for _____   D   Game _____

Present for _____   E   Game _____

Present for _____   F   Game _____

Present for _____   G   Game _____

Present for _____   H   Game _____

Starting tip: Work out for whom present H is intended.

605 MATCH BLOCKS

There are three identical squares in the grid below. Can you spot them? Watch out though, they may not be the same way up!

606 BATTLE GROUND

Each figure features one detail that is not present in the other three. Can you spot all four extra details?

607 SCATTER-PILLAR

Can you rearrange the six fragments below to form two identical pillars?

608 SQUARE NUMBERS

The digits, ranging from 1 to 9, in each of the five lines and columns in this square add up to 23; three have been inserted. From the clues given below, can you fill in the rest?

CLUES

1 In every line there are three odd and two even digits, as there are also in columns 1, 3 and 4; column 2 has four even and column 5 five odd digits. There are no repeated digits in any line, but column 1 has a repeated odd digit, like column 5; the other columns have no repeated digits.
2 The two 9s are in lines 1 and 4, the two 8s are in two other successive lines and the two lines which contain a 7 have a line separating them; the three 1s are in successive lines and the three 2s are in odd-numbered lines; only in line 3 is there no 3 and only in line 4 is there no 5; there are no 5s in columns 1 and 2.
3 In lines 2 and 3 the highest digit immediately precedes the lowest but in line 4 the lowest immediately precedes the highest. In line 1 the second digit is one higher than the fourth, but in line 5 the second is lower than the fourth.
4 The square at the intersection of line 3 and column 4 does not contain 5; the square at the end of line 3 contains an odd digit.

Starting tip: Work out in which lines the 8s appear.

	1	2	3	4	5
1					5
2					
3					
4					
5	3				5

609 LITTLE AND LARGE

In this puzzle, the little numbers are large and the large numbers are little! Each little number from 1 to 9 is to be placed into the boxes, one per box. Each larger number in the boxes is the sum of the little number that goes in it plus the little number in each box with which it shares an edge.

So the corner squares have two neighbours, the rest along the sides, three and the square in the middle has four. From the little larger numbers given, and the large little numbers already placed, can you fill in the rest?

14 **7**	16	14
25	22	18
19	18	14 **2**

610 ISLAND HOPPING

Each circle containing a number represents an island. The object is to connect each island with vertical or horizontal bridges so that:
* The number of bridges is the same as the number inside the island.
* There can be up to two bridges between two islands.
* Bridges cannot cross islands or other bridges.
* There is a continuous path connecting all the islands.

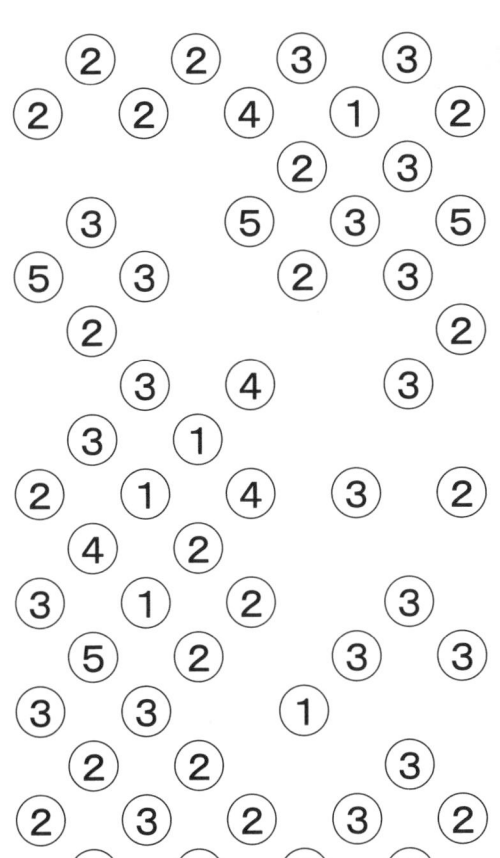

611 DOT-TO-DOT

Join the dots from 1 to 38 to reveal the hidden picture.

614 DIGIT FIDGET

The 10 digits are rewritten so that none is in its correct position, counting, 0–9 from the left.

1 is two places right of 0,
5 two places right of 4,
2 two places right of 8,
9 two places right of 7,
6 three left of 2,
4 three left of 3.

Can you rewrite the number?

613 MIRROR IMAGE

Can you work out which reflection belongs to each of the hat wearers, Andy, Ben and Colin, who are shown at the top?

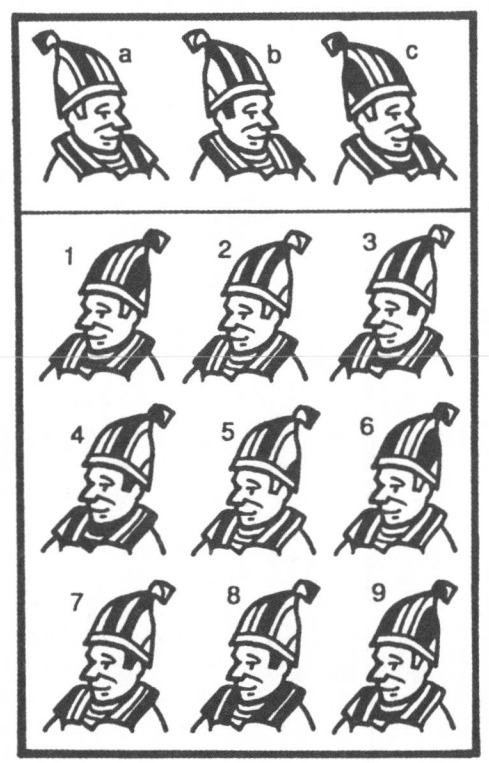

612 STRIP TRICK

Can you arrange the numbered strips in order to create the coiled strip shown at the top?

175

615 NUMBER KROSS

See how quickly you can fit all these numbers into the grid. We've filled one number in to start you off.

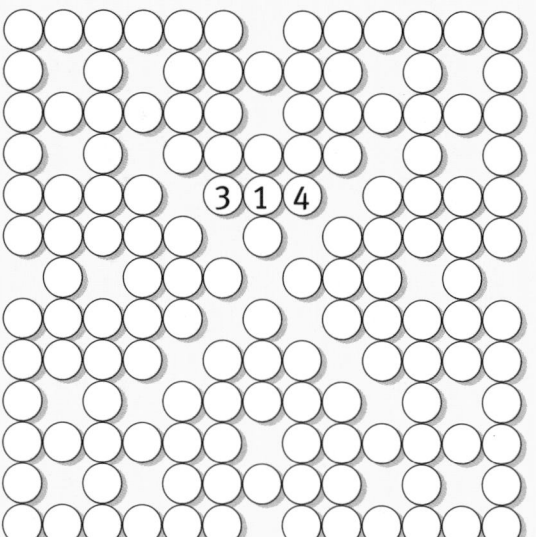

3 figures	5 figures	6 figures
209	13129	140415
~~314~~	15521	180356
504	23328	283913
526	27138	294897
620	34005	345950
731	34452	394352
832	40226	453124
915	54501	494874
	60926	566157
4 figures	64894	568265
1971	75233	587001
2295	75740	636031
3640	83992	678565
4981	87437	841807
5863	93620	860221
7042	94339	984942
8406		
9758		

616 SAFE BET

This is an odd safe. Solve all the clues and find the combination in the shaded squares.

ACROSS

1. Subtract 68,017 from *4 down*
3. Half of *1 across*
5. Twice *3 down*
6. First three digits of *25 across*
8. Next in series 595, 664, 733,…, then add 40
10. Subtract 204 from *22 down*
11. Square first four digits of *1 across*
17. Add 567,971 to *11 across*
19. Last three digits of *17 across*
20. Reverse digits of *23 across*
21. Square root of 259,081
23. Add 300 to *21 across*
24. Subtract 30 squared from *6 across* squared, then add 40
25. 3 per cent of 410,700

DOWN

1. Add *3 across* to *24 across*
2. Subtract 40 from *8 across*
3. Square root of *25 across*
4. Add 82,986 to *24 across*
5. Subtract 1,511,194 from *7 down*
7. Add 3,780,988 to *9 down*
9. Subtract 5,000 from *18 down*
12. Add 90 to *13 down*
13. Subtract 96,834 from *4 down*
14. Subtract 10 from *22 down*
15. Square root of 40,000
16. Add 1,000 to *18 down*
18. 3 per cent of 603,700
22. Multiply *3 down* by 9
23. Subtract 99 from *19 across*

618 SCOOP

At Justa Conesa Italian ice cream parlour, combinations of cones, scoops and chocolate bars are charged per item:

Chocca Likka –
1 cone, 1 scoop,
2 chocolate bars 80 cents
Coola Cona –
1 cone, 2 scoops, 1 chocolate bar
95 cents
Plain –
1 cone, 1 scoop 40 cents
From this – can you work out the cost of one scoop of ice cream?

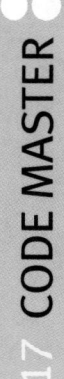

617 CODE MASTER

Just follow the rules of that classic puzzle, Master Mind, to crack the colour code. The first number tells you how many of the pegs are exactly correct – the right colour in the right place (✓✓). The second number tells you how many pegs are the correct colour but are not in the right place (✓). Colours may be repeated in the answer. By comparing the information given by each line, can you work out which colour goes in which place?

✓✓ ✓

1 0
0 1
1 0
1 0
0 0
4 0

619 TWOS AND THREES

Which of the articles below appear four times?

620 IT FIGURES

Place a number from 1 to 9 in each empty cell so that the sum of each vertical or horizontal block equals the number at the top or on the left of that block. Numbers may only be used once in each block.

621 NUMBER SQUARES

Can you complete the grids with the aid of the numbers given, so that all sums, whether horizontal or vertical, are correct? (Please note that each sum should be treated separately.)

12	×		=		+	20	=	
+		×		÷		+		−
	÷	10	=		+		=	
=		=		=		=		=
	−		=	12	+			=
÷		−		+		÷		−
	+		=		−	2	=	
=		=		=		=		=
	+	14	=		−		=	22

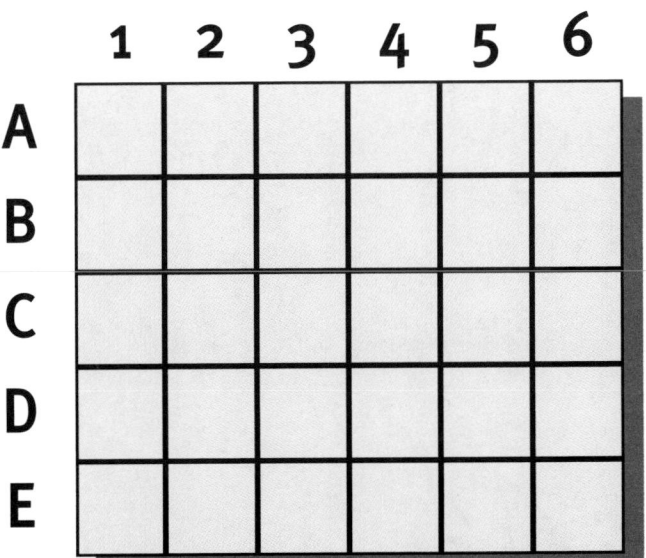

622 THIRTY DAYS HATH NOVEMBER

Each of the thirty days of November is inscribed in a different box in the diagram. From the clues given below, can you insert the correct date in each of the boxes?

Clues

1 The 15th, 23rd and 4th of the month are in consecutive boxes reading from left to right in the same horizontal row.

2 The 1st is in box C3; the only other single-digit date in row C is its immediate left-hand neighbour, and there are no more such dates at all in column 3.

3 The 11th is in the box immediately below the 21st, and the 24th is diagonally adjacent, below right, to the 22nd.

4 Box B4 contains a date five days after the one in A2.

5 The 30th is immediately below the 28th.

6 The 3rd, the 20th and the 9th are, reading from top to bottom, in the top three boxes of one vertical column.

7 The two days which immediately follow the one in B2 are, respectively, in D6 and D3.

8 Box A6 contains a two-digit even-numbered date, which is half the one to be found in C5.

9 One horizontal row begins with the 6th and ends with the 25th.

10 The 26th is two boxes above the 7th in the same column.

11 The 2nd, which has the 16th immediately to its left, is in the row above the 5th, which is two boxes right of the 13th, which is in the same vertical column as the 29th.

12 The 17th is somewhere in column 1, the 27th in column 2, and the 19th somewhere in row B.

13 The 10th is in a higher row than the 12th, but not in the same column.

Dates:

1	2	3	4
5	6	7	8
9	10	11	12
13	14	15	16
17	18	19	20
21	22	23	24
25	26	27	28
29	30		

Starting tip: Begin by placing the 9th in its correct box.

	1	2	3	4	5	6
A						
B						
C						
D						
E						

623 LUDO ●●●

Four little girls sat down one rainy day to play a traditional game of ludo. From the clues given below, can you say who sat in each of positions 1 to 4, decide which colour of counters each had chosen for the game, and work out what number of spots on the dice each had obtained with her most recent throw?

Clues

1 No player had a number of spots on the dice which corresponded with the number indicating her position at the table.

2 Rachel, who threw a three, was next clockwise from the player using the yellow counters.

3 The red counters on the board belonged to Theresa.

4 The player in seat 2 had just thrown a six.

5 It was a blue counter which was moved four squares after one player's last throw; this was not Angela.

6 Yvonne was not sitting in seat 3.

Names: Angela; Rachel; Theresa; Yvonne
Counters: blue; green; red; yellow
Spots on dice: 1; 3; 4; 6

Name: _____
Counters: _____   1
Spots: _____

Name: _____
Counters: _____   4
Spots: _____

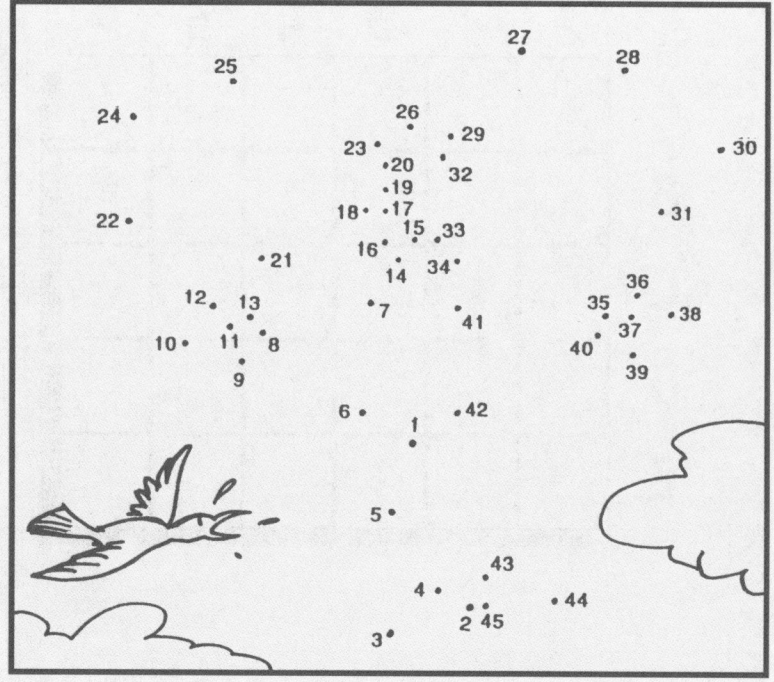

2 _____
_____
_____

3
Name: _____
Counters: _____
Spots: _____

Starting tip: Start by working out the colour of Rachel's counters.

624 NUMBER KROSS ●●

See how quickly you can fit all these numbers into the grid. We've filled one number in to start you off.

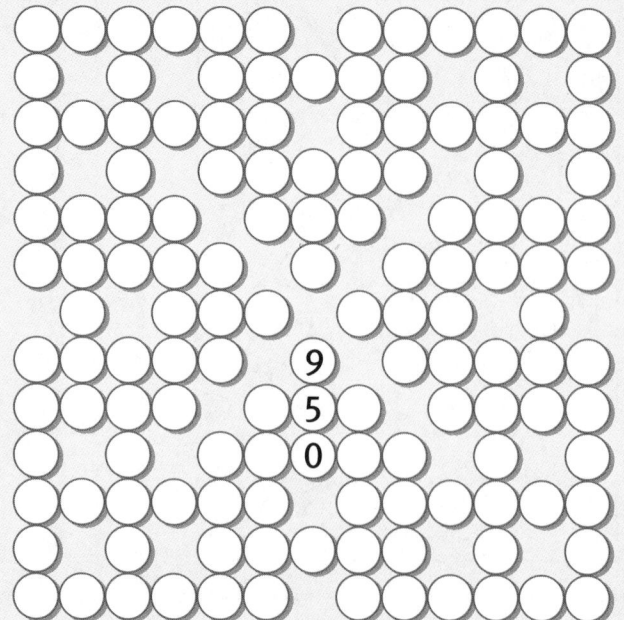

3 figures	5 figures	6 figures
147	14214	101723
257	17012	107028
348	21234	201034
439	27893	279469
527	30514	304050
731	39130	317029
823	43297	417924
950	50781	450353
	54829	557894
4 figures	69483	575859
1735	71335	610778
2007	71827	721707
3976	80724	771644
4041	82133	809010
5923	93009	817345
6125	94345	971872
7409		
8422		

625 DOT-TO-DOT

Join the dots from 1 to 45 to reveal the hidden picture.

626 FIGURE IT OUT

Each digit from 1–9 appears four times in the square, no similar digits being diagonally adjacent. Where the same digit appears more than once in any row or column, this is stated. Can you complete the square?

Row
1 Two 4s and two 9s; total 34
2 One even, two odd, two even, one odd digit from left to right; lowest is 2; total 37
3 Two 1s separated by an 8; two 5s but no 4s
4 Two adjacent 6s with an odd digit and two 8s
5 Two 3s separated by a 6; highest is a 7; total 22
6 Two adjacent 7s; total 24

Column
1 Two 8s separated by an odd digit; total 29
2 Two adjacent 9s; the other digits also total 18
3 Two adjacent 2s; total 27
4 Two 9s separated by two digits; total 31
5 Two 6s separated by two digits, all bracketed by two odd digits
6 Total 22

	1	2	3	4	5	6
1						
2						
3						
4						
5						
6						

627 ON SITE

Four couples are having a holiday in their caravans on a popular seaside site. From the clues given below, can you name the couple in each of the caravans numbered 1 to 4, and say where each pair is from?

Clues

1 Paul's caravan is somewhere to the right of the one being used by Alicia, from Cardiff, and her partner.
2 Esme and her partner are separated from Desmond and his partner only by the couple from Belfast.
3 Sebastian and Zoe have a lower-numbered caravan than the couple from London.
4 Miranda is staying in caravan 3, but not with Luther.

Males: Desmond; Luther; Paul; Sebastian
Females: Alicia; Esme; Miranda; Zoe
Cities: Belfast; Cardiff; Edinburgh; London

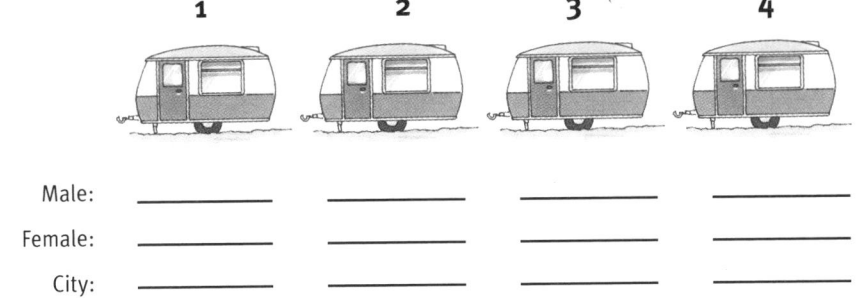

Male: ____ ____ ____ ____
Female: ____ ____ ____ ____
City: ____ ____ ____ ____

Starting tip: Start by naming the woman in caravan 4.

628 NUMBER TREE

Sixteen leaves are on the eight branches of the tree and each contains a different number from 1 to 16. Using the following clues, can you determine which number is on which leaf? All the totals of two leaves at the same height are different (leaf 2 is at the same height as leaf 9, 3 is the same as 10 and so on). Four of the totals of the leaves on each branch are unique but the other two totals each appear twice. No number is the same as the leaf that it is on and no two consecutive numbers are on the same branch or at the same height. The seven prime numbers, including 1, are all on leaves which have prime numbers. 2 and 14 are on the same branch and the number on leaf 14 is a multiple of that on 12. A leaf containing a square number is immediately above another with a square number, neither of the square numbers being 9. Number 7 is higher than number 9 which is higher than number 10, which is immediately below number 1. The total of leaf 9 (which does not contain 15) and leaf 11 is the same as the total of the numbers on leaves 5 and 7. Number 13 is at the same height as number 4 which is somewhere higher than number 16. Number 1 is immediately below an odd number. Only two branches contain two odd numbers and the total of the numbers on leaves 6 and 8 is a prime number, which is also the same as the total of one of the branches. Number 3 is somewhere below number 11.

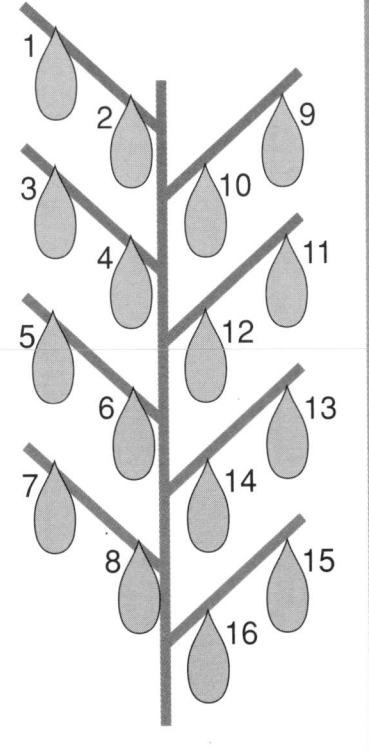

629 TWINNED UP

The twins would like to buy matching belts. Which two will they choose?

630 MODERN ART

Having bought one of the abstract paintings, the art-lover can't remember which one it is or which way up it should go. Can you help him?

631 CODE MASTER

Just follow the rules of that classic puzzle, Master Mind, to crack the colour code. The first number tells you how many of the pegs are exactly correct – the right colour in the right place (✓✓). The second number tells you how many pegs are the correct colour but are not in the right place (✓). Colours may be repeated in the answer. By comparing the information given by each line, can you work out which colour goes in which place?

				✓✓	✓
				0	3
				0	2
				2	0
				0	2
				1	0
				4	0

632 MATCH-BLOCKS

Can you spot which three squares in the picture below are identical? Watch out, though – they may not be the same way up!

633 CROSS-SUMS

With the help of the number already in place in the grid, see if you can fill in the cell, using the numbers listed below. The rule which decides what goes where is that the number in the top square of each cross of five squares must equal the total of the numbers in the square of that cross for instance

$X + A = B = C = D$

```
  X
A B C
  D
```

1	2	3	4	5	6	7
8	9	10	11	12	31	48
51	51	61	74	109	121	181
~~399~~	427	462	1469			

399

634 SQUARE NUMBERS

The numbers 1–25 are entered randomly in a 5 x 5 square so that no two consecutive numbers are adjacent in any direction, or included in any row, column or long diagonal. The four corner numbers are all two-digit prime numbers increasing each time clockwise starting from one of the corners. E4 is twice that in C1 but only half B3. D5 is twice C5 but only half A2. A4 is twice D3 but only half B2. B1 and D4 are both prime, the latter being five higher than D5; C1 and C4 total 25; E2 plus E3 equals C1, the former being less than the latter. B1 plus B5 equals D2. Can you locate each number?

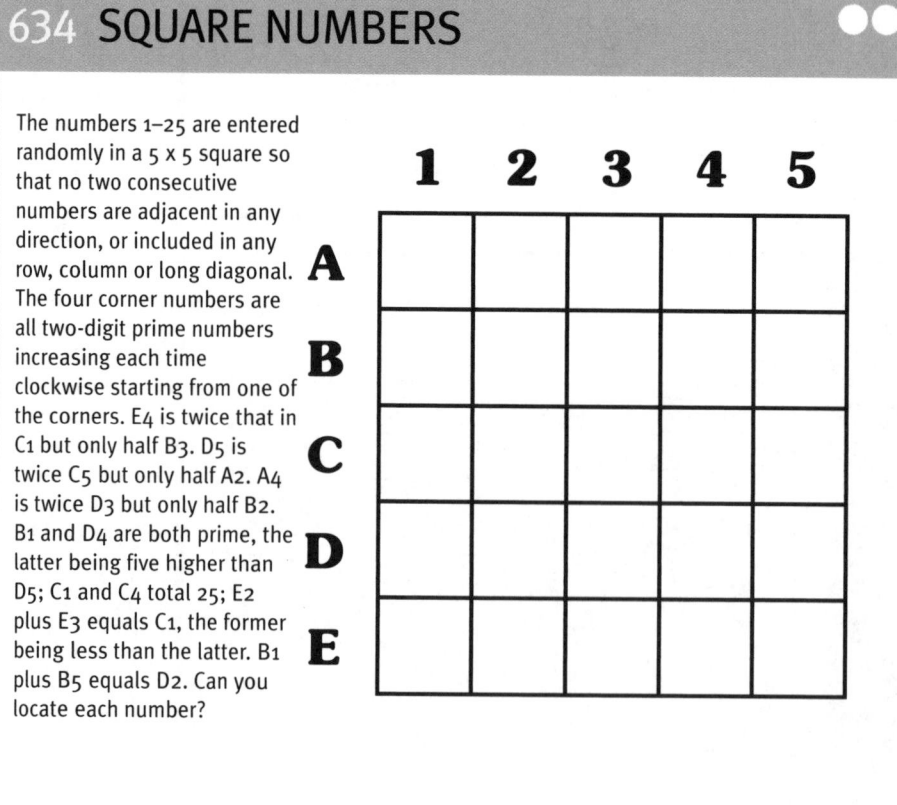

635 IN THE LOCKER ROOM

The diagram shows a block of lockers in the men's changing room at the squash club. From the clues given below, can you fully identify and describe the men who are currently using each of the lockers numbered 1 to 4?

First name: _____   _____
Surname: _____   _____
Description: _____   _____

Clues
1 The priest is using the locker immediately above Melvin's.
2 Denzil's locker is the one immediately to the right of Fettle's.
3 The bank manager is using locker number 4.
4 Gareth's locker is in diagonal alignment with the one the lecturer is using.
5 Kieron's locker is on the same level as the lawyer's.
6 Spry's locker has a number one lower than Hardy's.

First names: Denzil; Gareth; Kieron; Melvin
Surnames: Fettle; Fitt; Hardy; Spry
Descriptions: bank manager; priest; lawyer; lecturer

Starting tip: Begin by working out the first name of the man using locker 1.

First name: _____   _____
Surname: _____   _____
Description: _____   _____

636 NINE NUMBERS

Place a number from 1 to 9 in each empty cell so that each row, each column and each 3 x 3 block contains all the numbers from 1 to 9.

						5	6	4
	1	2	9					
		3		8				
		6						3
	2		6		5		7	
7						8		
			4			1		
					7	6	9	
2	5	8						

637 BATTLESHIPS

Do you remember the old game of battleships? These puzzles are based on that idea. Your task is to find the vessels in the diagram. Some parts of boats or sea squares have already been filled in, and a number next to a row or column refers to the number of occupied squares in that row or column. The boats may be positioned horizontally or vertically, but no two boats or parts of boats are in adjacent squares – horizontally, vertically or diagonally.

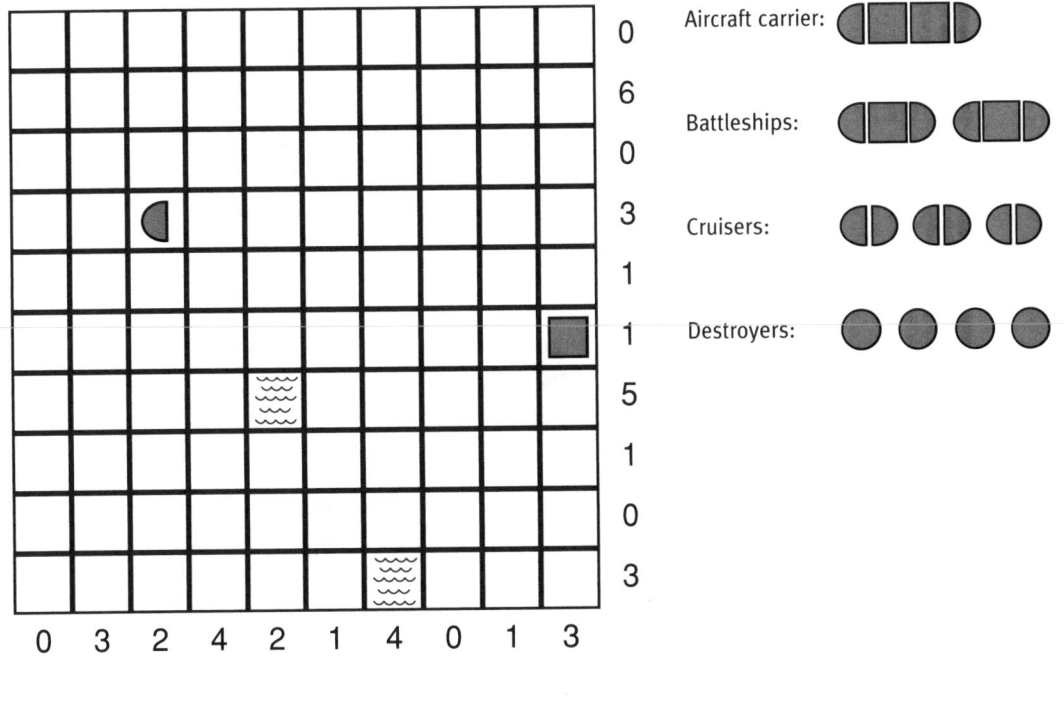

Aircraft carrier:
Battleships:
Cruisers:
Destroyers:

Row numbers (top to bottom): 0, 6, 0, 3, 1, 1, 5, 1, 0, 3
Column numbers (left to right): 0, 3, 2, 4, 2, 1, 4, 0, 1, 3

638 COSTUME DRAMA

Each picture contains a detail that is not present in the other three. Can you spot all four extra details?

639 ALL SQUARE

Each of the 16 small squares making up the large square in the diagram contains either one of the numbers 1 to 8 or the square of one of these numbers. From the clues given below, can you place the correct number in each square? NB The numbers 1 and 4 will, of course, each appear twice.

Clues

1 The numbers in the four corner squares, which are all different, total 21 when added together.

2 16 is immediately to the right of 64, and immediately below 49.

3 The 9 and 6 are both in column A.

4 Squares B2 and C4 both contain single-digit numbers, the former being an even number.

5 The total of the four numbers in row 1 is one higher than the number in square A2.

6 The number in square D2 is twice the one in C1.

7 The number in square B3 is the square of the one in D1.

8 The 25 and the 8 are on the same horizontal row of squares.

9 One of the 1s is in column B.

10 The number in C4 is the square root of one of the other numbers in column C.

Numbers: 1; 1; 2; 3; 4; 4; 5; 6; 7; 8; 9; 16; 25; 36; 49; 64

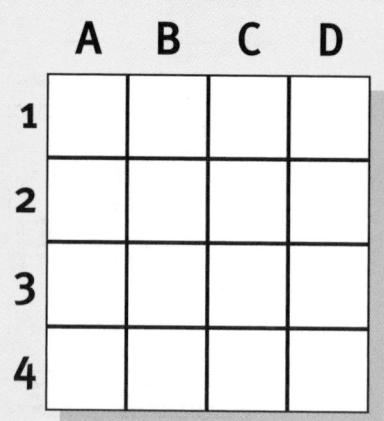

Starting tip: Begin by working out where to put the 16.

640 SILHOUETTE

Shade in every fragment containing a dot – and what have you got?

641 IT FIGURES

Place a number from 1 to 9 in each empty cell so that the sum of each vertical or horizontal block equals the number at the top or on the left of that block. Numbers may only be used once in each block.

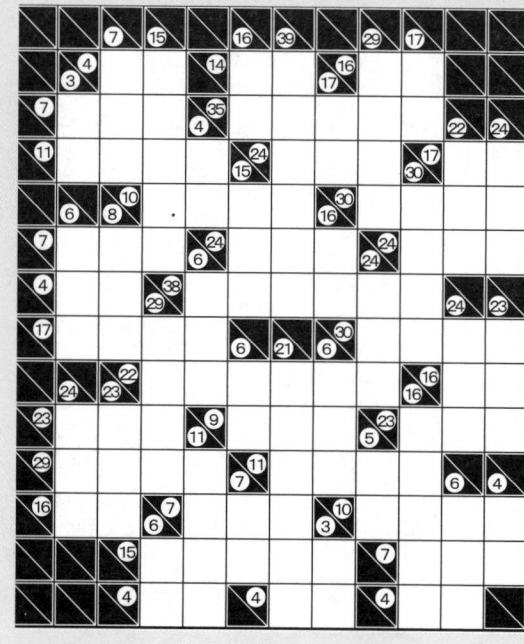

642 SALLY'S GUESTS

Young Sally was allowed to invite three of her friends who live in the same street to stay at her house for lunch. At the end of the meal, each child was asked to choose which flavour of yoghurt she would like. From the clues given below, can you work out who sat in which position at the table, say at which number in the street she lives, and name her chosen yoghurt flavour?

Clues

1 The meal was served at an odd-numbered house.

2 Sally sat directly opposite Jenny, who chose cherry as her yoghurt flavour.

3 The strawberry yoghurt was consumed by the girl on chair number 3, whose home is not at number 11.

4 The girl on chair 4 lives at number 20.

5 The peach yoghurt was eaten by the girl who lives at number 15, whose counterclockwise neighbour at the table was Rosie.

6 Helen was not sitting in position 2.

Names: Helen; Jenny; Rosie; Sally
House numbers: 8; 11; 15; 20
Flavours: cherry; peach; pineapple; strawberry

Name: _____
House no.: _____
Flavour: _____

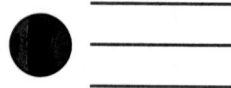

Starting tip: First work out who was sitting on chair 2.

Name: _____
House no.: _____
Flavour: _____

643 MAZE MYSTERY

Travel from the entrance to the exit of the maze, filling the path completely to create a picture.

644 SILHOUETTE

Shade in every fragment containing a dot – and what have you got?

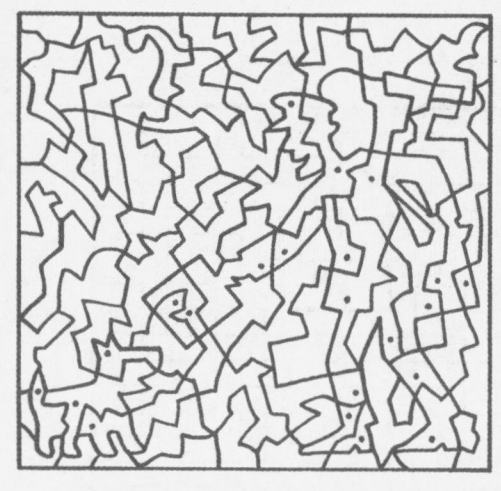

646 SUM-UP

Calculate the price of each pawn, castle, knight and king using the given totals.

$ 18-00

$ 14-50

$ 13-50

$ 15-50

645 TROPHIES

Karen Mills is 17, and a talented athlete. On the mantelpiece of her parents' home are displayed the three trophies which she's won this year. From the clues below, can you fill in on the diagram the details of each trophy: her placing, the event, the competition, and the month?

Clues

1 The 1,500 metres trophy was won the month after she received the third-place award, which isn't Trophy A.
2 Her discus trophy stands to the left of the one she won in July.
3 Trophy B was won at the County Amateur Athletics Association meeting, for a placing one higher than she achieved in the high jump.
4 It was in the annual town sports that she took a first place.

Placings: First; Second; Third
Events: Discus; 1,500 metres; high jump
Meetings: County; inter-schools; town
Months: May; June; July

Starting tip: Work out for which place Trophy B was awarded.

Placing:	_____	_____	_____
Event:	_____	_____	_____
Meeting:	_____	_____	_____
Month:	_____	_____	_____

A   B   C

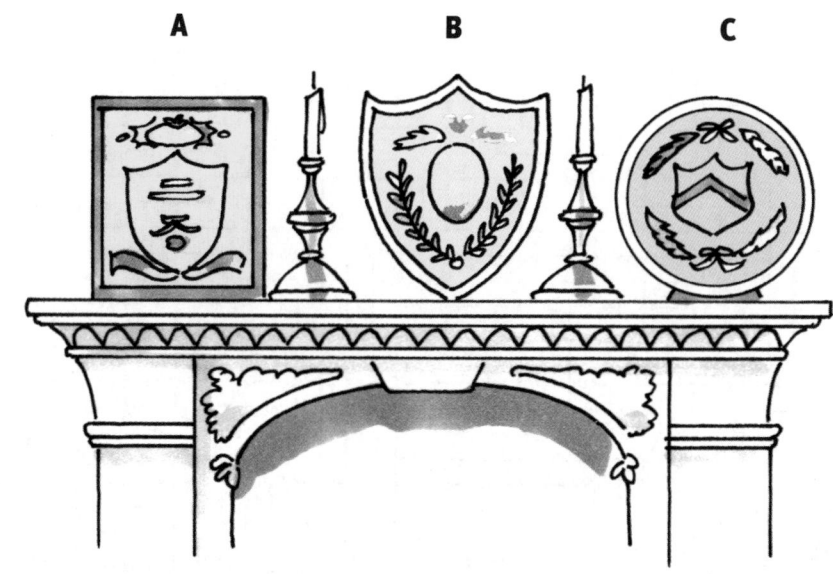

647 TROUBLESOME TRIANGLE

The numbers 1–15 are to be inserted into the grid. No two consecutive numbers are in the same row or arrowed diagonal. The numbers on the left show the total in the horizontal row and those below show the total of the diagonal.

If squares 5 and 8 total 16, and in the diagonal totalling 27 only one is an even number, can you complete the grid?

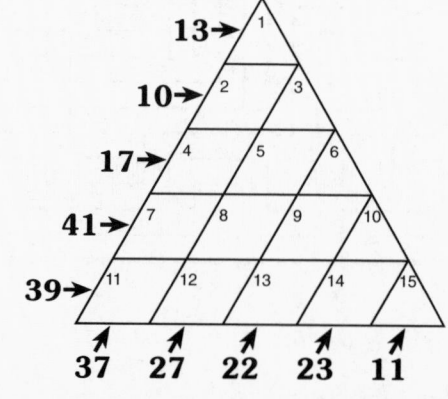

648 FIGURE WORK

Each figure contains a detail that is not present in the other three. Can you spot all four details?

650 DOT-TO-DOT

Join the dots from 1 to 36 to reveal the hidden picture.

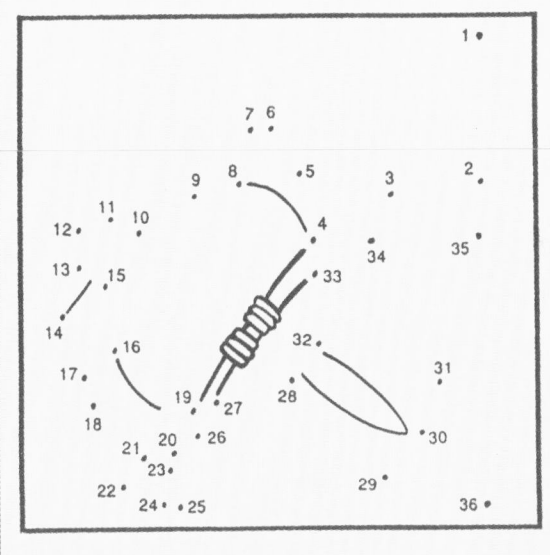

649 RED, WHITE AND BLUE

Each of the squares numbered 1 to 13 is coloured red, white or blue, one colour being represented five times, and the other two colours, four times each. From the clues given below, can you insert the correct colour in each of the squares?

Clues
1 No two adjacent squares vertically or horizontally are the same colour.
2 There is a white square directly to the left of a blue square in the middle horizontal row, which has no other white squares.
3 None of the four isolated squares (numbers 1, 5, 9 and 13) is blue.
4 Two of the four squares denoted by a double-digit number are red.
5 There is just one red square in the horizontal row numbered from 2 to 4.
6 Central square number 7 is red.
7 Squares 1 and 12 are the same colour.
8 One white square has a number which is twice that of a red square.

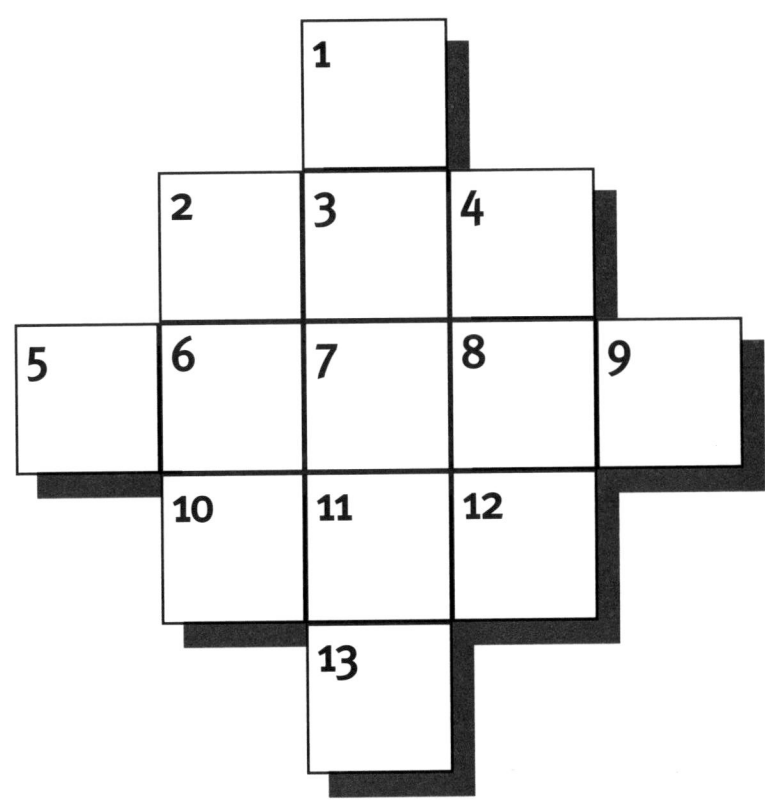

Starting tip: Begin by identifying the blue squares.

651 CUBIT

The square contains the first 16 numbers which are either a square or cube (or both) from 1–169 inclusive. Each row and column contains a one-digit number. When all of the numbers in each row or column are added together, the final digit of the total is shown next to the appropriate row or column. C2 plus A4 equals C3; B4 plus D2 plus one equals A1; C3 has three digits; all in column 1 are odd and all in column 4 are even; A3 is three times C1 and D2 is a multiple of A2.

Can you place each number in the grid?

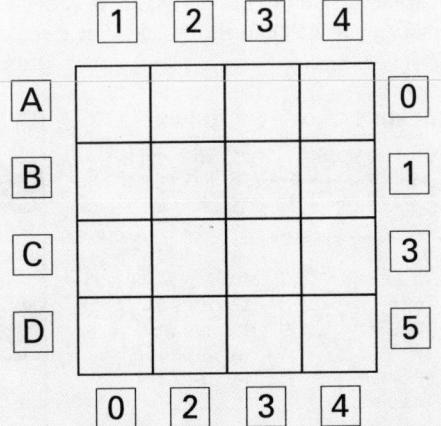

652 WHO'S WHO?

From the information given below can you match each girl to her sister?

653 DROP-OUT

In the top picture, the man is kicking a ball. In the bottom picture, the ball has gone. Which ball did he kick away?

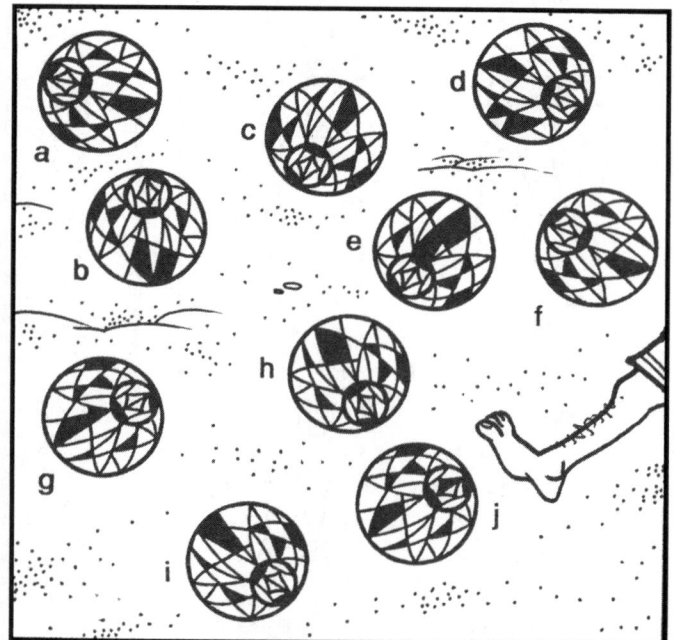

654 CROSSNUMBER

Just like a crossword – but the answer to each clue is a number which is entered by putting one digit into each square. See if you can fill all these empty squares:

ACROSS
1. 7 x 8 – 9
3. 9 x 8 – 7
6. 3 x 3 x 3 x 3
8. 4 x 5 x 6
10. 93 + 99
11. 2 x 2 x 2 x 3
12. 96 / 6
14. 102 – 38
17. 97 – 59
19. 387 – 93
21. 18 x 20
23. 1986 / 3
24. (12 x 8) + 1

DOWN
2. 1000 – 211
4. 29 x 11 – 10
5. 200 / 4
7. 11 x 11
9. 71 + 82 + 93
10. 24 – 8
13. 101 – 38
15. 20 x 20
16. 14 x 14
18. 364 + 475
19. 52 / 2
20. 6 x 7
22. (3 x 9) + (5 x 8)

655 CHRISTMAS PUDDING

The 16 squares in the large square in the diagram each contain one of the letters which make up the phrase CHRISTMAS PUDDING. From the clues given below, can you put the right letter into each of the squares?

Clues

1 None of the three letters which occur twice in the phrase is in the same vertical, horizontal or diagonal line as its twin.
2 Square A4 contains a letter from the first half of the alphabet.
3 The letter in square D3 is a vowel.
4 The A is immediately to the left of the C, and immediately above one of the Ds.
5 The letter in square B2 is an S, while the T is somewhere in column D.
6 The letter in C3 is not the initial letter of either of the words in the phrase.
7 Both the U and the N are in row 2, the former being further left.
8 The letter in square C4 immediately precedes in the alphabet its neighbour in B4.
9 The letter in square D4 comes earlier in the alphabet than the one in D1.
10 The R can be seen two places to the left of an I.
11 The M and the H appear in the same horizontal row as each other.

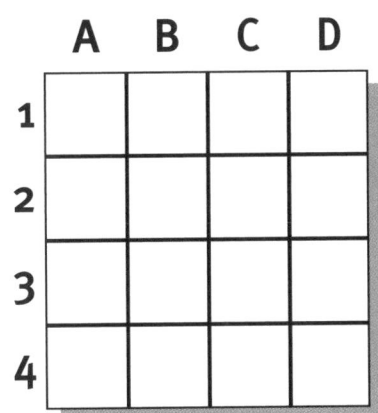

Starting tip: Start by placing both of the letters S.

656 SILHOUETTE

Shade in every fragment containing a dot – and what have you got?

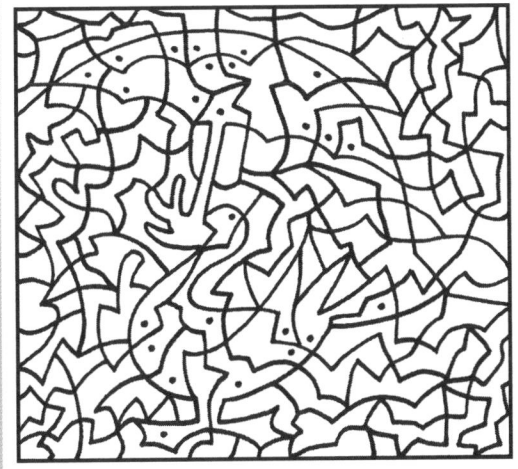

657 CODE MASTER

Just follow the rules of that classic puzzle, Master Mind, to crack the colour code. The first number tells you how many of the pegs are exactly correct – the right colour in the right place(✓✓).

The second number tells you how many pegs are the correct colour but are not in the right place(✓). Colours may be repeated in the answer.

By comparing the information given by each line, can you work out which colour goes in which place?

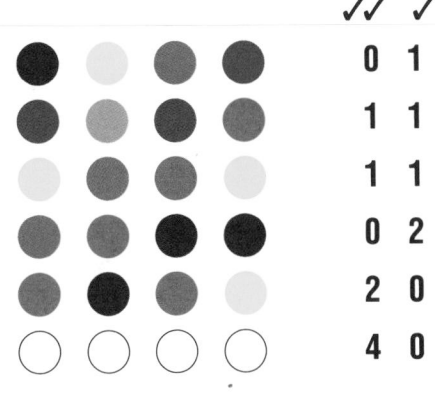

	✓✓	✓
	0	1
	1	1
	1	1
	0	2
	2	0
	4	0

658 ISLAND HOPPING

Each circle containing a number represents an island. The object is to connect each island with vertical or horizontal bridges so that:
• The number of bridges is the same as the number inside the island.
• There can be up to two bridges between two islands.
• Bridges cannot cross islands or other bridges.
• There is a continuous path connecting all the islands.

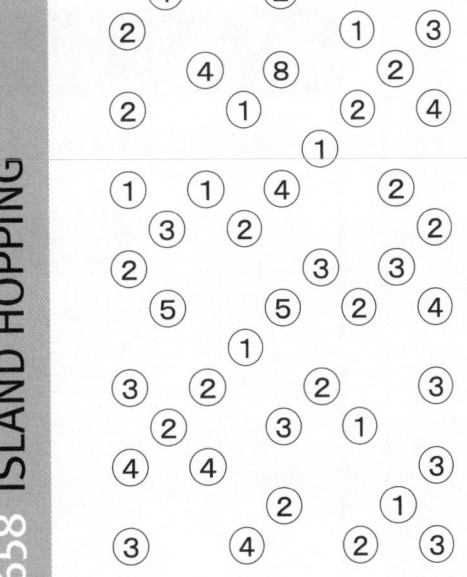

659 SILHOUETTE

Shade in every fragment containing a dot – and what have you got?

187

660 NUMBER KROSS

See how quickly you can fit all these numbers into the grid. We've filled one number in to start you off.

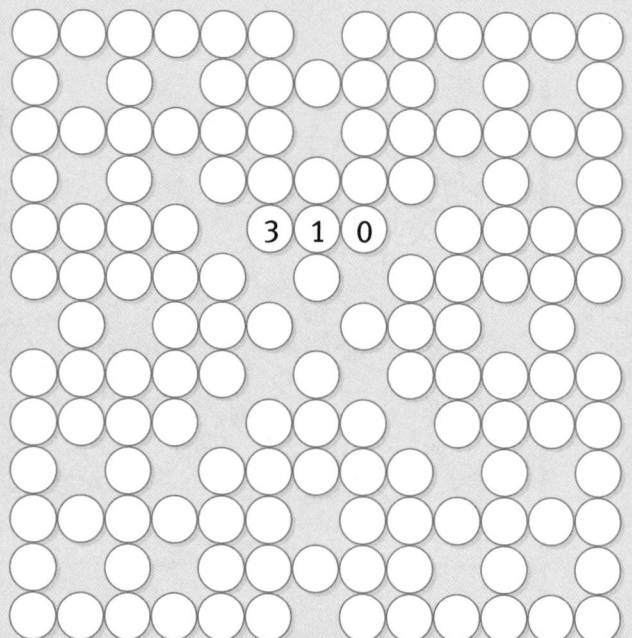

3 figures	5 figures	6 figures
132	12154	107237
217	19143	204155
~~310~~	22677	291193
428	25298	319623
543	32453	383823
638	35590	434658
748	44590	487064
920	49822	510035
	54376	567089
4 figures	56789	610987
2165	68492	620101
3312	72197	754054
4052	72346	762930
5836	84789	810501
6679	86543	885467
7096	99587	991764
8468		
9162		

661 WHICH CAR?

The game 'Which Car?' is a card game using 36 different cards. Each card depicts a car of a particular make, either a Ford, a Lincoln, or a Chevrolet, a particular model, a sports car, a saloon, or an estate, and the cars are red, green, blue or silver. In this particular game five children took part. They were each dealt seven cards, with the seventh being dealt face up. The 36th card was placed face down on the table. Each player in turn then stated (more or less!) which cards he or she did not have, and then gave an indication of the most or least numbers of cards held of any combination of make, model, or colour. In this game no-one held more than three cards in any category. George's exposed card was a green Ford saloon. He said he had no red and no blue Fords, no Chevrolet sports and no Ford estates.

Anna's exposed card was a green Chevrolet estate. She said she had no Ford sports, no silver Fords, no Ford estates, no red Lincolns and no Chevrolet saloons. Katy's exposed card was a blue Chevrolet saloon. She said she had no red cars, no silver Lincolns and no blue Fords. Richard's exposed card was a silver Lincoln saloon. He said he had no Chevrolet estates, no Lincoln sports, no Ford saloons.

Jane's exposed card was a red Ford sports car. She said she had no red Chevrolet, no Ford saloons, no green Fords, no Chevrolet sports and no silver Lincolns. George then said that he had more blue cars than any other colour and more Lincolns than any other make. He said he had one saloon car, one green car and one silver. Anna said she had more Lincolns than any other make and more saloon cars than any other model, all different colours. She said she had one blue car. Katy said she had more green cars than any other colour and one sports car. She said she had more Chevrolets than any other make, all different models and colours. Richard said he had more Fords than any other make, all different colours. He said he had more estates than any other model, only one green car and more reds than any other colour, plus one silver sports car. Jane said she had more Ford cars than any other make, all different colours, and only one blue car.

At this stage, Richard was able to identify the 36th card because he had failed to declare a further single card of a particular colour. Can you now evaluate each hand and the 36th?

	Ford			Lincoln			Chevrolet		
	Sp	Sa	Es	Sp	Sa	Es	Sp	Sa	Es
Red									
Green									
Blue									
Silver									

662 BREAKTHROUGH

See how quickly you can break this grid down into the 28 dominoes from which it is formed.

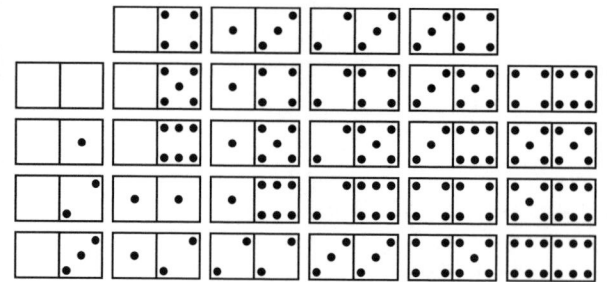

663 BOTTLED UP

Can you help the shop assistant find four identical bottles?

664 WHO AND HOW FAR?

These facts deal with four men:
1 The carpenter lives due East of Jack.
2 Mr Gainor is older than the dentist.
3 The tallest man lives due North of Len.
4 Mr Fulton lives exactly three miles from the dentist.
5 The artist is taller than Karl.
6 Len is heavier than Mr Fulton.
7 Mr Elton lives exactly two miles from the artist.
8 Jack lives due North of Karl.
9 Mr Gainor is younger than the artist.
10 Mr Fulton is shorter than Karl.
11 Mr Harkness is older than Ike.
12 Mr Fulton lives exactly five miles from the builder.

Exactly how far does the oldest man live from the builder?

665 IN THE FRAME

There were only four runners in the 3.30 at Shingledown the other day. The diagram shows a head-on view of them lined up for the start. From the clues given below, can you name the horse in each of the starting-stalls lettered A to D, and fully identify its jockey?

Clues
1 As they wait for the off in the starting-stalls Jackie has Mr Jingle immediately on one side of him and the rider named Silk immediately on the other.
2 Derek Raynes is riding a horse somewhere to the left of Placebo as you look at the diagram.
3 Nigel, who is ready for the off in stall C, is not riding Sea Fret.
4 Paddy, whose surname is not Mount, is riding Saturday Night.

Horses: Mr Jingle; Placebo; Saturday Night; Sea Fret
First names: Derek; Jackie; Nigel; Paddy
Surnames: Mount; Raynes; Ryder; Silk

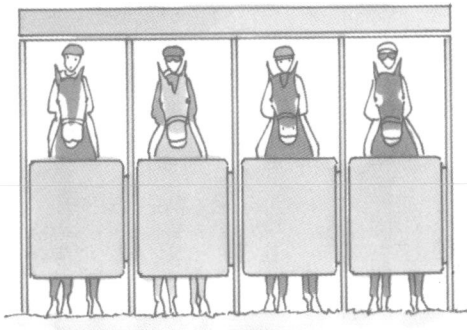

	A	B	C	D
Horse:	___	___	___	___
First name:	___	___	___	___
Surname:	___	___	___	___

Starting tip: First work out which stall Jackie is in.

666 ISLAND HOPPING

Each circle containing a number represents an island. The object is to connect each island with vertical or horizontal bridges so that:
• The number of bridges is the same as the number inside the island.
• There can be up to two bridges between two islands.
• Bridges cannot cross islands or other bridges.
• There is a continuous path connecting all the islands.

189

The artist has made five mistakes while trying to paint an exact portrait of the woman. Can you see what they are?

667 POSER

668 NUMBER KROSS

See how quickly you can fit all these numbers into the grid. We've filled one number in to start you off.

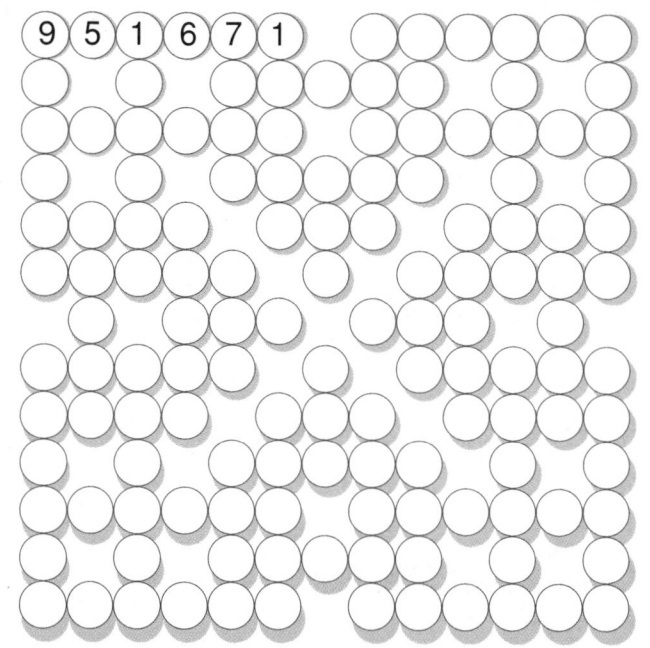

9 5 1 6 7 1

3 figures	5 figures	6 figures
103	10549	160056
208	19353	176802
321	20291	246795
435	32433	263857
530	37064	302960
645	41183	381526
847	47890	410430
923	55213	423557
	56658	504879
4 figures	64755	520128
1707	64980	614809
2067	70310	690560
3214	79287	746740
4134	84332	842710
5670	88017	951671
6786	90021	982912
7998		
8112		

669 ROLL UP

Which one of the seven impressions was made by the roller?

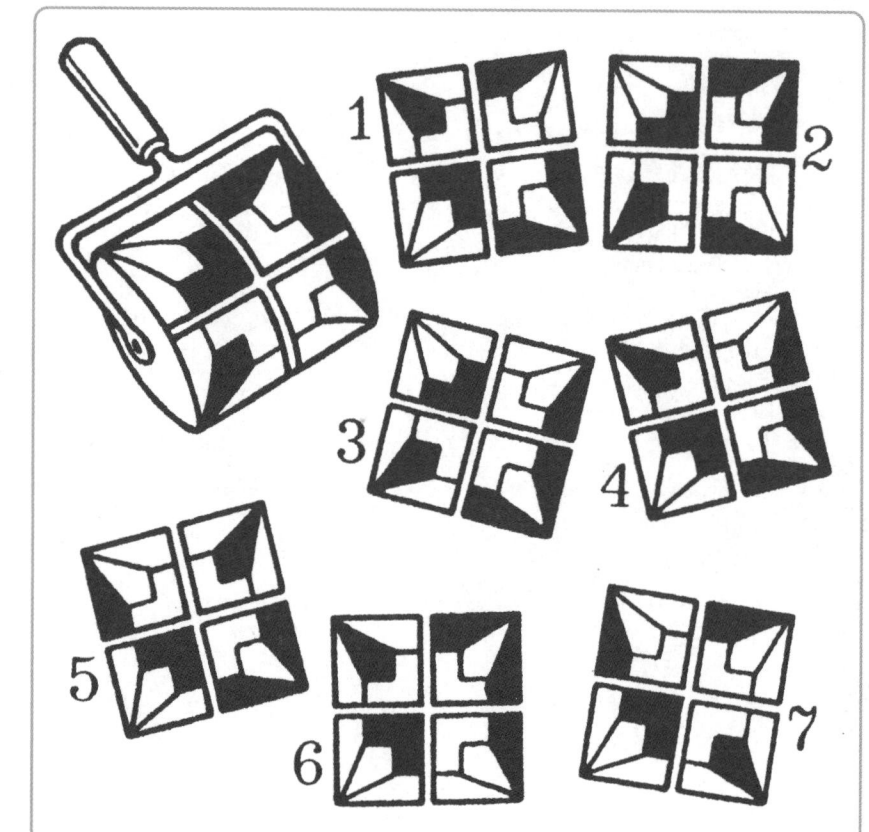

670 SIGHTSEEING

While on holiday in North Africa, four friends went sightseeing round four towns. Can you spot them in all four places?

672 TIME OUT

This digital display in Look-No-Hands Watch and Clock Emporium confuses many a passer-by. But if we tell you that one clock is 3 mins out, another is 7 mins out, a third is 14 mins out and the fourth is 20 minutes out you'll soon be able to tell anyone who asks the right time won't you?

671 ONBOARD TROUBLE

A dartboard has been divided into eight segments, each with an inner and outer number. The outer numbers are 1–8 and the inner are numbers 9–16. From the following clues, can you determine which number is in each segment? No numbers are the same as the segment number, and none of the outer numbers in a segment are a factor of the inner number of the same segment, except for the number one of course. Twice, the two numbers in a segment add up to 11 and the highest total is 22 which only appears once. The 7 is two places clockwise from the 5 and is diagonally opposite the 2. 1 is on the right-hand side of the board, three places clockwise from the 3. Segment 5 is the only one to contain two even numbers and segment 8, the only one with two odd numbers. The 7 and 16 are in the top half of the board and 15 is in the bottom half. Only one of the inner numbers is twice the segment number. On only one occasion do the two numbers in a segment add up to 19, but never do they total 20.

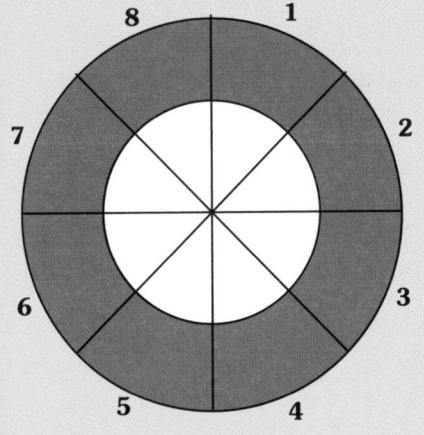

673 SET SQUARE

All the digits from 1 to 9 are used in this grid, but only once. Can you work out their positions in the grid and make the sums work? We've given two numbers to start you off.

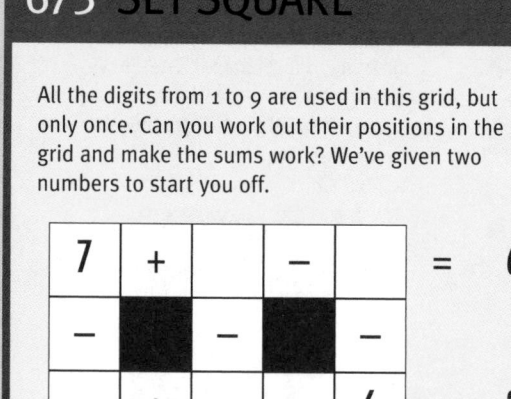

674 MISSING ONE

In the five puzzles A, B, C, D and E, can you replace each ? with the right number which fits the pattern?

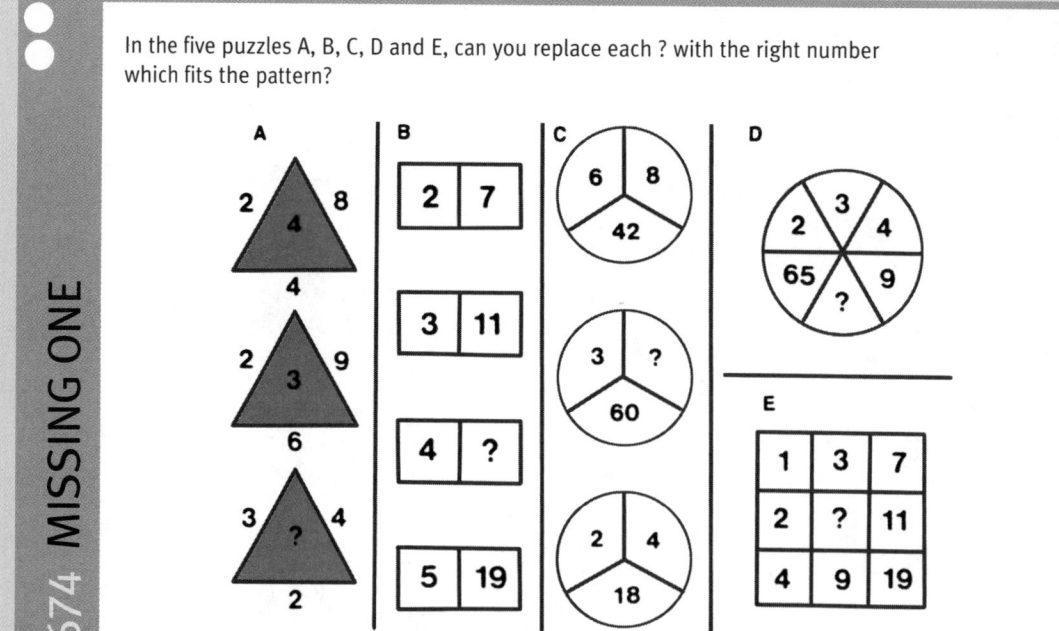

676 ISLAND HOPPING

Each circle containing a number represents an island. The object is to connect each island with vertical or horizontal bridges so that:
• The number of bridges is the same as the number inside the island.
• There can be up to two bridges between two islands.
• Bridges cannot cross islands or other bridges.
• There is a continuous path connecting all the islands.

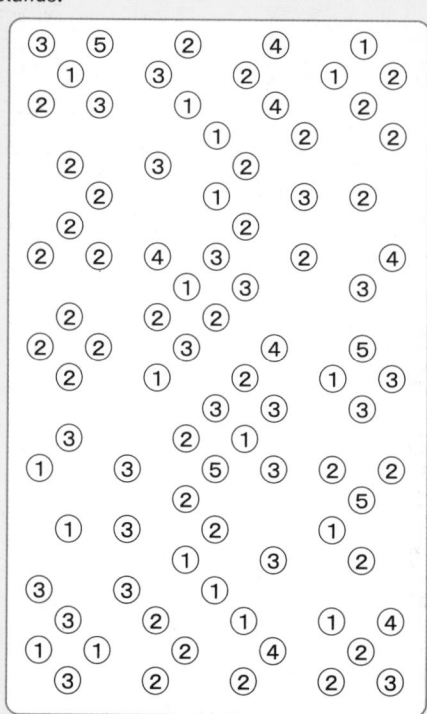

675 HIT AND MISMATCHES

The letters A–J are entered randomly in the top row so that none is in its correct position, counting left to right, and no two consecutive letters are adjacent. The numbers 2–11 are entered randomly on the bottom row and no two consecutive numbers are adjacent.

The centre row contains pairs of symbols, one plain and one coloured each of type ▭ ▬ ▢ ◼ ⬭ ⬬ ○ ● △ ▲ Two coloured symbols occupy the first two squares from the left, and two plain ones are adjacent in the 7th and 8th squares from the left. Elsewhere plain and coloured symbols alternate with no two similar shapes adjacent. A is somewhere left of B and right of G; C is not at either end. I and G are above plain symbols. 6 is below the coloured triangle, and somewhere left of both 9 and the plain rectangle, which are not in the same column. J is above the coloured square which is to the left of both the plain circle and 8 which are not in the same column; 4 is somewhere between 5 to its left, and 11, although not adjacent to either, and is below a coloured symbol. The fourth and fifth letters from the left are vowels; the second and eighth numbers from the left total 14; the coloured circle is three places to the left of the coloured triangle. One column reads H ● 3. F is to the immediate left of B and ● to the immediate left of ▭; 2 is to the immediate left of 6; D is somewhere left of E; ▬ is somewhere to the right of ▢; ○ is above 7.

Can you match letters, symbols and numbers?

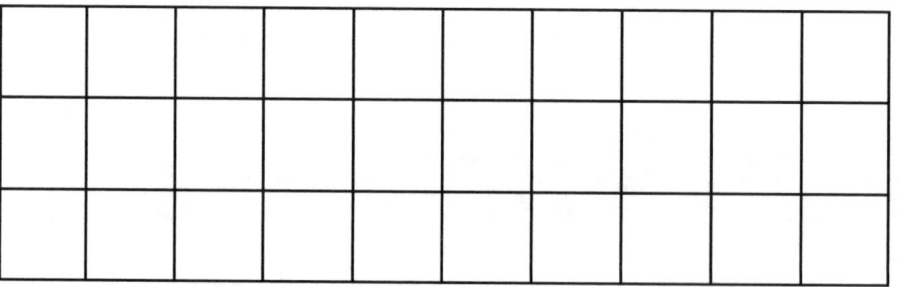

677 LOGISTICAL

Dr Featherbrane, the eminent naturalist and author of The Butterfly in Winter, was the proverbial absent-minded professor. Last week he mislaid his diary, and consequently got his timetable in a complete muddle. Can you sort out which vital item was missing on each day, which appointment he should have kept each day and which one he mistakenly went to on each day?

Clues

A Thursday was the actual day of the awards ceremony, but not the day the professor turned up, minus his notes, to give a lecture to an empty hall. The latter occasion occurred later in the week than the day he mistakenly set off for the awards ceremony.

B Professor Featherbrane spent Wednesday afternoon searching for his missing spectacles whilst waiting in vain for his students to turn up for tutorials. The interview board did not feature in any way on either this day or Friday, when he left his briefcase at home.

C On the day the professor should have gone to the faculty meeting, he travelled up to New York for an awards ceremony. Not an easy operation, as this was the day he had left his wallet behind!

Record in this grid all the information obtained from the clues, by using a cross to indicate a definite 'no' and a tick to show a definite 'yes'. Transfer these to all sections of the grid thus eliminating all but one possibility, which must be the correct one.

Day	Missing item	Appointment	Error

678 NETWORK TV

Can you spot the eight differences between these two pictures?

679 FILLING IN

Each of the letters in the boxes contains a different digit from 1 to 9. As is our usual practice, each calculation is to be treated sequentially rather than according to the 'multiplication first' system. Can you fill in the empty boxes?

```
[ ] + [ ] − [ ]  = 5
 +       ×     −
[ ] + [ ] × [ ] − [ ]  = 3
         ×     −
[ ] ÷ [ ] − [ ] × [ ]  = 2
         ×     ÷
   =     =     =
   3     8     9
```

680 MONSTER MATCH

Which two of these monsters are exactly the same?

681 SQUARE NUMBERS

The numbers 1–25 are arranged randomly so that no two consecutive numbers are adjacent in any direction. One number has been entered for you. The four corner numbers are all multiples of three and no other multiples of three are adjacent to them or to each other. The long diagonal from top left to bottom right totals 72 and the other from top right to bottom left totals 61, each diagonal containing two consecutive numbers. In column 1 the lowest number is 8; 25 is somewhere in column 2; in row E the highest number is 17. The number in B2 is twice D2 and half of E2. The number in D4 is four higher than that in D1, and equals B4 plus D3, the latter being half B5. C1 is five higher than D1; A3 plus A4 totals 23; and 24 is a chess knight's move from the 25. 10 is further left than 11 although they are in the same row; 13 and 19 are in the row below.

Can you locate each number?

	1	2	3	4	5
A					
B					
C				3	
D					
E					

683 SQUARED OFF

This empty 4 x 4 grid was originally filled with the numbers from 1 to 16 inclusive. No two consecutive numbers were adjacent (including diagonally) or in the same row or column. Each of the sixteen numbers given in the full grid is the sum of the horizontal and vertical neighbours of the corresponding square in the original grid. Can you work out where the sixteen numbers originally were?

20	21	24	17
23	41	40	25
39	28	40	28
5	37	14	19

682 ISLAND HOPPING

Each circle containing a number represents an island. The object is to connect each island with vertical or horizontal bridges so that:
• The number of bridges is the same as the number inside the island.
• There can be up to two bridges between two islands.
• Bridges cannot cross islands or other bridges.
• There is a continuous path connecting all the islands.

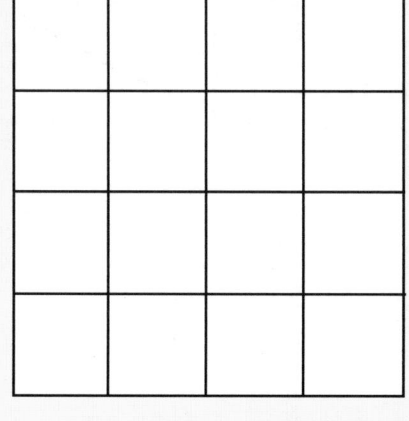

684 FILLING IN

Each of the nine empty boxes contains a digit from 1 to 9. The same digit can be used several times. As is our usual practice, each calculation is to be treated sequentially rather than according to the 'multiplication first' system. Can you fill in the empty boxes so that the calculations are correct both vertically and horizontally?

$$\square + \square \times \square = 9$$
$$\times \qquad \times \qquad \times$$
$$\square - \square - \square = 3$$
$$\div \qquad \times \qquad -$$
$$\square \times \square - \square = 6$$
$$= 6 \qquad = 6 \qquad = 9$$

685 CELL STRUCTURE

The object is to create white areas surrounded by black walls, so that:
• Each white area contains only one number.
• The number of cells in a white area is equal to the number in it.
• The white areas are separated from each other with a black wall.
• Cells containing numbers must not be filled in.
• The black cells must be linked into a continuous wall.
• Black cells cannot form a square of 2 x 2 or larger.

3			4	3			
	2						
							2
	4				2	4	
			3				
2					1		
				2			
			4		4		2

686 FIGURE IT OUT

Each figure from 1–9 appears four times in the square, no two similar digits being diagonally adjacent; where the same digit appears more than once in any row or column, this is stated. Can you complete the square?

Row
1 Two 4s and two 9s alternating; total 34
2 One even, two odd, two even, one odd digit, from left to right; lowest is 2; total 37
3 Two 1s separated by an 8; two 5s but no 4s
4 Two adjacent 6s with an odd digit and two 8s
5 Two 3s separated by a 6; highest is a 7; total 22
6 Two adjacent 7s; total 24

Column
1 Two 8s separated by an odd digit; total 29
2 Two adjacent 9s; the other digits also total 18
3 Two adjacent 2s; total 27
4 Two 9s separated by two digits; total 31
5 Two 6s separated by two digits, all bracketed by two odd digits
6 Total 22

	1	**2**	**3**	**4**	**5**	**6**
1						
2						
3						
4						
5						
6						

687 SNAIL TRAIL

Can you find a path through the maze, starting from the snail's nose and finishing in the bottom right-hand corner.

688 MAZE MYSTERY

Travel from the entrance to the exit of the maze, filling the path completely to create a picture.

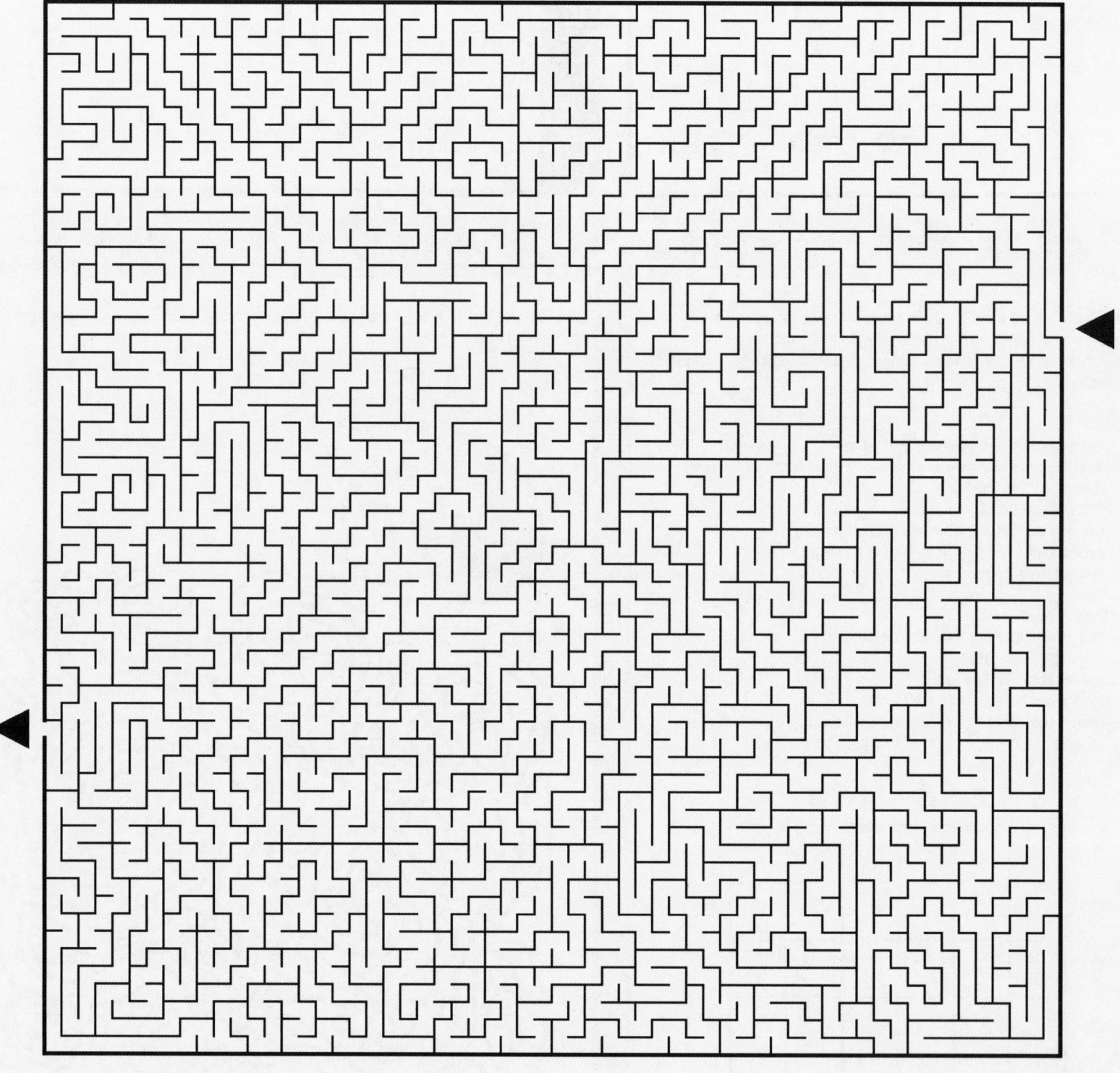

689 CARDS ON THE TABLE

The 13 cards of a suit are shuffled and dealt out in a row, and it is found that none is in its correct numerical position (Ace left, King right), and the court cards are not at either end or adjacent to each other. The Ace is between 9 (left) and 8, 4 between Queen (left) and Jack, 2 two places left of 10, 7 two places left of 3, the left-hand card one higher than the right-hand card, and the King is left of the Queen. The 9th and 10th cards from the left total 9, the 9th being of lower value. Can you locate each card?

690 NUMBER KROSS

See how quickly you can fit all these numbers into the grid. We've filled one number in to start you off.

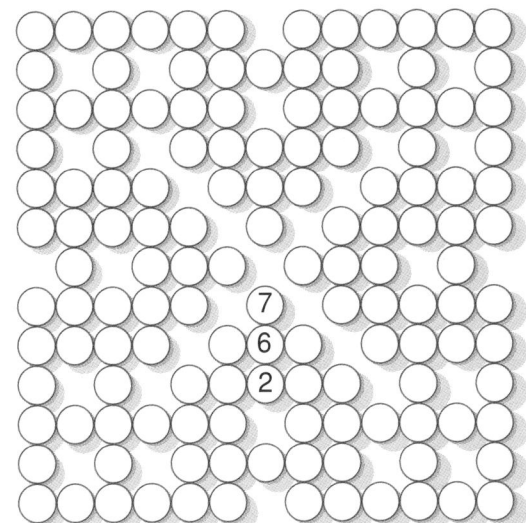

3 figures	5 figures	6 figures
184	10179	123579
287	20507	166266
395	22458	220179
499	30254	223344
571	31007	345678
672	47555	357913
762	47742	441133
863	50923	443322
	51206	556677
4 figures	62918	566333
1918	63459	601714
2016	78957	678135
3172	81633	721233
4958	84156	765432
5661	92107	803917
6294	97980	912005
7676		
9737		

691 FIGURE IT OUT

The digits 1–9 each appear four times in the grid, and no two squares which are adjacent horizontally or vertically contain the same digit. Every instance of a digit's occurring more than once in a row or column is mentioned in the clues.

Across
1 A pair of 3s; the last three digits reversed are one-third of the first three digits
2 A pair of 1s but no 4s; the total is 19
3 A pair of 2s enclosing an 8; the total is 30
4 A pair of 4s; the total is 35
5 A pair of 8s but no 6s; the total is 41
6 8 is the highest number and 1 the lowest; the total is 31

Down
1 A pair of 9s; the total is 42
2 A pair of 6s enclosing a 3; there are no 8s
3 A pair of 4s; the total is 19
4 A pair of 1s; the total is 28
5 A pair of 2s but no 4s; the total is 25
6 A pair of 9s but no 1s; the total is 35

	1	2	3	4	5	6
1						
2						
3						
4						
5						
6						5

692 A BARGIN TO BOOT

The diagram shows four neighbouring stalls at a car boot sale each selling an assortment of bric-a-brac. From the clues given below, can you identify the person in charge of each of the stalls lettered A to D and say which customer was buying which item from which stall at the particular moment in question?

Clues
1 Lesley bought something from Ken, whose stall was separated by just one other from the one where the fire irons were offered for sale.
2 The vase was sold at stall B.
3 Norman, who did not buy the paperback books, was the customer at stall C, which was not run by Ted.
4 Elsie's stall is lettered A in the diagram; her customer was not Ray.

Stall-holders: Elsie; Ken; Mary; Ted
Customers: Lesley; Norman; Penny; Ray
Item bought: books; fire irons; radio; vase

Starting tip: Begin by working out which stall sold the fire irons.

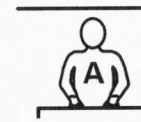 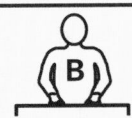  

Customers: _____ _____ _____ _____
Purchase: _____ _____ _____ _____

693 MONKEY PUZZLE

In a negative, everything which is really black appears white and everything which is really white appears black. Can you tell which one of the six monkeys is shown as a negative in the top left-hand corner?

694 CUT THE DEAL

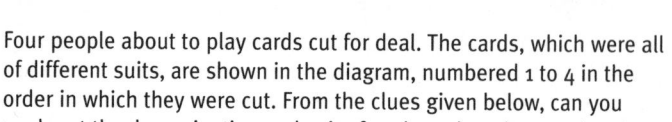

Four people about to play cards cut for deal. The cards, which were all of different suits, are shown in the diagram, numbered 1 to 4 in the order in which they were cut. From the clues given below, can you work out the denomination and suit of each card, and name the player who drew it?

Clues

1 Clara made her cut immediately before the King was drawn.
2 The Diamond was cut next but one after the 3, a male player making the intervening cut.
3 Betty's card, which was not a Club, was a lower one than card 4.
4 Adam, whose card was a Heart, drew it some time before the 10 was cut.
5 The second card to be drawn was a black one.

Denominations: 3; 7; 10; King
Suits: Clubs; Diamonds; Hearts; Spades
Players: Adam; Betty; Clara; Dave

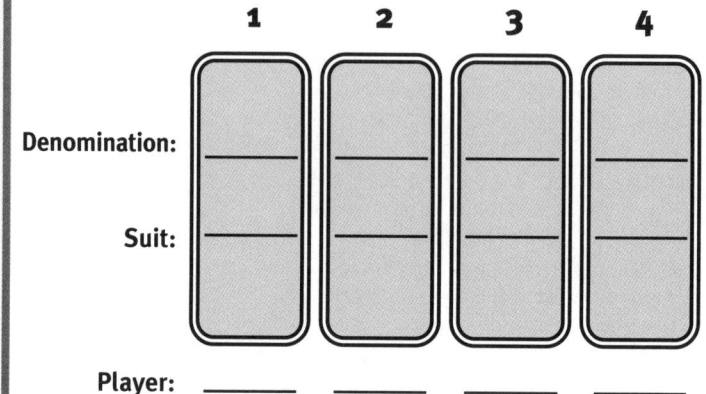

Starting tip: Begin by working out who cut card 4.

695 SYMBOLIC

Can you see which two small rectangles contain the same four symbols?

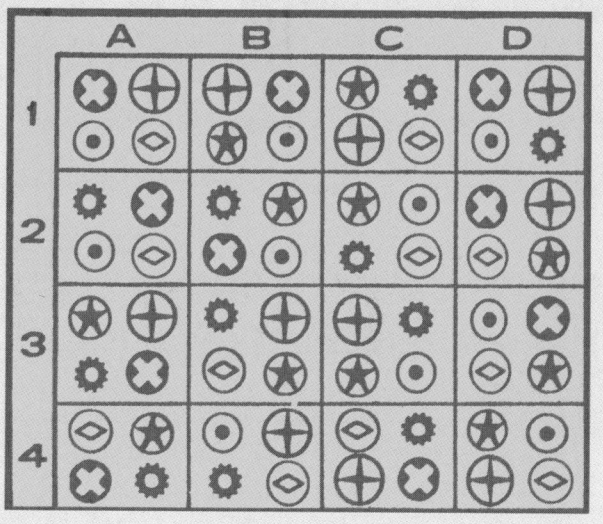

696 BLACK OUT

Which one of these letters was printed with the reverse stamp shown at the top?

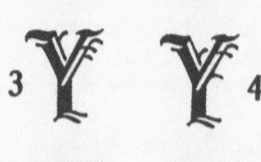

697 SPOT THE DIFFERENCE

See how quickly you can spot the ten differences between these two clowns.

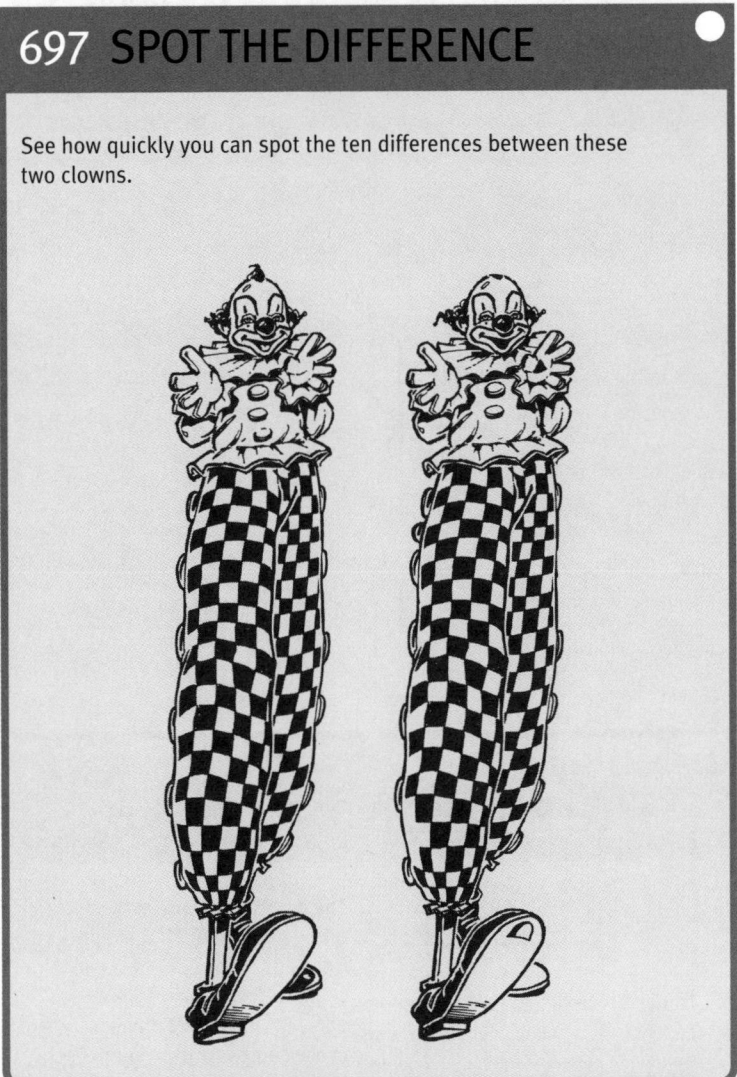

There are eight differences between the two cartoons. Can you spot them?

698 THAT LITTLE BIT OF DIFFERENCE

699 ORIENT EXPRESS ALIASES

One day in the late 1920s, the *chef de train* of the Orient Express received a discreet warning that the passengers in the first four sleeping compartments were – well, not all they appeared to be. From the clues given below, can you work out the name in which each compartment had been reserved, and uncover the real name of its occupant?

Clues

1 Maxwell Van Skyler, the notorious American confidence trickster, occupied the compartment next to that of the man masquerading as Danish physicst professor Nils Knudsen.
2 The man in compartment 4, who was not Russian spy Boris Zugov, was not posing as Middle Eastern playboy Prince Karim Al-Aziz.
3 Compartment 2 had been booked in the name of Sir Percival Gascoyne, described as a British diplomat.
4 Enrico Leone, the Italian jewel thief, travelled in compartment 1.
5 Franz Schmidt, the German anarchist, had the next compartment but one to the man posing as French aristocrat the Duc de Chomette.

Assumed names: Duc de Chomette; Prince Karim Al-Aziz; Professor Nils Knudsen; Sir Percival Gascoyne.
Real names; Boris Zugov; Enrico Leone; Franz Schmidt; Maxwell Van Skyler

	1	2	3	4
Alias:				
Real name:				

Starting tip: First work out the real name of the passenger in compartment 4.

700 PLUGGED IN

Which one of the four leads should the guitarist plug into the loudspeaker?

A
B
C
D

701 CIRCLE ROUND

The diagram shows four straight lines whose extremities are numbered I to VIII. Each of the arms numbered I to VIII has two circles, in the inner of which appears a different one of the numerals 1 to 8 and in the outer of which is contained a different one of the letters A to H. From the clues given below can you fill in correctly all the numbers and letters?

Clues

1 The word HAG may be read anti-clockwise on the outer ring; all of its letters are accompanied by even digits on the inner ring.

2 The 8 and the 7 are on the same straight line which bears even Roman numerals at each end, the 8 end having a higher numeral than the 7 end.

3 The letter at position III is the B.

4 The numeral on arm V and the one on the arm directly opposite the one bearing the A total the number on arm IV.

5 The 5 is on the arm numbered I in the diagram.

6 The letter in position VI is a vowel.

7 The 1, which is not on the same straight line as the 6, is on an arm numbered two higher than the one occupied by the C.

8 The letter on arm IV has an earlier position in the alphabet than the one on arm II, but does not come immediately before it.

Letters: A; B; C; D; E; F; G; H
Numerals: 1; 2; 3; 4; 5; 6; 7; 8

Starting tip: Begin by positioning the H.

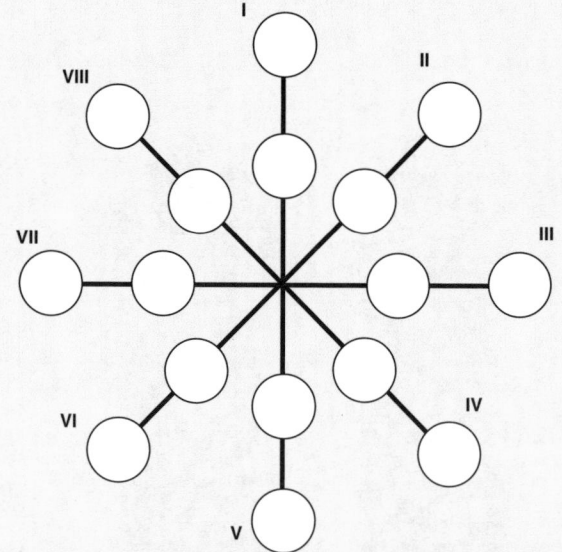

702 CELL STRUCTURE

The object is to create white areas surrounded by black walls, so that:
* Each white area contains only one number
* The number of cells in a white area is equal to the number in it
* The white areas are separated from each other with a black wall
* Cells containing numbers must not be filled in
* The black cells must be linked into a continuous wall
* Black cells cannot form a square of 2 x 2 or larger

(Grid with numbers: 5; 4; 5, 3, 2; 6, 2; 5, 2; 3, 2; 3; 4)

703 SQUARED OFF

The empty 4 x 4 grid was originally filled with the numbers from 1 to 16 inclusive. No two consecutive numbers were adjacent (including diagonally) or in the same row or column. Each of the sixteen numbers given in the full grid is the sum of the horizontal and vertical neighbours of the corresponding square in the original grid. Can you work out where the sixteen numbers originally were?

20	23	15	25
17	37	37	20
42	23	41	21
11	41	13	24

704 DARTING ABOUT

A dart player scores 85 with three darts hitting a treble, a double and a single (no bulls). Given that the three numbers that he hits add up to 43 and that the difference between the largest and smallest numbers is 6, can you work out how his score is made up?

Treble   Double   Single

705 SILHOUETTE

Shade in every fragment containing a dot – and what have you got?

706 IT'S MAGIC ⚪⚪

This magic square can be completed using every other number from 23 to 71. To give you a start, we have entered every digit 3 and all the numbers which are multiples of 3. Can you complete the square so that the five numbers in each row, column and diagonal add up to the magic total? That total – and close your eyes now if you don't want to be told – is 235.

707 EURO SQUARE ⚫⚫⚫

Each of the sixteen small squares in the diagram contains one of the numbers 1 to 4 in words, in either English, French, German or Italian, as listed below. From the clues given below, can you write the correct word in each square?

Clues

1 Each of columns A, B, C and D contains one number in each of the four different languages.

2 Quatre is the number in square B2.

3 The number in B1 is twice that in D2, both being in the same language.

4 Two is in the horizontal row above the one containing both zwei and due.

5 The even number in D3 is not in French.

6 Tre is immediately to the right of four, and immediately above vier.

7 Quattro is somewhere in column D.

8 The German number in column C is drei; but its right-hand neighbour is not in German; D1 does not contain eins.

9 The number in A4 is one higher than the one in A1, though, of course, the language is different.

10 The numbers in D1 and C3 are in the same language, the former being the higher of the two.

English: one; two; three; four
French: un; deux; trois; quatre
German: eins; zwei; drei; vier
Italian: uno; due; tre; quattro

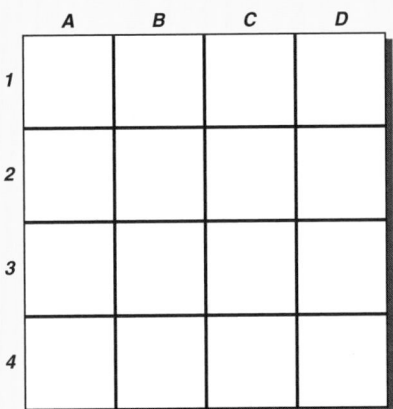

Starting tip: Begin by identifying the number in B1.

708 SYMBOLISM ⚪⚪

Each of the four symbols (Heart, Club, Diamond and Spade) represents a certain number in all the rows across – and the totals refer to the sum of the symbols shown on that row using these numbers.

Each symbol also refers to a number (it may or may not be the same number as that in the rows across!) when used in the sums downwards, with totals at the bottom of the grid – the symbols in each column add up to the totals at the bottom; and each symbol is the same number for all the downwards sums.

Can you work out the value of the symbols shown, both horizontally and vertically?

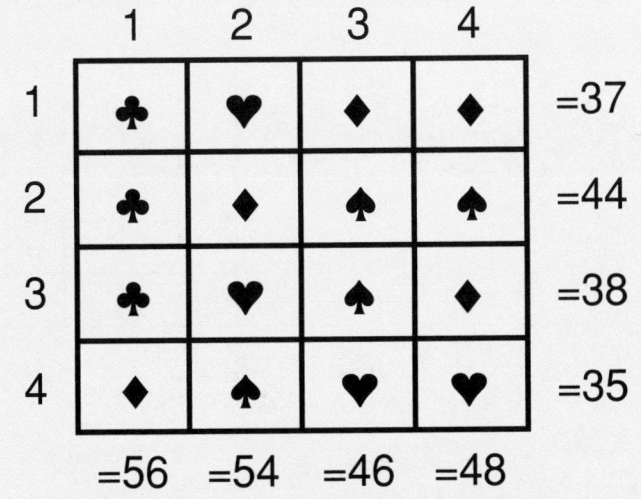

709 CELL STRUCTURE ⚪

The object is to create white areas surrounded by black walls, so that:
* Each white area contains only one number.
* The number of cells in a white area is equal to the number in it.
* The white areas are separated from each other with a black wall.
* Cells containing numbers must not be filled in.
* The black cells must be linked into a continuous wall.
* Black cells cannot form a square of 2 x 2 or larger.

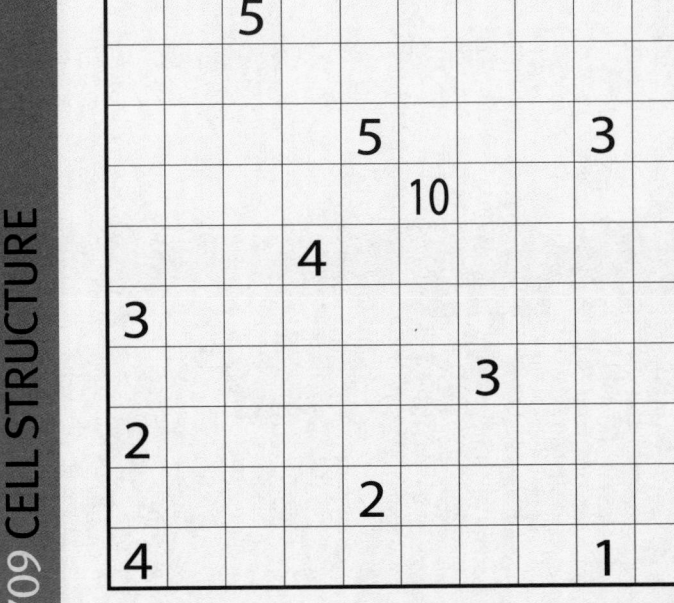

710 DOT-TO-DOT

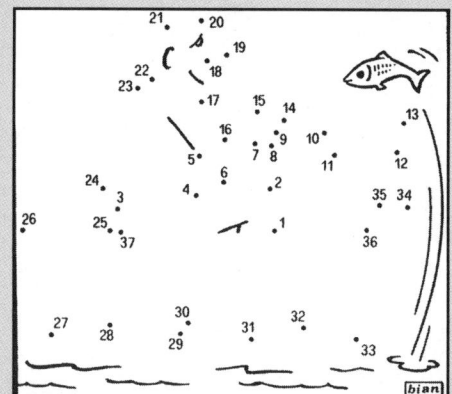

Join the dots from 1 to 37 to reveal the hidden picture.

711 GHOST STOREYS

Ghastleigh Castle has four towers, and each tower has a haunted room. From the clues below, can you fill in on the plan the name of each tower and its haunted room, and identify the ghost that manifests itself there?

Clues

1 The so-called King's Chamber (Charles II spent a night there while hiding from The Roundheads) is in tower C.

2 The Sorcerer's Den is, unsurprisingly, in the Sorcerer's Tower, which is the next in alphabetical order after the New Tower (built in 1340) where Lady Edith's ghost haunts the scene of her murder.

3 The Whistling Room – the sound comes from the badly-built chimney, not the resident phantom – isn't in Drogo's Tower, named after the original builder of the castle.

4 Brother Luke appears in the tower marked A on the plan; Tower B isn't haunted by Lord Ivo, and isn't the location of the Treasure Room, where the Ghastleigh family silver is still stored.

Tower Names: Black Tower; Drogo's Tower; New Tower; Sorcerer's Tower
Room Names: King's Chamber; Sorcerer's Den; Treasure Room; Whistling Room
Ghosts: Brother Luke; Lady Edith; Lord Ivo; Old Meg

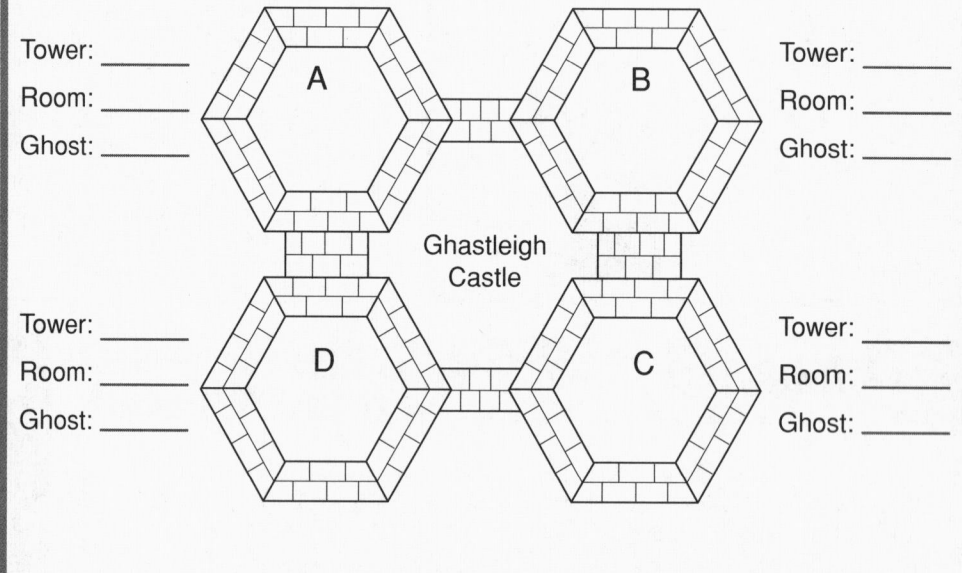

Tower: _____
Room: _____
Ghost: _____

Tower: _____
Room: _____
Ghost: _____

Tower: _____
Room: _____
Ghost: _____

Tower: _____
Room: _____
Ghost: _____

Starting tip: Work out the position of the Sorcerer's Tower.

712 ISLAND HOPPING

Each circle containing a number represents an island. The object is to connect each island with vertical or horizontal bridges so that:

* The number of bridges is the same as the number inside the island.
* There can be up to two bridges between two islands.
* Bridges cannot cross islands or other bridges.
* There is a continuous path connecting all the islands.

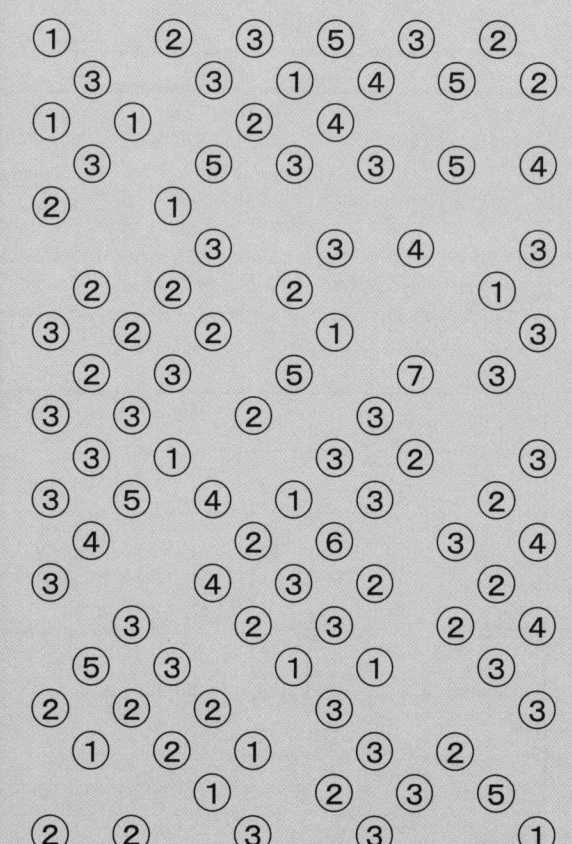

713 FILLING IN

Each of the letters in the boxes contains a different digit from 1 to 9. As is our usual practice, each calculation is to be treated sequentially rather than according to the 'multiplication first' system. Can you fill in the empty boxes?

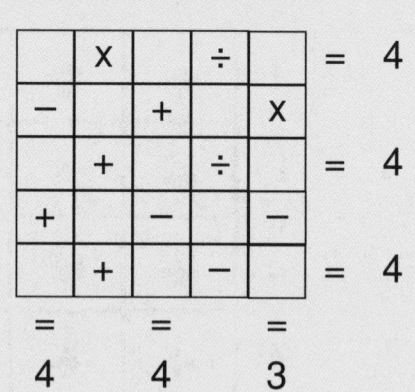

714 SKELETON SUMS

●●

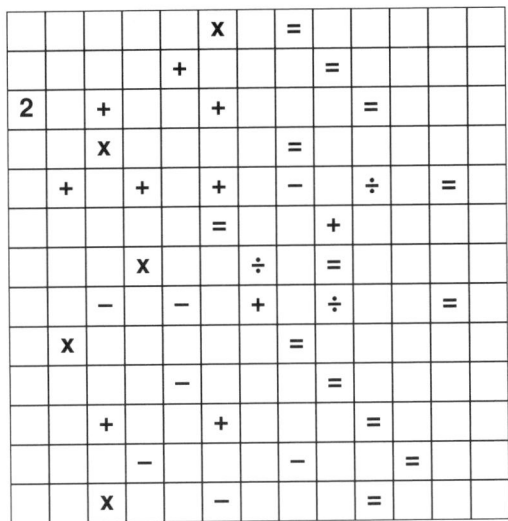

Insert the following numbers into the spaces on each horizontal line so as to form thirteen valid equations, treating each calculation sequentially rather than according to the 'multiplication first' system. When the numbers are correctly placed, the digits in each vertical column will total 45.

2 2 3 4 5 5 6 7 7 7 8 9 9 9

14 18 18 19 24 25 30 36 39 42 45 90 96

168 200 249 397 439 439 566 574 622 675 700

1089 1425 1711 2323 2587 2889 9991

10009 11545 36218 42546 69270 85092

715 BY THE SEASIDE

The diagram shows four children paddling in the sea, while their respective mothers sit in deck-chairs on the beach keeping a watchful eye on them. From the clues given below, can you identify the four children lettered A to D and the four mothers numbered 1 to 4, and match them up correctly?

Clues

1 None of the children is indicated by a letter whose position in the alphabet is equivalent to the number denoting his or her mother.

2 As they sit facing out to sea Jill is immediately to the right of Emma's mum, and immediately to the left of the mother of child D.

3 Jack is the son of Francesca, who is not in deck-chair 3.

4 Karen is paddling two positions to the left (facing the sea) of Lesley's child.

Children: Damien; Emma; Jack; Karen
Mothers: Francesca; Jill; Lesley; Sally

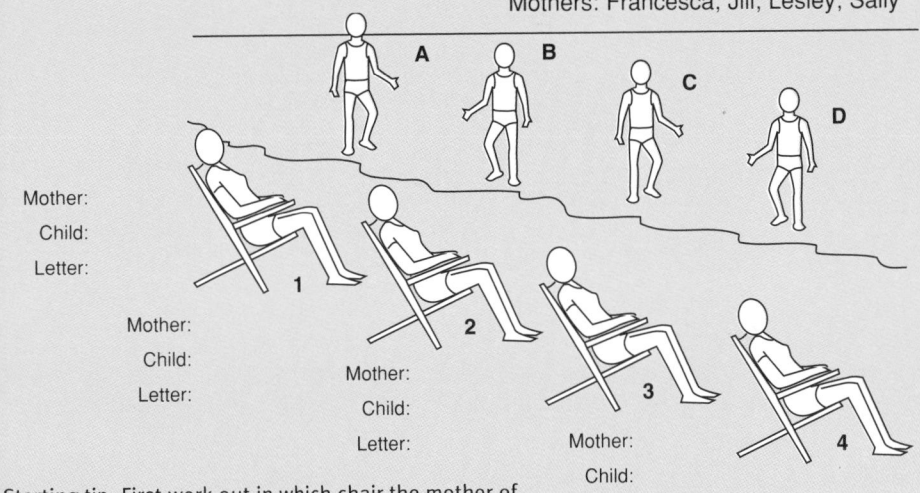

Mother:
Child:
Letter:

Mother:
Child:
Letter:

Mother:
Child:
Letter:

Mother:
Child:
Letter:

Starting tip: First work out in which chair the mother of child D is sitting.

717 SQUARED OFF ●●●

The (almost) empty 4 x 4 grid was originally filled with the numbers from 1 to 16 inclusive. No two consecutive numbers were adjacent horizontally, vertically or diagonally. Each of the sixteen numbers given in the full grid is the sum of the horizontal and vertical neighbours of the corresponding square in the original grid. Given the starter 1, can you work out where the sixteen numbers originally were?

		1	

28	21	27	8
18	35	30	25
33	28	25	31
6	25	32	18

716 CARDS ON THE TABLE

●●

The 13 cards of a suit are shuffled and dealt in a line. None is in its correct position counting from the Ace left to right, no court cards are at either end, but two of the court cards are adjacent, with the other three places to the right. 4 is two places left of 9, 5 two places left of 8, 10 two places left of 6, 7 two left of the Ace, the King three left of 2, the Queen two left of 3, and the Jack three right of the Ace. The centre card is not a court card. Where the Jack equals 11, the Queen equals 12, the King equals 13, the two end cards total 13 and the 3rd and 4th total 10. Can you locate each card?

718 KRIS KROSS

Fit the numbers into the grid. To get you started, one has been done for you.

2 figures	~~955~~
10	
21	**4 figures**
33	1276
42	2245
54	3093
56	5386
79	6482
87	7910
88	8218
95	9977

3 figures	5 figures
170	16650
186	20476
222	68308
260	90759
306	
402	**6 figures**
519	154564
548	338085
663	416707
791	720503
884	896952
889	919350
917	

7 figures	9 figures
1469353	624114298
3857292	967753780
4629390	
4959018	**11 figures**
5267489	36870152598
6357655	41479036525
	70264293061
	96762458813

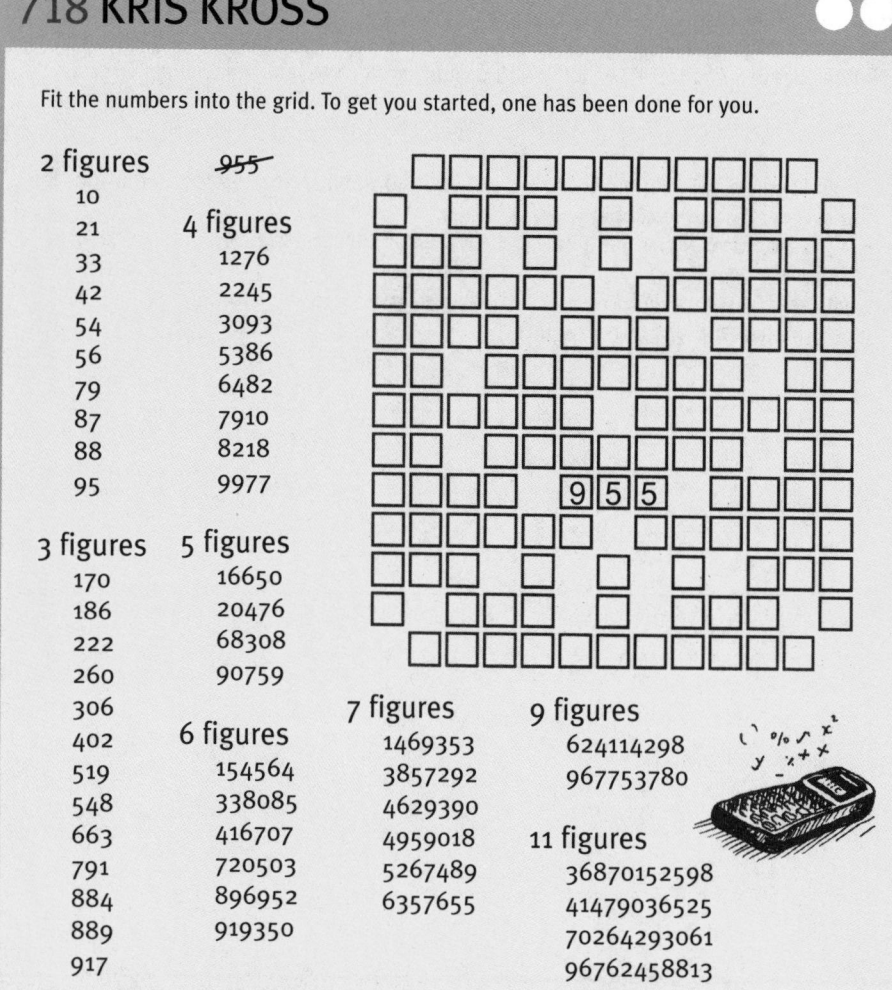

719 ISLANDS IN THE SUN

Four couples booked holidays on different islands for themselves and their two children. From the clues given below, can you match the couples, work out their surnames and the names of their children, and say which island paradise each foursome visited?

Clues

1 Rebecca is Charles' sister.

2 Keith and Angela's son is not the boy named Darren Morris.

3 Judy Langton's holiday location was not Cyprus, and her son's name is not Ian.

4 Chris is Garry's father, and Gail is the daughter of Lance, who did not visit the Canaries.

5 Violet is Fiona's mother; she is not married to Perry, and she is not Mrs Chadwick, who spent her holiday in Crete.

6 Bridget and her husband took their children to Majorca.

Husband	Wife	Surname	Son	Daughter	Location

720 A CRY FOR HELP

The 12 small squares each contain one of the letters of the phrase MAYDAY, MAYDAY, the international distress signal. From the clues given below, can you insert the correct letter in each of the squares?

Clues

1 No identical letter appears in adjacent squares vertically or horizontally.

2 The combination A above D can be seen in one vertical column.

3 Letter Y occurs once only in column 2.

4 The letter M is to be inserted in square B2.

5 No D appears in horizontal row D.

6 All four letters in column 1 are different.

7 The different letters in B3 and D3 are not repeated elsewhere in that column.

Letters check-list: A; A; A; A; D; D; M; M; Y; Y; Y; Y

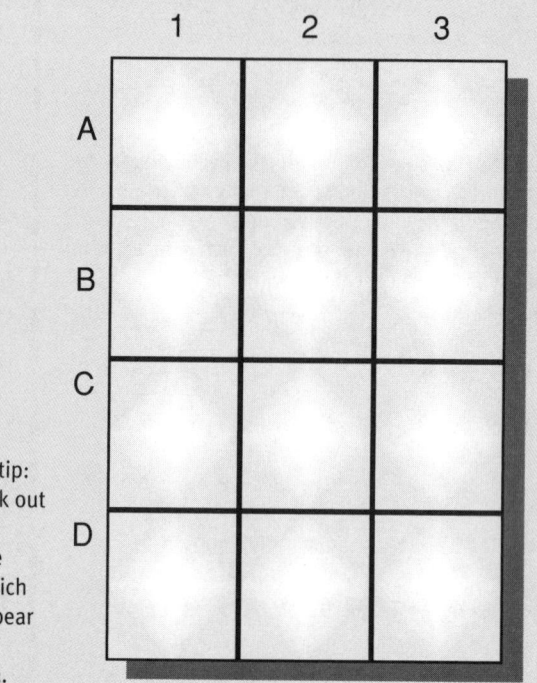

Starting tip: First work out and then place the letter which must appear twice in column 3.

721 CELL STRUCTURE

The object is to create white areas surrounded by black walls, so that:

* Each white area contains only one number
* The number of cells in a white area is equal to the number in it
* The white areas are separated from each other with a black wall
* Cells containing numbers must not be filled in
* The black cells must be linked into a continuous wall
* Black cells cannot form a square of 2 x 2 or larger

722 IT FIGURES

Place a number from 1 to 9 in each empty cell so that the sum of each vertical or horizontal block equals the number at the top or on the left of that block. Numbers may only be used once in each block.

725 SUM WAY DOWN

In the top line, the circles, A to E, are to be filled with two digits each, using between them, each digit (0,1,2,3,4,5,6,7,8,9) just once only; so 0,1,3,8 need placing. From then on, the number in each circle is the sum of the digits in the two circles which are above it and joined to it by a line. Thus circle H will contain the answer to 5+2+6+7. When filled in correctly, the circles will contain fifteen different numbers.

Given those already in position, can you complete the picture?

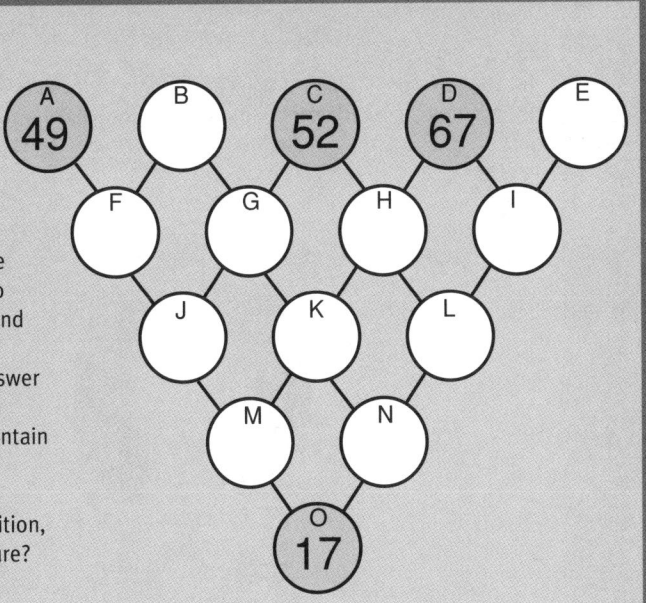

723 CELL STRUCTURE

The object is to create white areas surrounded by black walls, so that:
* Each white area contains only one number.
* The number of cells in a white area is equal to the number in it.
* The white areas are separated from each other with a black wall.
* Cells containing numbers must not be filled in.
* The black cells must be linked into a continuous wall.
* Black cells cannot form a square of 2 x 2 or larger.

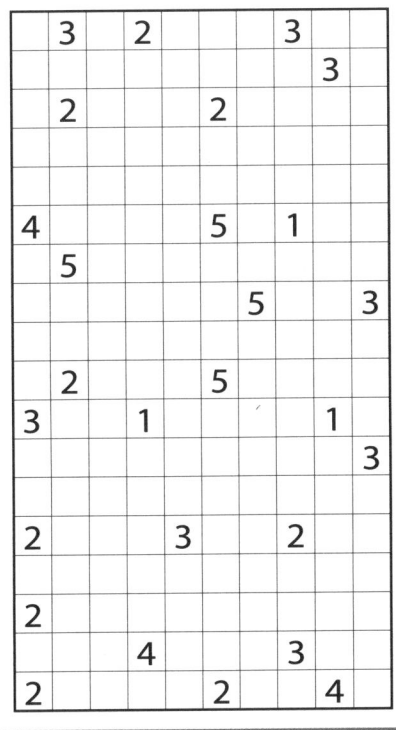

724 PAIRED UP

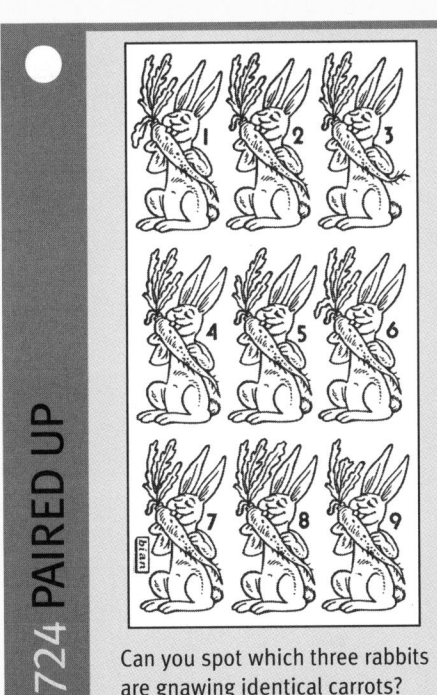

Can you spot which three rabbits are gnawing identical carrots?

726 WEIGHED UP

How many suitcases are needed to make the third pair of scales balance?

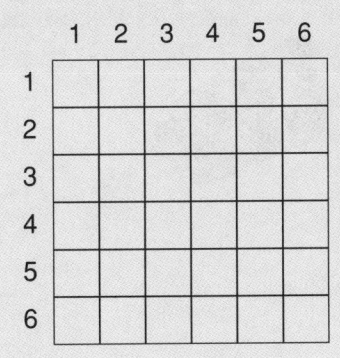

727 FIGURE IT OUT

The digits 1–9 each appear four times in the grid, and no two squares which are adjacent horizontally or vertically contain the same digit. Each instancce of a digit occurring more than once in a row or column is mentioned in the clues.

ACROSS
1 A pair of 6s; but no 9; the sum is 36
2 A pair of 1s; 7 is the second highest number; the sum is 23
3 A pair of 5s; but no 7s; the sum is 34
4 A pair of 2s, but no 7s; the sum is 28
5 A pair of 8s; the sum is 36
6 A pair of 1s; 9 is the highest number

DOWN
1 A pair of 6s; the sum is 41
2 A pair of 5s enclosing a 1
3 A pair of 7s; the sum is 35
4 A pair of 6s and a pair of 4s; the sum is 25
5 A pair of 9s; the sum is 39
6 A pair of 1s; the sum is 16

	1	2	3	4	5	6
1						
2						
3						
4						
5						
6						

728 PILE UP

These piles of bricks aren't the random results of a child's play but clues to a final, at present blank, pile on the right. Like the rest, that one has six bricks each with a different one of the six letters. The numbers below the heaps tell you two things:

(a) The number of adjacent pairs of bricks in that column which also appear adjacent in the final pile.
(b) The number of adjacent pairs of bricks that make a correct pair but the wrong way up.

So:

would score one in the 'Correct' row if the final heap had an A directly above a C and a one in the 'Reversed' row if the final heap had a C on top of an A. From all this, can you create the final pile before it topples?

Correct	2	0	0	0	5
Reversed	0	0	0	1	0

731 SQUARED OFF

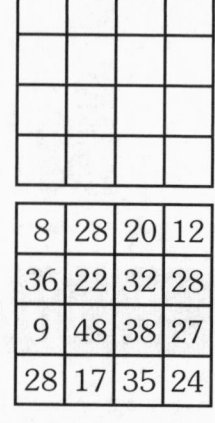

The empty 4 x 4 grid was originally filled with the numbers from 1 to 16 inclusive. No two consecutive numbers were adjacent (including diagonally) or in the same row or column. Each of the sixteen numbers given in the full grid is the sum of the horizontal and vertical neighbours of the corresponding square in the original grid. Can you work out where the sixteen numbers originally were?

8	28	20	12
36	22	32	28
9	48	38	27
28	17	35	24

729 CAN YOU DIGIT?

ACROSS

1 Add 1 to the square of (6 across + 7 across + 2 down + 11 down)
6 Subtract (4 down plus 1) from 7 across
7 Multiply 2 down's second digit by 19
8 Cube (11 down minus 1)
9 First two digits of 8 across
11 Add 3 to the square of 4 down's first digit
12 Square (11 across + 2 down)

DOWN

1 Square (7 across + 4 down + 10 down)
2 Reverse (7 across reversed minus 1)
3 Cube 11 down
4 Reverse (7 across plus 1)
5 Square (7 across + 11 across + 10 down + 11 down)
10 Third and fourth digits of 3 down
11 Subtract 2 from 11 across

1	2	3	4	5
6			7	
8				
9	10		11	
12				

732 BACKHANDER

Which one of these five archers is seen from the back in the top left-hand corner?

730 DARTING ABOUT

A dart player scores 85 with three darts hitting a treble, a double and a single (no bulls). Given that the three numbers he hits add up to 40 and that the difference between the largest and smallest numbers is 6, can you work out how his score is made up?

Treble   Double   Single

733 LENGTH IS STRENGTH

Four bridge players, seated in the traditional positions North, South, East and West (the two former being partners against the two latter), each picked up a hand with a different long suit, but a different length in each case. From the clues given below, can you name the player in each seat, match him with his long suit, and say how many cards of that suit he held?

Clues

1 Ruff had more of his suit than his partner had in Clubs, which was his long suit.

2 Trumpet had a suit longer than that of the player who held the long Diamonds.

3 South's long suit had only five cards in it.

4 East's suit was Hearts.

5 Pass was the player in the North seat.

6 It was Bidding's partner at the table who had the longest suit of all.

Names: Bidding; Pass; Ruff; Trumpet
Suits: Clubs; Diamonds; Hearts; Spades
Length: 5; 6; 7; 8

Starting tip: Begin by working out Ruff's seat.

Name: _____
Suit: _____
Length: _____

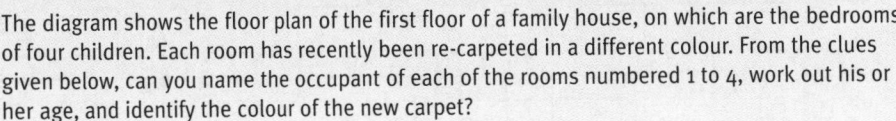

Name: _____
Suit: _____
Length: _____

Name: _____
Suit: _____
Length: _____

Name: _____
Suit: _____
Length: _____

734 SNAPPY

Which one of the six photographs of the model was taken as she posed below?

735 FLOOR SHOW

The diagram shows the floor plan of the first floor of a family house, on which are the bedrooms of four children. Each room has recently been re-carpeted in a different colour. From the clues given below, can you name the occupant of each of the rooms numbered 1 to 4, work out his or her age, and identify the colour of the new carpet?

Clues

1 Gemma's new blue carpet is in one of the front bedrooms.

2 James, who is 13, has a room numbered two lower on the plan than the one in which the green carpet has just been laid, whose occupant is 11.

3 The oldest of the four children, who is not Liam, has bedroom number 3.

4 Colette's room does not have the brown carpet.

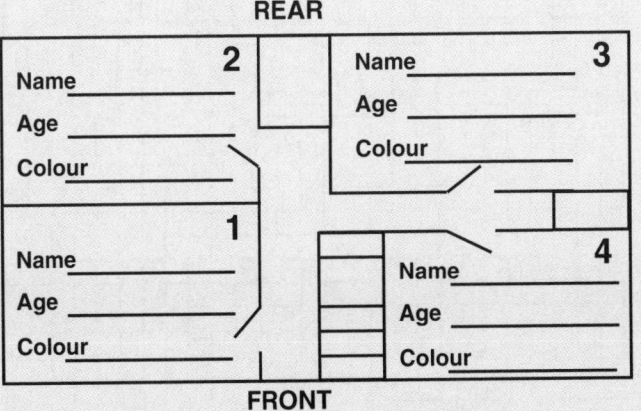

Names: Colette; Gemma; James; Liam
Ages: 11; 13; 15; 17
Colours: blue; brown; green; grey

Starting tip: Start by working out the number of the youngest child's room.

736 MAZE MYSTERY

Travel from the entrance to the exit of the maze, filling the path completely to create a picture.

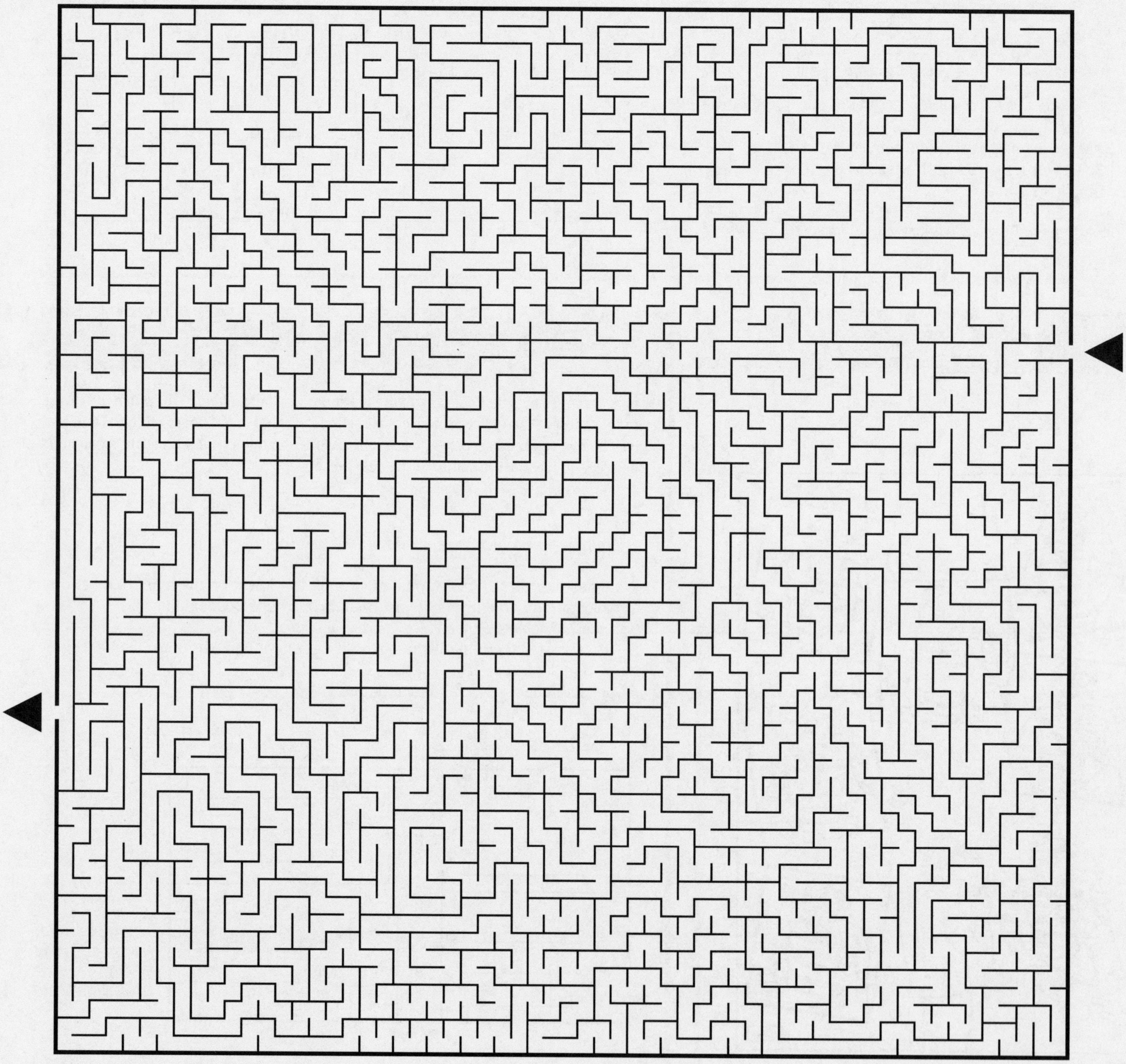

737 IT FIGURES

Place a number from 1 to 9 in each empty cell so that the sum of each vertical or horizontal block equals the number at the top or on the left of that block. Numbers may only be used once in each block.

739 LOTTERY, EXTRA, EXTRA

Here's a chance to get your own back on those unkind lottery numbers – at least you can cross a lot of them out and score points! Start by choosing a number and circling it, then cross out every other number that divides exactly into it. If, say, your first choice were 12, you would have to cross out 1, 2, 3, 4 and 6 as they all go into 12 exactly. There is only one rule governing your choice of number – it must be such that at least one other number, which has not been crossed out before, is now crossed out. The game ends when you cannot circle any further numbers.

Your points total is the sum of all the numbers you have circled.

What is the greatest possible score?

1	2	3	4	5	6	7
8	9	10	11	12	13	14
15	16	17	18	19	20	21
22	23	24	25	26	27	28
29	30	31	32	33	34	35
36	37	38	39	40	41	42
43	44	45	46	47	48	49

738 CELL STRUCTURE

The object is to create white areas surrounded by black walls, so that:
* Each white area contains only one number.
* The number of cells in a white area is equal to the number in it.
* The white areas are separated from each other with a black wall.
* Cells containing numbers must not be filled in.
* The black cells must be linked into a continuous wall.
* Black cells cannot form a square of 2 x 2 or larger.

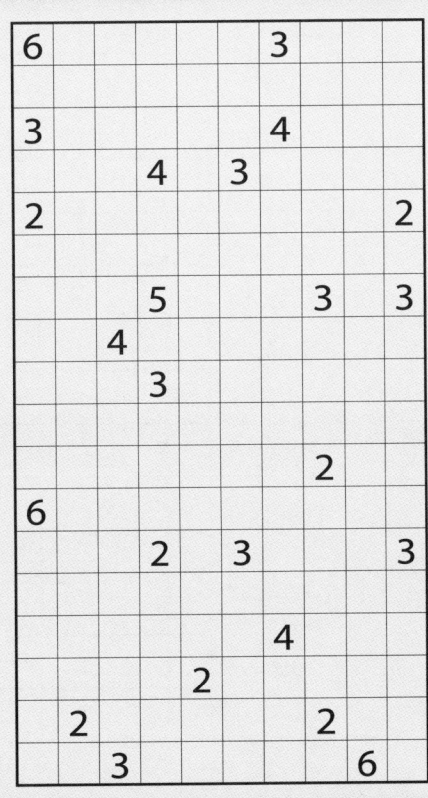

740 NUMBER HEX

What number belongs in the hexagon marked '?'?

14 6
5 22 2 9
8 1
10 16 7 2 18 16
15 4
4 13
5 22 ? 11
4 10

741 IDENTICAL TWINS

Mr Fix-it is doing some work in his garden. Can you spot the two numbered pictures which are identical?

742 BOX CLEVER

Which one of the numbered boxes will be formed when the pattern is folded up correctly?

743 LOGISTICAL

Five novels make up Letitia Perowne's Malthouse Saga, which tells the story of a landowning New England family from 1780 to 1977. From the clues below, can you work out the period covered by each title, and the forenames of the family members who are the book's main male and female characters?

Clues

1 *Chronicle*, which deals with the life and adventures of Vaughan Malthouse and his headstrong wife, is not the novel covering the period 1938–1977 which features Claudia Malthouse as its heroine.

2 Joseph and Miriam appear first as childhood sweethearts, then lovers, and finally husband and wife.

3 *Birthright*, which begins on the eve of the First World War, doesn't tell the story of Eugenie's rebellion against her overbearing husband.

4 Major Lambert Malthouse isn't the hero of *Testament*.

5 *Heritage*, the volume of the saga which features the tragic story of Rosalind Malthouse and her faithless husband, neither begins nor ends in 1830, the year of Samuel's birth.

6 Hannah Malthouse features in a volume two earlier in the series than the one which details the life and mysterious death of Esmond.

Title	Period	Male character	Female character

	1780–1830	1830–1881	1881–1914	1914–1938	1938–1977	Esmond	Joseph	Lambert	Samuel	Vaughan	Claudia	Eugenie	Hannah	Miriam	Rosalind
Birthright															
Chronicle															
Domain															
Heritage															
Testament															
Claudia															
Eugenie															
Hannah															
Miriam															
Rosalind															
Esmond															
Joseph															
Lambert															
Samuel															
Vaughan															

Record in this grid all the information obtained from the clues, by using a cross to indicate a definite 'no' and a tick to show a definite 'yes'. Transfer these to all sections of the grid thus eliminating all but one possibility, which must be the correct one.

744 DAILY DOZEN

● ● ●

Here's a gentle mental exercise. Each of the 12 squares contains a different one of the numbers 1 to 12. From the clues given below, can you place them correctly?

Clues

1 The 12 is in square B2; the numbers immediately to its left and diagonally below it to the left are both factors of it, one being an odd number (although not 1).

2 The 6 is adjacent to the 10 in the same row, and is to be found in the same vertical column as the 8.

3 The numbers in squares A1 and C3, added together, give the one in square C4.

4 The 7 is immediately below the 4, and immediately to the right of the 5.

5 Neither the 2 nor the 1 is in column 1, though the 2 is in a column further left than the one containing the 11.

Numbers: 1; 2; 3; 4; 5; 6; 7; 8; 9; 10; 11; 12

Starting tip: First place the numbers referred to in clue 1.

NB The numbers which are factors of 12 are 1, 2, 3, 4 and 6.

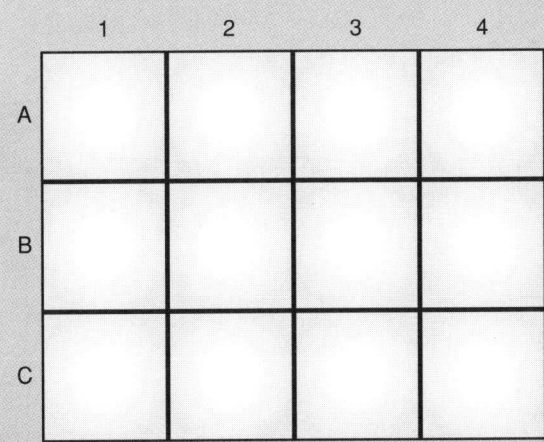

	1	2	3	4
A				
B				
C				

745 IT FIGURES

● ●

Place a number from 1 to 9 in each empty cell so that the sum of each vertical or horizontal block equals the number at the top or on the left of that block. Numbers may only be used once in each block.

746 SHADOWS

●

There's nothing a dragon likes better than a mug of cocoa to round off a meal of tasty take-away knight! Can you tell which one of the numbered shadows has been cast by this dragon?

747 PILE UP

These piles of bricks aren't the random results of a child's play but clues to a final, at present blank, pile on the right. Like the rest, that one has six bricks each with a different one of the six letters. The numbers below the heaps tell you two things:

(a) The number of adjacent pairs of bricks in that column which also appear adjacent in the final pile.

(b) The number of adjacent pairs of bricks that make a correct pair but the wrong way up.

So:

would score one in the 'Correct' row if the final heap had an A directly above a C and a one in the 'Reversed' row if the final heap had a C on top of an A. From all this, can you create the final pile before it topples?

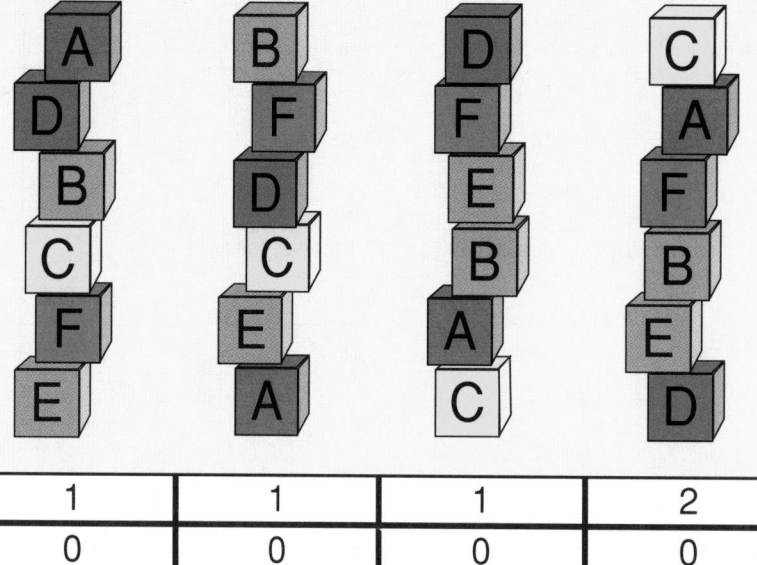

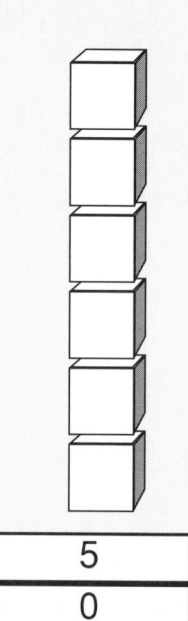

Correct	1	1	1	2		5
Reversed	0	0	0	0		0

748 SPOT THE DOG

Can you tell which of these happy hounds is the odd one out?

749 SET SQUARE

All the digits from 1 to 9 are used in this grid, but only once. Can you work out their positions in the grid and make the sums work? We've given two numbers to start you off.

	x		÷		=	3
−	■	+	■	+		
4	+		÷		=	4
÷	■	−	■	−		
	x	7	−		=	2
=		=		=		
5		3		4		

750 MAZE MYSTERY

Travel from the entrance to the exit of the maze, filling the path completely to create a picture.

751 SIX-PACK ●●

By packing numbers in the empty spaces, can you make the numbers in each of the 16 hexagons add up to 25? No two numbers in each hexagon may be the same and you can't use zero. We've started you off.

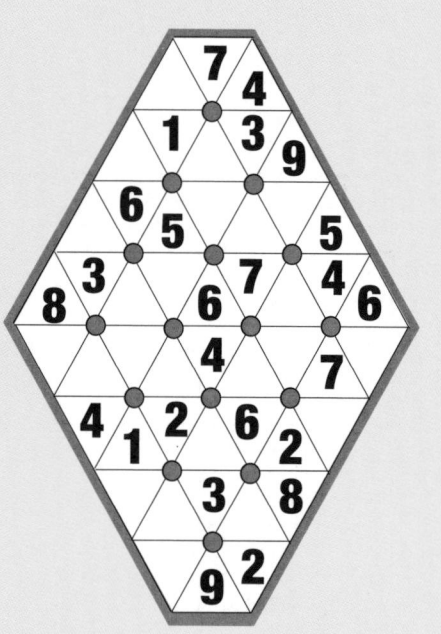

752 IT FIGURES ●●

Place a number from 1 to 9 in each empty cell so that the sum of each vertical or horizontal block equals the number at the top or on the left of that block. Numbers may only be used once in each block.

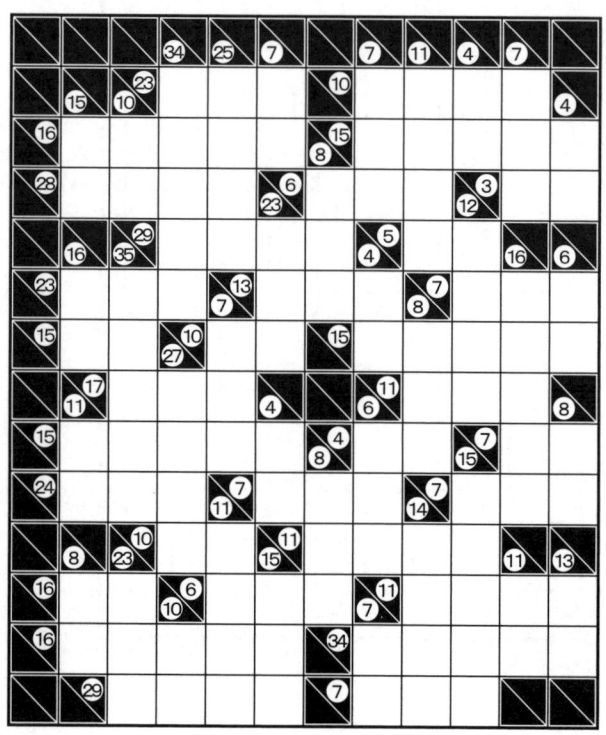

753 CELL STRUCTURE ●

The object is to create white areas surrounded by black walls, so that:
* Each white area contains only one number
* The number of cells in a white area is equal to the number in it
* The white areas are separated from each other with a black wall
* Cells containing numbers must not be filled in
* The black cells must be linked into a continuous wall
* Black cells cannot form a square of 2 x 2 or larger

754 LOST IN SPACE ●

Can you show this astronaut the way to his spaceship?

755 LOGISTICAL ●●●

At a recent 'point to point' horse-racing meeting in the country one of the most exciting events was the Ladies' Race. From the clues given below, can you work out in which order the five runners finished, and the name and occupation of the amateur jockey who rode each?

1 The doctor rode her mount into second place.

2 Di Richards didn't finish first, nor immediately in front of the secretary.

3 Captain Candy, which finished ahead of Drummer Boy, wasn't ridden by Sue Archer.

4 Lesley Carson, on Popcorn, finished immediately behind the vet.

5 Jane Piggott is a student at the local agricultural college.

6 The fifth horse to finish was the big grey called Snowstorm.

7 The woman who runs a farm isn't Vicky Mercer, whose horse brought her home in fourth place.

	Captain Candy	Drummer Boy	Eastern Star	Popcorn	Snowstorm	Di Richards	Jane Piggott	Lesley Carson	Sue Archer	Vicky Mercer	Farmer	Doctor	Secretary	Student	Vet
First															
Second															
Third															
Fourth															
Fifth															
Farmer															
Doctor															
Secretary															
Student															
Vet															
Di Richards															
Jane Piggott															
Lesley Carson															
Sue Archer															
Vicky Mercer															

Record in this grid all the information obtained from the clues, by using a cross to indicate a definite 'no' and a tick to show a definite 'yes'. Transfer these to all sections of the grid thus eliminating all but one possibility, which must be the correct one.

Place	Horse	Jockey	Occupation

756 GOLF LINK ●●●

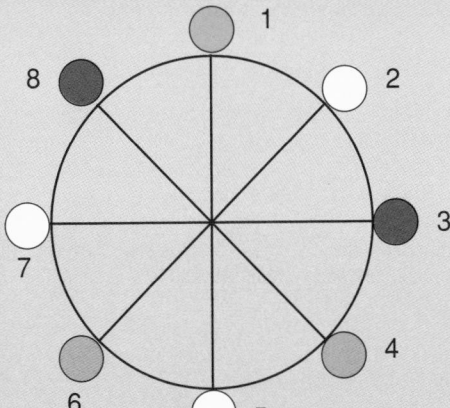

No.	Name	Shots	Prize
1			
2			
3			
4			
5			
6			
7			
8			

Eight people took part in a golf competition. Each person took his or her turn by standing on the tee, at the centre of a large circle, and putting a golf ball into one of the numbered holes. No two people putted the ball into the same hole and each person took a different number of shots to sink the ball into the hole he or she had chosen, the number of shots ranging from one to eight. In no case did the number of shots taken by a person match the number of the hole into which he or she putted the ball. Each person won a different prize. Gemma, who won the holiday vouchers, putted the ball into a white hole which was two counterclockwise of the hole at which the parasol was won. At the latter hole, two more shots were taken than at the former hole. Seven shots were taken to win the sombrero at a hole which was two clockwise of the hole at which John won his prize. Four shots were taken at a black hole, which was diametrically opposite the hole at which Jane won her prize.

The white hole at which the swimsuit was won was diametrically opposite the hole at which Mary won her prize. At the latter hole, six more shots were taken than at the former hole.

The greatest number of shots were taken to win the beachball, at a hole one counterclockwise of the black hole at which Edward won his prize. The number of shots taken to win the deckchair was more than the number of shots taken at the hole one counterclockwise of the hole at which the deckchair was won. Carol's hole had a higher number than Mike's. Donald won his prize at a hole whose number was half the number of the hole at which the beach towel (which was not Mike's prize) was won. One of the prizes won was a pair of sunglasses, and hole no. 8 was selected by a man.

Can you determine which person putted the ball into each hole, the prize each won and the number of shots taken by each?

757 INDEPENDENCE DAY

The twelve small squares each contain one of the letters or numbers making up the phrase USA 4 JULY, 1776. From the clues given below, can you place the correct number or letter in each of the squares?

Clues

1 Horizontal row B contains three numbers, but only one letter, which is not a vowel.

2 No letter or number occurs twice in any row or column.

3 The column in which a 7 appears immediately above the A is next right from the one containing the S, which is not the horizontal neighbour of either.

4 The L, which has a number in the square to its right, is in a square immediately above the 6.

5 One of the Us is immediately below the J, and immediately to the left of the 1.

6 Square A2 contains a number, and C4 contains a letter.

Letters: A; J; L; S; U; U; Y
Numbers: 1; 4; 6; 7; 7

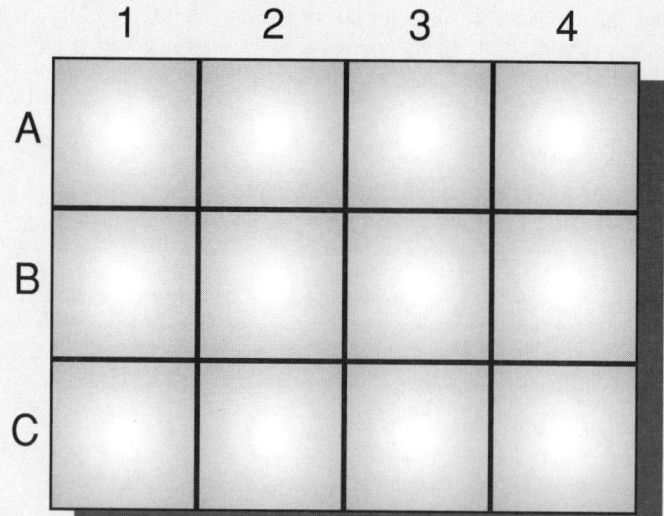

Starting tip: Begin by working out which is the letter in row B.

758 ZEROING IN

Twenty of the twenty-five squares in the diagram each contain a different one of the numbers 1 to 20, while each of the other five squares contains a zero. From the clues given below, can you place the correct number in each square? NB Where the phrase 'number' or 'single-digit number' occurs in a clue, this does not include zeros.

Clues

1 No row, column or diagonal (long or short) contains more than one zero.

2 The 19 in square B3 is the only two-digit number in that row, while the 7 is the only single-digit number in row 2.

3 The 9 is immediately below the 16, and immediately left of the 12.

4 The numbers in column E total 45, and those in row 2 total 51.

5 The number in A4 is five higher than the one in E5, which is itself one higher than the one in C2.

6 The 11 is immediately to the right of the 5 in row 4, while the 2 is to be found in a higher row than the 4.

7 The 17 appears in column D, somewhere below a zero, and somewhere above the 8.

8 The four numbers in column C are all even numbers, but do not include the 18.

9 The number 1 can be found in row 5, and the 6 in row 1.

10 The 10 is in the same column as the 3, but higher up.

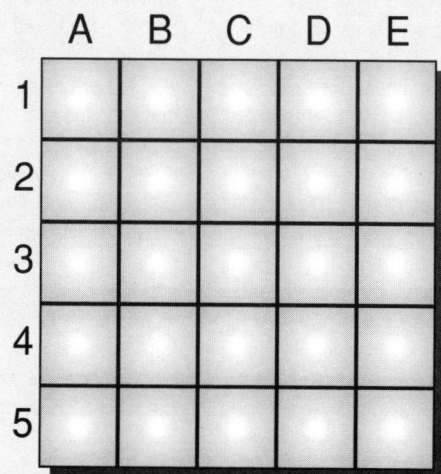

Starting tip: Begin by placing the 9.

759 LET'S FACE IT

Four children were each given a picture of a man's face, and invited to adorn it in a different manner. From the clues given below, can you work out the name and age of the child who was given each of pictures 1 to 4, and complete them by drawing in the missing detail in each picture?

Clues

1 Picture 2, which is clean-shaven, was produced by the artist a year older than Mary.

2 The oldest child produced picture 1.

3 Silas gave his character a monocle; this picture is somewhere to the right of the one produced by the artist aged 8.

4 Alistair is 9; his picture is not immediately to the right of the one with a moustache.

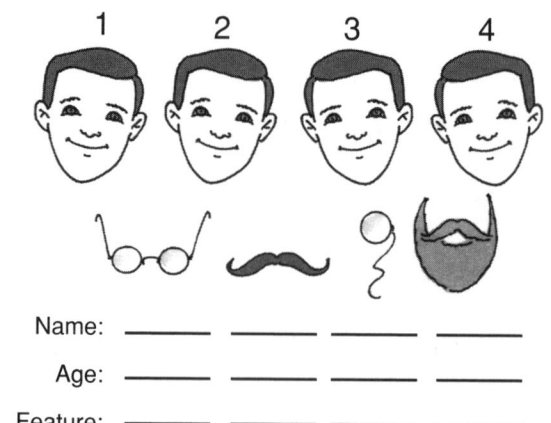

Name: —— —— —— ——

Age: —— —— —— ——

Feature: —— —— —— ——

Names: Alistair; Jennifer; Mary; Silas
Ages: 8; 9; 10; 11
Features: beard; monocle; moustache; spectacles

Starting tip: Begin by naming the child aged 11.

760 IT FIGURES

●●●

Place a number from 1 to 9 in each empty cell so that the sum of each vertical or horizontal block equals the number at the top or on the left of that block. Numbers may only be used once in each block.

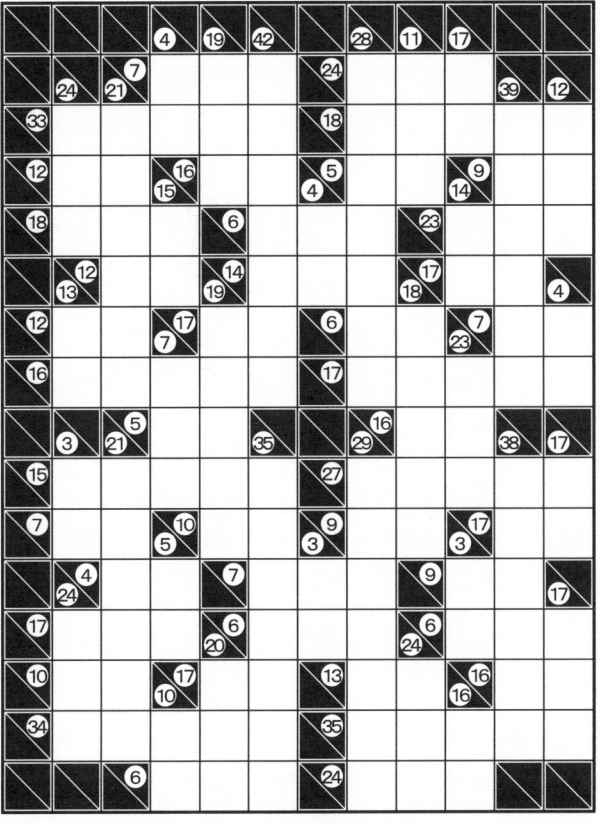

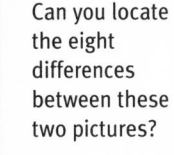

Can you locate the eight differences between these two pictures?

762 FOOT FAULT

761 TALK TURKEY

These crafty turkeys are avoiding Thanksgiving by hiding in the woods. How many can you see in this picture?

763 IT FIGURES

●●●

Place a number from 1 to 9 in each empty cell so that the sum of each vertical or horizontal block equals the number at the top or on the left of that block. Numbers may only be used once in each block.

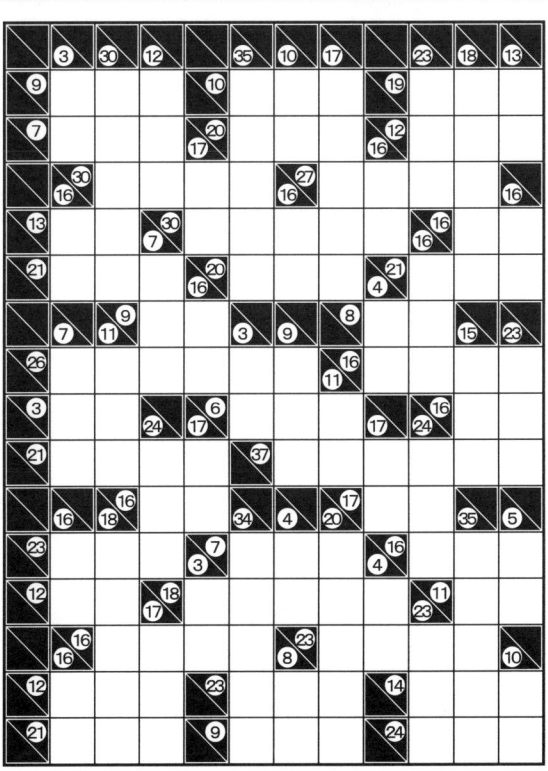

217

764 LOGISTICAL

A new production of Shakespeare's *Measure For Measure* is being put on at a London theatre, and none of the five female parts in this play is being taken by a British actress. From the clues given, can you work out the full name of each actress, the part she's playing, and where she comes from?

	Atkinson	Byrne	Edmunds	Potter	Thornhill	Francisca	Isabella	Juliet	Mariana	Mistress Overdone	Australia	Canada	Eire	USA	Zimbabwe
Amanda															
Gail															
Melanie															
Susan															
Wilma															
Australia															
Canada															
Eire															
USA															
Zimbabwe															
Francisca															
Isabella															
Juliet															
Mariana															
Mistress Overdone															

Record in this grid all the information obtained from the clues, by using a cross to indicate a definite 'no' and a tick to show a definite 'yes'. Transfer these to all sections of the grid thus eliminating all but one possibility, which must be the correct one.

Forename	Surname	Role	Country

1 The actress playing Mistress Overdone, who comes from Eire, isn't Ms Atkinson.

2 Gail Thornhill isn't Canadian.

3 Miss Byrne, who comes from New York, isn't playing Francisca.

4 Miss Potter isn't playing Juliet, which isn't Susan's role either.

5 Amanda, who's appearing as Mariana, has a shorter surname than Wilma.

6 Both Melanie, the Zimbabwean actress, and the woman who's playing Francisca have surnames which begin with consonants.

765 IT FIGURES

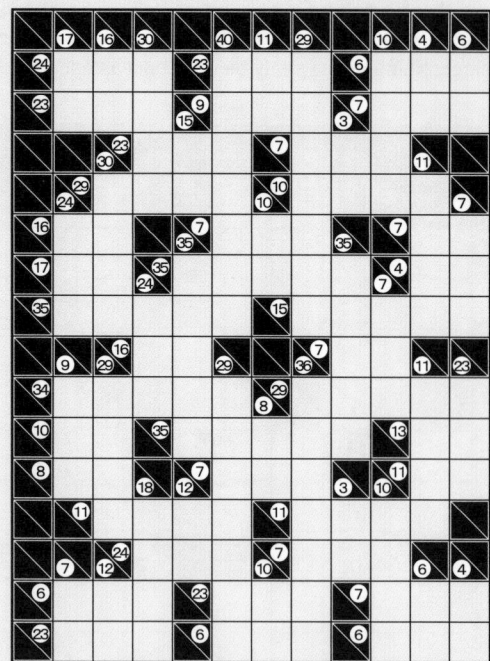

Place a number from 1 to 9 in each empty cell so that the sum of each vertical or horizontal block equals the number at the top or on the left of that block. Numbers may only be used once in each block.

766 DOUBLE TROUBLE

Which of these two students are identical?

767 SWORD PLAY

Big Eric's in a spot of bother! He's invited Even Bigger Eric round for some sword-fighting practice, but he's lost the swords. How many can you find for him in the picture?

769 TAKE THREE

The numbered pictures each differ from picture A in three unique ways. Can you find these differences?

768 SNACK TIME

As Tommy walked down the street he met in fairly quick succession four of his friends, each of whom was eating something different. As it was a rather chilly day, each lad was wearing a sweater. From the clues given below, can you name each of the boys numbered 1 to 4 in the diagram in the order in which they were met, and say what coloured sweater each was wearing and what item each was eating?

Clues

1 Tommy met Kevin, who was wearing the blue sweater, some time later than he came across the lad who was eating a lollipop.

2 The boy in the beige sweater was the third friend Tommy met.

3 The youth eating a banana, who was not Simon, was encountered next after the one wearing the green sweater.

4 The lad in the red sweater, who was not Danny, was encountered some time after Lewis, whose snack was the chocolate bar.

Names: Danny; Kevin; Lewis; Simon
Sweaters: beige; blue; green; red
Snacks: apple; banana; chocolate bar; lollipop

Starting tip: First name the boy in the red sweater.

Tommy

Name: _____ _____ _____ _____

Sweater: _____ _____ _____ _____

Snack: _____ _____ _____ _____

219

770 SET SQUARE ●●

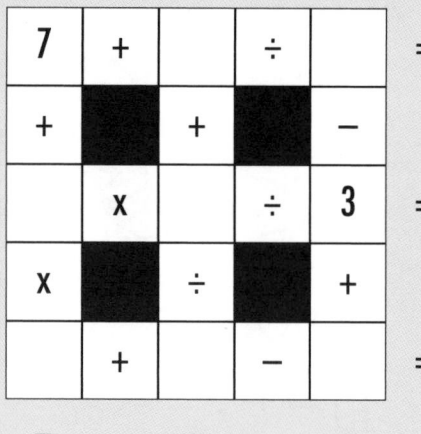

All the digits from 1 to 9 are used in this grid, but only once. Can you work out their positions in the grid and make the sums work? We've given two numbers to start you off.

771 SIX PACK ●●

By inserting numbers in the empty spaces, can you make the numbers in each of the 16 hexagons add up to 25? No two numbers in each hexagon may be the same and you can't use zero. We've started you off.

772 DIGITAL TIME ●●

Place eight of the digits 1 to 9 once each in the squares so that multiplying the three in each line produces the number shown in the circle on the end.

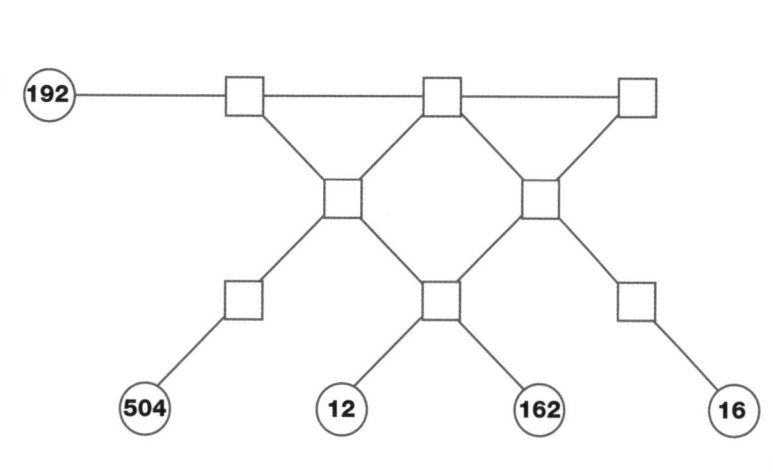

773 LOGIQUATIONS ●●

In the following problems the digits 0 to 9 are represented by letters. Within each separate puzzle the same letter always represents the same digit. Can you find the correct values each time so that all sums, both horizontal and vertical, are correct? There is a clue to help start you off.

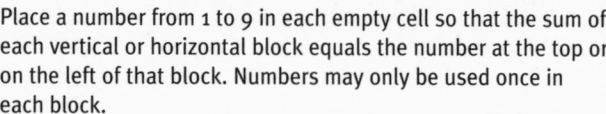

Clue: JK ÷ KH = G

774 IT FIGURES ●●●

Place a number from 1 to 9 in each empty cell so that the sum of each vertical or horizontal block equals the number at the top or on the left of that block. Numbers may only be used once in each block.

775 LOGISTICAL ●●●

In Hollywood's heyday, Bitt Player was a character actor specializing in playing Latin types, and, though he never had a major role, he was seldom out of work. In one week he played scenes for five different movies; from the clues below, can you work out the nationality and occupation of the character he played each day, and say which film it was for?

Clues

1 It wasn't on Sunday (the first day of the week) that Bitt played an Italian.

2 The scene in which Bitt played a corrupt policeman was shot three days after the one for *The Storm*

3 Bitt played a dying soldier on Saturday.

4 On Friday, Bitt played a Spanish part, but not for *Dead End*.

5 It was for *Web Of Fear* that Bitt played a Brazilian.

6 Bitt's Mexican character was a bandit.

7 It was on an odd-numbered day of the week that Bitt took on the role of a sailor for *Hunted Man*; this wasn't the Greek character, who wasn't the one Bitt played on Wednesday.

	Brazilian	Greek	Italian	Mexican	Spanish	Bandit	Policeman	Sailor	Soldier	Waiter	Dead End	Hunted Man	Split Seconds	The Storm	Web Of Fear
Sunday															
Tuesday															
Wednesday															
Friday															
Saturday															
Dead End															
Hunted Man															
Split Seconds															
The Storm															
Web Of Fear															
Bandit															
Policeman															
Sailor															
Soldier															
Waiter															

Record in this grid all the information obtained from the clues, by using a cross to indicate a definite 'no' and a tick to show a definite 'yes'. Transfer these to all sections of the grid thus eliminating all but one possibility, which must be the correct one.

Working day	Role Nationality	Role Occupation	Film

776 TROMBONES ○

Which one of the numbered pictures has been developed from the negative of this trombone? Remember – in a negative, any area which is really white appears black, and any area which is really black appears white!

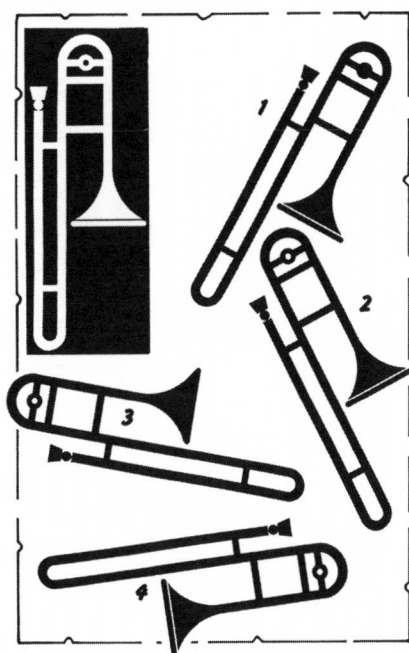

There are eight differences between these two pictures – can you find them?

778 TRAIL BLAZING ●

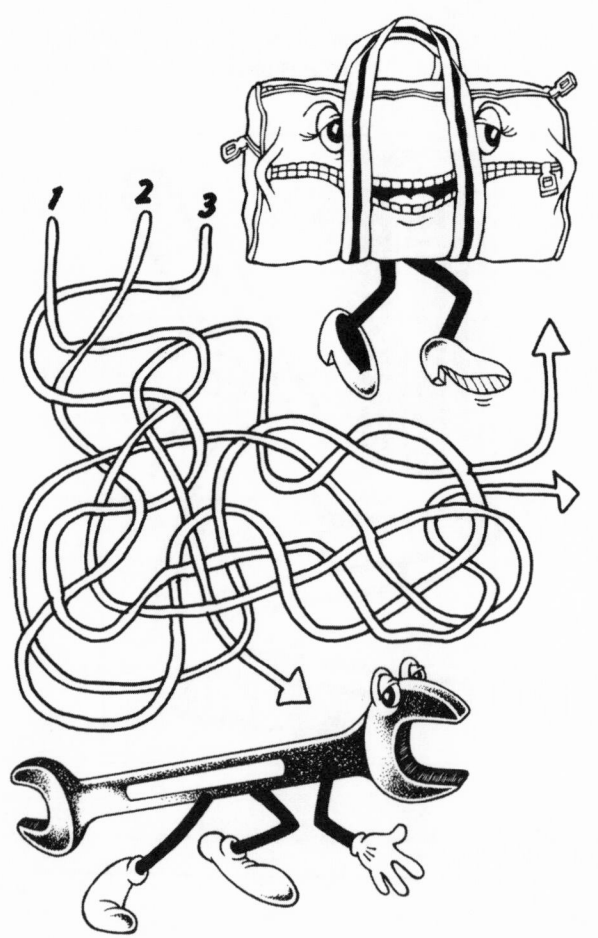

Can you tell which numbered trail will lead the toolbag to the wrench?

779 STAMPS OF VALUE

A new set of stamps has just been issued in Philatelia, and four of the values are shown here. From the clues given below, can you work out the design on each stamp, its face value, and the colour in which its frame and figures of value are printed?

Clues

1 The figure 5 does not appear in brown on any of the four stamps.
2 The stamp depicting the cathedral, which has a zero in its value panel, is shown immediately to the right of the stamp with a brown frame.
3 Stamp 4 has a 1 in its value panel, while the harbour is not the design featured on stamp 3.
4 The 15 cents stamp is shown in a position directly above or below the blue one.
5 The stamp with the red frame bears the value next higher than the one depicting the mountains, which is not in position 1.

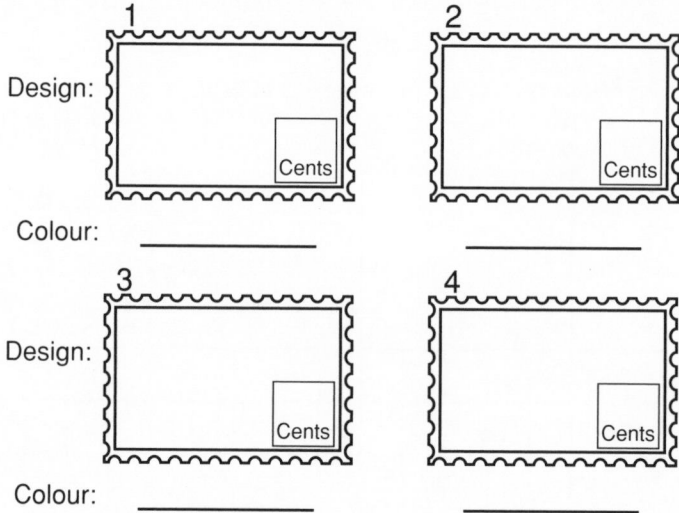

Designs: cathedral; harbour; mountains; waterfall
Values: 10 cents; 15 cents; 25 cents; 50 cents
Colours: blue; brown; green; red

Starting tip: Begin by working out the value on the brown stamp.

780 LOGISTICAL ● ● ●

Five women have each built up an extensive collection of pottery figurines of different creatures. From the clues below, can you work out each collector's full name, the type of figure she collects, and how many she has amassed?

Clues

1 It isn't Mrs Iveagh who has collected 91 pottery dogs of different breeds and sizes.
2 The cat-collector hasn't accumulated exactly 79 of them.
3 It's Ms Wallace who has collected 118 figurines, and Mrs Tate who collects pottery teddy-bears.
4 Janet is very proud of her collection of dragons.
5 Monica has the smallest collection, but it isn't Veronica who has the largest; Mrs Hayward has more than one hundred figurines displayed in the front room of the home.
6 Cynthia's surname is Iveagh; Ruth doesn't collect cats.

Forename	Surname	Figurine	Number

	Courtauld	Hayward	Iveagh	Tate	Wallace	Cats	Dogs	Dragons	Pigs	Teddy-bears	63	79	91	107	118
Cynthia															
Janet															
Monica															
Ruth															
Veronica															
63															
79															
91															
107															
118															
Cats															
Dogs															
Dragons															
Pigs															
Teddy-bears															

Record in this grid all the information obtained from the clues, by using a cross to indicate a definite 'no' and a tick to show a definite 'yes'. Transfer these to all sections of the grid thus eliminating all but one possibility, which must be the correct one.

781 MAZE MYSTERY

Travel from the entrance to the exit of the maze, filling the path completely to create a picture.

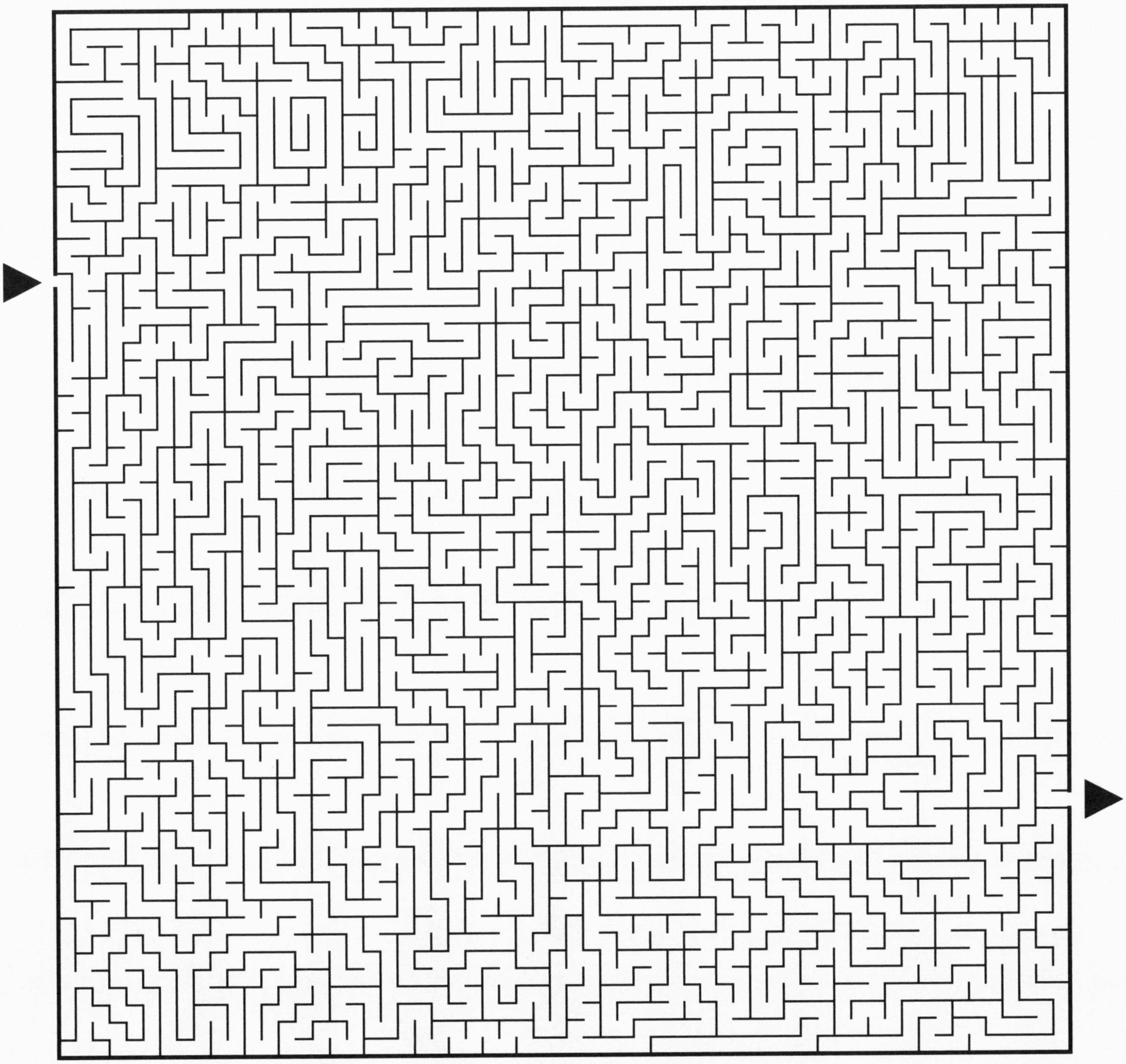

782 ROMEO AND JULIET ⬤

See if you can help Romeo reach Juliet by finding a path through this maze, from start to finish.

783 SIX-PACK ⬤⬤

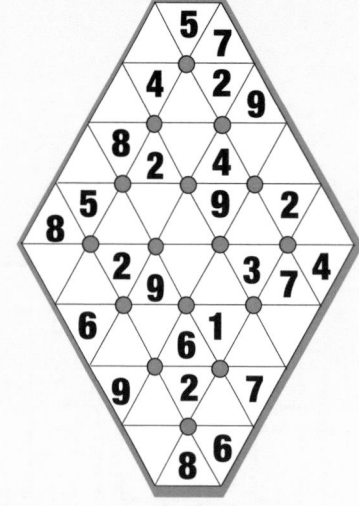

By packing numbers in the empty spaces, can you make the numbers in each of the 16 hexagons add up to 25? No two numbers in each hexagon may be the same, and you can't use zero. We've started you off.

784 SET SQUARE ⬤⬤

All the digits from 1 to 9 are used in this grid, but only once each. Can you work out their positions in the grid and make the sums work? We've given two numbers to start you off.

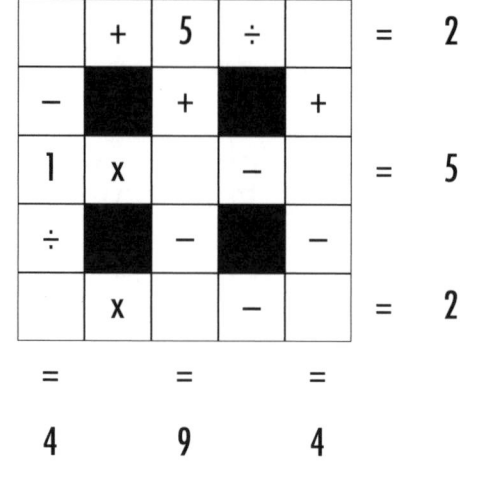

785 WHATEVER NEXT? ⬤⬤

Which two numbers continue this sequence?

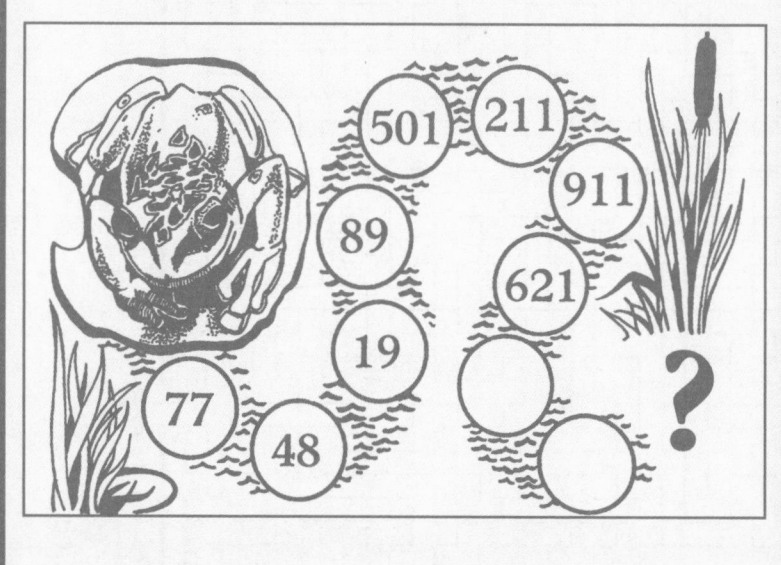

786 TOTTERING TOWERS ⬤⬤

These piles of bricks aren't the random results of child's play but clues to the final, at present, blank tower on the right. Like the rest, that tower has one brick in each of the six colours.

The numbers below each heap tell you two things:
(a) How many adjacent pairs of bricks are actually correct in the final tower.
(b) How many adjacent pairs of bricks make a correct pair but the wrong way up.

So:

would score one on the first number if the final tower had green directly above yellow. It would score one on the second number if the final tower had yellow on top of green.

From all of this, can you create the tower before it finally topples?

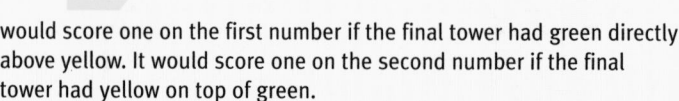

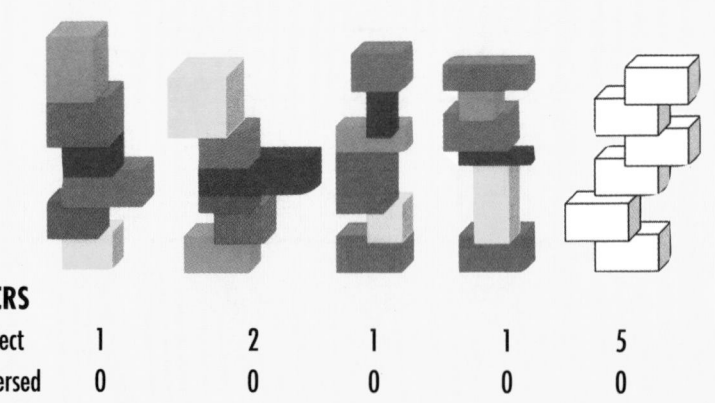

PAIRS					
Correct	1	2	1	1	5
Reversed	0	0	0	0	0

787 LOGISTICAL

●●●

At a craft fair in the village hall, five large and impressive matchstick models were on display, each having been painstakingly constructed by a local person. From the clues given below, can you work out which model was made by which man, and can you also determine how many matches were used and how much time was taken to build each object?

Clues

1 Derek Burns took less than five months to construct his windmill.

2 Charlie Head used more matchsticks than any of the other four men, but his was not the model that took the greatest number of months to build.

3 The cathedral is made up of just 4,000 matchsticks, which is more than were used to construct the steam-roller.

4 The model that was built in exactly four months comprises just 3,500 matchsticks, which is fewer matchsticks than were used by Alec Wood.

5 Brian Box took just two months to complete his model and used more than 3,000 matchsticks to do so.

6 The Ferris wheel was built in just three months and is made up of fewer than 5,000 matchsticks.

Model	Maker	No. of matches	Time taken

	Alec Wood	Brian Box	Charlie Head	Derek Burns	Eric Striker	3,000 matches	3,500 matches	4,000 matches	4,500 matches	5,000 matches	Two months	Three months	Four months	Six months	Seven months
Cathedral															
Ferris wheel															
Ship															
Steam-roller															
Windmill															
Two months															
Three months															
Four months															
Six months															
Seven months															
3,000 matches															
3,500 matches															
4,000 matches															
4,500 matches															
5,000 matches															

Record in this grid all the information obtained from the clues, by using a cross to indicate a definite 'no' and a tick to show a definite 'yes'. Transfer these to all sections of the grid thus eliminating all but one possibility, which must be the correct one.

788 SMILE PLEASE ●

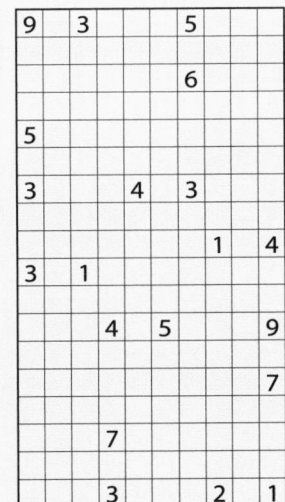

The top left-hand picture of this face is complete, but all the others have at least one detail missing. Can you add the missing details to make all the pictures the same?

789 CELL STRUCTURE ●

The object is to create white areas surrounded by black walls, so that:

* Each white area contains only one number
* The number of cells in a white area is equal to the number in it.
* The white areas are separated from each other with a black wall.
* Cells containing numbers must not be filled in.
* The black cells must be linked into a continuous wall.
* Black cells cannot form a square of 2 x 2 or larger.

9	3			5		
					6	
5						
3			4		3	
					1	4
3		1				
		4		5		9
						7
	7					
3				2	1	

790 STAMP DUTY ●

Which of these numbered prints was made by the stamp featured here?

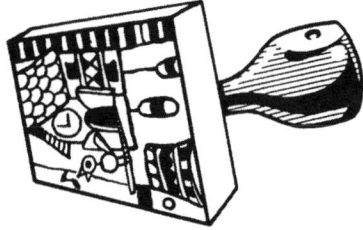

791 EASTER BUNNY ●

One of these Easter bunnies is different from all the others. Can you tell which one?

792 PARROT PIECES ●

These nine pieces can be fitted together to make a complete outline of the parrot, but three of the pieces are slightly wrong. Can you see which three they are?

793 RAT'S TRAIL ●

Can you help this rat find its way to the cheese?

794 PILE UP ●●

These piles of bricks aren't the random results of a child's play but clues to a final, at present blank, pile on the right. Like the rest, that one has six bricks each with a different one of the six letters. The numbers below the heaps tell you two things:

(a) The number of adjacent pairs of bricks in that column which also appear adjacent in the final pile.

(b) The number of adjacent pairs of bricks that make a correct pair but the wrong way up.

So:

would score one in the 'Correct' row if the final heap had an A directly above a C and a one in the 'Reversed' row if the final heap had a C on top of an A. From all this, can you create the final pile before it topples?

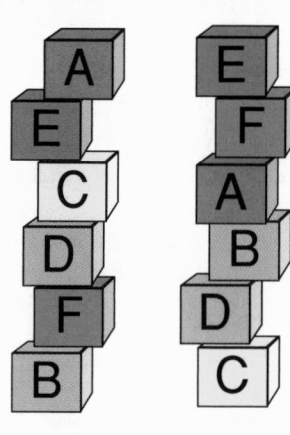   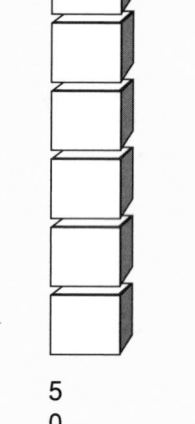

Correct	1	0	0	0	5
Reversed	0	0	2	2	0

795 SET SQUARE ●●

All the digits from 1 to 9 are used in this grid, but only once. Can you work out their positions in the grid and make the sums work? We've given two numbers to start you off.

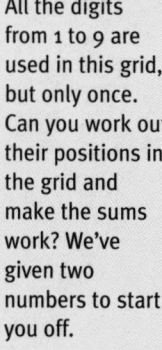

796 SET SQUARE ●●

All the digits from 1 to 9 are used in this grid, but only once each. Can you work out their positions in the grid and make the sums work? We've given two numbers to start you off.

797 LOGISTICAL

In a new science fiction movie, some of the main characters are a family of robots, identical except for the colours of their casings. From the clues below, can you work out the colour of each robot's casing, and the full name of the actor who's inside it?

Clues

1 The actor who plays 'Roxanne', who does not have a four-letter surname, isn't Phil.
2 The yellow robot is played by the actor surnamed Jenkins, while the one called Marvin appears as 'Ramona'.
3 Claudia, whose surname isn't Link, appears in the movie as the silver robot, which has a male name.
4 'Romulus', the robot played by Selena, doesn't have a green casing.
5 George's surname is Krag.
6 'Remus' is the robot with the red casing.

Record in this grid all the information obtained from the clues, by using a cross to indicate a definite 'no' and a tick to show a definite 'yes'. Transfer these to all sections of the grid thus eliminating all but one possibility, which must be the correct one.

Robot	Colour	Forename	Surname

798 LOGISTICAL

Five children who lived in Softwood Cuttings were allowed a few square feet in which to grow their own choice of seeds. From the information given, can you work out their full names, plot area and variety of seeds?

Clues

1 One boy intended to sell his 7 square feet of rocket leaves to the local supermarket, while Martine was looking forward to eating all her radishes.
2 Kylie's plot was twice as big as Dibber's poppy garden.
3 Shovell's area was larger than Jack's but smaller than the candytuft.
4 Miss Potts' flowers occupied an area of 4 square feet.
5 Dean's surname wasn't Trowell.

Record in this grid all the information obtained from the clues, by using a cross to indicate a definite 'no' and a tick to show a definite 'yes'. Transfer these to all sections of the grid thus eliminating all but one possibility, which must be the correct one.

First name	Surname	Plot area	Seed type

799 SPACE CHASE

This astronaut doesn't like the idea of becoming a spaceman sandwich, so he's clearing off back to his rocket! He wishes he could find his stun-gun. How many stun-guns can you find in this picture?

800 TENT FLAP

Which of the lettered paths will lead this confused camper back to his tent?

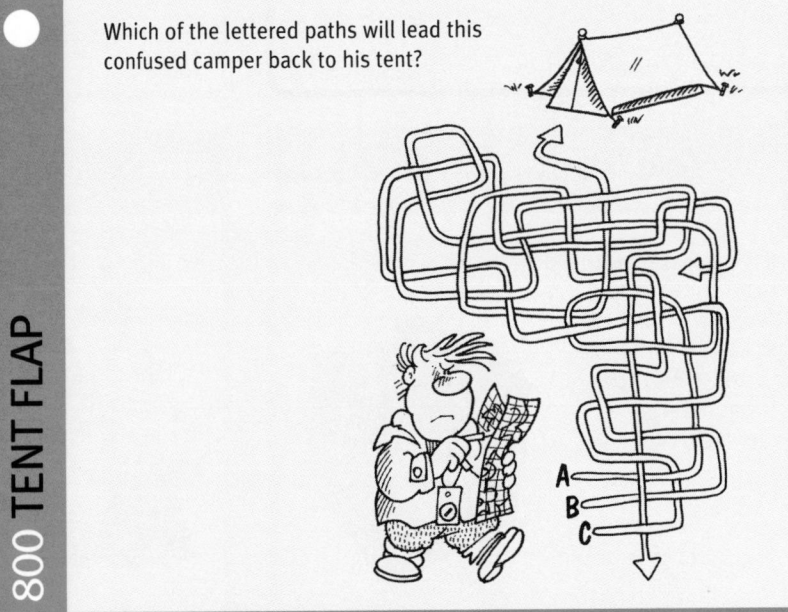

801 CELL STRUCTURE

The object is to create white areas surrounded by black walls, so that:
• Each white area contains only one number
• The number of cells in a white area is equal to the number in it
• The white areas are separated from each other with a black wall
• Cells containing numbers must not be filled in
• The black cells must be linked into a continuous wall
• Black cells cannot form a square of 2x2 or larger

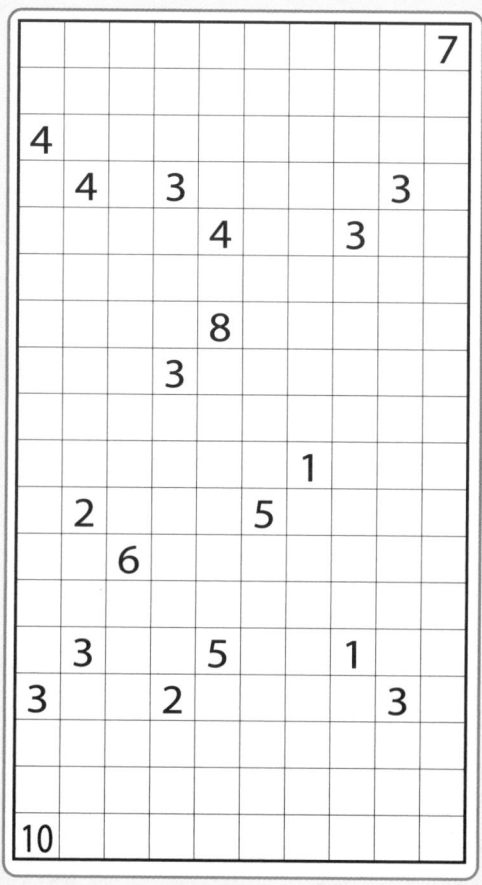

802 SIX-PACK

By packing numbers in the empty spaces, can you make the numbers in each of the 16 hexagons add up to 25? No two numbers in each hexagon may be the same and you can't use zero. We've started you off.

803 DARTING ABOUT

A dart player scores 60 with three darts hitting a treble, a double and a single (no bulls). Given that the three numbers that he hits add up to 31 and that the difference between the largest and smallest numbers is 11, can you work out how his score is made up?

804 STRIP TRICK

In what order must the five pieces below be arranged to form the complete strip shown above?

805 PARTY TIME

If it happens to be true that:
MONDAY = TODAY
TUESDAY = JUNE DAY
SUNDAY = THURSDAY
FRIDAY = BIRTHDAY
Then what day was yesterday?

806 IT'S MAGIC

Can you complete this Magic Square so that every row, column and diagonal adds up to the magic total? To help you we have placed figures above 5 in rows 1, 3, 5 and figures below 5 in rows 2 & 4.

HINT: Every row has units 1, 3, 5, 7, 9 once.

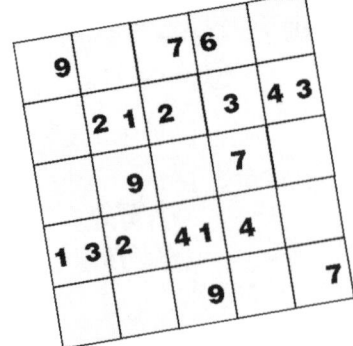

228

807 LOGIQUATIONS

In the following problems the digits 0 to 9 are represented by letters. Within each separate puzzle the same letter always represents the same digit. Can you find the correct values each time so that all sums, both horizontal and vertical, are correct? There is a clue to help start you off.

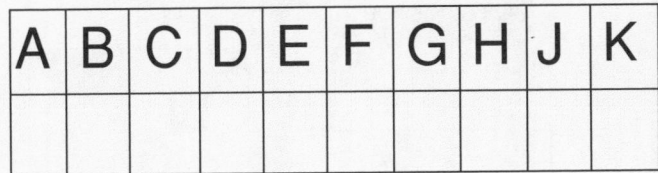

$$AB \times CD = DBEB$$
$$+ \qquad +\qquad -$$
$$\underline{FGHJ + FHJE = EGEC}$$
$$FFCD + BGFH = EFHK$$

A	B	C	D	E	F	G	H	J	K

CLUE: 2 X FD = EB

808 WHATEVER NEXT?

Which two numbers continue this sequence?

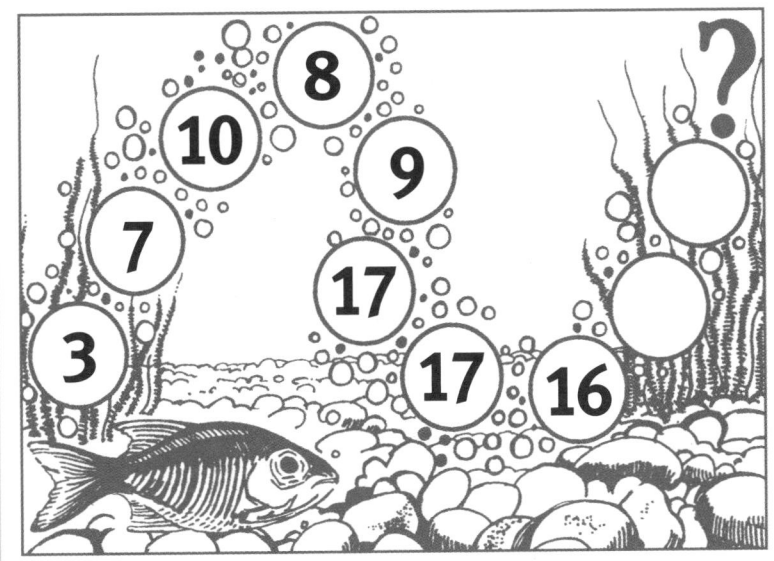

809 IN THE MAIL

Four housewife neighbours in a suburban area of an American town each had a different coloured mailbox at the entrance to their property. From the clues given below, can you work out the name of the woman who lives at each address, and work out the colour of her mailbox?

Clues
1 The green mailbox is next to Gemma's on one side, and Mrs Gerber's on the other.
2 Arlene chose the yellow mailbox for her gate, at a house with a higher number than Mrs Fishbein's.
3 The red mailbox is at Mrs Baron's house.
4 The blue mailbox is on the gate of number 232, which is not Louise's home.

First names: Arlene; Gemma; Kate; Louise
Surnames: Baron; Fishbein; Flint; Gerber
Mailboxes: blue; green; red; yellow

Starting tip: Begin by placing the green mailbox.

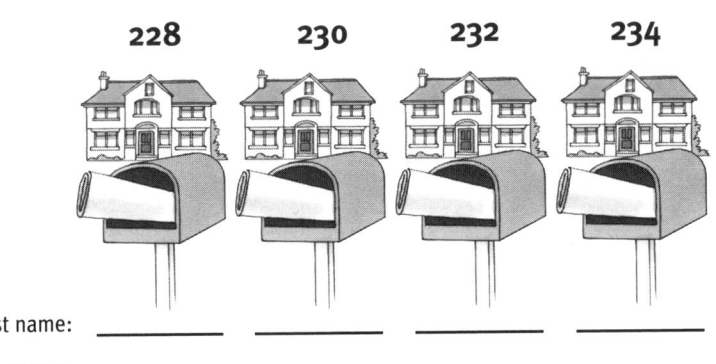

228   230   232   234

First name: ___ ___ ___ ___
Surname: ___ ___ ___ ___
Colour: ___ ___ ___ ___

810 GAME ON

What game is involved here?

JZQONU   LHKDR   ROZRRJX   EHRGDQ   JZROZQNU

811 SPOT THE DIFFERENCE

One of these scruffy birds is different from the rest. Can you tell which?

812 IT FIGURES

Place a number from 1 to 9 in each empty cell so that the sum of each vertical or horizontal block equals the number at the top or on the left of that block. Numbers may only be used once in each block.

813 ISLAND HOPPING

Each circle containing a number represents an island. The object is to connect each island with vertical or horizontal bridges so that:
• The number of bridges is the same as the number inside the island.
• There can be up to two bridges between two islands.
• Bridges cannot cross islands or other bridges.
• There is a continuous path connecting all the islands.

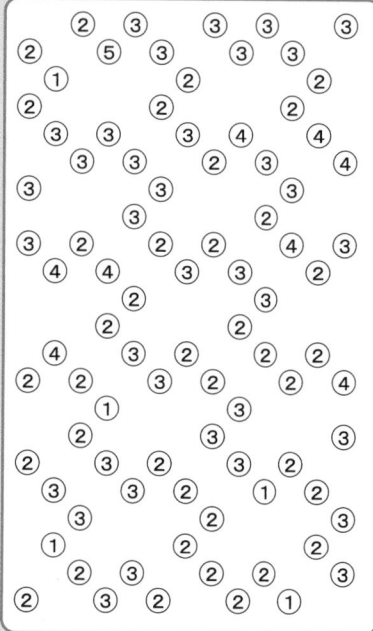

814 WEIGHED UP

Hats must be in heavy wool this year and the snow fall is light! As you can see, two sets of seesaws in the park balance beautifully. How many hats are needed to make the third seesaw level?

815 TELL THE UNTRUTH

The four girls depicted in the diagram are all, I'm afraid, inveterate little liars. From the clues given below, bearing in mind that every statement they make is untrue, can you correctly name the girl in each position, work out her true age, and describe the pet she owns?

Clues
1. Jenny says, "Hello, I'm nine, and I'm sitting in position 4."
2. Josie says, "Hi, I'm sitting next to my friend whose pet is a cat."
3. Jemima says, "Hello, I'm sitting next to Julie, whose pet is a tortoise, and my friend who owns the cat is nine."
4. Julie says, "Hi, my pet is the budgie, and I'm eight years old. I'm in position 2 in the line."
5. To help you out, we'll tell you that the girl aged 10 is in position 3, Josie's pet is a puppy, and the girl numbered 4 in the diagram has a budgie.

Names: Jemima; Jenny; Josie; Julie
Ages: 8; 9; 10;11
Pets: budgie; cat; puppy; tortoise

Starting tip: Begin by identifying Julie's pet.

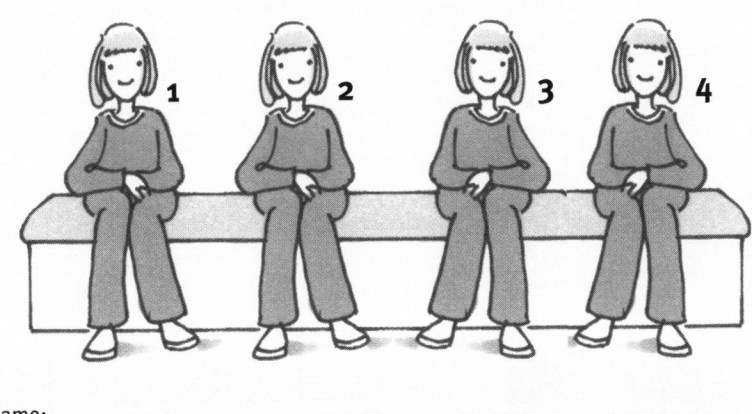

Name: _____ _____ _____ _____

Age: _____ _____ _____ _____

Pet: _____ _____ _____ _____

817 SIX-PACK

By packing numbers in the empty spaces, can you make the numbers in each of the 16 hexagons add up to 25? No two numbers in each hexagon may be the same, and you can't use zero. We've started you off.

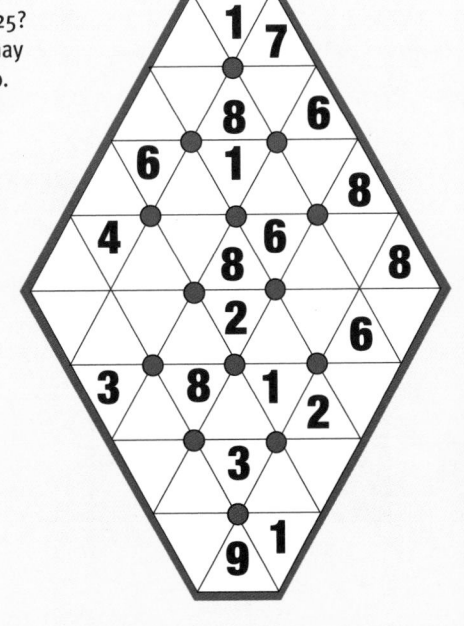

816 NEGATIVE

In a negative, everything which is really white appears black and everything which is really black appears white. Can you tell which one of the six karate experts is shown as a negative in the top left-hand corner?

818 DOT-TO-DOT

Join the dots from 1 to 31 to reveal the hidden picture.

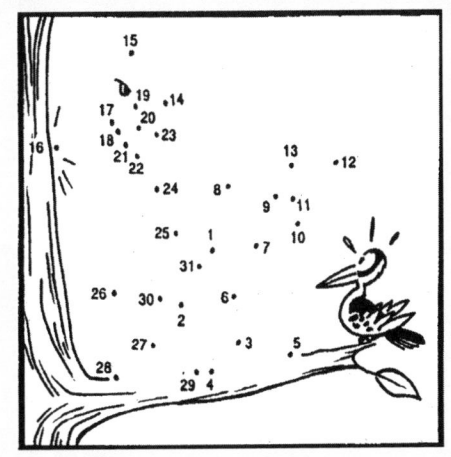

819 WEB MAZE

See if you can find a path through this web which will lead one spider to the other.

820 VIVE LA FRANCE

Each of the seventeen squares in the figure in the diagram contains one of the letters which form the name NAPOLEON BONAPARTE, in recognition of the French Fête Nationale celebrated on July 14. From the clues given below, can you insert all seventeen letters in their correct squares?

Clues

1 None of the letters which occur more than once in the name is immediately adjacent in any direction, including diagonally, to one of its duplicates.
2 The letter in the centre of the middle row is T; it has a consonant directly above it.
3 The diagonal sequence O P A appears somewhere in the layout reading downwards from right to left.
4 Neither of the two end squares of the middle row contains a vowel.
5 The letters at the left-hand end of both the top and bottom rows are identical.
6 The three As are all in different rows, and two of them have an N diagonally immediately above and to the left of them.
7 Both Es are in the same row.
8 The pairing N P occurs in one of the rows, reading left to right.
9 None of the columns reading downwards forms an English three-letter word.
10 The L, which has a consonant as its right-hand neighbour, is in the row above the B.

Letters to be inserted: A; A; A; B; E; E; L; N; N; N; O; O; O; P; P; R; T

Starting tip: Begin by placing the sequence referred to in clue 3.

821 SQUARING THE CIRCLE

What, logically, comes next?

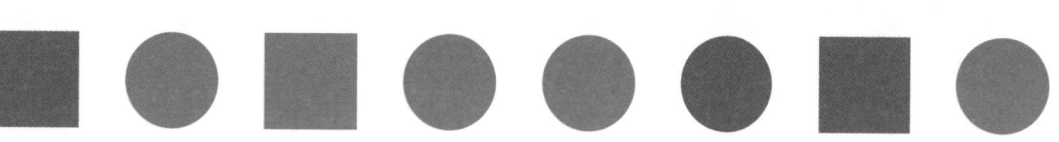

822 FREAK CONVERSION

Can you find the unique fraction

$$\frac{AB}{BC}$$

which when converted to a decimal

$$= 0.BCA\ ?$$

823 MAZE

Can you find a path through this maze?

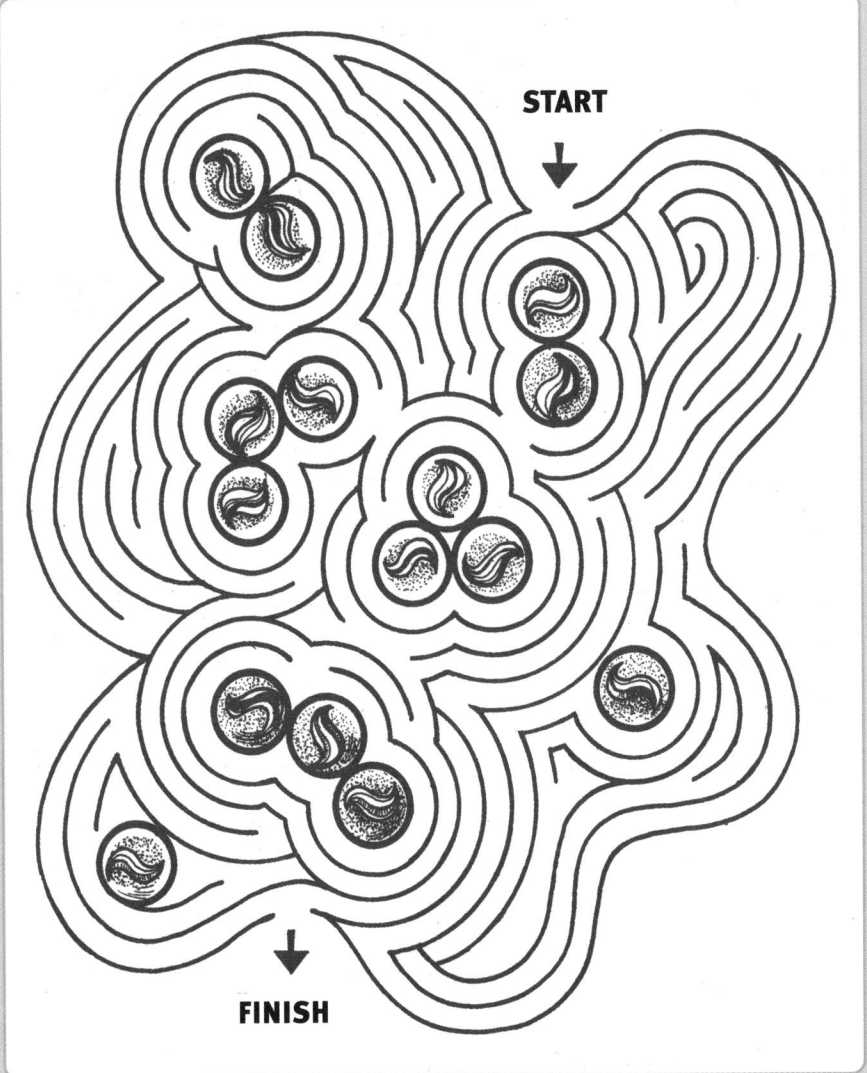

824 DARTING ABOUT

A dart player scored 91 with three darts hitting a treble, a double and a single (no bulls). Given that the three numbers that he hits add up to 47 and that the difference between the largest and smallest numbers is 5 can you work out how his score is made up?

Treble   Double   Single

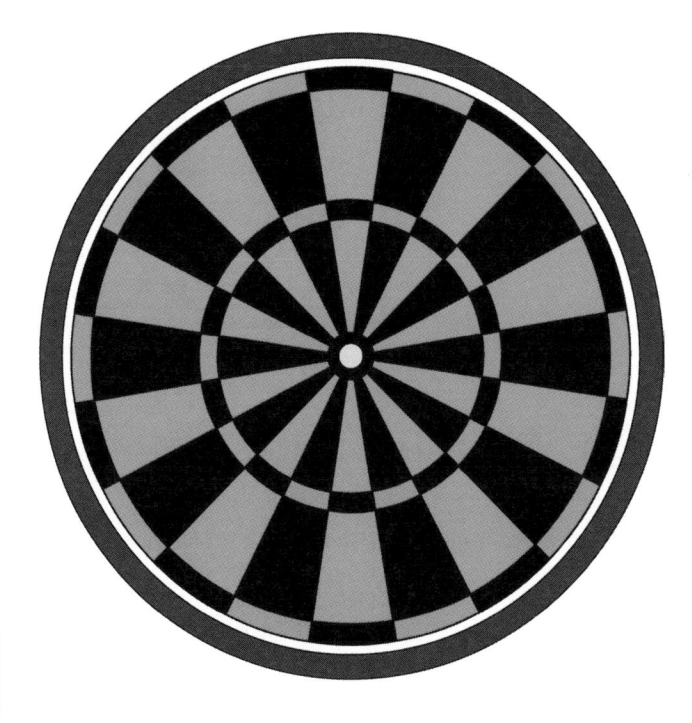

825 ON THE FLY

One day, a young Biggles took Algy on a training flight round a square course. On the first leg they averaged 100mph: on the second leg 200 mph. Gaining confidence, they did the third leg at 300mph and finished with a strut-shattering 400mph along the last leg. Algy reckons their average speed for the whole journey must be 250mph. Is he right?

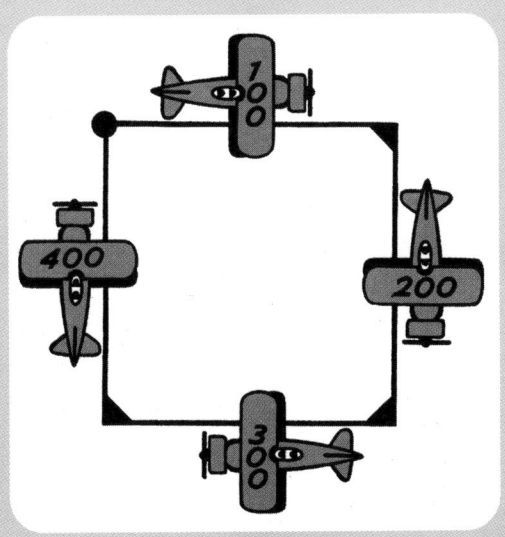

826 WEIGHED UP

How many cats are needed to balance the bottom set of scales?

827 BATTLE ZONE

Each of the figures shown differs slightly from the other three in one small detail. Can you spot all four extra details?

829 A BOX IN THE SHED

When Joe needed something for a job about the house, he would say "They're in a box in the shed". The four boxes shown in the diagram standing next to each other on a shelf, all of different colours, each contain a different number of useful items. From the clues given below, can you work out the full details?

Clues
1 The 43 nails of assorted sizes are not in the brown box.
2 There are 58 items in the blue box.
3 The screws are in the green box, one of whose immediate neighbours on the shelf contains the washers, and the other the largest number of items.
4 The carpet tacks are in box C.

Box colours: blue; brown; green; red
Number: 39; 43; 58; 65
Items: carpet tacks; nails; screws; washers

Colour: _____ _____ _____ _____

Number: _____ _____ _____ _____

Items: _____ _____ _____ _____

Starting tip: First work out the colour of the box containing the nails.

828 SPIDER SCARE

There's nothing Clarissa hates more than big spiders – except for even bigger spiders, of course! Which two pictures of Clarissa are exactly the same?

830 SIX-PACK

By packing numbers in the empty spaces, can you make the numbers in each of the 16 hexagons add up to 25? No two numbers in each hexagon may be the same and you can't use zero. We've started you off.

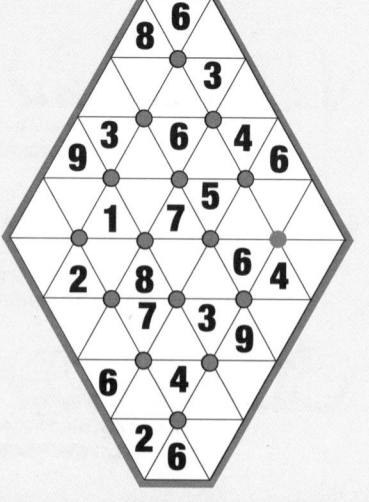

831 ALL CHANGE

At the height of Victorian England a lady of quality could only enjoy seaside bathing by hiring a bathing-machine from which she could descend modestly into the water wearing an ankle-length one-piece bathing dress. This problem features four such machines. From the clues given below, can you fully identify the lady who changed in each machine, and work out the colour of the striped bathing-costume in which she stepped into the sea?

Clues

1 Bertha's machine was immediately to the right of the one used by Miss Marchbanks.
2 Machine C was the one Miss Langthorpe hired.
3 Miss Carstairs wore the green and white striped costume.
4 Euphemia Ponsonby used a machine separated from the one whose occupant wore the orange and white bathing suit only by the one hired by Lavinia.
5 It was in machine B that one lady changed into her red and white bathing-costume.

First names: Bertha; Euphemia; Lavinia; Victoria
Surnames: Carstairs; Langthorpe; Marchbanks; Ponsonby
Costumes: blue and white; green and white; orange and white; red and white

First name: _____ _____ _____ _____

Surname: _____ _____ _____ _____

Costume: _____ _____ _____ _____

Starting tip: Start by working out the first name of the lady who hired machine D.

832 IT FIGURES

Place a number from 1 to 9 in each empty cell so that the sum of each vertical or horizontal block equals the number at the top or on the left of that block. Numbers may only be used once in each block.

833 DOT-TO-DOT

Join the dots from 1 to 46 to reveal the hidden picture.

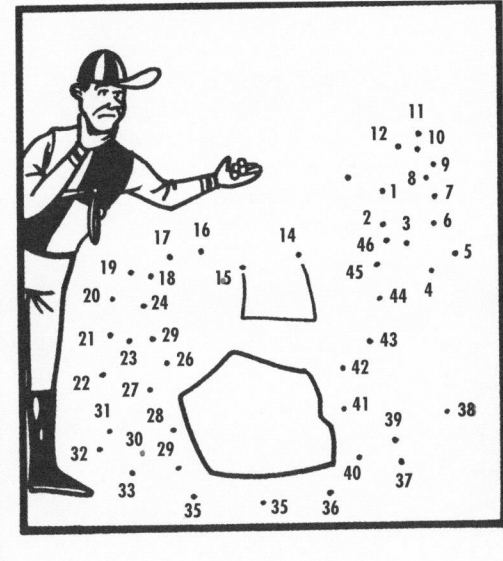

834 SILHOUETTE

Shade in every fragment containing a dot – and what have you got?

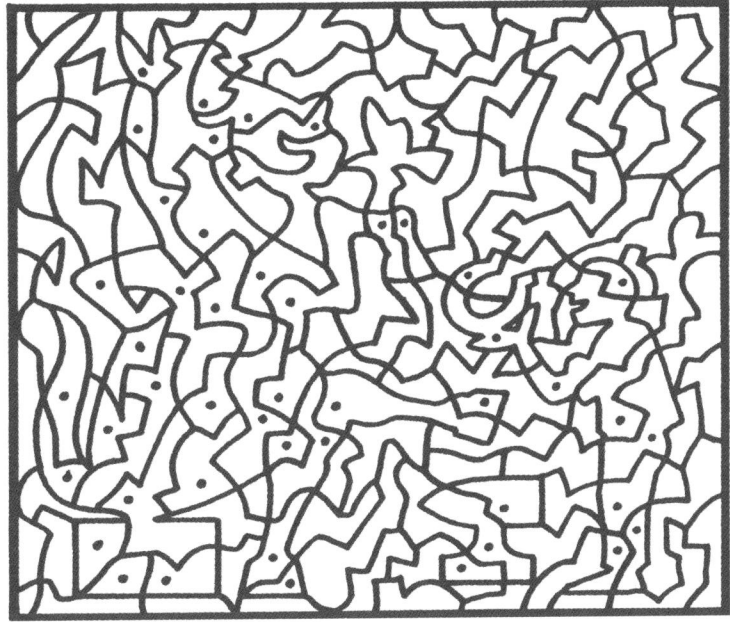

835 ACES HIGH

The four bridge players sitting round the table each had the Ace of a different suit in his or her hand on the deal in question. From the clues given below, can you fully identify the player in each of the four seats, and work out which Ace each holds? NB North and South play as partners against East and West.

Clues

1 Richard's Ace was the same colour as the one held by Ruff, who was in the North seat.
2 Martina's partner was holding the Ace of Hearts.
3 The woman sitting West, whose surname is not Tenace, had the Ace of Spades.
4 Paul Hand was partnering Esther.
5 The Ace of Clubs was not held by the player sitting South.

First names: Esther; Martina; Paul; Richard
Surnames: Hand; Ruff; Tenace; Trick
Aces: Clubs; Diamonds; Hearts; Spades

First name: _____
Surname: _____
Ace: _____

First name: _____
Surname: _____
Ace: _____

First name: _____
Surname: _____
Ace: _____

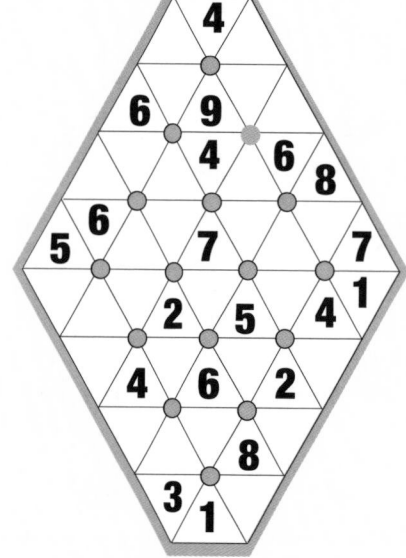

First name: _____
Surname: _____
Ace: _____

Starting tip: Begin by working out which Ace Richard held.

836 TRIO

Which three vases are identical?

837 BLACK OUT

Can you decide which two of the ten stereos are shown in silhouette at the top?

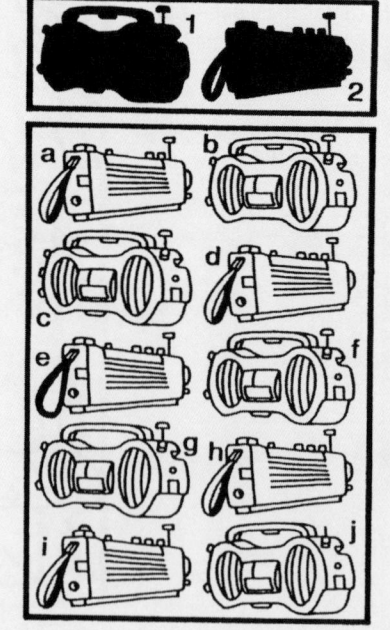

838 SIX-PACK

By packing numbers in the empty spaces, can you make the numbers in each of the 16 hexagons add up to 25? No two numbers in each hexagon may be the same and you can't use zero. We've started you off.

4
6 9
4 6
6 8
6 7 7
5 7 1
2 5 4
4 6 2
8
3 1

839 MAZE MYSTERY

Travel from the entrance to the exit of the maze, filling the path completely to create a picture.

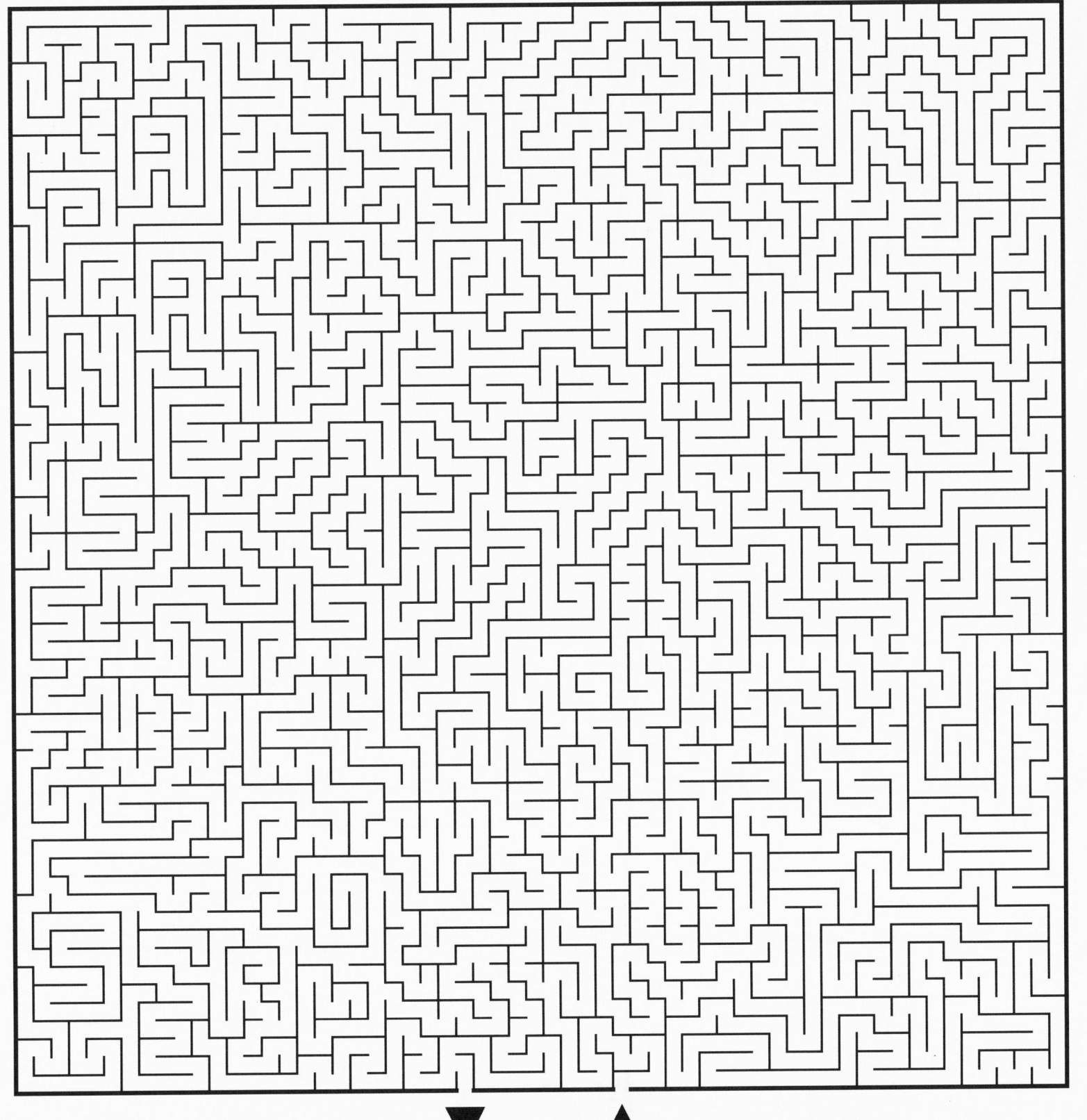

840 SILHOUETTE

Shade in every fragment containing a dot – and what have you got?

841 IN THE STALLS

The four central seats in each of the first three rows of the stalls at the theatre were all occupied at a recent performance. From the clues given below, can you place each of the listed people in their correct seats?

Clues
1 Peter was sitting directly behind Angela, and somewhere diagonally in front of Henry.
2 Nina had the ticket for seat 12 in row B.
3 The four seats featured in each row are occupied by two males and two females.
4 Maxine is two places to the right of Robert in the same row of the stalls.
5 Judy, who is immediately behind Charles, has her husband Vincent as her right-hand neighbour.
6 One of the men in the audience is sitting in seat 13 of row A.
7 Tony, Janet and Lydia all have seats in different rows of the stalls, the latter having a male neighbour to her left.

Names: Angela; Charles; Henry; Janet; Judy; Lydia; Maxine; Nina; Peter; Robert; Tony; Vincent

Name:

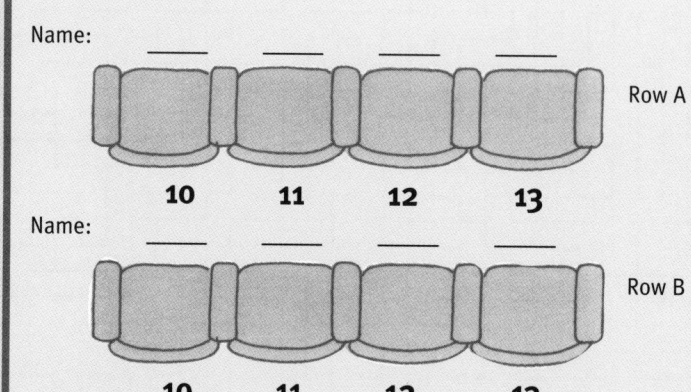

Row A

10   11   12   13

Name:

Row B

10   11   12   13

Name:

Row C

10   11   12   13

Starting tip: Begin by naming the man in seat 13 of row A.

842 ISLAND HOPPING

Each circle containing a number represents an island. The object is to connect each island with vertical or horizontal bridges so that:
• The number of bridges is the same as the number inside the island.
• There can be up to two bridges between two islands.
• Bridges cannot cross islands or other bridges.
• There is a continuous path connecting all the islands.

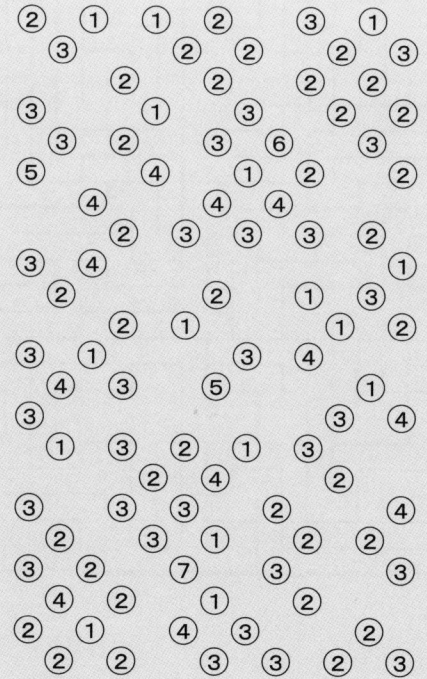

843 DARTING ABOUT

A dart player scores 66 with three darts hitting a treble, a double and a single (no bulls). Given that the three numbers that he hits add up to 31 and that the difference between the largest and smallest numbers is 10 can you work out how his score is made up?

Treble   **Double**   **Single**

844 CELL STRUCTURE

The object is to create white areas surrounded by black walls, so that:
• Each white area contains only one number
• The number of cells in a white area is equal to the number in it
• The white areas are separated from each other with a black wall
• Cells containing numbers must not be filled in
• The black cells must be linked into a continuous wall
• Black cells cannot form a square of 2 x 2 or larger

3						
		3		3		
1						
				3		
	2					
					9	
1		5				
		9				
				6		4
3	5		10			
9						
		5				
						4

845 DON'T PAY THE PIPER...

The diagram shows the Pied Piper leading away the children of Hamelin after the town refused to pay him for ridding it of rats. From the clues given below, can you name the first four children in the line, work out their ages, and say what work their father does in the town?

Clues
1 The cowherd's child is directly behind six-year-old Gretchen as they follow the Piper.
2 Hans is younger than Johann.
3 The boy who leads the line is not immediately followed by the butcher's child.
4 The child aged seven is number 3 in the line.
5 Maria, whose father is an apothecary, is younger than the child in position 2.

Names: Gretchen; Hans; Johann; Maria
Ages: 5; 6; 7; 8
Fathers: apothecary; butcher; cowherd; woodcutter

Name: ___ ___ ___ ___
Age: ___ ___ ___ ___
Father: ___ ___ ___ ___

Starting tip: Start by placing Gretchen.

846 SIX-PACK

By packing numbers in the empty spaces, can you make the numbers in each of the 16 hexagons add up to 25? No two numbers in each hexagon may be the same and you can't use zero. We've started you off.

847 MAZE MYSTERY

Travel from the entrance to the exit of the maze, filling the path completely to create a picture.

848 PANDORA'S BOXES

Pandora Persimmons is the presenter of a quiz show in which successful contestants earn the right to open one of the boxes displayed as in the diagram, the contents of which may prove to be worth having or virtually worthless. Pandora tempts the contestants to forfeit the right to open by offering sums of money, which, in this instance, were refused. From the clues given below, can you indicate in the diagram in what order each of our six qualified to open a box, which box each chose and what it contained?

Clues

1 The order of the contestants did not tally with the number of the box each chose to open.

2 Lynne, who opened box 2, won a cash prize but less than that won by Sharon, whose turn was more than one earlier.

3 Michael, whose turn was next after that of the winner of $100, opened a box more than one place further right than the winner's.

4 The box containing the bar of soap turned out to be next left to the one opened by the fifth contestant; the box chosen by Jim was further left than either.

5 The turn of the contestant who collected the wooden spoon was next before that of the one who was less than ecstatic at winning 50 cents; the box with the spoon in it was next right to the one holding $1,000.

6 Susan opened the box next right to that chosen by Rob, whose turn immediately followed hers.

7 No two men opened adjacent boxes; the winner of the star prize of $5,000 was the only person whose box was between a man's, on the left, and a woman's, on the right.

Contestants: Jim; Lynne; Michael; Rob; Sharon; Susan
Contents: 50 cents; $100; $1,000; $5,000; bar of soap; wooden spoon

Name: _____

Order: _____

Prize: _____

Starting tip: Work out in which box the $5,000 was hidden.

851 SIX-PACK

By packing numbers in the empty spaces, can you make the numbers in each of the 16 hexagons add up to 25? No two numbers in each hexagon may be the same and you can't use zero. We've started you off.

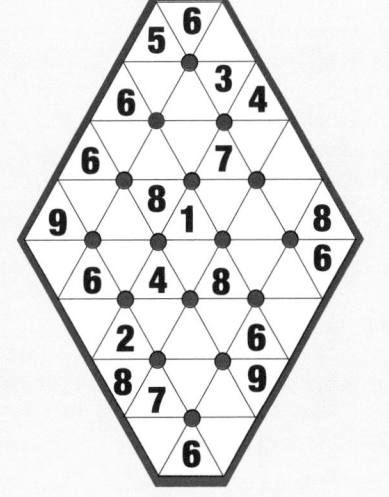

849 DICEY BUSINESS

In order to answer that all-important social question, how many flies are there round the grease spot, six dice are thrown. The answers to the first three throws are given. So what is the answer for the fourth throw?

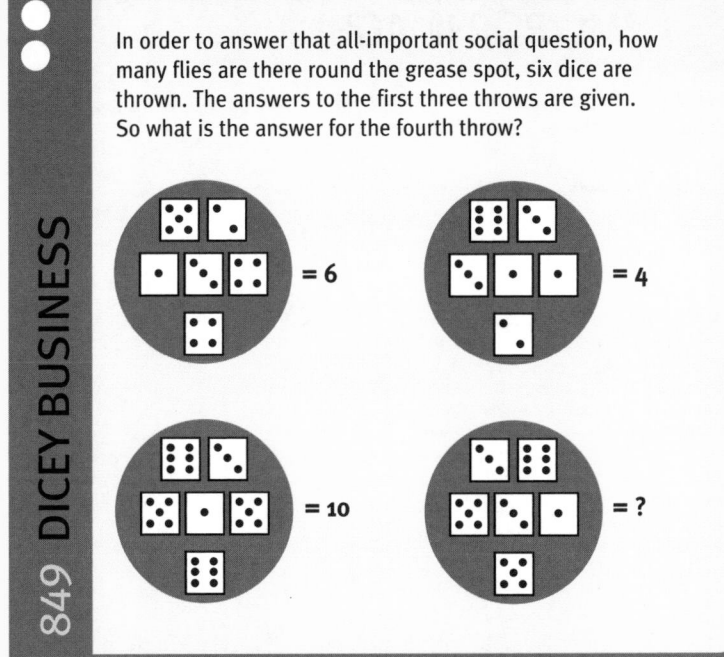

850 GUYS IN THE BLACK HATS

The four posters on the wall of the Sheriff's office in the Wild West town of Redrock show the members of the notorious Black Hat Gang of train-robbers. From the clues given below, can you fill in on the drawing each outlaw's forename, nickname and surname?

Clues

1 Herbert's picture is horizontally adjacent to that of 'Butch' McColl.

2 Poster A shows Jacob, but Silvester Jaggard isn't depicted on poster C.

3 The poster with a picture of the man surnamed Wolf is horizontally adjacent to the one which shows the one nicknamed 'Pony'.

4 Churchman, who appears on poster D, isn't the outlaw nicknamed 'Apache'.

First names: Herbert; Jacob; Matthew; Silvester
Nicknames: 'Apache'; 'Butch'; 'Pony'; 'Rio'
Surnames: Churchman; Jaggard; McColl; Wolf

First name: _____ A WANTED WANTED B _____
Nickname: _____ _____
Surname: _____ $ $ _____

First name: _____ C WANTED WANTED D _____
Nickname: _____ _____
Surname: _____ $ $ _____

Starting tip: Work out the first name of the baddie on poster C.

852 MIRROR IMAGE

There are four pairs of mirror images below. Can you identify the pairs, and find the odd-one-out?

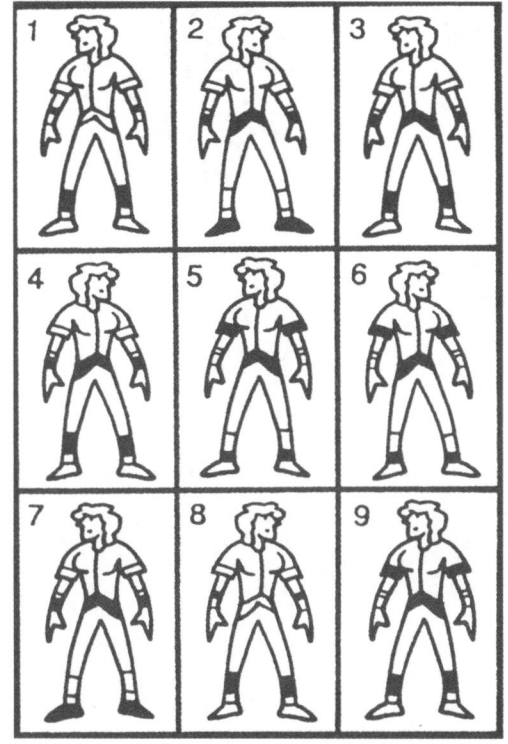

854 TWIN SET

Two of the pictures below are identical. Can you spot the 'twins' and identify what is different about the two remaining pictures?

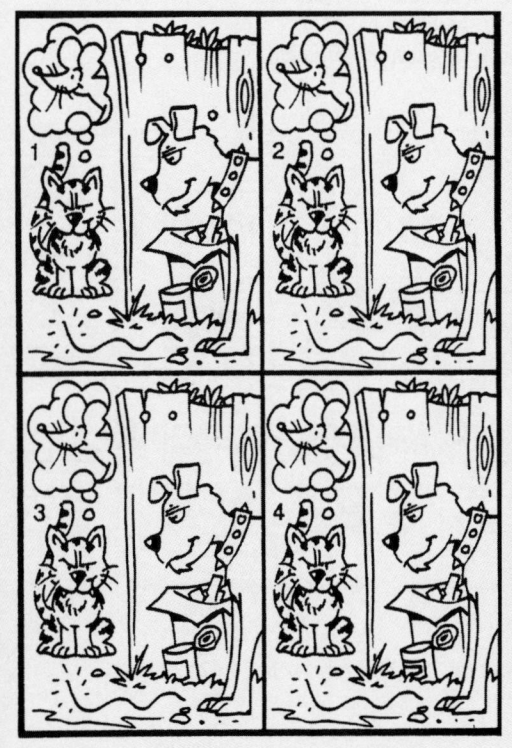

853 ALL SQUARE

A garden square in the city centre has a large hotel occupying each of its sides, as shown numbered 1 to 4 in the diagram. From the clues given below, can you name each hotel and its manager, and say how many rooms it boasts?

Clues

1 The hotel run by Max is directly across the square from the Majestic, which has more rooms, and which is not managed by Rupert.
2 The hotel on the western side of the square does not have 203 rooms.
3 The hotel with the fewest rooms occupies the north side of the square.
4 Guy runs the Castle Hotel, which is next counterclockwise round the square from the one with 197 rooms.
5 Perry is the manager of the hotel numbered 3 on the plan, which has fewer rooms than the Excelsior.

Hotels: Castle; Excelsior; Grand; Majestic
Managers: Guy; Max; Perry; Rupert
Rooms: 158; 197; 203; 224

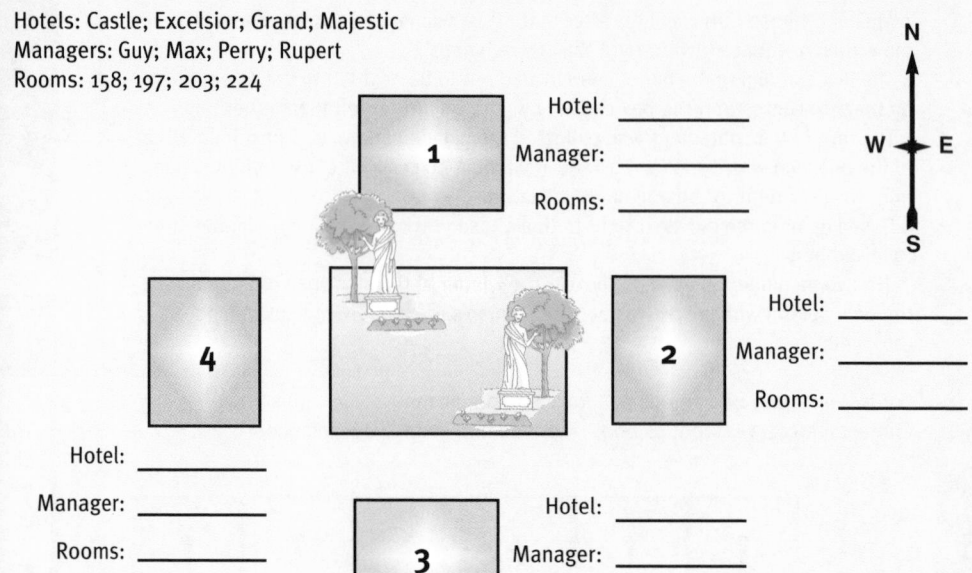

Hotel: _____
Manager: _____
Rooms: _____

Hotel: _____
Manager: _____
Rooms: _____

Hotel: _____
Manager: _____
Rooms: _____

Hotel: _____
Manager: _____
Rooms: _____

Starting tip: Begin by working out how many rooms there are in hotel 4.

855 UNLUCKY FOR SOME

Each of the white squares in the diagram contains a different one of the numbers 1 to 13. From the clues given below, can you place the correct number in each of the squares?

Clues

1 There are no two-digit numbers in rows A or D, or in columns 1 or 4.
2 The 9 does not occupy a corner square.
3 The 6 is in direct line below the 2.
4 The number in E5 is one below the one in A3.
5 The 1 is diagonally below and to the left of the 12, and diagonally above and to the right of the 10.
6 The number in square B4 is two higher than the one in square D2.
7 The 8 is in direct line above the number 13.

Numbers: 1; 2; 3; 4; 5; 6; 7; 8; 9; 10; 11; 12; 13

Starting tip: Start by placing the 1 in its correct position.

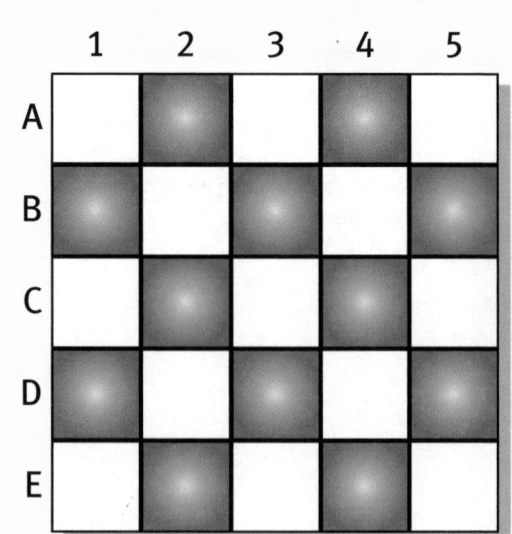

856 MAZE MYSTERY

Travel from the entrance to the exit of the maze, filling the path completely to create a picture.

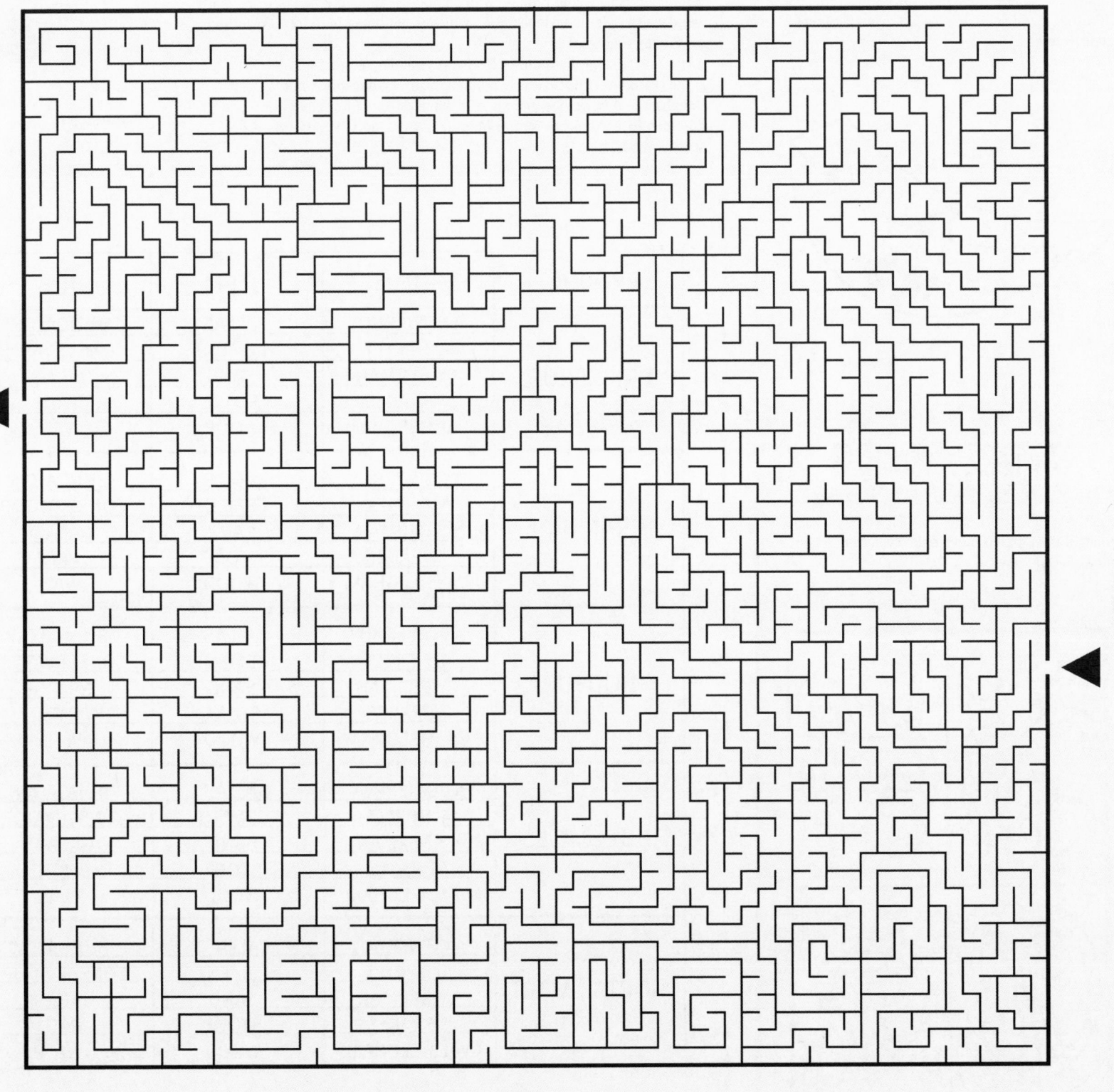

857 COFFIN'S CANOE

This extraordinary little puzzle was made by Stuart Coffin –a world-renowned puzzle craftsman. The 'canoe' has two recesses, one at each end, into which the balls will fit. A divider separates the two balls. If you think that the problem of rolling balls into the holes is just too easy, let us point out that you must pop them into place *Simultaneously*! Now that might seem impossible – but it can be done. How?

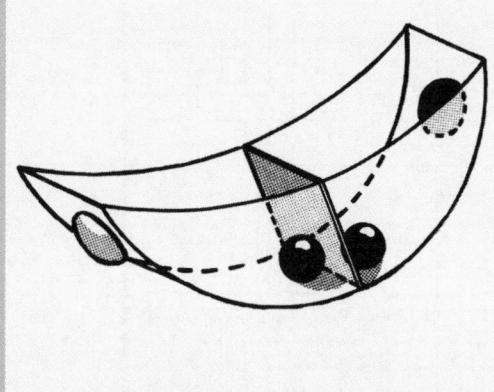

859 KNOT SO

Which of the tangled ropes below will form a knot, and which will not?

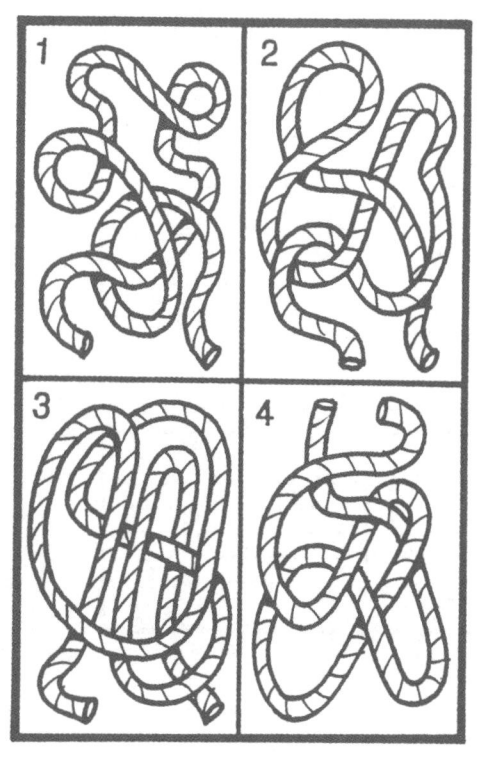

858 JOB IN HAND

Although it's a quiet time for building works, these five merchants are busy supplying the needs of five builders who each need a different item for a different project.

Can you put the facts into place?

1 Alf Pryce is calling at Hodsup who do not sell stone but he does not want wood which is for the conservatory which is not being built by A Cowerboy.
2 T Brakes wants sand.
3 The ballast is for the path. Cy Berman is building a bungalow.
4 The customer at BricksRus is building a garage but this is not Val Heegham or A Cowerboy and none of these three wants cement or stone.
5 Neither Just Slates nor Mortar Mart sells stone and the latter does not supply wood.

PRODUCT	CUSTOMER	ITEM	JOB
BRICKSRUS	A COWERBOY	BALLAST	BUNGALOW
	ALF PRYCE	CEMENT	CONSERVATORY
	CY BERMAN	SAND	GARAGE
	T BRAKES	STONE	PATH
	VAL HEEGHAM	WOOD	WALL
HIRAN HIRE	A COWERBOY	BALLAST	BUNGALOW
	ALF PRYCE	CEMENT	CONSERVATORY
	CY BERMAN	SAND	GARAGE
	T BRAKES	STONE	PATH
	VAL HEEGHAM	WOOD	WALL
HODSUP	A COWERBOY	BALLAST	BUNGALOW
	ALF PRYCE	CEMENT	CONSERVATORY
	CY BERMAN	SAND	GARAGE
	T BRAKES	STONE	PATH
	VAL HEEGHAM	WOOD	WALL
JUST SLATES	A COWERBOY	BALLAST	BUNGALOW
	ALF PRYCE	CEMENT	CONSERVATORY
	CY BERMAN	SAND	GARAGE
	T BRAKES	STONE	PATH
	VAL HEEGHAM	WOOD	WALL
MORTAR MART	A COWERBOY	BALLAST	BUNGALOW
	ALF PRYCE	CEMENT	CONSERVATORY
	CY BERMAN	SAND	GARAGE
	T BRAKES	STONE	PATH
	VAL HEEGHAM	WOOD	WALL

860 FOURSOME

This couple would like to buy four identical ornaments. Which design will they choose?

862 SIXTH LETTER

Which of the following five letters logically belongs in the circle marked (?)

1) H   2) Z   3) R   4) O   5) J

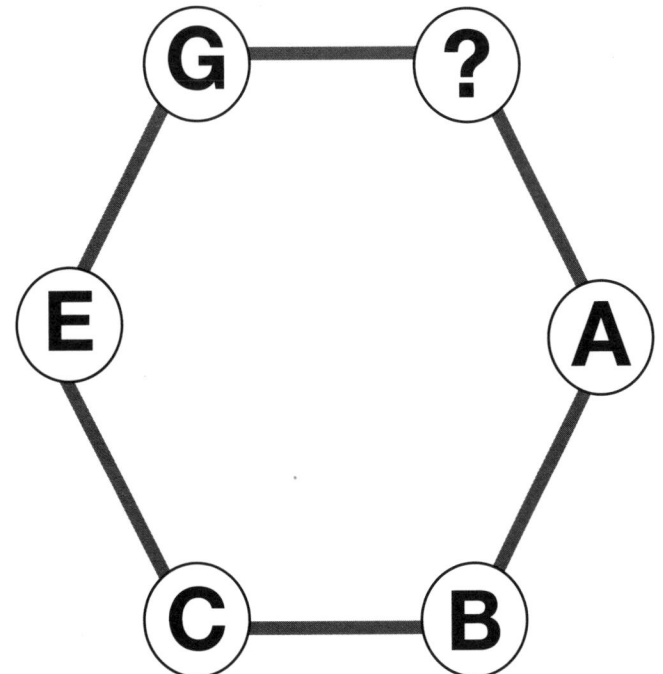

861 CELL STRUCTURE

The object is to create white areas surrounded by black walls, so that:

• Each white area contains only one number
• The number of cells in a white area is equal to the number in it
• The white areas are separated from each other with a black wall
• Cells containing numbers must not be filled in
• The black cells must be linked into a continuous wall
• Black cells cannot form a square of 2 x 2 or larger

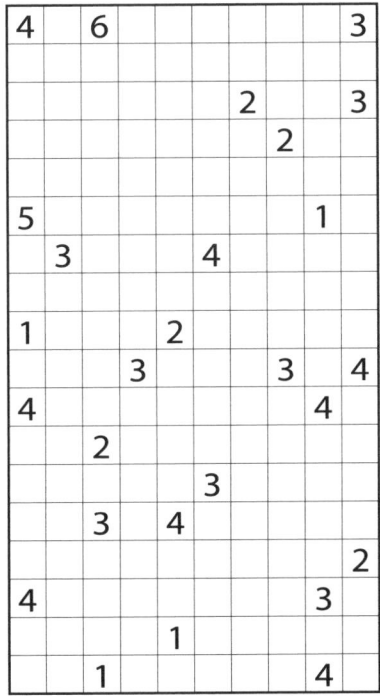

863 IT'S A GIFT

It's that time of year when we should spare a thought for that poor, lovesick male who spent the festive season lugging gifts along to his beloved during the 12 days of Christmas. You'll recollect he dragged a partridge in a pear tree to her house on day one. On day two it was two calling birds and another partridge in another tree. By day twelve the street must have been closed to pedestrians and traffic. The intriguing question is – just how many gifts in total did he foist upon the object of his affections?

864 LOGISTICAL ●●●

Five companies have offices in seven-storey Boreham House, and each has a receptionist in their foyer – which is on the lower floor if they occupy two. From the clues below, can you identify the company occupying each floor or floors, their business, and their receptionist?

Clues

1 The lawyers, whose offices aren't on the fourth floor, don't employ John King.

2 The architects for whom Keith Lyons works have offices higher up the building than those in which Ann Blake is on reception.

3 Gail Hood works for Lorrel & Hardie, whose offices aren't on the seventh floor.

4 Sue Tyler's desk is on a floor two above that of the receptionist who works for publishers Cheape & Chirfle.

5 The fifth and sixth floors of Boreham House are occupied by Kopz & Roberts.

6 Bredd & Cheise aren't the accountants with offices on the third floor.

	Bredd & Cheise	Cheape & Chirfle	Kopz & Roberts	Lorrel & Hardie	Rocke & Rowle	Accountants	Architects	Publishers	Lawyers	Stockbrokers	Ann Blake	Gail Hood	John King	Keith Lyons	Sue Tyler
First/second															
Third															
Fourth															
Fifth/sixth															
Seventh															
Ann Blake															
Gail Hood															
John King															
Keith Lyons															
Sue Tyler															
Accountants															
Architects															
Publishers															
Lawyers															
Stockbrokers															

Record in this grid all the information obtained from the clues, by using a cross to indicate a definite 'no' and a tick to show a definite 'yes'. Transfer these to all sections of the grid thus eliminating all but one possibility, which must be the correct one.

Office floor	Company name	Business	Receptionist

867 DICEY BUSINESS ●●

In order to answer that all-important social question – how many are out to lunch? – four dice are thrown. The answers to the first two throws are given. So what is the answer for the third throw?

= 3   **= 30**   **= ?**

865 SIX-PACK ●●

By packing numbers in the empty spaces, can you make the numbers in each of the 16 hexagons add up to 25? No two numbers in each hexagon may be the same and you can't use zero. We've started you off.

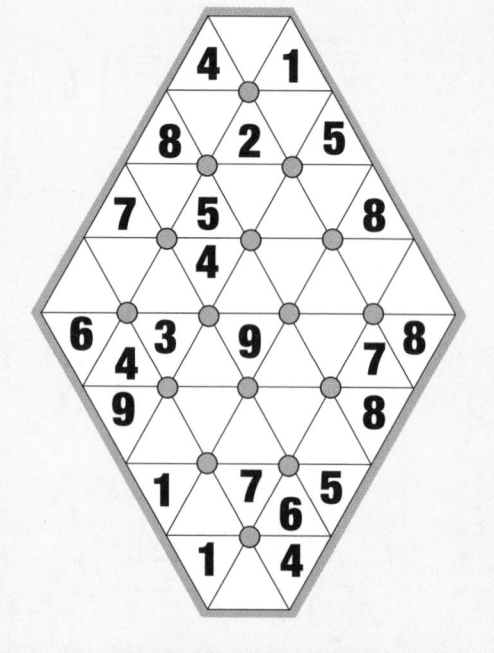

866 NUMBER SQUARES ●●

Can you complete the grid below with the aid of the numbers given, so that all sums, whether horizontal or vertical, are correct? (Please note that each sum should be treated separately.)

48	÷		=		+		=	44
−		+		×		÷		−
	÷	4	=		÷			
=		=		=		=		=
	+		=	32	+		=	
×		+		+		+		+
	+		=		+	1	=	
=		=		=		=		=
64	−		=		+		=	53

868 BOARD STIFF ●●●

Five firms have handed a directorship to a knight, in order to add that little something to the headed notepaper. Can you complete the details?

1 Sir John Snyfe has joined neither the insurance firm or KGH and R T Fish is chairman of none of these three. A C Maynes is not on the board of KGH which is not the construction company.
2 B N Kew is chairperson of neither the banking firm nor PNT and none of these three has added Sir Jestife to the strength.
3 Neither OBD nor the public relations firm is the one which has taken on Sir Tayne-Lee and LD Rhado chairs none of these three companies.
4 Sir Vance-Hall has joined neither PNT nor the construction company nor is any of these three connected with R T Fish or T D Huss who chairs LTP.
5 A C Maynes does not chair the public relations company or the insurance company which is not the one with L D Rhado on its board and none of these four firms has signed up Sir Fitz-Tension who has not joined the banking firm.

SIR	COMPANY	BUSINESS	CHAIRPERSON
FITZ-TENSION	KGH	BANKING	A C MAYNES
	LTP	CONSTRUCTION	B N KEW
	OBD	INSURANCE	L D RHADO
	PNT	P.R.	R T FISH
	RTC	TRAVEL	T D HUSS
JESTIFE	KGH	BANKING	A C MAYNES
	LTP	CONSTRUCTION	B N KEW
	OBD	INSURANCE	L D RHADO
	PNT	P.R.	R T FISH
	RTC	TRAVEL	T D HUSS
JOHN SNYFE	KGH	BANKING	A C MAYNES
	LTP	CONSTRUCTION	B N KEW
	OBD	INSURANCE	L D RHADO
	PNT	P.R.	R T FISH
	RTC	TRAVEL	T D HUSS
TAYNE-LEE	KGH	BANKING	A C MAYNES
	LTP	CONSTRUCTION	B N KEW
	OBD	INSURANCE	L D RHADO
	PNT	P.R.	R T FISH
	RTC	TRAVEL	T D HUSS
VANCE-HALL	KGH	BANKING	A C MAYNES
	LTP	CONSTRUCTION	B N KEW
	OBD	INSURANCE	L D RHADO
	PNT	P.R.	R T FISH
	RTC	TRAVEL	T D HUSS

869 DARTING ABOUT ●●

A dart player scores 75 with three darts hitting a treble, a double and a single (no bulls). Given that the three numbers that he hits add up to 35 and that the difference between the largest and smallest numbers is 14, can you work out how his score is made up?

Treble   **Double**   **Single**

870 TOTALIENS ●●

Each Seasonal Sign has a value in the range 1 to 8 and has the same value wherever it occurs. The numbers around two edges give the total of the values in each row or column. Can you work out the correct value for each symbol which will give these totals?

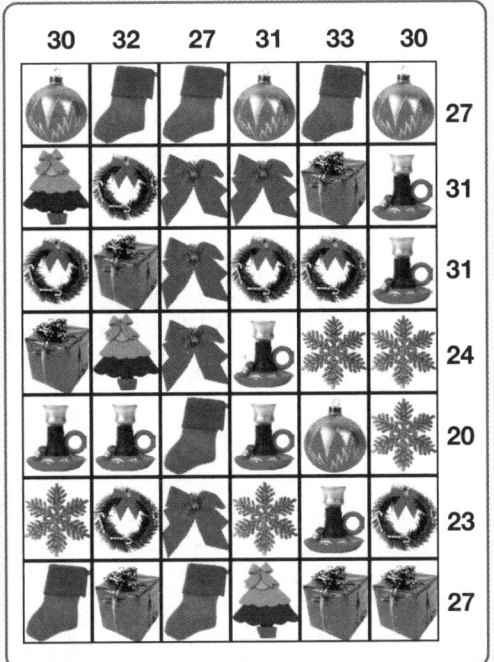

871 MIND JOGGER ●●

Can you find five consecutive numbers that add up to 490?

490

247

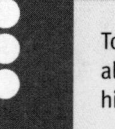
To the untutored eye the houses on the Merryview estate look pretty much alike. Which is why Don, a trainee realtor's tea maker, made plenty of notes on his few excursions.

Clues

1 Houses with double-glazing have central heating.
2 Houses with red roofs have front gardens.
3 Odd numbered houses have green doors.
4 Houses with iron gates have fierce dogs.
5 Houses with green doors have red roofs.
6 Houses with few visitors have white paintwork.
7 Houses without chimneys have leaded windows.
8 Houses with fierce dogs have few visitors.
9 Houses with plastic gnomes have double-glazing.
10 Detached houses have iron gates.
11 Houses with central heating do not have chimneys.
12 Houses with front gardens have plastic gnomes.
13 Even numbered houses are detached.

When asked, by a prospective client, what sort of house number 51 was, the only reply received was an 'umm', an 'agh' and a quick, nervous wipe round the inside of a hot collar. How much of a description can you give from this informative set of notes?

872 HOUSE THAT AGAIN

874 ARROW NUMBERS

Each number already in the grid shows the sum of the digits in the line whose direction is shown by the arrow. Only one digit can be placed in each square. There are no zeros. For each sum, each digit can only appear once – e.g., 8 cannot be completed with 44. A sequence of digits forming a sum can only appear once in the grid. If 8 is 53 somewhere then another 8 cannot also be 53. Nor could it be 35, but must contain a different set of digits, such as 71/17, or 62/26. Can you put logic, rather than higher maths, to work and find the unique solution?

	17	7	43	27		41	10	13
13 ▶					6			
23 ▶					24 / 23 ▾			
44 ▶								
	30	12 / 15 ▶					20	14
19 ▶			14 / 9 ▶					
14 ▶					22 / 35 ▶			
37 ▶								
21 ▶				12 / 13 ▶			29	11
13 ▶		17 / 10 ▶			8 / 9 ▶			
	4	26 / 16 ▶						
11 ▶				14 ▶				
18 ▶				28 ▶				

873 NUMBERCROSTIC

The two lower grids contain 12 equations, only the answers to which are given. These answers (without altering the order of their digits) also fit randomly into the 12 spaces in the first column of the right-hand grid (to read downwards), and thus form the first digits of the answers to the clues. As you start to fill in the answers, transfer each digit to the corresponding square in the lower grids and begin to piece together the equations.

Clues

A Both digits are the same
B Square of A; reverse of the square of Z
C B – Z
D A x 4
E C – D; palindromic number
F D x 5; two-thirds of C
G First and second digits are 4 times the third digit
H G + A
J F – G – H
K First digit is the square root of the second and third
L J + K; N x 7
M Digits of L rearranged, each in a different position
N G – Z
P M – N
Q Second digit is the sum of the first and third digits
R N + P + Q
S All the digits are the same
T D x 2
U S – T
V Second and third digits are 5 times the first digit
W Descending consecutive odd digits
X Third digit is the sum of the first and second digits
Y B x 6
Z A x 3

A	39	62		
B	5	48	28	64
C	6	43	32	
D	16	41	10	
E	36	67	60	
F	21	53	56	
G	23	30	47	
H	66	27	44	
J	29	51	8	
K	17	57	13	
L	46	63	7	
M	40	11	65	
N	34	42	4	
P	58	12	45	
Q	71	25	54	
R	37	18	3	
S	59	72	38	
T	69	33	26	
U	9	22	50	
V	55	15	52	
W	70	1	35	
X	49	68	14	
Y	61	24	19	2
Z	20	31		

W1	Y2	+	R3	N4	+	B5	C6	=	6	9
L7	J8	+	U9	D10	+	M11	P12	=	9	1
K13	X14	+	V15	D16	–	K17	R18	=	3	8
Y19	Z20	+	F21	U22	–	G23	Y24	=	7	4
Q25	T26	–	H27	B28	+	J29	G30	=	5	6
Z31	C32	–	T33	N34	+	W35	E36	=	4	7

R37	S38	–	A39	M40	–	D41	N42	=	2	2
C43	H44	–	P45	L46	–	G47	B48	=	3	1
X49	U50	+	J51	V52	–	F53	Q54	=	1	3
V55	F56	+	K57	P58	–	S59	E60	=	2	5
Y61	A62	–	L63	B64	+	M65	H66	=	8	6
E67	X68	–	T69	W70	+	Q71	S72	=	6	2

875 IDENTIGRIDS

Can you spot which three squares are identical? Watch out – they may not be the same way up!

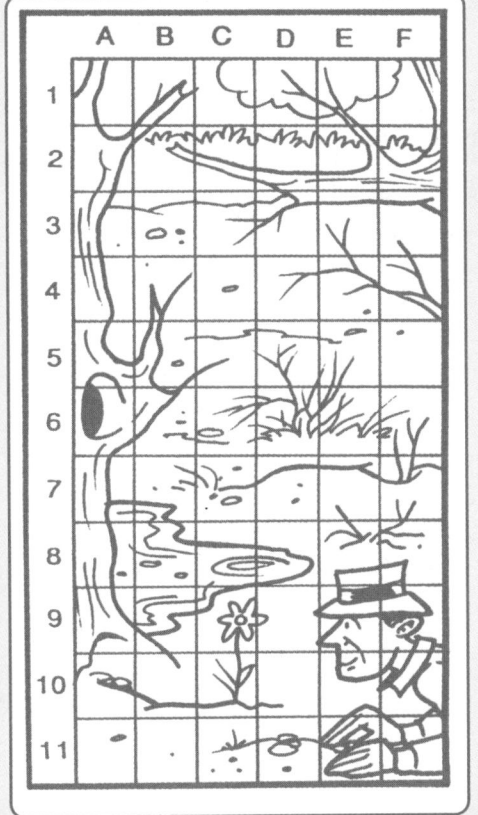

876 SEARCH PARTY

Four of the six shapes at the top are hidden in the main picture. Can you spot which four and whereabouts they are?

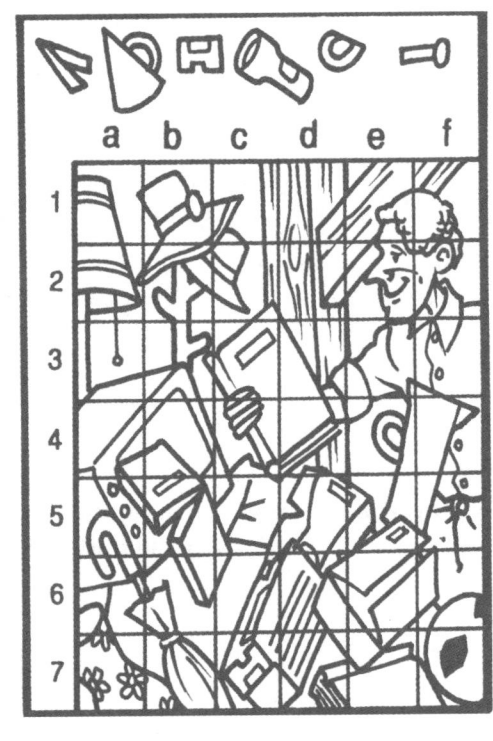

877 DARTING ABOUT

A dart player scores 83 with three darts hitting a treble, a double and a single (no bulls). Given that the three numbers that he hits add up to 36 and that the difference between the largest and smallest numbers is 16, can you work out how his score is made up?

Treble   **Double**   **Single**

878 CAROUSEL

The Carousel is a popular ride with the toddlers at Orles Fair. There are eight different animals on it and so that the children don't get bored with it Sid Slick, the owner, changes the positions of the animals each day. With the position of the horse given and the knowledge that the animals face and move in a clockwise direction, see if you can use the clues to work out the positions of each animal and child on today's ride.

Clues
1 No child is next to or opposite another with the same number of letters in his/her name.
2 Each neighbour has a different number of letters in his/her name.
3 Both mythical animals have boys on them and both birds have girls on them.
4 Bob is opposite the emu and two places behind Chloe, whose neighbours are both boys.
5 The zebra is two places in front of the dragon.
6 Sue is opposite the camel and Alan is opposite the elephant.
7 David is two places in front of the horse but is not next to the emu.
8 There are also a unicorn and a peacock, and the other riders are Edward, Helena and Joan.

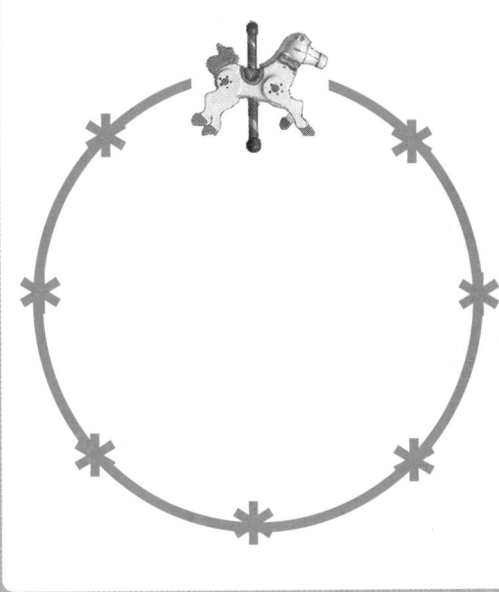

879 SEARCH FOR A RAINBOW

The seven colours of the rainbow (red, orange, yellow, green, blue, indigo, violet) appear just once in the correct order in this grid, running in either a forward or backward direction, either vertically, horizontally or diagonally. Can you locate the rainbow?

880 MIXED PAIRS

● ● ●

For their annual bowls tournament this year, the Tisbury club has arranged a novel competition. Four married couples, that had fought their way through earlier rounds playing with their spouses, now played three final rounds without them. In each round, nobody played with his/her spouse and each partnered a different member of the opposite gender in each round. After the three rounds, each individual player counted up the points (shots, for the bowls-literate) his/her pair had scored in each round. Each married couple then added their two totals together. The couple with the highest combined total score won the competition. From the facts shown on the master scoreboard, can you name each couple, give their occupations and then name the eventual winners?

	Round 1			Round 2			Round 3	
SHE	SCORE	AND HE	SHE	SCORE	AND HE	SHE	SCORE	AND HE
Caterer's wife	15	Mr Kelly	Thelma	11	Director's husband	Mechanic's wife	17	Teacher's husband
	v			v			v	
Mail lady	10	Butcher	Brenda	8	Sculptor's husband	Director	16	Mr Watson

Ann	14	Pete	Clive's wife	12	Jack	Len's wife	14	Clive Dawson
	v			v			v	
Vet's wife	6	Len	Rose	5	Mechanic	Teacher	14	Mr Morris

881 DOT-TO-DOT

Join the dots from 1 to 51 to reveal the hidden picture.

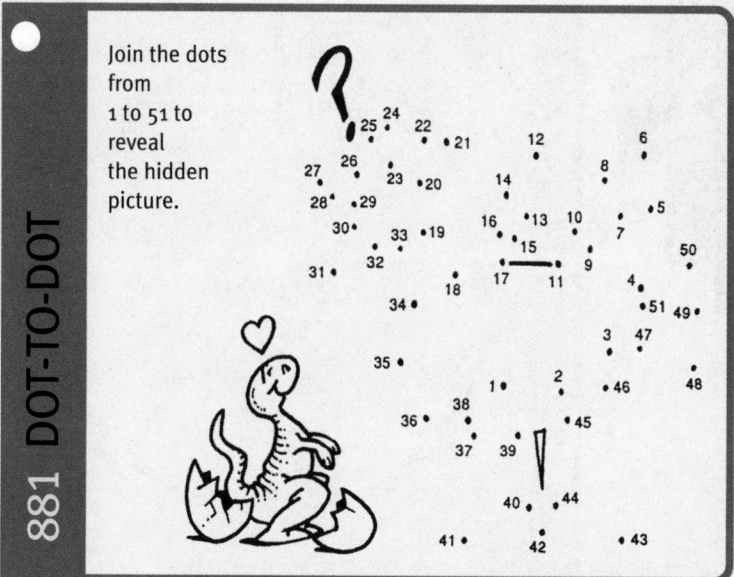

882 NUMBER SQUARES

● ●

Can you complete the grid with the aid of the numbers given, so that all sums, whether horizontal or vertical, are correct? (Please note that each sum should be treated separately.)

36	+		=		−		=	22
−	■	−	■	−	■	−	■	−
	+		=	25	−		=	
=	■	=	■	=	■	=	■	=
	+	7	=		−	9	=	
+	■	+	■	+	■	+	■	+
	+		=	26	−		=	
=	■	=	■	=	■	=	■	=
31	+		=		−		=	37

883 TRYING TIMES

Substitute each letter with a digit (0–9) so that this long multiplication sum works out correctly.

```
      A B C D
      F E F E   x
    G E D F F
    E H B G E
    G E D F F
    E H B G E
  E A E C J K J F
```

885 IDENTIGRIDS

Which of the three small squares are exactly the same? Watch out, they may not be the same way up!

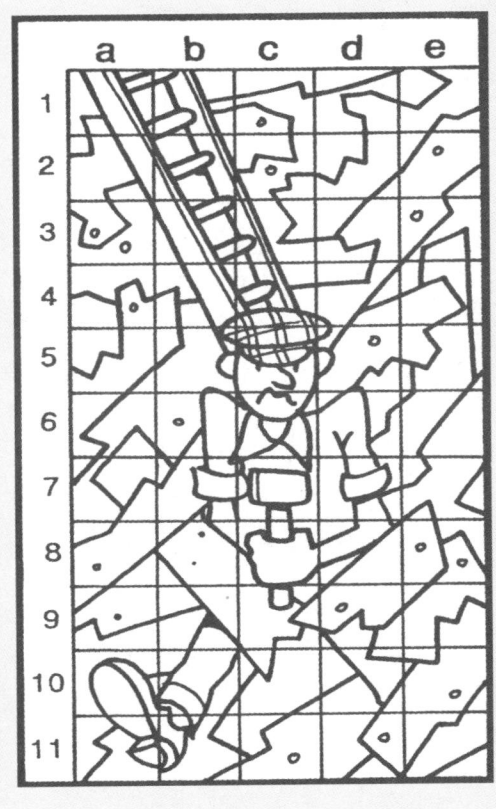

884 FIDDLEHAM APARTMENTS

The super of these notorious apartments continues to confuse visitors with his addiction to Invicta's game Master Mind. Instead of "Smith's in Apartment X, buddy," he hands the visitor a list of current residents and asks him to make guesses as to who is in each apartment. He then marks the line of guesses with two numbers:

First: how many are exactly right – the correct name on the right door.
Second: how many of the names are correct for that floor but are on the wrong door. The only other information he gives is that each surname can only occur on one floor – if Smith is on the ground floor, that name can't be on either of the other two floors. However, the same name can occur more than once on the same floor.

From the 12 guesses below and the list of names on the right, can you work out the correct name for each apartment?

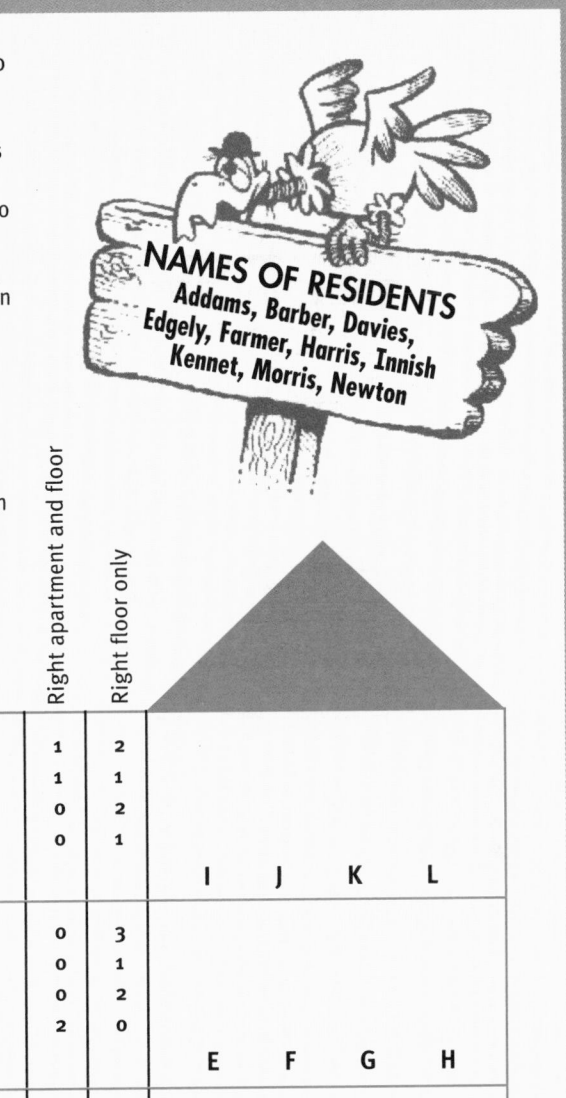

NAMES OF RESIDENTS
Addams, Barber, Davies,
Edgely, Farmer, Harris, Innish
Kennet, Morris, Newton

					Right apartment and floor	Right floor only		I	J	K	L
1	Newton	Harris	Innish	Newton	1	2					
2	Davies	Newton	Davies	Newton	1	1					
3	Kennet	Davies	Edgely	Innish	0	2					
4	Innish	Harris	Barber	Davies	0	1					
	I	J	K	L							

					Right apartment and floor	Right floor only		E	F	G	H
5	Morris	Barber	Addams	Innish	0	3					
6	Davies	Davies	Farmer	Kennet	0	1					
7	Kennet	Innish	Morris	Newton	0	2					
8	Addams	Farmer	Harris	Barber	2	0					
	E	F	G	H							

					Right apartment and floor	Right floor only		A	B	C	D
9	Davies	Kennet	Davies	Harris	1	2					
10	Harris	Davies	Barber	Morris	2	0					
11	Farmer	Barber	Harris	Newton	0	2					
12	Addams	Davies	Newton	Kennet	1	0					
	A	B	C	D							

886 NUMBER SQUARES

Can you complete the grids below with the aid of the numbers given, so that all sums, whether horizontal or vertical, are correct? (Please note that each sum should be treated separately.)

72	÷		=		+		=	39
−		−		×		−		+
	÷		=		×	4	=	
=		=						=
	+		=	30	+		=	
+		+						+
	+	4	=		−		=	
=		=		=				=
38	+		=		+		=	61

887 MAZE MYSTERY

Travel from the entrance to the exit of the maze, filling the path completely to create a picture.

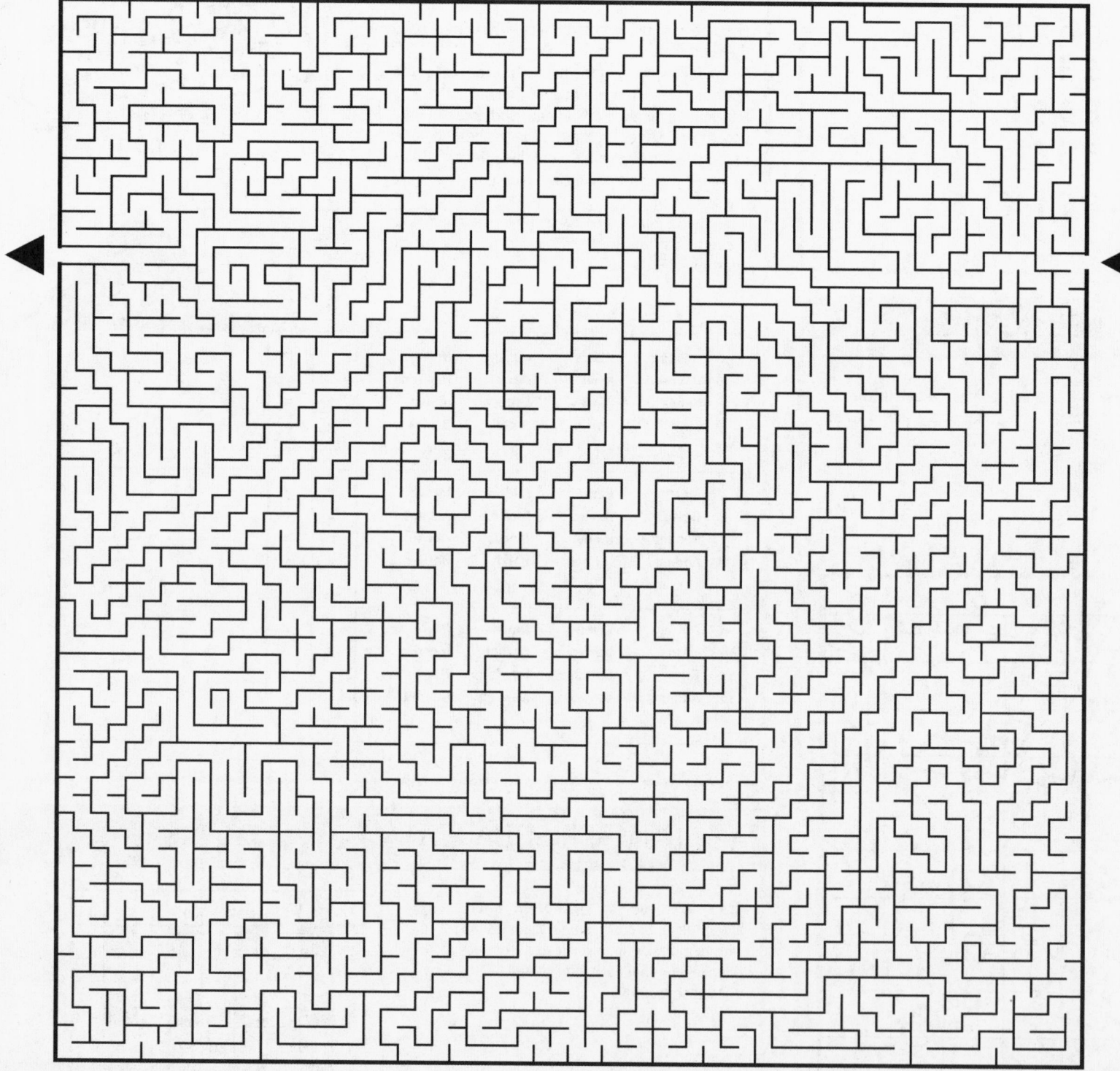

888 WALKIES

Four of the six shapes at the top are hidden in the main picture. Can you spot which four and whereabouts they are?

889 STRESSED MANAGEMENT

Four stressed executives have each taken up with a relaxation system having an oriental flavour. If it is not too much of a strain, can you work out the name of each tense soul, the company each suffers at and the method being tried?

Clues
1 Dee rolls Chinese iron balls in his hand and is known around his office as 'Captain Queeg' but he is not Nathan who works for Just Loans.
2 Poppin can, appropriately, be found looking like a sick hedgehog with acupuncture needles sticking out in all directions. She is not the one with the forename of Ellis.
3 Elsa does not work for J C Nutts and neither of these two is the one who listens to sitar music all day.
4 The employee at U B Loopy does yoga and can be found upside down on her monitor most afternoons. She is not Tewitt. Val Heegham does not work for Hi-Fi Nants.

ACUPUNCTURE

ELLIS	ELSA	FORENAME
NATHAN	VAL	
~~DEE~~	HEEGHAM	SURNAME
POPPIN	TEWITT	
HI-FI NANTS	JC NUTTS	COMPANY
JUST LOANS	U B LOOPY	

CHINESE BALLS

ELLIS	~~ELSA~~
~~NATHAN~~	VAL
(DEE)	~~HEEGHAM~~
~~POPPIN~~	~~TEWITT~~
HI-FI NANTS	JC NUTTS
~~JUST LOANS~~	U B LOOPY

SITAR MUSIC

ELLIS	ELSA	FORENAME
NATHAN	VAL	
~~DEE~~	HEEGHAM	SURNAME
POPPIN	TEWITT	
HI-FI NANTS	JC NUTTS	COMPANY
JUST LOANS	U B LOOPY	

YOGA

ELLIS	ELSA
NATHAN	VAL
~~DEE~~	HEEGHAM
POPPIN	TEWITT
HI-FI NANTS	JC NUTTS
JUST LOANS	U B LOOPY

890 CELL STRUCTURE

The object is to create white areas surrounded by black walls, so that:
• Each white area contains only one number
• The number of cells in a white area is equal to the number in it
• The white areas are separated from each other with a black wall
• Cells containing numbers must not be filled in
• The black cells must be linked into a continuous wall
• Black cells cannot form a square of 2 x 2 or larger

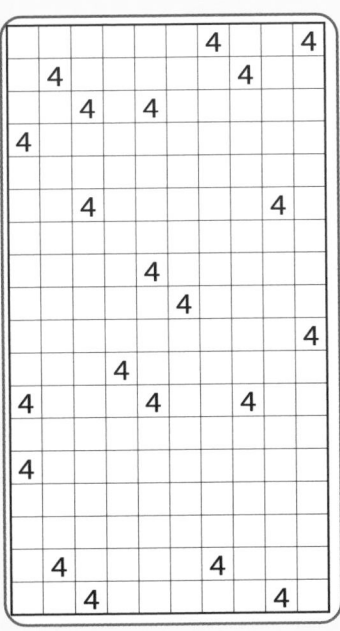

891 THAT LITTLE BIT OF DIFFERENCE

There are eight differences between the two cartoons. Can you spot them?

892 SCATTERPILLAR

Can you reconstruct the six fragments into two identical pillars?

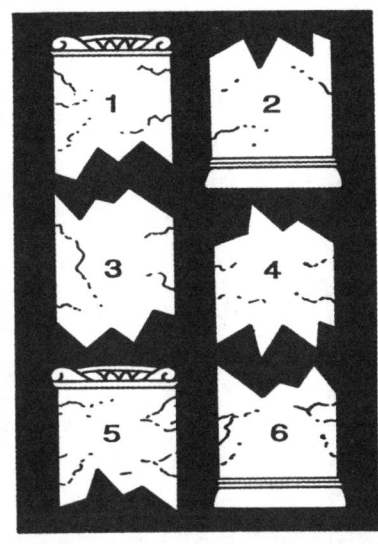

893 HEADLINES ●●●

When Pop Star Harry Splitter throws a party the world soon knows about it. Five papers have reported on his latest gathering. In the clues below the papers and headlines are muddled, so that none of the words belong with any of the other three. Can you put the right headlines back into their respective papers?

1. The Daily Standard said Hilarious Romp
2. The Morning Argus said Outrageous Orgy
3. The Daily Chronicle said Hilarious Antics
4. The Evening Chronicle said Mad Party
5. The Weekly Echo said Wild Antics
6. The Sunday News said Outrageous Binge
7. The Daily Argus said Jolly Antics
8. The Sunday Standard said Wild Romp
9. The Weekly News said Jolly Party
10. The Evening News said Outrageous Antics

HINT: What title goes with Antics? So which paper is it in?

PAPER	PAPER	HEADLINE	HEADLINE
DAILY	ARGUS	HILARIOUS	ANTICS
	CHRONICLE	JOLLY	BINGE
	ECHO	MAD	ORGY
	NEWS	OUTRAGEOUS	PARTY
	STANDARD	WILD	ROMP
EVENING	ARGUS	HILARIOUS	ANTICS
	CHRONICLE	JOLLY	BINGE
	ECHO	MAD	ORGY
	NEWS	OUTRAGEOUS	PARTY
	STANDARD	WILD	ROMP
MORNING	ARGUS	HILARIOUS	ANTICS
	CHRONICLE	JOLLY	BINGE
	ECHO	MAD	ORGY
	NEWS	OUTRAGEOUS	PARTY
	STANDARD	WILD	ROMP
SUNDAY	ARGUS	HILARIOUS	ANTICS
	CHRONICLE	JOLLY	BINGE
	ECHO	MAD	ORGY
	NEWS	OUTRAGEOUS	PARTY
	STANDARD	WILD	ROMP
WEEKLY	ARGUS	HILARIOUS	ANTICS
	CHRONICLE	JOLLY	BINGE
	ECHO	MAD	ORGY
	NEWS	OUTRAGEOUS	PARTY
	STANDARD	WILD	ROMP

894 DOT-TO-DOT ●

Join the dots from 1 to 41 to reveal the hidden picture.

895 IDENTIGRIDS ●

Which of the three small squares are exactly the same. Watch out, they may not be the same way up.

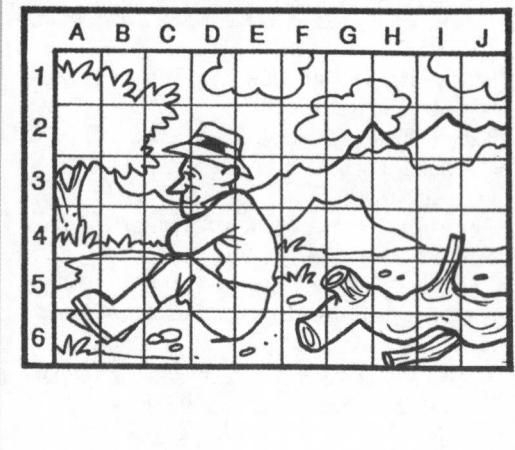

896 FOURSOME

This man would like to buy four identical vases. Which design will he choose?

897 TAG GRAPPLERS

Four wrestlers are in the ring ready for a tag wrestling event. The clues are waiting for you to make the introductions.

Clues
1 The Crusader is in purple trunks and Jack the Warrior will take on a Caped opponent.
2 Tom – who calls himself the Secret – is opposing the black-trunked Avenger.
3 Fred's partner is the Masked Gladiator who is not in silver trunks.
   Clue 1 has been entered for you

DON
CAPED	HOODED	TITLE
MASKED	SECRET	
AVENGER	CRUSADER	TITLE
GLADIATOR	~~WARRIOR~~	
BLACK	ORANGE	TRUNKS
PURPLE	SILVER	

FRED
CAPED	HOODED	
MASKED	SECRET	
AVENGER	CRUSADER	
GLADIATOR	~~WARRIOR~~	
BLACK	ORANGE	
PURPLE	SILVER	

JACK
~~CAPED~~	HOODED	TITLE
MASKED	SECRET	
~~AVENGER~~	~~CRUSADER~~	TITLE
~~GLADIATOR~~	(WARRIOR)	
BLACK	ORANGE	TRUNKS
~~PURPLE~~	SILVER	

TOM
CAPED	HOODED	TITLE
MASKED	SECRET	
AVENGER	CRUSADER	TITLE
GLADIATOR	~~WARRIOR~~	
BLACK	ORANGE	TRUNKS
PURPLE	SILVER	

---

898 QUEENS HIGH

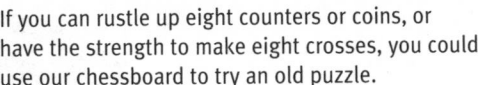

If you can rustle up eight counters or coins, or have the strength to make eight crosses, you could use our chessboard to try an old puzzle.

Place the eight counters so that no two are in the same line across or down or diagonally. If you choose, say, A3 then you could not put a mark in any other square in column A or in row 3 nor in squares like C1 and D6 which are in a diagonal line from A3.

The real puzzle, though, is to choose your eight squares, according to the rule, so that the total of the eight numbers you mark is as high as possible. Just how many can you score with your eight queens on each of these chessboards?

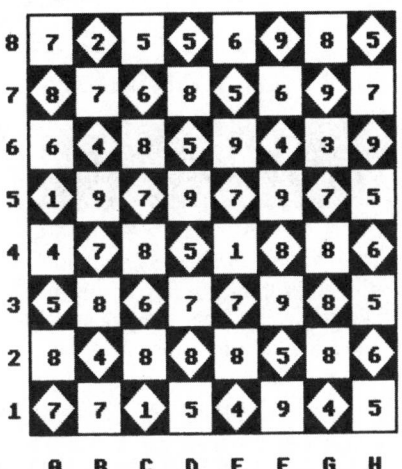

	A	B	C	D	E	F	G	H
8	7	2	5	5	6	9	8	5
7	8	7	6	8	5	6	9	7
6	6	4	8	5	9	4	3	9
5	1	9	7	9	7	9	5	5
4	4	7	8	5	1	8	6	3
3	5	8	6	7	7	8	5	5
2	8	4	8	8	8	5	6	6
1	7	7	1	5	4	9	4	5

---

899 QUILTESSENTIAL

In this patchwork quilt, squares of material have been sewn together – each square being either Blue, Green, Lavender or Red. The numbers in the squares tell you how many of that square and its neighbours are of each colour. A square can have up to eight neighbours:

1	2	3
8	x	4
7	6	5

30 / 10		40 / 02		11 / 04		14 / 01	42 / 00	40 / 02	01 / 03
	40 / 41		31 / 14		14 / 04	45 / 00	52 / 02		22 / 05
10 / 41		40 / 41		23 / 13		43 / 02		43 / 11	20 / 34	03 / 12
	01 / 53		13 / 41		24 / 21		61 / 11	21 / 33	03 / 42
03 / 12		01 / 35		05 / 31		22 / 32	30 / 15	01 / 62	04 / 20
	05 / 04		13 / 14		23 / 40		10 / 44	30 / 24	33 / 30
04 / 02		24 / 03		43 / 02		13 / 41	10 / 44	51 / 21	42 / 00
	13 / 05		52 / 02		35 / 10		04 / 41	31 / 41	60 / 30
01 / 03		31 / 02		33 / 00		05 / 10	02 / 40	20 / 40	20 / 20

Sadly, there is no pretty picture – just chunks of colours. Using brain power alone, can you work out the colour of each patch?

---

900 BALANCING THE SCALES

How many forks are needed to balance scale C?

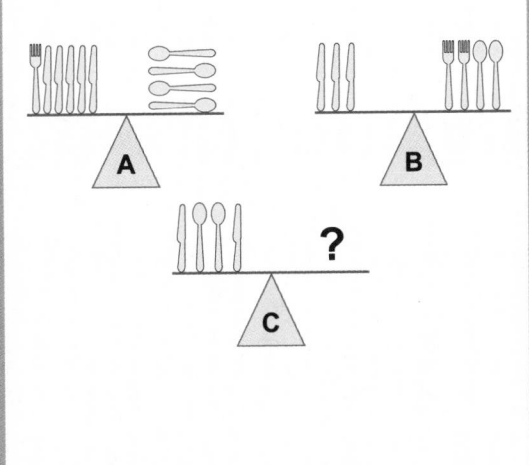

901 DARTING ABOUT

A dart player scores 77 with three darts hitting a treble, a double and a single (no bulls). Given that the three numbers that he hits add up to 41 and that the difference between the largest and smallest numbers is 12, can you work out how his score is made up?

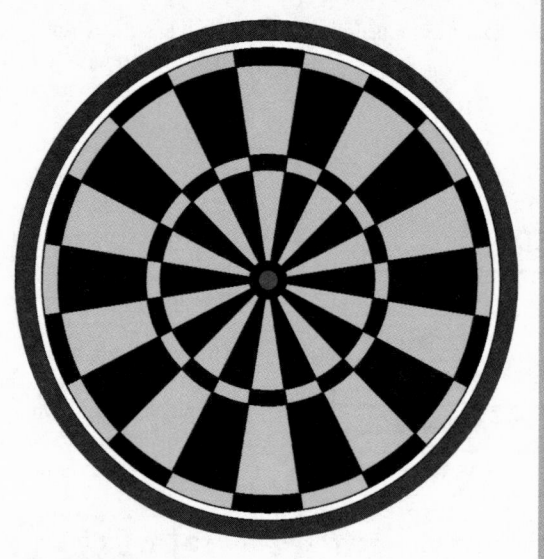

Treble   Double   Single

902 SHELLING OUT

In an effort to distract the children from playing with an incoming oil slick, Mrs Mumble persuaded them to gather up a pile of relatively clean shells and play a simple game. The two players would take turns to remove one, two, or three shells from the pile and add them to their own store. When all the shells had been taken, the child with the *odd number* of shells would be the winner.

Later, while poring over the holiday snaps, nobody could remember, in this particular game, whose turn it was next. In fact, it doesn't matter! Whoever is next to play, there is a quantity of shells that can be taken, which will ensure that player wins the game. How many is that – one, two or three?

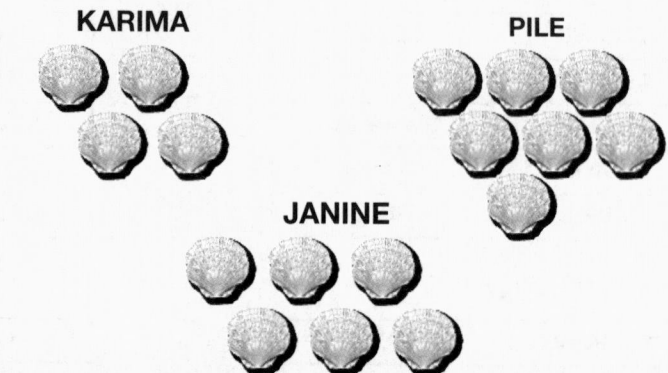

KARIMA   PILE

JANINE

903 CELL STRUCTURE

The object is to create white areas surrounded by black walls, so that:
* Each white area contains only one number.
* The number of cells in a white area is equal to the number in it.
* The white areas are separated from each other with a black wall.
* Cells containing numbers must not be filled in.
* The black cells must be linked into a continuous wall.
* Black cells cannot form a square of 2 x 2 or larger.

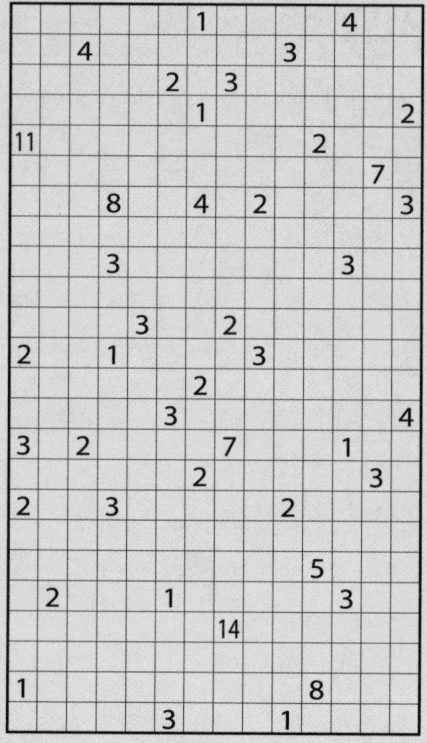

904 SHARP'S SUPERSTORE

When Mr Smith was appointed manager of a brand new Sharp's supermarket, he was faced with the task of stocking the shelves, following guidelines given by the area manager. Can you help Smith sort stock on Sharp's shelves?

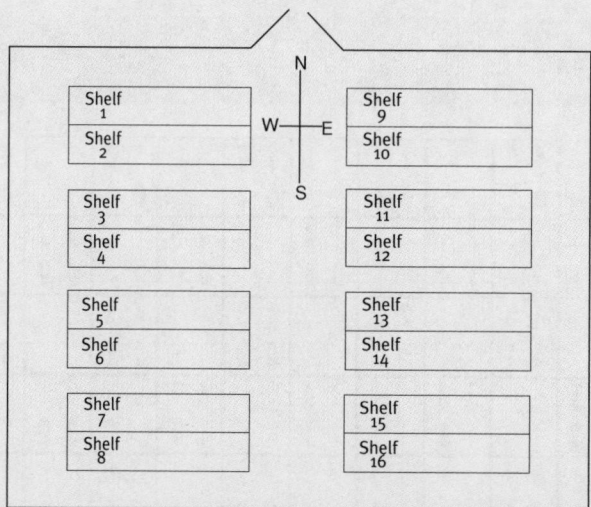

"Don't mix commodities up on the shelves. The cookies and frozen vegetables must face the wall, but put them on opposite sides of the store. Obviously, both fridges should be back to back, with the fruit juices/cordials facing the frozen meat."

"All the non-consumable items including the pet food should be stocked in the same area. I suggest the far south-west corner. The soap powder should be opposite the cleaning fluids and back to back with the pet food."

"All the tinned produce must be on the east side of the store, with the tinned meat and tinned vegetables back to back. Put the tinned fruit on a north-facing shelf and the tinned meat on a south-facing shelf, opposite the home baking produce. The home baking produce should be in the same row as the pet food."

"Cakes and cookies should be back to back, with the candy in the same row as the cakes and facing south."

"Reserve shelf 3 for the tea and coffee and remember to find shelves for the bread and kitchen ware."

905 COACH AND FOUR

Anyone who has tuned into American Football lately will have noticed that more people are directly involved in each pile-up than the overgrown King Kongs on the pitch. Radio links join coach to spy-in-stand; video films are made – and why do you think the Shuttle has been up so often launching all those satellites?

Even at local level, knowing the opposition is everything. Mary's son, Fred, is a player in a four team mini-league. His friend Ed plays for a different team.

The keen coaches have scouted the other teams so well that each coach has a sure technique which will enable his team to defeat one of the others. Which means, in turn, that he knows his team will be defeated by one other team. This leaves one team to play where the outcome is debatable. Four players, one from each team, are involved in the following facts concerning forename, surname, mother and father. (No, there are no tricks using divorces or parentage!)

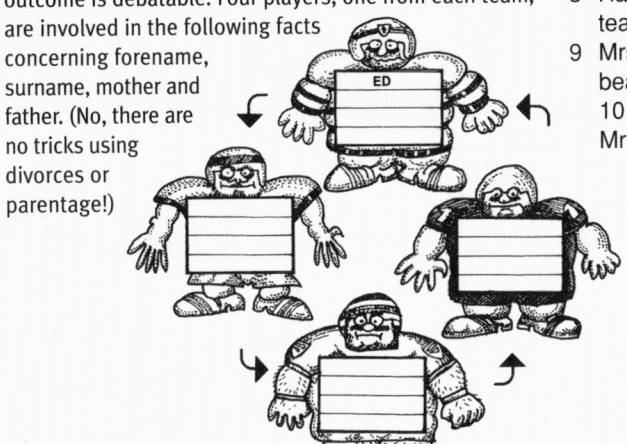

1 George's team can regularly beat Jim's son's team.
2 Mr Clark's son's team can regularly beat the Davis boy's team.
3 Karl's son's team can regularly beat Nancy's son's team.
4 Mrs Davis's son's team can regularly beat Harry's team.
5 Leonard's son's team can regularly beat Ivan's son's team.
6 Pamela's son's team can regularly beat Ornella's son's team.
7 Jim's son's team can regularly beat Mary's son's team.
8 Harry's team can regularly beat Karl's son's team.
9 Mrs Beacham's son's team can regularly beat Mr Clark's son's team.
10 Mary's son's team can regularly beat Mr Clark's son's team.

As a test of your ability to identify all four players, you are asked to identify the Alston boy's parents.

906 DOT-TO-DOT

Join the dots from 1 to 36 to reveal the hidden picture.

907 TWINNED UP

The little girl would like a top identical to the one she is holding. Which one will she choose?

908 ISLAND HOPPING

Each circle containing a number represents an island. The object is to connect each island with vertical or horizontal bridges so that:
* The number of bridges is the same as the number inside the island.
* There can be up to two bridges between two islands.
* Bridges cannot cross islands or other bridges.
* There is a continuous path connecting all the islands.

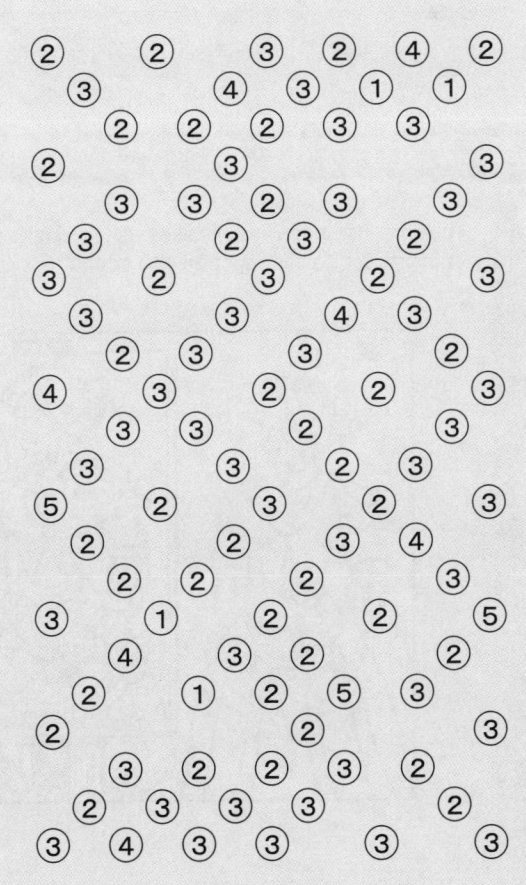

909 QUEENS HIGH

If you can rustle up eight counters or coins, or have the strength to make eight crosses, you could use our chessboard to try an old puzzle. Place the eight counters so that no two are in the same line across or down or diagonally. If you choose, say, A3 then you could not put a mark in any other square in column A or in row 3 nor in squares like C1 and D6 which are in a diagonal line from A3. The real puzzle, though, is to choose your eight squares, according to the rule, so that the total of the eight numbers you mark is as high as possible. Just how many can you score with your eight queens on each of these chessboards?

911 BY DEGREES

Four of the six objects lined up at the top are hidden in the picture. Can you see which ones and whereabouts they are?

DOT-TO-DOT

Join the dots from 1 to 34 to reveal the hidden picture.

910 POSER

The artist has made five mistakes while trying to paint an exact portrait of the model. Can you spot the five errors?

913 CELL STRUCTURE

The object is to create white areas surrounded by black walls, so that:
* Each white area contains only one number.
* The number of cells in a white area is equal to the number in it.
* The white areas are separated from each other with a black wall.
* Cells containing numbers must not be filled in.
* The black cells must be linked into a continuous wall.
* Black cells cannot form a square of 2 x 2 or larger.

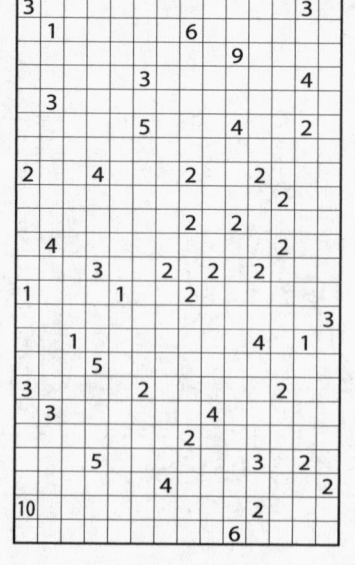

914 IT'S MAGIC ●●

This magic square can be completed using the numbers from 39 to 63 inclusive. To give you a start, looking at the thing as if it was divided into ten columns of digits, we have entered the even digits in the first column, the odd in the second, the even in the third and so on. Can you complete the square so that the five numbers in each row, column and diagonal add up to the magic total? The total – and close your eyes now if you don't want to be told – is 255.

4 5			6 1	4 3
	9 4	1 4		7
	3	5 6	9 4	
4	4	1		6
	6 3	4	4 7	4 9

916 DARTING ABOUT ●●

A dart player scores 71 with three darts hitting a treble, a double and a single (no bulls). Given that the three numbers that he hits add up to 35 and that the difference between the largest and smallest numbers is 9, can you work out how his score is made up?

Treble   Double   Single

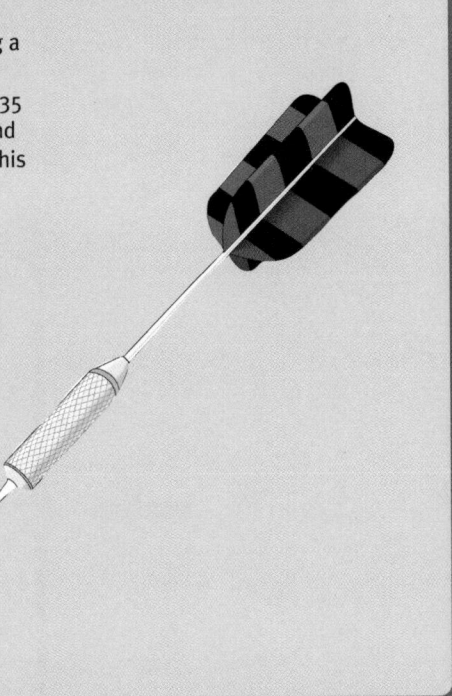

915 LOGIQUATIONS ●●

In the following problem the digits 0 to 9 are represented by letters. Within each separate puzzle the same letter always represents the same digit. Can you find the correct values each time so that all sums, both horizontal and vertical, are correct? With each separate puzzle, there is a clue to help start you off.

ABC	x	DE	=	CEFC
+		+		–
GHJK	+	DGBB	=	KFGH
BBBG	+	DGKJ	=	KACD

A	B	C	D	E	F	G	H	J	K

Clue: BG + KE = HC

917 LATIN SQUARE ●●

The grid is to be filled with the numbers 1 to 6 so that each number appears exactly once in each row and column. The clues refer to the digit totals in the squares mentioned. For example, DEF2 = 9 would mean that the numbers in D2, E2 and F2 add up to 9.

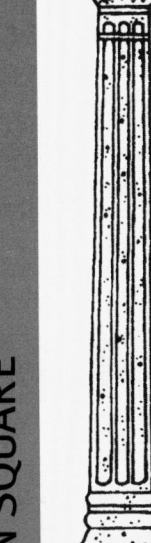

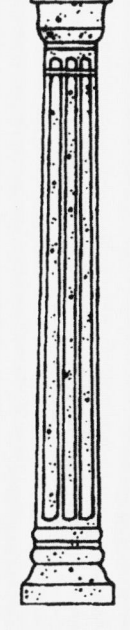

	A	B	C	D	E	F
6						
5						
4						
3						
2						
1						

A34 = 5   DE1 = 7
ABC5 = 10   DE5 = 10
B45 = 8   E456 = 7
BC6 = 7   EF6 = 3
C23 = 10   F234 = 15
CDE3 = 14

918 LABYRINTH ●●●

Starting at the left hand side, moving forward at each go, try to work your way to the other side. At each step, you must follow the instruction for that column (such as + 4). There are, of course, dead ends. Go on – be amazed!

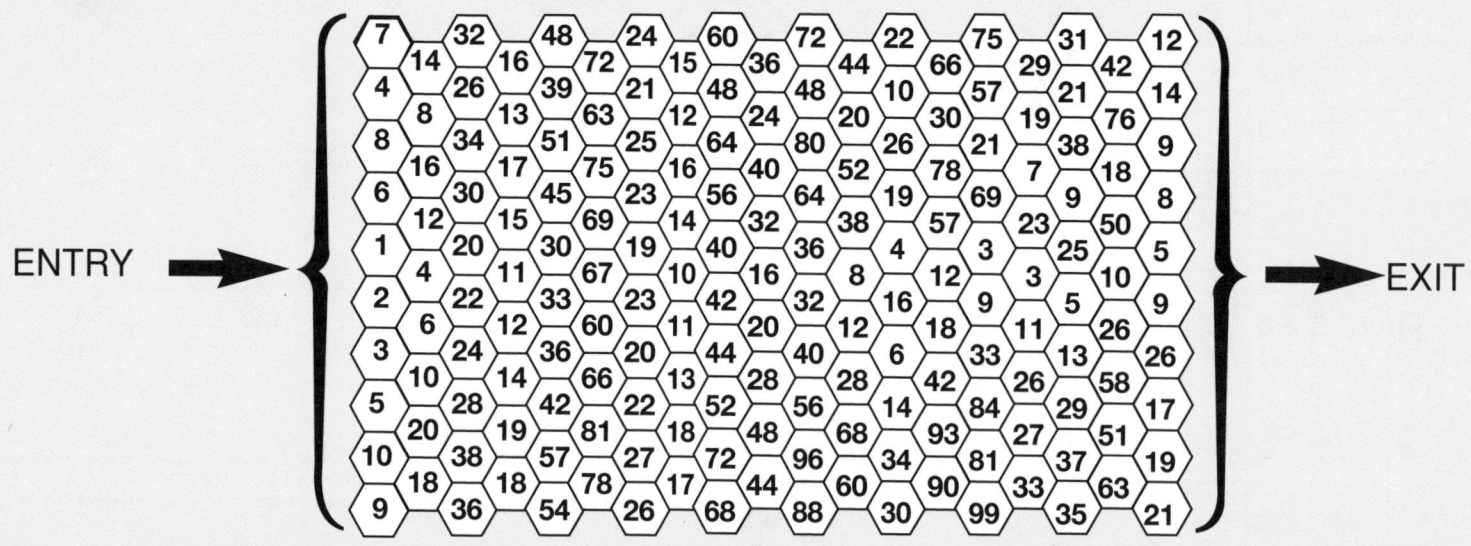

919 LATIN SQUARE ●●

Each cell of the square below has one of the digits from 1 to 7. Each row and each column has exactly one of each digit. The clues below give the sum total of the digits in two or more cells. From these clues, can you figure out what number is in each cell?

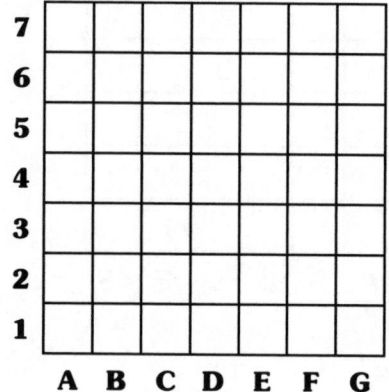

A12=6   C234=16   EFG4=16
ABCD7=10 CD7=5   F23=8
B123=15   DEF6=18   G23=7
B567=12   DEFG3=11 G4567=18
BCD5=18   EFG1=6

920 CELL STRUCTURE ●●

The object is to create white areas surrounded by black walls, so that:
* Each white area contains only one number.
* The number of cells in a white area is equal to the number in it.
* The white areas are separated from each other with a black wall.
* Cells containing numbers must not be filled in.
* The black cells must be linked into a continuous wall.
* Black cells cannot form a square of 2 x 2 or larger.

921 HIDE 'N' SEEK

Four of the six objects shown at the top can be found hidden in the picture. Can you see which ones and whereabouts they are?

922 TWIN-SET

Two of the pictures shown form a matching pair, while the other two contain one difference each. Can you identify the 'twins' and spot the differences?

923 HIGH FLIERS

Various performers are gathering in London to appear in the Command Performance next week. From the clues given about five of them, can you say on which day they flew into Heathrow, work out the country in which they were previously appearing, and name the airline on which they flew?

Clues

1 Tina Turkey, who did not arrive on a Lo-Cal flight, arrived two days before the Aer Fungus flight from Eire.
2 Sister Sludge arrived on Wednesday, but not from France. The Sabrena flight arrived on Tuesday.
3 Maradonna flew in from the USA two days before the Virgo flight arrived.
4 Englebert Pumpernickel was not the one who arrived on Friday from Germany.
5 Beers For Dears arrived on a Lefthanda flight.

ACT	DAY	COUNTRY	AIRLINE
BEERS FOR DEARS	MONDAY	CANADA	AER FUNGUS
	TUESDAY	EIRE	LEFTHANDA
	WEDNESDAY	FRANCE	LO-CAL
	THURSDAY	GERMANY	SABRENA
	FRIDAY	USA	VIRGO
ENGELBERT PUMPERNICKEL	MONDAY	CANADA	AER FUNGUS
	TUESDAY	EIRE	LEFTHANDA
	WEDNESDAY	FRANCE	LO-CAL
	THURSDAY	GERMANY	SABRENA
	FRIDAY	USA	VIRGO
MARADONNA	MONDAY	CANADA	AER FUNGUS
	TUESDAY	EIRE	LEFTHANDA
	WEDNESDAY	FRANCE	LO-CAL
	THURSDAY	GERMANY	SABRENA
	FRIDAY	USA	VIRGO
SISTER SLUDGE	MONDAY	CANADA	AER FUNGUS
	TUESDAY	EIRE	LEFTHANDA
	WEDNESDAY	FRANCE	LO-CAL
	THURSDAY	GERMANY	SABRENA
	FRIDAY	USA	VIRGO
TINA TURKEY	MONDAY	CANADA	~~AER FUNGUS~~
	TUESDAY	~~EIRE~~	LEFTHANDA
	WEDNESDAY	FRANCE	~~LO-CAL~~
	~~THURSDAY~~	GERMANY	SABRENA
	~~FRIDAY~~	USA	VIRGO

924 BLOOMERS ●●●

Charlie Dimwit's garden centre, Bloomers, has a fine display of pot plants for sale. Four gardeners each took ten pots from the stand. Each gardener took a different number of pots of the colours they selected. After they had taken their pots there were an equal number of each colour left over. From the information given can you work out what each gardener selected?

The only colours to be bought by all four gardeners were red and violet and at least two people bought each colour. Rosie bought all colours except blue; she bought one less red than Geoff's greens and two more reds than Ellen's violets. The two ladies bought half the total number of yellow flowers between them. Percy bought all colours except green as did Ellen who bought twice as many blues as Rosie bought yellows. Geoff bought the same number of reds as Percy did violets and together these totalled the same as Rosie's yellows.

925 LATIN SQUARE ●●

Each cell of the square below has one of the digits from 1 to 7. Each row and each column has exactly one of each digit. The clues below give the total of two, three or four cells. From these clues, can you figure out what number is in each cell?

A1234 = 13   D123 = 10
ABC4 = 7   DE3 = 11
ABCD1 = 10   E567 = 6
B567 = 15   EFG2 = 10
BCD6 = 17   EFG5 = 13
C12 = 7   F3456 = 10
CDEF7 = 14   G123 = 11

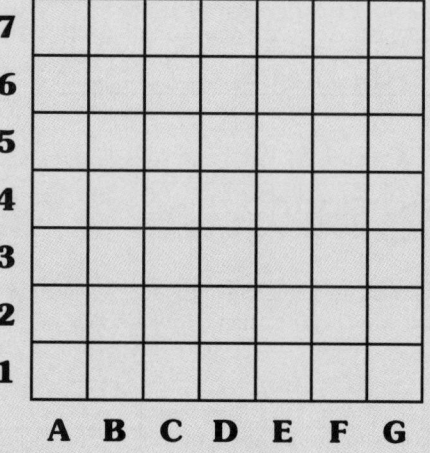

926 SQUARE NUMBERS ●●

The numbers 1 to 25 are arranged randomly in a 5 x 5 square so that no two consecutive numbers are adjacent in any direction or in the same row, column or long diagonal. The corner numbers are all prime; A4 is twice A3; E2 is four times E3, and E4 is twice C4. The single-digit numbers in C2 and D2 appear in the same order reproduced in the number in B1, which is prime; B3 is five times B2. The single-digit number in B5 is ten lower than the number in C5 and six higher than that in B4. D1 is three times D3 but eleven lower than D5. D4 is an odd number. Can you locate each number?

927 WEIGHED UP

How many inkpots are needed to make the third pair of scales balance?

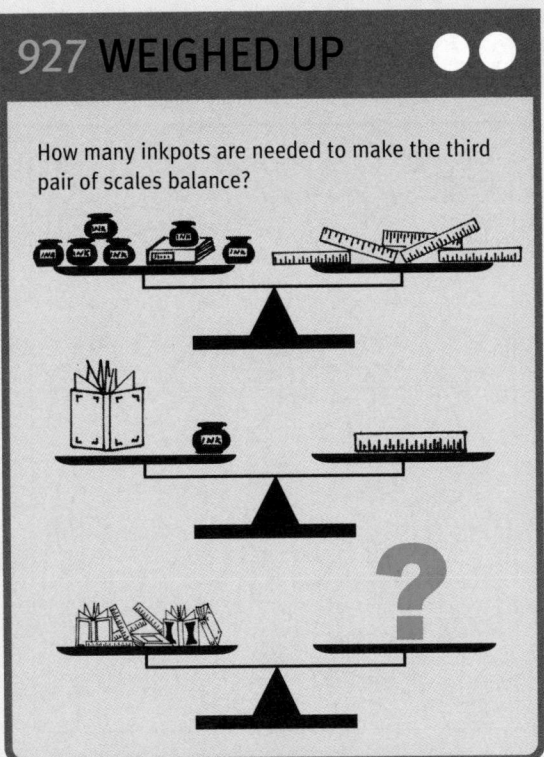

928 LOGIQUATIONS

In the following problem the digits 0 to 9 are represented by letters. Within each separate puzzle the same letter always represents the same digit. Can you find the correct values each time so that all sums, both horizontal and vertical, are correct? With each separate puzzle, there is a clue to help start you off.

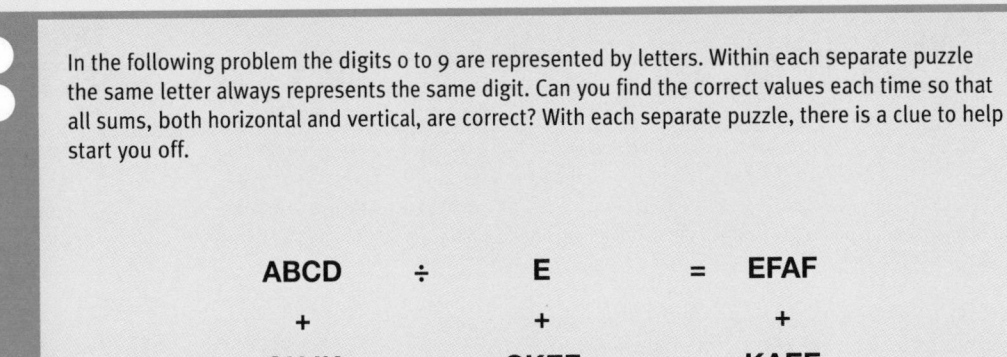

ABCD	÷	E	=	EFAF
+		+		+
GHJK	+	CKEF	=	KAEE
FFCH	−	CKGH	=	BGFH

A	B	C	D	E	F	G	H	J	K

Clue: 3 x CD = KF

929 PIECES OF EIGHT

Which pieces (four red and four yellow) can be used to make a square, where all four sides are of equal length? Any piece may be rotated, but not flipped over.

A B C D E F G H I J K L M N O P Q

930 WHO WON?

● ● ●

Quite a few race-goers decided to have a drink in the bar and listen to the commentary on the next race through the Tannoy system. Just as the race started, the system went faulty and the commentary was broken up by a series of crackles and whistles. Would you have known from what follows who rode which horse, what number it had and most importantly, *the result?*

"And they're off. Four runners for the *@*@* Chase, Swift Lad, the outsider takes an early lead, *@*@* is second and Willie Parsons on *@*@* third.
@@!?/@@.&!*@@*!**·**@!!?/%**·!@@@**!*@**

Steve Caution on No. 2, *!@*@* now leads, Mother's Joy has taken second place and Crazy Lad is improving –
'@@!?/@@.&!*'@@*!**·**'@!!?/%**·!@@@**!*@**

No. 1, *!@* Lad, is running on well and Pat Ellery on *!@*!@* is making a fine challenge.
'@@!?/*@@.&!*@@*!·**'@!!?/**·!@@@**!*@**

Silver Streak is coming up on the rails and is catching Joe Percer on –
'!?/*@@.&!*@@*!**·**'@!!?/%**·!@@@**!*@**

Into the final furlong now and No. *!@*!@*!@*!@* has been pulled up. No. 1, *!@*!@* is leading by a short head from Silver Streak. Willie Parsons is a close third.
'@@!?/@@.&!*@@*!**·**'@!!?/%**·!@@@**!*@**

Coming to the line and *!@*!@*!@*!@ wins; No. 2, *!@*!@*!@* the favourite is second and No. 4,*!@* Lad is the last to finish."

932 SILHOUETTE

○

Shade in every fragment containing a dot – and what have you got?

931 FIDDLEHAM APARTMENTS

● ● ●

The super of these notorious apartments continues to confuse visitors with his addiction to Invicta's game Master Mind. Instead of "Smith's in Apartment X", he hands the visitor a list of current residents and asks him to make guesses as to who is in each apartment. He then marks the line of guesses with two numbers:

First: how many are exactly right with the correct name on the right door?

Second: how many of the names are correct for that floor but are on the wrong door?

The only other information he gives is that each surname can only occur on one floor – if Smith is on the ground floor, that name can't be on either of the other two floors.

However, the same name can occur more than once on the same floor.

From the 12 guesses below and the list of names on the right, can you work out the correct name for each flat?

NAMES OF RESIDENTS
Barber   Farmer   Quirke
Carrol   Harris   Newton
Davies   Jenkin

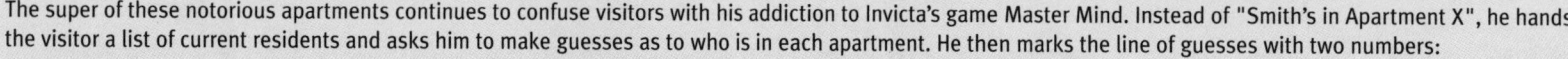

					Right apartment & floor	Right floor only				
1	Farmer	Carrol	Barber	Barber	2	1				
2	Barber	Jenkin	Harris	Davies	1	1				
3	Newton	Farmer	Barber	Harris	0	2				
4	Newton	Barber	Barber	Harris	0	2				
	I	J	K	L			I	J	K	L
5	Barber	Harris	Harris	Barber	2	0				
6	Harris	Barber	Barber	Quirke	1	1				
7	Quirke	Newton	Farmer	Farmer	0	1				
8	Harris	Newton	Jenkin	Quirke	1	2				
	E	F	G	H			E	F	G	H
9	Barber	Farmer	Newton	Farmer	1	2				
10	Jenkin	Farmer	Jenkin	Farmer	1	1				
11	Newton	Harris	Harris	Newton	2	0				
12	Carrol	Farmer	Carrol	Farmer	1	1				
	A	B	C	D			A	B	C	D

933 FITBITS

Can you identify the two fragments on the left that form part of the main picture?

934 POSER

The artist has made five mistakes while trying to paint an exact portrait of the model. Can you spot the five errors?

935 BORDER DISPUTE

Each of these unhappy souls is having trouble with a neighbour. We can't expect you to sort out their problem – doubtless you've enough of your own – but you are invited to discover who is battling with whom, where the warring parties live and the cause of the upset.

Clues

1 The couple at *Justus* are having trouble with the couple at *Wee Kendos*. Those involved are not the Daveys or the Mulveys as these two are, in one way or another, having trouble with the Brewers and the Fletchers neither of whom is responsible for the noise or the slugs.

2 The couple at *Dream Gnome* who are not the Careys or the Daveys are in dispute with the Chaters. The other house involved is not *Wear Ear* where the tree overhangs the neighbouring patio which does not belong to the Daveys.

3 The *Gurneys* at *Our Patch* are the neighbours of neither the Hunters nor the couple at *Pamensam* one of whom is responsible for the slugs flying over the wall and the other for throwing noisy parties.

4 The Fletchers do not live next to *Mortar Pay*. The two with animal problems are the Barneys and the couple living at *Last Stop*. Neither is in dispute with the Packers who live at *The Blotts*.

Name	House	Neighbour	House	Problem

	DREAM GNOME	JUSTUS	LAST STOP	MORTAR PAY	OUR PATCH	BREWER	CHATER	FLETCHER	HUNTER	PACKER	PAMENSAM	SCURGES	THE BLOTTS	WEAR EAR	WEE KENDOS	CATS	FENCE	NOISE	SLUGS	TREE
BARNEY																				
CAREY																				
DAVEY																				
GURNEY																				
MULVEY																				
CATS																				
FENCE																				
NOISE																				
SLUGS																				
TREE																				
PAMENSAM																				
SCURGES																				
THE BLOTTS																				
WEAR EAR																				
WEE KENDOS																				
BREWER																				
CHATER																				
FLETCHER																				
HUNTER																				
PACKER																				

936 SQUARE NUMBERS ● ●

The numbers 1–25 are entered randomly in a 5 x 5 square so that there are no two consecutive numbers in any row, column or long diagonal.

The numbers in squares A1 and A4 are prime, the former being two higher than the number in E5. B2 is also prime, and thirteen higher than E1, which is twice D1. D3 is twice D2, which is one lower than B5, which is four higher than C4, which is three times A5. B3 is one higher than C5 but two lower than E3. D5 is twice A4, which is eight lower than C1. A3 is twice D4, and E2 is twice E1. 9 is vertically between 18 and 7, and 6 is one row higher than 8. Can you locate each number?

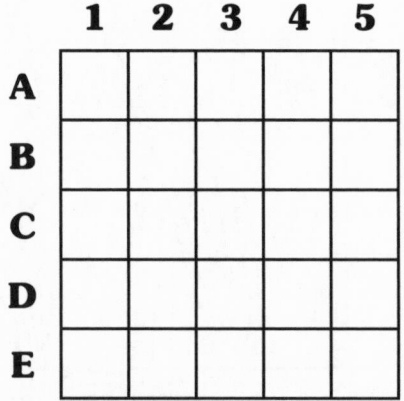

937 LATIN SQUARE ● ●

Each cell of the square below has one of the digits from 1 to 7. Each row and each column has exactly one of each digit. The clues below give the total of two, three or four cells. From these clues, can you figure out what number is in each cell?

A567=11 D67=9

ABC2=12 DEFG1=10

AB5=10   DEFG3=22

B456=7   DEF7=6

C123=9   E2345=22

CDE6=15 F456=9

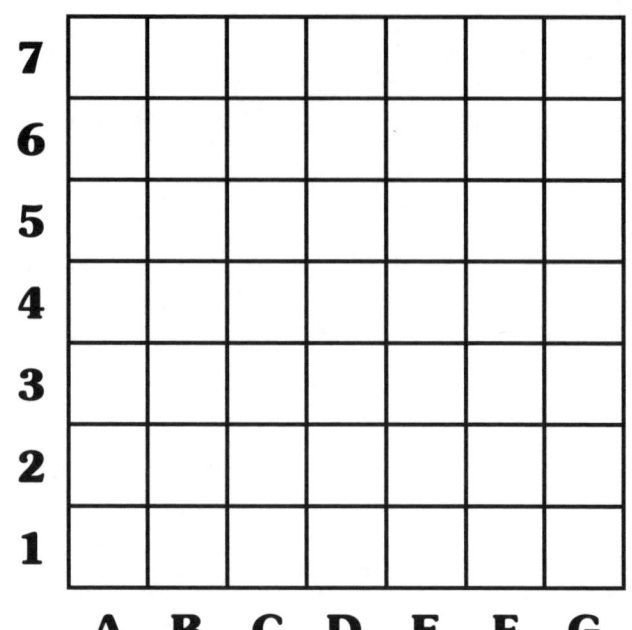

938 BARRELS OF FUN ● ●

The 15 barrels in the pub cellar each contain a different whole number of gallons from 6 to 20, none containing the same number as its numerical position counting from the left, and no two consecutive amounts are adjacent. No. 13 contains one gallon more than no. 6, no. 10 one more than no. 1, no. 7 one more than no. 4, no. 14 one more than no. 11, no. 12 one more than no. 9, and no. 3 one more than no. 8. No. 3 contains two more than no. 15, no. 2 two more than no. 9, no. 14 two more than no. 3, and no. 11 two more than no. 8. No. 1 contains three more than no. 2, no. 5 three more than no. 14, no. 7 three more than no. 11, and no. 10 three more than no. 6. If no. 15 does not contain 6 gallons, how much does each contain?

939 SET SQUARE ● ● ●

All the digits from 1 to 9 are used in this grid, but only once each. Can you work out their positions in the grid and make the sums work? We've given two numbers to start you off.

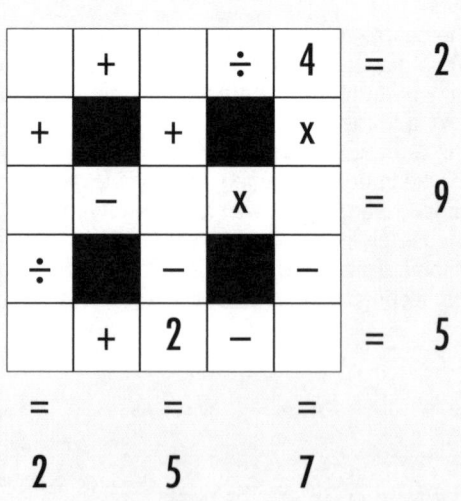

940 SAFE BET

This is a strange safe. Solve all the clues and the combination appears in the shaded squares.

ACROSS

1   Reverse digits of *3 across*
3   Square root of 1,745,041
5   Divide *8 down* by 213,326
6   Multiply *29 across* by *22 down*
9   Divide *10 down* by *29 across*
11 Add 4,875 to *13 across*
13 Multiply *29 across* by 178
15 Cube of *3 down*
19 Cube of *2 down*
21 Multiply *29 across* by 526
23 Subtract *1 down* from *22 down*, then add 10
25 Square root of 7,921
26 15 per cent of 343,400
29 Cube root of 1,728
30 Multiply *1 down* by 2
31 Add 6,000 to *24 down*

DOWN

1   Multiply *5 across* by 50
2   Half of *5 down*
3   Half of *10 down*
4   Anagram of digits of *3 across*
5   Multiply 16 by 17
6   25 per cent of 16,486,100
7   Add 3,925,005 to *8 down*
8   Add 144,995 to *6 down*
10 Multiply the last two digits of *24 down* by 8
12 Add 9,809 to *23 across*
14 Square *28 down*
16 Next in series 614, 713, 812,...
17 Add 73 to *16 down*
18 Add *2 down* to *3 down*
20 Add *27 down* to *9 across*
22 Square root of 15,225,604
24 Square root of 1,283,689
27 Multiply *5 across* by 5
28 Divide 1,644 by *29 across*

941 SILHOUETTE

Shade in every fragment containing a dot – and what have you got?

942 TWINNED UP

The twins would like to buy identical vases. Which two will they choose?

943 LIGHT WORK

●●●

After summer lightning caused havoc in Cable Street, five residents each had to call in an electrical firm and have work done before power could safely be restored. Can you sort out positive from negative and bring a summary to earth?

Clues

1 New lights were needed at the house numbered three higher than the one to which LiveWires were called. Neither of these is the house where A C Maynes lives.

2 Eartha Green lives at No. 6 – she did not need rewiring nor did she call in Glowball Services who replaced a fusebox.

3 Lottie Watts called in Pluggins. Bill Quarterley's house number is four higher than Phil O'Ment's.

4 The wiring was replaced by ShocksRus and the new main installed by Just Sparks. Neither firm visited No. 4.

Hint: Which firm replaced the lights – and at which house?

RESIDENT	NO.	FIRM	PROBLEM
A C MAYNES	3	GLOWBALL SVCS	FUSEBOX
	4	JUST SPARKS	LIGHTS
	6	LIVEWIRES	NEW RING MAIN
	7	PLUGGINS	REWIRING
	10	SHOCKSRUS	SOCKETS
BILL QUARTERLEY	3	GLOWBALL SVCS	FUSEBOX
	4	JUST SPARKS	LIGHTS
	6	LIVEWIRES	NEW RING MAIN
	7	PLUGGINS	REWIRING
	10	SHOCKSRUS	SOCKETS
EARTHA GREEN	3	GLOWBALL SVCS	FUSEBOX
	4	JUST SPARKS	LIGHTS
	6	LIVEWIRES	NEW RING MAIN
	7	PLUGGINS	REWIRING
	10	SHOCKSRUS	SOCKETS
LOTTIE WATTS	3	GLOWBALL SVCS	FUSEBOX
	4	JUST SPARKS	LIGHTS
	6	LIVEWIRES	NEW RING MAIN
	7	PLUGGINS	REWIRING
	10	SHOCKSRUS	SOCKETS
PHIL O' MENTS	3	GLOWBALL SVCS	FUSEBOX
	4	JUST SPARKS	LIGHTS
	6	LIVEWIRES	NEW RING MAIN
	7	PLUGGINS	REWIRING
	10	SHOCKSRUS	SOCKETS

944 WIRED UP

●

Which of the four plugs should be inserted in the socket to operate the shaver?

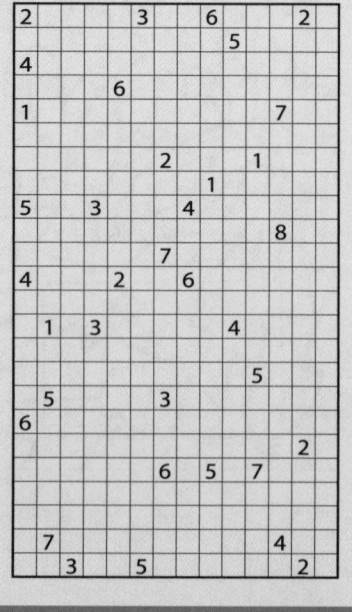

945 CELL STRUCTURE

●●

The object is to create white areas surrounded by black walls, so that:
* Each white area contains only one number.
* The number of cells in a white area is equal to the number in it.
* The white areas are separated from each other with a black wall.
* Cells containing numbers must not be filled in
* The black cells must be linked into a continuous wall.
* Black cells cannot form a square of 2 x 2 or larger.

946 GARDENER'S WORLD

The large picture has been reproduced underneath in twelve pieces. However, three of the pieces contain an extra detail, while four pieces have a detail missing. Can you spot all the extra and missing details?

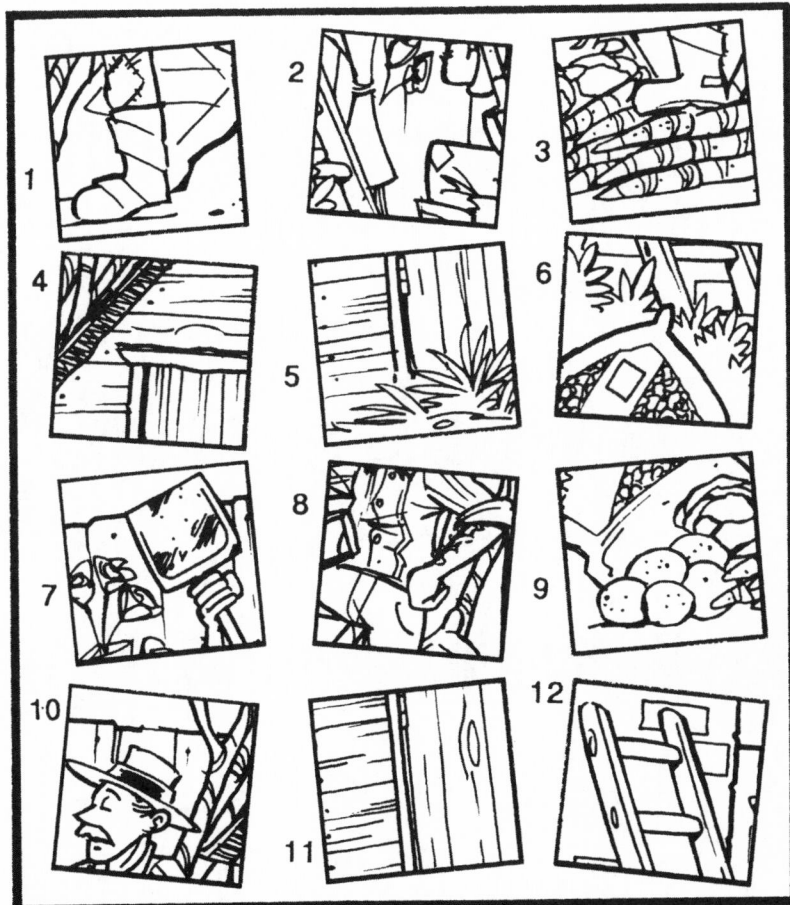

947 PICNIC PARTY

Four happy couples are out for a picnic on Whistleberry Hill. See if you can manage to pair up husband and wife before the rain comes.

THIS CUP OF TEA IS STONE COLD!

DAPHNE

HE MIGHT LET ME SIT DOWN FOR A BIT!

ENID

GERTIE

I COULD DO WITH A SIT DOWN!

LAURA

GOSH HE'S SCOFFING YET ANOTHER CAKE!

FRANK

JUST WAIT TIL THE ANTS ARRIVE!

SHE STILL HASN'T FINISHED THAT CUP OF TEA!

GEORGE

LARRY

I DON'T KNOW WHY WE'VE BOTH GOT TO STAND!

JACK

I MUST SAY THIS CAKE IS JOLLY GOOD

948 DROP OUT

The man is choosing a jar. In the bottom picture, he has taken his chosen jar away. Which one?

949 CRIME SQUAD

The criminals involved in the four scenes on the left below were soon arrested by a smart detective who spotted them in the larger picture. Can you spot them as well?

950 LOGIQUATIONS

In the following problem the digits 0 to 9 are represented by letters. Within each separate puzzle the same letter always represents the same digit. Can you find the correct values each time so that all sums, both horizontal and vertical, are correct? With each separate puzzle, there is a clue to help start you off.

AB	x	CDE	=	FCBB
x		+		–
GHJ	+	GDBB	=	GABA
BFKA	+	GCKD	=	EGDA

A	B	C	D	E	F	G	H	J	K

Clue: GH is a prime number

951 LATIN SQUARE

Each cell of the square below has one of the digits from 1 to 7. Each row and each column has exactly one of each digit. The clues below give the total of two, three or four cells. From these clues, can you figure out what number is in each cell?

ABC4=6   DE7=3
B2345=10 E1234=13
BCD1=16   F456=11
BCD6=9   FG2=5
CDE3=10   FG4=12
D567=9   G3456=13

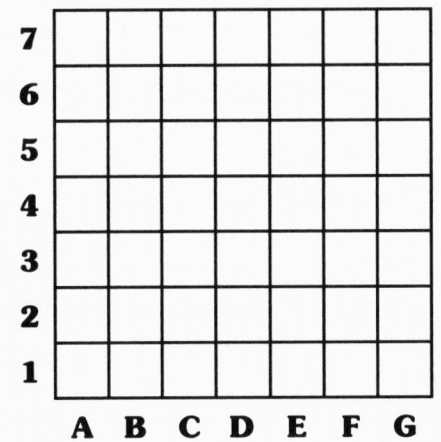

952 ARROW NUMBERS

Each number already in the grid shows the sum of the digits in the line whose direction is shown by the arrow. Only one digit can be placed in each square. There are no zeros. For each sum, each digit can only appear once – e.g., 8 cannot be completed with 44. A sequence of digits forming a sum can only appear once in the grid. If 8 is 53 somewhere then another 8 cannot also be 53. Nor could it be 35, but must contain a different set of digits, such as 71/17, or 62/26. Can you put logic, rather than higher maths, to work and find the unique solution?

	14	29	23	16		25	4	11
26					10 / 14			
43			4					
	11			8			11	8
30		8			10			
12					24	9		

953 TENTACKLE

Eight children are camping, two to each tent, and some have given us a couple of clues as to how to find them. The trouble is their directions are as bad as their cooking and in each case only one direction is true whilst the other is an exact opposite, so that East should read West etc. Directions are not necessarily exact so North could be North, Northeast or Northwest. To help you one child is already tucked into a sleeping bag.

Alice says: "I'm North of Fiona and West of Beth."
Carol says: "I'm South of Helen and East of Gina."
Fiona says: "I'm North of Gina and East of Carol."
Helen says: "I'm South of Daisy and West of Enid."

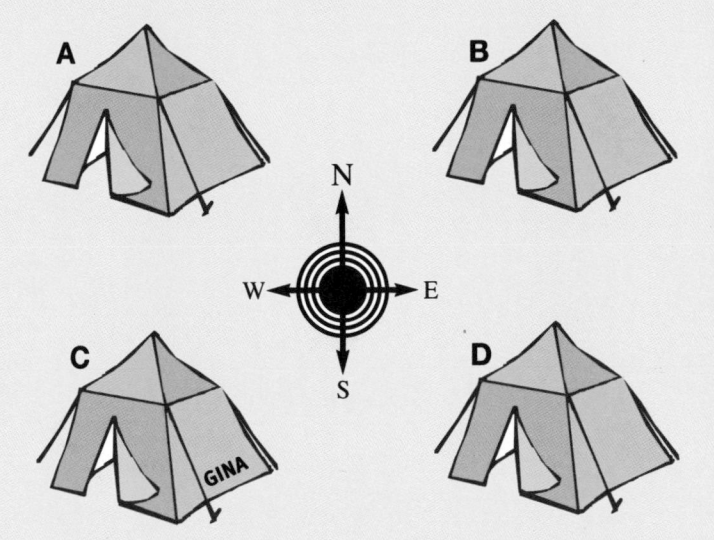

954 FIND THE FAKES

The proud owners of the famous artist's paintings (shown at the top) are showing off their new acquisitions (shown below). Unfortunately, however, five of these are not the artist's original work, but are clever fakes. Which are the five fakes and how can you identify them?

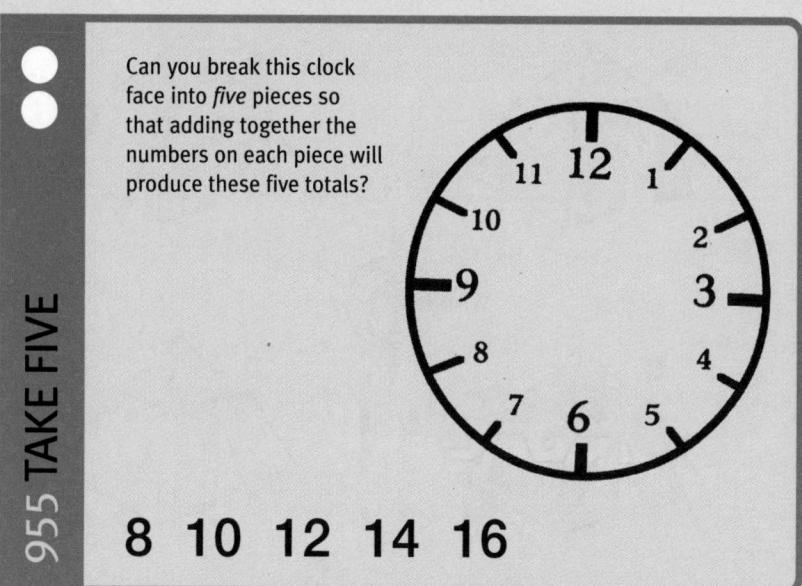

955 TAKE FIVE

Can you break this clock face into *five* pieces so that adding together the numbers on each piece will produce these five totals?

8 10 12 14 16

956 PRIZE DRAW

As usual, there was a prize draw held as part of the local fair and this year all the major prizes went to local people. From the clues below, can you say in what order the prizes were drawn, which were the winning tickets and who bought them?

Clues

1 The second prize drawn, which was the six bottles of home-made wine, went to one of the men.

2 Ticket 161 won the prize which was awarded just before the camera.

3 Ticket 198 won the bicycle; it was not sold to Mrs Smart, who did not hold the highest-numbered ticket.

4 Father Murphy's ticket was number 242.

5 The fifth prize to be drawn went to Mr White.

6 The hair drier went to Mr Copper, whose ticket was drawn just after Mrs Evans'.

	Bicycle	Camera	Food hamper	Hair drier	Wine	161	198	242	504	625	Father Murphy	Mrs Smart	Mr White	Mrs Evans	Mr Copper
First															
Second															
Third															
Fourth															
Fifth															
Father Murphy															
Mrs Smart															
Mr White															
Mrs Evans															
Mr Copper															
161															
198															
242															
504															
625															

Record in this grid all the information obtained from the clues, by using a cross to indicate a definite 'no' and a tick to show a definite 'yes'. Transfer these to all sections of the grid thus eliminating all but one possibility, which must be the correct one.

Order	Prizes	Ticket numbers	Ticket holders

957 TREASURE HUNT

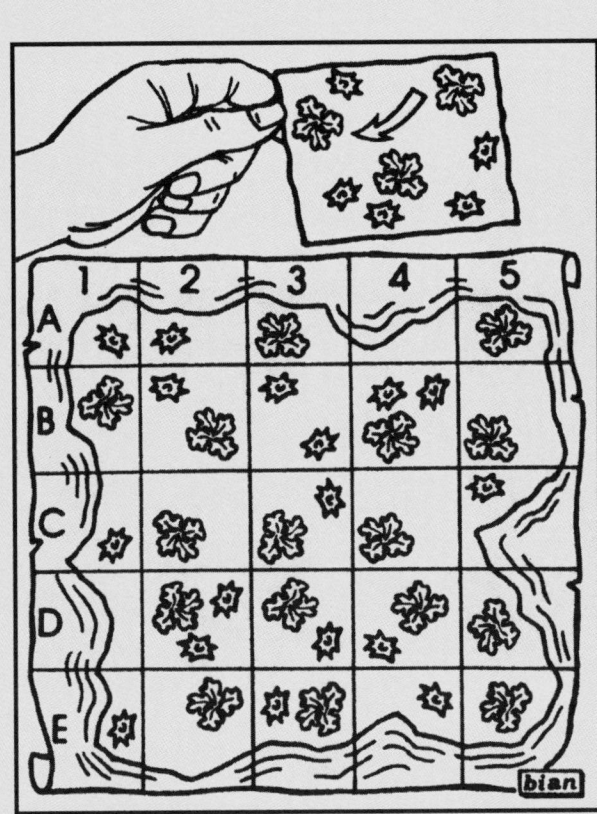

The small piece of the map at the top shows under which large bush the treasure is buried. Can you work out in which square this is in the larger map?

958 SILHOUETTE

Match the picture of gardening tools with its silhouette.

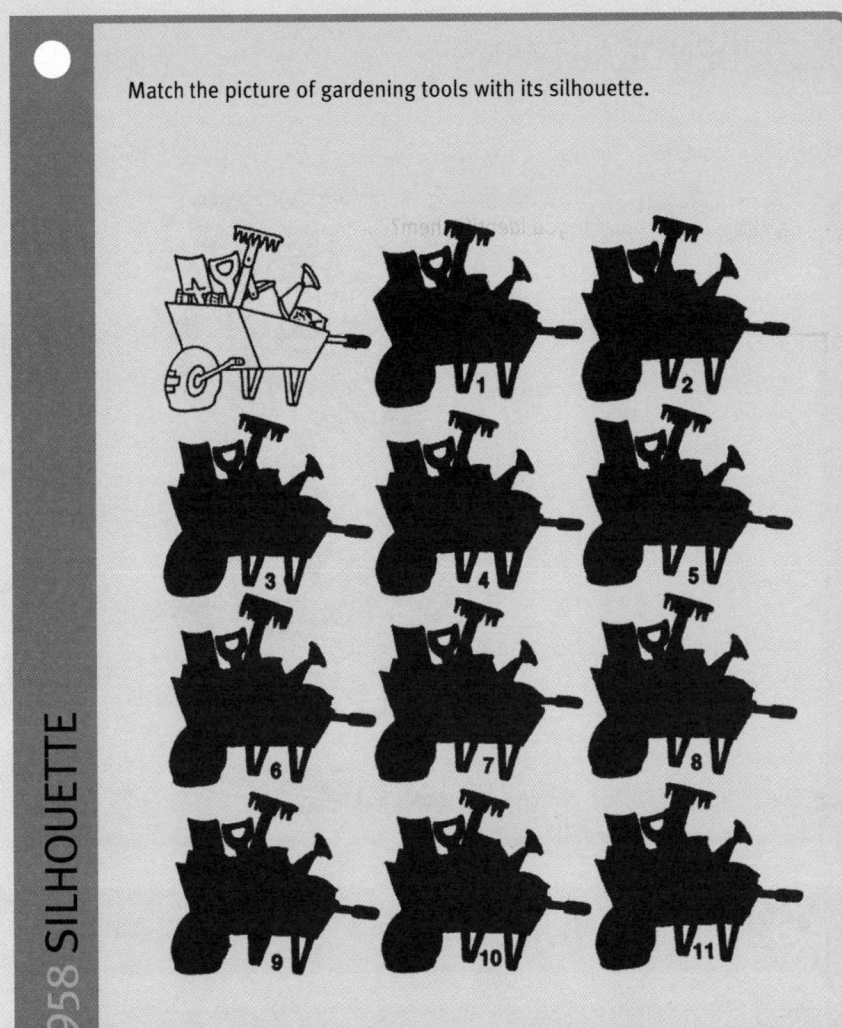

959 LABYRINTH

●●●

Starting at the left hand side, moving forward at each go, try to work your way to the other side. At each step, you must follow the instruction for that column (such as x 4). There are, of course, dead ends. Go on – be amazed!

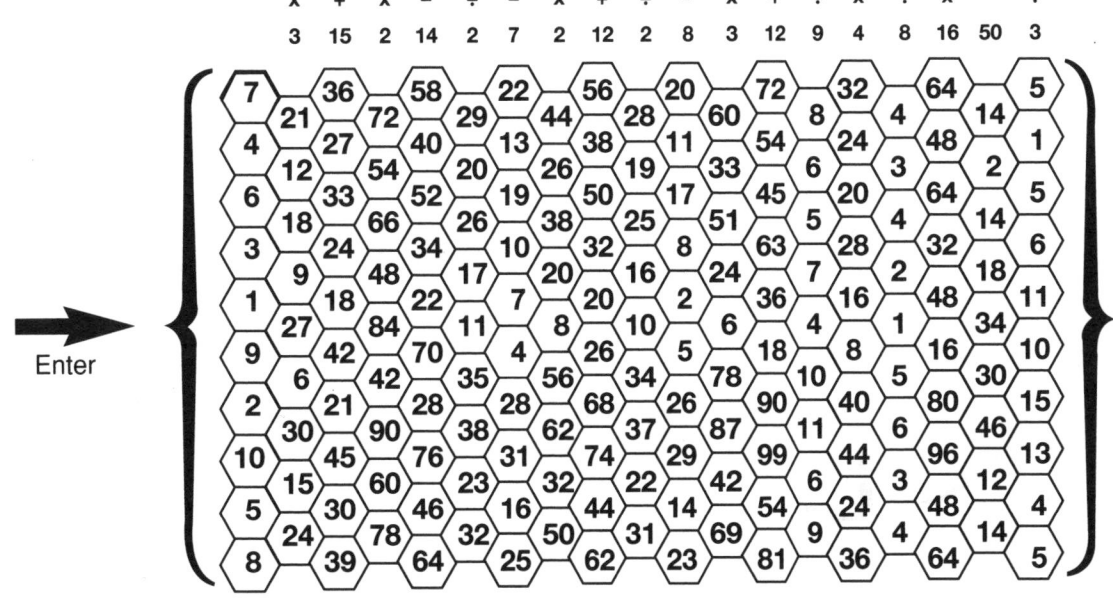

?

960 IDENTICAL TWINS

Two of these go-karters are identical. Which two?

1.

3.

4.

5.

6.

961 ARROW NUMBERS

● ● ●

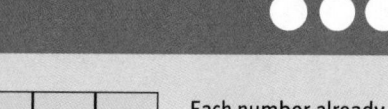

Each number already in the grid shows the sum of the digits in the line whose direction is shown by the arrow. Only one digit can be placed in each square. There are no zeros. For each sum, each digit can only appear once – e.g., 8 cannot be completed with 44. A sequence of digits forming a sum can only appear once in the grid. If 8 is 53 somewhere then another 8 cannot also be 53. Nor could it be 35, but must contain a different set of digits, such as 71/17, or 62/26. Can you put logic, rather than higher maths, to work and find the unique solution?

Top headers: 11, 19, 17, [ ], 6, 18, 21, 16, 11, 8

Left headers (by row): 14, 24, 15, [ ], 18, 4, 18, [ ], 9, 10, 30, [ ], 33, 15

Interior clues:
39; 23/13; 7/18, 20, 6; 10, 22/20, 8/22; 8/10, 11/12; 14/9, 18/11; 21/14, 10, 17; 12, 11/23, 15/16; 10/16, 12/29; 12/21, 13/9; 9/17, 19, 11; 10, 12/7, 13/5; 18; 28

962 ARROW PUZZLE

Can you help the ship reach America by following the arrows, being careful not to land on Australia by mistake?

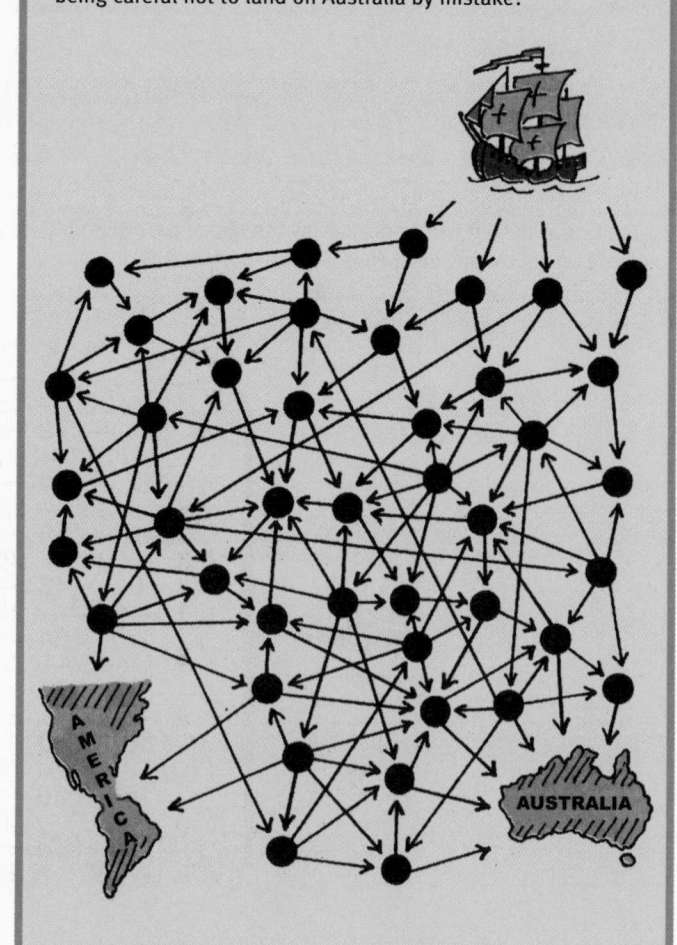

AMERICA

AUSTRALIA

963 TOOL BAG

Four of the six shapes shown at the top can be found hidden in the picture. Which ones and whereabouts are they?

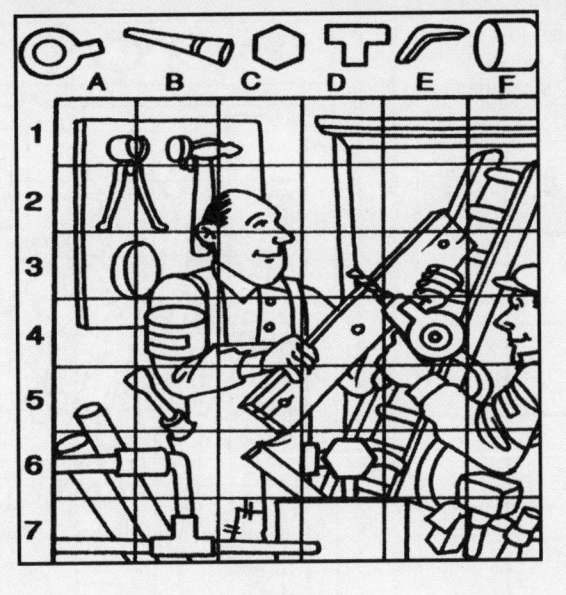

964 FOURSOME

The shopper is looking for four identical books. Which will he select?

965 BLACK OUT

Which three creatures are shown in silhouette at the top?

966 WHO'S WHO?

The five top models parade down the catwalk in turn. Amy, who is immediately in front of Bridget and immediately behind Claudia, is wearing a short skirt and the same belt as Deborah; Elaine is modelling a long skirt. Name the numbers!

967 ARROW NUMBERS

Each number already in the grid shows the sum of the digits in the line whose direction is shown by the arrow. Only one digit can be placed in each square. There are no zeros. For each sum, each digit can only appear once – e.g., 8 cannot be completed with 44. A sequence of digits forming a sum can only appear once in the grid. If 8 is 53 somewhere then another 8 cannot also be 53. Nor could it be 35, but must contain a different set of digits, such as 71/17, or 62/26. Can you put logic, rather than higher maths, to work and find the unique solution?

	10	28	22		19	7	22		28	27
17				9				12 / 9		
21			37 / 12							
26						25				
12			11			14				

968 ARROW NUMBERS

Each number already in the grid shows the sum of the digits in the line whose direction is shown by the arrow. Only one digit can be placed in each square. There are no zeros. For each sum, each digit can only appear once – e.g., 8 cannot be completed with 44. A sequence of digits forming a sum can only appear once in the grid. If 8 is 53 somewhere then another 8 cannot also be 53. Nor could it be 35, but must contain a different set of digits, such as 71/17, or 62/26. Can you put logic, rather than higher maths, to work and find the unique solution?

(Grid:)

	19	35	13		19	11		37	8	13
7				15			20/11			
21			24/15							
15		10/10			20/20					
	10/9			12/9					6	11
27						9				
13		22			21					

969 MISGIVINGS

Of the six objects shown at the top, four are to be found hidden in the main picture. Which ones, and where are they?

970 LATIN SQUARE

Each cell of the square below has one of the digits from 1 to 7. Each row and each column has exactly one of each digit. The clues below give the total of two, three or four cells. From these clues, can you figure out what number is in each cell?

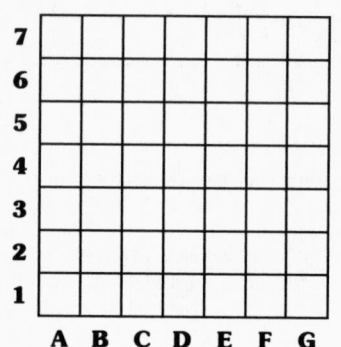

A567=9
AB4=9
ABCD2=21
C234=18
C567=7

CDE3=18
CDE7=6
D4567=12
DE4=3
DEF1=14

DEFG5=21
E1234=13
F234=7
G123=9

971 LOGIQUATIONS

In the following problem the digits 0 to 9 are represented by letters. Within each separate puzzle the same letter always represents the same digit. Can you find the correct values each time so that all sums, both horizontal and vertical, are correct? With each separate puzzle, there is a clue to help start you off.

ABC	+	DEF	=	GBFH
+		−		+
JDGH	−	GCK	=	JGJE
DBJJ	+	GFA	=	DGCK

Clue: DF is a square

A	B	C	D	E	F	G	H	J	K

972 TOTTERING TOWER

These piles of bricks aren't the random results of child's play – but clues to the final, at present, blank tower on the right. Like the rest, that tower has one brick with each of the six letters. The numbers below each heap tell you two things:
(a) How many adjacent pairs of bricks are actually correct in the final tower.
(b) How many adjacent pairs of bricks make a correct pair but the wrong way up.

So:

would score one on the first number if the final tower had an A directly above a C. It would score one on the second number if the final tower had C on top of A. From all of this, can you create the tower before it finally topples?

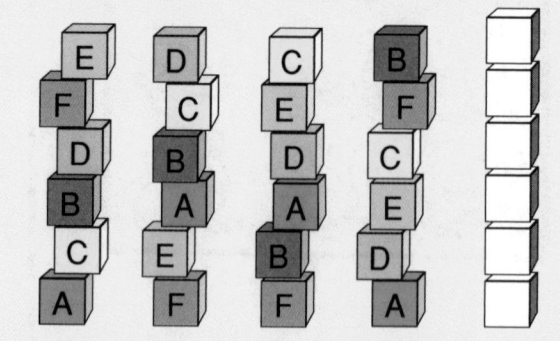

PAIRS					
Correct	0	1	0	1	5
Reversed	2	0	0	0	0

973 URNS-INGS

Which three urns are identical?

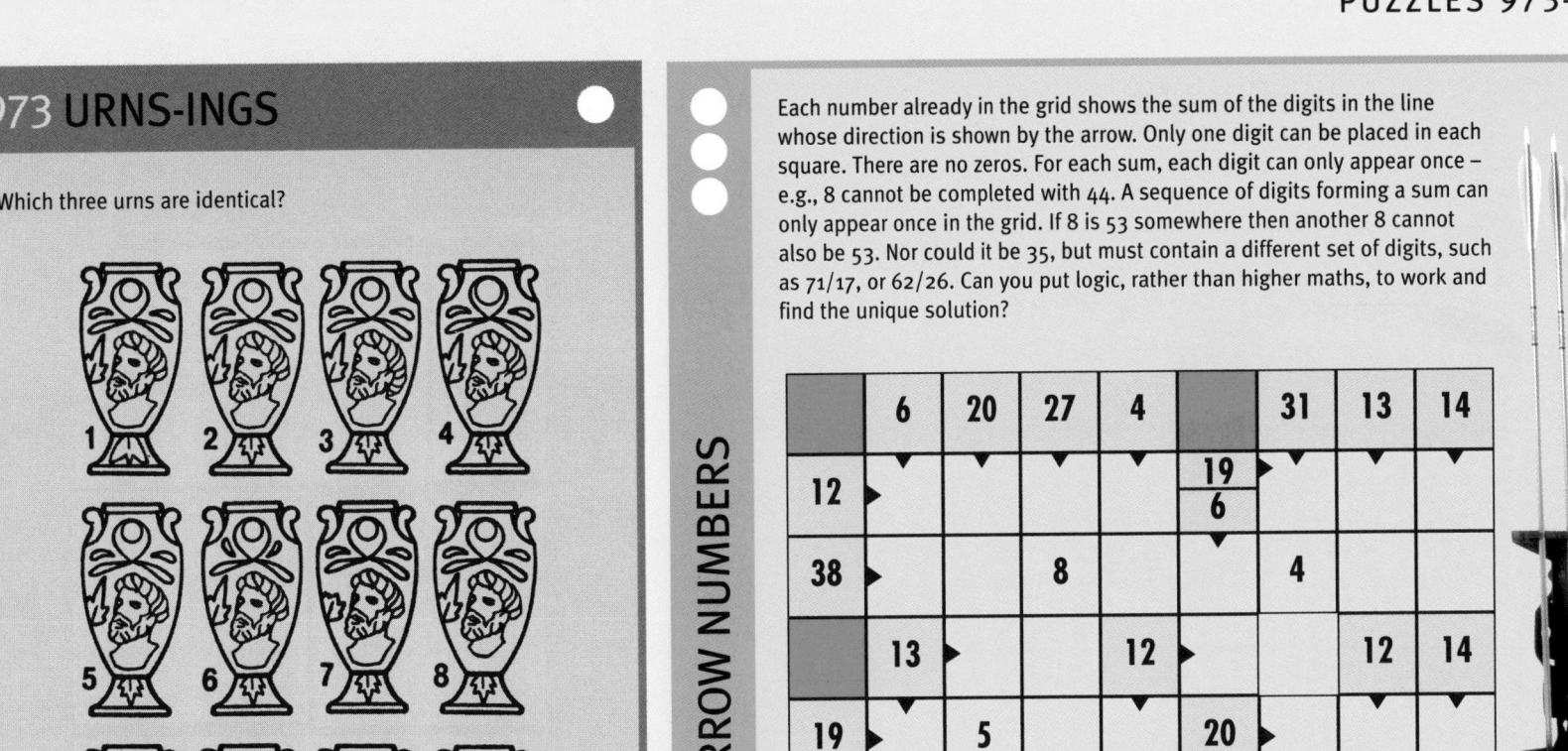

974 FIX THE PIC

Basher has broken all the Easter eggs. Can you put them back together again?

975 ARROW NUMBERS

Each number already in the grid shows the sum of the digits in the line whose direction is shown by the arrow. Only one digit can be placed in each square. There are no zeros. For each sum, each digit can only appear once – e.g., 8 cannot be completed with 44. A sequence of digits forming a sum can only appear once in the grid. If 8 is 53 somewhere then another 8 cannot also be 53. Nor could it be 35, but must contain a different set of digits, such as 71/17, or 62/26. Can you put logic, rather than higher maths, to work and find the unique solution?

976 SQUARES

The six squares seen highlighted at the top right-hand corner of the grid are repeated in only one other place. Can you see where?

977 SPOT THE DIFFERENCE

Can you spot the eight differences between the two drawings?

978 WEB BROWSING

The spiders are identical, but only three have spun precisely the same web – which three?

979 ICELANDS

Our walrus has completely gone to pieces! Can you put him back together again?

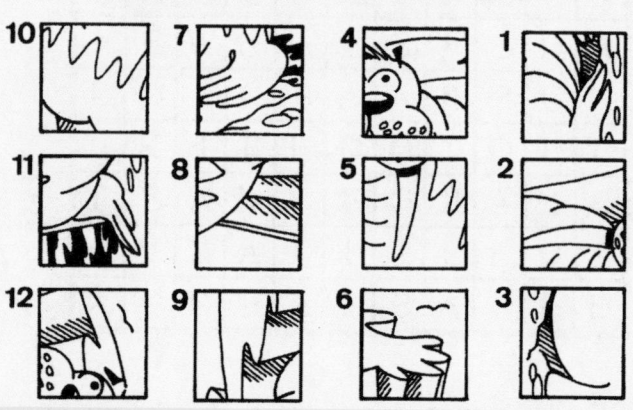

980 ARROW NUMBERS

Each number already in the grid shows the sum of the digits in the line whose direction is shown by the arrow. Only one digit can be placed in each square. There are no zeros. For each sum, each digit can only appear once – e.g., 8 cannot be completed with 44. A sequence of digits forming a sum can only appear once in the grid. If 8 is 53 somewhere then another 8 cannot also be 53. Nor could it be 35, but must contain a different set of digits, such as 71/17, or 62/26. Can you put logic, rather than higher maths, to work and find the unique solution?

	9	20	19	14		24	4	12
22 ▶					17 ▶ / 16			
37 ▶		4			▼			
	9 ▶			12 ▶			9	14
22 ▶			5		17 ▶	2		
14 ▶		6			12 ▶			

981 NUMBER SEARCH

The number 31425 appears just once in this grid, running in either a forward or backward direction, either verically, horizontally or diagonally. Can you locate it?

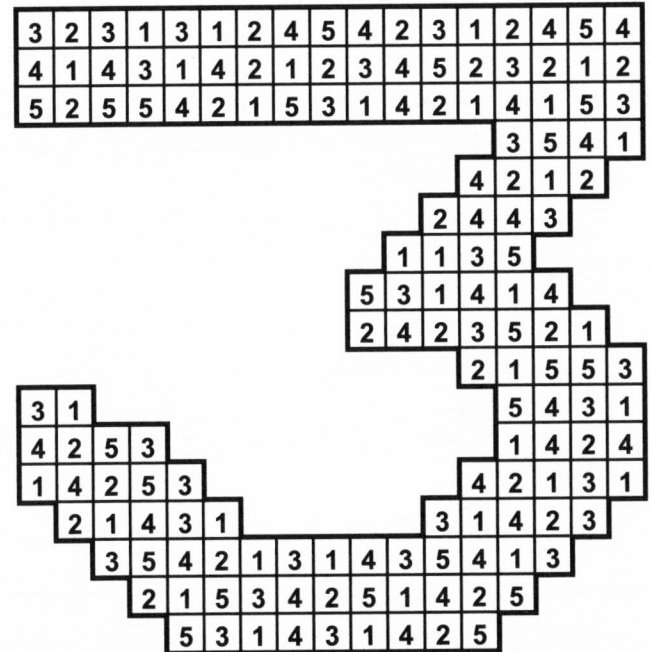

982 TAKE ONE

Remove just one letter and leave all 26 letters of the alphabet...

X	J	N	D	O
K	G	W	P	L
S	C	Q	V	H
R	B	Z	F	T
E	Y	M	U	I	A

984 LATIN SQUARE

Each cell of the square below has one of the digits from 1 to 7. Each row and each column has exactly one of each digit. The clues below give the total of two, three or four cells. From these clues, can you figure out what number is in each cell?

A1234=14
AB1=12
B456=8
BCD3=15
C123=13
C67=9
CDE5=10
D456=18

DEFG2=17
DEFG7=10
E567=7
EFG4=15
F345=12
FG1=5
G567=13

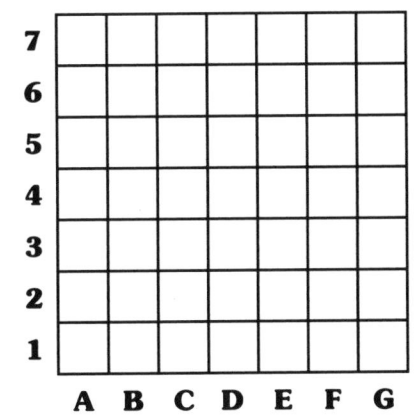

983 CELL STRUCTURE

The object is to create white areas surrounded by black walls, so that:
* Each white area contains only one number
* The number of cells in a white area is equal to the number in it
* The white areas are separated from each other with a black wall
* Cells containing numbers must not be filled in
* The black cells must be linked into a continuous wall
* Black cells cannot form a square of 2x2 or larger

985 PIECES OF EIGHT

Which pieces (four red and four yellow) can be used to make a square, where all four sides are of equal length? Any piece may be rotated, but not flipped over.

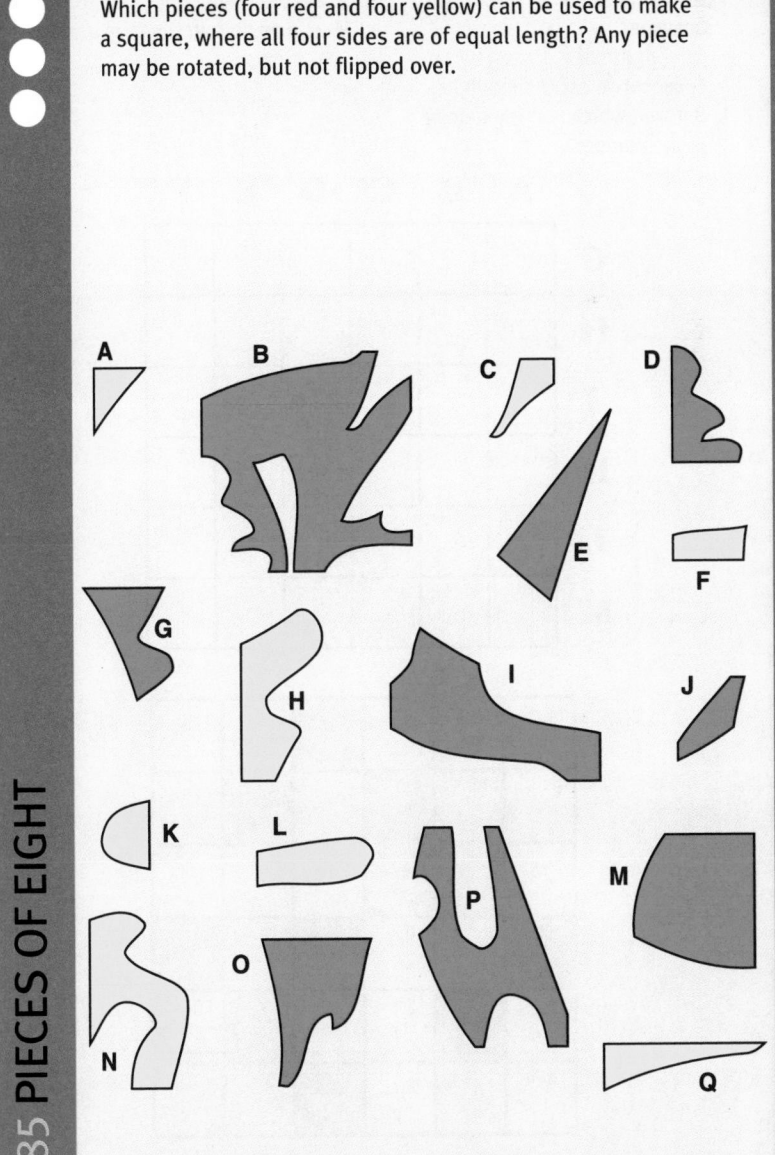

986 2 x 6 x 6

●●●

All the clues lead to single or two-digit answers to be filled into the main grid. You must also complete the crossword grid which will help you complete the main grid. Where there are two single-digit answers, they are not adjacent in that row or column. The clues are in no particular order for the indicated row or column. The digit zero only appears in the main grid. Good luck!

COLUMN

A Square root of *2 down*; first two digits of *1 across*; *9 across*, which is twice *11 down*; one less than the other single digit

B Two-digit cube number; two consecutive digits multiplied together; *11 down*, which is a prime number; all digits are different

C Half of *12 across*; half of *14 across*; two more than *5 across*; all digits are different

D Half of *12 across*; first digit is three times the second; five times the first two digits of column A

E (*3 across* reversed) minus one; *6 down*; total of the other two answers

F One-eighth of *7 across*; two consecutive ascending digits; *8 down*, which is three times a prime number

ROW

G Three times *3 across*; square root of *1 across*; two single digits which are consecutive numbers

H Half of *4 down*; quarter of *1 down*; two single digits which total 5

J Cube number, which is also one-quarter of *7 across*; prime number, which is two more than *11 down*; cube number

K *8 down* plus *13 down*, which is also two consecutive numbers multiplied together; three times a cube number; two consecutive numbers multiplied together

L Half a square number; *6 down*; square number

M *15 across*; four times *15 across*; *5 across*

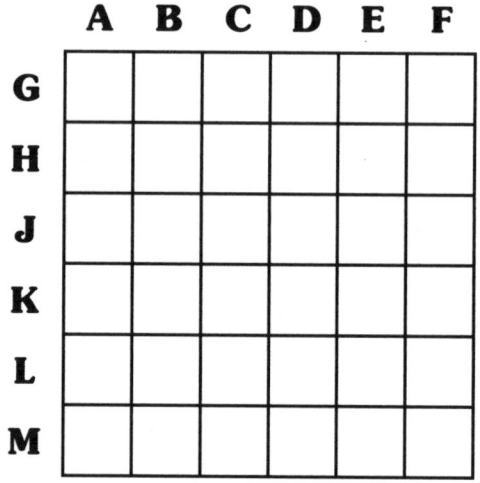

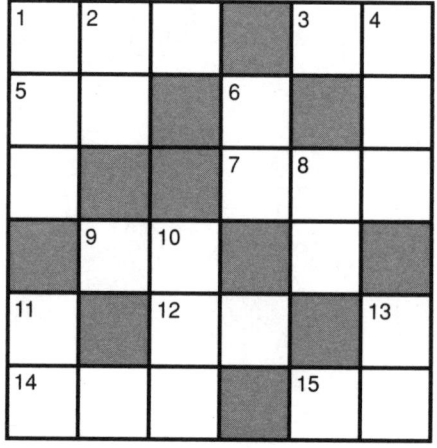

987 STONED

●●

"Here, Harry. Can you place these four stones so that every one is the same distance from the other three?"
"Dunno, Bert. I'll try."
"You'll have a bit of a job on the patio – but you can do it in the garden." How?

988 DOMINO DEAL

●●

A standard set (0 – 0) to (6 – 6) is laid out below. Each domino is placed so that the larger number will be on the bottom:
ie,　　3　　not　　6
　　　　6　　　　　　3
Those top numbers show the four numbers which form the top half of each domino in that column. The bottom numbers, below the grid, give the four bottom numbers for that column. The seven numbers on the left show the numbers which belong in that row. Can you cross-reference the facts and deduce where each domino had been placed? 1*2 is given as a start.

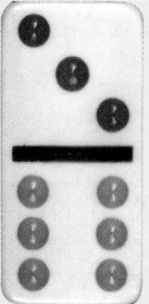

'TOP' NUMBERS

	01	00	03	01	02	12	0~~7~~
	35	12	36	22	34	45	14
0 ~~1~~ 1 1 2 3 4							1
0 1 ~~2~~ 2 6 6 6							2
0 0 1 1 2 3 5							
2 3 3 4 4 4 6							
0 0 1 2 3 4 6							
3 4 4 5 5 5 6							
0 0 2 2 3 4 5							
1 3 5 5 5 6 6							
	25	04	34	13	34	25	1~~7~~
	56	56	66	46	56	56	34

'BOTTOM' NUMBERS

989 OFF FORM

Which one of the eight numbered pieces is the one which is missing from the broken bench?

990 WRAPPED UP

Which of the four numbered cubes is identical to the one held by the boy?

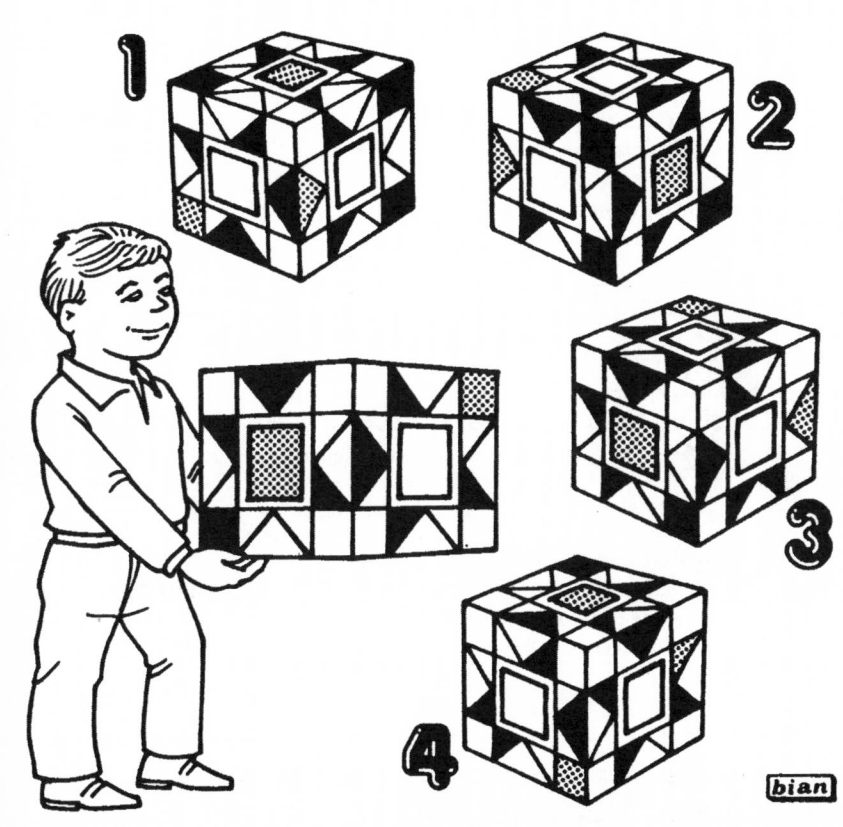

991 POT LUCK

Which of the numbered pots should logically occupy the empty square?

992 WHATEVER NEXT?

Can you give the next letter in this sequence?

A D O P Q ?

993 PILE UP

These piles of bricks aren't the random results of child's play – but clues to the final, at present, blank tower on the right. Like the rest, that tower has one brick with each of the six letters.

The numbers below each heap tell you two things:
(a) How many adjacent pairs of bricks are actually correct in the final tower.
(b) How many adjacent pairs of bricks make a correct pair but the wrong way up.

So:

would score one on the first number if the final tower had an A directly above a C. It would score one in the second number if the final tower had C on top of A. From all of this, can you create the tower before it finally topples?

PAIRS					
Correct	0	0	0	0	5
Reversed	0	1	2	2	0

994 CROSS NUMBERWORD

This puzzle uses the device of expressing a three-letter word as a number. This is done by replacing each letter with the number which is its position in the alphabet, A=1, Z=26 so DOG=4157 and PUT=162120. When transposing the numbers back into letters to make a three-letter word, there may be more than one possibility e.g. 22114 could be BUN (2, 21,14) or VAN (22,1,14)

The aim of the puzzle is to complete the crossword grid with three-letter words. You will need to look at the numerical clues to find the numbers to translate into letters for the words in the grid, but you will also need to keep switching to the grid and to any completed words to eliminate impossibilities.

ACROSS
1 Digit total is 17
3 Multiple of 6; can be expressed as three letters in two ways
5 45 times a number which is less than 500
6 75 times a number which is greater than 2,500
8 Less than 1000; digit total is 10
10 Ignoring the first digit, a multiple of 14
12 Four digits
14 Four digits; five times a cube number
15 Less than 14 across; digit total is 19
16 Less than 12 across

DOWN
1 Six digits; 40 times a number which is less than 4000

2 75 times a number which is less than 500; it can be expressed as three letters in three ways
3 Four digits; multiple of 24; letters are in reverse alphabetical order
4 Greater than 2000
7 15 times a number which is greater than 1100; digit total is 21
9 Four digits; not a multiple of 25; 15 times a number which is less than 80
10 Six digits; letters in alphabetical order
11 Less than 14 across
12 Multiple of five; digit total is 17
13 Digit total is 20; five times a number which is greater than 50,000

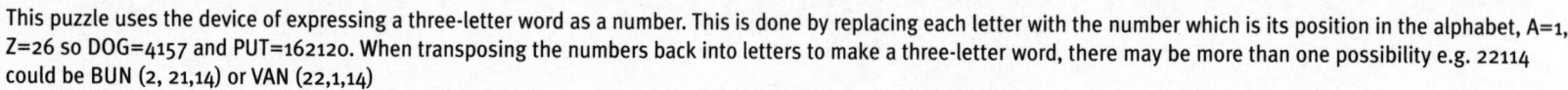

995 25 OF THE BEST

Twenty-five of the numbers between 1 and 49 have been inserted in the grid. Clues to each of the answers in each row and column are given below, but I must add that the numbers in the long diagonal from top left to bottom right total 112, and the other long diagonal from top right to bottom left totals 137. No two consecutive numbers are in the same row, column or diagonal. Using this information can you complete the original grid?

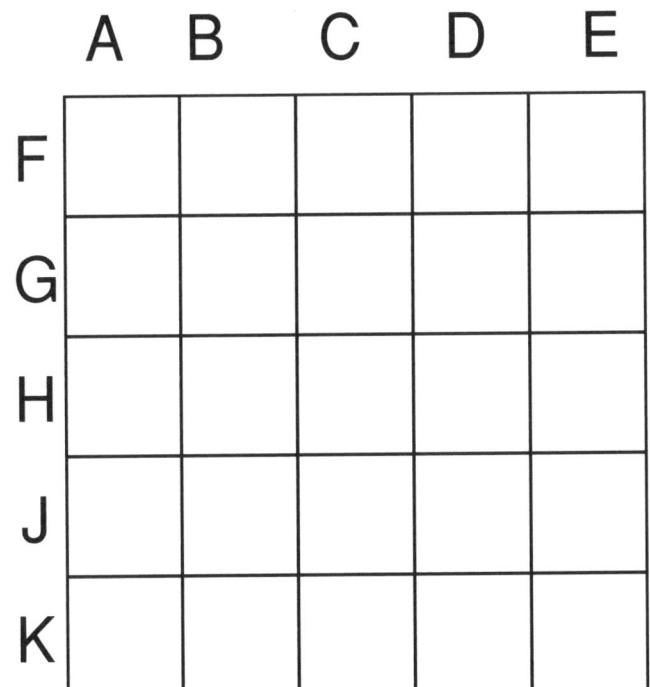

ACROSS

F D equals twice E; D plus E equals twice A; B equals C plus 9

G C plus E equals B plus D; total equals 116

H B plus D equals E; only one odd number

J A equals seven times C; E equals twice C

K D equals three times B

COLUMN

A G equals twice H

B F plus K equals H plus J; total equals 123

C F plus G equals J plus K; K is a cube number; total equals 84

D K equals twice (F plus H); J is the second highest number

E H equals three times F

996 NUMBERS UP

Can you discover the logical sequence shown here and work out what number should replace the question-mark?

997 AMAZING

Can you work your way from the entrance at the top to the exit at the bottom of this maze?

998 BLACK OUT

Can you see which two dinosaurs are shown in silhouette at the top?

999 WALKIES

Each picture is missing a detail that is present in the other seven. Can you spot all eight missing details?

1000 ON THE LINE

Seven travellers using a provincial city's underground railway alighted at successive stations on their journey from west to east. From the clues given below, can you name each of the stations numbered 1 to 7 (interchange stations being denoted by a circle), and name the passenger who got out there?

Clues

1 Libby had already left the train by the time Nigel got out at King's Grove, which is not an interchange station, though the station where Tessa alighted is.

2 Howard got off the train two stations before Peel Park.

3 Station 3 on the plan is Maple Street.

4 It was a woman who alighted at station 5.

5 Eileen got out at the station before Red Lion.

6 Bradley left the train at station 6, which is further east than Market Cross.

7 One of the men got out at Museum station, which is not numbered 7 on the plan.

Stations: Central Station; King's Grove; Maple Street; Market Cross; Museum; Peel Park; Red Lion

Travellers: Bradley; Conrad; Eileen; Howard; Libby; Nigel; Tessa

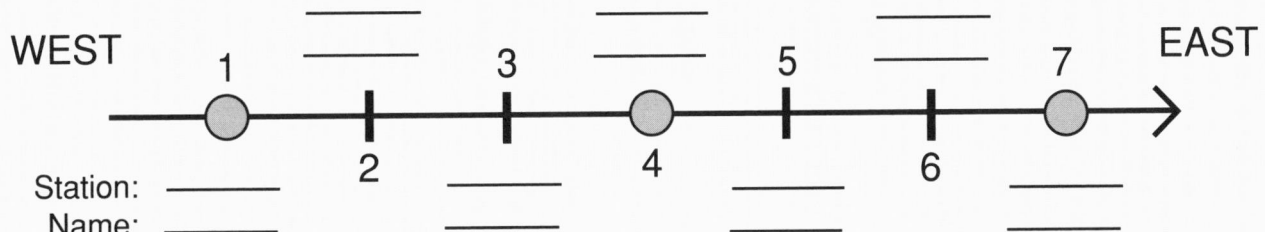

Starting tip: Begin by working out the number indicating King's Grove station.

1001 THANKS FOR THE MEMORY

On top of her bookcase Alice has six photographs taken on some of her favourite holidays over the years. From the clues given below, can you indicate in the spaces provided the location and date of each of the photographs lettered A to F in the diagram?

Clues

1 None of the photographs is in its correct chronological position, reading from left to right.

2 The snapshot taken on Lake Garda is next left to the souvenir of Alice's 1959 holiday, while the scene from Cornwall is next right to the picture taken in 1963.

3 The Isle of Man photograph, whose date is earlier than that of the one in position C, is next but one right from the 1975 one.

4 The photo in position E was taken next after the one marked C, while the one bringing back memories of Tenby dates from a later holiday than the one on which photo A, which does not depict a scene from Brittany, was taken.

5 The picture labelled D was taken in the same decade as the one in position B, but in an earlier year.

Location: Assisi; Brittany; Isle of Man; Lake Garda; Tenby
Year: 1959; 1963; 1971; 1972; 1975; 1979

Starting tip: Begin by working out the position of the photo taken in 1959.

SOLUTIONS

1

A – Maria – heraldic dragon – 1825;
B – William V – shield – 1745;
C – Karl II – crossed swords – 1865;
D – Josef III – wreath of laurels – 1785.

2

5	0	1	2	0	3	2
5	2	4	6	4	6	2
5	2	2	3	0	2	6
6	3	5	4	6	4	6
3	1	0	0	1	3	0
5	3	1	0	2	3	3
1	4	4	1	4	1	0
5	5	6	6	4	1	5

3

From	Al	Bob	Chris	Don	Ed
Al Harkness		2	4	1	3
Bob Jarrett	3		2	4	1
Chris Farley	1	3		2	4
Don Insley	4	1	3		2
Ed Gainor	2	4	1	3	

4

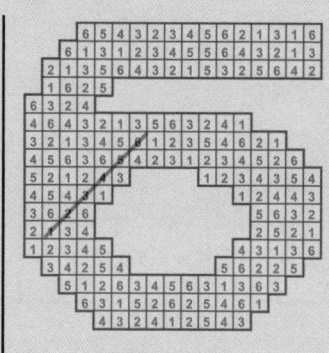

5

Pictures 3 and 5

6

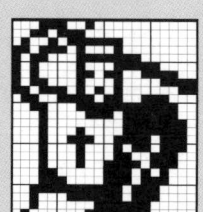

7

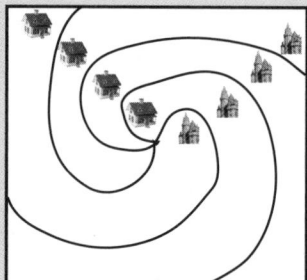

8

9

1 BE DE BG BE **2** DF AF BF(Down) **3** BG CG DF BF CF **4** AG DF(Down) AG **5** BG BF AF BF **6** CG DG AE CE DG **7** AE DE BE AF DE **8** CE CG **9** BE DF **10** CG DG CF

10

Waistcoat g

11

13 red, 3 yellow, 3 brown, 3 blue, 4 pink

12

a – The spots become the same colour as the central colour of the wing of the previous butterfly.

13

3	0	1	0	1	4	6
4	1	5	6	3	4	6
5	3	2	2	3	1	2
5	5	2	3	6	2	5
5	0	1	2	2	0	3
6	5	6	6	4	2	3
1	1	0	4	0	4	0
4	1	3	6	0	5	4

14

15

16

C			A	B
	B	C		A
A		B		C
	C	A	B	
B	A		C	

17

Red = $0.72
Blue = $0.68
Yellow = $2.00
Green = $0.88

18

The cactus in the top-right corner was left.

The purchases were:

Madge	Kim	Laura	Jackie	Cactus
Laura	Laura given	Kim	Madge	Jackie
Jackie	Laura	Jackie given	Kim	Madge
Kim	Jackie	Madge	Kim given	Laura
Madge given	Madge	Jackie	Laura	Kim

19

PERSON	JOB	FEATURE
ALF	BLACKSMITH	MONOCLE
FRED	LAWYER	PANAMA
GEORGE	MAIL MAN	BEARD
TOM	DOCTOR	CRAVAT

20

21

89. If you work out the ways for forming 5 cents, 10 cents, 15 cents, 20 cents, 25 cents ... you get this famous sequence:
1, 2, 3, 5, 8 ... the Fibonacci Series, where each number is the sum of the previous two. Continuing the sequence is a lot quicker than counting all the ways for 50 cents.

22

| 6 | 3 | 2 | 5 | 0 | 4 | 3 |
| 6 | 5 | 2 | 5 | 4 | 5 | 3 |

| 5 | 1 | 4 | 1 | 3 | 2 | 2 |
| 6 | 6 | 4 | 5 | 4 | 6 | 3 |

| 0 | 0 | 0 | 3 | 0 | 2 | 2 |
| 5 | 3 | 6 | 6 | 2 | 5 | 4 |

| 1 | 1 | 0 | 4 | 0 | 1 | 1 |
| 1 | 3 | 1 | 6 | 0 | 4 | 2 |

23

24

25

| 1 | 1 | 1 | 1 | 4 | 3 | 2 |
| 3 | 6 | 2 | 5 | 4 | 4 | 4 |

| 0 | 3 | 3 | 0 | 5 | 5 | 1 |
| 5 | 3 | 5 | 4 | 5 | 6 | 1 |

| 0 | 2 | 0 | 2 | 0 | 1 | 3 |
| 1 | 5 | 0 | 3 | 3 | 4 | 6 |

| 4 | 0 | 2 | 2 | 6 | 0 | 4 |
| 6 | 2 | 2 | 6 | 6 | 6 | 5 |

26

| Mr Grey | Mr Pink | Mr Green |
| Opel White | VW Grey | Skoda Red |

| Mr Blue | Mr White |
| Lancia Green | Jaguar Blue |

27

A FELIX	B ISAAC	C KEITH	D CLIVE
E LYDIA	F HENRY	G AGNES	H DAVID
I GRACE	J JOYCE	K BERYL	L EMILY

28

```
5 2 1 0 4   3   2   3 2 1 9 4
3   3   8   1 2 6 6 3     9   0
6   0   1   0   2   0   3   1
0   0   8 7 6   0   6   0   3
6 2 2 7 1     9 3 5     2 9 9 9 4
    7       2       7     2
6 5 0 1 8     5 0 2 4 2     1
7     2 0 3 9 3   1   5 8 8
1 1 0 3 7 5         9       4 6 3
    9     4 5 2 7 0 6     9
9 1 2 0 3     4 1 9     8 3 1 1 8
3     1   6 9 0     0   0
9 3 6 6 1     3   0     9 0 4 6 0
0       5 0 7   2 3 3     3
6 0 8 8 5   1 3 0     5 0 5 5 1
```

29

The begonia in the middle of the back row was left. The plants were purchased or given as follows:

NORMA	LEN	BEGONIA LEFT	KEVIN	MARY
MARY	LEN GIVEN	NORMA	LEN	KEVIN
LEN	KEVIN	MARY GIVEN	KEVIN	NORMA
NORMA GIVEN	NORMA	KEVIN	MARY	LEN
KEVIN	MARY	LEN	NORMA	MARY GIVEN

30

10	21	23	7	4
25	1	18	13	16
5	14	20	9	2
8	11	6	22	19
15	24	3	17	12

31

A	B	E	C	D
D	A	B	E	C
C	D	A	B	E
E	C	D	A	B
B	E	C	D	A

32

Oxford

33

DAY	FROM SHE	& HE	TO SHE	& HE
THURSDAY	PAM	TOM	FAY	LES
FRIDAY	MAY	JIM	SUE	BOB
SATURDAY	JOY	SAM	KAY	DON
SUNDAY	LIZ	ALF	DOT	TIM

34

7	2	6	4	9	3	8	1	5
3	1	5	7	2	8	9	4	6
4	8	9	6	5	1	2	3	7
8	5	2	1	4	7	6	9	3
6	7	3	9	8	5	1	2	4
9	4	1	3	6	2	7	5	8
1	9	4	8	3	6	5	7	2
5	6	7	2	1	4	3	8	9
2	3	8	5	7	9	4	6	1

35

36

| Mr Black | Mr White | Mr Green | Mr Grey | Mr Red |
| Lada Grey | Renault Blue | Ford Red | Nissan White | Toyota Black |

37

38

39

6	1	0	3	4	3	4	1
1	6	6	3	6	5	2	2
2	0	3	1	2	3	5	1
1	3	4	2	6	1	1	0
5	4	2	6	0	5	2	5
3	0	4	0	4	6	4	4
0	3	6	0	2	5	5	5

40

41

| Mr Green | Mr Brown | Mr White | Mr Grey | Mr Black |
| BMW Grey | Audi Green | Volvo Black | Fiat Red | Ford Brown |

42

43

4	6	4	3
3	3	2	2
5	5	5	4
6	4	2	6
5	6	3	2

44

1	4	2		3	2	1	8		7	1
4	3	1		8	5	7	9		8	2
	5	7	8	9		2	4	1	6	3
1	2		1	6	2	3		6	9	8
3	1	2	5		1	5	2	3		
		1	2	3	5		4	2	5	1
1	2	4		1	3	2	5		9	6
3	1	5	6	2		4	1	6	2	3
2	4		7	4	6	1		7	1	2
5	6	8	9		8	5	6	9		
	7	8	9	5		9	8	4	7	
5	8	9		8	9	3	7		8	9
3	2	4	1	6		6	8	9	7	
2	9		4	7	1	2		6	9	7
1	3		2	4	3	1		8	6	9

45

Boot C

46

Going clockwise starting with the host, the players are: Syd, Mail man (1). Malcolm, Baker (4). Lionel, Jockey (3). Keith, Doctor (5). Jerry, Bookmaker (2). Gus, Financier (7). Wilf, Salesman (6). The number indicates the player's position in the line.

47

No. 4

48

49

Figure 1 has an extra fold of material on his arm. Figure 2 has an extra detail on his right sandal. Figure 3 has more hair. Figure 4 has a wristband.

50

Andrew and Dolly Gould, Kansas City. Brian and Edna Hedges, New York. Colin and Floe Jacobs, New Orleans.

51

0	0	1	5	4	5	2	6
1	0	5	3	6	1	4	2
3	5	0	4	5	3	4	1
2	5	6	5	6	1	3	6
2	3	2	3	2	4	3	6
0	0	5	0	2	1	0	6
4	3	6	1	1	4	2	4

52

Red, Blue, Lavender, Blue

53

54

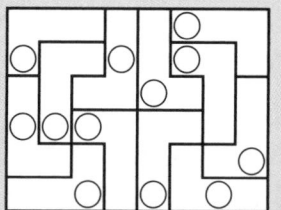

55

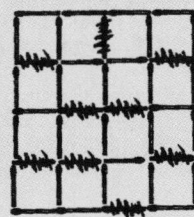

56

CONTACT	EMPLOYEE	METHOD	PLACE
BOOKMAKER	TANIA	E-MAIL	BURNLEY
CAR SALES	WILF	INTERNET	DENMARK
MOTHER	SEAN	FAX	ACCRINGTON
PARTNER	RHODA	PHONE	CANADA

57

58

Print 3

59

D. Each square has the top right quarter cut off. This leaves three smaller squares. In the next picture each of those has its top right quarter removed and so on.

60

```
2 8 1 4 6    3  3    4 1 7 0 3
4   8   0   4 3 3 1 2    3   2
9   2   0         2   0 2   4 8
7   0   4 0 7   6    3 6 2   4
1 4 0 9 9   9 6 4   6 3 4 9 1
    2           6         4
8 1 9 5 5       1 8 8 0 8    4
2   3 1 9 2 7   5    1 9 0   4
5 5 2 8 1       7     3 7 2
9         1 4 2 8 0 7   6
5 3 9 0 4   3 7    8 3 0 1 3
0   3   1 0 2   4   3
7 0 9 5 0   2       3 6 6 3 8
      2   2 9 9   6 0 9     1
1 2 7 5 6   6 5 6   9 4 2 7 0
```

61

One of the green books is missing.

62

5	6	3	7	9	2	4	1	8
4	9	1	5	6	8	3	2	7
8	7	2	1	4	3	9	5	6
9	8	7	6	2	5	1	4	3
1	5	6	9	3	4	8	7	2
3	2	4	8	1	7	6	9	5
7	3	9	2	8	1	5	6	4
6	4	5	3	7	9	2	8	1
2	1	8	4	5	6	7	3	9

63

64

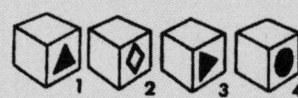

65

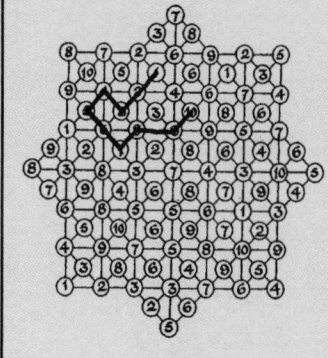

66

8	0	3	2	7	9	8	0	9	7	9
7	4	7	1	1	2	2	4	9	3	6
8	3	0	5	2	3	0	9	0	5	0
4	4	9	8	2	4	3	7	8	3	
8	0	0	3	8	1	6	0	8	6	3
4	1	8	9	2	5	8	5	8	9	2
1	2	3	5	9	5	7	2	3	1	4
5	7	5	7	6	7	1	6	1	6	6
1	7	9	6	5	4	5	2	0	3	1
0	5	0	7	6	6	9	4	2	1	4

67

68

Chuck's date isn't Beth (clue 3) or Cathy (clue 4), so is Alice. Thus Art is heavier than Chuck (1), who (3) is heavier than Beth's date; so Beth's date isn't Art - he's Bill. By elimination, Art's date is Cathy. Since Art is heavier than Chuck, who is heavier than Bill (above), Art is man F, Chuck is E and Bill is D. Bill's date is Beth and Chuck's is Alice (above); so Beth is taller than Alice (2), who is taller than Cathy – thus Beth is woman C, Alice is A and Cathy is B.

69

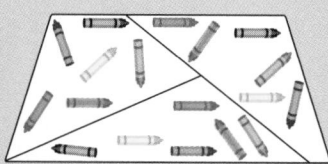

70

1	3			2	1	4		9	3
2	1	3		7	4	9	6		8	2
4	2	5	3	6	1		9	8	7	1
		2	1	5		9	8	6		
4	2	1		8	9	7		9	8	7
1	4		7	9	6	8	4		9	2
3	1	2	6	4		6	2	4	3	1
		1	9			3	1			
6	1	3	4	2		5	1	2	3	4
9	7		8	5	7	9	6		1	9
8	3	1		3	1	6		9	2	8
		2	3	1		8	9	7		
8	9	7	5		1	7	5	4	3	2
9	7		2	1	4	3		8	1	4
7	1			1	3	2			7	1

71

11 red, 3 brown, 2 blue, 1 pink, 5 black.

72

$6 \times 3 + 9 - 6 = 21$
$4 \times 4 + 2 + 3 = 21$
$3 \times 5 + 10 - 4 = 21$

73

The lines should be drawn from 6 to 36, 8 to 29 and 19 to 45.

74

D and J

75

E	C	B	D	A
B	A	C	E	D
A	E	D	C	B
D	B	E	A	C
C	D	A	B	E

76

	A		C	B
C		B	A	
A	B	C		
	C		B	A
B	A		C	

77

Each square tile has neighbours – tiles that share an edge. Look at the number of each colour, red or blue, in the tile and its neighbours. Whichever colour occurs most often, that is the new colour of the cell. If the number of neighbouring colours is the same, the square is left empty.

78

```
6 7 9 0 7 3     3 2 4 3 1 8
2       2 0 5 8 5 1       5
5 0 6 3 4 2     2 8 6 1 4 1   1
3   1 3   1 7 8     3 5     4
3 8 0         1 3     5 8 3
1 2 5 5 0 7   8 0 2 2 0 2   6
    9       2 1       3 4 8
  8 7   8 7 8 3 2 1 9 2
3   2 3 4 0 0 6       2 1
1 1 0 9 1         3       6 1 9 3
    2   4 4 3 9 1 1 4   9
5 3 0 4 6   0 0       5 3 2 5
1   5       1   9 1 6 2       2
9 3 8 3     9 0 4       3   2 8 1
0   5       6   2 2 3 1       8
```

79

80

```
2 5 9 8 4 6 3 7 1
7 4 3 9 5 1 6 8 2
8 1 6 3 7 2 5 4 9
5 6 7 2 3 4 9 1 8
4 8 1 5 9 7 2 6 3
3 9 2 6 1 8 4 5 7
1 7 5 4 2 3 8 9 6
9 2 8 7 6 5 1 3 4
6 3 4 1 8 9 7 2 5
```

81

1	+	4	÷	5	= 1
+		×		×	
9	+	3	÷	2	= 6
−		−		−	
7	+	6	−	8	= 5
=		=		=	
3		6		2	

82

John and Zoe Young, Jester and Ballerina.
Mark and Ann Turner, King and Fairy.
Norman and Leila West, Pirate and Nurse.
Steve and Rose Downs, Eskimo and Cowgirl.

83

	B	A		C	D
D	A			B	C
		C	D	A	
	C	D	A		B
A	D	B	C		
B		C	D	A	
C			B	D	A

84

```
7 8 1 2 9 5 6 4 3
5 9 4 6 3 1 7 8 2
6 3 2 8 7 4 9 1 5
8 4 6 1 2 3 5 9 7
2 7 9 4 5 6 1 3 8
3 1 5 7 8 9 2 6 4
4 5 8 9 1 7 3 2 6
1 2 3 5 6 8 4 7 9
9 6 7 3 4 2 8 5 1
```

85

2 Diamonds, 3 Hearts, 6 Clubs,
8 Spades, 9 Hearts

86

UP = A, D, E: DOWN = B, C

87

```
5 0 1 0 6   7   6   7 1 2 0 9
0   5 0   1 0 2 1 1   7   0
6 7   3     2 3   1   7 8 0
6   7 4 0 0   2   0 6     0
2 0 1 8 5   6 1 0   1 5 1 3 1
    0     3       1   4
8 9 9 0 5     3 2 9 0 9   8
8   3 9 2 4 6   5   3 6 4
3 3 0 5 1 4       5     9 8 3
8     8 6 1 2 3 4   1
9 1 2 0 6   1 6 8   8 3 2 4 7
1     8     5 5 0     3
3 5 0 1 6   2   3   3 2 1 9 8
2     8 9 2   7 0 2       0
4 0 1 1 8   9 5 6   1 0 8 6 0
```

88

Girls 4 and 6.

89

90

91

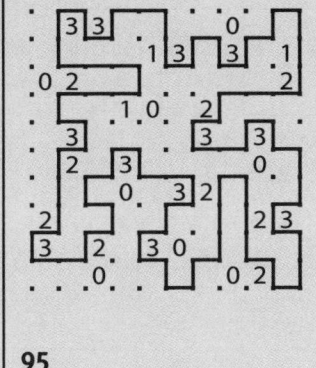

92

93

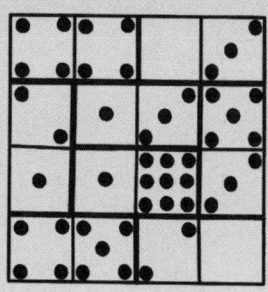

94

A crossword-style grid of numbers.

95

```
0 2 | 1 2 | 0 3 | 1
2 4 | 1 5 | 5 5 | 6
0 6 | 1 1 | 1 2 | 1
0 6 | 5 4 | 3 6 | 2
3 0 | 4 2 | 0 4 | 5
4 3 | 4 2 | 6 6 | 6
0 0 | 3 4 | 5 2 | 3
4 1 | 6 5 | 5 3 | 3
```

96

```
7 2 6 4 9 3   5 2 4 6 3 1 9
7   1 0   2   1 1   1     3
8 3 0 2 2 6 9   5 1 9 9 5
3   1 6     4     7   5 3 0 2
9 3 0 3   8 0 3 1 0 3   6   6
1 1   3 9 6     5 2 5 0 0 8
4   7     5   3 3 5 4   2
  9 3 8 1 1 8     1 4 3 8 1 1 6
3   0     6       8   4
4 0 3 6 2 5   0     1
1   3     5 8 6   3 2 1 6 5
1 2 8   1 2 5 8 9   2 8 5   4
0   1 2 2 5 8 9     9   5 3
7 9 3   1   6 2 3 3   1 8 0 9
4   9 2 8 5 1   7   0
```

97

BOX	BIRD	EGGS
1	BRENDA	5
2	FELICITY	2
3	DEIRDRE	6
4	EDWINA	4
5	ABIGAIL	1
6	CLARISSA	3

98

A and E

99

```
1 9 2 8 1   4   5   6 7 7 6 8
5   4 3   9 2 2 0 0   1   2
3 4   5   6 7 8   9     0
4 6   9 5 4   3 2 1   0
8 3 7 2 8   7 7 9   6 3 0 9 1
    5     4     3 3
5 2 6 7 3     4 8 1 9 0   0
5   3 5 5 4 3   2   2 4 1
1 1 6 2 3 8       9     2 4 9
  7     2 6 8 9 8 2   4
3 0 7 1 4   4 2 3   5 3 5 0 9
6     4 6 1 4 0   0     0
7 9 8 0 5   9   5   8 2 6 9 7
7     9 7 0   1 1 6       2
2 8 9 0 6   3 0 6   7 4 7 8 3
```

100

```
2 6 7 4 9 3 8 5 1
9 5 1 2 8 6 4 3 7
4 8 3 7 5 1 9 6 2
1 7 6 3 2 8 5 4 9
3 9 5 1 4 7 2 8 6
8 4 2 9 6 5 7 1 3
7 1 8 5 3 2 6 9 4
6 2 4 8 1 9 3 7 5
5 3 9 6 7 4 1 2 8
```

101

2	1	1	3
3	5	2	2
3	3	5	2
1	2	5	5
5	1	1	3

102

Flying saucer 4.

103

Up = A, D and E
Down = B and C

104

Hiatus could not have served for twelve years (clue 4). Nor could this have been Blunderbuss or Rictus (clue 1), so the man with that length of service must have been Voluminus. He could not have been from Syria (clue 2) or Germania (clue 4) and the man from Africa had 11 years' service, so Voluminus must have been from Gallia and must therefore have been stationed on the west wall (clue 3). Blunderbuss must therefore have been on the east wall (clue 1). The man on the north wall had served for nine years in the legion (clue 3). He could not have been Hiatus (clue 4), so must have been Rictus and Hiatus must consequently have been on the south wall and, from clue 4, the man from Germania must have been Blunderbuss on the east wall. By elimination, he must have served for ten years. Finally, Rictus, with his nine years' service, cannot have been from Africa (clue 3), so he must have been from Syria, leaving Hiatus on the south wall as the African with eleven years of service.

In summary:
North, Rictus, Syria, nine years.
East, Blunderbuss, Germania, ten years.
South, Hiatus, Africa, eleven years.
West, Voluminus, Gallia, twelve years.

105

D	A	C	E	B
E	C	B	D	A
A	B	D	C	E
C	E	A	B	D
B	D	E	A	C

106

4	2	0	4	3	9	3	1	3	8
8	3	5	8	5	1	2	4	0	4
9	1	4	6	1	8	2	0	5	7
2	7	3	7	0	3	8	9	3	9
5	0	9	6	8	2	4	2	1	4
9	7	2	1	7	5	3	6	5	8
3	1	4	9	2	8	0	2	3	2

107

7	+	1	–	5	=	3
+		+		x		
4	+	8	÷	2	=	6
–				÷		
6	x	3	–	9	=	9
=		=		=		
5		3		1		

108

8	9	3	1	7	6	5	4	2
1	7	6	4	5	2	8	9	3
4	5	2	8	3	9	7	1	6
6	1	7	5	8	4	3	2	9
2	4	5	3	9	1	6	8	7
9	3	8	2	6	7	1	5	4
7	2	4	6	1	8	9	3	5
5	8	9	7	2	3	4	6	1
3	6	1	9	4	5	2	7	8

109

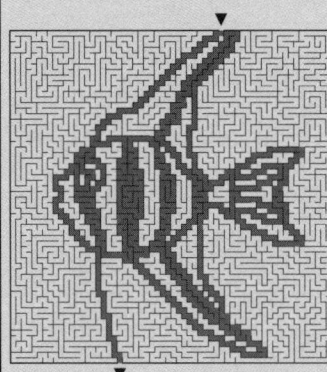

110

111

HE	JOB	SHE	JOB	PLOY
A HOUND	DIRECTOR	H BEE-P	PERSONNEL	GET DRUNK
B PUSHIE	ACCOUNTANT	G PURRS	SECRETARY	PLAY TAPE
C NUTTING	CLERK	I NOAH	TYPIST	MEET HUS.
D VEEUS	SALESMAN	J BEECY	GEN. MAN	TAKE PIC
E STENDER	DRIVER	F ISHENT	DIRECTOR	SHOW FILE

112

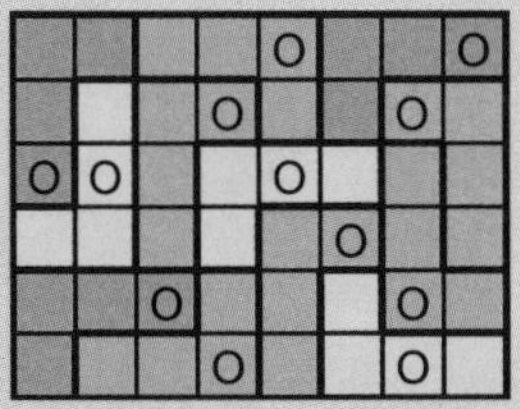

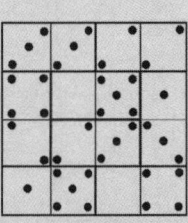

113

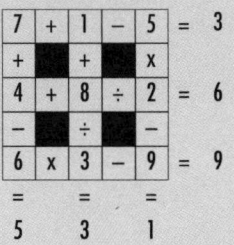

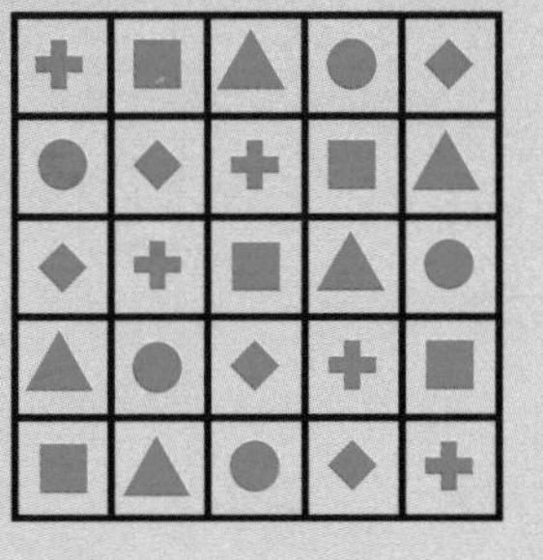

114

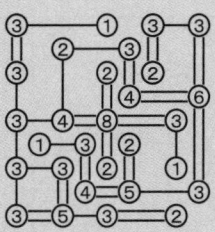

115

2	9	3	0	6		4		9		7	2	4	3	1
6		0		7		2	9	3	1	7		8		4
8		1		1		6		7		2		8		7
1		1			5	4	1		7	1		8		1
7	3	5	3	8		8	2	0		3	9	7	9	2
				9			9			9	2			
7	5	3	6	8			3	7	3	0	4		0	
0		1	1	9	0	3		4		3	6	6		
7	6	3	0	8	1		6			5	5	2		
2			4	9	3	9	1	8		1				
5	2	7	8	9		4	1	3		7	2	4	2	2
0			3		6	7	3		6		1			
4	0	0	1	3		1		0		4	9	9	8	0
6				7	4	5		1	7	2			1	
8	6	2	6	1		2	9	6		1	5	7	0	4

116

E and G

117

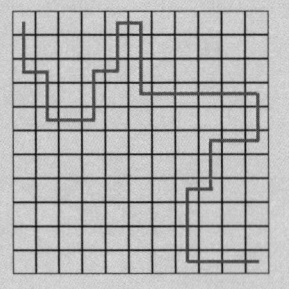

118

E	B	C	A	D
A	E	B	D	C
D	C	A	E	B
C	D	E	B	A
B	A	D	C	E

119

LADY	ORANGES	DATES	TOPS
MRS FEATHERBED	0	1	2
MRS FLOWERPOT	1	1	1
MRS GREENGAGE	2	1	0

120

	B	A		C
A	C		B	
	A	B	C	
B		C		A
C			A	B

121

E, L and O

122

1	Jerry	9	Jack
2	Alice	10	Christine
3	Daisy	11	Enid
4	Mary	12	Charley
5	Tom	13	George
6	Bernard	14	Kate
7	Joan	15	Lottie
8	Freddy	16	Peter

123

			7	9			1	3	
1	2		9	8	7		4	2	
3	1	2	5		5	3	2	1	
			4	8		9	1		
2	3	1		3	6	2	1	4	
1	9		3	1	8		7	1	
4	7	8	6	9		1	3	2	
		9	4		3	2			
9	3	6	1		2	4	3	1	
8	2		2	3	1		9	8	
6	1			1	5				

124

Hein was with Rudig and Jan was with Wouter. Hence it was Roel who had no alibi.

125

[grid puzzle with path]

126

9, 13, 3, 10, 1, 11, 6, 7, 14, 2, 12, 8, 4, 5

127

[maze illustration]

128

[dot grid puzzle]
```
.0 1  3 .0 2    2
        3 .   3
.0 2  2  2    3
    3 3  3  3 1
2 0.   2 0  .0 1.
  2    2 0    1
      3  1
.0 1  2 3      3
.1  1  3  3 .0 1.
```

129

[circle network puzzle]

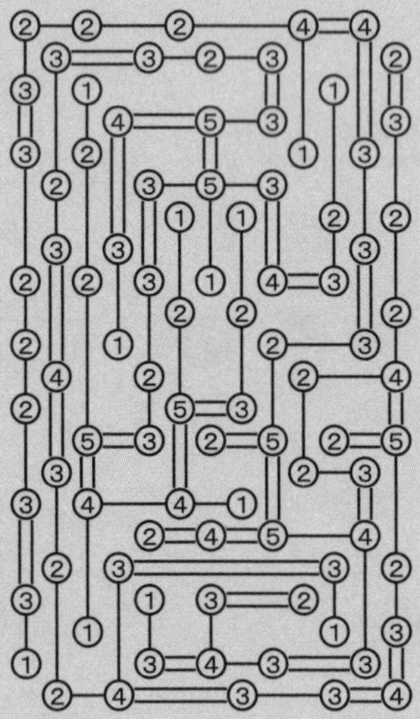

130

12 reds, 2 yellows, 3 browns, 4 blues, 3 blacks.

131

B	C	E	A	D
D	A	B	E	C
E	D	A	C	B
C	E	D	B	A
A	B	C	D	E

132

```
3 4 1 7 1 2   5 2 7 3 5 5 9
8 3 7 2     4 7     1
6 1 5 7 2 4 8   2 8 1 3 5   0
2   1   6   4     2   1 6 2 2
5 9 2 1   6 3 7 9 0 1   1   6
6   7   9 4 3     7 2 9 3 6 2
1     1   3   8 2 7 3   9   6
  3 1 4 5 1 7       0   8
  9   6   1   9 9 2 1 3 4 9
4 1 0 3 5 5     5   7 1   1
6   0     1 5 0   2 7 4 0 3
7 8 2   5     9   9   8   2
1   1 8 7 3 3 2   8 8 8     6
6 2 9   6   4 5 7 0     3 1 6 0
9   1 3 8 0 4     1   6
```

133

134

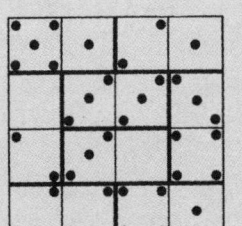

135

136

	C	B		A
A			C	B
B		A		C
	A	C	B	
C	B		A	

137

BEAR	SLEEPER	CEREAL	BROKE
CARMEN	WYN	CHAFFLAKES	CHAIR
FRED	GOLDIE	RICYPOPS	SIDEBOARD
MAMA	CHER	MUESLI MUNCH	BOOKCASE
PAPA	DAWN	WEETY BRICKS	TABLE
TEDDY	CILLA	BRAN BITS	DESK

138

GIRL	BOY	BOY	BOY
AVA	BRIAN	ERIC	GARY
GLADYS	COLIN	DAVID	HENRY
MARIAN	ALAN	FRANK	IAN

139

1	8	3	4	9	6	5	2	7
2	5	4	3	7	8	9	6	1
9	7	6	5	1	2	4	3	8
8	1	2	7	3	5	6	4	9
6	9	5	8	2	4	1	7	3
4	3	7	1	6	9	8	5	2
5	2	1	6	8	3	7	9	4
3	6	8	9	4	7	2	1	5
7	4	9	2	5	1	3	8	6

140

```
1 2 1 2 ■ 1 ■ 2 2 1 2
■ 0 ■ 1 0 0 0 0 ■ 1 ■
■ 2 ■ 0 ■ 0 ■ 9 ■ 7 ■
3 5 1 ■ 3 ■ 5 ■ 1 0 3
5 ■ 1 4 6 8 9 4 4 ■ 5
1 ■ 2 9 8 1 8 9 0 ■ 1
4 ■ 4 8 9 2 9 4 4 ■ 0
5 3 1 ■ 1 ■ 1 ■ 3 1 0
■ 4 ■ 1 ■ 4 ■ 2 ■ 8 ■
■ 2 ■ 1 1 0 0 3 ■ 8 ■
4 4 1 7 ■ 4 ■ 4 3 1 2
```

The combination is 2981890.

141

3	1		3	4		1	3		1	4
1		4	1		4		5	6		6
1		3	5	0		5	2	6		5
6	5		4		6		4		6	3
0		0		2	5	0		5	5	0
6	4		0	6		2	5	6		0
1	4		2	1		2		3	3	3

142

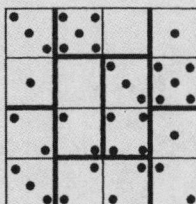

143

Up = B and C and E
Down = A and D

144

Seven bunches have all three colours

145

14 reds, 4 yellows, 3 greens, 2 blues, 5 pinks

146

0	1	3	2
1	2	3	2
2	2	0	0
1	1	1	0
3	3	0	3

147

Picture 4

148

4	2	2	3
4	2	5	5
4	5	3	5
5	2	3	4
3	2	3	4

149

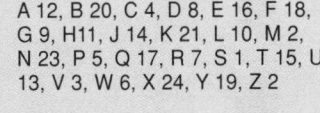

	Eagle	Birdie	Par	Bogey	Double Bogey	FINAL SCORE
PARNELL DARMA	4	1	6	5	2	72
NICK JACKLISS	3	5	7	2	1	65
BARRY CLAYER	1	8	2	3	4	73

150

C		A	B	
B		C	A	
	A		C	B
	C	B		A
A	B			C

151

$9 + (3 \times 2) + 6 = 21$
$7 - 4 + 9 + 9 = 21$
$3 \times 5 - 8 \times 3 = 21$

152

2	+	8	÷	5	=	2
÷		+		x		
1	+	7	−	3	=	5
+		−		−		
4	x	9	÷	6	=	6

| = | | = | | = | | |
| 6 | | 6 | | 9 | | |

153

2	4	3	3	0	3	3	1
4	1	1	6	1	6	4	3
5	2	4	5	4	4	1	5
4	2	0	1	5	3	5	2
3	6	2	0	4	6	0	1
3	2	1	0	0	5	5	2
6	6	2	6	5	0	6	0

154

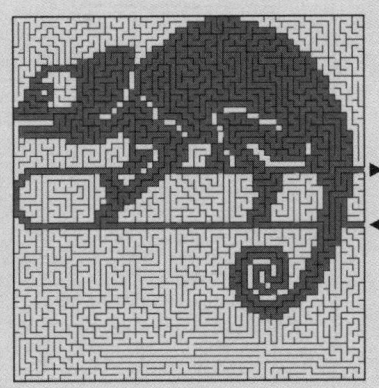

155

A 12, B 20, C 4, D 8, E 16, F 18, G 9, H 11, J 14, K 21, L 10, M 2, N 23, P 5, Q 17, R 7, S 1, T 15, U 13, V 3, W 6, X 24, Y 19, Z 2

156

A is 35, B is 40, C is 25 and D is 20.

157

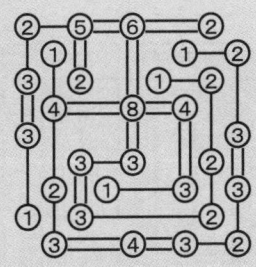

158

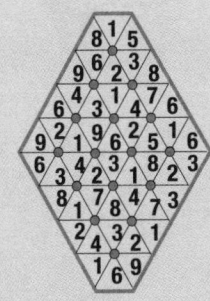

159

Alan – 2B, 1Y, 7V.
Dawn – 3R, 1B, 4G, 2Y.
John – 2R, 5B, 3Y.
Mary – 3R, 4G, 2Y, 1V.

160

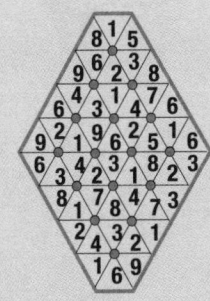

161

77	84	61	68	75
66	73	80	82	64
85	62	69	71	78
74	76	83	65	67
63	70	72	79	81

162

6	+	4	−	5	=	5
+		+		−		
9	−	8	+	1	=	2
÷		−		×		
3	+	7	÷	2	=	5
=		=		=		
5		5		8		

163

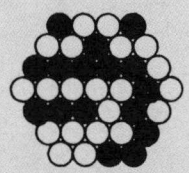

164

2	1	1	3	5	7	4	7
1	6	3	4	7	5	2	6
4	2	2	3	2	6	1	6
6	3	5	7	2	3	7	
1	4	4	1	4	3	6	6
5	7	4	5	3	6	5	7
5	1	2	2	4	5	2	7

165

166

| 5 | 4 | 3 | 7 | 4 | 8 | | 9 | 7 | 8 | 3 | 2 | 8 | 8 |
| 9 | 2 | 4 | 1 | | | 0 | 4 | 1 | | | | | |

(etc.)

167

(grid of numbers)

168

1 Crazy Carvellos
2 Fred the Fire-eater
3 Madame Poll's Parrots
4 Clever Clowns
5 Jim the Juggler
6 Senor Pedro's Poodles
7 Flying Fortresses
8 Agilles Acrobats

169

6	7	6	7	6	6	6	3
2	4	2	7	5	1	5	1
1	3	1	4	5	2	5	4
2	6	4	7	5	3	4	7
2	1	7	1	5	2	1	1
7	6	2	7	4	3	6	5
5	5	3	4	3	4	4	4

170

Ten bunches have all three colours.

171

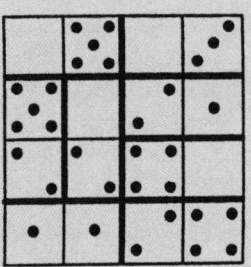

172

(dominoes / dice grid)

173

F, J, C, I, A, H, B, G, E, L, D, K

174

2	7	3	5	8	4	9	1	6
6	8	5	1	3	9	2	7	4
4	1	9	7	6	2	3	8	5
3	5	4	9	7	6	1	2	8
9	6	8	2	5	1	4	3	7
1	2	7	8	4	3	6	5	9
8	3	2	4	9	7	5	6	1
7	9	6	3	1	5	8	4	2
5	4	1	6	2	8	7	9	3

175

(grid of numbers)

176

(grid of numbers)

177

(grid of numbers)

178

Seven bunches have all three colours.

179

Each square tile has neighbours – tiles that share an edge. The corners have just two neighbours, those along the edge have three and the ones in the middle have four.

For each square, check its neighbours' colours (red or black) – whichever colour occurs least often that is the new colour of the cell. If the number of neighbouring colours is the same, the square is left empty.

180

1—D, 2—B, 3—A, 4—C

181

1	JESSE JONES	WELLS FARGO
2	FRANK FOSTER	JAIL
3	CHUCK CARSON	SALOON
4	DAVE DALTON	BANK
5	ROCKY RAWLINGS	TRADING POST

182

3	5	7	1	9	6	8	2	4
6	9	8	2	5	4	7	1	3
1	4	2	8	3	7	5	9	6
2	3	5	7	8	9	6	4	1
7	6	4	3	1	2	9	8	5
9	8	1	4	6	5	2	3	7
4	7	6	9	2	1	3	5	8
8	1	9	5	7	3	4	6	2
5	2	3	6	4	8	1	7	9

183

D	B	A	C		
A	D		B		C
		C	D	A	B
	B	A	C	D	
C	A	D		B	
B	C			D	A

184

(triangular number grid)

185

4	+	7	-	9	=	2
+		+		-		
6	+	3	-	8	=	1
-		÷		+		
1	×	5	-	2	=	3
=		=		=		
9		2		3		

186

	B	D		A	C
D			A	C	B
		C	A	D	B
A		B	C	D	
C	D		B		A
B	A	C			D

187

Tangles a, b and d will not form a knot. Tangle c will form a knot.

188

Pictures 2 and 3

189

28 triangles

190

1+7, 2+4, 3+6, 5+8

191

13 red, 2 green, 3 blue, 5 pink, 3 black

192

3	6	6	5
4	4	3	4
0	0	0	5
6	5	3	3
0	6	4	5

193

Johnny is number 3 (clue 3). Number 1 cannot be Darren Poole (clue 2), or Shaun (clue 1), so he must be Garry. So, from clue 4, boy number 2 must have green boots. Those of lad number 4 cannot be red (clue 1), or brown (clue 2), so they must be black. So, from clue 4, Johnny, in position 3, must be Waters. Shaun's surname is not Brook (clue 1), so it must be Burne, leaving Garry's as Brook. So Shaun is not in position 2 (clue 3), and must be lad 4, wearing the black boots. By elimination, this leaves boy 2, in the green boots, as Darren Poole. So, from clue 2, the brown boots must belong to the lad in position 1, Garry, leaving Johnny Waters wearing the red boots.

In summary:
1, Garry Brook, brown.
2, Darren Poole, green.
3, Johnny Waters, red.
4, Shaun Burne, black.

194

```
  7 1 3 6 4 8    1 6 3 8 4 2 5
5 7 3 1      5 3      9
2 1 5 2 2 6 0    7 3 0 1 4    9
4 0  3 1      9  3 2 5 0
9 0 5 4    3 2 6 4 1 9      3
3  0  4 8 3      1 0 3 6 0 0
9    9  4   2 9 2 1    9  4
    5 3 8 0 1 8      3 0
    6  3  0    6 6 0 3 2 9 9
4 0 9 2 1 4    4      0      3
0  6      8 0 9    2 7 3 2 8
3 5 8    6      8 1 1    1
6    2 3 5 7 9 8    1 6 1  0
4 4 4    1    4 2 3 0      6 3 0 7
7    3 9 9 0 2      8    6
```

195

Horse 3

196

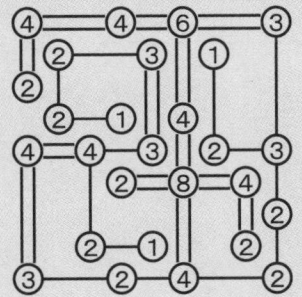

197

Albert – 1R, 3B, 6V
Anne – 4B, 3G, 1Y, 2V
Barbara – 4R, 5G, 1Y
George – 3R, 1B, 6Y

198

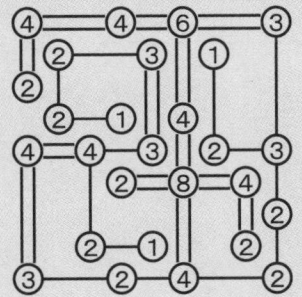

199

1	2	4	5	2	3	2	3
1	5	6	4	4	2	3	1
1	4	2	2	1	0	3	4
2	5	1	6	5	6	3	3
3	5	4	6	6	2	5	1
0	5	3	6	4	6	1	0
0	4	5	0	6	0	0	0

200

201

202

1, 3 and 4 will knot, 2 will not.

203

Apart from the nine smaller squares, there is a tenth to be seen in 1/2/4/5, an eleventh in 2/3/5/6, a twelfth in 4/5/7/8, a thirteenth in 5/6/8/9 and one large square made up of all nine s m a l l e r squares.

1	2	3
4	5	6
7	8	9

204

J	W	G	Z	U	P	E
B	R	N	P	X	H	U
D		Y	K	S	F	M
V	F	D	M	I	Y	S
L		A	R	E		W
G		K	I	O	T	C
Q	B	V	X	Z	J	O
N	I	Q	C	A	L	H

205

206

Susan's surname is Niven (clue 4) and Knight is the quiz host (clue 2), so Laura the newsreader (clue 3) must be Robins, and Knight's first name must be Donna. By elimination, Susan Niven must be the presenter. She didn't train to be a nurse (clue 4) or a teacher (clue 5), so must have trained as a lawyer. Donna Knight didn't train to be a teacher (clue 1), so must have trained as a nurse, leaving newsreader Laura Robins as the former student teacher.

In summary:
Donna Knight, quiz host, nurse.
Laura Robins, newsreader, teacher.
Susan Niven, presenter, lawyer.

207

41. In order, the numbers are 1, 4, 7, 11, 14, 17... numbers that are made from straight lines only. The shop only stocks 1s, 4s and 7s!

208

60. It was, as suggested, worth finding out how many squares there are altogether, which is the sum of 1+4+9+16+25+36+49+64– square numbers. Only squares with an odd number of cells along a side can be more of one colour than the other so we need half of every other number in that series ie, 2+8+18+32=60.

209

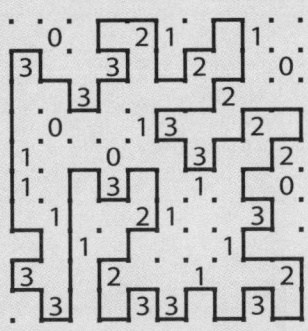

210

211

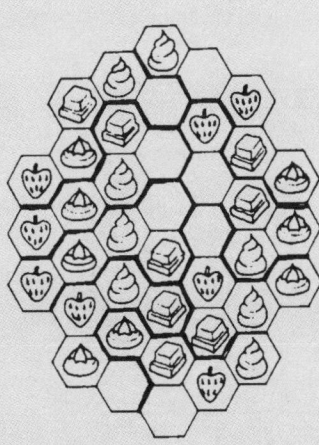

212

3 and 8

213

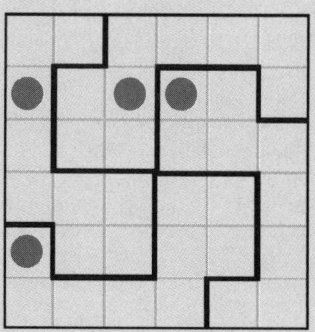

214

A Owen and Vince
B Nick and Rob
C Pete and Tom
D Sam and Will

215

216

217

The clocks add on an hour and ten minutes each time, so the final clock will show the time as half past twelve.

218

1	2	4	5	1	1	1	3
6	2	2	5	6	2	5	3
2	1	2	5	6	3	6	3
2	6	4	5	0	4	0	4
0	3	0	5	6	0	0	0
5	3	6	5	4	4	6	3
3	1	4	1	4	0	1	2

219

9	+	4	–	7	=	6
–		+		+		
5	+	6	–	3	=	8
+		–		–		
2	+	8	–	1	=	9
=		=		=		
6		2		9		

220

Rosalind painted in oils (clue 2), so the watercolour painting of the windmill, which was not by Nadine (clue 3), must have been done by Josephine, leaving Nadine as the artist who used pen and ink. So she did not draw the pond (clue 4), and must have depicted the local church, so she is Ms Frame (clue 1). By elimination, Rosalind's oil painting must be of the pond. Her surname is not Canvass (clue 2), so it must be Pallett, leaving Canvass as the surname of Josephine.

In summary:
Josephine Canvass, windmill, watercolour.
Nadine Frame, local church, pen and ink.
Rosalind Pallett, pond, oils.

221

11 bunches have all three colours.

222

1	2	3	5	9	7	4	6	8
7	6	8	2	1	4	3	5	9
5	4	9	8	3	6	2	7	1
8	7	5	6	4	1	9	2	3
3	1	6	9	8	2	5	4	7
4	9	2	3	7	5	1	8	6
9	3	7	4	5	8	6	1	2
2	5	1	7	6	3	8	9	4
6	8	4	1	2	9	7	3	5

223

224

Dogs A and D.

225

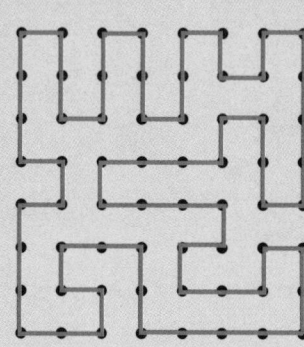

226

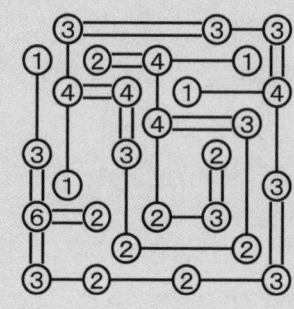

227

Box 1

228

9	4	3	2	0	1		5	1	7	3	4	8	4
9	6	7	0		3		3	7		2		1	
2	3	6	1	7	1	2		4	8	2	0	6	1
0		2	3		3		2		7	3	2	6	
3	9	7	9		7	3	9	9	8		0		2
0		8		4	2	1		1	9	3	7	6	7
7		4	1		1	7	6	2		0		2	
	6	1	8	2	4	3			0	0	2		
	3		2	2		2	7	1	9	3	8	3	
4	7	6	2	3	6		1		7			3	1
0		1			7	2	9		3	7	0	2	2
3		7	6	0	6	3	6		2	1	4		9
3	1	1		1	6	9	1	3		9	0	3	2
1		4	8	8	7	2		3		3	1		

229

1	x	4	÷	2	=	2
+		x		x		
9	÷	3	+	7	=	10
÷		÷		–		
5	+	6	–	8	=	3
=		=		=		
2		2		6		

230

Beth – 1R, 2G, 4Y, 3V
Brian – 4R, 3B, 2G, 1V
Gloria – 3R, 4B, 1G, 2Y
Pete –1B, 3G, 2Y, 4V

231

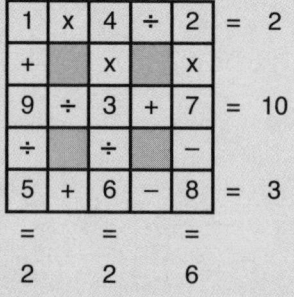

232

3	0	0	3
3	3	3	2
5	5	0	5
5	2	2	2
2	0	0	5

233

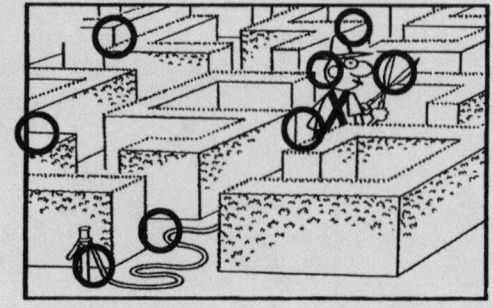

234

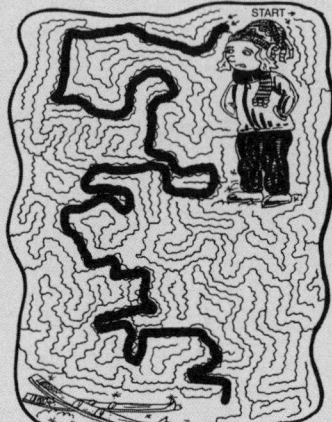

235

No. 1

236

		A	B	D	C
C	D			A	B
B	A		D	C	
A		B	C		D
	C	D		B	A
D	B	C	A		

237

1	x	2	+	5	=	7
x		+		+		
9	+	4	–	7	=	6
–		÷		÷		
8	x	3	÷	6	=	4
=		=		=		
1		2		2		

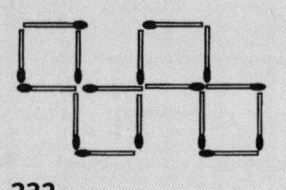

238

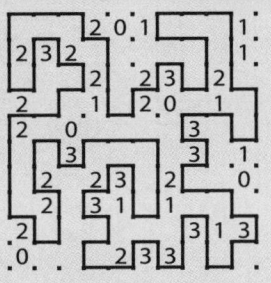

239

35

240

29

241

Arthur–2 begonias, 3 cyclamen, 1 gardenia and 4 jasmines
Barry–1 African violet, 4 cyclamen, 3 gardenias and 2 jasmines.
Connie–6 African violets, 3 begonias and 1 cyclamen.
Debbie–1 African violet, 3 begonias, 4 gardenias and 2 jasmines

242

4–8, 1–10, 5–7, 3–9, 2–6

243

A	B	C	D
ALAN	FRED	LUCY	CLEO
E	F	G	H
IRMA	EDNA	JOHN	GWEN
I	J	K	L
BABS	HUGH	KARL	DAVE

244

Rabbit C

245

246

247

248

CRACKER	FORENAME	SURNAME	GIFT	DECOR	COLOUR
1	AUDREY	YAPP	KNIFE	REINDEER	SILVER
2	JOCK	LEWIS	SCARF	CAKES	RUBY
3	PAUL	WILLIAMS	BIRO	STARS	GOLD
4	TRICIA	COLE	PIC.	TINSEL	BRONZE

249

Weights 1 and 4 will fall, and weights 2 and 3 will rise.

250

9 bunches have all three colours.

251

Print No 4

252

253

2	÷	1	+	5		= 7
x		+		+		
6	x	8	÷	4		= 12
−		÷		÷		
7	+	3	−	9		= 1
=		=		=		
5		3		1		

254

Box D

255

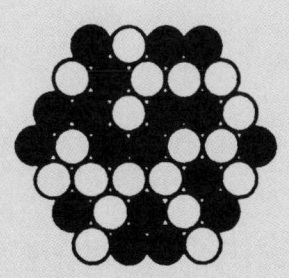

256

257

258

2 x (12 + 3) − 9 = 21
2 x 11 − 11 + 10 = 21
5 x 3 + 8 − 2 = 21
12 x 10 ffi 5 − 3 = 21

259

260

261

1	2	7	9	3	6	8	5	4
9	5	4	7	1	8	6	3	2
3	8	6	2	5	4	7	9	1
5	6	9	1	7	3	2	4	8
4	1	8	5	6	2	9	7	3
7	3	2	8	4	9	1	6	5
6	4	1	3	2	7	5	8	9
8	7	5	4	9	1	3	2	6
2	9	3	6	8	5	4	1	7

262

1 Senor Pedro's Poodles
2 Fred the Fire-eater
3 Crazy Carvellos
4 Clever Clowns
5 Jim the Juggler
6 Flying Fortresses
7 Agilles Acrobats
8 Madame Poll's Parrots

263

Pictures 2 and 5

264

Q	8	T	J	J
D	D	D	S	D
T	8	K	J	A
C	C	D	H	H
J	9	K	K	T
C	H	S	H	S
Q	9	Q	8	8
C	D	S	S	H
K	9	Q	T	9
C	S	H	H	C

265

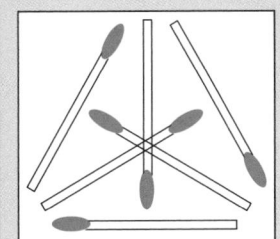

266

267

Billiard room – Lance O'Boyle;
Lounge – Wicklow, the maid;
Card room – Hon. Reginald Ackney;
Morning room – Reverend Rash;
Cloak room – Lady Mole;
Study – Spott, the butler;
Library – Miss Felicity Bytes.

268

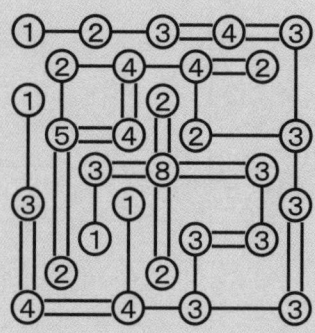

269

After numbering the squares 1 to 25 in the conventional manner – arbitrarily assign A to square 10. This means that square 1 is also A since squares 2, 3, 4 or 5 cannot be A as they are in the same shape as square 10 – and square 14 is an A, as squares 9, 15, 20 and 25 are in the same row or column as square 10. Similarly, square 17 has an A, so the remaining A is in square 23. Assigning arbitrary letter B to square 5 means that square 9 must also contain a B. In turn, this means that square 11 also has a B. Thus neither squares 12, 13, 16 or 21 has a B – and since there is an A in square 17 (above), this means that the requirement cannot be met.

1	2	3	4	5
6	7	8	9	10
11	12	13	14	15
16	17	18	19	20
21	22	23	24	25

270

3, 0, 6, 2, 8, 5, 4, 9, 7, 1

271

Pictures 4 and 5

272

Television 3

273

64,512 Multiply the figures that form the numbers
2 x 3 x 4 x 7 = 168.

274

A Donner B Cupid C Dancer
D Vixen E Prancer F Cornet
G Dasher H Blitzen

275

Weights A and B will rise, and weights C and D will fall.

276

C		B		A	D
D			C	B	A
	B	A	D		C
A	C		B	D	
	A	D		C	B
B	D	C	A		

277

The matching ducks are: 1+8, 2+3 and 4+6; so the different ducks are 5 and 7.

278

```
9 9 2 8 3     4     5     6 7 7 6 8
5   4     8   1 2 1 0 1     2 0     3
4   5     6   7     8   9   5 0     1
2   3     2 4 7     4     5     6 4 0
2 8 9 3 0     3 1 8     3 1 2 4 3
      4           5           6   7
5 8 9 0 7     7 1 2 3 4     5     3
6           7 7 6 7 8     1     6 3 0
2 9 3 4 9 2           0         7 4 1
      6           8 6 8 7 8 9   0
8 2 1 2 9     1 5 3     1 3 4 5 2
6           7 7 5 6 4     8     6   0
1 0 1 2 3     4     5     4 6 7 8 9
1         1 2 8 5     3 9 6       0
5 1 2 3 4     4 0 7     6 5 6 7 8
```

279

A Kate & Naomi
B Jenny & Lisa
C Megan & Sally
D Paula & Rita

280

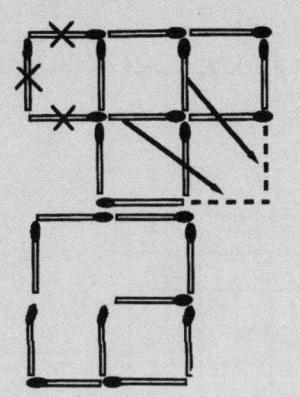

281

	2nd floor:	Carrol	Farmer	Jenkin	Innish
	1st floor:	Grimes	Edgely	Davies	Harris
	Ground floor:	Levers	Grimes	Edgely	Levers

282

283

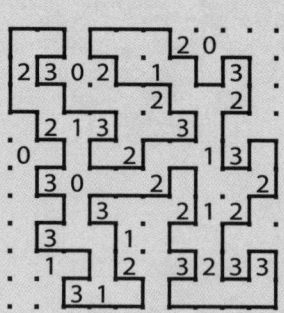

284

285

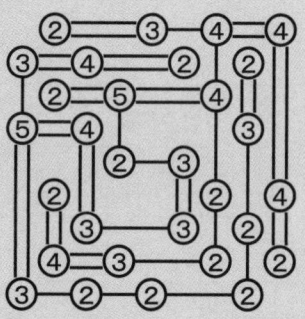

286

Eye colour changed, sign on window missing, wheel nut missing, handle different colour, driver's tie missing and tyre tread missing.

287

Frown now a smile, shadow on jumper missing, shadow under foot missing, collar now yellow, seed shadow missing, two eyebrows.

288

6	8	7	2	4	9	1	5	3
5	4	2	1	3	6	8	7	9
3	1	9	7	5	8	4	6	2
2	9	5	6	8	1	3	4	7
7	3	1	5	2	4	9	8	6
8	6	4	3	9	7	2	1	5
4	5	3	8	6	2	7	9	1
9	7	6	4	1	3	5	2	8
1	2	8	9	7	5	6	3	4

289

Shape D

290

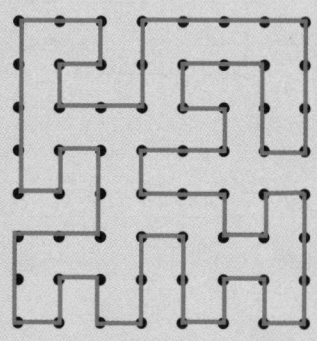

291

292

293

294

3	3	4		6			2	7	3
6	7	1		6	1	1	9	8	7
1	2	9		6	2	0	6	5	1
2	7	3	6	1	1	7	7	3	
	2	6	1	8	2	8	2		
1	8	2	7	6	3	5	4	4	
2	1	6		6	1	9	2	1	9
9	0	5		1	7	2	1	7	3
2	7	2			7	1	6		

295

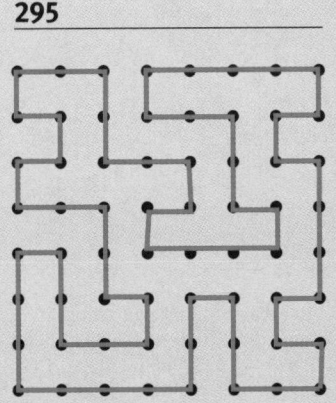

296

T	8	8	K	T
S	D	H	D	C
J	A	K	8	Q
S	H	C	C	S
T	9	K	8	9
D	C	H	S	S
T	K	Q	Q	9
H	S	D	C	H
J	J	J	Q	9
C	H	D	H	D

297

Footballer D

298

Pieces 2 and 6

299

2	4	1	■	6	9	8	■		
8	7	3	■	8	7	9	6		
■	8	5	9	7	■	7	9	8	
7	9	■	6	9	8	■	8	6	
9	6	8	■	5	9	■	7	9	
■	9	3	■	■	7	1	■		
1	2	■	1	2	■	2	4	1	
2	3	■	2	4	1	■	1	3	
4	1	2	■	1	3	5	2	■	
■	4	1	2	3	■	1	3	7	
■	3	1	5	■	8	6	9		

300

| 2 | 0 | 1 | 5 | 4 | 4 | 6 |
| 5 | 5 | 1 | 6 | 5 | 6 | 6 |

| 3 | 0 | 3 | 1 | 1 | 1 | 0 |
| 6 | 2 | 5 | 2 | 5 | 3 | 0 |

| 0 | 2 | 2 | 3 | 0 | 0 | 2 |
| 1 | 4 | 2 | 4 | 4 | 3 | 3 |

| 1 | 5 | 0 | 3 | 2 | 1 | 4 |
| 6 | 5 | 6 | 3 | 6 | 4 | 4 |

301

Betty, surgeon, and Alice, lawyer, are sisters. Frank, surgeon, and Dave, accountant, are brothers. Carol, accountant, and Ed, lawyer are siblings. Marriages are: Betty and Ed; Alice and Dave; and Carol and Frank.

302

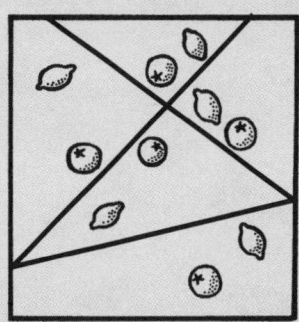

303

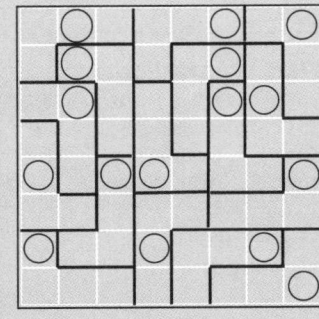

304

Nos. 3, 4 and 9

305

T	9	K	J	8
C	H	C	S	H
T	8	Q	9	Q
D	D	C	S	D
8	8	K	Q	A
C	S	H	S	H
T	K	J	J	J
H	S	H	C	D
Q	9	J	9	K
H	C	T	D	D

306

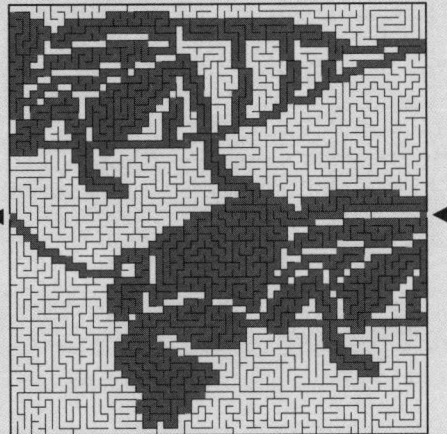

307

B	A	E	C	D
E	C	A	D	B
D	E	C	B	A
C	B	D	A	E
A	D	B	E	C

308

309

ZULU = 83 (A=15, B=10, C=4, D=24, E=7, F=16, G=17, H=21, I=6, J=25, K=20, L=8, M=1, N=5, O=13, P=9, Q=14, R=2, S=22, T=3, U=26, V=19, W=12, X=18, Y=11, Z=23)

310

311

C	D			B	A
A	D	B		C	A
B	C		A	D	
D	A		B		C
		C	D	A	B
	B	A	C		D

312

2	5	2	7	2	3	1	5
6	5	6	4	2	5	6	5
4	1	1	1	3	4	3	1
3	5	4	6	2	7	4	1
2	1	4	2	7	3	3	6
1	5	3	3	7	4	2	4
7	5	7	7	6	6	6	7

313

2 and 5

314

Piece no. 4

315

5 is the innermost number on strap D (clue 4), so that cannot be the strap referred to in clue 5, nor can strap E (clue 3), or strap C (clue 7), while the outermost numbers on both straps A and F must be single-digit numbers (clue 2), so the strap referred to in clue 5 must be strap B. Clue 8 tells us the 17 is not the innermost number, so, from clue 5, the strap B numbers, reading outwards, must be 12, 1 and 17. So, from clue 8, the innermost number of strap E must be 18, and that on strap 8 therefore 8. We have now placed four innermost numbers, which total 43, so, from clue 1, the other two must total 21. From numbers already placed, we know these cannot be 18 and 3, 17 and 4, 16 and 5, 13 and 8, or 12 and 9, and clue 6 rules out both 15 and 6 and 11 and 10, so they must be 14 and 7. So, from clue 4, the 7 must be on strap C, and the 14 on strap A. We now know the single-digit number in the middle of strap A (clue 2) is not 1, 5, 7 or 8, nor, since the 15 is not an innermost number, can it be 6 (clue 6). It clearly cannot be 2 (clue 2). If it were 3 or 4, then, from clue 2, one of the other two numbers referred to would have to be 1, but we have already placed that number elsewhere, so, by elimination, it must be 9. We know the number outside it is not 7 or 8, nor, since we have placed 7 and 8, can it be 1 or 2 (clue 2). We also know that it is not 5, and, since we

have placed the 5, it cannot be 4 (clue 2), so it must be 3 or 6, and so must the outermost number of strap F (clue 2). But we have placed the only even number on strap F (clue 3), so its outermost number must be 3, and the 6 must be on strap A. We know the 15 is not on strap B, so, from clue 6, it must be the middle number on strap F. Clue 6 now reveals the 10 as an outermost number. The middle number next to it is 16 (clue 6), so they Cannot be on strap E, which already has one even number (clue 3), or on C, which has only one two-digit number (clue 7), so they must be on strap D. Since the 2 is not on strap C (clue 7), it must be one of the two even numbers on strap E (clue 3), which leaves the 4 on strap C. Clue 7 also places the 13 on strap C, leaving the 11 on strap E. From clue 3, the 2 must be the outermost number of strap E, and the 13 therefore is the outermost on strap C (clue 7), leaving the 11 and the 4 as the central numbers on their respective straps.

In summary: (Reading outwards)
Strap A: 14, 9, 6.
Strap B: 12, 1, 17.
Strap C: 7, 4, 13.
Strap D: 5, 16, 10.
Strap E: 18, 11, 2.
Strap F: 8, 15, 3.

316

7	6	5	4	4	5	6	
6	2	5		6	2	3		8	9	4
7		7	4	5	0	9	7	5		5
4	3	1	3	6	7	7	7	7	8	6
		4	3	2	1	3	4	5		
7	4	2		5		9		8	5	3
		4	2	2	4	5	4	5		
5	5	4	4	3	1	3	5	6	6	6
6		5	4	4	3	0	9	9		6
5	2	2		5	2	1		4	3	2
		4	3	1	2	3	4	4		

317

Man H is the wanted man.

318

13

319

320

Numbering the positions 1 (left end) to 5 (right end);
Snuffy is not in positions 1 or 5. Snuffy is not in position 2 as that would put Basher on the left end and Wilf would have to be next door to either Clogger or Alf, which he cannot be. Snuffy is not in position 4 as that would put Clogger in 5 but he cannot be next to Snuffy. So Snuffy is in position 3. Clogger is in position 5. Wilf cannot be in 2 or 4 and must be in 1. So Alf is in 4 and Basher in 2. Alf was the cloth-headed thief.

321

322

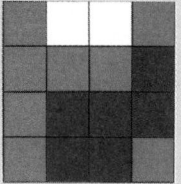

323

SKIP	LEAD	TWO	THREE
REG	PETE	JOAN	DORIS
RITA	PAULINE	JIM	DAVE
RON	PAMELA	JANET	DENNIS
ROSE	PHILIP	JOHN	DEIRDRE

Reg 24 – Rose 21
Rita 17 – Ron 12

324

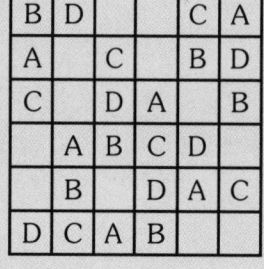

B	D			C	A
A		C		B	D
C		D	A		B
	A	B	C	D	
	B		D	A	C
D	C	A	B		

325

2	7	3	4	1	9	5	8	6
9	5	6	8	7	3	4	2	1
1	4	8	5	2	6	7	9	3
7	8	1	9	5	4	6	3	2
6	2	4	3	8	7	1	5	9
5	3	9	1	6	2	8	7	4
4	1	7	2	9	5	3	6	8
3	9	5	6	4	8	2	1	7
8	6	2	7	3	1	9	4	5

326

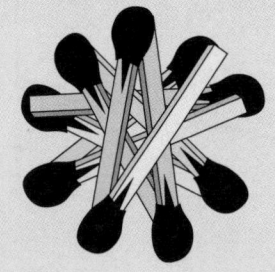

Each square tile has neighbours – tiles that share an edge. The corners have just two neighbours, those along the edge have three and the ones in the middle have four. For each square, check how many of its neighbours are in the same state (empty, red or blue) as the cell itself. If the score is 0 – the cell becomes empty; if it is 1 or 2 – colour it red and if it is 3 or 4 colour it blue.

327

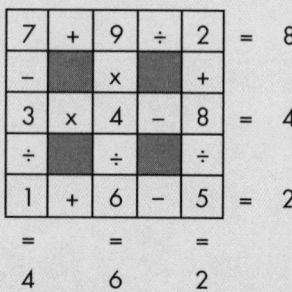

328

GHOST	OF	AT	FEATURE
A	DYSART	HAM HOUSE	PAPERS
B	WINDHAM	FELBRIGG	BOOKS
C	BOLEYN	BLICKLING	HEADLESS
D	VERNEY	CLAYDON	HAND
E	LEGH	LYME PARK	FUNERAL

329

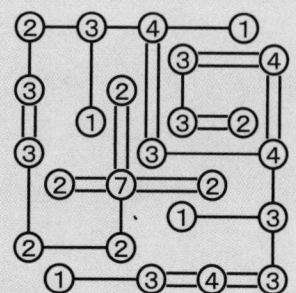

330

7	+	9	÷	2	=	8
−		×		+		
3	×	4	−	8	=	4
÷				÷		
1	+	6	−	5	=	2
=		=		=		
4		6		2		

331

The weights that will go up are 1 and 4 and the weights that will go down are 2, 3 and 5.

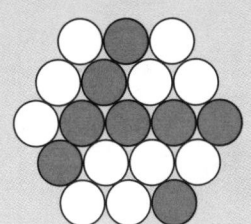

332

333

334

5	5	7	5	6	5	7	5
3	3	3	1	1	2	1	2
3	4	6	2	6	7	3	1
6	1	5	7	1	1	7	7
2	7	7	4	4	2	6	1
5	4	4	2	3	2	4	6
3	6	4	1	2	1	3	6

335

	B	A		C	D
D	A			B	C
	C	D	A		B
A	D	B	C		
B		C	D	A	
C			B	D	A

336

FINISH LINE

337

338

2

339

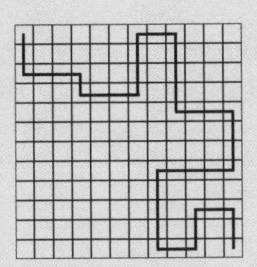

340

Piece b

341

FORENAME	SURNAME	FORENAME	SURNAME
JUAN	FIGN-DIAZ	ISABELLA	DA BOLLA
MANUEL	GHIAZ	MARIA	NIDJOTA
PANCHO	HEROLE	JUANITA	MEEYA
SANCHO	MUCHO	ROSA	SUTAZ

342

C		D		B	A
C	A	D	B		C	A
B	C		A	D	
D	A		B		C
		C	D	A	B
	B	A	C		D

343

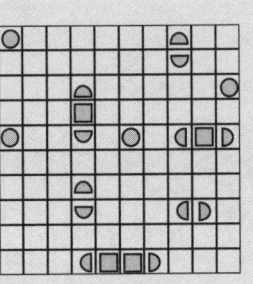

344

345

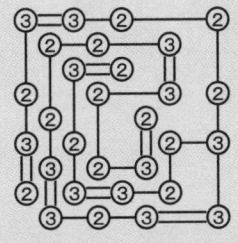

346

Rabbit D

347

5	+	7	÷	6	=	2
+		−		÷		
8	−	4	x	2	=	8
−		x		+		
9	÷	3	−	1	=	2
=		=		=		
4		9		4		

348

PANELLIST	GUEST	OCCUPATION	OCCUPATION
GERTA	KEN	FLEDGER'S	CRINGE
MILES	CONNIE	GRUTTLER'S	HOCKER
NOAH	ANN	CRIMPER'S	SLANT
WANDA	ENA	TADDLER'S	POSSE

349

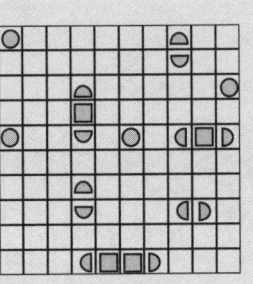

350

A = 2
B = 3
C = 1

351

352

TURNIPS	GRAPES	POTATOES	BANANAS
DATES	YAMS	FIGS	RADISHES
W'CRESS	APPLES	MARROWS	KUMQUATS
LYCHEES	PEAS	CHERRIES	ONIONS

353

Flag, fork, candle

354

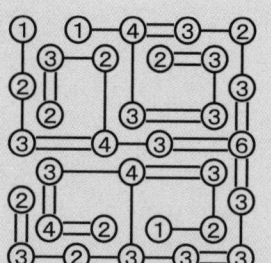

355

356

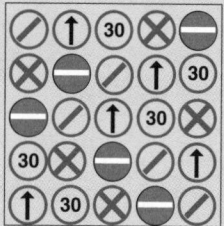

357

A1=B5, A2=F1, C1=E5,
D5=E2, F2=F5

358

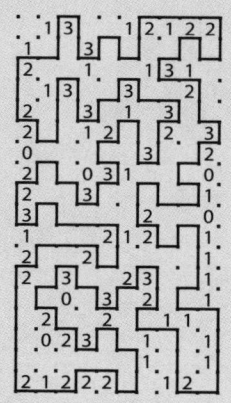

359

Letter E

360

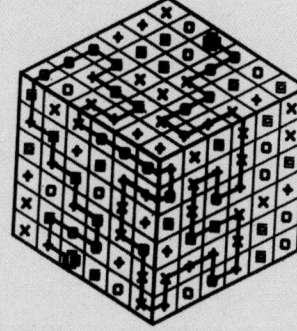

361

2 and 4

362

Shop	Customer	Video
Just Flicks	C Nitt	Gosh!
More Movies	B Dee-High	Whew!
Nite Rates	A Blinkon	Wow!
Rent 'n' Rave	D Cryer	Hey!

363

E inner is given as 4, so C inner, which must be an even number (clue 4) cannot be 4 or 8. If it were 2 and D inner 1, from clue 2, B outer and H inner would both be 3 and, from clue 3, the inner 6 could only be in segment G. C outer would therefore also be 6 as would F middle (clue 4). In that case F outer would have to be 12, which is impossible. So C inner must be 6 and D inner 3 (clue 4). So, from clue 2, B outer must be 7, H middle 8 and H inner 7, and since those two H numbers add up to 15, H outer must be 0. With the inner 6 being in C, the outer 6 must be in G (clue 3) and B inner must therefore be 5

(clue 2). To complete the B quota, B middle must be 3. We know D inner is 3, and since, from clue 4, D outer is double D middle, those numbers must be 8 and 4 respectively. F outer must be four times G middle (clue 4) and since the outer circle already has an 8, F outer must be 4, G middle 1 and F middle, from the same clue, 2. To complete their quotas, F inner must be 9 and G inner 8. C outer must be 2 (clue 4) and C middle 7. All inner numbers have now been inserted except in A, which is an odd number (clue 2), so it must be 1. To make up A's quota, the remaining odd numbers must be 5 and 9 and from clue 1, the 9 must be A outer and 5 A middle. Therefore E outer must also be 5 (clue 4) and E middle 6.

In summary:
Numbers given as outer, middle, inner.
A, 9, 5, 1.
B, 7, 3, 5.
C, 2, 7, 6.
D, 8, 4, 3.
E, 5, 6, 4.
F, 4, 2, 9.
G, 6, 1, 8.
H, 0, 8, 7.

364

C		B		A	D
D			C	B	A
	B	A	D		C
A	C		B	D	
	A	D		C	B
B	D	C	A		

365

Print 3

366

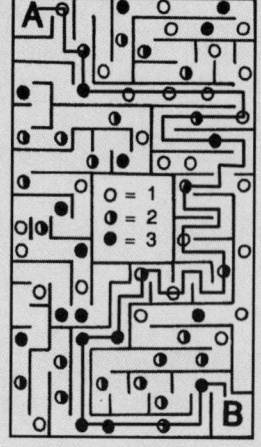

367

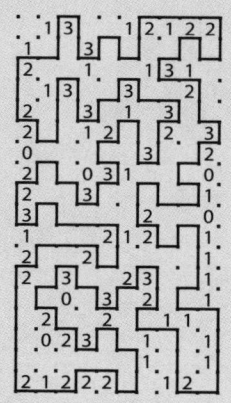

368

369

	Table 1	Table 2	Table 3	Table 4
N	Harry	Babs	Tessa (dummy)	Fred
E	Susie (dummy)	Kate	Connie	Lola
S	Jane	Roger (dummy)	Dot	Gordon
W	Peter	Alan	Michael	Eddie (dummy)
Contract	2 Diamonds	4 Spades	1 Heart	3 Clubs

370

	Eagle	Birdie	Par	Bogey	Double Bogey	FINAL SCORE
Darma	2	5	1	6	4	77
Jackliss	4	2	8	3	1	67
Clayer	1	4	6	2	5	78

371

A	E	D	B	C
B	D	C	E	A
D	C	E	A	B
E	A	B	C	D
C	B	A	D	E

372

373

4	+	6	−	1	=	9
÷		+		×		
2	×	8	−	9	=	7
+		÷		÷		
5	+	7	÷	3	=	4
=		=		=		
7		2		3		

374

0	4	1	5	0	0	0	1
5	5	1	2	5	6	0	1
5	2	0	4	3	3	0	4
6	4	2	4	3	3	4	4
1	4	2	0	1	3	1	5
1	6	2	3	6	6	6	5
1	1	2	0	1	2	2	3
4	3	5	6	6	5	6	3

375

C	D	E	A	B
E	A	B	D	C
B	C	A	E	D
A	B	D	C	E
D	E	C	B	A

376

NAME	SANDWICH	CRISPS	FRUIT
FELICITY	EGG	PRAWN	PEACH
FELIX	HAM	SALTED	ORANGE
FIONA	CHICKEN	CHEESE	BANANA
FREDDIE	CHEESE	S & V	APPLE

377

A – The Old Mill – 1964
B – St Aidan's Church – 1981
C – Crane Bay – 1976
D – Lower Wood – 1992
E – Fiddler's Brook – 1988

378

1 and 7
2 and 4
3 and 6
5 and 8

379

A – H   D – G
B – F   E – J
C – I

380

Quarter-Finals	Semi-Finals	Final	Winner
Chelsea v Norwich	Chelsea		
		Arsenal	
Spurs v Arsenal	Arsenal		
			EVERTON
Everton v Watford	Everton		
		Everton	
Liverpool v Southampton	Liverpool		

381

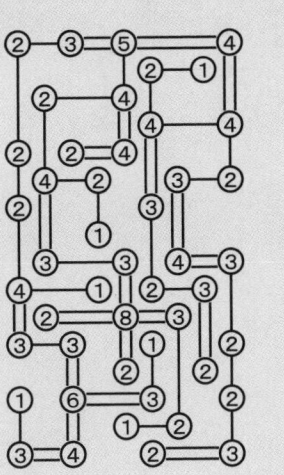

382

J	Q	J	T	9
C	S	H	S	S
Q	8	J	T	9
C	C	D	D	D
K	9	Q	Q	9
H	H	D	H	C
T	K	8	A	K
C	S	D	H	C
T	8	J	8	K
H	H	S	S	D

383

6	0	5	1	1	4	1
6	2	5	1	3	6	4
1	2	3	1	3	3	4
5	3	5	2	6	4	5
2	2	4	5	0	0	1
2	4	4	6	1	5	6
0	0	2	0	2	0	3
3	6	5	4	6	0	3

384

385

Weights 3 and 4 will rise, and weights 1, 2 and 5 will fall.

386

Rocking-horse D

387

Shape D

388

Pattern	Flyer	Advert	Basket
Stars	C Vyewes	Tea	Straw
Spots	D Hytes	Chocolate	Wood
Stripes	E Bargum	Coffee	Fibreglass
Tartan	F Tathort	Cars	Plastic
Brickwork	G. Nears	Gas	Burlap

389

9	8	7	5	6	1	3	2	4
1	2	4	3	7	8	9	5	6
5	3	6	9	2	4	7	1	8
8	9	5	7	1	2	4	6	3
4	7	1	6	3	9	5	8	2
2	6	3	8	4	5	1	7	9
3	5	9	1	8	6	2	4	7
6	1	2	4	9	7	8	3	5
7	4	8	2	5	3	6	9	1

390

0	0	3	6	4	2	3
3	4	4	4	4	5	2
0	5	5	0	5	5	6
4	3	3	6	6	6	2
4	5	3	0	5	1	3
6	2	2	0	1	1	1
1	5	2	0	2	4	1
1	3	6	6	2	1	0

391

9	+	7	−	8	= 8
−		+		x	
6	−	2	x	1	= 4
+		÷		÷	
5	−	3	x	4	= 8
= 8		= 3		= 2	

392

1,7,3,4,2,0,5,8,9,6

393

3 and 7

394

A – G
B – E
C – D
F – H

395

From left to right:
King of Spades – Queen of Spades – King of Clubs – King of Hearts.

396

397

398

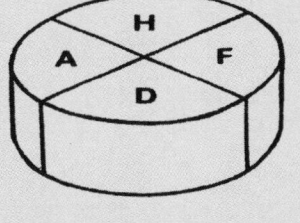

399

SEAT	FORENAME	SURNAME	BUSINESS
1	Ella	Vatripp	Tourist
2	Ron	Waylite	Director
3	Adelia	Baddand	Croupier
4	Mahatma	Ghote	Magician
5	Stewart	Hess	Male Model
6	Lady	Smayde	Author

400

14 red, 4 yellow, 2 green, 5 blue, 3 pink.

401

There are 54 missing bricks.

402

7	3	5	8	6	9	2	1	4
9	8	1	7	2	4	6	3	5
2	6	4	1	3	5	8	9	7
8	5	7	9	4	1	3	2	6
3	4	2	6	8	7	9	5	1
1	9	6	3	5	2	7	4	8
6	2	3	4	1	8	5	7	9
4	7	8	5	9	3	1	6	2
5	1	9	2	7	6	4	8	3

403

404

A	E	B	D	C
C	B	D	E	A
D	A	E	C	B
E	C	A	B	D
B	D	C	A	E

405

There are four knots.

406

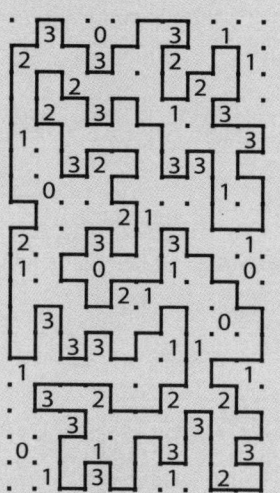

407

Weights A and C will rise, and weights E, B and D will fall.

408

From the top: blue, red, yellow, lavender, green, orange.

409

If you were on the near side of the Moon – the Earth would always be up and never set. If you were on the far side of the Moon – the Earth would never rise and you would not directly know it existed. It just so happens that, as the Moon takes about 29 days to orbit the Earth, so, too it takes the same time to spin once on its axis. So it presents the same side to the Earth all the time.

410

From the left: Rachel, blonde, programmer; Teresa, brunette, saleslady; Mavis, redhead, secretary.

411

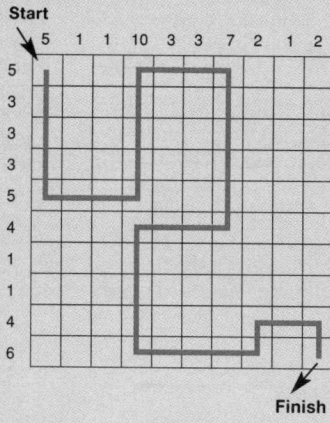

412

Card 1

413

Pictures 6 and 8.

414

	Eagle	Birdie	Par	Bogey	Double Bogey	FINAL SCORE
Darma	3	5	7	2	1	65
Jackliss	1	4	8	3	2	73
Clayer	2	7	5	1	3	68

415

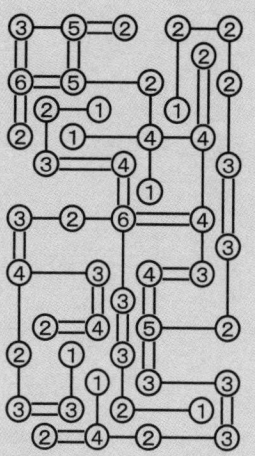

416

Diagram 1–16 triangles
Diagram 2–10 triangles
Diagram 3–18 triangles
Diagram 4–12 triangles
Ostrich 3 is holding the diagram with the most triangles.

417

418

1 Madame Poll's Parrots
2 Agilles Acrobats
3 Jim the Juggler
4 Flying Fortresses
5 Clever Clowns
6 Fred the Fire-eater
7 Crazy Carvellos
8 Senor Pedro's Poodles

419

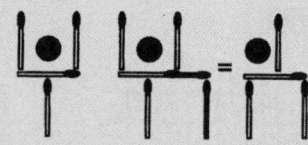

420

They match up as follows:
A6, B4, C5, D1, E2, F8, G3, H7.

421

Make a circular cut around the inside of the pie, then cut into quarters.

422

2	6	1	4	4	3	0	3
2	3	5	5	6	6	4	2
0	1	0	2	1	1	1	4
5	3	0	0	5	3	0	5
0	6	1	2	1	6	4	1
4	3	3	4	0	5	5	6
2	4	6	3	2	2	6	5

423

Blocks 1 and 3.

424

425

Arrange to have your body flown eastwards across the International Date Line (where it is still the day before!) and buried immediately.

426

Path B

427

8	2	5	3	7	1	9	6	4
9	4	3	6	2	5	8	7	1
1	6	7	8	9	4	2	5	3
3	5	9	2	8	7	1	4	6
6	1	2	4	5	3	7	8	9
4	7	8	1	6	9	5	3	2
5	8	4	9	1	6	3	2	7
7	9	6	5	3	2	4	1	8
2	3	1	7	4	8	6	9	5

428

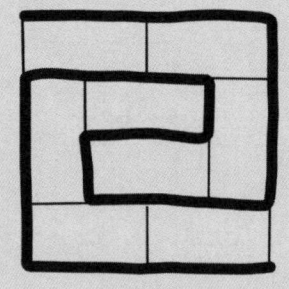

429

Amy – orange, Bob – yellow, Chloe – blue, Fiona – violet, Jack – pink, Martin – red, Paul – brown, Sharon – green.

430

1	0	7	9	8	9		2	1	2	8	0	6
3		1		3	0	9	4	7		1		6
4	5	3	5	2	7		5	8	1	9	4	1
8		9		6	1	5	1	3		2		6
7	6	5	7		8	7	4		9	0	8	3
1	0	4	3	9		2		2	7	1	9	0
	1		3	0	4		4	2	1		2	
5	7	1	4	7		2		6	7	3	2	9
7	5	7	6		8	1	5		9	4	4	7
2		2		1	4	7	5	6		1		5
2	1	3	0	7	1		3	1	6	2	9	3
1		5		4	6	0	2	3		6		2
5	5	1	1	0	8		6	7	6	8	6	9

431

From the top: blue, orange, yellow, lavender, green.

432

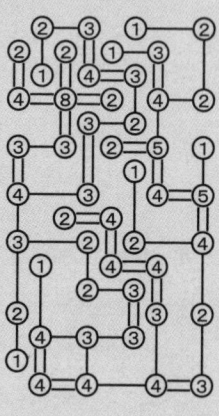

433

Kettledrum 7

434

2	0	2	1	1	0	1
6	6	3	3	2	2	0
4	3	5	4	2	6	6
0	0	0	4	4	6	3
1	6	5	4	5	5	1
6	0	3	5	2	5	4
0	4	3	5	5	1	2
3	4	1	3	2	1	6

435

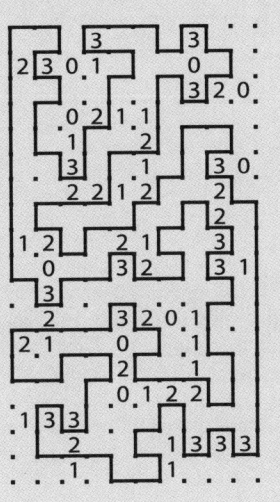

436

7	6	8	3	4	1	2	9	5
9	3	2	8	6	5	7	4	1
5	1	4	9	2	7	6	8	3
2	8	9	1	5	3	4	7	6
3	5	7	4	9	6	1	2	8
1	4	6	7	8	2	5	3	9
6	7	5	2	3	9	8	1	4
8	2	3	6	1	4	9	5	7
4	9	1	5	7	8	3	6	2

437

	B	C	A	D	
A	D			C	B
	C	A	B		D
B		D		A	C
C		B	D		A
D	A		C	B	

438

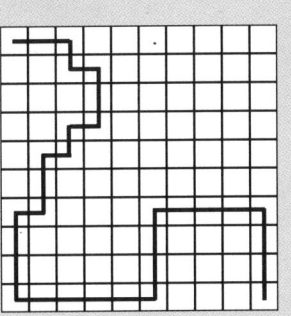

439

Alien 4

440

The order is:
9, 1, 11, 5, 14, 7, 10, 2, 12, 3, 13, 8, 4, 6.

441

442

2	6	0	6	0	5	3
3	3	3	5	5	6	5
6	2	0	4	1	6	6
3	2	1	4	4	3	4
5	2	4	1	1	1	6
2	3	0	2	3	2	4
5	4	1	0	0	1	6
5	0	1	0	4	5	2

443

5	0	4	1	1	9		8	2	4	3	3	2
1		0		7	1	0	5	0		4		1
1	8	3	5	4	7		9	0	1	5	7	0
4		5		6	1	1	4	0		6		9
3	5	8	4		7	5	7		4	7	3	8
3	1	2	5	5		5		1	2	8	0	7
	7		6	6	2		3	7	7		4	
8	2	7	1	0		4		9	1	6	0	6
5	6	6	6		2	8	1		6	6	5	6
6		6		7	4	8	2	8		5		7
7	4	5	6	4	8	9		3	1	7	5	0	6
7		6		6	3	4	2	2		4		8
2	1	5	0	3	2		1	2	3	4	5	6

444

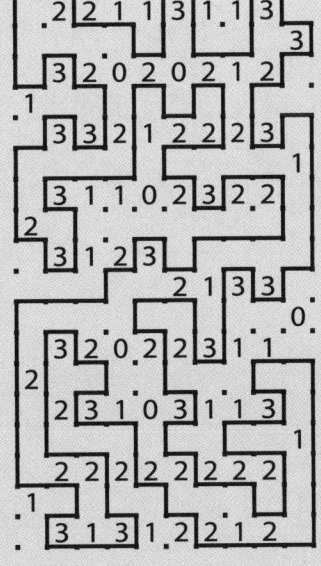

445

	B		D	C	A
C	A	B		D	
A		D	B		C
B		C	A		D
	D	A	C	B	
D	C			A	B

446

9	8	5	3	1	4	2	6	7
6	3	1	7	2	5	9	4	8
7	4	2	8	9	6	1	5	3
8	7	3	9	5	2	6	1	4
4	2	9	1	6	3	8	7	5
5	1	6	4	8	7	3	9	2
2	5	4	6	3	9	7	8	1
1	9	7	2	4	8	5	3	6
3	6	8	5	7	1	4	2	9

447

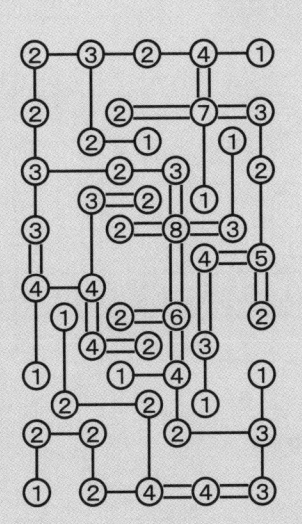

448

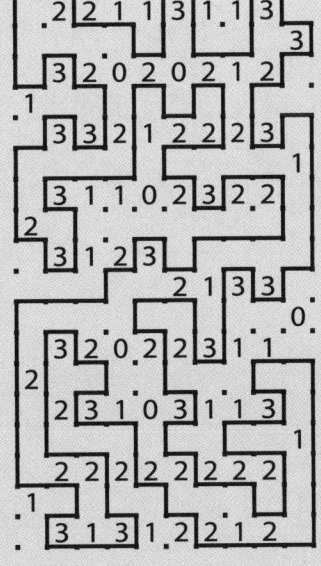

449

From the top: A, C, E, B, D, F

450

451

452

Number 3

453

6	4	3	9	5	7	2	8	1
8	5	2	4	3	1	6	9	7
9	1	7	8	6	2	5	3	4
2	8	9	1	7	3	4	5	6
5	3	1	2	4	6	9	7	8
4	7	6	5	9	8	3	1	2
7	9	5	6	8	4	1	2	3
3	2	4	7	1	9	8	6	5
1	6	8	3	2	5	7	4	9

454

Architect: Mark Jones; Barber: Neil Franklin; Critic: Luke Harkness; Dentist: Otto Ives; Economist: Karl Gainor.

455

456

457

N	F	Y	K	C
Q	J	W	H	T
G	U	R	B	M
A	L	D	V	O
X	P	I	S	E

458

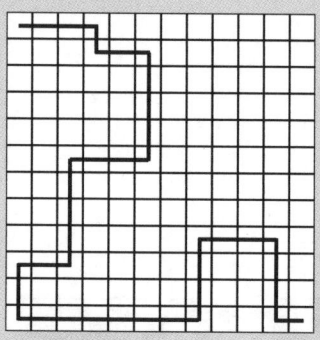

459

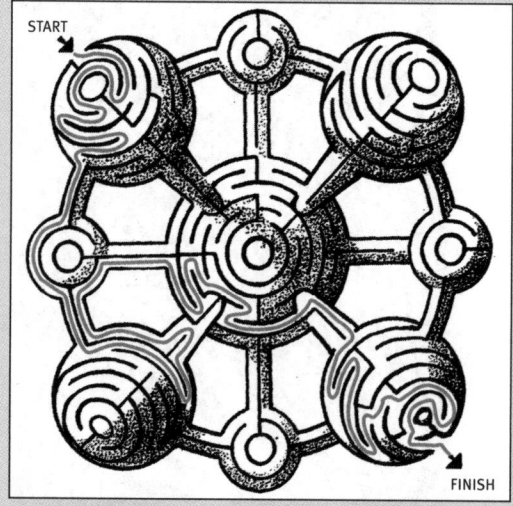

START

FINISH

460

A Hebe   B Cary
C Alan   D Fred
E Bess   F Enid
G Dave   H Gina

461

462

7	0	3	8	9	1		8	8	4	2	7	1
7		4		2	9	0	1	7		1		0
6	2	4	8	9	6		5	4	3	2	1	0
9		0		3	5	7	0	9		2		2
7	4	7	5		8	3	7		7	2	8	0
6	9	1	7	7		6		9	1	3	7	0
	8		6	2	3		5	4	7		1	
4	3	5	8	1		4		1	0	6	7	9
6	2	1	9		2	1	3		5	3	4	2
3		5		4	0	2	3	3		5		1
3	1	2	1	1	1		4	5	3	5	3	2	4
2		5		7	8	9	0	5		4		0
2	4	3	4	4	4		1	2	1	3	1	4

463

3	6	8	4	4	0	4
6	2	5	9	0	3	3
8	5	6	2	7	5	1
4	9	2	4	8	4	3
4	0	7	8	0	2	1
0	3	5	4	2	4	3
4	3	1	3	1	3	2

464

PLOT	FAMILY	FROM	SIZE
WEST	LARKITTS	FRUMLEY	4
NORTH	SPENCERS	CHEAPHILL	3
EAST	GROVES	WELMSIDE	6
SOUTH	HUGGINS	TYNEHAM	5

465

466

Q	T	T	Q	9
C	H	S	S	H
K	9	T	J	J
C	C	T	S	C
K	8	J	9	J
D	S	H	D	D
9	Q	8	K	Q
S	H	H	S	D
K	A	8	T	8
H	H	C	D	D

467

468

FORENAME	SURNAME	SUBJECT	UNIVERSITY
ANNA	JONES	MATHS	YALE
BARBARA	BROWN	PHYSICS	HARVARD
CLARE	TAYLOR	CHEMISTRY	MIT
DIANA	MOORE	BIOLOGY	PRINCETON

469

6	4	9	2	5	1	7	8	3
5	1	8	4	7	3	9	6	2
3	7	2	9	8	6	1	4	5
8	2	4	6	1	7	3	5	9
7	6	3	5	4	9	2	1	8
1	9	5	3	2	8	6	7	4
2	5	6	1	3	4	8	9	7
9	3	7	8	6	5	4	2	1
4	8	1	7	9	2	5	3	6

470

1 Crazy Carvellos
2 Agilles Acrobats
3 Clever Clowns
4 Fred the Fire-eater
5 Jim the Juggler
6 Senor Pedro's Poodles
7 Flying Fortresses
8 Madame Poll's Parrots

471

3	1	9	6	7	5	8	4	2
5	8	2	3	9	4	6	7	1
6	7	4	2	1	8	9	3	5
4	6	7	5	2	9	1	8	3
1	2	3	7	8	6	4	5	9
8	9	5	4	3	1	2	6	7
9	3	1	8	4	7	5	2	6
2	4	6	1	5	3	7	9	8
7	5	8	9	6	2	3	1	4

472

3	6	10	1	8	4	9	2	7	5
I	C	G	E	B	J	A	D	H	F

473

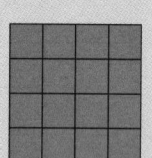

474

Each square tile has neighbours – tiles that share an edge. The corners have just two neighbours, those along the edge have three and the ones in the middle have four. For each square, check how many of it and its neighbours are not white. If the score is 0 or 1 – colour it red; if it is 2 or 3 – colour it black and if it is 4 or 5 leave it empty.

475

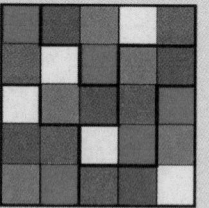

476

477

9018

478

From the top: B, E, D, C, F, A

479

Piece 8

480

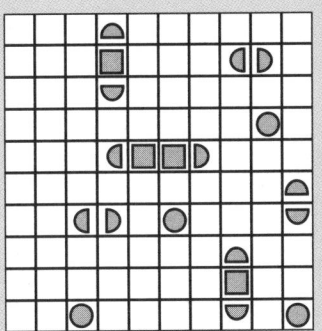

481

7	3	5	9	2	1	4	8	6
6	1	4	5	7	8	2	9	3
9	8	2	6	4	3	5	7	1
4	9	6	1	5	2	8	3	7
3	5	1	7	8	6	9	4	2
8	2	7	3	9	4	6	1	5
2	6	9	8	1	7	3	5	4
5	7	3	4	6	9	1	2	8
1	4	8	2	3	5	7	6	9

482

7	5	9	6	5	7		1	6	2	5	6	4
1		5		2	9	1	1	0		8		7
5	3	8	4	5	8		8	4	3	3	5	8
2		5		4	2	4	0	7		2		4
2	6	5	6		8	3	2		1	1	3	3
7	0	5	9	6		0		3	0	8	7	9
	4		2	5	6		7	7	7		2	
4	1	2	9	6		1		8	0	9	0	3
1	7	6	2		5	6	2		3	6	7	5
2		3		8	9	1	3	4		7		7
2	1	6	4	3	2		3	8	4	8	5	8
4		4		9	7	1	2	6		6		7
1	1	6	2	8	5		6	4	5	4	4	4

483

She's blown 79 bubbles.

484

485

6	2	9	3	1	3		4	2	8	4	9	6
0		9		1	3	1	3	1		1		5
1	7	0	1	5	4		5	4	3	7	1	6
5		1		2	0	4	1	5		9		6
3	5	7	6		3	0	9		4	3	3	6
7	0	3	9	5		5		9	0	4	1	7
	2		1	8	0		7	4	7		0	
8	2	7	0	1		6		1	5	2	0	9
5	1	7	4		2	1	5		6	7	1	3
4		0		7	1	8	7	8		9		1
3	5	1	0	5	7		3	1	3	1	0	8
5		9		6	7	8	9	0		5		6
2	7	8	1	4	5		1	5	1	6	1	7

486

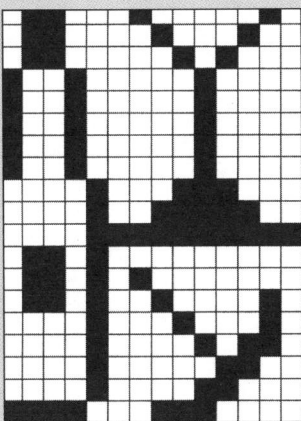

487

	C		D	A	B
B	D	C			A
A		B		D	C
D		A	C	B	
C	B		A		D
	A	D	B	C	

488

72694

489

6	5	7	1	2	3	4	9	8
1	9	4	5	6	8	3	7	2
2	3	8	7	9	4	5	1	6
5	8	1	6	3	2	7	4	9
9	4	2	8	7	5	1	6	3
3	7	6	4	1	9	8	2	5
4	2	9	3	8	7	6	5	1
8	1	5	9	4	6	2	3	7
7	6	3	2	5	1	9	8	4

490

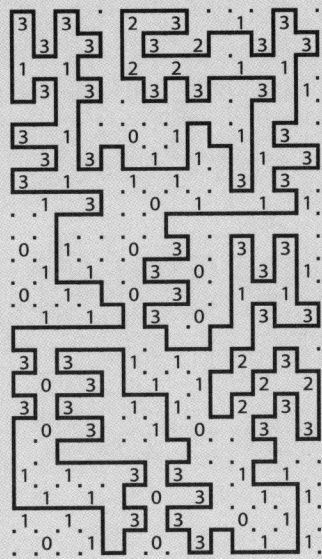

491

From the top: green, yellow, red, blue, orange, lavender.

492

493

1 – 9, 2 – 4, 3 – 10, 5 – 8, 6 – 7

494

Path 3

495

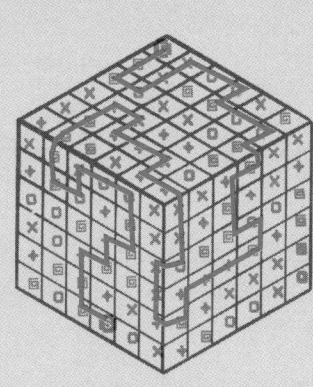

496

SHE	SURNAME	HE	SURNAME
ANN	BRAKES	GARY	STAMPS
BELLA	NOBLE	HORACE	LYNES
CHER	DABALL	ED	COPES
DAWN	CHOVIES	FRANK	BALDY

497

Horse/Robin
Unicorn/Simon
Peacock/Biddie
Zebra/Sheila
Dragon/Tom
Emu/Rose
Camel/Tess
Elephant/Brian

498

499

3D	8C	7D
10S	6H	2S
5D	4C	9D

500

Simply move the 1 in the right-hand column to the left of any number in the left-hand column. e.g, turn the 0 into 10! Then both columns will total 27.

501

A Elmer & Harvey
B Alvin & Frank
C Conrad & Dexter
D Brad & Gary

502

41967

503

B	A	C		D	
	A	C		D	B
D			B	C	A
B	C	D	A		
A	D			B	C
C		B	D	A	

504

6 JK 10 A 7 Q 4 9 K 2 J 8 JK 5 3

505

1 D	5 I	9 G	13 C
2 O	6 B	10 K	14 E
3 F	7 P	11 H	15 N
4 L	8 A	12 J	16 M

506

507

Winner to 6th, the order is: escapologist, magician, comedian, impressionist, dancer, baritone.

508

1 Empty.
2 Empty.
3 Informer.
4 Gunman.
5 Gunman.

509

Dan – blue, Dick – violet, Gwen – yellow, Jenny – pink, John – orange, Lisa – brown, Moira – red, Tom – green

510

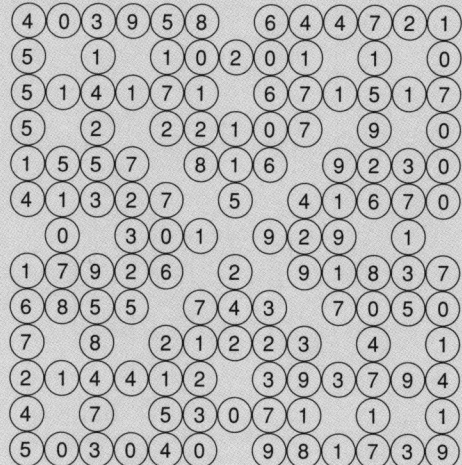

4	0	3	9	5	8		6	4	4	7	2	1
5		1		1	0	2	0	1		1		0
5	1	4	1	7		6	7	1	5	1	7	
5		2		2	2	1	0	7		9		0
1	5	5	7		8	1	6		5	9	2	3
4	1	3	2	7		5		4	1	6	7	0
	0		3	0	1		9	2	9		1	
1	7	9	2	6		2		9	1	8	3	7
6	8	5	5		7	4		3	7	0	5	0
7		8		2	1	2	3		4		3	1
2	1	4	1	2		3	9	3	7	9	4	
4		7		5	3	0	7	0	1		1	1
5	0	3	0	4	0		9	8	1	7	3	9

511

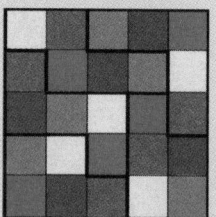

512

513

514

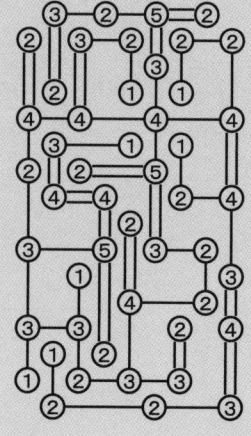

515

B	C		A	D	
	A	B		D	C
C	D		A		B
D	C	A	B		
		B		D	C	A
A		D	C	B	

516

YAMS	FIGS	TURNIPS	DATES
LYCHEE	MARROWS	CHERRIES	RADISH
POTATOES	BANANAS	PEAS	GRAPES
APPLES	W'CRESS	KUMQUAT	ONIONS

517

9	1	8	3	1	7		6	2	5	7	7	3
9		1		9	1	5	3	2		7		0
5	3	7	2	1	9		4	2	0	3	9	5
0		5		8	0	8	1	7		3		3
3	5	1	4		2	3	4		4	5	3	0
3	0	2	1	3		4		1	0	5	7	6
	1		4	8	9		6	5	0		7	
2	3	3	2	7		7		2	0	2	3	1
5	9	9	5		5	1	6		6	1	3	0
2		5		7	0	3	1	8		0		1
4	1	4	3	4	2		5	1	5	2	5	3
2		4		7	8	4	7	0		1		1
6	3	6	6	6	9		7	4	7	1	7	6

518

519

520

Since the pink elephant is on the top row (clue 1), the dragon, being immediately to the right of the blue creature must be in quarter 4. Therefore, from clue 4, the blue creature must be in quarter 3. We know the lion is not pink, nor, since it represents the Muddelkopf alliance (clue 3), can it be black, which is the colour of the creature inherited from the von Plonka arms (clue 2). Nor is it orange (clue 3), so, by elimination, it must be blue, and it is therefore in quarter 3. Now, from clue 1, the pink elephant cannot be in quarter 1, and must be in quarter 2, and the dragon in quarter 4 must be from the Klotzky arms (clue 1). Now, by elimination, the eagle must be in quarter 1. We have matched three quarters with a colour or a family, so the black creature of the von Plonkas must be the eagle in quarter 1, and, by elimination, the pink elephant must be inherited from the Nitwitz family, and the dragon in quarter 4 must be orange.

In summary:
1, eagle, black, von Plonka.
2, elephant, pink, Nitwitz.
3, lion, blue, Muddelkopf.
4, dragon, orange, Klotzky.

521

	Eagle	Birdie	Par	Bogey	Double Bogey	FINAL SCORE
PARNELL DARMA	1	5	7	3	2	72
NICK JACKLISS	3	2	8	1	4	73
BARRY CLAYER	2	6	5	4	1	68

522

Shadow C

523

2	1			3	4	
2	5	3	1		5	1	2	4
1	3		2	1	4		5	1
4	1	5	3	2		2	1	3
4	1		5	4	1	3	
	2	1		5	3	
2	4	3	1		5	3	
2	1	3		4	2	5	1	3
1	3		5	3	1		4	2
5	4	3	2		4	3	2	1
	5	2			1	5	

524

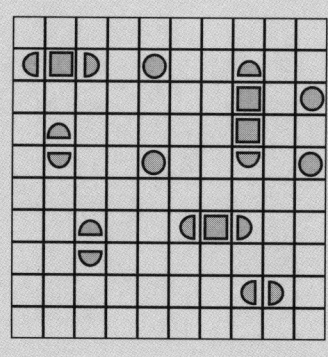

525

526

Brian Holmes,
Novice Newsgroups, $600.
Dougal Dalgliesh,
Advanced Surfing, $550.
Florence Wexford,
Speedy Searching, $400.
Zebedee Brown,
Beginners Browsing, $350.

527

K 7 10 A 8 3 9 Q 4 J 6 Jo 2 Jo 5

528

0	5	6	3	2	5	4
0	5	6	2	2	1	5
2	0	0	6	5	2	1
1	5	5	3	3	2	3
5	1	4	2	3	2	6
4	0	4	3	4	4	4
0	6	1	3	0	1	6
6	6	1	1	3	4	0

529

C		D	B		A
	B	C	A	D	
A			C	B	D
B	A			D	C
D		C	B		A
	D	A		C	B

530

An elephant

531

Sam is 42.

532

Since sculpture B is *Dichotomy* (clue 1), from clue 4, *Revenge* must be sculpture C, so, from that clue, sculpture D must have been completed in Spring. Also, from clue 4, *Revenge* must have been produced in either 1992 or 1994. But *Dichotomy* was not sculpted in a leap year (clue 1), so, from clue 4, it must have been completed in 1990, and *Revenge* in 1992. We have named sculptures B and C, and we know sculpture D was produced in Spring, so, from clue 2, *Enchantment*, completed in Fall, must be sculpture A, and, by elimination, sculpture D is *Sorrow*. This was not Ivor's 1994 work (clue 3), so it must have been produced in 1996, leaving *Enchantment* as the 1994 work. Finally, from clue 5, *Revenge* was not completed in Summer, so it must have been the Winter sculpture, leaving Summer 1990 as the time when *Dichotomy* was completed.

In summary:
A, *Enchantment*, Fall, 1994.
B, *Dichotomy*, Summer, 1990.
C, *Revenge*, Winter, 1992.
D, *Sorrow*, Spring, 1996.

533

Balloon C

534

29179

535

3	x	8	÷	6	= 4
x		−		+	
2	x	7	−	9	= 5
−		+		÷	
1	+	4	÷	5	= 1
=		=		=	
5		5		3	

536

1	3	4	2
5	6		0
1		1	1
5	6	5	6

537

Not quite – one party should have received 72 and the other 864!

538

Line 2

539

540

The red line must be either line 3 or line 4 (clue 3), so Riverhead must be on either line 1 or line 2 (clue 3). But line 2 does not have an eastern terminus, so, from clue 3, Riverhead must be station E on line 1, and the red line is therefore line 3. Therefore the diagonal line running between Gradwell and The Unicorn (clue 1), must be line 3. Since the blue line intersects at an angle of 90 degrees the one with a western terminus at Molton Park (clue 2), which, we know by elimination, must be either station A or station H, it must be line 2 or line 3, but we know that line 3 is red, so the blue line must be line 2, and Molton Park must be station H on line 4. From clue 4, Potterfield cannot be either station A or station B, and we know it is not any of stations C, G, E or H, so it must be either station D or station F, and Lampwick is therefore either station B or station D. But Wallgate must be either station B or station F (clue 1), so Lampwick, whose name is the same length, cannot be station B (clue 6), and must be station D, and therefore Potterfield must be station F, and Wallgate station B. Now, from clue 1, Gradwell must be station C and The Unicorn is therefore station G. So, by elimination, station A must be Castlebridge. So line 1 is not the green one (clue 5), and must be the yellow one, leaving line 4 as the green line.

In summary:
Line 1, yellow, Castlebridge (A) to Riverhead (E).
Line 2, blue, Wallgate (B) to Potterfield (F).
Line 3, red, Gradwell (C) to The Unicorn (G).
Line 4, green, Molton Park (H) to Lampwick (D).

541   **542**

06243   Cat 5

543

Seven of these @ 7 pennies each makes 49 pennies and 6 of those @ 8 pennies each makes 48 pennies for a total of 97 pennies.

544

Just write out this pattern of 49s and add the columns!
```
      49
    4949
  494949
    4949
      49
  603729
```

545

4	+	7	−	3	= 8
×		+		+	
6	×	1	+	1	= 7
÷		÷		+	
3	−	2	×	5	= 5

= 8   = 4   = 9

546

He's met a fire-breathing dragon!

547

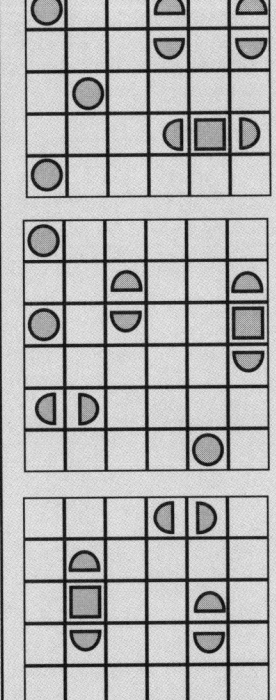

548

The actor sitting at D could not have been Lime (clue 1), Pitt (clue 2), Lynes (clue 4), or Green (clue 5), so must have been Flood. The one at B could not have been Lime (clue 1), Pitt (clue 2) or Green (clue 5), so must have been Lynes. Therefore the one who wanted to play Bottom must have been at C and the one who was cast as Quince at F (clue 4). So, from clue 5, Green's position was not at F and must have been either C or E. From clue 3, the man cast as Oberon was not at F, so he must have been at D (clue 5), with Green therefore at C. Now, from clue 5, the actor cast as Bottom must have sat at B, while the place of the man chosen to be Demetrius must have been C (clue 3). By elimination, the one selected for the role of Lysander must have been at E and Pitt's place must accordingly have been F (clue 2). By elimination, Lime must have sat at E. The would-be Lysander was opposite Pitt (clue 2), so must have been Lynes and the would-be Oberon must have been Lime (clue 3). From clue 4, Green at C must have hankered after the part of Bottom. Finally Flood must have yearned to be Quince (clue 5) and, by elimination, Pitt must have wanted the role of Demetrius.

In summary:
(hoped for parts are in brackets)
B, Lynes, Bottom, (Lysander)
C, Green, Demetrius, (Bottom)
D, Flood, Oberon, (Quince)
E, Lime, Lysander, (Oberon)
F, Pitt, Quince (Demetrius)

549

3	4	2	7	9	1	5	6	8
7	5	9	6	8	2	3	1	4
6	1	8	3	4	5	2	9	7
4	6	1	2	5	3	8	7	9
9	7	5	8	6	4	1	3	2
8	2	3	1	7	9	6	4	5
2	9	7	5	3	6	4	8	1
5	8	6	4	1	7	9	2	3
1	3	4	9	2	8	7	5	6

550

Mark 5

551

552

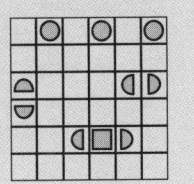
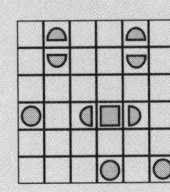

553

Print 5

554

From clue 1, the 3 cannot be in square 3, so, from clue 4, the Roman VI must be in either square 4 or square 5, but clue 6 rules out square 5, so the VI must be in square 4, and the 3 in square 1 (clue 4). Since the B cannot be in square 2 (clue 1), clue 3 now places the III in square 6, and the B in square 3. The Roman numeral in square 1 cannot be I (clue 1), nor can it be II (clue 2). The V shares a square with the 6 (clue 5), and we have placed the III and the VI, so square 1 must contain the IV, and therefore also the F (clue 5). We have now placed letters in squares 1 and 3, so, from clue 3, the D must be in square 2, and the 4 therefore in square 5. We now know the C must be in the bottom row. From clue 2, it cannot be in squares 5 or 6, so it must be in square 4, and the II is therefore in square 5 (clue 2). The E cannot be in that square (clue 1), and we have placed four other letters, so it must be in square 6, and therefore so is the 1 (clue 5). This leaves the A, by elimination, in square 5. The 2 cannot be in square 2 or in square 3, which contains the B (clue 1), so it must be with the C and the VI in square 4. Nor is the 5 in square 2 (clue 4), so it must be in square 3, which leaves the 6, and therefore also the Roman V (clue 5), in square 2, so, by elimination, the Roman number in square 3 must be the I.

In summary:
Square 1, 3, F, IV.
Square 2, 6, D, V.
Square 3, 5, B, I.
Square 4, 2, C, VI.
Square 5, 4, A, II.
Square 6, 1, E, III.

555

87612

556

3 2	3 9	4 6	4 8	5 5
5 1	5 3	3 5	3 7	4 4
4 0	4 2	4 9	5 6	3 3
5 4	3 6	3 8	4 5	4 7
4 3	5 0	5 2	3 4	4 1

557

Cube C

558

The cushion originally at F could not have been gold or green (clue 1), blue (clue 2) or turquoise (clue 3). If it had been pink with the blue one at E (clue 3), it would have been impossible for the turquoise cushion to replace the blue one (clue 2), so it must have been red. The original cushion at E couldn't have been gold (clue 1), blue (clue 2), green (clue 3), or pink (clue 4), so must have been turquoise, and the green one, which should have been at D (clue 3), finished up at E (clue 2). The turquoise cushion was never at A (clue 3), and the cleaner can't have moved it two places to C (clue 2), so she must have moved it three places to B, instead of the blue one, which she moved four places. From clue 1, the gold cushion can't have been moved from C to D, so it must have started at A, leaving C for the pink one. Again from clue 1, the pink cushion must have moved to A and the red one to C, leaving D as the new position for the gold one.

In summary:
A, gold, pink.   B, blue, turquoise.
C, pink, red.   D, green, gold.
E, turquoise, green.   F, red, blue.

559

9	0	4	1	1	1	■	8	2	2	5	3	8
4	■	5	■	9	6	7	8	0	■	1	■	6
1	3	4	5	6	5	■	6	7	8	9	0	2
1	■	2	■	8	3	4	4	5	■	6	■	7
5	4	8	3	■	9	2	0	■	6	1	2	2
7	3	8	4	2	■	5	■	6	6	9	7	8
■	0	■	5	1	1	■	7	3	2	■	3	■
7	4	2	5	6	■	8	■	5	7	1	8	2
7	9	0	1	■	1	4	2	■	8	2	3	4
5	■	6	■	3	7	8	9	4	■	0	■	1
4	2	3	4	5	8	■	7	6	7	8	9	3
0	■	1	■	4	2	3	4	5	■	1	■	2
6	3	7	4	5	2	■	3	6	7	6	8	7

560

Eight

561

These are multiples of seven, but they are reversed on the lower line so 56 becomes 65.

562

The shapes appear in squares b3, c6, e5 and f1.

563

D is the correct plug.

?

564

The team's goalkeeper who started the move off cannot be Garry (clue 1), Clyde Johnson (clue 2), Mike (clue 4), or Peter (clue 4). Steve is number 2 (clue 3), so, by elimination, the goalkeeper must be Darren. So, from clue 2, number 1 is Clyde Johnson, and number 2, Steve, is Marchant. Swann, who is number 3 (clue 6), cannot be Mike, who received a pass from David (clue 4) or Peter, who was passed to by Glenn (clue 5), nor can he be Garry (clue 1), and we know he is not Clyde, Darren or Steve, so, by elimination, he must be David. So, from clue 4, Mike must be number 4, and, from the same clue, Bennett must be Darren, the goalkeeper. The player numbered 6, at the end of the move, cannot be O'Casey (clue 1), or Glenn (clue 5), so he must be Donovan. Therefore, from clue 5, Peter is not player 5, and must be player 6, Donovan. This places Glenn as player 5 (clue 5), and, by elimination, his first name must be Garry. Now, by elimination and from clue 1, Mike, number 4, must be the player named O'Casey.

In summary:
Goalkeeper, Darren Bennett.
1, Clyde Johnson. 2, Steve Marchant.
3, David Swann. 4, Mike O'Casey.
5, Garry Glenn. 6, Peter Donovan.

565

566

Silhouette 1 is vase g, silhouette 2 is vase n and silhouette 3 is vase j.

567

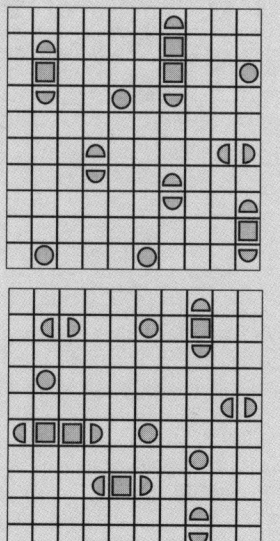

568

31970

569

16. The next number is double the difference between the previous two.

570

571

Plug c is attached to the chainsaw.

572

The student in seat C wanted to play Scrabble (clue 4). Since seat A was Beverly McBain's (clue 5), from clue 1, the student who favoured Monopoly can't have been in seat B, nor did the student in B want to play Trivial Pursuit (clue 3), so he or she must have favoured mah-jong, and was therefore from Canada (clue 2). He or she wasn't Matt Scott (clue 2) or Rajendra Patel, who's from India (clue 1), so, as we know Beverly McBain was in seat A, seat B must have been Jayne Bailey's. We now know the countries for two students, so the Australian, who's not Beverly McBain (clue 5), must be Matt Scott, and by elimination Beverly McBain must be from Barbados. Her favoured game wasn't Trivial Pursuit (clue 3), so must have been Monopoly, and it must have been the student in seat D who favoured Trivial Pursuit; from clue 1 this was Rajendra Patel, from India. Finally, by elimination, Matt Scott from Australia must have been in seat C and wanted to play Scrabble.

In summary:
A, Beverly McBain, Barbados, Monopoly.
B, Jayne Bailey, Canada, mah-jong.
C, Matt Scott, Australia, Scrabble.
D, Rajendra Patel, India, Trivial Pursuit.

573

574

North, Mrs Scott, 4 Diamonds.
East, Mrs Evans, 5 Hearts.
South, Mrs Jennings, 3 no Trumps.
West, Mrs Ryan, 6 Spades.

575

4	7	1	0	1	7	■	5	2	0	2	9	3
0	■	5	■	9	6	1	4	5	■	7	■	0
2	4	6	6	4	7	■	5	8	8	2	8	9
6	■	4	■	8	5	1	7	7	■	6	■	2
3	1	1	8	■	6	1	8	■	7	7	3	2
1	6	4	2	2	■	0	■	5	0	4	5	0
■	3	■	7	2	0	■	9	3	5	■	0	■
6	3	9	5	8	■	8	■	4	9	8	8	7
4	4	1	9	■	3	4	2	■	8	3	1	3
0	■	3	■	9	2	0	5	6	■	4	■	1
6	3	0	5	8	0	■	7	7	2	0	4	2
5	■	9	■	2	2	2	1	2	■	1	■	9
8	9	7	6	1	3	■	9	0	0	5	1	0

576

577

(crossword grid of numbers)

578

Soap	Dove	Peach	Avocado	Rose	Mango	Lemon
Waters	Peach	Mango	Rose	Dove	Lemon	Avocado
Flannell	Avocado	Dove	Peach	Lemon	Rose	Mango
Tubbs	Rose	Lemon	Mango	Avocado	Dove	Peach
Lather	Mango	Rose	Lemon	Peach	Avocado	Dove
Faucett	Lemon	Avocado	Dove	Mango	Peach	Rose

579

Michel dropped out at point 4 (clue 6). The rider at point 6 cannot have been Yves, who had a flat tyre (clues 2 and 5), so, from clue 5, the latter must have left the race at point 2. We now know Dirk did not drop out at point 2 or point 4, and clue 1 rules out points 6 and 7. Since the rider at point 3 twisted his ankle (clue 4), Dirk cannot have withdrawn at point 1 (clue 1), so he must have abandoned the race at point 3 or point 5. But clue 7 rules him out as the man at point 5, so he must have dropped out at point 3, and the pedal therefore snapped at point 5 (clue 1). The rider whose knee gave way is not Bjorn, and cannot be Michel, Roland or Victor (clue 7), and we know he was not Dirk or Yves, so he must have been Gino. We now

know the rider whose chain broke must be one of Bjorn, Michel, Roland or Victor, but clue 2 rules out Bjorn. So, from clue 2, the rider at point 6 must be one of Gino, Michel or Roland. We know he is not Michel, and, from clue 3, he cannot be Roland, so he must be Gino. Therefore, from clue 2, it must be Michel whose chain broke. Clue 3 rules out positions 1 or 7 as the one where Roland dropped out, so he must have done so at point 5, and, from clue 3, it must have been the rider at point 7 whose wheel buckled. This leaves point 1 as the location of the migraine attack. The sufferer was not Victor (clue 8), so he must have been Bjorn, leaving Victor as the rider whose wheel buckled at point 7.

In summary:
1, Bjorn, migraine attack.
2, Yves, flat tyre.
3, Dirk, twisted ankle.
4, Michel, chain broke.
5, Roland, pedal snapped.
6, Gino, knee gave way.
7, Victor, buckled wheel.

580

d is the 'twin' top.

581

J	Q	9	K	T
C	C	D	D	S
8	T	J	9	K
C	H	H	S	H
K	8	Q	8	9
S	S	H	H	H
T	Q	A	Q	K
D	D	H	S	C
J	J	8	T	9
S	D	D	C	C

582

1 Jewel on the turban is missing 2 Triangle on the model's left shoulder pad is missing 3 Band beneath medal is missing 4 Bottom left of tunic pattern is different 5 Middle tassel is missing.

583

Objects appear in squares 2b, 2d, 5a and 7e.

584

Yellow, Magenta, Blue, Orange

585

Shield C is green (clue 4). Shield A cannot be blue (clue 1), or yellow (clue 2), so it must be red. Since the owner of this shield is Lord Liversedge (clue 5), from clue 1, the blue shield cannot be shield B, so, by elimination, it must be shield D, leaving shield B as the yellow one. Therefore, from clue 2, the eagle is

the device on Lord Liversedge's red shield in position A. Now, from clue 2, shield B must belong to Lord Bertram. Lord Rackham's shield bearing a turkey cannot be in position D (clue 1), so it must be shield C. This leaves shield D as Lord Mallender's. Its device is not the lion (clue 3), so it must be the stag, leaving the lion as the device on Lord Bertram's yellow coat of arms.

In summary:
A, Lord Liversedge, eagle, red.
B, Lord Bertram, lion, yellow.
C, Lord Rackham, turkey, green.
D, Lord Mallender, stag, blue.

586

Pictures 3 and 4 are the same. Picture 1 has an extra leaf and picture two is missing a flower petal.

587

588

(crossword grid of numbers)

589

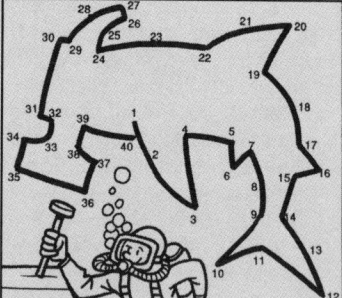

590

591

Green, Orange, Orange, Yellow

592

593

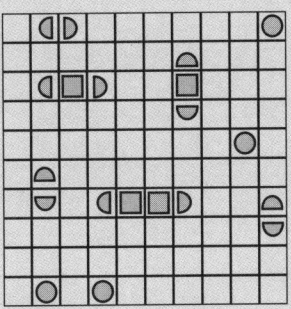

594

Letter 1, Jill Dukes, Cardiff.
Letter 2, Sally Markham, Nantwich.
Letter 3, Jenny Hardy, Ipswich.
Letter 4, Betty Riley, Hull.

595

596

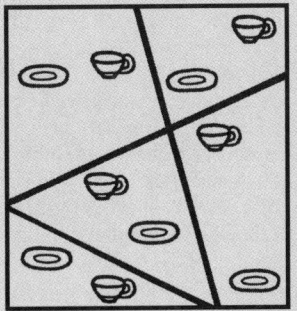

597

Photograph H is the exact replica.

598

The red was at C on Tuesday (clue 4) so since it was obviously not there on Thursday, the blue could not have been at D on that day (clue 1). Nor, by the same clue, was the red there and since also the green could not have been there (clue 3), D must have been the black's Thursday place. So D on Wednesday could not have been black, nor blue (clue 1) or green (clue 3), so must have been red and D on Monday must have been green (clue 2). By elimination, Tuesday's D must have been blue and, from clue 1, C on Wednesday must have been blue. From what we have already placed, C on Monday can't be any of red, blue or green, so must have been black, leaving C on Thursday as green. From clue 1, blue on Monday must have been A and red at B. Now, from clue 3, green must have been at B on Tuesday and A on Wednesday with black at A on Tuesday and B on Wednesday. By elimination, on Thursday, red must have been at A and blue at B.

In summary:
Monday: blue, red, black, green.
Tuesday: black, green, red, blue.
Wednesday: green, black, blue, red.
Thursday: red, blue, green, black.

599

Cake 3 was the ginger sponge (clue 4). The chocolate cake cannot have been cake 4 (clue 1), nor, since cake 2 was made by Eileen (clue 3), can it have been cake 1 (clue 1). So it must have been cake 2, made by Eileen. Therefore, from clue 1, the ginger sponge must have been made by Mary, and bought by Thelma. Betty did not make the fruit cake (clue 2), so her cake must have been the jelly sponge, leaving Jean as the woman who made the fruit cake. This was not cake 4 (clue 2), so it must have been cake 1, leaving cake 4 as Betty's jelly sponge. So, from clue 5, Hilary must have bought Eileen's chocolate cake in position 2. Therefore, from clue 2, Linda, who did not buy Jean's fruit cake, must have bought Betty's jelly sponge, leaving Sarah as the woman who bought cake 1.

In summary:
1, fruit, Jean, Sarah.
2, chocolate, Eileen, Hilary.
3, ginger sponge, Mary, Thelma.
4, jelly sponge, Betty, Linda.

600

6, Molly Bird, duck.
8, Denise Carver, goose.
10, Beryl Legge, chicken.
12, Elaine Fowler, turkey.

601

602

14	16	15
3	5	1
24	29	21
6	7	9
16	21	15
8	2	4

603

Green, Green, Blue, Red

604

A, Fields, *Advantage*.
B, Woods, chess.
C, Kings, *Stonewall*.
D, Allens, *X-Words*.
E, Smiths, backgammon.
F, Browns, *Grand Tour*.
G, Dixons, *Terminator*.
H, Longs, *Hippodrome*.

605

The three identical squares are f4, i2 and j4.

606

a Extra jewel on scabbard.
b Extra band on right leg.
c Extra stud on shield.
d Extra detail on helmet.

607

Fragments 4, 3 and 1 and fragments 5, 6 and 2 will form two identical pillars.

608

4	3	9	2	5
6	8	1	5	3
7	2	5	8	1
3	4	6	1	9
3	6	2	7	5

609

14	16	14
7	1	5
25	22	18
6	3	8
19	18	14
9	4	2

610

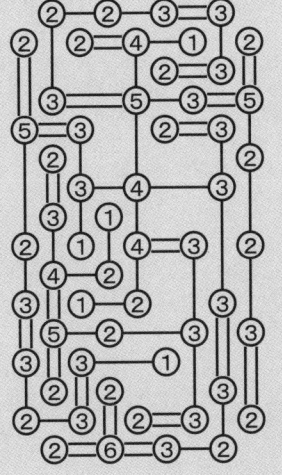

611

612

3 – 4, 8 – 7, 1 – 2, 6 – 5, 10 – 9.

613

Andy – 5, Ben – 7, Colin – 9.

614

6 8 0 2 1 7 4 9 5 3

615

2	9	4	8	9	7		6	7	8	5	6	5
8		9		7	5	7	4	0		6		8
3	9	4	3	5	2		8	4	1	8	0	7
9		8		8	3	9	9	2		2		0
1	9	7	1		3	1	4		3	6	4	0
3	4	4	5	2		5		4	5	4	0	1
	3		5	0	4		6	2	0		2	
1	3	1	2	9		7		6	0	9	2	6
4	9	8	1		8	3	2		5	8	6	3
0		0		2	7	1	3	8		4		6
4	5	3	1	2	4		3	4	5	9	5	0
1		5		9	3	6	2	0		4		3
5	6	6	1	5	7		8	6	0	2	2	1

616

2	9	2	3	8		1	4	6	1	9
8			0	1			7			7
8		2	2	2		1	2	3		2
8	4	2		1			7	9	5	
8		8	5	4	3	9	2	9		5
		2	1	2	1	8	0	4		
1		9	1	1	1	9	0	0		1
9	0	0		1			9	0	8	
1		5	0	9		8	0	9		1
1			9	0			1			1
1	4	2	6	9		1	2	3	2	1

The combination is:
2121804

617

Lavender, Orange, Lavender, Lavender

618

Take the third price (40 cents) away from the first (80 cents) and you have the price of two chocolate bars. So one costs 20 cents. So, from the middle price, a cone and two scoops costs 75 cents, therefore, using the third price a scoop costs 35 cents.

619

The skittle, pipe and pencil appear four times.

620

9	7		2	3		2	9		1	3	
6	8	9	7	5		4	8	7	6	9	
8	9	7		2	4	1	5	6	3		
	6	4	3	1	2		7	9			
		8	4			7	6	8	9		
1	6	2		1	9		5	0	9		
3	4		1	2	4	8	3		6	7	
1	2		3	2		1	2	7			
3	2	5	1		2	4					
	1	2		8	9	7	6	4			
8	5	4	6	9	7		3	1	2		
4	6	3	1	2		5	3	1	2	4	
1	9		3	1		8	2		3	1	

621

12	×	4	=	48	+	20	=	68
+		×		÷		+		
40	÷	10	=	4	+	16	=	20
=		=		=		=		
52	−	40	=	12	+	36	=	48
÷		−		+		÷		
2	+	26	=	28	+	-	=	26
=		=		=		=		
26	+	14	=	40	−	18	=	22

622

17	3	15	23	4	14
6	20	29	8	19	25
26	9	1	18	28	10
16	2	22	12	30	21
7	27	13	24	5	11

623

Theresa had the red counters (clue 3). Rachel, who threw a three, was not using the yellow counters (clue 2), and the player with the blue counters threw a four (clue 5), so Rachel must have been playing with the green counters. It was not Angela who had the blue counters (clue 5), so it must have been Yvonne, leaving Angela with the yellow ones. Yvonne, who threw a four, cannot have been in seat 4 (clue 1), and the player in seat 2 threw a six (clue 4), so Yvonne must have been in either seat 1 or seat 3. But clue 6 rules out seat 3, so she must have been in seat 1. We now know Rachel, who threw a three, was not in seat 1 or seat 2, and clue 1 rules out seat 3, so she must have had seat 4, and Angela, with the yellow counters, was therefore in seat 3 (clue 2), leaving Theresa as the player in seat 2 who threw a six. So, by elimination, it must have been Angela who threw the one.

In summary:
1, Yvonne, blue, 4.
2, Theresa, red, 6.
3, Angela, yellow, 1.
4, Rachel, green, 3.

624

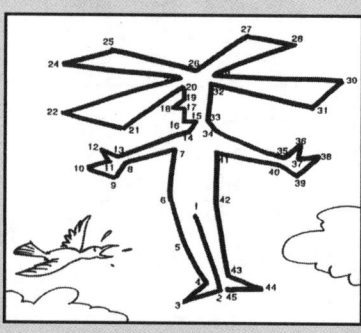

625

626

4	9	4	9	3	5
8	9	5	2	6	7
5	1	8	1	5	2
8	6	6	9	8	4
1	7	2	3	6	3
3	4	2	7	7	1

627

Miranda is in caravan 3 (clue 4), so the woman in caravan 4, who cannot be Alicia from Cardiff (clue 1), or Zoe, the companion of Sebastian (clue 3), must be Esme. Therefore, from clue 2, Miranda, in caravan 3, is from Belfast, and Desmond is in caravan 2. So Sebastian and Zoe, whose caravan we know is not 3 or 4, must be in caravan 1, and, by elimination, Alicia from Cardiff must be sharing caravan 2 with Desmond. Sebastian and Zoe are not from London (clue 3), so they must be from Edinburgh, leaving London as Esme's home city. Miranda's partner is not Luther (clue 4), so he must be Paul, leaving Esme with Luther.

In summary:
1, Sebastian and Zoe, Edinburgh.
2, Desmond and Alicia, Cardiff.
3, Paul and Miranda, Belfast.
4, Luther and Esme, London.

628

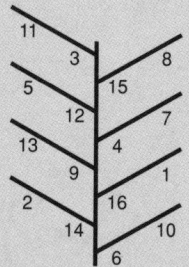

629

Belts 3 and 9 are identical.

630

The top right picture should be hung with side A facing north.

631

Lavender, Green, Orange, Yellow

632

The three identical squares are: 3a, 4d and 11c.

633

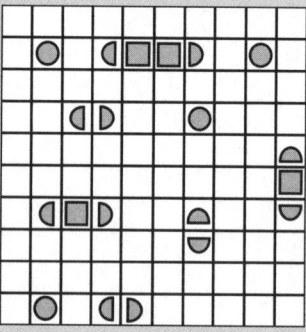

634

13	24	22	10	19
7	20	16	14	2
4	18	25	21	6
15	9	5	17	12
11	1	3	8	23

635

1, Kieron Spry, priest.
2, Gareth Hardy, lawyer.
3, Melvin Fettle, lecturer.
4, Denzil Fitt, bank manager.

636

9	8	7	3	1	2	5	6	4
4	1	2	9	5	6	7	3	8
5	6	3	7	8	4	2	1	9
1	9	6	2	7	8	4	5	3
8	2	4	6	3	5	9	7	1
7	3	5	4	9	1	8	2	6
6	7	9	5	4	3	1	8	2
3	4	1	8	2	7	6	9	5
2	5	8	1	6	9	3	4	7

637

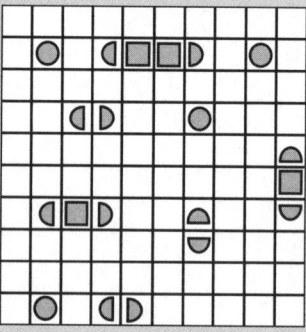

638

Figure 1 has a band on his right foot. Figure 2 has a bar in the diamond chest pattern. Figure 3 has a band on his hat. Figure 4 has a band on his right arm.

639

3	25	1	8
36	4	49	2
9	64	16	5
6	1	7	4

640

641

642

1, Rosie, number 11, pineapple.
2, Sally, number 15, peach.
3, Helen, number 8, strawberry.
4, Jenny, number 20, cherry.

643

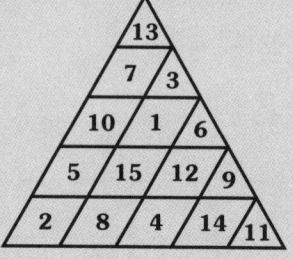

644

645

The first place was achieved in the town sports (clue 4), so trophy B, won at the county meeting for a higher placing than the high jump trophy (clue 3), must have been for second place, and the high jump must be the event for which Karen was awarded third place. The latter isn't trophy A (clue 1), so must be C, and, by elimination, must have been won at the inter-schools sports. If it had been won in May, then, from clue 1, the 1,500 metres trophy would have been won in June, leaving the discus trophy as the one awarded in July. From clue 2, this isn't the case, so the 1,500 metres trophy, which can't have been won in May (clue 1), must have been awarded in July, and third place in the high jump must have been achieved in June (clue 1). From clue 2, the 1,500 metres trophy must be trophy B, leaving A as the one awarded for the discus. By elimination, this must have been awarded in May and must have been for first place at the town sports.

In summary:
A, First place, discus, town, May.
B, Second place, 1,500 metres, county, July.
C, Third place, high jump, inter-schools, June.

646

Pawn – $2.50; castle – $4.50; knight – $5.00; king – $6.00.

647

(pyramid)
13
7, 3
10, 1, 6
5, 15, 12, 9
2, 8, 4, 14, 11

648

Figure a has a bracelet, figure b has a necklace, figure c has a head band and figure d has a band on her sandal.

649

None of the four isolated squares is blue (clue 3), so, since the centre square, number 7, is red (clue 6), and no two adjacent squares horizontally or vertically are the same colour (clue 1), and there must be at least four blue squares (intro), these must be either numbers 2, 4, 10 and 12, or numbers 3, 6, 8 and 11. Two of the four squares numbered 10 to 13 are red (clue 4). If one of these is 13, the other cannot be 11 (clue 1), so it must be either 10 or 12, which would rule out the blues as 2, 4, 10 and 12. If 13 was not a red square, then the red squares would have to be 10 and 12 (clue 1), which also rules out the blues as 2, 4, 10 and 12, so, as we have seen above, they must be 3, 6, 8 and 11. Since the blue square numbered 8 has a red square to its left, from clue 2, square 5 must be white. From the same clue, square 9 cannot be white, nor can it be blue (clue 1), so it must be red. We have placed two red squares in that row, and there is another in the row above (clue 5). We also know there are two amongst squares 10 to 13, which makes five in all, so there cannot be any more red squares (intro), and there must be four each of the blue and white, so we have placed all the blue squares too. Therefore square 1 must be white, so square 12 must be white as well (clue 7). Therefore the red squares referred to in clue 4 must be 10 and 13. We have identified three of the four white squares as 1, 5 and 12. Since square 6 is blue, none of these white squares can be the one referred to in clue 8. Only the colours of squares 2 and 4 remain to be identified. From clue 8, the fourth white square must be 4 and square 2 must be red.

In summary:
1, white.
2, red, 3 blue, 4 white.
5, white, 6 blue, 7 red, 8, blue, 9 red.
10, red, 11 blue, 12 white. 13, red.

650

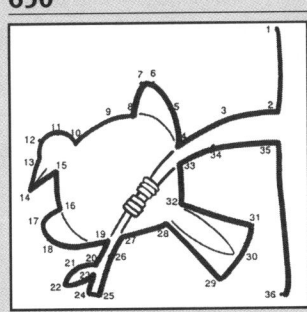

651

81	8	27	144
49	125	1	16
9	25	169	100
121	64	36	4

652

Mia – 2, Judy; Gill – 1, Kylie; Kay – 3, Mel; Jane – 4, Linda.

653

Ball f was kicked away.

654

4	7		6	5		5
	8	1		1	2	0
1	9	2		2	4	
6		1	6		6	4
	1		3	8		0
2	9	4			3	6	0
6	6	2		9	7	

655

B2 contains an S (clue 5), so, from clue 1, the other S cannot be in row 2 or column B, or in any of squares A1, C3, D4, C1 or A3. This leaves only A4, C4, D1 and D3. The latter contains a vowel (clue 3), and the letter in A4 is from the first half of the alphabet (clue 2). Since the T is in column D (clue 5), from clue 8, the second S cannot be in C4 either, so, by elimination, it must be in D1. So, from clue 9, the T in column D cannot be in D4, nor, as we know, is it in D3, which contains a vowel, so it must be in D2. From clue 7, we can now place the U in A2, and the N in C2. From clue 4, it is now clear that the A must be in row 3, but not in D3. The D below it (clue 4) cannot be in C4 (clue 8), since there is no E in the phrase, so this rules out C3 for the A. Nor is the C in C3 (clue 6), so the A cannot be in B3, and must be in A3, placing the C in B3, and a D in A4 (clue 4). We have now placed the A and the U, so the vowel in D3 (clue 3) must be an I. This cannot be the I referred to in clue 10, since the C is in B3, nor can that I be in D4 (clue 1), so, by elimination, it must be in C1, and the R in A1 (clue 10). The letters now remaining to be placed are D, G, H, M and P. So we can see from clue 8 that the G must be in C4 and the H in B4. So, from clue 11, the M must be in D4. Clue 6 rules out the P for C3, which must therefore contain the second D, leaving the P in B1.

In summary:

	A	B	C	D
1	R	P	I	S
2	U	S	N	T
3	A	C	D	I
4	D	H	G	M

656

657

Red, Orange, Red, Green

658

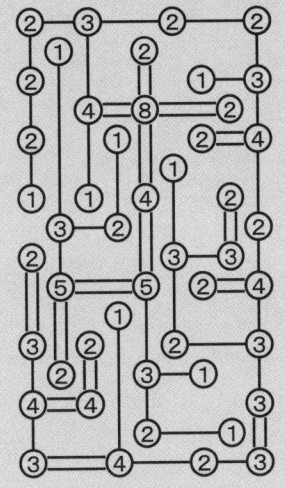

659

660

2	9	1	1	9	3		3	8	3	8	2	3
0		0		1	2	1	5	4		1	1	
4	8	7	0	6	4		5	6	7	0	8	9
1		2		5	2	9	8		5		5	6
5	8	3	6		3	1	0		4	0	5	2
5	6	7	8	9		7		1	9	1	4	3
	5		4	2	8		6	3	8		3	
4	4	5	9	0		5		2	2	6	7	7
3	3	1	2		7	4	8		2	1	6	5
4		0		7	2	3	4	6		0		4
6	2	0	1	0	1		7	6	2	9	3	0
5		3		9	9	5	8	7		8		5
8	8	5	4	6	7		9	9	1	7	6	4

661

FORD	Sp	Sa	Es
Red	J	A	R
Green	R	G	K
Blue	J	A	R
Silver	G	K	J
LINCOLN	Sp	Sa	Es
Red	G	J	R
Green	J	A	K
Blue	G	K	G
Silver	A	R	A
CHEVROLET	Sp	Sa	Es
Red	A	R	G
Green	K	J	A
Blue	*	K	G
Silver	R	J	K

662

6	4	3	1	4	6	5
1	2	1	1	2	0	6
3	6	1	3	5	1	0
6	4	1	3	2	6	0
6	6	5	2	3	0	4
5	0	5	5	3	0	3
0	2	4	3	4	1	2
2	2	4	5	4	5	0

663

The third from the left on the top shelf, the second from the right on the second shelf down, the fifth from the left on the third shelf down and the third from the left on the bottom shelf.

664

The following steps refer to the given facts and to truths established in earlier steps.
13 Mr Fulton is not the artist (5, 10).
14 Mr Fulton is the carpenter (4, 12, 13).
15 The carpenter is not Karl (1, 8).
16 The carpenter is not Len (6, 12).
17 The carpenter is Ike (1, 15, 16).
18 Mr Harkness is the artist (7, 9, 14).
19 Mr Gainor is the builder (2, 9, 14).
20 Mr Elton is the dentist. (14, 18, 19).
21 Len is not the tallest (3).
22 Karl is not the tallest (5).
23 Ike Fulton (14, 17) is not the tallest (10).
24 Jack is the tallest. (21, 22, 23).
25 Ike Fulton is not the oldest (11).
26 Mr Gainor is not the oldest (9).
27 Mr Elton, the dentist (20), is not the oldest (2).
28 Mr Harkness is the oldest (25, 26, 27).

Now consider the geography. Jack is the tallest man (24), and lives due North of both Len (3) and Karl (8), and due West of Ike Fulton, the carpenter (1, 14, 17). Ike lives exactly three miles from the dentist, and five miles from the builder, both of whom live in the North-South line which includes Jack, Len and Karl. The three-mile distance must be either to Jack or to the northernmost of the other two. The two possibilities can be sketched, and some distances can be computed, on the basis of the relationship between legs and hypotenuse of right triangles. Here are the choices:

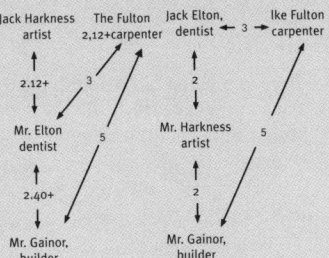

Statement 7 says that Elton and the artist are two miles apart. The second sketch is therefore the only acceptable one. We can complete the identification of Len Harkness and Karl Gainor by using given fact 5. The question of the puzzle is thus solved by saying that the oldest (Len Harkness) lives exactly two miles from Karl Gainor, the builder.

665

Nigel is in stall C (clue 3), so, from clue 1, Jackie must be in stall B. Derek Raynes is not in stall D (clue 2), so he must be in stall A, and the jockey in stall D must be Paddy, riding Saturday Night (clue 4). Now, from clue 1, Silk must be Nigel in stall C, and Mr Jingle must be the mount of Derek Raynes in stall A. Nigel's horse is not Sea Fret (clue 3), so it must be Placebo, leaving Sea Fret as Jackie's horse. Finally, Paddy, who is not Mount (clue 4), must be Ryder, leaving Jackie as Mount.

In summary:
A, Mr Jingle, Derek Raynes.
B, Sea Fret; Jackie Mount.
C, Placebo, Nigel Silk.
D, Saturday Night, Paddy Ryder.

666

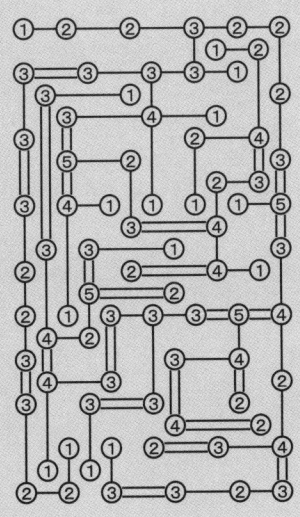

667

The five mistakes are: 1 different style shoulder pad; 2 different style necklace; 3 detail on front of dress is a circle (not diamond); 4 hair at back is different; 5 stripe is missing on right forearm.

668

9	5	1	6	7	1		3	8	1	5	2	6
8	7		9	0	0	2	1		1	0	9	
2	4	6	7	9	5		4	1	0	4	3	0
9		8		8	4	3	3	2		8		5
1	7	0	7		9	2	3		6	7	8	6
2	0	2	9	1		1		6	4	9	8	0
	3		2	0	8		8	4	7		0	
4	1	1	8	3		5		5	5	2	1	3
2	0	6	7		4	3	5		5	6	7	0
3		0		3	7	0	6	4		3		2
5	2	0	1	2	8		6	1	4	8	0	9
5		5		1	9	3	5	3		5		6
7	4	6	7	4	0		8	4	2	7	1	0

669

No. 4

670

671

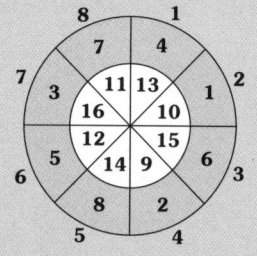

672

Take any three clocks and work out all the possible times each can be, e.g. 9.01 – 3 mins, +3 mins, –7 mins, +7 mins ... and find the time common to all three, which is 9.15.

673

7	+	8	–	9	=	6
–		–		–		
4	+	5	–	6	=	3
÷		+		÷		
1	x	2	x	3	=	6
=		=		=		
3		5		1		

674

A 6. Multiply the number on the left by the number on the right then divide by the number below the triangle 3 x 4/2=6.

B 15. Multiply the number on the left by 4 then subtract 1.

C 17. Divide the bottom number by 3 then subtract the number on the left to give the number on the right 60/3=20–3=17.

D 28. Each number in the bottom half is one more than the cube of the number opposite to it in the top half. 33=27+1=28.

E 5. In each row, from left to right, the second and third numbers are found by multiplying the previous number by 2 then adding 1. 2x2=4+1=5, 2x5=10+1=11.

675

D	J	G	A	I	C	F	B	H	E
●	■	⬭	▲	▢	▬	○	△	⬬	▭
10	5	2	6	8	4	7	9	3	11

676

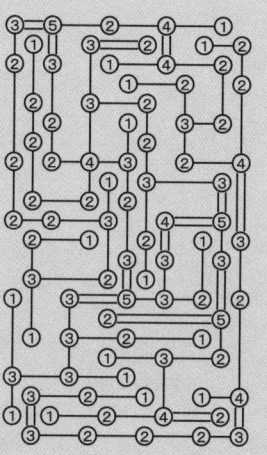

677

Monday, wallet, faculty meeting, awards ceremony. Tuesday, notes, interview board, lecture. Wednesday, spectacles, lecture, tutorials. Thursday, pens, awards ceremony, interview board. Friday, briefcase, tutorials, faculty meeting.

678

679

8	+	2	–	5	=	5
+		x		–		
1	x	7	–	4	=	3
÷		–		x		
3	x	6	÷	9	=	2
=		=		=		
3		8		9		

680

Monsters 3 and 5 are the same.

681

21	25	18	5	9
8	2	22	16	14
24	10	20	3	11
19	1	7	23	13
15	4	12	17	6

682

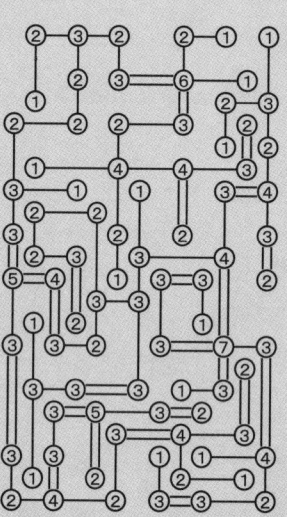

683

6	11	2	8
9	13	5	15
4	16	10	12
14	1	7	3

684

2	+	1	x	3	=	9
x		x		x		
9	–	2	–	4	=	3
÷		x		–		
3	x	3	–	3	=	6
=		=		=		
6		6		9		

685

686

4	9	4	9	3	5
8	9	5	2	6	7
5	1	8	1	5	2
8	6	6	9	8	4
1	7	2	3	6	3
3	4	2	7	1	1

687

688

689

6 K 9 A 8 Q 4 J 2 7 10 3 5

690

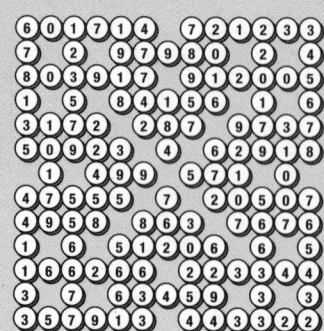

691

9	6	3	1	2	3
7	3	1	5	1	2
3	6	2	8	2	9
9	5	4	6	7	4
8	4	5	7	8	9
6	7	4	1	5	8

692

The vase was sold at stall B (clue 2). Since Elsie was running stall A (clue 4), and Norman was the customer at stall C (clue 3), from clue 1, the fire irons cannot have been sold at stall A or stall C, so they must have been on stall D. Therefore, from clue 1, it must have been stall B which was Ken's, and his customer Lesley must have bought the vase. Ted's stall was not C (clue 3), so it must have been D, leaving stall C as Mary's. Norman, her customer, did not buy books (clue 3), so he must have bought a radio from her stall, leaving the books as the item sold by Elsie on stall A. Her customer was not Ray (clue 4), so she must have been Penny, leaving Ray as the man who bought the fireirons from Ted.

In summary:
A, Elsie, Penny, books. B, Ken, Lesley, vase. C, Mary, Norman, radio. D, Ted, Ray, fire irons.

693

Monkey E is the same.

694

The fourth card cut cannot have been cut by Clara (clue 1), Betty (clue 3), or Adam (clue 4), so it must have been Dave's. So the man referred to in clue 2 must be Adam, whose card was a Heart (clue 4). He must have made the second or third cut (clue 2), but the second card was a black one (clue 5). Therefore Adam made the third cut. So, from clue 2, Dave's card must have been a Diamond, and, from clue 4, it must have been the 10. Also, from clue 2, card 2 must have been the 3. So, from clue 1, Clara cannot have drawn card 1, and must have cut card 2, and Adam's Heart, card 3, must have been the King, leaving card 1 as the 7, which, by elimination, must have been cut by Betty. So it was not a Club (clue 3), and must have been a Spade, leaving Clara's 3 as a Club.

In summary:
Card 1, 7 of Spades, Betty.
Card 2, 3 of Clubs, Clara.
Card 3, King of Hearts, Adam.
Card 4, 10 of Diamonds, Dave.

695

1-C and 3-B.

696

No. 5

697

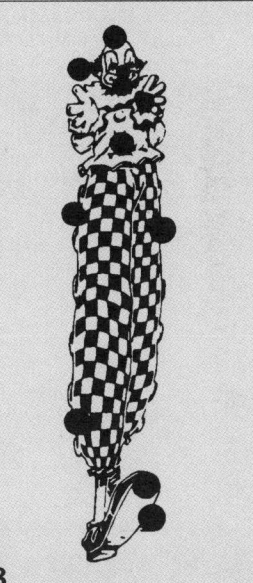

698

699

Enrico Leone was in compartment 1 (clue 4). As 'Sir Percival Gascoyne' was in compartment 2 (clue 3), Franz Schmidt cannot have been in compartment 4 (clue 5), nor was Boris Zugov (clue 2), so Maxwell Van Skyler must have been, and 'Professor Nils Knudsen' therefore in compartment 3 (clue 1). Van Skyler was not posing as Prince Karim Al-Aziz (clue 2), so he must have called himself the 'Duc de Chomette', and therefore Franz Schmidt was in compartment 2 (clue 5), posing as 'Sir Percival Gascoyne'. By elimination, 'Professor Knudsen', in compartment 3, must really have been Boris Zugov, and Enrico Leone in compartment 1 must have been posing as 'Prince Karim Al-Aziz'.

In summary:
Compartment 1, 'Prince Karim Al-Aziz', Enrico Leone,
Compartment 2, 'Sir Percival Gascoyne', Franz Schmidt.
Compartment 3, 'Professor Nils Knudsen', Boris Zugov.
Compartment 4, 'Duc de Chomette', Maxwell Van Skyler.

700

Lead B

701

The letter at III is the B (clue 3) and the 5 is on arm I (clue 5), so the letter at I cannot be any of the HAG combination, each of which is paired with an even digit (clue 1). This also rules out the letter at II as one of the combination. We now know that the H is not at any of points I, II or III, nor can it be at either point IV or point V, since the B is at point III (clue 1). The letter at VI is a vowel (clue 6), which rules out both VI and VIII for the H (clue 1), so it must be in position VII and from clue 1 the A is at VI and the G at V. So the number on arm II, which is directly opposite the A, cannot be the 7, since if it were the number on arm V would have to be the 1 and the one on arm IV the 8 (clue 4), but clue 2 tells us the 7 and the 8 are on the same straight line. So the straight line whose extremities both bear an even Roman numeral referred to in clue 2 cannot be II–VI and must be IV–VIII. So from clue 2 the 7 must be on arm IV and the 8 on arm VIII. Now from clue 4 the numbers on arms V and II, which total 7, must be either 4 and 3 or 6 and 1, since we have placed the 5 on arm I. All three numbers on arms V, VI and VII are even (clue 1), so the odd number must be on arm II. This cannot be the 1 (clue 7), so it must be the 3. Therefore the number on arm V must be the 4 (clue 4). Since arms VI and VII both bear an even digit (clue 1) by elimination the 1 must be on arm III, so from clue 7 the C is on arm I. We are now left with D, E and F for arms II, IV and VIII. Therefore from clue 8 the D must be on arm IV and the F on arm II, leaving the E on arm VIII. Finally, from clue 7 the 6 cannot be on arm VII, so it must be on arm VI, leaving the 2 on arm VII.

In summary:
Arm I: C, 5. Arm II: F, 3. Arm III: B, 1.
Arm IV: D, 7. Arm V: G, 4. Arm VI: A, 6.
Arm VII; H, 2. Arm VIII: E, 8.

702

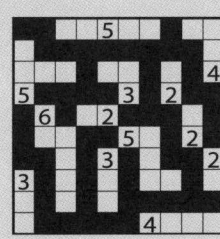

703

3	8	15	6
12	5	1	10
9	16	7	13
14	2	11	4

704

Treble 12   Double 18   Single 13

705

706

6	7	3	1	3	5	4	9	5	3
4	5	5	9	6	3	2	7	4	1
2	3	3	7	5	1	5	5	6	9
6	1	6	5	2	9	3	3	4	7
3	9	4	3	5	7	7	1	2	5

707

The number in B1 must be 2 or 4 in one of the four languages (clue 3), but this cannot be French, since quatre is in B2 (clues 1 and 2). Clue 7 rules out quattro, and clue 6 rules out vier. Since the German drei is in column C (clue 8), vier cannot be in that column (clue 1), so, from clue 6, four cannot be in B1 either. So B1 must contain a 2. Clue 4 rules out both zwei and due, and we have already ruled out the French deux, so two must be in B1, and one therefore in D2 (clue 3). Now, from clue 4, zwei and due must both be in row 2. Clues 1 and 8 rule out C2 for zwei, so zwei must be in A2, and due in C2. It is now clear, from clue 6, that tre must be in row 3, but it cannot be in column A (clue 6), or column C (clue 1). D3 contains an even number (clue 5), so, by elimination, tre must be in B3. So, from clue 6, four must be in A3, and vier in B4. We have now placed all the 2s except deux, and all the 4s except quattro. The even number in D3 is not French (clue 5), so it must be quattro. We have now placed three of the Italian numbers, so the remaining one, uno, must be in column A (clue 1). It cannot be in A4 (clue 9), so it must be in A1. We have also placed three 2s, so, from clue 9, the remaining one, deux, must be in A4. Now, from clues 1 and 8, eins must be in column D but not in D1, so must be in D4. Now, from clue 1, the number in D1 must be in French. Only trois and un remain, so, from clue 10, trois must be in D1, and un in C3. Finally, from clue 8, drei cannot be in C4, so it must be in C1, and, by elimination, C4 must contain the number three.

In summary:

uno	two	drei	trois
zwei	quatre	due	one
four	tre	un	quattro
deux	vier	three	eins

708

Across
A Spade is worth one more than a Diamond (rows 1 and 3) and six more than a Heart (rows 2 and 3); thus a Diamond is worth five more than a Heart. So (4) four Hearts + 5 + 6 = 35: thus four Hearts = 24, so a Heart = 6. A Spade = 12 and a Diamond = 11 (above), so (2) a Club = 9.
Thus: Heart = 6, Club = 9, Diamond = 11 and Spade = 12.
Down
A Heart is worth eight more than a Spade (columns 2 and 3) and a Diamond two more than a Spade (3 and 4). Thus (3) four Spades + 10 = 46, so four Spades = 36, thus a Spade = 9. A Heart =17 (above) and a Diamond = 11 (above), so (1) a Club = 15.
Thus: Heart = 17, Club = 15, Diamond = 11 and Spade = 9.

709

710

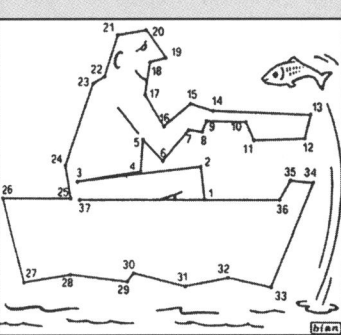

711

Brother Luke appears in tower A (clue 4). The New Tower is haunted by Lady Edith (clue 2), so, from clue 2, the Sorcerer's Tower, location of the Sorcerer's Den, can't be tower A or tower B. The room in tower C is the King's Chamber (clue 1), so the Sorcerer's Tower must be tower D, and, from clue 2, the New Tower is tower C and Lady Edith must haunt the King's Chamber. The room in tower B isn't the Treasure Room (clue 4), so it must be the Whistling Room. Therefore tower B isn't Drogo's Tower (clue 3) and must be the Black Tower. By elimination, Drogo's Tower must be tower A, and Brother Luke, who haunts it, must appear in the Treasure Room. Finally, from clue 4, the ghost of tower B, who isn't Lord Ivo (clue 4), must be Old Meg, and Lord Ivo must haunt tower D, the Sorcerer's Tower.

In summary:
A, Drogo's Tower, Treasure Room, Brother Luke.
B, Black Tower, Whistling Room, Old Meg.
C, New Tower, King's Chamber, Lady Edith.
D, Sorcerer's Tower, Sorcerer's Den, Lord Ivo.

712

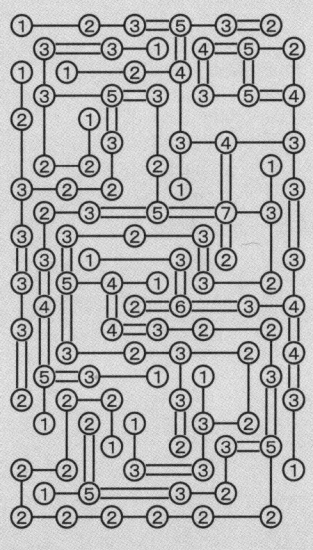

713

8	x	1	÷	2	=	4
−		+		x		
7	+	9	÷	4	=	4
+		−		−		
3	+	6	−	5	=	4
=		=		=		
4		4		3		

714

4	2	5	4	6	x	2	=	8	5	0	9	2
1	0	8	9	+	6	2	2	=	1	7	1	1
2	4	+	1	8	+	3	9	7	=	4	3	9
1	4	x	2	5	8	7	=	3	6	2	1	8
5	+	9	+	4	+	5	−	9	÷	2	=	7
1	0	0	0	9	=	1	8	+	9	9	9	1
6	7	5	x	1	9	÷	9	=	1	4	2	5
9	6	−	7	−	7	+	8	÷	3	0	=	3
6	x	1	1	5	4	5	=	6	9	2	7	0
2	8	8	−	5	6	6	=	2	3	2	3
4	5	+	9	0	+	4	3	9	=	5	7	4
2	4	9	−	1	6	8	−	3	9	=	4	2
2	5	x	3	6	−	2	0	0	=	7	0	0

715

From clue 2, the mother of child D cannot be in deckchairs 1 or 2, and clue 1 rules out chair 4, so she must be in chair 3. So, from clue 2, Jill is in chair 2, and Emma's mum in chair 1. Since Jack is the son of Francesca (clue 3), she cannot be in chair 1, nor is she in chair 3 (clue 3), so she must be in chair 4. We now know child D, whose mother is in chair 3, is not Emma or Jack, and clue 4 rules out Karen, so child D must be Damien. We have now matched chair numbers with three children, so the child of Jill, in chair 2, must be Karen. So she cannot be child B (clue 1). Therefore, from clue 4, she must be child A, and Lesley must be the mother of child C. We know this is not Damien or Karen, and that Jack is the son of Francesca, so child C must be Emma. Now, by elimination, Damien's mother in chair 3 must be Sally, and Francesca's son Jack must be child B.

In summary:
A, Karen, Jill, 2.
B, Jack, Francesca, 4.
C, Emma, Lesley, 1.
D, Damien, Sally, 3.

716

Solution: 7 4 A 9 Q J 3 5 K 8 10 2 6

717

7	12	5	14
16	9	1	3
2	6	13	10
11	4	8	15

718

	3	6	8	7	0	1	5	2	5	9	8	
9		8	8	9		7		2	6	0		4
6	6	3		1		0		4		7	9	1
7	2	0	5	0	3		1	5	4	5	6	4
6	4	8	2		8	8	4		9	9	7	7
2	1		6	3	5	7	6	5	5		7	9
4	1	6	7	0	7		9	1	9	3	5	0
5	4		4	6	2	9	3	9	0		3	3
8	2	1	8		9	5	5		1	2	7	6
8	9	6	9	5	2		3	3	8	0	8	5
1	8	6		3		2		0		4	0	2
3		5	4	8		2		9	1	7		5
	7	0	2	6	4	2	9	3	0	6	1	

719

Keith's wife is Angela (clue 2), and Lance is Gail's father (clue 4), so, from clue 5, Violet, whose daughter is Fiona, and whose husband is not Perry, must be the wife of Chris. So their son is Garry (clue 4). We know Darren is not Violet's son, nor is he Angela's (clue 2). Since his surname is Morris (clue 2), he cannot be the son of Judy Langton (clue 3), so, by elimination, his mother must be Bridget. So they went to Majorca (clue 6). Violet is not Mrs Chadwick, whose holiday location was Crete (clue 5), so, by elimination, she must be Mrs Durham, leaving Mrs Chadwick as Angela. We now know Judy Langton's holiday was not in Crete or Majorca, nor was it in Cyprus (clue 3), so she must have visited the Canaries, and, by elimination, the Durhams' holiday island must have been Cyprus. Now, from clue 4, Lance's wife is not Judy Langton, who had the holiday in the Canaries, so she must be Bridget, and he is therefore Mr Morris. Now, by elimination, Perry must be Mr Langton, Judy's husband. Their son is not Ian (clue 3), so he must be Charles, and their daughter is therefore Rebecca (clue 1). So, by elimination, Keith and Angela Chadwick's children must be Ian and Janet.

In summary:
Chris & Violet Durham, Cyprus. Garry & Fiona, Keith & Angela Chadwick, Ian & Janet, Crete. Lance & Bridget Morris, Darren & Gail, Majorca. Perry & Judy Langton, Charles & Rebecca, Canaries.

720

B2 contains an M (clue 4). Column 1 contains one each of the letters A, D, M and Y (clue 6), and Y occurs only once in column 2 (clue 3), so there must be two Ys in column 3. Neither can be in B3 or D3, which each contain a different letter not repeated in that column (clue 7), so they must be in A3 and C3. D3 does not contain a D (clue 5), and we already know the two Ms are in columns 1 and 2 (clues 4 and 6), so there must be an A in D3. The letter in B3 cannot be another A or Y (clue 7), and we know it is not an M, so it must be a D. The second D we know is in column 1 (clue 6), so, since there is only one Y in column 2 (clue 3), and we know there is only one M there, the other two squares must each contain an A. Neither of these can be in D2 (clue 1), so they must be in A2 and C2, and the Y is therefore in D2. We can now see that the combination A above D (clue 2), must be in column 1. From letters already placed, this A cannot be in A1 or C1 (clue 1), so it must be in B1, with the D in C1. The remaining Y in column 1 (clue 6), cannot be in D1 (clue 1), so it must be in A1, and D1 must contain the second M (clue 6).

In summary:

Y	A	Y
A	M	D
D	A	Y
M	Y	A

721

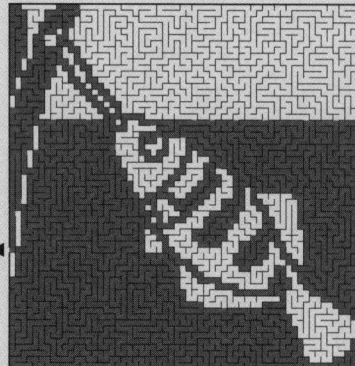

722

723

724

Nos. 2, 4 and 7.

725

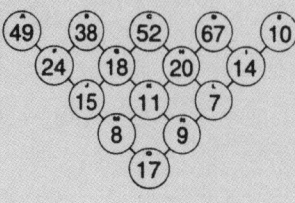

726

31 suitcases are needed.

727

6	5	8	6	7	4
9	1	7	3	2	1
8	5	3	4	9	5
5	2	9	6	4	2
6	8	7	4	8	3
7	3	1	2	9	1

728

From the top: F, D, B, C, A, E

729

5	8	5	6	5
2	5	0	9	5
4	6	6	5	6
4	6	5	3	9
1	5	3	7	6

730

Treble 17   Double 11   Single 12

731

10	7	4	2
1	14	11	8
12	3	6	15
5	16	9	13

732

No. 4

733

Pass was North (clue 5). South, whose long suit had only five cards (clue 3), cannot have been Ruff (clue 1), and, since East's suit was Hearts (clue 4), clue 1 also rules out West for Ruff, whose partner had the Clubs. So, by elimination, he must have been East, and his suit was Hearts. Now, from clue 1, West's suit must have been Clubs. We know the South player with the five-card suit was not Pass or Ruff, nor can he have been Trumpet (clue 2), so, by elimination, he must have been Bidding. So, from clue 6, his partner, Pass, in the North seat, must have had an eight-card suit. Now, by elimination, Trumpet must have been West, and his suit was therefore Clubs. Pass' eight-card suit cannot have been Diamonds (clue 2), so it must have been Spades, leaving Diamonds as Bidding's five-card suit. Now, from clue 1, Ruff must have had seven Hearts, and Trumpet six Clubs.

In summary:
North, Pass, Spades, 8.
East, Ruff, Hearts, 7.
South, Bidding, Diamonds, 5.
West, Trumpet, Clubs, 6.

734

No. 4

735

The youngster aged 17 has room 3 (clue 3), so, from clue 2, the green carpet in the room occupied by the 11 year old must be in room 4. So James, aged 13, must have room 2 (clue 2), and, from clue 1, Gemma's blue carpet must be in room 1, so, by elimination, she must be 15. Liam is not 17 (clue 3), so he must be 11, leaving Colette as 17. Her carpet is not brown (clue 4), so it must be grey, leaving the brown carpet in room 2, occupied by James.

In summary:
1, Gemma, 15, blue.
2, James, 13, brown.
3, Colette, 17, grey.
4, Liam, 11, green.

736

737

738

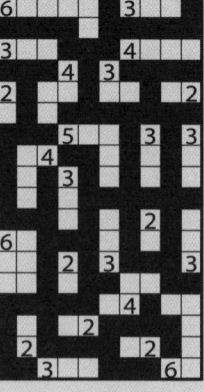

739

The best we know of is 700. In turn choose: 49, 47, 14, 35, 46, 38, 34, 28, 44, 26, 39, 27, 42, 36, 45, 32, 48, 30, 40.

740

In each triangle the centre number is the sum of the three corner numbers less the number nearest the middle of the opposite triangle. So 11 + 10 + 4 − 7 = 18.

741

Pictures 1 and 7

742

Cube 3

743

Birthright, 1914 – 1938, Joseph, Miriam.
Chronicle, 1780 – 1830, Vaughan, Hannah.
Domain, 1938 – 1977, Lambert, Claudia.
Heritage, 1881 – 1914, Esmond, Rosalind.
Testament, 1830 – 1881, Samuel, Eugenie.

744

The 12 is in square B2 (clue 1). Since neither the 2 nor the 1 is in column 1 (clue 5), neither can be one of the factors of 12 referred to in clue 1. Nor is the 4 in column 1 (clue 4), so the two numbers in question must be 3 and 6. Since the 6 is next to the 10 in the same horizontal row (clue 2), it cannot be in B1, so, from clue 1, the 6 must be in C1, and the 10 in C2 (clue 2), while, from clue 1, the 3 must be in B1, and, from clue 2, the 8 must be in A1. We have placed the 3 and the 10, so, from clue 3, the number in C3 cannot be 2 or 3, nor can it be 4 (clue 7), so, since the highest number in the layout is 12, from clue 3, the 1 must be in C3, and the 9 therefore in C4. Clue 4 now places the 7 in B4, the 4 in A4, and the 5 in B3. Clue 5 therefore tells us the 2 is in A2, and the 11 in A3.

	1	2	3	4
A	8	2	11	4
B	3	12	5	7
C	6	10	1	9

745

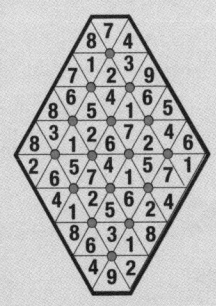

746

Shadow 5

747

From the top: C, E, D, B, A, F

748

Hound 4

749

9	×	2	÷	6	=	3
−		+		+		
4	+	8	÷	3	=	4
÷		−		−		
1	×	7	−	5	=	2
=		=		=		
5		3		4		

750

751

752

753

754

755

First, Eastern Star, Sue Archer, vet.
Second, Popcorn, Lesley Carson, doctor.
Third, Captain Candy, Jane Piggott, student.
Fourth, Drummer Boy, Vicky Mercer, secretary.
Fifth, Snowstorm, Di Richards, farmer.

756

No.	Name	Shots	Prize
1	Mary	7	sombrero
2	Gemma	3	holiday vouchers
3	Donald	6	deckchair
4	Jane	5	parasol
5	Mike	1	swimsuit
6	Carol	2	beach towel
7	John	8	beachball
8	Edward	4	sunglasses

757

Since the only letter in row B is not a vowel (clue 1), from clue 5, the U in question cannot be in row A or row B, and must be in row C, which places the J as the letter in row B. Similarly, from clues 1 and 3, the A must be in row C and the 7 in row B, so the S must be in row A. This cannot be in A4 (clue 3) or A2 (clue 6). If it was in A1, the A would be in C2 (clue 3), and the only positions for the U and the 1 would be C3 and C4. But C4 contains a letter (clue 6). Therefore the S must be in A3, and, from clue 3, B4 must contain a 7, and C4 the A. We know the J is the only letter in row B, so, from clue 4, the L must be in row A. We know it is not in A3, and the fact that the S is there also rules out the L for A2 (clue 4). Since we know a 7 is in B4, the L cannot be in A4 (clue 4), so it must be in A1, and the 6 in B1 (clue 4). Clue 5 now places the J in B2, a U in C2, and the 1 in C3. We have now placed three of the five numbers, leaving a 7 and a 4, one of which must be in B3 (clue 1). This cannot be the 7 (clue 2), so it must be the 4. So, from clue 4, the number in A2 must be the second 7. Clue 2 now rules out the second U for C1, so it must be in A4, leaving the Y in C1.

In summary:

	1	2	3	4
A	L	7	S	U
B	6	J	4	7
C	Y	U	1	A

758

The 19 in B3 is row 3's only two-digit number (clue 2), so the 9 cannot be in any of rows 1, 3 or 4 (clue 3), while the only single-digit number in row 2 is the 7 (clue 2), so the 9 must be in row 5, but not in square E5 (clue 3). Since the 11 is in row 4 (clue 6), clue 5 rules out the 16 for A4, so the 9 cannot be in A5. Nor can it be in C5 (clue 8). Since the 17 is in column D (clue 7), clue 5 rules out the 12 for E5, so, from clue 3, the 9 cannot be in D5, and, by elimination, must be in square B5. Therefore, from clue 3, the 16 must be in B4, and the 12 in C5. There must be exactly one zero in each row and each column (clue 1). We know the one in row 5 is not in B5 or C5, nor can it be in D5 (clue 7), or E5 (clue 5), so it must be in A5. The 1 in row 5 (clue 9) cannot be in E5, since the 6 is in row 1 (clues 5 and 9), so, by elimination, it must be in D5. The 17 in column D cannot be in D1 or D4 (clue 7), and clue 2 rules out D3. Therefore it must be in D2, and D1 therefore contains a zero (clue 7). The zero in row 3 cannot be in A3, C3 or D3 (clue 1), and we know it is not in B3, so it must be in E3. Clue 1 now rules out A4, D4 and E4 for the zero in row 4, which therefore must be in C4. The one in column B cannot be in B1 (clue 1), so it must be in B2. Clue 6 now places the 11 in E4, and the 5 in D4, so, from clue 7, the 8 must be in D3. The number in E5 cannot be any of 16 to 20 (clue 5), and we know it is not any of 1, 5, 6 (clue 9), 7 (clue 2), 8, 9, 11 or 12, so it must be one of 2, 3, 4, 10, 13, 14 or 15. Clue 5 rules out 3, 4 and 14, since we have placed 8, 9 and 19, and also rules out 2, 10 or 13, since we know none of 1, 9 or 12 is in C2, so, by elimination, 15 must be in E5, and, from clue 5, 20 must be in A4, and 14 in C2. Since the numbers in column E total 45 (clue 4), those in E1 and E2 must total 19. Therefore, since we have placed the 12, the 7 cannot be in E2, and therefore must be in A2 (clue 2). Now, from clue 4, the 13 must be in E2, so, from that clue, E1 must contain the 6. The 3 cannot be in C3 (clue 8), so, from clue 10, it must be in A3, and the 10

in A1. The 18 is not in C1 or C3 (clue 8), so it must be in B1. Clue 6 now places the 2 in C1, and the 4 in C3.

In summary:

	A	B	C	D	E
1	10	18	2	0	6
2	7	0	14	17	13
3	3	19	4	8	0
4	20	16	0	5	11
5	0	9	12	1	15

759

Alistair is 9 (clue 4). The oldest child, who produced picture 1 (clue 2), cannot be Mary (clue 1), or Silas, whose monocled character is somewhere to the right of another (clue 3), so she must be Jennifer. We now know Silas is not 9 or 11, nor is he 8 (clue 3), so he must be 10, leaving Mary as 8. So, from clue 1, picture 2 must have been drawn by Alistair, aged 9. This face is clean-shaven (clue 1), but does not have the monocle, so it must be wearing spectacles. From clue 3, Mary must have drawn picture 3, and Silas picture 4. From clue 4, picture 1 does not have a moustache, so it must have a beard, leaving the moustache adorning picture 3.

In summary:
1, Jennifer, 11, beard.
2, Alistair, 9, spectacles.
3, Mary, 8, moustache.
4, Silas, 10, monocle.

760

761

There are thirteen turkeys in the picture.

762

763

764

Amanda Byrne, Mariana, USA.
Gail Thornhill, Francisca, Australia.
Melanie Potter, Isabella, Zimbabwe.
Susan Edmunds, Mistress Overdone, Eire.
Wilma Atkinson, Juliet, Canada.

765

766

Students 3 and 6

767

There are eight swords in the picture.

768

The boy in the red sweater was not Danny or Lewis, who had the chocolate bar (clue 4), and Kevin's sweater was blue (clue 1), so the red sweater must have been Simon's. The first friend met did not have the red sweater (clue 4), or the blue one (clue 1), and number 3 wore the beige sweater (clue 2), so number 1 must have been in the green one. So, from clue 3, it was boy 2 who was eating a banana. We know his sweater was not beige or green, and he was not Simon, in the red sweater (clue 3), so he must have worn the blue sweater, and is therefore Kevin. So, from clue 1, boy 1, in the green sweater, was eating a lollipop. This rules out Kevin, Lewis and Simon, so he must have been Danny. By elimination, Simon must have been eating an apple, and Lewis must have been the third friend Tommy met, wearing the beige sweater, which leaves Simon as friend number 4.

In summary:
1, Danny, green, lollipop.
2, Kevin, blue, banana.
3, Lewis, beige, chocolate bar.
4, Simon, red, apple.

769

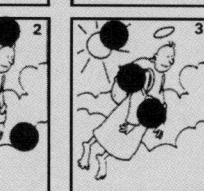

770

7	+	9	÷	8	=	2
+		+		−		
2	x	6	÷	3	=	4
x			÷		+	
1	+	5	−	4	=	2
=		=		=		
9		3		9		

771

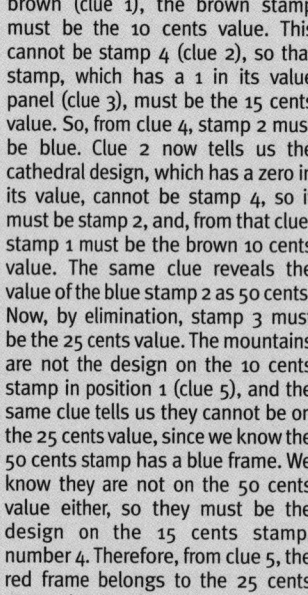

772

192 — 6 — 8 — 4
9 — 1
7 — 3 — 2
504 — 12 — 162 — 16

773

8, 9, 0, 4, 2, 6, 3, 7, 5, 1

774

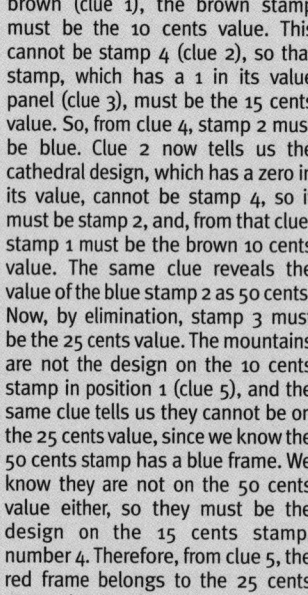

775

Sunday, Mexican bandit, *The Storm*. Tuesday, Italian sailor, *Hunted Man*. Wednesday, Brazilian policeman, *Web Of Fear*. Friday, Spanish waiter, *Split Seconds*. Saturday, Greek soldier, *Dead End*.

776

Picture 2

777

778

Trail 2

779

Since the figure 5 is not printed in brown (clue 1), the brown stamp must be the 10 cents value. This cannot be stamp 4 (clue 2), so that stamp, which has a 1 in its value panel (clue 3), must be the 15 cents value. So, from clue 4, stamp 2 must be blue. Clue 2 now tells us the cathedral design, which has a zero in its value, cannot be stamp 4, so it must be stamp 2, and, from that clue, stamp 1 must be the brown 10 cents value. The same clue reveals the value of the blue stamp 2 as 50 cents. Now, by elimination, stamp 3 must be the 25 cents value. The mountains are not the design on the 10 cents stamp in position 1 (clue 5), and the same clue tells us they cannot be on the 25 cents value, since we know the 50 cents stamp has a blue frame. We know they are not on the 50 cents value either, so they must be the design on the 15 cents stamp, number 4. Therefore, from clue 5, the red frame belongs to the 25 cents stamp, leaving the 15 cents value as the green stamp. Clue 3 tells us stamp 3 does not depict the harbour, so its subject must be the waterfall, leaving the harbour as the design on stamp 1, the brown 10 cents value.

In summary:
1, harbour, 10 cents, brown.
2, cathedral, 50 cents, blue.
3, waterfall, 25 cents, red.
4, mountains, 15 cents, green.

780

Cynthia Iveagh, pigs, 79.
Janet Wallace, dragons, 118.
Monica Tate, teddy-bears, 63.
Ruth Courtauld, dogs, 91.
Veronica Hayward, cats, 107.

781

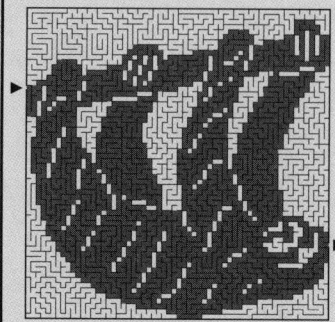

782

783

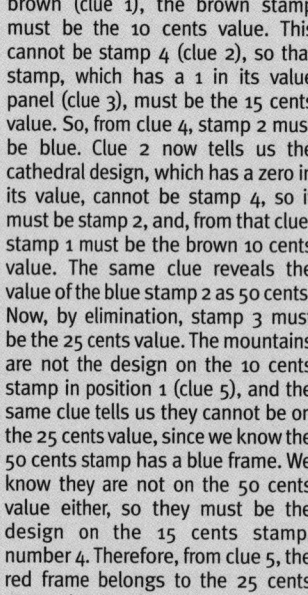

784

9	+	5	÷	7	=	2
−			+		+	
1	x	8	−	3	=	5
÷			−		−	
2	x	4	−	6	=	2
=		=		=		
4		9		4		

785

331, 041
These are multiples of 7 with the figures reversed. 77 (!), 84, 91....

786

From the top: orange, red, green blue, yellow, lavender.

787

Cathedral, Brian Box, 4,000 matches, two months.
Ferris wheel, Alec Wood, 4,500 matches, three months.
Ship, Charlie Head, 5,000 matches, six months.
Steam-roller, Eric Striker, 3,000 matches, seven months.
Windmill, Derek Burns, 3,500 matches, four months.

788

No solution needed to this problem.

789

790

Print 2

791

Bunny 2 is different.

792

The three pieces are: 1, 6 and 9.

793

794

From the top: D, A, E, B, C, F

795

1	+	2	+	4	= 7
+		x		+	
8	+	7	÷	5	= 3
÷		–		÷	
3	x	6	÷	9	= 2
=		=		=	
3		8		1	

796

6	+	7	–	5	= 8
x				x	
4	+	3	+	2	= 9
÷		x			
8	+	1	÷	9	= 1
=		=		=	
3		4		1	

797

Ramona, green, Phil Marvin.
Remus, red, George Krag.
Ricky, silver, Claudia Score.
Romulus, blue, Selena Link.
Roxanne, yellow, Gregory Jenkins.

798

Chloe Potts, 4, sunflowers.
Dean Barrow, 7, rocket.
Jack Dibber, 3, poppies.
Kylie Trowell, 6, candytuft.
Martine Shovell, 5, radishes.

799

There are seven stun guns in the picture.

800

Path B

801

802

803

6 + 8 + 17 = 31. Treble 6 = 18, double 17 = 34, single 8 = 8; thus 18 + 34 + 8 = 60.

804

Order 4 – 3, 7 – 8, 2 – 1, 5 – 6, 9 – 10.

805

Wednesday. Each answer has the same vowels as the day with which it is associated.

806

29	33	47	61	15
57	21	25	39	43
35	49	53	17	31
13	27	41	45	59
51	55	19	23	37

807

8, 2, 7, 6, 3, 1, 0, 9, 4, 5

808

15 and 13.
Each new number is the sum of the digits in the previous two circles; thus 3 + 7 = 10, 7 + 1 + 0 = 8, 8 + 1 + 0 = 9, 8 + 9 = 17, 9 + 1 + 7 = 17 and 1 + 7 + 1 + 7 = 16 – so the sequence continues: 1 + 7 + 1 + 6 = 15 and 1 + 6 + 1 + 5 = 13.

809

The green mailbox cannot belong to number 228 or number 234 (clue 1), and the one at number 232 is blue (clue 4), so the green one must be at number 230. Arlene cannot live at 228 (clue 2), and, since her box is yellow (clue 2), this rules out numbers 230 and 232, so her home must be number 234. Now, by elimination, Mrs Baron's red mailbox (clue 3) must be at number 228. So, from clue 1, Mrs Gerber must live at number 232, and Gemma must be Mrs Baron at number 228. Arlene is not Mrs Fishbein (clue 2), so she must be Mrs Flint, leaving Mrs Fishbein at number 230. From clue 4, Louise is not Mrs Gerber, so she must be Mrs Fishbein, leaving Mrs Gerber as Kate.

In summary:
228, Gemma Baron, red.
230, Louise Fishbein, green.
232, Kate Gerber, blue.
234, Arlene Flint, yellow.

810

Chess. Replace each letter by the one that follows it in the alphabet (with A following Z) and the 'words' spell out: Karpov, Miles, Spassky, Fisher, Kasparov.

811

Bird 4

812

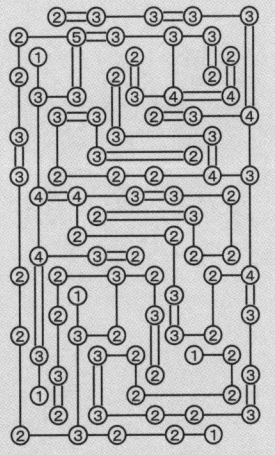

813

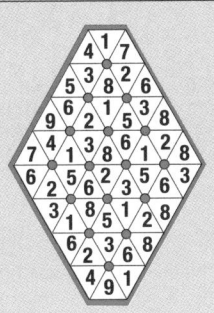

814

22 hats

815

Josie's pet is a puppy (clue 5). Julie's cannot be a budgie (clue 4), or a tortoise (clue 3), so it must be a cat. So she is not the girl in position 4, who has a budgie (clue 5). This fact also rules out Josie as girl 4, and clue 1 rules out Jenny, so it must be Jemima who is in position 4. By elimination, the tortoise must belong to Jenny. Since Jemima is in position 4, Julie cannot be in position 3 (clue 3).

Nor can she be in position 2 (clue 4), so she must be in position 1. So, since Julie's pet is the cat, Josie cannot be in position 2 (clue 2). Therefore she must be in position 3, and position 2 must be occupied by Jenny. Clue 5 now tells us Josie is ten. Julie cannot be eight (clue 4), or nine (clue 3), so she must be eleven. Jenny cannot be nine (clue 1), so she is eight. Jemima is nine.

In summary:
1, Julie, 11, cat.
2, Jenny, 8, tortoise.
3, Josie, 10, puppy.
4, Jemima, 9, budgie.

816

Karate expert number 6.

817

818

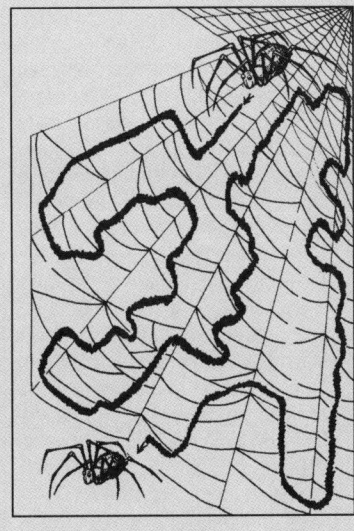

819

820

The central letter is T (clue 2), so the O referred to in clue 3, which must be in the top row, cannot be immediately above it (clue 2), nor can it be in any of the first, second or fourth squares in the top row (clue 3), so it must be in the right-hand square. So, from clue 3, a P is immediately right of the T, and an A immediately below it. So, from clue 6, one of the Ns must be immediately to the left of the T, and another N must be diagonally above left of the middle row A (clue 6). This fact rules out the first two squares of the middle row and the right-hand end square for the A, and we have placed letters in the third, fourth and fifth, so the A must be in the sixth square, immediately below the O, which places an N immediately to the left of the latter (clue 6). We have now placed two As, two Ns and one P and the two Es are both in the same row (clue 7), so the identical letters referred to in clue 5 must be the remaining two Os. The two Es in the same row cannot be the first and second letters of the top row, whose other letters are all in place (clue 1), nor can they be the first or last letters of the middle row (clue 4), which leaves only one square available in that row, so they must both be in the bottom row. But they cannot occupy the two last squares of that row either (clue 1), so one of them must be in its second square. Since the third square of the middle row contains an N, the pairing N P (clue 8) cannot be in the two remaining top row squares (clue 1), and we know one of the two unfilled squares in the bottom row contains an E, so, by elimination, the N must be in the first square of the middle row, and the P in the second. The L cannot be in the right-hand end square of the middle row, nor can it be in the bottom row (clue 6), so it must be in the top row, but, if it were in the second square, the A would have to be in the third (clue 6), which clue 10 denies, so the L must be in the third square, and the A therefore in the second (clue 6). Clue 10 now places the B at the right-hand end of the middle row. So the other letter in the bottom row, along with the second E, must, by elimination, be the R. This cannot be in the right-hand end square, where it would complete the word Oar reading downwards (clue 9), so it must be in the fourth square, and the E in the one to its right.

In summary:

O	A	L	N	O
N	P	N	T	P	A	B
O	E	A	R	E

821

Given the first two, each subsequent item is formed from the previous two: if they are both the same colour, the next shape is a circle: if not, it is a square. If they are both the same shape, the next colour is blue: if not, it is green.

822

13/36 = 0.36111...

823

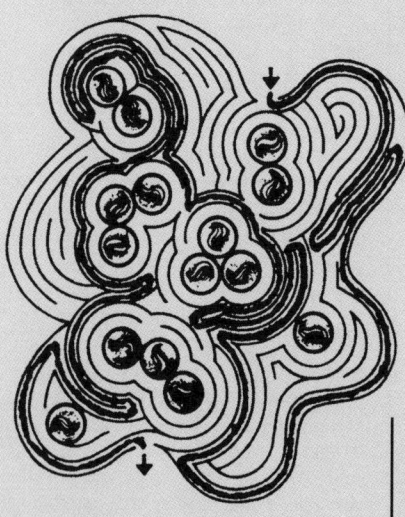

824

Treble 13 Double 18 Single 16

825

No. The average is 192mph. Suppose each leg is 100 miles. The first took them one hour. The next leg took half an hour, the third a third of an hour and the fourth a quarter of an hour. The total distance is 400 miles and the total time taken is two and one twelfth hours. That's 192 miles per hour.

826

37

827

1 Extra jewel on sword, 2 Detail on helmet, 3 Spike on right knee, 4 Detail on sword handle.

828

Pictures 1 and 4

829

The blue box contains 58 items (clue 2), and the green box contains the screws (clue 3), so the 43 nails, which are not in the brown box (clue 1), must be in the red one. We know the green box does not contain 43 or 58 items, and clue 3 rules out 65, so it must

contain 39 screws. So, by elimination, the contents of the brown box must be 65 items. These are not washers (clue 3), so they must be carpet tacks, and they are in box C (clue 4), which leaves the blue box containing 58 washers. The green box cannot be box D (clue 3), since it has two neighbours, so that clue places it as box B, and the blue box containing the washers must be box A (also clue 3), leaving the red box as box D.

In summary:
A, blue, 58 washers.
B, green, 39 screws.
C, brown, 65 carpet tacks.
D, red, 43 nails.

830

831

Since machine B was used by the lady with the red and white costume (clue 5), clue 4 rules out machine D for Euphemia Ponsonby, who hired a machine next but one to the one used by the lady in the orange and white costume. Since Miss Langthorpe used machine C (clue 2), Euphemia's machine must have been either A or B. Therefore Lavinia's must have been B or C (clue 4), so she did not use machine D either. Nor, since we know Miss Langthorpe used machine C, can Bertha have changed in machine D (clue 1). Therefore, by elimination, Victoria must have done so. So her surname cannot have been Marchbanks (clue 1). We know it was not Ponsonby or Langthorpe, so it must have been Carstairs, and her costume was therefore green and white (clue 3). Therefore Euphemia cannot have used machine B (clue 4), and, as we have seen, she must therefore have changed in machine A, which leaves machine B as the one used by Miss Marchbanks. So, from clue 1, Bertha must have been Miss Langthorpe in machine C, and, from clue 4, Lavinia was Miss Marchbanks who used machine B. Clue 4 also identifies Bertha Langthorpe, in machine C, as the lady in the orange and white bathing-suit, so, by elimination, Euphemia Ponsonby must have worn the blue and white striped one.

In summary:
A, Euphemia Ponsonby, blue and white. B, Lavinia Marchbanks, red and white. C, Bertha Langthorpe, orange and white. D, Victoria Carstairs, green and white.

832

833

834

835

Paul Hand was Esther's partner (clue 4), so Martina must have been partnered by Richard. So he held the Ace of Hearts (clue 2). Therefore, from clue 1, Ruff had the Ace of Diamonds in the North hand. We now know Paul Hand did not have the Aces of Diamonds or Hearts, and it was a woman who was in the West seat with the Ace of Spades (clue 3), so Paul must have had the Ace of Clubs. So he was not South (clue 5). We know he was not North, and he cannot have been West (clue 3), so he must have been East, and Esther was therefore West, who had the Ace of Spades (clues 3 and 4). By elimination, Richard, who we know was not North, must have been South, and Ruff, in the North seat, was

therefore Martina. Esther's surname is not Tenace (clue 3), so it must be Trick, leaving Tenace as Richard.

In summary:
North, Martina Ruff, Ace of Diamonds. East, Paul Hand, Ace of Clubs. South, Richard Tenace, Ace of Hearts. West, Esther Trick, Ace of Spades.

836

The three identical vases are the middle vase on the top line, the end vase on the third line and the end vase on the bottom line.

837

Silhouette 1 is stereo f and silhouette 2 is stereo h.

838

839

840

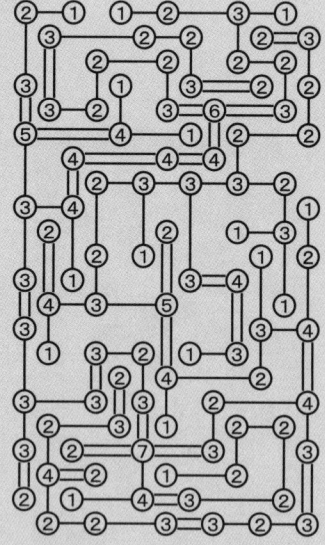

841

The man in seat 13 of row A (clue 6) cannot be Peter or Henry (clue 1), or Robert (clue 4). Judy cannot have a seat numbered 13 (clue 5), so that clue rules out seat 13 in row

A for both Charles and Vincent, so, by elimination, the man in that seat must be Tony. Angela is also in row A (clue 1), which must also seat one more woman (clue 3). This is not Nina, who has seat 12 in row B (clue 2), and it cannot be Janet or Lydia (clue 7). Clue 5 rules out Judy, so, by elimination, Maxine must have a front row seat. This cannot be numbered 10 or 11 (clue 4), and we know it is not 13, so it must be 12. Therefore Robert has seat 10 in that row (clue 4), which leaves Angela in seat 11. So, from clue 1, Peter has seat 11 in row B. There must be a second man in that row (clue 3). This is not Henry, who must be in row C (clue 1), and clue 5 rules out Vincent for either seat 10 or seat 13 in that row, which are the only two still vacant. We know Tony and Robert are in row A, so, by elimination, Charles must be in row B. He cannot be in seat 13 (clue 5), so he must be in seat 10. Therefore, from clue 5, Judy must be in seat 10 of row C, and Vincent in seat 11 of that row. So, from clues 1 and 7, Henry must have seat 12 of row C, and Lydia seat 13 of the same row, leaving seat 13 in row B occupied by Janet.

In summary:
Row A: 10, Robert; 11, Angela; 12, Maxine; 13, Tony. Row B; 10, Charles; 11, Peter; 12, Nina; 13, Janet. Row C: 10, Judy; 11, Vincent; 12, Henry; 13, Lydia.

842

843

Treble 15 Double 5 Single 11

844

845

Gretchen, who is 6, cannot be number 4 (clue 1), and number 3 is 7 (clue 4). Number 1 is a boy (clue 3), so, by elimination, Gretchen must be number 2. So, from clue 1, the child aged 7 in position 3 is the cowherd's child. Maria, whose father is an apothecary (clue 5), cannot be number 1 (clue 3), so she must be number 4, and, from clue 5, she is 5, leaving the boy in position 1 as 8. So he is not Hans (clue 2), and must be Johann, leaving Hans as the seven-year-old son of the cowherd. From clue 3, Gretchen's father cannot be the butcher, so he must be the woodcutter, leaving Johann as the butcher's son.

In summary: 1, Johann, 8, butcher. 2, Gretchen, 6, woodcutter. 3, Hans, 7, cowherd. 4, Maria, 5, apothecary.

846

847

848

The $5,000 prize cannot have been in box 1 or 6 (clue 7) or 2, from which Lynne got a smaller sum (clue 2), or 3 (clue 7 again) or 5 (clue 3), so must have been in box 4. From clue 7, a man opened box 3 and a woman box 5, and since no two men opened adjacent boxes, the remaining two females, Sharon and Susan, must have opened boxes 4 and 5. From clue 6, it was Susan who opened the winner's box 4, while Rob opened box 3, Sharon box 5 and, by elimination Jim box 1. Both Lynne and Sharon won cash (clue 2), so, from clue 5, the box with the spoon was opened by either Michael or Rob. But, from clue 4, neither Michael nor Jim can have found the soap, so Rob must have done so, leaving Michael with the spoon and Jim with some cash. Therefore, from clue 5, Sharon must have struck lucky with $1,000. Now, from clue 4, Susan was the fifth contestant, and from clue 6, Rob was the sixth. The first contestant wasn't him (clue 1), or Lynne (clue 2), or Michael (clue 3), so must have been Sharon. From clues 2 and 3, either Michael or Lynne must have opened third or fourth, so Jim must have been second. He didn't collect 50 cents (clue 5), so Lynne must have done so, leaving Jim with $100, Michael as the third contestant (clue 3), and Lynne as the fourth.

In summary: 1, second, Jim, $100. 2, fourth, Lynne, 50 cents. 3, sixth, Rob, bar of soap. 4, fifth, Susan, $5,000. 5, first, Sharon, $1,000. 6, third, Michael, wooden spoon.

849

12. Count the die spots you can see which are placed around a central spot. Thus 3 is worth 2 and 5 is worth 4. The other die spots 2, 4 and 6 are worth nothing – they do not surround a central spot. 1 is just a grease spot with nothing around it.

850

Poster A shows Jacob (clue 2) and poster D shows Churchman, so Herbert, who's shown on the poster horizontally adjacent to the one showing 'Butch' McColl (clue 1), can't be shown on poster C, nor does poster C show Silvester Jaggard (clue 2), so it must show Matthew. We now know that Silvester Jaggard isn't shown on poster A, C or D, so he must be on poster B. By elimination, Herbert must be on poster D, and, from clue 1, Matthew, on poster C, must be 'Butch' McColl. By elimination, Jacob's surname must be Wolf. So, from clue 3, 'Pony' must be Silvester Jaggard on poster B. Herbert Churchman on poster D isn't 'Apache' (clue 4), so his nickname must be 'Rio', and 'Apache' must be Jacob Wolf on poster A.

In summary:
A, Jacob 'Apache' Wolf.
B, Silvester 'Pony' Jaggard.
C, Matthew 'Butch' McColl.
D, Herbert 'Rio' Churchman.

851

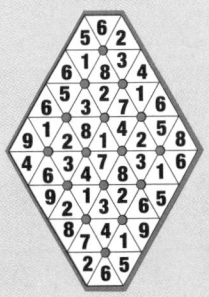

852

1 and 8, 2 and 7, 3 and 4, 5 and 6 are pairs; 9 is the odd-one-out.

853

Hotel 1 has 158 rooms (clue 3). Since Perry manages hotel 3 (clue 5), clue 4 rules out hotel 4 as the one with 197 rooms, which is next clockwise from Guy's Castle Hotel, nor does hotel 4 have 203 rooms (clue 2), so it must have 224. Its manager cannot be Guy (clue 4), and we know he is not Perry. Clue 1 rules out Max, whose hotel has fewer rooms than the Majestic, so he must be Rupert. We know the Majestic is not managed by Guy, and clue 1 rules out both Max and Rupert, so it must be Perry's hotel, number 3. So, from clue 1, Max must run hotel 1, the smallest, which leaves Guy's Castle Hotel as number 2 on the plan. So, from clue 4, the Majestic must have 197 rooms, leaving the Castle with 203. Clue 5 tells us the Excelsior cannot be Max's hotel, so it must be Rupert's, leaving Max's as the Grand.

In summary:
1, Grand, Max, 158 rooms. 2, Castle, Guy, 203 rooms. 3, Majestic, Perry, 197 rooms. 4, Excelsior, Rupert, 224 rooms.

854

2 and 3 are twins, 1 has an extra nail in the fence, 4 has an extra label on the tin.

855

From clue 5, the 1 cannot be in column 1 or column 5, and, since there are no two-digit numbers in columns 1 or 4 (clue 1), the 1 cannot be in column 2 or column 3 (clue 5), so it must be in column 4. But it cannot be in B4 (clue 6), so it must be in D4. So, from clue 5, the 12 must be in C5, and the 10 in E3. The 8 is directly above the 13 (clue 7). This cannot be in column 1 or column 4 (clue 1), nor, since the 13 cannot be in square D2 (clue 1), can they be in column 2 either. Nor can the number 13 be in E5 (clue 4), which rules out column 5. Therefore, from clue 7, the 8 must be in A3, and the 13 in C3. So, from clue 4, square E5 must contain the 7. The 11 cannot be in column 1 or column 4 (clue 1), nor can it be in square A5 (clue 1), so it must be in column 2. But it cannot be in D2 (clue 1), so it must be in B2. The 9 is not in a corner square (clue 2), which leaves only squares B4, C1 or D2. But it cannot be in B4 or D2 (clue 6), so it must be in C1. Since the 6 is directly below the 2 (clue 3), it cannot be in D2, B4, A1 or A5, so it must be in E1. The 2 is therefore in A1 (clue 3). The remaining numbers to be placed are 3, 4 and 5. So, from clue 6, the 5 must be in B4 and the 3 in D2, which leaves the 4 in A5.

In summary:

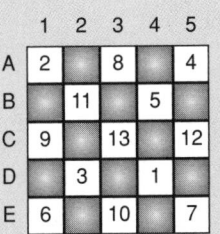

856

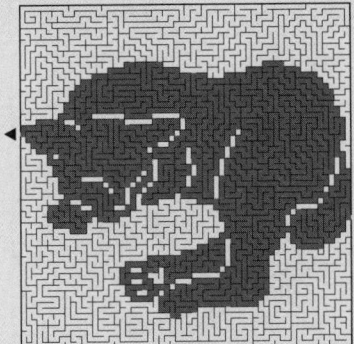

857

Just place the canoe on a flat surface and *spin* it. Centri-whatsisname (petal not fugal?) force will carry the balls up and away at the same time.

858

MERCHANT	CUSTOMER	ITEM	JOB
BRICKSRUS	T BRAKES	SAND	GARAGE
HIRAN HIRE	C Y BERMAN	STONE	BUNGALOW
HODSUP	ALF PRYCE	CEMENT	WALL
JUST SLATES	VAL HEEGHAM	WOOD	CONSERV.
MORTAR MART	A COWERBOY	BALLAST	PATH

859

1 and 2 will knot; 3 and 4 will not.

860

861

862

O. Clockwise from A, the letters have straight lines, then straight and curve then curved only and this pattern repeats.

863

364 – one for every day of the year – except Christmas Day, perhaps. He brings the first present 12 times and the twelfth present once, so that's 1 x 12 twice. He brings the second present 11 times and the eleventh present twice, so that's 2 x 11 twice. So the total is twice (1 x 12 + 2 x 11 + 3 x 10 + 4 x 9 + 5 x 8 + 6 x 7) = 2 x 182 = 364.

864

1st/2nd floors, Cheape & Chirfle, publishers, John King. 3rd floor, Rocke & Rowle, accountants, Sue Tyler. 4th floor, Lorrel & Hardie, stockbrokers, Gail Hood. 5th/6th floors, Kopz & Roberts, lawyers, Ann Blake. 7th, Bredd & Cheise, architects, Keith Lyons.

865

866

48	÷	12	=	4	+	40	=	44
–		+		x		÷		–
32	÷	4	=	8	÷	4	=	2
=		=		=		=		=
16	+	16	=	32	+	10	=	42
x		+				+		+
4	+	6	=	10	+	1	=	11
=		=		=		=		=
64	–	22	=	42	+	11	=	53

867

24. There are six numbers on a die. In each picture, just multiply the values of all the die numbers you cannot see (they've 'gone to lunch'). In the third picture you have 1, 2, 3 and 5. So 4 and 6 are missing.

868

SIR	COMPANY	BUSINESS	CHAIR
FITZ-TENSION	OBD	CONSTRUCTION	B N KEW
JESTIFE	RTC	P R	R T FISH
JOHN SNYFE	PNT	TRAVEL	A C MAYNES
TAYNE-LEE	LTP	INSURANCE	T D HUSS
VANCE-HALL	KGH	BANKING	L D RHADO

869

Treble 18   Double 4   Single 13

870

8	1	1	8	1	8
4	5	6	6	7	3
5	7	6	5	5	3
7	4	6	3	2	2
3	3	1	3	8	2
2	5	6	2	3	5
1	7	1	4	7	7

871

96 – 97 – 98 – 99 – 100

872

Using just initial leters, such as DG for double glazing and DG' for NOT double glazing, the clues can be charted as follows:
1 DG---CH   2 RR---FG   3 ON---GD
and so on. Now form the longest chain of linked facts: clues 1 and 11, for instance, give DG---CH---C' which says that houses with double glazing

have central heating and do not have chimneys. Number 51, being an odd numbered house, gives this chain:
ON---GD---RR---FG---PG---DG---CH---C'---LW.
3 5 2 12 9 1 11 7 (clue number).
So number 51 has a green door, red roof, front garden, plastic gnomes, double glazing, central heating, no chimney and leaded windows.

873

A 33 B 1089 C 990 D 132 E 858 F 660
G 205 H 238 J 217 K 525 L 742 M 427
N 106 P 321 Q 374 R 801 S 666 T 264
U 402 V 735 W 531 X 617 Y 6534 Z 99

34 + 16 + 19 = 69   86 – 34 – 30 = 22
27 + 42 + 22 = 91   98 – 17 – 50 = 31
57 + 31 – 50 = 38   62 + 15 – 64 = 13
39 + 60 – 25 = 74   70 + 23 – 68 = 25
74 – 38 + 20 = 56   63 – 49 + 72 = 86
90 – 61 + 18 = 47   51 – 25 + 36 = 62

874

	17	7	43	27		41	10	13
13	2	1	3	7	6	3	1	2
23	8	2	4	9	24/23	9	7	8
44	7	4	5	8	9	6	2	3
	30	12/15	1	3	6	2	20	14
19	7	3	9	14/9	8	1	9	2
14	2	1	7	4	22/35	5	8	9
37	4	2	6	5	1	7	9	3
21	9	4	8	12/13	4	8	29	11
13	8	5	17/10	9	8	8/7	3	
	4	26/16	1	4	7	2	9	3
11	1	7	3	14	5	1	5	2
18	3	9	6	28	9	6	8	5

875

The three squares the same are 3F, 7E and 10B.

876

Objects are in squares 1b, 4e, 5b and 7c.

877

Treble 14   Double 19   Single 3

878

Horse/Sue – Peacock/Joan
Elephant/David – Dragon/Bob
Camel/Edward – Zebra/Chloe
Unicorn/Alan – Emu/Helen

879

880

Winners: Ann and Clive Dawson, Director, Butcher, 77.
The rest were: Brenda and Pete Morris, Mail lady, Mechanic, 68.
Rose and Len Watson, Sculptor, Caterer, 64. Thelma and Jack Kelly, Teacher, Vet, 75.

881

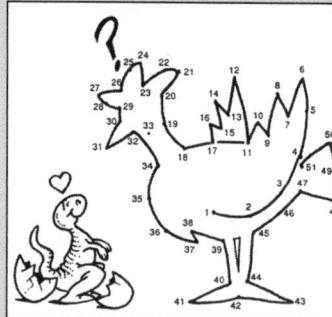

882

36	+	12	=	48	–	26	=	22
–								–
20	+	5	=	25	–	17	=	8
=				=				=
16	+	7	=	23	–	9	=	14
+				+				+
15	+	11	=	26	–	3	=	23
=				=				=
31	+	18	=	49	–	12	=	37

883

4659
7373
13977
32613
13977
32613
34350807

884

2nd Floor, Edgely, Innish, Newton Newton
1st Floor, Addams, Morris, Kennet, Barber
G.Floor, Harris, Davies, Davies, Farmer

885

Squares 2d, 5a and 9e are the same.

886

72	÷	12	=	6	+	33	=	39
–		–		x		–		+
45	÷	9	=	5	x	4	=	20
=		=		=		=		=
27	+	3	=	30	+	29	=	59
+		+				–		+
11	+	4	=	15	–	13	=	2
=		=		=		=		=
38	+	7	=	45	+	16	=	61

887

888

The four shapes appear in squares 1b, 2f, 6b and 7e.

889

METHOD	FORENAME	SURNAME	COMPANY
ACUPUNCTURE	ELSA	POPPIN	HI-FI NANTS
CHIN. BALLS	ELLIS	DEE	J C NUTTS
SITAR MUSIC	NATHAN	TEWITT	JUST LOANS
YOGA	VAL	HEEGHAM	U B LOOPY

890

891

892

Fragments 1, 3 and 6 and fragments 5, 4 and 2 form the two pillars.

893

PAPER	PAPER	HEADLINE	HEADLINE
DAILY	NEWS	WILD	ORGY
EVENING	ECHO	JOLLY	BINGE
MORNING	STANDARD	MAD	ANTICS
SUNDAY	ARGUS	HILARIOUS	PARTY
WEEKLY	CHRONICLE	OUTRAGEOUS	ROMP

894

895

Squares the same are: 5B, 2I and 6G.

896

897

Don – Masked – Gladiator – orange trunks; Fred – Caped – Avenger – black trunks; Jack – Hooded – Warrior – silver trunks; Tom – Secret Crusader – purple trunks.

898

A7 B4 C2 D5 E8 F1 G3 H6 Score 64

899

30 10	40 02	11 04	14 01	42 00	40 02
40 41	31 14	14 04	45 00	52 02	22 05
10 41	40 41	23 13	43 02	43 11	20 34
01 53	13 41	24 21	61 11	21 33	03 42
05 04	01 35	05 31	22 32	30 15	01 62
04 02	24 03	43 41	13 41	10 44	51 21
13 05	52 02	35 10	04 41	31 41	60 30
01 03	31 02	33 00	05 10	02 40	20 40

900

23. Four spoons balance 26 forks, so 2 spoons balance 13 forks; thus one knife balances 5 forks, so 2 knives balance 10 forks.

901

Treble 8 Double 20 Single 13

902

Take two.
Since each player has an even number, she can be sure of winning by having an even total and leaving five shells. Whatever the other player then does, she can be sure to *take an odd number* on her last turn and so win the game. By taking two and leaving five, if the other child takes one or two, take three. If she takes three, then take one. If one is left, the other player has to take it, making her score even again.

903

904

1 Cookies 2 Cakes 3 Tea/Coffee 4 Bread 5 Pet food 6 Soap Powder 7 Cleaning fluids 8 Kitchen ware 9 Tinned fruit 10 Candy 11 Tinned veg. 12 Tinned meat 13 Home baking 14 Fruit juices 15 Frozen meat 16 Frozen veg.

905

906

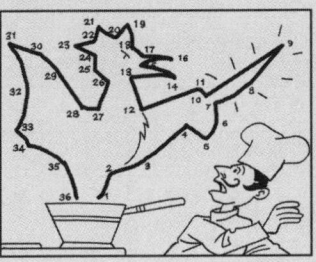

907

No. 6 is the matching top.

908

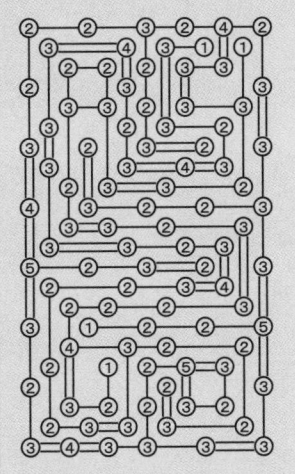

909

A6 B4 C7 D1 E3 F5 G2 H8 Score 58

910

The five errors are:
1 The model's earring is missing. 2 The frill on the model's right shoulder is different. 3 The model's left sleeve has thinner bands. 4 The central design under the waistband of the skirt is not pointed. 5 The skirt has an extra band on it.

911

The four objects appear in squares b1, b6, e5 and f2.

912

913

914

4	5	5	2	5	4	6	1	4	3
5	9	4	1	4	8	5	0	5	7
5	3	5	5	6	2	3	9	4	6
4	2	4	4	5	1	5	8	6	0
5	6	6	3	4	0	4	7	4	9

915

A	B	C	D	E	F	G	H	J	K
5	3	8	1	6	0	2	7	9	4

916

Treble 15   Double 6   Single 14

917

6	4	3	5	1	2
5	3	2	6	4	1
3	5	1	4	2	6
2	1	6	3	5	4
1	6	4	2	3	5
4	2	5	1	6	3

918

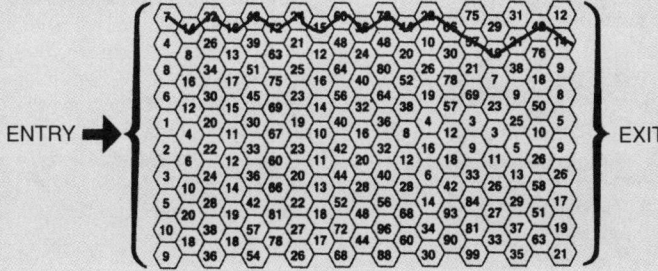

ENTRY ➤ · EXIT

919

3	2	1	4	7	5	6
4	3	2	5	6	7	1
2	7	5	6	1	3	4
6	1	3	2	5	4	7
7	4	6	1	3	2	5
1	5	7	3	4	6	2
5	6	4	7	2	1	3

920

921

The objects are hidden in squares d2, g2, e5 and b4.

922

Pictures 1 and 2 are twins. Picture 3 has an extra label on the large bag behind the chef. Picture 4 is missing a piece of rubbish from the bin.

923

ACT	DAY	FROM	AIRLINE
BEERS	FRIDAY	GERMANY	LEFTHANDA
ENGELBERT	THURSDAY	EIRE	AER FUNGUS
MARADONNA	MONDAY	USA	LO-CAL
SISTER	WEDNESDAY	CANADA	VIRGO
TINA	TUESDAY	FRANCE	SABRENA

924

Ellen – 1R, 4B, 3Y, 2V.
Geoff – 1R, 5G, 4V.
Percy – 2R, 4B, 3Y, 1V.
Rosie – 4R, 3G, 2Y, 1V.

925

7	5	1	4	3	6	2
5	4	6	7	1	2	3
3	6	5	1	2	4	7
4	1	2	6	7	3	5
2	3	7	5	6	1	4
6	7	3	2	4	5	1
1	2	4	3	5	7	6

926

7	16	11	22	13
19	5	25	2	8
14	1	21	10	18
12	9	4	15	23
17	24	6	20	3

927

Six inkpots. Four rulers balance five inkpots and four folders balance one inkpot.

928

A	B	C	D	E	F	G	H	J	K
5	7	1	6	2	8	3	0	9	4

929

A, B, D, F, H, M, N and Q

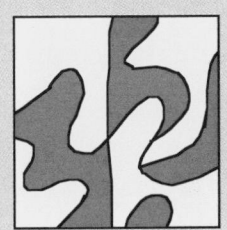

930

1st – No 1 – Swift Lad – Joe Percer;
2nd – No 2 – Silver Streak – Steve Caution;
3rd – No 4 – Crazy Lad – Willie Parsons;
4th – No 3 – Mother's Joy – Pat Ellery.

931

Second floor: Barber Carrol Davies Barber
First floor: Jenkin Harris Harris Quirke
Ground floor: Newton Farmer Farmer Newton

932

933

Fragments 2 and 3 are taken from the main picture.

934

The mistakes are: 1 An extra plume on the hat. 2 The beauty spot is missing. 3 The left shoulder flap is different. 4 The belt buckle is black. 5 An extra flower on the right sleeve.

935

NAME	HOUSE	NEIGHBOUR	HOUSE	PROBLEM
BARNEY	DREAM GNOME	CHATER	PAMENSAM	SLUGS
CAREY	JUSTUS	HUNTER	WEE KENDOS	NOISE
DAVEY	LAST STOP	FLETCHER	SCURGES	CATS
GURNEY	OUR PATCH	PACKER	THE BLOTTS	FENCE
MULVEY	MORTAR PAY	BREWER	WEAR EAR	TREE

936

17	6	14	11	3
8	23	2	18	13
19	16	21	9	1
5	12	24	7	22
10	20	4	25	15

937

4	6	7	2	1	3	5
1	2	5	7	3	6	4
6	4	3	5	7	1	2
5	1	4	3	6	2	7
2	3	1	4	5	7	6
3	7	2	6	4	5	1
7	5	6	1	2	4	3

938

1 11 2 8 3 15 4 18 5 20 6 9 7 19 8 14 9 6 10 12 11 16 12 7 13 10 14 17 15 13

939

7	+	1	÷	4	= 2
+		+		x	
9	−	6	x	3	= 9
÷				−	
8	+	2	−	5	= 5
=		=		=	
2		5		7	

940

■	1	2	3	1	■	1	3	2	1	■
■	0	■	3	3	■	■	1	■
2	0	■	4	6	8	2	4	■	2	2
7	0	1	1	■	1	■	2	1	3	6
2	■	2	2	9	9	6	8	■	4
■	■	7	1	1	1	8	6	7	■	■
2	■	2	5	1	5	4	5	6	■	1
6	3	1	2	■	2	■	2	9	1	2
8	9	■	5	1	5	1	0	■	1	2
■	0	■	0	■	3	■	3	■
■	2	0	0	0	■	7	1	3	3	■

The combination is 7111867.

941

942

Vases c and j are identical.

943

RESIDENT	HOUSE NO.	FIRM	JOB
A C MAYNES	4	GLOWBALL	FUSEBOX
BILL Q.	7	LIVEWIRES	SOCKETS
EARTHA GREEN	6	JUST SPARKS	NEW RING
LOTTIE WATTS	10	PLUGGINS	LIGHTS
PHIL O'MENT	3	SHOCKSRUS	REWIRING

944

Plug B

945

946

Picture 1 is missing the heel of the boot. Picture 4 is missing a knot in the wood. Picture 9 is missing a potato. Picture 12 is missing a brick to the left of the ladder. Picture 2 has a patch on the knee. Picture 6 has a label on the bag. Picture 8 has a pocket on the trousers.

947

DAPHNE – GEORGE
ENID – FRANK
GERTIE – LARRY
LAURA – JACK

948

The man bought jar h.

949

950

A	B	C	D	E	F	G	H	J	K
2	4	3	0	6	7	1	9	8	5

951

3	6	4	1	2	7	5
6	5	1	3	7	4	2
4	1	7	5	6	2	3
1	3	2	6	4	5	7
7	4	3	2	5	6	1
5	2	6	7	3	1	4
2	7	5	4	1	3	6

952

■	14	29	23	16	■	25	4	11
26	6	4	7	9	10/14	2	3	5
43	8	3	4	7	9	5	1	6
■	11	9	2	8	5	3	11	8
30	7	8	9	6	10	6	3	1
12	4	5	1	2	24	9	8	7

953

A Enid and Fiona   B Carol and Daisy
C Alice and Gina   D Beth and Helen

954

The five fakes are: the picture of the house, where the gatepost is too tall; the picture of the clown, where the decoration on his hat is too high; the picture of the horse and cart, where the cart's side is too low; the picture of the seagull, where the gull's right wing is too low; and the picture of the ballerina, where part of her skirt is missing.

955

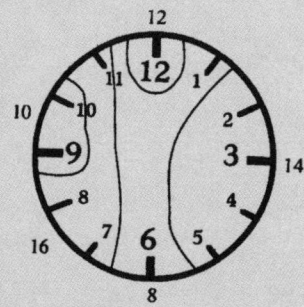

956

First, food hamper, 504, Mrs Smart.
Second, wine, 242, Father Murphy.
Third, bicycle, 198, Mrs Evans.
Fourth, hair drier, 161, Mr Copper.
Fifth, camera, 625, Mr White.

957

The treasure is buried under the large bush in square B5.

958

8

959

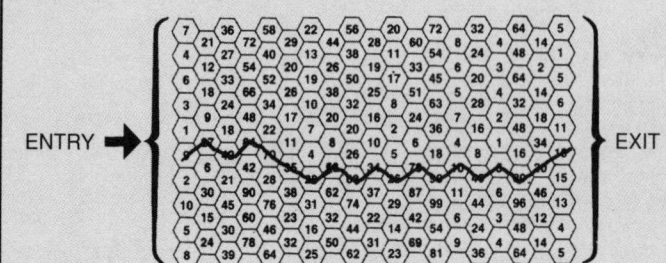

ENTRY ➤ ◀ EXIT

960

Karts 2 and 6

961

	11	19	17		6	18	21	16	11	8
14	2	8	4	39	5	4	9	8	7	6
24	8	9	7	23/13	1	3	8	5	4	2
15	1	2	3	9	7/18	1	4	2	20	6
	10	22/20	1	4	9	8/22	1	4	3	
18	7	9	2	8/10	1	2	5	11/12	9	2
4	1	3	14/9	6	8	18/11	8	2	7	1
18	2	8	5	21/14	9	7	10	17		
	12	11/23	3	1	5	2	15/16	3	9	7
9	2	6	1	10/16	1	4	5	12/29	3	9
10	1	9	12/21	4	13/7	7	3	2	1	
30	9	8	7	6	9/17	4	2	19	11	
10	10	12/7	2	7	4	13/5	7	5	1	
33	7	6	8	3	9	18	1	8	6	3
15	3	1	4	2	5	28	4	9	8	7

962

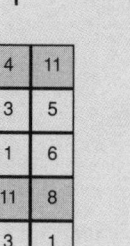

963

The four objects are in squares 4B, 4E, 7B and 6D.

964

965

1k, 2d, 3j

966

1 Elaine
2 Deborah
3 Claudia
4 Amy
5 Bridget.

967

	10	28	22		19	7	22		28	27
17	2	7	8	9	1	3	5	12/9	8	4
21	4	8	9	37/12	3	4	7	6	9	8
26	1	4	5	7	9	25	8	2	6	9
12	3	9	11	5	6	14	2	1	5	6

968

19	35	13		19	11		37	13
7	2	1	4	15	7	8	20/11	8	5	7
21	8	4	9	24/9	3	4	1	5
15	9	6	10/7	7	2	20/20	8	9	1
10/7	7	2	1	12/8	8	1	3	6	11
27	4	9	8	2	1	9	6	1	2
13	5	8	22	5	8	9	21	5	9

969

The carrot is at E3, the bottle is at E5, the cheese-wire is at C3, and the pencil is at F2.

970

4	6	1	2	3	5	7
3	7	2	4	5	6	1
2	1	4	5	7	3	6
6	3	7	1	2	4	5
1	4	5	7	6	2	3
7	5	6	3	4	1	2
5	2	3	6	1	7	4

971

A	B	C	D	E	F	G	H	J	K
7	0	8	3	5	6	1	4	2	9

972

From the top: A, E, B, D, F, C

973

Nos 2, 5 and 10

974

1–12, 2–11, 3–16, 4–15, 5–13, 6–10, 7–9, 8–14.

975

6	20	27	4		31	13	14
12	4	2	5	1	19/6	6	8	5
38	2	6	8	3	1	4	5	9
	13	4	9	12	5	7	12	14
19	7	5	3	4	20	5	9	6
19	6	3	2	8	20	9	3	8

976

C	B	A	H	G	F	E	D	C	B	A
F	E	D	E	F	J	I	E	K	E	D	B
A	J	U	V	H	F	U	C	H	I	H
F	D	B	I	E	A	Q	I	D	F	J
A	U	P	E	F	C	B	A	O	E	A
P	J	B	N	F	E	D	C	B	V	M
A	B	C	Y	H	P	E	F	O	K	N
F	E	D	P	K	J	P	D	C	B	A
E	D	C	B	E	P	O	K	C	E
V	F	M	U	Y	O	P	S	I	M	N
Q	R	E	C	U	A	P	O	K	C	N
F	E	W	N	G	E	S	F	E	D	A
D	D	A	C	B	A	A	R	B	C	A
C	K	J	F	E	D	O	T	D	E	F
F	E	A	X	V	F	C	B	A	X	E
D	I	Q	V	Y	A	F	I	L	E	D	I
A	C	D	F	E	C	B	A	B	F	E	D

977

978

1, 7, 9

979

12	4	9	6
2	5	10	8
11	3	1	7

980

	9	20	19	14		24	4	12
22	8	2	7	5	17/16	9	1	7
37	1	4	2	9	7	6	3	5
	9	5	4	12	9	3	9	14
22	6	3	5	8	17	2	1	4
14	3	6	1	4	12	4	2	5

981

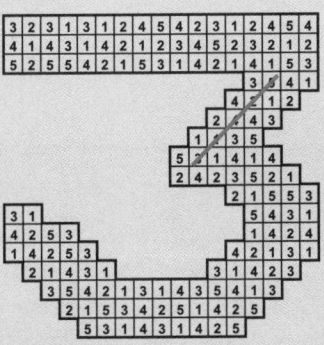

3	2	3	1	3	1	2	4	5	4	2	3	1	2	4	5	4
4	1	4	3	1	4	2	1	2	3	4	5	3	2	3	2	1	2
5	2	5	5	4	2	1	5	3	1	4	2	1	4	1	5	3

982

X	J	N	D	O
K	G	W	P	L
S	C		V	H
R	B	Z	F	T
E	Y	M	U	I	A

983

984

7	5	6	3	4	1	2
1	4	3	5	2	6	7
2	1	4	6	7	5	3
3	6	7	2	5	4	1
4	2	5	1	3	7	6
5	7	1	4	6	2	3

985

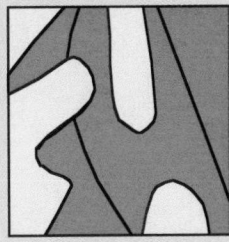

A, E, G, H, J, K, L and P

986

1	2	6	9	3	5
4	7	8	3	2	1
6	4	2	7	4	3
8	1	9	0	4	2
2	5	3	2	1	8
7	6	1	9	2	9

1	4	4		3	1
2	9		3		5
8			2	5	6
	8	2		1	
4		5	8		3
1	3	6		1	9

987

Put three on the ground to form an equilateral triangle then dig a hole to put the fourth one the same distance from each of the others. If you don't want to have holes in the garden, pile the earth up to make a pyramid and put the stone on top.

988

1	0	3	1	4	2	1
6	0	6	1	6	2	2
0	1	0	2	3	1	0
2	4	4	3	4	6	3
3	0	6	2	0	1	4
5	5	6	4	3	5	4
5	2	3	0	2	0	1
5	6	3	6	5	5	1

989

The missing piece is no. 6.

990

Cube no. 2

991

Pot no. 5. The bottom pot in each column has a lid like the top pot and a label like the middle one.

992

R – These are the letters of the alphabet, in order, that have just one region (or enclosed area) inside the letter.

993

From the top: D, B, A, E, C, F

994

O	R	B		W	A	R
U		U	S	E		U
T	R	Y		B	A	G
	Y				R	
M	E	N			F	E	Z
O		A	G	O		O
P	E	G		E	G	O

995

15	41	32	20	10
22	9	1	38	46
11	26	18	4	30
42	31	6	45	12
40	16	27	48	25

996

The missing number is 4. In each tile, the lower figure is obtained by multiplying the two digits of the upper number.

997

998

Silhouette 1 is picture f, and silhouette 2 is picture i.

999

Picture 1 is missing a nail in the fence. Picture 2 is missing a stone on the pavement. Picture 3 is missing a leaf. Picture 4 is missing a brick. Picture 5 is missing a patch on the dog. Picture 6 is missing a nut on the wheel. Picture 7 is missing a leg on the dog. Picture 8 is missing a shirt pocket.

1000

Bradley got out at station B (clue B), and station 3 is Maple Street (clue 3). A woman passenger got out at station B (clue 4), so King's Grove, where Nigel alighted, which is not an interchange station (clue 1), and therefore cannot be numbered 1, 4 or 7, must be station 2. Therefore, from clue 1, Libby must have got out at station 1. Tessa left the train at an interchange station (clue 1), so the woman who descended at station B must be Eileen. So station B is Red Lion (clue B). Therefore Howard cannot have alighted at station 4 or station 7 (clue 2), and must have done so at station 3. Therefore Peel Park must be station B (clue 2). Museum cannot be station 1, where Libby alighted, nor is it station 7 (clue 7), so it must be station 4. By elimination, the man who got out there (clue 7) must have been Conrad, leaving station 7 as the one where Tessa got out. This cannot be Market Cross (clue B), so it must be Central Station, leaving Market Cross as station 1.

In summary:
1, Market Cross, Libby. 2, King's Grove, Nigel. 3, Maple Street, Howard. 4, Museum, Conrad. 5, Peel Park, Eileen. 6, Red Lion, Bradley. 7, Central Station, Tessa.

1001

The photo from the 1959 holiday cannot be in positions A (clue 1), C (clue 3), E (clue 4), B or D (clue 5), so it must be F. The one taken at Lake Garda must be photo E (clue 2). Since photo E was not taken in the Isle of Man, the date of photo C cannot be 1975 (clue 3), nor, therefore, was that of photo E 1979 (clue 4). It cannot be 1975 (clue 1), and since photo C cannot have been taken in 1971 (clue 1), photo E cannot date from 1972 (clue 4). Since we know photo C was not taken in 1959, photo E cannot be from 1963 (clue 4), so it must be the one taken in 1971, and picture C must have been taken in 1963 (clue 4). Therefore the Isle of Man photo must have been taken in 1959 (clue 3), and is picture F. So D must have been taken in 1975 (clue 3), and, from clue 2, it must be the scene from Cornwall. Clue 5 now reveals the date of photo B as 1979, leaving that of picture A as 1972. Now, from clue 4, Tenby must be the location of picture B, taken in 1979. Brittany was not the location of picture A (clue 4), so the latter must be a photo of Assisi, leaving Brittany as the scene in photo C.

Thus:
A – Assisi – 1972. B – Tenby – 1979. C – Brittany –1963. D – Cornwall – 1975. E – Lake Garda – 1971. F – Isle of Man - 1959.